Lecture Notes in Computer Science 12038

More information about this series at http://www.springer.com/series/7407

Alberto Leporati · Carlos Martín-Vide ·
Dana Shapira · Claudio Zandron (Eds.)

Language
and Automata Theory
and Applications

14th International Conference, LATA 2020
Milan, Italy, March 4–6, 2020
Proceedings

 Springer

Editors
Alberto Leporati (iD)
University of Milano-Bicocca
Milan, Italy

Carlos Martín-Vide (iD)
Rovira i Virgili University
Tarragona, Spain

Dana Shapira (iD)
Ariel University
Ariel, Israel

Claudio Zandron (iD)
University of Milano-Bicocca
Milan, Italy

ISSN 0302-9743   ISSN 1611-3349   (electronic)
Lecture Notes in Computer Science
ISBN 978-3-030-40607-3   ISBN 978-3-030-40608-0   (eBook)
https://doi.org/10.1007/978-3-030-40608-0

LNCS Sublibrary: SL1 – Theoretical Computer Science and General Issues

This Springer imprint is published by the registered company Springer Nature Switzerland AG
The registered company address is: Gewerbestrasse 11, 6330 Cham, Switzerland

Preface

These proceedings contain the papers that should have been presented at the 14th International Conference on Language and Automata Theory and Applications (LATA 2020) which was planned to be held in Milan, Italy, during March 4–6, 2020. The conference was postponed due to the coronavirus pandemic and will be merged with LATA 2021.

The scope of LATA is rather broad, including: algebraic language theory; algorithms for semi-structured data mining; algorithms on automata and words; automata and logic; automata for system analysis and program verification; automata networks; automatic structures; codes; combinatorics on words; computational complexity; concurrency and Petri nets; data and image compression; descriptional complexity; foundations of finite state technology; foundations of XML; grammars (Chomsky hierarchy, contextual, unification, categorial, etc.); grammatical inference, inductive inference, and algorithmic learning; graphs and graph transformation; language varieties and semigroups; language-based cryptography; mathematical and logical foundations of programming methodologies; parallel and regulated rewriting; parsing; patterns; power series; string processing algorithms; symbolic dynamics; term rewriting; transducers; trees, tree languages, and tree automata; and weighted automata.

LATA 2020 received 59 submissions. Each paper was reviewed by three Program Committee members. There were also some external experts consulted. After a thorough and vivid discussion phase, the committee decided to accept 26 papers (which represents an acceptance rate of about 44%). The conference program included six invited talks as well.

The excellent facilities provided by the EasyChair conference management system allowed us to deal with the submissions successfully and handle the preparation of these proceedings in time.

We would like to thank all invited speakers and authors for their contributions, the Program Committee and the external reviewers for their cooperation, and Springer for its very professional publishing work.

December 2019

Alberto Leporati
Carlos Martín-Vide
Dana Shapira
Claudio Zandron

Organization

Program Committee

Jorge Almeida	University of Porto, Portugal
Franz Baader	Technical University of Dresden, Germany
Alessandro Barenghi	Polytechnic University of Milan, Italy
Marie-Pierre Béal	University of Paris-Est, France
Djamal Belazzougui	CERIST, Algeria
Marcello Bonsangue	Leiden University, The Netherlands
Flavio Corradini	University of Camerino, Italy
Bruno Courcelle	University of Bordeaux, France
Laurent Doyen	ENS Paris-Saclay, France
Manfred Droste	Leipzig University, Germany
Rudolf Freund	Technical University of Vienna, Austria
Paweł Gawrychowski	University of Wroclaw, Poland
Amélie Gheerbrant	Paris Diderot University, France
Tero Harju	University of Turku, Finland
Jeffrey Heinz	Stony Brook University, USA
Lane A. Hemaspaandra	University of Rochester, USA
Marcin Jurdziński	University of Warwick, UK
Juhani Karhumäki	University of Turku, Finland
Jarkko Kari	University of Turku, Finland
Dexter Kozen	Cornell University, USA
François Le Gall	Kyoto University, Japan
Markus Lohrey	University of Siegen, Japan
Parthasarathy Madhusudan	University of Illinois at Urbana-Champaign, USA
Sebastian Maneth	University of Bremen, Germany
Nicolas Markey	Irisa, Rennes, France
Carlos Martín-Vide (Chair)	Rovira i Virgili University, Spain
Giancarlo Mauri	University of Milano-Bicocca, Italy
Victor Mitrana	University of Bucharest, Romania
Paliath Narendran	University at Albany, USA
Gennaro Parlato	University of Molise, Italy
Dominique Perrin	University of Paris-Est, France
Nir Piterman	Chalmers University of Technology, Sweden
Sanguthevar Rajasekaran	University of Connecticut, USA
Antonio Restivo	University of Palermo, Italy
Wojciech Rytter	University of Warsaw, Poland
Kai Salomaa	Queen's University, Canada
Helmut Seidl	Technical University of Munich, Germany
William F. Smyth	McMaster University, Canada

Jiří Srba	Aalborg University, Denmark
Edward Stabler	University of California, Los Angeles, USA
Benjamin Steinberg	City University of New York, USA
Frank Stephan	National University of Singapore, Singapore
Jan van Leeuwen	Utrecht University, The Netherlands
Margus Veanes	Microsoft Research, USA
Tomáš Vojnar	Brno University of Technology, Czech Republic
Mikhail Volkov	Ural Federal University, Russia
James Worrell	University of Oxford, UK

Additional Reviewers

Berdinsky, Dmitry
Boigelot, Bernard
Boker, Udi
Bollig, Benedikt
Bosma, Wieb
Cacciagrano, Diletta Romana
Carpi, Arturo
Chaiken, Seth
Choudhury, Salimur
Dolce, Francesco
Erbatur, Serdar
Fahrenberg, Uli
Fici, Gabriele
Gagie, Travis
Ganardi, Moses
Giammarresi, Dora
Grabolle, Gustav
Guaiana, Giovanna
Havlena, Vojtěch
Holík, Lukáš
Holt, Derek
Hunter, Tim
Jain, Chirag
Jančar, Petr
Janczewski, Wojciech
Jeż, Artur
K. S., Thejaswini
Keeler, Chris
Kiefer, Sandra
Lemay, Aurélien

Lengál, Ondrej
Lipták, Zsuzsanna
Loreti, Michele
Madonia, Maria
Maletti, Andreas
Mhaskar, Neerja
Mostarda, Leonardo
Muniz, Marco
Peltomäki, Jarkko
Popa, Alexandru
Rogers, John
Rosenkrantz, Daniel
Rowland, Eric
Saarela, Aleksi
Salmela, Leena
Sankur, Ocan
Sawada, Joe
Sciortino, Marinella
Semukhin, Pavel
Sernadas, Cristina
Shur, Arseny
Skrzypczak, Michał
Sohrabi, Mahmood
Staiger, Ludwig
Tesei, Luca
Tesson, Pascal
van Gool, Sam
Williams, Ryan
Winter, Sarah

Contents

Complexity

Grammars

Languages

Invited Papers

The New Complexity Landscape Around Circuit Minimization

Eric Allender$^{(\boxtimes)}$

Rutgers University, New Brunswick, NJ 08854, USA
allender@cs.rutgers.edu
http://www.cs.rutgers.edu/~allender

Abstract. We survey recent developments related to the Minimum Circuit Size Problem.

Keywords: Complexity theory · Kolmogorov complexity · Minimum Circuit Size Problem

1 Introduction

Over the past few years, there has been an explosion of interest in the Minimum Circuit Size Problem (MCSP) and related problems. Thus the time seemed right to provide a survey, describing the new landscape and offering a guidebook so that one can easily reach the new frontiers of research in this area.

It turns out that this landscape is extremely unstable, with new features arising at an alarming rate. Although this makes it a scientifically-exciting time, it also means that this survey is doomed to be obsolete before it appears. It also means that the survey is going to take the form of an "annotated bibliography" with the intent to provide many pointers to the relevant literature, along with a bit of context.

The title of this article is "The *New* Complexity Landscape around Circuit Minimization" (emphasis added). This means that I will try to avoid repeating too many of the observations that were made in an earlier survey I wrote on a related topic [1]. Although that article was written only three years ago, several of the open questions that were mentioned there have now been resolved (and some of the conjectures that were mentioned have been overturned).

2 Meta-complexity, MCSP and Kolmogorov Complexity

The focus of complexity theory is to determine how hard problems are. The focus of *meta-complexity* is to determine how hard it is to determine how hard problems are. Some of the most exciting recent developments in complexity theory have been the result of meta-complexity-theoretic investigations.

Supported in part by NSF Grant CCF-1909216.

A. Leporati et al. (Eds.): LATA 2020, LNCS 12038, pp. 3–16, 2020.
https://doi.org/10.1007/978-3-030-40608-0_1

The Minimum Circuit Size Problem (MCSP) is, quite simply, the problem of determining the circuit complexity of functions. The input consists of a pair (f, i), where f is a bit string of length $N = 2^n$ representing the truth-table of a Boolean function, and $i \in \mathbb{N}$, and the problem is to determine if f has a circuit of size at most i. The study of the complexity of MCSP is therefore the canonical meta-complexity-theoretic question. Complexity theoreticians are fond of complaining that the problems they confront (showing that computational problems are hard to compute) are notoriously difficult. But is this really true? Is it hard to show that a particular function is difficult to compute? This question can be made precise by asking about the computational complexity of MCSP. (See also [44] for a different approach.)

A small circuit is a short description of a large truth-table f; thus it is no surprise that investigations of MCSP have made use of the tools and terminology of Kolmogorov complexity. In order to discuss some of the recent developments, it will be necessary to review some of the different notions, and to establish the notation that will be used throughout the rest of the article.

Let U be a Turing machine. We define $K_U(x)$ to be $\min\{|d| : U(d) = x\}$. Those readers who are familiar with Kolmogorov complexity[1] will notice that the definition here is for what is sometimes called "plain" Kolmogorov complexity, although the notation $K_U(x)$ is more commonly used to denote what is called "prefix-free" Kolmogorov complexity. This is intentional. In this survey, the distinctions between these two notions will be blurred, in order to keep the discussion on a high level. Some of the theorems that will be mentioned below are only known to hold for the prefix-free variant, but the reader is encouraged to ignore these finer distinctions here, and seek the more detailed information in the cited references. For some Turing machines U, $K_U(x)$ will not be defined for some x, and the values of $K_U(x)$ and $K_{U'}(x)$ can be very different, for different machines U and U'. But the beauty of Kolmogorov complexity (and the applicability of of the theory it gives rise to) derives from the fact that if U and U' are *universal* Turing machines, then $K_U(x)$ and $K_{U'}(x)$ differ by at most $O(1)$. By convention, we select one particular universal machine U and define $K(x)$ to be equal to $K_U(x)$.

The function K is not computable. The simplest way to obtain a computable function that shares many of the properties of K is to simply impose a time bound, leading to the definition $K^t(x) := \min\{|d| : U(d) = x \text{ in time } t(|x|)\}$ where t is a computable function. Although it is useful in many contexts, $K^t(x)$ does not appear to be closely connected to the circuit size of x (where x is viewed as the truth-table of a function). Thus we will frequently refer to two additional resource-bounded Kolmogorov complexity measures, Kt and KT.

Levin defined $\mathrm{Kt}(x)$ to be $\min\{|d| + \log t : U(d) = x \text{ in time } t\}$ [32]; it has the nice property that it can be used to define the optimal search strategy to use, in searching for accepting computations on a nondeterministic Turing machine. $\mathrm{Kt}(x)$ also corresponds to the circuit size of the function x, but not on

---

[1] If the reader is not familiar with Kolmogorov complexity, then we recommend some excellent books on this topic [17, 33].

"normal" circuits. As is shown in [2], $\mathsf{Kt}(x)$ is roughly the same as the size of the smallest *oracle* circuit that computes x, where the oracle is a complete set for EXP. (An oracle circuit has "oracle gates" in addition to the usual AND, OR, and NOT gates; an oracle gate for oracle A has k wires leading into it, and if those k wires encode a bitstring y of length k where y is in A, then the gate outputs 1, otherwise it outputs 0.)

It is clearly desirable to have a version of Kolmogorov complexity that is more closely related to "ordinary" circuit size, instead of oracle circuit size. This is accomplished by defining $\mathsf{KT}(x)$ to be $\min\{|d| + t : U(d, i) = x_i \text{ in time } t\}$. (More precise definitions can be found in [2,10].)

We have now presented a number of different measures $\mathsf{K}_\mu \in \{K, K^t, \mathsf{Kt}, \mathsf{KT}\}$. By analogy with MCSP, we can study K_μ in place of the "circuit size" measure, and thus obtain various problems of the form $\mathsf{MK}_\mu\mathsf{P} = \{(x, i) : \mathsf{K}_\mu(x) \le i\}$, such as MKTP, $\mathsf{MK}^t\mathsf{P}$ and MKtP. If $t(n) = n^{O(1)}$, then $\mathsf{MK}^t\mathsf{P}$ is in NP, and several theorems about MKTP yield corollaries about $\mathsf{MK}^t\mathsf{P}$ in this case. (See, e.g. [2]). Similarly, if $t(n) = 2^{n^c}$ for some $c > 0$, then $\mathsf{MK}^t\mathsf{P}$ is in EXP, and several theorems about MKtP yield corollaries about $\mathsf{MK}^t\mathsf{P}$ for t in this range [2].

In order to highlight some of the recent developments, let us introduce some notation that is somewhat imprecise and which is not used anywhere else, but which will be convenient for our purposes. Let K^{poly} serve as a shorthand for K^t whenever $t = n^{O(1)}$, and similarly let K^{exp} serve as a shorthand for K^t whenever $t = 2^{n^c}$ for some $c > 0$. We will thus be referring to $\mathsf{MK}^{poly}\mathsf{P}$ and $\mathsf{MK}^{exp}\mathsf{P}$. Doing so will enable us to avoid some confusing notation surrounding the name $MINKT$, which was introduced by Ko [31] to denote the set $\{x, 1^t, 1^i : \exists d\, U(d) = x \text{ in at most } t \text{ steps and } |d| \le i\}$. That is, $(x, i) \in \mathsf{MK}^{poly}\mathsf{P}$ iff $(x, 1^{n^c}, i) \in MINKT$ (where the time bound $t(n) = n^c$). Hence these sets have comparable complexity and results about $MINKT$ can be rephrased in terms of $\mathsf{MK}^{poly}\mathsf{P}$ with only a small loss of accuracy. In particular, some recent important results [19,20] are phrased in terms of $MINKT$, and as such they deal with K^{poly} complexity, and they are not really very closely connected with the KT measure; the name $MINKT$ was devised more than a decade before KT was formulated. The reader who is interested in the details should refer to the original papers for the precise formulation of the theorems. However, the view presented here is "probably approximately correct".

Frequently, theorems about MCSP and the various $\mathsf{MK}_\mu\mathsf{P}$ problems are stated not in terms of *exactly* computing the circuit size or the complexity of a string, but in terms of *approximating* these values. This is usually presented in terms of two thresholds $\theta_1 < \theta_2$, where the desired solution is to say *yes* if the complexity of x is less than θ_1, and to say *no* if the complexity of x is greater than θ_2, and any answer is allowed if the complexity of x lies in the "gap" between θ_1 and θ_2. In the various theorems that have been proved in this setting, the choice of thresholds θ_1 and θ_2 is usually important, but in this article those details will be suppressed, and all of these approximation problems will be referred to as GapMCSP, GapMKtP, GapMKTP, etc.

At this point, the reader's eyes may be starting to glaze over. It is natural to wonder if we really need to have all of these different related notions. In particular, there does not seem to be much difference between MCSP and MKTP. Most hardness results for MCSP actually hold for GapMCSP, and if the "gap" is large enough, then MKTP is a solution to GapMCSP (and vice-versa). Furthermore it has frequently been the case that a theorem about MCSP was first proved for MKTP and then the result for MCSP was obtained as a corollary. However, there is no efficient reduction known (in either direction) between MCSP and MKTP, and there are some theorems that are currently known to hold only for MKTP, although they are suspected to hold also for MCSP (e.g., [4,6,23]). Similarly, some of the more intriguing recent developments can only be understood by paying attention to the distinction between different notions of resource-bounded Kolmogorov complexity. Thus it is worth making this investment in defining the various distinct notions.

3   Connections to Learning Theory

Certain connections between computational learning theory and Kolmogorov complexity were identified soon after computational learning theory emerged as a field. After all, the goal of computational learning theory is to find a satisfactory (and hence succinct) explanation of a large body of observed data. For instance, in the 1980s and 1990s there was work [40,41] showing that it is NP-hard to find "succinct explanations" that have size somewhat close to the optimal size, if these "explanations" are required to be finite automata or various other restricted formalisms. Ko studied this in a more general setting, allowing "explanations" to be efficient programs (in the setting of time-bounded Kolmogorov complexity).

Thus Ko studied not only the problem of computing $K^{poly}(x)$ (where one can consider x to be a completely-specified Boolean function), but also the problem of finding the smallest description d such that $U(d)$ agrees with a given list of "yes instances" Y and a list of "no instances" N (that is, x can be considered as a partial Boolean function, with many "don't care" instances). Thus, following [28], we can call this problem Partial-MK^{poly}P. In the setting that is most relevant for computational learning theory, the partial function x is presented compactly as separate lists Y and N, rather than as a string of length 2^n over the alphabet $\{0, 1, *\}$.

Ko showed in [31] that relativizing techniques would not suffice, in order to settle the question of whether MK^{poly}P and Partial-MK^{poly}P are NP-complete. That is, by giving the universal Turing machine U that defines Kolmogorov complexity access to an oracle A, one obtains the problems MK^{poly}P^A and Partial-MK^{poly}P^A, and these sets can either be NP^A-complete or not, depending on the choice of A.

Thus it is noteworthy that it has recently been shown that Partial-MCSP is NP-complete under $\leq_m^P$ reductions [28]. I suspect (although I have not verified) that the proof also establishes that Partial-MKTP is NP-complete under $\leq_m^P$ reductions. One lesson to take from this is that KT and K^{poly} complexity differ from each other in significant ways. There are other recent examples of related phenomena, which will be discussed below.

There are other strong connections between MCSP and learning theory that have come to light recently. Using MCSP as an oracle (or even using a set that shares certain characteristics with MCSP) one can efficiently learn small circuits that do a good job of explaining the data [11]. For certain restricted classes of circuits, there are sets in P that one can use in place of MCSP to obtain learning algorithms that don't require an oracle [11]. This connection has been explored further [12, 36].

4 Completeness, Hardness, Reducibility

The preceding section mentioned a result about a problem being NP-complete under $\leq_m^P$ reductions. In order to discuss other results about the complexity of MCSP and related problems it is necessary to go into more detail about different notions of reducibility.

Let $\mathcal{C}$ be either a class of functions or a class of circuits. The classes that will concern us the most are the standard complexity classes $\mathsf{L} \subseteq \mathsf{P} \subseteq \mathsf{NP}$ as well as the circuit classes (both uniform and nonuniform):

$$\mathsf{NC}^0 \subsetneq \mathsf{AC}^0 \subsetneq \mathsf{AC}^0[p] \subsetneq \mathsf{NC}^1 \subseteq \mathsf{P/poly}.$$

We refer the reader to the text by Vollmer [46] for background and more complete definitions of these standard circuit complexity complexity classes, as well as for a discussion of uniformity.

We say that $A \leq_m^{\mathcal{C}} B$ if there is a function $f \in \mathcal{C}$ (or f computed by a circuit family in $\mathcal{C}$, respectively) such that $x \in A$ iff $f(x) \in B$. We will make use of $\leq_m^{\mathsf{L}}, \leq_m^{\mathsf{AC}^0}$ and $\leq_m^{\mathsf{NC}^0}$ reducibility. The more powerful notion of Turing reducibility also plays an important role in this work. Here, $\mathcal{C}$ is a complexity class that admits a characterization in terms of Turing machines or circuits, which can be augmented with an "oracle" mechanism, either by providing a "query tape" or "oracle gates". We say that $A \leq_T^{\mathcal{C}} B$ if there is a oracle machine in $\mathcal{C}$ (or a family of oracle circuits in $\mathcal{C}$) accepting A, when given oracle B. We make use of $\leq_T^{\mathsf{P/poly}}, \leq_T^{\mathsf{RP}}, \leq_T^{\mathsf{ZPP}}, \leq_T^{\mathsf{BPP}}, \leq_T^{\mathsf{P}}$, and $\leq_T^{\mathsf{NC}^1}$ reducibility; instead of writing $A \leq_T^{\mathsf{P/poly}} B$ or $A \leq_T^{\mathsf{ZPP}} B$, we will sometimes write $A \in \mathsf{P}^B/\mathsf{poly}$ or $A \in \mathsf{ZPP}^B$. Turing reductions that are "nonadaptive" – in the sense that the list of queries that are posed on input x does not depend on the answers provided by the oracle – are called *truth table reductions*. We make use of $\leq_{tt}^{\mathsf{P}}$ reducibility.

Not much has changed, regarding what is known about the "hardness" of MCSP, in the three years that have passed since my earlier survey [1]. Here is what I wrote at that time:

Table 1 presents information about the consequences that will follow if MCSP is NP-complete (or even if it is hard for certain subclasses of NP). The table is incomplete (since it does not mention the influential theorems of Kabanets *and Cai [30] describing various consequences if MCSP were complete under a certain restricted type of $\leq^{P}_{m}$ reduction). It also fails to adequately give credit to all of the papers that have contributed to this line of work, since – for example – some of the important contributions of [35] have subsequently been slightly improved [7,25]. But one thing should jump out at the reader from Table 1: All of the conditions listed in Column 3 (with the exception of "FALSE") are widely believed to be true, although they all seem to be far beyond the reach of current proof techniques.*

Table 1. Summary of what is known about the consequences of MCSP being hard for NP under different types of reducibility. If MCSP is hard for the class in Column 1 under the reducibility shown in Column 2, then the consequence in Column 3 follows.

Class $\mathcal{C}$	Reductions $\mathcal{R}$	Statement $\mathcal{S}$	Reference
TC^0	$\leq^{n^{1/3}}_{m}$	FALSE	[35]
TC^0	$\leq^{AC^0}_{m}$	LTH[a] $\not\subseteq$ io-SIZE$[2^{\Omega(n)}]$ and P = BPP	[7,35]
TC^0	$\leq^{AC^0}_{m}$	NP $\not\subseteq$ P/poly	[7]
P	$\leq^{L}_{m}$	PSPACE $\neq$ P	[7]
NP	$\leq^{L}_{m}$	PSPACE $\neq$ ZPP	[35]
NP	$\leq^{P}_{tt}$	EXP $\neq$ ZPP	[25]

[a]LTH is the linear-time analog of the polynomial hierarchy. Problems in LTH are accepted by alternating Turing machines that make only $O(1)$ alternations and run for linear time.

It is significant that neither MCSP nor MKTP is NP-complete under $\leq^{n^{1/3}}_{m}$ reductions, since SAT and many other well-known problems are complete under this very restrictive notion of reducibility – but it would be more satisfying to know whether these problems can be complete under more widely-used reducibilities such as $\leq^{AC^0}_{m}$. These sublinear-time reductions are so restrictive, that even the PARITY problem is not $\leq^{n^{1/3}}_{m}$-reducible to MCSP or MKTP. In an attempt to prove that PARITY is not $\leq^{AC^0}_{m}$-reducible to MKTP, we actually ended up proving the opposite:

Theorem 1 [6]. MKTP *is hard for* DET *under non-uniform* NC^0 *reductions. This also holds for* MKtP *and* MKP.

Here, DET is the class of problems NC^1-Turing-reducible to computing the determinant. It includes the well-known complexity classes L and NL. This remains the only theorem that shows hardness of $MK_{\mu}P$ problems under any kind of $\leq^{\mathcal{C}}_{m}$ reductions.

As a corollary of this theorem it follows that MKTP is not in $AC^0[p]$ for any prime p. This was mentioned as an open question in [1] (see footnote 2 in [1]). (An alternate proof was given in [23].) It remained open whether MCSP was in $AC^0[p]$ until a lower bound was proved in [18].

It is *still* open whether MCSP is hard for DET. The proof of the hardness result in [6] actually carries over to a version of GapMKTP where the "gap" is quite small. Thus one avenue for proving a hardness result for MCSP had seemed to be to improve the hardness result of [6], so that it worked for a much larger "gap". This avenue was subsequently blocked, when it was shown that PARITY is not AC^0-reducible to GapMCSP (or to GapMKTP) for a moderate-sized "gap" [8]. Thus, although it is still open whether MCSP is NP-complete under $\leq_m^{AC^0}$ reductions, we now know that GapMCSP is not NP-complete under this notion of reducibility.

When a *much* larger "gap" is considered, it was shown in [6] that, if cryptographically-secure one-way functions exist, then GapMCSP and GapMKTP are NP-intermediate in the sense that neither problem is in P/poly, and neither problem is complete for NP under P/poly-Turing reductions.

The strongest hardness results that are known for the $MK_\mu P$ problems in NP remain the results of [3], where it was shown that MCSP, MKTP, and $MK^{poly}P$ are all hard for SZK under $\leq_T^{BPP}$ reductions. SZK is the class of problems that have statistical zero knowledge interactive proofs; SZK contains most of the problems that are assumed to be intractable, in order to build public-key cryptosystems. Thus it is widely assumed that MCSP and related problems lie outside of P/poly, and cryptographers hope that it requires nearly exponential-sized circuits. SZK also contains the Graph Isomorphism problem, which is $\leq_T^{RP}$-reducible to MCSP and MKTP. In [4], Graph Isomorphism (and several other problems) were shown to be $\leq_T^{ZPP}$ reducible to MKTP; it remains unknown if this also holds for MCSP. In fact, there is no interesting example of a problem A that is not known to be in NP ∩ coNP that has been shown to be $\leq_T^{ZPP}$ reducible to MCSP.

We close this section with a discussion of a very powerful notion of reducibility: SNP reductions. (Informally A is SNP reducible to B means that A is (NP ∩ coNP)-reducible to B.) Hitchcock and Pavan have shown that MCSP is indeed NP-complete under SNP reductions if NP ∩ coNP contains problems that require large circuits (which seems very plausible) [25]. It is interesting to note that, back in the early 1990's, Ko explicitly considered the possibility that computing $MK^{poly}P$ might be NP-complete under SNP reductions [31].

4.1   Completeness in **EXP** and Other Classes

There are problems "similar" to MCSP that reside in many complexity classes. We can define $MCSP^A$ to be MCSP for oracle circuits with A-oracle gates. That is, $MCSP^A = \{(f,i) : f$ has an A-oracle circuit of size at most $i\}$. When A is complete for EXP, then $MCSP^A$ is thought of as being quite similar to MKtP. Both of these problems, along with $MK^{exp}P$, are complete for EXP under $\leq_T^{P/poly}$ and $\leq_T^{NP}$ reductions [2].

It is still open whether either of MKtP or $MCSP^A$ is in P, and it had been open if MK^tP is in P for "small" exponential functions t such as $t(n) = 2^{n/2}$. But there is recent progress:

Theorem 2 [20]. $MK^{exp}P$ *is complete for* EXP *under* $\leq_T^P$ *reductions.*

This seems to go a long way toward addressing Open Question 3.6 in [1].

As a corollary, $MK^{exp}P$ is not in P. In fact, a much stronger result holds. Let t be any superpolynomial function. Then the set of K^t-random strings $\{x : K^t(x) < |x|\}$ is *immune* to P (meaning: it has no infinite subset in P) [20]. The proof does not seem to carry over to Kt complexity, highlighting a significant difference between Kt and K^{exp}.

Although it remains open whether MKtP $\in$ P, Hirahara does show that MKtP is not in P-uniform ACC^0, and in fact the set of Kt-random strings is immune to P-uniform ACC^0. Furthermore, improved immunity results for the Kt-random strings are in some sense possible *if and only if* better algorithms for CircuitSAT can be devised for larger classes of circuits.

Oliveira has defined a randomized version of Kt complexity, which is conjectured to be nearly the same as Kt, but for which he is able to prove unconditional intractability results [37].

$MCSP^{QBF}$ was known to be complete for PSPACE under $\leq_T^{ZPP}$ reductions [2]. In more recent work, for various subclasses $\mathcal{C}$ of PSPACE, when A is a suitable complete problem for $\mathcal{C}$, then $MCSP^A$ has been shown to be complete for $\mathcal{C}$ under $\leq_T^{BPP}$ reductions [29]. Crucially, the techniques used by [29] (and, indeed, by any of the authors who had proved hardness results for $MCSP^A$ previously for various A) failed to work for any A in the polynomial hierarchy. We will return to this issue in the following section.

In related work, it was shown [6] that the question of whether $MKTP^A$ is hard for DET under a type of uniform AC^0 reductions is equivalent to the question of whether DSPACE(n) contains any sets that require exponential-size A-oracle circuits. Furthermore, this happens if and only if PARITY reduces to $MKTP^A$. Note that this condition is *more likely* to be true if A is easy, than if A is complex; it is false if A is complete for PSPACE, and it is probably true if $A = \emptyset$. Thus, although $MKTP^{QBF}$ is almost certainly more complex than MKTP (the former is PSPACE-complete, and the latter is in NP), a reasonably-large subclass of P probably reduces to MKTP via these uniform AC^0 reductions, whereas hardly anything AC^0-reduces to $MKTP^{QBF}$. The explanation for this is that a uniform AC^0 reduction cannot formulate any useful queries to a complex oracle, whereas it (probably) can do so for a simpler oracle.

4.2 NP-Hardness

Recall from the previous section that there were no NP-hardness results known for any problem of the form $MCSP^A$ where A is in the polynomial hierarchy.

This is still true; however, there is some progress to report. Hirahara has shown that computing the "conditional" complexity $K^{poly}(x|y)$ relative to SAT (i.e., given (x, y), finding the length of the shortest description d such that $U^{SAT}(d, y) = x$ in time n^c) is NP-hard under $\leq_{tt}^P$ reductions [20].

It might be more satisfying to remove the SAT oracle, and have a hardness result for computing $K^{poly}(x|y)$ – but Hirahara shows that this can't be shown to be hard for NP (or even hard for ZPP) under $\leq_{tt}^P$ reductions without first separating EXP from ZPP.

In a similar vein, if one were to show that MCSP or MKTP (or MCSP^A or MKTP^A for any set $A \in$ EXP) is hard for NP under $\leq_{tt}^P$ reductions, then one will have shown that ZPP $\neq$ EXP [20].

A different kind of NP-hardness result for conditional Kolmogorov complexity was proved recently by Ilango [27]. In [2], conditional KT complexity $KT(x|y)$ was studied by making the string y available to the universal Turing machine U as an "oracle". Thus it makes sense to consider a "conditional complexity" version of MCSP by giving a string y available to a circuit via oracle gates. This problem was formalized and shown to be NP-complete under $\leq_T^{ZPP}$ reductions [27].

Many of the functions that we compute daily produce more than one bit of output. Thus it makes sense to study the circuit size that is required in order to compute such functions. This problem is called Multi-MCSP in [28], where it is shown to be NP-complete under $\leq_T^{RP}$ reductions. It will be interesting to see how the complexity of this problem varies, as the number of output bits of the functions under consideration shrinks toward one (at which point it becomes MCSP).

It has been known since the 1970's that computing the size of the smallest DNF expression for a given truth-table is NP-complete. (A simple proof, and a discussion of the history can be found in [5].) However, it remains unknown what the complexity is of finding the smallest depth-three circuit for a given truth table. (Some very weak intractability results for minimizing constant-depth circuits can be found in [5], giving subexponential reductions from the problem of factoring Blum integers.) The first real progress on this front was reported in [22], giving an NP-completeness result (under $\leq_m^P$ reductions) for a class of depth three circuits (with MOD gates on the bottom level). Ilango proved that computing the size of the smallest depth-d *formula* for a truth-table lies outside of AC$^0[p]$ for any prime p [27], and he has now followed that up with a proof that computing the size of the smallest depth-d *formula* is NP-complete under $\leq_T^{RP}$ reductions [26]. Note that a constant-depth circuit can be transformed into a formula with only a polynomial blow-up; thus in many situations we are able to ignore the distinction between circuits and formulas in the constant-depth realm. However, the techniques employed in [26,27] are quite sensitive to small perturbations in the size, and hence the distinction between circuits and formulae is important here. Still, this is dramatic progress on a front where progress has been very slow.

5   Average Case Complexity, One-Way Functions

Cai and Kabanets gave birth to the modern study of MCSP in 2000 [30], in a paper that was motivated in part by the study of Natural Proofs [42], and which called attention to the fact that if MCSP is easy, then there are no cryptographically-secure one-way functions. In the succeeding decades, there has been speculation about whether the converse implication also holds. That is, can one base cryptography on assumptions about the complexity of MCSP?

First, it should be observed that, in some sense, MCSP is very easy "on average". For instance the hardness results that we have (such as reducing SZK to MCSP) show that the "hard instances" of MCSP are the ones where we want to distinguish between n-ary functions that require circuits of size $2^n/n^2$ (the "NO" instances) and those that have circuits of size at most $2^{n/3}$ (the "YES" instances). However, an algorithm that simply says "no" on all inputs will give the correct answer more than 99% of the time.

Thus Hirahara and Santhanam [23] chose to study a different notion of heuristics for MCSP, where algorithms must always give an answer in {Yes, No, I don't know}, where the algorithm never gives an incorrect answer, and the algorithm is said to perform well "on average" if it only seldom answers "I don't know". They were able to show unconditionally that MCSP is hard on average in this sense for $AC^0[p]$ for any prime p, and to show that certain well-studied hypotheses imply that MCSP is hard on average.

More recently, Santhanam [43] has formulated a conjecture (which would involve too big of a digression to describe more carefully here), which – if true – would imply that a version of MCSP is hard on average in this sense if and only if cryptographically-secure one-way functions exist. That is, Santhanam's conjecture provides a framework for believing that one can base cryptography on the average-case complexity of MCSP.

But how does the average-case complexity of MCSP depend on its worst-case complexity? Hirahara [19] showed that GapMCSP has no solution in BPP if and only if a version of MCSP is hard on average. A related result stated in terms of K^{poly} appears in the same paper. These results attracted considerable attention, because prior work had indicated that such worst-case-to-average-case reductions would be impossible to prove using black-box techniques. Additional work has given further evidence that the techniques of [19] are inherently non-black-box [24].

6   Complexity Classes and Noncomputable Complexity Measures

The title of this section is the same as the title of Sect. 4 of the survey that I wrote three years ago [1]. In that section, I described the work that had been done, studying the classes of sets that are reducible to the (non-computable) set of Kolmogorov-random strings R_K, and to MKP, including the reasons why it seemed reasonable to conjecture that BPP and NEXP could be characterized in terms of different types of reductions to the Kolmogorov-random strings.

I won't repeat that discussion here, because both of those conjectures have been disproved (barring some extremely unlikely complexity class collapses). Taken together, the papers [21,24], and [20] give a much better understanding of the classes of languages reducible to the Kolmogorov-random strings.

Previously, it was known that $PSPACE \subseteq P^{R_K}$, and $NEXP \subseteq NP^{R_K}$. Hirahara [20] has now shown $NEXP \subseteq EXP^{NP} \subseteq P^{R_K}$.

This same paper also gives a surprising answer to Open Question 4.6 of [1], in showing that Quasipolynomial-time nonadaptive reductions to R_K suffice to capture NP (and also some other classes in the polynomial hierarchy).

7 Magnification

Some of the most important and exciting developments relating to MCSP and related problems deal with the emerging study of "hardness magnification". This is the phenomenon whereby seemingly very modest lower bounds can be "amplified" or "magnified" and thereby be shown to imply superpolynomial lower bounds. I was involved in some of the early work in this direction [9] (which did not involve MCSP), but much stronger work has subsequently appeared.

It is important to note, in this regard, that lower bounds have been proved for MCSP that essentially match the strongest lower bounds that we have for any problems in NP [16]. There is now a significant body of work, showing that slight improvements to those bounds, or other seemingly-attainable lower bounds for GapMKtP or GapMCSP or related problems, would yield dramatic complexity class separations [12–15, 34, 38, 39, 45].

This would be a good place to survey this work, except that an excellent survey already appears in [12]. Igor Carboni Oliveira has also written some notes entitled "Advances in Hardness Magnification" related to a talk he gave at the Simons Institute in December, 2019, available on his home page. These notes and [12] describe in detail the reasons that this approach seems to avoid the Natural Proofs barrier identified in the work of Razborov and Rudich [42]. But they also describe some potential obstacles that need to be overcome, before this approach can truly be used to separate complexity classes.

References

1. Allender, E.: The complexity of complexity. In: Day, A., Fellows, M., Greenberg, N., Khoussainov, B., Melnikov, A., Rosamond, F. (eds.) Computability and Complexity. LNCS, vol. 10010, pp. 79–94. Springer, Cham (2017). https://doi.org/10.1007/978-3-319-50062-1_6
2. Allender, E., Buhrman, H., Koucký, M., van Melkebeek, D., Ronneburger, D.: Power from random strings. SIAM J. Comput. **35**, 1467–1493 (2006). https://doi.org/10.1137/050628994
3. Allender, E., Das, B.: Zero knowledge and circuit minimization. Inf. Comput. **256**, 2–8 (2017). https://doi.org/10.1016/j.ic.2017.04.004. Special issue for MFCS 2014
4. Allender, E., Grochow, J., van Melkebeek, D., Morgan, A., Moore, C.: Minimum circuit size, graph isomorphism and related problems. SIAM J. Comput. **47**, 1339–1372 (2018). https://doi.org/10.1137/17M1157970
5. Allender, E., Hellerstein, L., McCabe, P., Pitassi, T., Saks, M.E.: Minimizing disjunctive normal form formulas and AC^0 circuits given a truth table. SIAM J. Comput. **38**(1), 63–84 (2008). https://doi.org/10.1137/060664537
6. Allender, E., Hirahara, S.: New insights on the (non)-hardness of circuit minimization and related problems. ACM Trans. Comput. Theory (ToCT) **11**(4), 27:1–27:27 (2019). https://doi.org/10.1145/3349616

7. Allender, E., Holden, D., Kabanets, V.: The minimum oracle circuit size problem. Comput. Complex. **26**(2), 469–496 (2017). https://doi.org/10.1007/s00037-016-0124-0

8. Allender, E., Ilango, R., Vafa, N.: The non-hardness of approximating circuit size. In: van Bevern, R., Kucherov, G. (eds.) CSR 2019. LNCS, vol. 11532, pp. 13–24. Springer, Cham (2019). https://doi.org/10.1007/978-3-030-19955-5_2

9. Allender, E., Koucký, M.: Amplifying lower bounds by means of self-reducibility. J. ACM **57**, 14:1–14:36 (2010). https://doi.org/10.1145/1706591.1706594

10. Allender, E., Koucký, M., Ronneburger, D., Roy, S.: The pervasive reach of resource-bounded Kolmogorov complexity in computational complexity theory. J. Comput. Syst. Sci. **77**, 14–40 (2010). https://doi.org/10.1016/j.jcss.2010.06.004

11. Carmosino, M., Impagliazzo, R., Kabanets, V., Kolokolova, A.: Learning algorithms from natural proofs. In: 31st Conference on Computational Complexity, CCC. LIPIcs, vol. 50, pp. 10:1–10:24. Schloss Dagstuhl - Leibniz-Zentrum fuer Informatik (2016). https://doi.org/10.4230/LIPIcs.CCC.2016.10

12. Chen, L., Hirahara, S., Oliveira, I.C., Pich, J., Rajgopal, N., Santhanam, R.: Beyond natural proofs: hardness magnification and locality. In: 11th Innovations in Theoretical Computer Science Conference (ITCS). LIPIcs, vol. 151, pp. 70:1–70:48. Schloss Dagstuhl - Leibniz-Zentrum fuer Informatik (2020). https://doi.org/10.4230/LIPIcs.ITCS.2020.70

13. Chen, L., Jin, C., Williams, R.: Hardness magnification for all sparse NP languages. In: Symposium on Foundations of Computer Science (FOCS), pp. 1240–1255 (2019)

14. Chen, L., Jin, C., Williams, R.: Sharp threshold results for computational complexity (2019). Manuscript

15. Chen, L., McKay, D.M., Murray, C.D., Williams, R.R.: Relations and equivalences between circuit lower bounds and Karp-Lipton theorems. In: 34th Computational Complexity Conference (CCC). LIPIcs, vol. 137, pp. 30:1–30:21. Schloss Dagstuhl - Leibniz-Zentrum fuer Informatik (2019). https://doi.org/10.4230/LIPIcs.CCC.2019.30

16. Cheraghchi, M., Kabanets, V., Lu, Z., Myrisiotis, D.: Circuit lower bounds for MCSP from local pseudorandom generators. In: 46th International Colloquium on Automata, Languages, and Programming, (ICALP). LIPIcs, vol. 132, pp. 39:1–39:14. Schloss Dagstuhl - Leibniz-Zentrum fuer Informatik (2019). https://doi.org/10.4230/LIPIcs.ICALP.2019.39

17. Downey, R., Hirschfeldt, D.: Algorithmic Randomness and Complexity. Springer, New York (2010). https://doi.org/10.1007/978-0-387-68441-3

18. Golovnev, A., Ilango, R., Impagliazzo, R., Kabanets, V., Kolokolova, A., Tal, A.: $AC^0[p]$ lower bounds against MCSP via the coin problem. In: 46th International Colloquium on Automata, Languages, and Programming, (ICALP). LIPIcs, vol. 132, pp. 66:1–66:15. Schloss Dagstuhl - Leibniz-Zentrum fuer Informatik (2019). https://doi.org/10.4230/LIPIcs.ICALP.2019.66

19. Hirahara, S.: Non-black-box worst-case to average-case reductions within NP. In: 59th IEEE Annual Symposium on Foundations of Computer Science (FOCS), pp. 247–258 (2018). https://doi.org/10.1109/FOCS.2018.00032

20. Hirahara, S.: Kolmogorov-randomness is harder than expected (2019). Manuscript

21. Hirahara, S.: Unexpected power of random strings. In: 11th Innovations in Theoretical Computer Science Conference, ITCS. LIPIcs, vol. 151, pp. 41:1–41:13. Schloss Dagstuhl - Leibniz-Zentrum fuer Informatik (2020). https://doi.org/10.4230/LIPIcs.ITCS.2020.41

22. Hirahara, S., Oliveira, I.C., Santhanam, R.: NP-hardness of minimum circuit size problem for OR-AND-MOD circuits. In: 33rd Conference on Computational Complexity, CCC. LIPIcs, vol. 102, pp. 5:1–5:31. Schloss Dagstuhl - Leibniz-Zentrum fuer Informatik (2018). https://doi.org/10.4230/LIPIcs.CCC.2018.5

23. Hirahara, S., Santhanam, R.: On the average-case complexity of MCSP and its variants. In: 32nd Conference on Computational Complexity, CCC. LIPIcs, vol. 79, pp. 7:1–7:20. Schloss Dagstuhl - Leibniz-Zentrum fuer Informatik (2017). https://doi.org/10.4230/LIPIcs.CCC.2017.7

24. Hirahara, S., Watanabe, O.: On nonadaptive reductions to the set of random strings and its dense subsets. In: Electronic Colloquium on Computational Complexity (ECCC), vol. 26, p. 25 (2019)

25. Hitchcock, J.M., Pavan, A.: On the NP-completeness of the minimum circuit size problem. In: Conference on Foundations of Software Technology and Theoretical Computer Science (FST&TCS). LIPIcs, vol. 45, pp. 236–245. Schloss Dagstuhl - Leibniz-Zentrum fuer Informatik (2015). https://doi.org/10.4230/LIPIcs.FSTTCS.2015.236

26. Ilango, R.: Personal communication (2019)

27. Ilango, R.: Approaching MCSP from above and below: Hardness for a conditional variant and $AC^0[p]$. In: 11th Innovations in Theoretical Computer Science Conference, ITCS. LIPIcs, vol. 151, pp. 34:1–34:26. Schloss Dagstuhl - Leibniz-Zentrum fuer Informatik (2020). https://doi.org/10.4230/LIPIcs.ITCS.2020.34

28. Ilango, R., Loff, B., Oliveira, I.C.: NP-hardness of minimizing circuits and communication (2019). Manuscript

29. Impagliazzo, R., Kabanets, V., Volkovich, I.: The power of natural properties as oracles. In: 33rd Conference on Computational Complexity, CCC. LIPIcs, vol. 102, pp. 7:1–7:20. Schloss Dagstuhl - Leibniz-Zentrum fuer Informatik (2018). https://doi.org/10.4230/LIPIcs.CCC.2018.7

30. Kabanets, V., Cai, J.Y.: Circuit minimization problem. In: ACM Symposium on Theory of Computing (STOC), pp. 73–79 (2000). https://doi.org/10.1145/335305.335314

31. Ko, K.: On the notion of infinite pseudorandom sequences. Theor. Comput. Sci. **48**(3), 9–33 (1986). https://doi.org/10.1016/0304-3975(86)90081-2

32. Levin, L.A.: Randomness conservation inequalities; information and independence in mathematical theories. Inf. Control **61**(1), 15–37 (1984). https://doi.org/10.1016/S0019-9958(84)80060-1

33. Li, M., Vitányi, P.M.B.: An Introduction to Kolmogorov Complexity and Its Applications. Texts in Computer Science, 4th edn. Springer (2019). https://doi.org/10.1007/978-3-030-11298-1

34. McKay, D.M., Murray, C.D., Williams, R.R.: Weak lower bounds on resource-bounded compression imply strong separations of complexity classes. In: Proceedings of the 51st Annual ACM SIGACT Symposium on Theory of Computing (STOC), pp. 1215–1225 (2019). https://doi.org/10.1145/3313276.3316396

35. Murray, C., Williams, R.: On the (non) NP-hardness of computing circuit complexity. Theory Comput. **13**(4), 1–22 (2017). https://doi.org/10.4086/toc.2017.v013a004

36. Oliveira, I., Santhanam, R.: Conspiracies between learning algorithms, circuit lower bounds and pseudorandomness. In: 32nd Conference on Computational Complexity, CCC. LIPIcs, vol. 79, pp. 18:1–18:49. Schloss Dagstuhl - Leibniz-Zentrum fuer Informatik (2017). https://doi.org/10.4230/LIPIcs.CCC.2017.18

37. Oliveira, I.C.: Randomness and intractability in Kolmogorov complexity. In: 46th International Colloquium on Automata, Languages, and Programming, (ICALP). LIPIcs, vol. 132, pp. 32:1–32:14. Schloss Dagstuhl - Leibniz-Zentrum fuer Informatik (2019). https://doi.org/10.4230/LIPIcs.ICALP.2019.32

38. Oliveira, I.C., Pich, J., Santhanam, R.: Hardness magnification near state-of-the-art lower bounds. In: 34th Computational Complexity Conference (CCC). LIPIcs, vol. 137, pp. 27:1–27:29. Schloss Dagstuhl - Leibniz-Zentrum fuer Informatik (2019). https://doi.org/10.4230/LIPIcs.CCC.2019.27

39. Oliveira, I.C., Santhanam, R.: Hardness magnification for natural problems. In: 59th IEEE Annual Symposium on Foundations of Computer Science (FOCS), pp. 65–76 (2018). https://doi.org/10.1109/FOCS.2018.00016

40. Pitt, L., Valiant, L.G.: Computational limitations on learning from examples. J. ACM **35**(4), 965–984 (1988). https://doi.org/10.1145/48014.63140

41. Pitt, L., Warmuth, M.K.: The minimum consistent DFA problem cannot be approximated within any polynomial. J. ACM **40**(1), 95–142 (1993). https://doi.org/10.1145/138027.138042

42. Razborov, A., Rudich, S.: Natural proofs. J. Comput. Syst. Sci. **55**, 24–35 (1997). https://doi.org/10.1006/jcss.1997.1494

43. Santhanam, R.: Pseudorandomness and the minimum circuit size problem. In: 11th Innovations in Theoretical Computer Science Conference (ITCS), LIPIcs, vol. 151, pp. 68:1–68:26. Schloss Dagstuhl - Leibniz-Zentrum fuer Informatik (2020). https://doi.org/10.4230/LIPIcs.ITCS.2020.68

44. Santhanam, R.: Why are proof complexity lower bounds hard? In: Symposium on Foundations of Computer Science (FOCS), pp. 1305–1324 (2019)

45. Tal, A.: The bipartite formula complexity of inner-product is quadratic. In: Electronic Colloquium on Computational Complexity (ECCC), vol. 23, p. 181 (2016)

46. Vollmer, H.: Introduction to Circuit Complexity: A Uniform Approach. Springer, New York Inc. (1999). https://doi.org/10.1007/978-3-662-03927-4

Containment and Equivalence of Weighted Automata: Probabilistic and Max-Plus Cases

Laure Daviaud[(✉)]

CitAI, Department of Computer Science, SMCSE, City University of London,
London, UK
laure.daviaud@city.ac.uk

Abstract. This paper surveys some results regarding decision problems for probabilistic and max-plus automata, such as containment and equivalence. Probabilistic and max-plus automata are part of the general family of weighted automata, whose semantics are maps from words to real values. Given two weighted automata, the equivalence problem asks whether their semantics are the same, and the containment problem whether one is point-wise smaller than the other one. These problems have been studied intensively and this paper will review some techniques used to show (un)decidability and state a list of open questions that still remain.

Keywords: Weighted automata · Probabilistic automata · Max-plus automata · Equivalence problem · Containment problem · Decidability

1 Introduction

Weighted automata have been introduced by Schützenberger in 1961 in [37] as a quantitative generalisation of non deterministic finite-state automata. While non deterministic finite automata have a Boolean behaviour (each word is mapped to 0 or 1), weighted automata allow a more fine grained output: each word is mapped to an element in a chosen semiring. This allows for example to map words with real values, modelling probabilities or costs. They have been intensively studied both:

1. in a general setting, i.e. giving frameworks and results that are valid for any semiring,
2. and on particular instances, for example when focusing on the classic semiring $\mathbb{R}$ with the standard addition and product operations.

For any semiring, a weighted automaton can be viewed as a graph with labelled transitions carrying weights, or as a morphism from words to matrices (both definitions are given in Sect. 2). Recently, Alur introduced another equivalent model, closer to the implementation level: the cost register automata [2,3].

A. Leporati et al. (Eds.): LATA 2020, LNCS 12038, pp. 17–32, 2020.
https://doi.org/10.1007/978-3-030-40608-0_2

These have engendered a lot of research works, in particular regarding questions around minimisation. Weighted automata also admit an equivalent logic [14] introduced by Droste and Gastin and while this paper focuses on weighted automata on words, they have also been generalised to other structures such as trees [4,29,38].

Specific instances that have been particularly studied are the probabilistic automata on the standard semiring $\mathbb{R}$ with operations $+$ and $\times$ (the exact definition is given in Sect. 2) [35]; and the max-plus (resp. min-plus) automata on the semiring $\mathbb{R}$ with operations max (resp. min) and $+$ [40].

They have been applied in image compression [25], natural language processing [6,32,33], model-checking of probabilistic systems [30,42], automatic analysis of complexity of programs [9], study of discrete event systems [18], and in the proofs of results in tropical algebra [10] and automata theory [21,39,40].

One of the first natural question which arises when dealing with computational models is the equivalence problem: in our case, this would ask whether two distinct weighted automata map words to the same values? Since probabilistic and max-plus automata compute functions from words to real values, another natural problem is to wonder whether the function computed by a given probabilistic (resp. max-plus) automaton is point-wise smaller than the function computed by another probabilistic (resp. max-plus) automaton. This is called the containment problem. These problems are highly dependant on the semiring under consideration and have originally been tackled using very different techniques for probabilistic and max-plus automata. We will however present one technique that can be used in both cases to show the undecidability of the containment problem for both max-plus and probabilistic automata which are linearly ambiguous.

Another mainstream topic that have been intensively studied is the one of determinisation. Weighted automata are not determinisable in general: there exist for example max-plus automata that do not have an equivalent deterministic one. This question is of particular interest for max-plus automata and is linked to the minimisation of cost register automata [11,13]. Deciding whether a given max-plus automaton is determinisable is still open. This topic is out of the scope of this paper but the interested reader is referred to [17,26,27].

In the rest of this paper, we will explain a way to prove undecidability of the containment problem for probabilistic and max-plus automata and discuss restricted classes as well as approximations to obtain more positive results and decidability in some cases.

2   Weighted Automata

In this section, we start by recalling basic notions used to define weighted automata. The paper should be self-contained but the reader is referred to [36] for a full exposition on the topic.

2.1 Preliminaries

Semiring. Given a set M, a binary operation $\cdot$ on M and an element 1 of M (called neutral element), $(M, \cdot, 1)$ is called a monoid if $\cdot$ is associative and $1 \cdot x = x \cdot 1 = x$ for all $x \in M$. The monoid is said to be commutative if $x \cdot y = y \cdot x$ for all $x, y \in M$.

A semiring $(S, \oplus, \otimes, 0, 1)$ is a set S equipped with two binary operations such that $(S, \oplus, 0)$ is a commutative monoid, $(S, \otimes, 1)$ is a monoid, $0 \otimes x = x \otimes 0 = 0$ and $x \otimes (y \oplus z) = (x \otimes y) \oplus (x \otimes z)$ and $(y \oplus z) \otimes x = (y \otimes x) \oplus (z \otimes x)$ for all $x, y, z \in S$. In the rest of the paper, we will simply use S to denote the semiring $(S, \oplus, \otimes, 0, 1)$. For x in S, we will use the standard notation x^k to denote the product $\underbrace{x \otimes \cdots \otimes x}_{k \text{ times}}$.

Matrices. Given a semiring S, we consider the set of matrices with coefficients in S. Given a matrix M, $M[i][j]$ denotes the coefficient at row i and column j of the matrix. For two matrices M and M', one defines the product $M \cdot M'$ provided the number of columns of M is equal to the number of rows of M' (denoted by N) by:

$$(M \cdot M')[i][j] = \bigoplus_{k=1,\ldots,N} (M[i][k] \otimes M'[k][j])$$

Given a positive integer N, the set of square matrices of dimension $N \times N$ with coefficients in S is denoted by $\mathcal{M}_N(S)$ or simply $\mathcal{M}_N$ when S is clear from context. The set $\mathcal{M}_N$ equipped with the binary operation $\cdot$ is a monoid with neutral element the identity matrix (the matrix with 1 on the diagonal coefficients and 0 everywhere else).

Words. In the rest of the paper, Σ denotes a finite alphabet, Σ^* the set of words on this alphabet, and ε the empty word. For a word w, $|w|$ denotes the length of w.

Notation. Given a finite set Q, $|Q|$ denotes the number of elements in Q.

2.2 Graphical Definition

We give now a first definition of weighted automata.

Definition 1. *A weighted automaton over a semiring S and alphabet Σ is a tuple (Q, Q_I, Q_F, T) where:*

- *Q is a finite set of states,*
- *$Q_I \subseteq Q$ is the set of initial states,*
- *$Q_F \subseteq Q$ is the set of final states,*
- *T is the transition function $Q \times \Sigma \times Q \to S$.*

Given $p, q \in Q$ and $a \in \Sigma$, whenever $T(p, a, q) \neq 0$, we say that (p, a, q) is a transition, $T(p, a, q)$ is its weight and we write:

$$p \xrightarrow{a:T(p,a,q)} q$$

A run on a word $w = w_1 w_2 \ldots w_n$ where for all $i = 1, \ldots, n$, $w_i \in \Sigma$ is a sequence of compatible transitions:

$$q_0 \xrightarrow{w_1:m_1} q_1 \xrightarrow{w_2:m_2} q_2 \xrightarrow{w_3:m_3} \cdots \xrightarrow{w_n:m_n} q_n$$

The weight of a run is the product of the weights of the transitions in the run i.e. $\bigotimes_{i=1}^{n} m_i$. A run is said to be accepting if $q_0 \in Q_I$ and $q_n \in Q_F$. The weight of a word in the automaton is the sum $\oplus$ of the weights of the accepting runs on w, and 0 if there is no such run. By convention, the weight of the empty word is 1 if there exist a state which is both initial and final and 0 otherwise.

Definition 2. *The semantics of a weighted automaton $\mathcal{A}$ over the semiring S and alphabet Σ is the function which maps every word of Σ^* to its weight in S. It is denoted by $[\![\mathcal{A}]\!]$.*

Variants. There exist several alternative definitions for weighted automata. A classic one allows also initial and final weights: each state q is associated with two elements i_q and f_q from S (possibly 0). The weight of a run:

$$q_0 \xrightarrow{w_1:m_1} q_1 \xrightarrow{w_2:m_2} q_2 \xrightarrow{w_3:m_3} \cdots \xrightarrow{w_n:m_n} q_n$$

is then the product $i_{q_0} \otimes m_1 \otimes \cdots \otimes m_n \otimes f_{q_n}$ and the weight of a word w the sum of the weights of the runs on w.

Adding initial and final weights does not increase the expressive power of weighted automata: the set of semantics is the same. The problems we are considering in this paper are also not affected by this: equivalence or containment will be decidable for both variants or for none.

However, these considerations will have to be taken into account when dealing with determinisation issues, but this is not in the scope of this paper.

Example 1. Figure 1 shows a weighted automaton on a semiring S and alphabet $\{a, b, t\}$. It has two initial states q_1 and q_2 and two final states q_3 and q_4. Let w be the word $a^{i_0} b^{j_0} t a^{i_1} b^{j_1} t \cdots t a^{i_k} b^{j_k}$ for some non negative integers $i_0, j_0, \ldots$ There are k accepting runs on w: each accepting run corresponds to read one of the occurrences of t from q_2 to q_3 and has weight $m^{i_\ell} \otimes n^{i_{\ell+1}}$ for some $\ell \in \{0, \ldots, k-1\}$. The weight of w is then:

$$\bigoplus_{\ell \in \{0, \ldots, k-1\}} m^{i_\ell} \otimes n^{i_{\ell+1}}$$

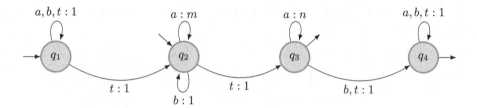

Fig. 1. Weighted automaton

Ambiguity. The notion of ambiguity that applies for finite non deterministic automata applies here too: A weighted automaton is said to be unambiguous is there is at most one accepting run on every word, and finitely ambiguous if there is an integer L such that for all words w, there are at most L accepting runs labelled by w. Finally, a run is polynomially ambiguous if there is a polynomial P such that for all words w, there are at most $P(|w|)$ accepting runs labelled by w, and linearly ambiguous whenever this polynomial is of degree 1.

2.3 Matrix Representation

An equivalent way to see weighted automata is by using a matrix representation.

Definition 3 (equivalent definition). *A weighted automaton over a semiring S and alphabet Σ is a tuple (N, I, F, μ) where N is an integer and:*

- *I is a set of matrices with 1 row and N columns, and coefficients in $\{0, 1\}$,*
- *F is a set of matrices with N rows and 1 column, and coefficients in $\{0, 1\}$,*
- *μ is a map $\Sigma \to \mathcal{M}_N(S)$.*

The semantics of a weighted automaton is a function mapping each word $w = w_1 w_2 \cdots w_n$, where for all i, $w_i \in \Sigma$ to:

$$I \cdot \mu(w_1) \cdot \mu(w_2) \cdots \mu(w_n) \cdot F$$

Note that the later is an element of S. There are easy translations to go from the graphical definitions to the matrix one and conversely:

- starting from (Q, Q_I, Q_F, T), set $N = |Q|$, and denote by $q_1, q_2, \ldots, q_N$ the states in Q. Set I with 1 row and N columns, defined by $I[1][j] = 1$ if $q_j \in Q_I$ and 0 otherwise. Similarly, set F with N rows and 1 column, defined by $F[j][1] = 1$ if $q_j \in Q_F$ and 0 otherwise. Finally, set μ such that for all $a \in \Sigma$, $\mu(a)[i][j] = T(q_i, a, q_j)$. It is easy to check that the semantics of the two weighted automata are the same. In particular, for any word w, $\mu(w)[i][j]$ is the sum of the weights of the runs labelled by w going from q_i to q_j.
- Similarly, starting from (N, I, F, μ), set $Q = \{q_1, q_2, \ldots, q_N\}$, $Q_I = \{q_j \mid I[1][j] = 1\}$, $Q_F = \{q_j \mid F[j][1] = 1\}$ and $T(q_i, a, q_j) = \mu(a)[i][j]$ for all $a \in \Sigma$, $i, j \in \{1, \ldots, N\}$.

Example 2. The weighted automaton from Fig. 1 is represented by the following set of matrices:

$$\mu(a) = \begin{pmatrix} 1 & 0 & 0 & 0 \\ 0 & m & 0 & 0 \\ 0 & 0 & n & 0 \\ 0 & 0 & 0 & 1 \end{pmatrix} \quad \mu(b) = \begin{pmatrix} 1 & 0 & 0 & 0 \\ 0 & 1 & 0 & 0 \\ 0 & 0 & 0 & 1 \\ 0 & 0 & 0 & 1 \end{pmatrix} \quad \mu(t) = \begin{pmatrix} 1 & 1 & 0 & 0 \\ 0 & 0 & 1 & 0 \\ 0 & 0 & 0 & 1 \\ 0 & 0 & 0 & 1 \end{pmatrix}$$

$$I = \begin{pmatrix} 1 & 1 & 0 & 0 \end{pmatrix} \quad F = \begin{pmatrix} 0 \\ 0 \\ 1 \\ 1 \end{pmatrix}$$

2.4   Classic Examples

In the rest of the paper, we will consider two classic examples of weighted automata: max-plus automata and probabilistic automata.

Non Deterministic Finite Automata (or Boolean Automata). Non deterministic finite automata can be seen as weighted automata over the Boolean semiring. They can also be seen as weighted automata in any semiring as follows: for a given Boolean automaton $\mathcal{B}$, and a semiring S, construct the weighted automaton $\mathcal{A}$ by giving weight 1 to transitions in $\mathcal{B}$ (and 0 to non-existing transitions). It is easy to see that for every word w, w is accepted by $\mathcal{B}$ if and only if $[\![\mathcal{A}]\!](w) = 1$ ($[\![\mathcal{A}]\!](w) = 0$ otherwise).

Max-Plus Automata. The semiring $\{\mathbb{R} \cup \{-\infty\}, \max, +, -\infty, 0\}$ is called the max-plus semiring. Max-plus automata are weighted automata over the max-plus semiring. Alternatively, the min-plus semiring is $\{\mathbb{R} \cup \{+\infty\}, \min, +, +\infty, 0\}$ and min-plus automata are weighted automata over this semiring. Given a max-plus automaton $\mathcal{A}$, it is easy to construct a min-plus automaton $\mathcal{B}$ by changing all the weights to their opposite to obtain $[\![\mathcal{A}]\!] = -[\![\mathcal{B}]\!]$. Most of the results later on given for max-plus automata can thus be easily translated for min-plus automata. However, when restricting the domain of the semiring to $\mathbb{N}$, the translation does not work anymore and for the results which are only valid in $\mathbb{N}$, one has to be more careful when translating from max-plus to min-plus and vice-versa.

Probabilistic Automata. Probabilistic automata are weighted automata over the semiring $\{\mathbb{R}, +, \times, 0, 1\}$ with the extra restriction that all the weights on transitions are in $[0, 1]$ and for a given state q and a given letter a of Σ, the weights of the transitions exiting q labelled by a have to sum to 1.

Example 3. Let us consider the weighted automaton given in Fig. 1 and the word w defined in Example 1. For S taken as the max-plus semiring, the weight of w would be:

$$\max_{\ell \in \{0, \dots, k-1\}} (i_\ell m + i_{\ell+1} n)$$

For S taken as the semiring $\{\mathbb{R}, +, \times, 0, 1\}$, the weight of w would be:

$$\sum_{\ell \in \{0,\ldots,k-1\}} m^{i_\ell} n^{i_{\ell+1}}$$

The later is not a probabilistic automaton, as for example there are two transitions labelled by t each of weight 1 exiting q_1.

3 Decision Problems

Many decision problems arise naturally when considering weighted automata. We will consider two of them (and their variants): the equivalence and the containment problems. Generally speaking, the decidability of these problems highly depends on the semiring under consideration, and there is no general results that would work for the whole class of weighted automata. However, we will see that some techniques can be used both for max-plus and for probabilistic automata.

3.1 The Equivalence and Containment Problems

The equivalence and containment problems are stated as follows:

> **Equivalence problem:** Given two weighted automata $\mathcal{A}$ and $\mathcal{B}$ over an alphabet Σ and a semiring S, is it true that $[\![\mathcal{A}]\!] = [\![\mathcal{B}]\!]$?

This problem has been known to be decidable for Boolean automata since the 50's and for probabilistic automata since the 70's. Surprisingly at the time, it was proved to be undecidable for max-plus automata, in the 90's.

> **Containment problem:** Given two weighted automata $\mathcal{A}$ and $\mathcal{B}$ over an alphabet Σ and a semiring S whose domain is equipped with an order $\leq$, is it true that for all $w \in \Sigma^*$, $[\![\mathcal{A}]\!](w) \leq [\![\mathcal{B}]\!](w)$?

This problem is the counterpart of the containment problem for Boolean automata: given two non deterministic finite automata $\mathcal{A}$ and $\mathcal{B}$, is it true that the regular language accepted by $\mathcal{A}$ is a subset of the regular language accepted by $\mathcal{B}$.

Several other problems of the same kind have been investigated: the boundedness problem for min-plus automata, the isolation, emptiness and value 1 problems for probabilistic automata. They will be discussed later on.

3.2 Undecidability of the Containment Problem

The containment problem is undecidable both for max-plus and for probabilistic automata and we will explain here one common idea used in specific proofs of this result in both cases.

Probabilistic Automata. The more specific emptiness problem:

> *Given a probabilistic automaton $\mathcal{A}$ and a constant c, is it true that for all $w \in \Sigma$, $[\![\mathcal{A}]\!](w) < c$?*

was proved to be undecidable by Paz in 1971 [34]. Other similar problems were also proved to be undecidable like the c-threshold problem [5]:

> *Given a probabilistic automaton $\mathcal{A}$ and a constant c, does there exist $\varepsilon > 0$ such that for all words w, $|[\![\mathcal{A}]\!](w) - c| \geq \varepsilon$?*

and the value 1 problem [19]:

> *Given a probabilistic automaton $\mathcal{A}$ and a constant c, for all $\varepsilon > 0$, does there exist a word w such that $[\![\mathcal{A}]\!](w) \geq 1 - \varepsilon$?*

Max-Plus Automata. Regarding max-plus automata, the undecidability of the containment problem was first proved in a seminal paper by Krob [28], by reduction from Hilbert's tenth problem: given a diophantine equation, is there a solution with only integral values?

More recently, a new proof has been given by reduction from the halting problem of two-counter machines [1].

More specifically, the two following problems are already undecidable:

- Given a max-plus automaton $\mathcal{A}$ with weights in $\mathbb{Z}$, is it true that for all words w, $[\![\mathcal{A}]\!](w) \geq 0$?
- Given a max-plus automaton $\mathcal{A}$ with weights in $\mathbb{N}$, is it true that for all words w, $[\![\mathcal{A}]\!](w) \geq |w|$?

Restricted Classes. Given the negative results stated above, restricted classes of weighted automata have been studied to get decidability. For probabilistic automata one can cite hierarchical [7] and leaktight [16] automata, and both for probabilistic and max-plus automata, classes of automata with restricted ambiguity (see Sect. 3.4).

However, even for the classes of linearly ambiguous max-plus automata and linearly ambiguous probabilistic automata the containment problem remains undecidable (it is proved in [12] for probabilistic automata, previous proofs were not attaining linear ambiguity - for max-plus automata, this could have already been deduced from the original proof of Krob). In both cases, one can use the reduction from the halting problem of a two counter machine.

Reduction from the Halting Problem of Two Counter Machines. Two counter machines or Minsky machines have many equivalent definitions. We consider here the following one: A two counter machine is a deterministic finite state machine with two non-negative counters which can be incremented, decremented and checked to be equal to 0. Transitions are of the form $(p, update_c, q)$ where p and q are states of the machine, $i \in \{1, 2\}$ and $update_c$ can be equal to:

- inc_c, meaning that the value of the counter c is incremented,

- dec_c meaning that the value of the counter c is decremented and that the transition can only be taken if the value of the counter c is not 0,
- $check_c$ meaning that the transition can only be taken if the value of the counter c is 0.

Determinism is guaranteed if for every state p, every two distinct transitions exiting from p are labelled by dec_c and $check_c$ respectively for $c = 1$ or $c = 2$. A run of the machine starts from an initial state, follows the unique transitions that can be taken and halts when a final state is reached. If the unique run halts, the machine is said to halt.

The halting problem, i.e. given a two-counter machine, does the unique run halts? Is undecidable [31].

Given a two counter machine $\mathcal{M}$, let $\Sigma_{\mathcal{M}}$ be the alphabet containing letters a, b and one letter for each transition of the two-counter machine. The idea is to encode the value of the first counter into the size of blocks of consecutive occurrences of the letter a and the value of the second counter into the size of blocks of consecutive occurrences of the letter b. More precisely, we say that a word on $\Sigma_{\mathcal{M}}$ encodes a halting run of the machine if it is of the form $a^{i_0} b^{j_0} t_1 a^{i_1} b^{j_1} t_2 \cdots t_k a^{i_k} b^{j_k}$ where:

1. $t_1, t_2, \ldots, t_k$ are transitions of the machine, such that the sequence forms a valid run with compatible states,
2. $i_0 = 0$, $j_0 = 0$, t_1 starts in the initial state,
3. t_k ends in a final state,
4. for all t_ℓ, if $t_\ell = (p, update_c, q)$, then $(i_{\ell-1}, i_\ell)$ and $(j_{\ell-1}, j_\ell)$ have to be compatible with $update_c$. For example, if $update_c = inc_1$, then we should have $i_\ell = i_{\ell-1} + 1$ and $j_{\ell-1} = j_\ell$. If $update_c = dec_2$ then we should have $i_\ell = i_{\ell-1}$, $j_{\ell-1} \neq 0$ and $j_\ell = j_{\ell-1} - 1$. And similarly for the other cases.

Clearly, a two-counter machine halts if and only if there exist a halting word on $\Sigma_{\mathcal{M}}$. In the case of max-plus automata and probabilistic automata, one can prove that:

Theorem 1 ([1]). *Given a two-counter machine, one can construct a linearly ambiguous max-plus automaton $\mathcal{A}$ such that a word $w \in \Sigma_{\mathcal{M}}$ encodes a halting run if and only if $[\![\mathcal{A}]\!](w) < 0$.*

Theorem 2 ([12]). *Given a two-counter machine, one can construct a linearly ambiguous probabilistic automaton $\mathcal{A}$ such that a word $w \in \Sigma_{\mathcal{M}}$ encodes a halting run if and only if $[\![\mathcal{A}]\!](w) > \frac{1}{2}$.*

This later theorem is also true for all the variants: $\geq, <, \leq$.

To prove the first result, one needs to construct a max-plus automaton which will give high value (greater than 0) to any word that does not encode a halting run. Or, in other words, a high value to any word that does not satisfy at least one of the conditions 1–4 above. This is done by taking the union of several max-plus automata, each giving high value to words not fulfilling one of the conditions. Conditions 1–3 are regular conditions, and such a construction will be straightforward. Conditions 4 will be dealt with by a similar automaton as the one given in Fig. 1.

For probabilistic automata, the idea is similar. However, the construction of an automaton giving high value (greater than $\frac{1}{2}$) to any word encoding a halting run, while ensuring the probabilistic condition is much more intricate than in the max-plus case.

Remark 1. By considering a universal two-counter machine, which encodes initially any two-counter machine in the value of the first counter, these two results prove that the containment problem is also undecidable on classes of max-plus (resp. probabilistic) automata with a bounded number of states.

3.3 Equivalence

For max-plus automata, it is easy to see that the equivalence problem is as difficult as the containment problem, and thus undecidable. This is due to the use of the operation max in the semiring. Indeed, given two automata $\mathcal{A}$ and $\mathcal{B}$, one has that $[\![\mathcal{A}]\!] \leq [\![\mathcal{B}]\!]$ if and only if $[\![\mathcal{B}]\!] = \max([\![\mathcal{A}]\!], [\![\mathcal{B}]\!])$. The later function is the semantics of a max-plus automaton constructible from $\mathcal{A}$ and $\mathcal{B}$ (just taking the union). These problems are also undecidable even when restricting the weights in $\mathbb{N}$.

This is a very different situation for probabilistic automata, as the equivalence is decidable (this is generally true when the domain of the semiring is a field). Tzeng gave an algorithm in PTIME to solve this problem [41].

3.4 Decidability: Restricting the Ambiguity

On the positive side, containment and equivalence are decidable when restricting sufficiently the ambiguity of the automaton:

Theorem 3 ([24,43]). *The containment and equivalence problems are decidable on the class of finitely ambiguous max-plus automata.*

For probabilistic automata, the situation is more complex and the decidability of the containment problem on the class of finitely ambiguous probabilistic automata is open. A restricted case is shown to be decidable in [12], and the proof of this result is mathematically difficult.

Theorem 4 ([12]). *If Schanuel's conjecture holds then the containment problem is decidable for the class of finitely ambiguous probabilistic automata, provided that at least one of the input automata is unambiguous.*

4 Approximations

Approximations of the containment and equivalence problems have also been studied, in the hope to get decidability, in particular considering algorithms that do not always output the correct result.

4.1 Probabilistic Case

Unfortunately, in the probabilistic case, even by allowing quite a lot of flexibility, undecidability persists. Fijalkow gives in [15] a result which subsumes all the results of undecidability for the problems mentioned above (emptiness, value 1 and isolation).

Theorem 5 ([15]). *There exists no algorithm such that: given a probabilistic automaton $\mathcal{A}$,*

- *if $sup_{w \in \Sigma^*} [\![\mathcal{A}]\!](w) = 1$ then the algorithm outputs "Yes",*
- *if $sup_{w \in \Sigma^*} [\![\mathcal{A}]\!](w) \leq \frac{1}{2}$, then the algorithm outputs "No".*

4.2 Approximating Max-Plus and Min-Plus Automata

For max-plus and min-plus automata, the situation is slightly different and one can obtain good approximations of their semantics provided the weights are restricted to be non-negative.

Since we are now considering only non-negative weights, it is unclear whether the results that are stated below for max-plus automata are also valid for min-plus automata and vice-versa.

Approximate Comparison. The following result shows that an approximation of the containment problem can be decided for min-plus automata. Given two min-plus automata with weights in $\mathbb{N}$, one can compare their semantics up to any small multiplicative error.

Theorem 6 ([8]). *There exist an algorithm which, given $\varepsilon > 0$, given two min-plus automata $\mathcal{A}$ and $\mathcal{B}$ with weights in $\mathbb{N}$, has the following behaviour:*

- *if $[\![\mathcal{A}]\!] \leq [\![\mathcal{B}]\!]$ then the algorithm outputs "Yes",*
- *if there is a word w such that $[\![\mathcal{A}]\!](w) \geq (1 + \varepsilon)[\![\mathcal{B}]\!](w)$, then the algorithm outputs "No".*

Note that in the remaining cases, the algorithm can answer "Yes" or "No". It is unclear whether a similar result holds for max-plus automata.

Boundedness and Asymptotic Descriptions. The semantics of a max-plus or min-plus automaton $\mathcal{A}$ with weights in $\mathbb{N}$ can be represented as follows (let us suppose that no word has weight $-\infty$ or $+\infty$ - it would be easy to reduce the problems to this case).

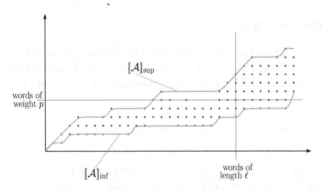

We are interested in describing the functions $\mathcal{A}_{\mathrm{sup}}$ and $\mathcal{A}_{\mathrm{inf}}$ defined by:

$$\mathcal{A}_{\mathrm{sup}} : \mathbb{N} \to \mathbb{N} \qquad\qquad \mathcal{A}_{\mathrm{inf}} : \mathbb{N} \to \mathbb{N}$$
$$n \mapsto \sup_{w \text{ s.t } |w|=n} [\![\mathcal{A}]\!](w) \qquad\qquad n \mapsto \inf_{w \text{ s.t } |w|=n} [\![\mathcal{A}]\!](w)$$

The function $\mathcal{A}_{\mathrm{sup}}$ is easy to described for max-plus automata, and similarly the function $\mathcal{A}_{\mathrm{inf}}$ is easy to describe for min-plus automata. However, the other way around is much more difficult.

The boundedness problem asks whether $\mathcal{A}_{\mathrm{sup}}$ is bounded for $\mathcal{A}$ a min-plus automaton. This problem was proved to be decidable by Hashiguchi is 1982 [20,22,23].

Theorem 7 ([20]). *The boundedness problem is decidable for min-plus automata with weights in* $\mathbb{N}$.

The function $\mathcal{A}_{\mathrm{inf}}$ can also be described for max-plus automata, and it was proved that this function is asymptotically equivalent to n^α for some rational α in $[0,1]$. Moreover, all the rationals α in $[0,1]$ can be attained by some max-plus automata.

Theorem 8 ([9]). *There exist an algorithm which, given a max-plus automaton $\mathcal{A}$ with weights in $\mathbb{N}$, such that no word is mapped to $-\infty$, computes the value $\alpha \in \{\beta \in \mathbb{Q} \; : \; \beta \in [0,1]\}$ such that: $\mathcal{A}_{\mathrm{inf}} = \Theta(n^\alpha)$.*

This result was applied in the automatic analysis of complexity of programs.

All the results given in this section were proved using the forest factorisation theorem and the matrix representation given in Sect. 2.

5   Conclusion

The containment and equivalence problems have been studied intensively for probabilistic and max-plus automata. Though many open questions remain. First, cost register automata gives an alternative model for weighted automata. Containment and equivalence could be studied on restricted classes of this model.

For probabilistic automata, the (un)decidability of the containment problem over the class of finitely ambiguous automata is unknown. For max-plus and min-plus automata, approximations should be generalised and it is unclear if the ones that are decidable for max-plus automata are also decidable for min-plus automata and vice-versa. Finally, generally speaking, complexity issues could be investigated.

References

1. Almagor, S., Boker, U., Kupferman, O.: What's decidable about weighted automata? In: Bultan, T., Hsiung, P.-A. (eds.) ATVA 2011. LNCS, vol. 6996, pp. 482–491. Springer, Heidelberg (2011). https://doi.org/10.1007/978-3-642-24372-1_37

2. Alur, R., D'Antoni, L., Deshmukh, J.V., Raghothaman, M., Yuan, Y.: Regular functions and cost register automata. In: 28th Annual ACM/IEEE Symposium on Logic in Computer Science, LICS 2013, New Orleans, LA, USA, 25–28 June 2013, pp. 13–22. IEEE Computer Society (2013). https://doi.org/10.1109/LICS.2013.65

3. Alur, R., Raghothaman, M.: Decision problems for additive regular functions. CoRR abs/1304.7029 (2013). http://arxiv.org/abs/1304.7029

4. Berstel, J., Reutenauer, C.: Recognizable formal power series on trees. Theor. Comput. Sci. **18**, 115–148 (1982). https://doi.org/10.1016/0304-3975(82)90019-6

5. Bertoni, A., Mauri, G., Torelli, M.: Some recursively unsolvable problems relating to isolated cutpoints in probabilistic automata. In: Salomaa, A., Steinby, M. (eds.) ICALP 1977. LNCS, vol. 52, pp. 87–94. Springer, Heidelberg (1977). https://doi.org/10.1007/3-540-08342-1_7

6. Buchsbaum, A.L., Giancarlo, R., Westbrook, J.R.: On the determinization of weighted finite automata. SIAM J. Comput. **30**(5), 1502–1531 (2000). https://doi.org/10.1137/S0097539798346676

7. Chadha, R., Sistla, A.P., Viswanathan, M., Ben, Y.: Decidable and expressive classes of probabilistic automata. In: Pitts, A. (ed.) FoSSaCS 2015. LNCS, vol. 9034, pp. 200–214. Springer, Heidelberg (2015). https://doi.org/10.1007/978-3-662-46678-0_13

8. Colcombet, T., Daviaud, L.: Approximate comparison of distance automata. In: Portier, N., Wilke, T. (eds.) 30th International Symposium on Theoretical Aspects of Computer Science, STACS 2013, Kiel, Germany, 27 February–2 March 2013, vol. 20, pp. 574–585. LIPIcs, Schloss Dagstuhl - Leibniz-Zentrum fuer Informatik (2013). https://doi.org/10.4230/LIPIcs.STACS.2013.574

9. Colcombet, T., Daviaud, L., Zuleger, F.: Size-change abstraction and max-plus automata. In: Csuhaj-Varjú, E., Dietzfelbinger, M., Ésik, Z. (eds.) MFCS 2014. LNCS, vol. 8634, pp. 208–219. Springer, Heidelberg (2014). https://doi.org/10.1007/978-3-662-44522-8_18

10. Daviaud, L., Guillon, P., Merlet, G.: Comparison of max-plus automata and joint spectral radius of tropical matrices. In: Larsen, K.G., Bodlaender, H.L., Raskin, J. (eds.) 42nd International Symposium on Mathematical Foundations of Computer Science, MFCS 2017, Aalborg, Denmark, 21–25 August 2017, vol. 83, pp. 19:1–19:14. LIPIcs, Schloss Dagstuhl - Leibniz-Zentrum fuer Informatik (2017). https://doi.org/10.4230/LIPIcs.MFCS.2017.19

11. Daviaud, L., Jecker, I., Reynier, P.-A., Villevalois, D.: Degree of sequentiality of weighted automata. In: Esparza, J., Murawski, A.S. (eds.) FoSSaCS 2017. LNCS, vol. 10203, pp. 215–230. Springer, Heidelberg (2017). https://doi.org/10.1007/978-3-662-54458-7_13

12. Daviaud, L., Jurdzinski, M., Lazic, R., Mazowiecki, F., Pérez, G.A., Worrell, J.: When is containment decidable for probabilistic automata? In: Chatzigiannakis, I., Kaklamanis, C., Marx, D., Sannella, D. (eds.) 45th International Colloquium on Automata, Languages, and Programming, ICALP 2018, 9–13 July 2018, Prague, Czech Republic, vol. 107, pp. 121:1–121:14. LIPIcs, Schloss Dagstuhl - Leibniz-Zentrum fuer Informatik (2018). https://doi.org/10.4230/LIPIcs.ICALP.2018.121

13. Daviaud, L., Reynier, P., Talbot, J.: A generalised twinning property for minimisation of cost register automata. In: Grohe, M., Koskinen, E., Shankar, N. (eds.) Proceedings of the 31st Annual ACM/IEEE Symposium on Logic in Computer Science, LICS 2016, 5–8 July 2016, New York, NY, USA, pp. 857–866. ACM (2016). https://doi.org/10.1145/2933575.2934549

14. Droste, M., Gastin, P.: Weighted automata and weighted logics. Theor. Comput. Sci. **380**(1–2), 69–86 (2007). https://doi.org/10.1016/j.tcs.2007.02.055

15. Fijalkow, N.: Undecidability results for probabilistic automata. SIGLOG News **4**(4), 10–17 (2017). https://dl.acm.org/citation.cfm?id=3157833

16. Fijalkow, N., Gimbert, H., Kelmendi, E., Oualhadj, Y.: Deciding the value 1 problem for probabilistic leaktight automata. Logical Methods Comput. Sci. **11**(2) (2015). https://doi.org/10.2168/LMCS-11(2:12)2015

17. Filiot, E., Jecker, I., Lhote, N., Pérez, G.A., Raskin, J.: On delay and regret determinization of max-plus automata. In: 32nd Annual ACM/IEEE Symposium on Logic in Computer Science, LICS 2017, Reykjavik, Iceland, 20–23 June 2017, pp. 1–12. IEEE Computer Society (2017). https://doi.org/10.1109/LICS.2017.8005096

18. Gaubert, S., Mairesse, J.: Modeling and analysis of timed petri nets using heaps of pieces. IEEE Trans. Automat. Contr. **44**(4), 683–697 (1999). https://doi.org/10.1109/9.754807

19. Gimbert, H., Oualhadj, Y.: Probabilistic automata on finite words: decidable and undecidable problems. In: Abramsky, S., Gavoille, C., Kirchner, C., Meyer auf der Heide, F., Spirakis, P.G. (eds.) ICALP 2010. LNCS, vol. 6199, pp. 527–538. Springer, Heidelberg (2010). https://doi.org/10.1007/978-3-642-14162-1_44

20. Hashiguchi, K.: Limitedness theorem on finite automata with distance functions. J. Comput. Syst. Sci. **24**(2), 233–244 (1982). https://doi.org/10.1016/0022-0000(82)90051-4

21. Hashiguchi, K.: Algorithms for determining relative star height and starheight. Inf. Comput. **78**(2), 124–169 (1988). https://doi.org/10.1016/0890-5401(88)90033-8

22. Hashiguchi, K.: Improved limitedness theorems on finite automata with distance functions. Theor. Comput. Sci. **72**(1), 27–38 (1990). https://doi.org/10.1016/0304-3975(90)90044-I

23. Hashiguchi, K.: New upper bounds to the limitedness of distance automata. In: Meyer, F., Monien, B. (eds.) ICALP 1996. LNCS, vol. 1099, pp. 324–335. Springer, Heidelberg (1996). https://doi.org/10.1007/3-540-61440-0_139

24. Hashiguchi, K., Ishiguro, K., Jimbo, S.: Decidability of the equivalence problem for finitely ambiguous finance automata. IJAC **12**(3), 445 (2002). https://doi.org/10.1142/S0218196702000845

25. Ii, K.C., Kari, J.: Image compression using weighted finite automata. Comput. Graph. **17**(3), 305–313 (1993). https://doi.org/10.1016/0097-8493(93)90079-0

26. Kirsten, D., Lombardy, S.: Deciding unambiguity and sequentiality of polynomially ambiguous min-plus automata. In: Albers, S., Marion, J. (eds.) 26th International Symposium on Theoretical Aspects of Computer Science, Proceedings, STACS 2009, Freiburg, Germany, 26–28 February 2009, vol. 3, pp. 589–600. LIPIcs, Schloss Dagstuhl - Leibniz-Zentrum fuer Informatik, Germany (2009). https://doi.org/10. 4230/LIPIcs.STACS.2009.1850

27. Klimann, I., Lombardy, S., Mairesse, J., Prieur, C.: Deciding unambiguity and sequentiality from a finitely ambiguous max-plus automaton. Theor. Comput. Sci. **327**(3), 349–373 (2004). https://doi.org/10.1016/j.tcs.2004.02.049

28. Krob, D.: The equality problem for rational series with multiplicities in the tropical semiring is undecidable. In: Kuich, W. (ed.) ICALP 1992. LNCS, vol. 623, pp. 101–112. Springer, Heidelberg (1992). https://doi.org/10.1007/3-540-55719-9_67

29. Kuich, W.: Formal power series over trees. In: Bozapalidis, S. (ed.) Proceedings of the 3rd International Conference Developments in Language Theory, DLT 1997, Thessaloniki, Greece, 20–23 July 1997, pp. 61–101. Aristotle University of Thessaloniki (1997)

30. Kwiatkowska, M., Norman, G., Parker, D., Qu, H.: Assume-guarantee verification for probabilistic systems. In: Esparza, J., Majumdar, R. (eds.) TACAS 2010. LNCS, vol. 6015, pp. 23–37. Springer, Heidelberg (2010). https://doi.org/10.1007/978-3-642-12002-2_3

31. Minsky, M.L.: Computation: Finite and Infinite Machines. Prentice-Hall Inc., Englewood Cliffs (1967). Prentice-Hall Series in Automatic Computation

32. Mohri, M.: Finite-state transducers in language and speech processing. Comput. Linguist. **23**(2), 269–311 (1997)

33. Mohri, M., Pereira, F., Riley, M.: Weighted finite-state transducers in speech recognition. Comput. Speech Lang. **16**(1), 69–88 (2002). https://doi.org/10.1006/csla. 2001.0184

34. Paz, A.: Introduction to Probabilistic Automata (Computer Science and Applied Mathematics). Academic Press Inc., Cambridge (1971)

35. Rabin, M.O.: Probabilistic automata. Inf. Control **6**(3), 230–245 (1963). https:// doi.org/10.1016/S0019-9958(63)90290-0

36. Sakarovitch, J.: Elements of Automata Theory. Cambridge University Press, Cambridge (2009). http://www.cambridge.org/uk/catalogue/catalogue.asp?isbn= 9780521844253

37. Schützenberger, M.P.: On the definition of a family of automata. Inf. Control **4**(2–3), 245–270 (1961). https://doi.org/10.1016/S0019-9958(61)80020-X

38. Seidl, H.: Finite tree automata with cost functions. Theor. Comput. Sci. **126**(1), 113–142 (1994). https://doi.org/10.1016/0304-3975(94)90271-2

39. Simon, I.: Limited subsets of a free monoid. In: 19th Annual Symposium on Foundations of Computer Science, Ann Arbor, Michigan, USA, 16–18 October 1978, pp. 143–150. IEEE Computer Society (1978). https://doi.org/10.1109/SFCS.1978.21

40. Simon, I.: Recognizable sets with multiplicities in the tropical semiring. In: Chytil, M.P., Koubek, V., Janiga, L. (eds.) MFCS 1988. LNCS, vol. 324, pp. 107–120. Springer, Heidelberg (1988). https://doi.org/10.1007/BFb0017135

41. Tzeng, W.: A polynomial-time algorithm for the equivalence of probabilistic automata. SIAM J. Comput. **21**(2), 216–227 (1992). https://doi.org/10.1137/ 0221017

42. Vardi, M.Y.: Automatic verification of probabilistic concurrent finite-state programs. In: 26th Annual Symposium on Foundations of Computer Science, Portland, Oregon, USA, 21–23 October 1985, pp. 327–338. IEEE Computer Society (1985). https://doi.org/10.1109/SFCS.1985.12
43. Weber, A.: Finite-valued distance automata. Theor. Comput. Sci. **134**(1), 225–251 (1994). https://doi.org/10.1016/0304-3975(94)90287-9

Approaching Arithmetic Theories with Finite-State Automata

Christoph Haase[✉][iD]

University College London, London, UK
`c.haase@ucl.ac.uk`

Abstract. The automata-theoretic approach provides an elegant method for deciding linear arithmetic theories. This approach has recently been instrumental for settling long-standing open problems about the complexity of deciding the existential fragments of Büchi arithmetic and linear arithmetic over p-adic fields. In this article, which accompanies an invited talk, we give a high-level exposition of the NP upper bound for existential Büchi arithmetic, obtain some derived results, and further discuss some open problems.

Keywords: Presburger arithmetic · Büchi arithmetic · Reachability · Automatic structures

1 Introduction

Finite-state automata over finite and infinite words provide an elegant method for deciding linear arithmetic theories such as Presburger arithmetic or linear real arithmetic. Automata-based decision procedures for arithmetic theories have also been of remarkable practical use and have been implemented in tools such as LASH [16] or TaPAS [10]. However, understanding the algorithmic properties of automata-based decision procedures turned out to be surprisingly difficult and tedious, see e.g. [3,6,9,19]. It took, for instance, 50 years to show that Büchi's seminal approach for deciding Presburger arithmetic using finite-state automata runs in triply-exponential time and thus matches the upper bound of quantifier-elimination algorithms [5,6]. Given this history, it is not surprising that, until recently, the author was of the opinion that automata should better be avoided when attempting to prove complexity upper bounds for arithmetic theories.

The author's opinion drastically changed when appealing to automata-based approaches recently allowed for settling long-standing open problems about the

This work is part of a project that has received funding from the European Research Council (ERC) under the European Union's Horizon 2020 research and innovation programme (Grant agreement No. 852769, ARiAT).

A. Leporati et al. (Eds.): LATA 2020, LNCS 12038, pp. 33–43, 2020.
https://doi.org/10.1007/978-3-030-40608-0_3

complexity of the existential fragments of Büchi arithmetic and linear arithmetic over p-adic fields, which were both shown NP-complete [8]. The NP upper bounds are the non-trivial part in those results, since, unlike, for instance, in existential Presburger arithmetic, the encoding of smallest solutions can grow super-polynomially. The key result underlying both NP upper bounds is that given two states of a finite-state automaton encoding the set of solutions of a system of linear Diophantine equations, one can decide whether one state reaches the other in NP in the size of the encoding of the system (and without explicitly constructing the automaton).

This article gives a high-level yet sufficiently detailed outline of how the NP upper bound for existential Büchi arithmetic can be obtained. We subsequently show how the techniques used for the NP upper bound can be applied in order to show decidability and complexity results for an extension of Presburger arithmetic with valuation constraints. Those results are somewhat implicit in [8] but seem worthwhile being explicated in written. We conclude with some observations and discussion of open problems.

2   Preliminaries

We denote by $\mathbb{R}$ the real numbers, by $\mathbb{R}_+$ the non-negative reals, by $\mathbb{Q}$ the rational numbers, by $\mathbb{Z}$ the integers, by $\mathbb{N}$ the non-negative integers, and by $\mathbb{N}_+$ the positive integers. For integers $a < b$, we write $[a, b]$ for the set $\{a, a+1, \ldots, b\}$. All numbers in this article are assumed to be encoded in binary. Given a matrix $\mathbf{A} \in \mathbb{Z}^{m \times n}$ with components $a_{ij} \in \mathbb{Z}$, $1 \leq i \leq m$, $1 \leq j \leq n$, the $(1, \infty)$-norm of $\mathbf{A}$ is $\|\mathbf{A}\|_{1,\infty} := \max_{i=1}^{m} \sum_{j=1}^{n} |a_{ij}|$. For $v \in \mathbb{R}^n$, we just write $\|v\|_\infty$.

2.1   Büchi Arithmetic

Throughout this article, let $p \geq 2$ be a base. Recall that Presburger arithmetic is the first-order theory of the structure $\langle \mathbb{N}, 0, 1, + \rangle$. Büchi arithmetic is the first-order theory of the structure $\langle \mathbb{N}, 0, 1, +, V_p \rangle$ obtained from endowing Presburger arithmetic with a functional binary predicate $V_p \subseteq \mathbb{N} \times \mathbb{N}$ such that $V_p(x, u)$ evaluates to true if and only if u is the largest power of p dividing x without remainder. This definition leaves the case $x = 0$ ambiguous. A sensible approach would be to introduce a special value ∞ and to assert $V_p(0, \infty)$ to hold, many authors choose to assert $V_p(0, 1)$, see e.g. [4]. However, the particular choice has no impact on the sets of naturals definable in Büchi arithmetic.

Atomic formulas of Büchi arithmetic are either linear equations $a \cdot x = c$ or Büchi predicates $V_p(x, u)$. Note that the negation of $a \cdot x = c$ is equivalent to $a \cdot x < c \vee a \cdot x > c$. Since we interpret variables over the non-negative integers, we have $a \cdot x > c \equiv \exists y \, a \cdot x - y = c + 1$. Consequently, we can, with no loss of generality, assume that negation symbols only occur in front of V_p predicates. Now if we consider a negated literal $\neg V_p(x, u)$, we have that $\neg V_p(x, u)$ evaluates to true if and only if either

(i) u is a power of p but not the largest power of p dividing x; or

(ii) u is not a power of p.

The case (i) can easily be dealt with, as it is definable by

$$\exists v\, V_p(u, u) \wedge V_p(x, v) \wedge \neg(u = v)$$

Moreover, $\neg V_p(u, u)$ asserts that u is not a power of p. Thus, we may, without loss of generality, assume that quantifier-free formulas of Büchi arithmetic are positive Boolean combinations of atomic formulas $\boldsymbol{a} \cdot \boldsymbol{x} = c$, $V_p(x, u)$ and $V_p(u, u)$.

2.2   Finite-State Automata and p-automata

It is well known that Büchi arithmetic can elegantly be decided using finite-state automata, see [2] for a detailed overview over this approach. In this section, we give a generic definition of deterministic automata and then define p-automata which are used for deciding Büchi arithmetic.

Definition 1. *A* deterministic automaton *is a tuple* $A = (Q, \Sigma, \delta, q_0, F)$, *where*

- Q *is a set of* states,
- Σ *is a finite* alphabet,
- $\delta \colon Q \times \Sigma \to Q \cup \{\bot\}$, *where* $\bot \notin Q$, *is the* transition function,
- $q_0 \in Q$ *is the* initial state, *and*
- $F \subseteq Q$ *is the set of* final states.

Note that this definition allows automata to have infinitely many states and to have partially defined transition functions (due to the presence of $\bot$ in the codomain of δ).

For states $q, r \in Q$ and $u \in \Sigma$, we write $q \xrightarrow{u} r$ if $\delta(q, u) = r$, and extend $\to$ inductively to finite words such that for $w \in \Sigma^*$ and $u \in \Sigma$, $q \xrightarrow{w \cdot u} r$ if there is $s \in Q$ such that $q \xrightarrow{w} s \xrightarrow{u} r$. Whenever $q \xrightarrow{w} r$, we say that A *has a run on w from q to r*. We write $q \xrightarrow{*} r$ if there is some $w \in \Sigma^*$ such that $q \xrightarrow{w} r$.

A *finite-state automaton* A is a deterministic automaton with a finite set of states that accepts finite words. The *language of A* is defined as

$$L(A) \overset{\text{def}}{=} \{w \in \Sigma^* : q_0 \xrightarrow{w} q_f, q_f \in F\}.$$

We now introduce p-automata, which are deterministic automata whose language encodes a set of non-negative integers in base p. Furthermore, we recall the construction of the key gadget underlying the automata-based decision procedures for Büchi arithmetic which provides a representation of the set of non-negative integer solutions of a system of linear equations as the language of a finite-state p-automaton.

Formally, a *p-automaton* is a deterministic automaton over an alphabet $\Sigma_p^n := \{0, 1, \ldots, p-1\}^n$ for some nonnegative integer n. A finite word over the alphabet Σ_p^n can naturally be seen as encoding an n-tuple of nonnegative integers in base p. There are two possible encodings: least significant digit first and most-significant digit first. We only consider the latter *msd-first encoding*, in which the most significant digit appears on the left. Formally, given a word $w = \boldsymbol{u}_0 \cdots \boldsymbol{u}_k \in (\Sigma_p^n)^*$, we define $[\![w]\!] \in \mathbb{N}^n$

$$[\![w]\!] := \sum_{j=0}^{k} p^{k-j} \cdot \boldsymbol{u}_j .$$

Note that for $w = \varepsilon$, the empty word, we have $[\![w]\!] = \boldsymbol{0}$.

A system S of *linear Diophantine equations* has the form $S \colon \mathbf{A} \cdot \boldsymbol{x} = \boldsymbol{c}$, where $\mathbf{A}$ is an $m \times n$ matrix with integer coefficients, $\boldsymbol{c} \in \mathbb{Z}^m$, and $\boldsymbol{x} = (x_1, \ldots, x_n)^\top$ is a vector of variables taking values in the nonnegative integers. We write $[\![S]\!] := \{\boldsymbol{u} \in \mathbb{N}^n : \mathbf{A} \cdot \boldsymbol{u} = \boldsymbol{c}\}$ for the set of all nonnegative integer solutions of S. We denote by $\langle S \rangle$ the size of the encoding of S, i.e., the number of symbols required to represent S assuming binary encoding of all numbers.

Following Wolper and Boigelot [19], we define a p-automaton whose language is the msd-first encoding all nonnegative integer solutions of systems of linear equations.

Definition 2. *Let $S \colon \mathbf{A} \cdot \boldsymbol{x} = \boldsymbol{c}$ be a system of linear equations with integer coefficients such that $\mathbf{A}$ has dimension $m \times n$. Corresponding to S, we define a p-automaton $A(S) := (Q, \Sigma_p^n, \delta, \boldsymbol{q}_0, F)$ such that*

- $Q = \mathbb{Z}^m$,
- $\delta(\boldsymbol{q}, \boldsymbol{u}) = p \cdot \boldsymbol{q} + \mathbf{A} \cdot \boldsymbol{u}$ *for all $\boldsymbol{q} \in Q$ and $\boldsymbol{u} \in \Sigma_p^n$,*
- $\boldsymbol{q}_0 = \boldsymbol{0}$, *and*
- $F = \{\boldsymbol{c}\}$.

Although the automaton $A(S)$ has infinitely many states, it defines a regular language since there are only finitely many *live states*, i.e., states that can reach the set F of accepting states. The reason is that no state $\boldsymbol{q} \in Q$ such that $\|\boldsymbol{q}\|_\infty > \|\mathbf{A}\|_{1,\infty}$ and $\|\boldsymbol{q}\|_\infty > \|\boldsymbol{c}\|_\infty$ can reach an accepting state [1,8], and hence Q can be restricted to a finite number of states. A rough upper bound on the number $\#Q$ of states of $A(S)$ is

$$\#Q \le 2^m \cdot \max(\|\mathbf{A}\|_{1,\infty}, \|\boldsymbol{c}\|_\infty)^m , \tag{1}$$

where m is the number of equations in the system S [8,19].

A key reachability property of the automaton $A(S)$ is the following: Let $\boldsymbol{q}, \boldsymbol{r} \in \mathbb{Z}^m$ be states of $A(S)$. Then for all $k \in \mathbb{N}$ and words $w \in (\Sigma_p^n)^k$ we have

$$\boldsymbol{q} \xrightarrow{w} \boldsymbol{r} \iff \boldsymbol{r} = p^k \cdot \boldsymbol{q} + \mathbf{A}\,[\![w]\!] \tag{2}$$

From this characterization, it follows that the language of $A(S)$ is an msd-first encoding of the set of solutions of the system $\mathbf{A} \cdot \boldsymbol{x} = \boldsymbol{c}$. Indeed, choosing $\boldsymbol{q}$ as $\boldsymbol{0}$ and the final state $\boldsymbol{c}$ as $\boldsymbol{r}$, we have that $\boldsymbol{0} \xrightarrow{w} \boldsymbol{c}$ if and only if $\mathbf{A} \cdot [\![w]\!]_m = \boldsymbol{c}$.

If we wish to emphasize the underlying system S of linear Diophantine equations of a p-automaton $A(S)$ we annotate the transition relation with the subscript S and, e.g., write $\boldsymbol{q} \xrightarrow{*}_S \boldsymbol{r}$.

2.3   Semi-linear Sets

Given a *base vector* $b \in \mathbb{N}^n$ and a finite set of period vectors $P = \{p_1, \ldots, p_m\} \subseteq \mathbb{N}^n$, define

$$L(b, P) := \left\{ b + \sum_{i=1}^{m} \lambda_i \cdot p_i : \lambda_i \in \mathbb{N} \right\}.$$

We call $L(b, P)$ a *linear set* and we say that a subset of $\mathbb{N}^n$ is *semi-linear* if it can be written as a finite union of linear sets. It is well-known that the set of nonnegative integer solutions of a system of linear Diophantine equations is a semi-linear set [7]. Also note that a linear set is definable by a formula of existential Presburger arithmetic of linear size.

A special subclass of semi-linear sets are ultimately periodic sets, which are an equivalent presentation of semi-linear sets in dimension one. A set $M \subseteq \mathbb{N}$ is *ultimately periodic* if there is a threshold $t \in \mathbb{N}$ and a period $\ell \in \mathbb{N}$ such that for all $a, b \in \mathbb{N}$ with $a, b \geq t$ and $a \equiv b \bmod \ell$ we have $a \in M$ if and only if $b \in M$.

3   Existential Büchi Arithmetic

One of the main results of [8] is that deciding existential formulas of Büchi arithmetic is NP-complete. A main obstacle is that the magnitude of satisfying variable assignments may grow super-polynomially. It is known that for infinitely many primes q the multiplicative order $\mathrm{ord}_q(2)$ of 2 modulo q is at least $\sqrt{q}$ [13]. For such a prime the predicate x *is a strictly positive power of* 2 *that is congruent to* 1 *modulo* q can easily be expressed as a formula of existential Büchi arithmetic of base 2:

$$\Phi(x) \stackrel{\text{def}}{=} \exists y \, x > 1 \land V_2(x, x) \land x = q \cdot y + 1$$

Observe that $\Phi(x)$ has a constant number of literals and that its length linear in the bit-length of q, while the smallest satisfying assignment is $x = 2^{\mathrm{ord}_q(2)}$. Thus satisfying assignments in existential Büchi arithmetic may have super-polynomial bit-length in the formula size, even for a fixed base and a fixed number of literals. This rules out the possibility of showing NP membership by a non-deterministic guess-and-check algorithm. We nevertheless have the following theorem:

Theorem 1 ([8]). *Existential Büchi arithmetic is NP-complete.*

Existential Büchi arithmetic inherits the NP lower bound from integer programming when the number of variables is not fixed. While existential Presburger arithmetic can be decided in polynomial time when the number of variables is fixed [15], showing such a result for Büchi arithmetic would likely require major breakthroughs in number theory, even when fixing the number of literals. Given $a, b, c \in \mathbb{N}$, we can express discrete logarithm problems of the kind, *does there exist* $x \in \mathbb{N}$ *such that* $a^x \equiv b \bmod c$, in a similar way as above:

$$\exists x \, \exists y \, V_a(x, x) \land x = c \cdot y + b$$

Such discrete logarithm problems are believed to possibly be even more difficult than those underlying the Diffie-Hellman key exchange [14]. Of course, it may well be that existential Büchi arithmetic with a fixed number of variables (and even literals) is NP-hard. For instance, existential Presburger arithmetic with a full divisibility predicate is NP-hard already for a fixed number of variables and literals [11], shown via a reduction from a certain NP-complete problem involving a special class of quadratic congruences [12].

We now give an exposition of the NP upper bound of Theorem 1 developed in [8]. It clearly suffices to only consider quantifier-free formulas. Let $\Phi(x)$ be a quantifier-free formula of Büchi arithmetic, and let us first consider the special case of a system of linear Diophantine equations together with a single V_p assertion

$$\Phi(x) \stackrel{\text{def}}{=} A \cdot x = c \wedge V_p(x, u),$$

where x and u are variables occurring in x. From Sect. 2.2, we know that we can construct a p-automaton $A(S)$ whose language encodes all solutions of $S \colon A \cdot x = c$. A key insight enabling showing decidability of Büchi arithmetic is that the set of solutions of $V_p(x, u)$ for $x > 0$ can be encoded by a regular language over the alphabet $\Sigma_p \times \Sigma_p$:

$$\begin{bmatrix} \Sigma_p \\ 0 \end{bmatrix}^* \begin{bmatrix} \Sigma_p \setminus \{0\} \\ 1 \end{bmatrix} \begin{bmatrix} 0 \\ 0 \end{bmatrix}^*$$

Thus, in order to decide whether $\Phi(x)$ is satisfiable, we can check whether we can find a run through the automaton $A(S)$ that can be partitioned into three parts. In the first part, x can have any digit and u has only zeros as digits. The second part is a single transition in which x can have any non-zero digit and u has digit one, and in the third part both x and u have digits zero.

To make this argument more formal, it will be useful to introduce a mild generalization of the reachability relation for p-automata. Suppose we are given a system of linear equations $S \colon \mathbf{A} \cdot x = c$ and an additional system of constraints $T \colon \mathbf{B} \cdot x = d$. For all pairs of states q, r of the automaton $A(S)$, write $q \xrightarrow{w}_{S[T]} r$ if $q \xrightarrow{w}_S r$ and $\mathbf{B} \cdot [\![w]\!] = d$. Plainly $q \xrightarrow{w}_{S[T]} r$ if and only if

$$\begin{pmatrix} q \\ 0 \end{pmatrix} \xrightarrow{w}_{S \wedge T} \begin{pmatrix} r \\ d \end{pmatrix},$$

where $S \wedge T$ is the system of equations

$$S \wedge T \colon \begin{pmatrix} \mathbf{A} \\ \mathbf{B} \end{pmatrix} x = \begin{pmatrix} c \\ d \end{pmatrix}.$$

With the new notation at hand, the observations made above now enable us to reduce satisfiability of $\Phi(x)$ to three reachability queries in p-automata: $\Phi(x)$ is satisfiable if and only if there are states d and e of $A(S)$, and $a \in \Sigma_p \setminus \{0\}$ such that

$$0 \xrightarrow{*}_{S[u=0]} d \to_{S[x=a, u=1]} e \xrightarrow{*}_{S[x=u=0]} c. \tag{3}$$

Note that by (1), the encoding of the binary representation of the states d and e of $A(S)$ is polynomial in the encoding of S, and hence both states can be guessed in NP.

The reduction to reachability queries in p-automata is easily seen to generalize to the case where we have an arbitrary number k of constraints $V_p(x_i, u_i)$ in $\Phi(x)$. To check satisfiability, all we have to do is to guess a relative order between the u_i, $a_i \in \Sigma_p \setminus \{0\}$, states d_i and e_i of $A(S)$, resulting in $O(k)$ reachability queries in p-automata. We illustrate the reachability queries for the case in which $u_i > u_{i+1}$ for all $1 \le i \le k$, the remaining cases follow analogously:

$$0 \xrightarrow{*} S[u_1,\ldots,u_k=0] \; d_1 \rightarrow S[x_1=a_1,u_1=1,u_2,\ldots,u_k=0] \; e_1$$
$$\xrightarrow{*} S[x_1,u_1,\ldots,u_k=0] \; d_2 \rightarrow S[x_2=a_2,u_2=1,x_1,u_1,u_3,\ldots u_k=0] \; e_2 \xrightarrow{*} S[x_1,x_2,u_1,\ldots,u_k=0] \cdots$$
$$\cdots d_k \rightarrow S[x_k=a_k,u_k=1,x_1,\ldots,x_{k-1},u_1,\ldots,u_{k-1}=0] \; e_k \xrightarrow{*} S[x_1,\ldots,x_k,u_1,\ldots,u_k=0] \; c \quad (4)$$

Finally, we observe that the set of solutions of a literal $\neg V_p(u, u)$, stating that u is not a power of p, is encoded by the regular language given by the following regular expression:

$$\overline{0^*10^*} \equiv 0^*(\Sigma_p \setminus \{0,1\})\Sigma_p^* + 0^*10^*(\Sigma_p \setminus \{0\})\Sigma_p^*$$

Observe that this regular expression induces a decomposition similar to (3). Hence, we can non-deterministically polynomially reduce deciding conjunctions of the form

$$\mathbf{A} \cdot \mathbf{x} = c \wedge \bigwedge_{i \in I} V_p(x_i, u_i) \wedge \bigwedge_{j \in J} \neg V_p(u_j, u_j) \quad (5)$$

for finite index sets I, J to a linear number of state-to-state reachability queries in p-automata implicitly given by systems of linear Diophantine equations. We now invoke the following theorem:

Theorem 2 ([8]). *Deciding state-to-state reachability in a p-automaton $A(S)$ given by a system of linear Diophantine equations S is in NP (with respect to the encoding of S).*

In particular, the NP upper bound does *not* require the explicit construction of $A(S)$. By application of this result and the arguments above, the NP upper bound for existential Büchi arithmetic follows. Given a quantifier-free formula $\Phi(x)$, as discussed in Sect. 2.1, we can assume that Φ is a positive Boolean combination of literals $a \cdot x = c$, $V_p(x, u)$ and $\neg V_p(u, u)$. Hence we can guess in NP a clause of the disjunctive normal form of Φ, which is of the form (5), and in turn check in NP a series of guessed reachability queries in p-automata induced by the guessed clause.

We close this section with a brief discussion of the main ideas behind the NP upper bound of Theorem 2. The first observation is that reachability in p-automata reduces to satisfiability in a certain class of systems of linear-exponential Diophantine equations. From (2), we can deduce that for a word $w \in (\Sigma_p^n)^k$,

$$q \xrightarrow{w} r \iff r = p^k \cdot q + \mathbf{A} \cdot [\![w]\!] \iff r = p^k \cdot q + \mathbf{A} \cdot x, \|x\|_\infty < p^k.$$

Let $\boldsymbol{x} = (x_1, \ldots, x_n)^\top$, replacing p^k by a fresh variable y, it follows that $q \xrightarrow{*} r$ if and only if the following system of linear Diophantine inequalities has a solution in which y is a power of p:

$$r = y \cdot q + \mathbf{A} \cdot \boldsymbol{x}, x_i < y, \ 1 \leq i \leq n.$$

This is now a problem that is not difficult to decide, since we can guess in NP a linear set $L(\boldsymbol{b}, P) \subseteq \mathbb{N}^m$ with a small description that generates a subset of the set of solutions of this system. Checking whether $L(\boldsymbol{b}, P)$ contains a point in which the y-coordinate is a power of p can easily be done in NP, we refer the reader to [8] for further details.

4   Presburger Arithmetic with Valuation Constraints

The definition of V_p ensures that p-recognizable sets are equivalent to those definable in Büchi arithmetic. Note that it is possible to enrich Presburger arithmetic with an even more general predicate which does, however, not change the definable sets of natural numbers, see e.g. [4, p. 209]. But the predicate V_p also has a close connection to the valuation function $v_p \colon \mathbb{Q} \to \mathbb{Z}$ underlying the definition of the p-adic numbers. Given a prime p and a non-zero rational number x, the p-adic valuation $v_p(x)$ is defined to be the unique integer $e \in \mathbb{Z}$ such that $x = p^e \cdot \frac{a}{b}$ with $a, b \in \mathbb{Z}$ and $p \nmid a, b$. Intuitively $v_p(x)$ is the exponent of the greatest power of p that divides x. Now the p-adic valuation v_p and the V_p predicate of Büchi arithmetic (viewing V_p as a function) are related as follows: for a natural number $n \in \mathbb{N}$ we have $V_p(n) = p^{v_p(n)}$. Thus, we could view $v_p(n)$ as a succinct representation of $V_p(n)$.

In arithmetic theories over p-adic numbers, it is common to consider two-sorted logics with one sort for the p-adic numbers and another sort for the valuation ring $\mathbb{Z}$, together with additional (restricted) arithmetic over the valuation ring, see e.g. [18]. One can naturally transfer this concept to arithmetic theories over numerical domains other than the p-adic numbers. The decompositions established in the previous section together with classical results on finite-state automata then give decidability and complexity results.

As a concrete illustrating example, we introduce in this section Presburger arithmetic with valuation constraints. Since $v_p(n) \in \mathbb{N}$ for all $n \in \mathbb{N}_+$, technically we are not dealing with a multi-sorted logic.[1] We use the following notational convention: a variable x is interpreted as a natural number, and $\overline{x} \overset{\text{def}}{=} v_p(x)$ is interpreted as the valuation of x. A formula $\varPhi$ of *Presburger arithmetic with valuation constraints* is then given by a tuple

$$\varPhi = (\varPsi(x_1, \ldots, x_n); \varGamma(\overline{x}_1, \ldots, \overline{x}_n)),$$

where both $\varPsi$ and $\varGamma$ are formulas of Presburger arithmetic. We say that $\varPhi$ is existential if both $\varPsi$ and $\varGamma$ are formulas of existential Presburger arithmetic.

---

[1] And for brevity, we do not delve into different ways of defining $V_p(0)$, the results given work for any sensible choice of defining $V_p(0)$.

Moreover, Φ is satisfiable with respect to a fixed $p > 1$ given as input whenever we can find a variable assignment $\sigma \colon \{x_1, \ldots, x_n\} \to \mathbb{N}$ such that both $\Psi(\sigma(x_1), \ldots, \sigma(x_n))$ and $\Gamma(v_p(\sigma(x_1)), \ldots, v_p(\sigma(x_n)))$ evaluate to true.

It is not surprising and easy to see that satisfying assignments are not semi-linear since, e.g.,

$$\Phi = (x > 0; \exists y \, \overline{x} = 2y \wedge y > 0)$$

has the set of all positive integers n with $v_p(n)$ even and greater than zero as its set of satisfying assignments, i.e., Φ defines the set $\{p^{2k} \cdot n : k, n \in \mathbb{N}_+, p \nmid n\}$ which, for any base $p > 1$, is obviously not ultimately periodic and hence not semi-linear.

We now show NP-completeness of existential formulas of Presburger arithmetic with valuation constraints from which we can then conclude decidability of the general case. Given $\Phi = (\Psi, \Gamma)$, let us first consider the case in which Ψ is a system of linear Diophantine equations $S \colon A \cdot \boldsymbol{x} = \boldsymbol{c}$ with $\boldsymbol{x} = (x_1, \ldots, x_n)$, and Γ is existential. A solution of S is encoded by a path in $A(S)$ from $\boldsymbol{0}$ to $\boldsymbol{c}$, and if we assume without loss of generality that $x_i > x_{i+1}$ for all $1 \leq i < n$ then similarly as in (4) we can decompose this path as

$$\boldsymbol{0} \xrightarrow{*} \boldsymbol{d}_1 \to_{S[x_1=a_1]} \boldsymbol{e}_1 \xrightarrow{w_1}_{S[x_1=0]} \boldsymbol{d}_2 \to_{S[x_2=a_2,x_1=0]} \boldsymbol{e}_2 \xrightarrow{w_2}_{S[x_1,x_2=0]} \cdots$$
$$\cdots \boldsymbol{d}_n \to_{S[x_n=a_n,x_1,\ldots,x_{n-1}=0]} \boldsymbol{e}_n \xrightarrow{w_n}_{S[x_1,\ldots,x_n=0]} \boldsymbol{c} \ (6)$$

for some $w_i \in (\Sigma_p^n)^*$ and with all $a_i \neq 0$. Note that this decomposition implies that $v_p(x_n) = |w_n| + 1$, $v_p(x_{n-1}) = |w_n| + |w_{n-1}| + 2$, etc. In particular, each $|w_i|$ is the length of a path between the states $\boldsymbol{e}_i$ and $\boldsymbol{d}_{i+1}$. It is well-known that the set of lengths of paths between two states in a non-deterministic finite-state automaton is semi-linear and that the encoding of each linear set in such a semi-linear set is logarithmic in the number states, see e.g. [17]. Moreover, semi-linear sets are closed under taking finite sums. Recall that by the estimation in Eq. (1) the number of states of a p-automaton $A(S)$ is exponentially bounded and that each state has an encoding linear in the encoding of S. It follows that given a decomposition as in (6), we can for each x_i guess in NP a linear set $L(b, P) \subseteq \mathbb{N}$ such that $v_p(x_i) \in L(b, P)$. Also recall from Sect. 2.3 that a linear set is definable by a formula of existential Presburger arithmetic of linear size. Consequently, we obtain the following non-deterministic polynomial-time algorithm deciding satisfiability of Φ above:

– guess the states occurring in a decomposition of a run from $\boldsymbol{0}$ to $\boldsymbol{c}$ in $A(S)$ of the form (6) (again note that this does not require constructing $A(S)$);
– from this decomposition, guess linear sets $L(b_i, P_i)$ such that $v_p(x_i) \in L(b_i, P_i)$ for each x_i;
– check whether Γ is satisfiable with each $v_p(x_i)$ constrained to lie in $L(b_i, P_i)$.

If $\Phi = (\Psi, \Gamma)$ is an arbitrary existential formula of Presburger arithmetic with valuation constraints, an NP upper bound also follows: we only need to guess a clause of the disjunctive normal form of Ψ and then proceed as before. The case where Φ is arbitrary obviously reduces to the existential case since Presburger arithmetic has quantifier elimination.

Theorem 3. *Presburger arithmetic with valuation constraints is decidable, and its existential fragment is NP-complete.*

5   Conclusion

This article provided an exposition of the results of [8] together with some results that follow but are not explicated in [8]. We described the proof of NP-completeness of existential Büchi arithmetic and showed how this proof can be applied to obtain decidability of Presburger arithmetic with valuation constraints and NP-completeness of its existential fragment. We close this article with a couple of remarks and open questions for future work:

- There is an analogue of Büchi arithmetic for the reals that was studied by Boigelot, Rassart and Wolper [1]. This analogue builds upon a predicate $X_p \subseteq \mathbb{R}_+ \times \mathbb{Q} \times [0, p-1]$ such that $X_p(x, u, k)$ is true if and only if u is a (possibly negative) integer power of p, and there is an encoding of x such that the digit at the position specified by u is k:

$$X_p(x, u, k) \iff \text{there are } \ell \in \mathbb{Z}, a_\ell, a_{\ell-1}, \ldots \in [0, p-1] \text{ s.t. } x = \sum_{i=\ell}^{-\infty} a_i p^i$$

$$\text{and there is } q \in \mathbb{Z} \text{ s.t. } q \leq \ell, u = p^q \text{ and } a_q = k.$$

  The real analogue of Büchi arithmetic is the first-order theory of the structure $\langle \mathbb{R}_+, 0, 1, +, X_p \rangle$ (*BRW arithmetic* after the authors of [1] for short).[2] Looking at the similarities of the definitions of $X_p(x, u, k)$ and V_p, it seems conceivable that existential BRW arithmetic is also NP-complete, though this is likely more tedious to prove mainly because some real numbers have multiple encodings (e.g., $1.0000 \cdots = 0.9999 \cdots$).
- Presburger arithmetic with valuation constraints is a powerful logic which can be used to reason about sets of integers which are not semi-linear. Decidability in such contexts is rare, and NP-completeness of its existential fragment means that this logic could potentially find practical applications in areas such as formal verification, as we seemingly can, for instance, express some problems typically arising in bit-vector arithmetic. Generally speaking, what are natural applications of Presburger arithmetic with valuation constraints?
- Is Büchi arithmetic with valuation constraints decidable? It can be derived from the approach presented in Sect. 4 that this is the case for existential Büchi arithmetic. However, the author is not aware of a quantifier-elimination procedure for Büchi arithmetic that given a formula of Büchi arithmetic allows for obtaining an equivalent formula of *existential* Büchi arithmetic.
- Is existential Büchi arithmetic with a fixed number of variables (and possibly even a fixed number of literals) NP-complete? As discussed in Sect. 3, showing membership in P would require breakthroughs that currently (and likely over the next decades) seem out of reach, and would moreover break some public key cryptographic systems.

---

[2] For presentational convenience, we chose $\mathbb{R}_+$ as the domain of BRW arithmetic, unlike [1] who actually use $\mathbb{R}$.

References

1. Boigelot, B., Rassart, S., Wolper, P.: On the expressiveness of real and integer arithmetic automata (extended abstract). In: Automata, Languages and Programming, ICALP. Lect. Notes Comp. Sci., vol. 1443, pp. 152–163. Springer (1998)
2. Boigelot, B., Wolper, P.: Representing arithmetic constraints with finite automata: An overview. In: Logic Programming, ICLP. Lect. Notes Comp. Sci., vol. 2401, pp. 1–19. Springer (2002)
3. Boudet, A., Comon, H.: Diophantine equations, presburger arithmetic and finite automata. In: Trees in Algebra and Programming - CAAP. Lect. Notes Comp. Sci., vol. 1059, pp. 30–43. Springer (1996)
4. Bruyère, V., Hansel, G., Michaux, C., Villemaire, R.: Logic and p-recognizable sets of integers. Bull. Belg. Math. Soc. Simon Stevin $1(2)$, 191–238 (1994)
5. Durand-Gasselin, A., Habermehl, P.: On the use of non-deterministic automata for presburger arithmetic. In: Concurrency Theory - CONCUR. Lect. Notes Comp. Sci., vol. 6269, pp. 373–387. Springer (2010)
6. Durand-Gasselin, A., Habermehl, P.: Ehrenfeucht-fraïssé goes elementarily automatic for structures of bounded degree. In: Symposium on Theoretical Aspects of Computer Science, STACS. LIPIcs, vol. 14, pp. 242–253. Schloss Dagstuhl - Leibniz-Zentrum fuer Informatik (2012)
7. Ginsburg, S., Spanier, E.H.: Bounded ALGOL-like languages. T. Am. Math. Soc. pp. 333–368 (1964)
8. Guépin, F., Haase, C., Worrell, J.: On the existential theories of Büchi arithmetic and linear p-adic fields. In: Logic in Computer Science, LICS. IEEE (2019)
9. Klaedtke, F.: Bounds on the automata size for presburger arithmetic. ACM Trans. Comput. Log. $9(2)$, 11:1–11:34 (2008)
10. Leroux, J., Point, G.: Tapas: The talence presburger arithmetic suite. In: Tools and Algorithms for the Construction and Analysis of Systems, TACAS. Lect. Notes Comp. Sci., vol. 5505, pp. 182–185. Springer (2009)
11. Lipshitz, L.M.: Some remarks on the Diophantine problem for addition and divisibility. Proc. Model Theory Meeting. **33**, 41–52 (1981)
12. Manders, K.L., Adleman, L.M.: NP-complete decision problems for binary quadratics. J. Comput. Syst. Sci. **16**(2), 168–184 (1978)
13. Matthews, C.R.: Counting Points Modulo p for some Finitely Generated Subgroups of Algebraic Groups. Bull. Lond. Math. Soc. **14**(2), 149–154 (1982)
14. McCurley, K.S.: The discrete logarithm problem. Proc. of Symp. in Applied Math. **42**, 49–74 (1990)
15. Scarpellini, B.: Complexity of subcases of Presburger arithmetic. T. Am. Math. Soc. **284**, 203–218 (1984)
16. The Liège automata-based symbolic handler (LASH): Available at http://www.montefiore.ulg.ac.be/~boigelot/research/lash/
17. To, A.W.: Unary finite automata vs. arithmetic progressions. Inf. Process. Lett. **109**(17), 1010–1014 (2009)
18. Weispfenning, V.: The complexity of linear problems in fields. J. Symb. Comput. **5**(1/2), 3–27 (1988)
19. Wolper, P., Boigelot, B.: On the construction of automata from linear arithmetic constraints. In: Tools and Algorithms for the Construction and Analysis of Systems, TACAS. Lect. Notes Comp. Sci., vol. 1785, pp. 1–19. Springer (2000)

Recompression: Technique for Word Equations and Compressed Data

Artur Jeż[(✉)] [ID]

University of Wrocław, Joliot-Curie 15, 50383 Wrocław, Poland
aje@cs.uni.wroc.pl

Abstract. In this talk I will present the recompression technique on the running example of word equations. In word equation problem we are given an equation $u = v$, where both u and v are words of letters and variables, and ask for a substitution of variables by words that equalizes the sides of the equation. The recompression technique is based on employing simple compression rules (replacement of two letters ab by a new letter c, replacement of maximal repetitions of a by a new letter), and modifying the equations (replacing a variable X by bX or Xa) so that those operations are sound and complete. The simple analysis focuses on the size of the instance and not on the combinatorial properties of words that are used. The recompression-based algorithm for word equations runs in nondeterministic linear space.

The approach turned out to be quite robust and can be applied to various generalized, simplified and related problems, in particular, to problems in the area of grammar compressed words. I will comment on some of those applications.

Keywords: Algorithms on automata and words · Word equations · Context unification · Equations in groups · Compression · SLPs

1 Introduction

1.1 Word Equations

The word equation problem, i.e. solving equations in the algebra of words, was first investigated by Markov in the fifties. In this problem we get as an input an equation of the form

$$u = v$$

where u and v are strings of letters (from a fixed alphabet) as well as variables and a *solution* is a substitution of words for variables that turns this formal equation into a true equality of strings of letters (over the same fixed alphabet). It is relatively easy to show a reduction of this problem to the Hilbert's 10-th problem, i.e. the question of solving systems of Diophantine equations. Already then it was generally accepted that Hilbert's 10-th problem is undecidable and Markov wanted to show this by proving the undecidability of word equations.

© Springer Nature Switzerland AG 2020
A. Leporati et al. (Eds.): LATA 2020, LNCS 12038, pp. 44–67, 2020.
https://doi.org/10.1007/978-3-030-40608-0_4

Alas, while Hilbert's 10-th problem is undecidable, the word equation problem is *decidable*, which was shown by Makanin [54]. The termination proof of his algorithm is very complex and yields a relatively weak bound on the computational complexity, thus over the years several improvements and simplifications over the original algorithm were proposed [27,29,43,79]. Simplifications have many potential advantages: it seems natural that simpler algorithm can be generalised or extended more easily (for instance, to the case of equations in groups) than a complex one. Moreover, simpler algorithm should be more effective in practical applications and should have a lower complexity bounds.

Subcases. It is easy to show NP-hardness for word equations, so far no better computational complexity lower bound is known. Such hardness stimulated a search for a restricted subclasses of the problem for which efficient (i.e. polynomial) algorithms can be given [4]. One of such subclasses is defined by restricting the amount of different variables that can be used in an equation: it is known that equations with one [11,45] and two [4,10,28] variables can be solved in polynomial time. Already for three variables it is not known, whether they are in NP or not [71] and partial results require nontrivial analysis [71].

Generalisations. Since Makanin's original solution much effort was put into extending his algorithm to other structures. Three directions seemed most natural:

- adding constraints to word equations;
- equations in free groups;
- partial commutation;
- equations in terms.

Constraints. From the application point of view, it is advantageous to consider word equations that can also use some additional constraints, i.e. we require that the solution for X has some additional properties. This was first done for regular constraints [79], on the other hand, for several types of constraints, for instance length-constraints, it is still open, whether the resulting problem is decidable or not (it becomes undecidable, if we allow counting occurrences of particular letter in the substitutions and arithmetic operations on such counts [3]).

Free groups. From the algebraic point of view, the word equation problem is solving equations in a free semigroup. It is natural to try to extend an algorithm from the free semigroup also to the case of free groups and then perhaps even to a larger class of groups (observe, that there are groups and semigroups for which the word problem is undecidable). The first algorithm for the group case was given by Makanin [55,56], his algorithm was not primitively-recursive [44]. Furthermore, Razborov showed that this algorithm can be used to give a description of all solutions of an equation [68] (more readable description of the Razborov's construction is available in [41]). As a final comment, note that such a description was the first step in proving the Tarski's Conjecture for free groups (that the theory of free groups is decidable) [42].

Partial commutation. Another natural generalization is to allow partial commutation between the letters, i.e. for each pair of letters we specify, whether $ab = ba$ or not. Such partially commutative words are usually called traces and the corresponding groups are usually known as Right-Angled Artin Groups, RAAGs for short. Decidability for trace equations was shown by Matiyasevich [57] and for RAAGs by Diekert and Muscholl [15]. In both cases, the main step in the proof was a reduction from a partially commutative case to a non-commutative one.

Terms. We can view words as very simple terms: each letter is a function symbol of arity 1. In this way word equations are equations over (very simple) terms. It is known, that term unification can be decided in polynomial time, assuming that variables represent closed (full) terms [69]; thus such a problem is unlikely to generalise word equations.

A natural generalisation of term unification and word equations is a *second-order unification*, in which we allow variables to represent functions that take arguments (which need to be closed terms). However, it is known that this problem is undecidable, even in many restricted subcases [16,26,47,49]. *Context unification* [7,8,74] is a natural problem 'in between': we allow variables representing functions, but we insist that they use their argument *exactly once*. It is easy to show that such defined problem generalises word equations, on the other hand, the undecidability proofs for second-order unification do not transfer directly to this model.

Being a natural generalisation is not enough to explain the interest in this problem, more importantly, context unification has natural connections with other, well-studied problems (equality up to constraints [61], linear second-order unification [47,50], one-step term rewriting [62], bounded second order unification [76], ...). Unfortunately, for over two decades the question of decidability of context unification remained open. Despite intensive research, not much is known about the decidability of this problem: only results for some restricted subcases are known: [8,19,47,48,51,75,77,78].

1.2 Compression and Word Equations

For more than 20 years since Makanin's original solution there was very small progress in algorithms for word equations: the algorithm was improved in many places, in particular this lead to a better estimation of the running time; however, the main idea (and the general complexity of the proof) was essentially the same.

The breakthrough was done by Plandowski and Rytter [67], who, for the first time, used the compression to solve word equations. They showed, that the shortest solution (of size N) of the word equation (of size n) has an SLP representation of size $\mathsf{poly}(n, \log N)$; here a *Straight Line Programme* (SLP for short) is simply a context free grammar generating exactly one word. Using the algorithm for testing the equality of two SLPs [63] this easily yields a (nondeterministic) algorithm running in time $\mathsf{poly}(n, \log N)$. Unfortunately, this work did not provide any bound on N and the only known bound (4 times exponential in n) came directly from Makanin's algorithm, together those two results yielded a 3NEXPTIME algorithm. Soon after the bound on the size of the short-est solution was improved to triply exponential [27], which immediately yielded an algorithm from class 2NEXPTIME, however, the same paper [27] improved Makanin's algorithm, so that it workd in EXPSPACE.

Next, Plandowski gave a better (doubly exponential) bound on the size of the shortest solution [64] and thus obtained a NEXPTIME algorithm, in particular, at that time this was the best known algorithm for this problem. The proof was based on novel factorisations of words. By better exploiting the interplay between factorisations and compression, he improved the algorithm so that it worked in PSPACE [65].

It is worth mentioning, that the solution proposed by Plandowski is essen-tially different than the one given by Makanin. In particular, it allowed gen-eralisations more easily: Diekert, Gutiérrez and Hagenah [13] showed, that Plandowski's algorithm can be extended to the case in which we allow regu-lar constraints in the equation (i.e. we want that the word substituted for X is from a regular language, whose description by a finite automaton is part of the input) and inversion; such an extended algorithm still works in polynomial space. It is easy to show that solving equations in free groups reduces to the above-mentioned problem of word equations with regular constraints and inver-sion [13] (it is worth mentioning, that in general we do not know whether solving equations in free groups is easier or harder than solving the ones in a free semi-group).

On the other hand, Plandowski showed, that his algorithm can be used to gen-erate a finite representation of all solutions of a word equation [66], which allows solving several decision problems concerning the set of all solutions (finiteness, boundedness, boundedness of the exponent of periodicity etc.). It is not known, whether this algorithm can be generalised so that it generates all solutions also in the case of regular constraints and inversion (or in a free group).

The new, simpler algorithm for word equations and demonstration of connec-tions between compression and word equations gave a new hope for solving the context unification problem. The first results were very promising: by using 'tree' equivalents of SLPs [2] computational complexity of some problems related to context unification was established [9,19,48]. Unfortunately, this approach failed to fully generalise Plandowski's algorithm for words: the equivalent of factorisa-tions that were used in the algorithm were not found for trees.

It is worth mentioning, that Rytter and Plandowski's approach, in which we compress a solution using SLPs (or in the non-deterministic case—we guess the compressed representation of the solution) and then perform the computa-tion directly on the SLP-compressed representations using known algorithm that work in polynomial time, turned out to be extremely fruitful in many branches of computer science. The recent survey by Lohrey gives several such successful applications [53].

1.3 Recompression

Recompression was developed for a specific problem concerning compressed data (fully compressed membership problem for finite automata [30]) and was later successfully applied to word equations [36] and other problems related to compressed representations. The usual approach for word equations (and compressed data in general) is that one tries to extract information about the combinatorics of the underlying words from the equation (compressed representation) and use this structure to solve the problem at hand. This is somehow natural: if the word can be represented compactly (be it as a solution of a word equation or using some compression mechanism) then it should have a lot of internal structure.

Recompression takes a different approach: our aim is to perform simple compression operations on the solution word of the word equation directly on the compressed representation. We need to modify the equation a bit in order to do that, however, the choice of the compression operation and the analysis focuses on the compressed representation and its properties and (almost) completely ignores the properties of the solution. The idea of performing the compression operation is somehow natural in view of the already mentioned Plandowski and Rytter result [67], that the (length-minimal) solution has a small SLP: since such an SLP exists, we can try to build it bottom-up, i.e. the SLP has a rule $a \to bc$ and so we will replace each bc in the solution by a. (There are some complications in case of $b = c$, as then the compression is ambiguous: we solve this by replacing the maximal repetitions of b letter instead of replacing bb).

Of course, performing such a compression on the equation might be difficult or even impossible at all and we sometimes need to modify the equation. However, it turns out that a greedy choice suffices to guarantee that the kept equation is of quadratic size. The correctness and size analysis turns out to be surprisingly easy. The method is also very robust, so that it can be applied to various scenarios related to word equations: one variable word equations [35], equations in free groups [14], twisted word equations [12], context unification [31], ... See the following Sections for details of some of those results.

1.4 Algorithms for Grammar-Based Compression

Due to ever-increasing amount of data, compression is widely applied in order to decrease the data's size. Still, the stored data is accessed and processed. Decompressing it on each such an occasion basically wastes the gain of reduced storage size. Thus there is a demand for algorithms dealing directly with the compressed data, without explicit decompression. Indeed, efficient algorithms for fundamental text operations (pattern matching, equality testing, etc.) are known for various practically used compression methods (LZ77, LZW, their variants, etc.) [20–25,63].

Note that above the compression can be seen as a source of problem that we want to overcome. However, as demonstrated by Plandowski and Rytter [67], the compression can also be seen as a solution to some problems, i.e. if we can show that the instance or its solutions is (highly) compressible, then we can compress it and, using the algorithms mentioned above, perform the computation on the compressed representation. See a recent survey of Lohrey [53], which gives examples of application of this approach in various fields, ranging from group theory, computational topology to program verification.

Compression standards differ in the main idea as well as in details. Thus when devising algorithms for compressed data, quite early one needs to focus on the exact compression method, to which the algorithm is applied. The most practical (and challenging) choice is one of the widely used standards, like LZW or LZ77. However, a different approach is also pursued: for some applications (and most of theory-oriented considerations) it would be useful to *model* one of the practical compression standard by a more mathematically well-founded and 'clean' method. The already mentioned Straight-Line Programs (SLPs), are such a clean formulation for many block compression methods: each LZ77 compressed text can be converted into an equivalent SLP of size $\mathcal{O}(n \log(N/n))$ and in $\mathcal{O}(n \log(N/n))$ time [5, 70] (where N is the size of the decompressed text), while each SLP can be converted to an equivalent LZ77-like of $\mathcal{O}(n)$ size in polynomial time. Other reasons of popularity of SLPs is that usually they compress well the input text [46, 60] Lastly, a greedy grammar compression can be efficiently implemented and thus can be used as a preprocessing to other compression methods, like those based on Burrows-Wheeler transform [39].

One can treat an SLP as a system of (very simple) word equations, i.e. a production $X \to \alpha$ is rewritten as $X = \alpha$, and so the recompression algorithm generalizes also to such setting. It can be then seen as a variant of *locally consistent parsing* [1, 58, 72], and indeed those techniques were one of the sources of the recompression approach.

It is no surprise that the highly non-deterministic recompression algorithm determinises when applied to SLPs, what is surprising is that it can be made efficient. In particular, it can be used to checking the equality of two SLPs in roughly quadratic time, which is the fastest known algorithm for this problem [33] (and also for the generalisation of this problem, the fully compressed pattern matching).

The main drawback of grammar compression is that the size of the smallest grammar cannot be even approximated within (small enough) constant factor [5, 80]. There are many algorithms that achieve a logarithmic approximation ratio [5, 70, 73], recompression can also be used to obtain one (in fact: two different). One of those algorithms [32] seems to have a slightly better practical behaviour than the other ones, the second has much simpler analysis than other approximation algorithms [34] (as it is essentially a greedy left-to-right scan).

Just as recompression generalizes from word equations to context unification (i.e. term equations), the approximation algorithm based on recompression for strings can be generalized to trees [38], in which case it produces a so-called tree SLP [2]. This was the first approximation algorithm for this problem.

Survey's Limitations

As this is an informal survey presentations, most of the proofs are only sketched or omitted. Due to space constraints, only some applications and results are explained in detail.

2   Recompression for Word Equations

We begin with a formal definition of the word equations problem: Consider a finite alphabet Σ and set of variables $\mathcal{X}$; during the algorithm Σ will be extended by new letters, but it will always remain finite. Word equation is of a form '$u = v$', where $u, v \in (\Sigma \cup \mathcal{X})^*$ and its solution is a homomorphism $S : \Sigma \cup \mathcal{X} \mapsto \Sigma^*$, which is constant on Σ, that is $S(a) = a$, and satisfies the equation, i.e. words $S(u)$ and $S(v)$ are equal. By n we denote the size of the equation, i.e. $|u| + |v|$. The algorithm requires only small improvements so that it applies also to systems of equations, to streamline the presentation we will not consider this case.

Fix any solution S of the equation $u = v$, without loss of generality we can assume that this is the *shortest solution*, i.e. the one minimising $|S(u)|$; let N denote the *length of the solution*, that is $|S(u)|$. By the earlier work of Plandowski and Rytter [67], we know that $S(u)$ (and also $S(X)$ for each variable X) has an SLP (of size $\mathsf{poly}(n, \log N)$), in fact the same conclusion can be to drawn from the later works of Plandowski [64–66]. Regardless of the form of S and SLP, we know, that at least one of the productions in this SLP is of the form $c \to ab$, where c is a nonterminal of the SLP while $a, b \in \Sigma$ are letters. Let us 'reverse' this production, i.e. replace in $S(u)$ all pairs of letters ab by c. It is relatively easy to formalise this operation for words, it is not so clear, what should be done in case of equations, so let us inspect the easier fragment first.

Algorithm 1. PairComp(ab, w) Compression of pair ab

1: let $c \in \Sigma$ be an unused letter
2: replace all occurrences of ab in w by c

Consider an explicitly given word w. Performing the 'ab-pair compression' on it is easy (we replace each pair ab by c), as long as $a \neq b$: replacing pairs aa is ambiguous, as such pairs can 'overlap'. Instead, we replace *maximal blocks* of a letter a: block a^ℓ is *maximal*, when there is no letter a to left nor to the right of it (in particular, there could be no letter at all).

Formally, the operations are defined as follows:

- *ab pair compression* For a given word w replace all occurrences of ab in w by a fresh letter c.
- *a block compression* For a given word w replace all occurrences of maximal blocks a^ℓ for $\ell > 1$ in w by fresh letters a_ℓ.

We always assume, that in the ab-pair compression the letters a and b are different.

Observe, that those operations are indeed 'inverses' of SLP productions: replacing ab with c corresponds to a production $c \to ab$, similarly replacing a^ℓ with a_ℓ corresponds to a production $a_\ell \to a^\ell$.

Algorithm 2. BlockComp(a, w) Block compression for a

1: **for** $\ell > 1$ **do**
2:     let $a_\ell \in \Sigma$ be an unused letter
3:     replace all maximal blocks a^ℓ in w by a_ℓ

Iterating the pair and blocks compression results in a compression of word w, assuming that we treat the introduced symbols as normal letters. There are several possible ways to implement such iteration, different results are obtained by altering the order of the compressions, exact treatment of new letters and so on. Still, essentially each 'reasonable' variant works.

Observe, that if we compress two words, say w_1 and w_2, in parallel then the resulting words w_1' and w_2' are equal if and only if w_1 and w_2 are. This justifies the usage of compression operations to both sides of the word equation in parallel, it remains to show, how to do that.

Let us fix a solution S, a pair ab (where $a \neq b$); consider how does a particular occurrence of ab got into $S(u)$.

Definition 1. *For an equation $u = v$, solution S and pair ab an occurrence of ab in $S(u)$ (or $S(v)$) is*

- explicit, *if it consists solely of letters coming from u (or v);*
- implicit, *if it consists solely of letters coming from a substitution $S(X)$ for a fixed occurrence of some variable X;*
- crossing, *otherwise.*

A pair ab is crossing *(for a solution S) if it has at least one crossing occurrence and* non-crossing *(for a solution S) otherwise.*

We similarly define explicit, implicit *and* crossing *occurrences for blocks of letter a; a is* crossing, *if at least one of its blocks has a crossing occurrence. (In other words: aa is crossing).*

Example 1. Equation

$$aaXbbababa = XaabbYabX$$

has a unique solution $S(X) = a$, $S(Y) = abab$, under which sides evaluate to

$$aaabbabababa = aaabbabababa.$$

Pair ba is crossing (as the first letter of $S(Y)$ is a and first Y is preceded by a letter b, moreover, the last letter of $S(Y)$ is b and the second Y is succeeded by a letter a), pair ab is non-crossing. Letter b is non-crossing, letter a is crossing (as X is preceded by a letter a on the left-hand side of the equation and on the right-hand side of the equation X is succeeded by a letter a).

Algorithm 3. PairComp(ab, '$u = v$') Pair compression for ab in an equation $u = v$

1: let $c \in \Sigma$ be a fresh letter
2: replace all occurrences of ab in '$u = v$' by c

Algorithm 4. BlockComp(a, '$u = v$') Block compression for a letter a in an equation '$u = v$'

1: **for** $\ell > 1$ **do**
2:     let $a_\ell \in \Sigma$ be a fresh letter
3:     replace all occurrences of maximal blocks a^ℓ in '$u = v$' by a_ℓ

Fix a pair ab and a solution S of the equation $u = v$. If ab is non-crossing, performing PairComp(ab, $S(u)$) is easy: we need to replace every explicit occurrence (which we do directly on the equation) as well as each implicit occurrence, which is done 'implicitly', as the solution is not stored, nor written anywhere. Due to the similarities to PairComp we will simply use the name PairComp(ab,'$u = v$'), when we make the pair compressions on the equation. The argument above shows, that if the equation had a solution for which ab is non-crossing then also the obtained equation has a solution. The same applies to the block compression, called BlockComp(a,'$u = v$') for simplicity. On the other hand, if the obtained equation has a solution, then also the original equation had one (this solution is obtained by replacing each letter c by ab, the argument for the block compressions the same).

Lemma 1. *Let the equation $u = v$ have a solution S, such that ab is non-crossing for S. Then $u' = v'$ obtained by* PairComp*(ab,'$u = v$') is satisfiable. If the obtained equation $u' = v'$ is satisfiable, then also the original equation $u = v$ is. The same applies to* BlockComp*(a,'$u = v$').*

Unfortunately Lemma 1 is not enough to simulate Compression(w) directly on the equation: In general there is no guarantee that the pair ab (letter a) is non-crossing, moreover, we do not know which pairs have only implicit occurrences. It turns out, that the second problem is trivial: if we restrict ourselves to the shortest solutions then every pair that has an implicit occurrence has also a crossing or explicit one, a similar statement holds also for blocks of letters.

Lemma 2 ([67]). *Let S be a shortest solution of an equation '$u = v$'. Then:*

- *If ab is a substring of $S(u)$, where $a \neq b$, then a, b have explicit occurrences in the equation and ab has an explicit or crossing occurrence.*
- *If a^k is a maximal block in $S(u)$ then a has an explicit occurrence in the equation and a^k has an explicit or crossing occurrence.*

The proof is simple: suppose that a pair has only implicit occurrences. Then we could remove them and the obtained solution is shorter, contradicting the assumption. The argument for blocks is a bit more involved, as they can overlap.

Getting back to the crossing pairs (and blocks), if we fix a pair ab (letter a), then it is easy to 'uncross' it: by Definition 1 we can conclude that the pair ab is crossing if and only if for some variables X and Y (not necessarily different) one of the following conditions holds (we assume that the solution does not assign an empty word to any variable—otherwise we could simply remove such a variable from the equation):

(CP1) aX occurs in the equation and $S(X)$ begins with b;
(CP2) Yb occurs in the equation and $S(Y)$ ends with a;
(CP3) YX occurs in the equation, $S(X)$ begins with b and b $S(Y)$ ends with a.

In each of these cases the 'uncrossing' is natural: in (1) we 'pop' from X a letter b to the left, in (2) we pop a to the right from Y, in (3) we perform both operations. It turns out that in fact we can be even more systematic: we do not have to look at the occurrences of variables, it is enough to consider the first and last letter of $S(X)$ for each variable X:

- If $S(X)$ begins with b then we replace X with bX (changing implicitly the solution $S(X) = bw$ to $S'(X) = w$), if in the new solution $S(X) = \epsilon$, i.e. it is empty, then we remove X from the equation;
- if $S(X)$ ends with a then we apply a symmetric procedure.

Such an algorithm is called Pop.

Algorithm 5. Pop($a, b, {}'u = v'$)

1: **for** X: variable **do**
2:     **if** the first letter of $S(X)$ is b **then**   ▷ Guess
3:         replace every X w '$u = v$' by bX
                          ▷ Implicitly change solution $S(X) = bw$ to $S(X) = w$
4:         **if** $S(X) = \epsilon$ **then**   ▷ Guess
5:             remove X from u and v
6:     ...   ▷ Perform a symmetric operation for the last letter and a

---

It is easy to see, that for appropriate non-deterministic choices the obtained equation has a solution for which ab is non-crossing: for instance, if aX occurs in the equation and $S(X)$ begins with b then we make the corresponding non-deterministic choices, popping b to the left and obtaining abX; a simple proof requires a precise statement of the claim as well as some case analysis.

Lemma 3. *If the equation 'u = v' has a solution S then for an appropriate run of* Pop$(a, b, 'u = v')$ *(for appropriate non-deterministic choices) the obtained equation* $u' = v'$ *has a corresponding solution* S', *i.e.* $S(u) = S'(u')$, *for which ab is a non-crossing pair. If the obtained equation has a solution then also the original equation had one.*

Thus, we know how to proceed with a crossing ab-pair compression: we first turn ab into a non-crossing pair (Pop) and then compress it as a non-crossing pair (PairComp).

We would like to perform similar operations for block compression. For non-crossing blocks we can naturally define a similar algorithm BlockComp$(a, 'u = v')$. It remains to show how to 'uncross' a letter a. Unfortunately, if aX occurs in the equation and $S(X)$ begins with a then replacing X with aX is not enough, as $S(X)$ may still begin with a. In such a case we iterate the procedure until the first letter of X is not a (this includes the case in which we remove the whole variable X). Observe, that instead of doing this letter by letter, we can uncross a in one step: it is enough to remove from variable X its whole a-prefix and a-suffix of $S(X)$ (if $w = a^\ell w' a^r$, where w' does not begin nor end with a, a-prefix w is a^ℓ and a-suffix is a^r; if $w = a^\ell$ then a-suffix and w' are empty). Such an algorithm is called CutPrefSuff.

Algorithm 6. CutPrefSuff$(a, 'u = v')$ Popping prefixes and suffixes

---
1: **for** X: variable **do**
2:　　guess the lengths ℓ, r of a-prefix and suffix of $S(X)$ 　　　　▷ $S(X) = a^\ell w a^r$
　　　　　　　　　　　　　　　　　　　　　　　　　　▷ If $S(X) = a^\ell$ then $r = 0$
3:　　replace occurrences of X in u and v by $a^\ell X a^r$
　　　　　　　　　　　　　　　　　　　　▷ a^ℓ, a^r are stored in a compressed way
4:　　　　　　　　　　　　▷ Implicitly change the solution $S(X) = a^\ell w b^r$ to $S(X) = w$
5:　　**if** $S(X) = \epsilon$ **then** 　　　　　　　　　　　　　　　　　　▷ Guess
6:　　　　remove X from u and v

Similarly as in Pop, we can show that after an appropriate run of CutPrefSuff the obtained equation has a (corresponding) solution for which a is non-crossing. Unfortunately, there is another problem: we need to write down the lengths ℓ and r of a-prefixes and suffixes. We can write them as binary numbers, in which case they use $\mathcal{O}(\log \ell + \log r)$ bits of memory. However in general those still can be arbitrarily large numbers. Fortunately, we can show that in *some* solution those values are at most exponential (and so their description is polynomial-size). This easily follows from the exponential bound on exponent of periodicity [43]. For the moment it is enough that we know that:

Lemma 4 ([43]). *In the shortest solution of the equation 'u = v' each a-prefix and a-suffix has at most exponential length (in terms of $|u| + |v|$).*

Thus in Pop we can restrict ourselves to a-prefixes and suffixes of at most exponential length.

Lemma 5. *Let S be a shortest solution of '$u = v$'. For some non-deterministic choices, i.e. after some run of* CutPrefSuff$(a, 'u = v')$, *the obtained equation '$u' = v''$ has a corresponding solution S', such that $S'(u') = S(u)$, and a is a non-crossing letter for S', moreover, the explicit a blocks in '$u' = v''$ have at most exponential length. If the obtained equation has a solution then also the original equation had one.*

After Pop we can compress a-blocks using BlockComp$(a, 'u = v')$, observe that afterwards long a-blocks are replaced with single letters.

We are now ready to simulate Compression directly on the equation. The question is, in which order we should compress pairs and blocks? We make the choice nondeterministically: if there are any non-crossing pairs or letters, we compress them. This is natural, as such compression decreases both the size of the equation and the size of the length-minimal solution of the equation. If all pairs and letters are crossing, we choose greedily, i.e. the one that leads to the smallest equation (in one step). It is easy to show that such a strategy keeps the equation quadratic, more involved strategy, in which we compress many pairs/blocks in parallel, leads to a linear-length equation.

Algorithm 7. WordEqSAT Deciding the satisfiability of word equations

---

1: **while** $|u| > 1$ or $|u| > 1$ **do**
2:     $L \leftarrow$ list of letters in u, v
3:         Choose a pair $ab \in P^2$ or a letter $a \in P$ ▷ Guess
4:         **if** it is crossing **then**   ▷ Guess
5:             uncross it
6:         compress it
7: Solve the problem naively

Call one iteration of the main loop a *phase*.

The correctness of the algorithm follows from the earlier discussion on the correctness of BlockComp, CutPrefSuff, PairComp and Pop. In particular, the length of the length-minimal solution drops by at least 1 in each iteration, thus the algorithm terminates.

Lemma 6. *Algorithm* WordEqSAT *has $\mathcal{O}(N)$ phases, where N is the length of the shortest solution of the input equation.*

Let us bound the space needed by the algorithm: we claim that for appropriate nondeterministic choices the stored equation has at most $8n^2$ letters (and n variables). To see this, observe first that each Pop introduces at most $2n$ letters, one at each side of the variable. The same applies to CutPrefSuff (formally, CutPrefSuff introduces long blocks but they are immediately replaced with single letters, and so we can think that in fact we introduce only $2n$ letters). By (1)–(3) we know that there are at most $2n$ crossing pairs and crossing letters (as each crossing pair/each crossing letter corresponds to one occurrence of a variable and one 'side' of such an occurrence). If the equation has m letters (and at most n occurrences of variables) and there is an occurrence of a non-crossing pair or block then we choose it for compression. Otherwise, there are m letters in the equation and each is covered by at least one pair/block, so for one of $2n$ choice at least $\frac{m}{2n}$ letters are covered, so at least $\frac{m}{4n}$ letters are removed by some compression. Thus the new equation has at most

$$\underbrace{m}_{previous} - \underbrace{\frac{m}{4n}}_{removed} + \underbrace{2n}_{popped} = m\left(1 - \frac{1}{4n}\right) + 2n$$

$$\leq 8n^2\left(1 - \frac{1}{4n}\right) + 2n$$

$$= 8n^2 - 2n + 2n = 8n^2$$

letters, where the inequality follows by the inductive assumption that $m \leq 8n^2$. Going for the bit-size, each symbol requires at most logarithmic number of bits, and so

Lemma 7. WordEqSAT *runs in* $\mathcal{O}(n^2 \log n)$ *(bit) space.*

With some effort we can make the above if analysis much tighter, see Sect. 4.1.

Theorem 1 ([36]). *The recompression based algorithm (nondeterministically) decides word equations problem in* $\mathcal{O}(n \log n)$ *bit-space; moreover, the stored equation has linear length.*

Moreover, with some extra effort one can remove also the logarithmic dependency, and show that satisfiability of word equations is in non-deterministic linear space, i.e. the problem is context sensitive. Surprisingly, it is enough to employ Huffman coding for the equation and run a variant of the algorithm. However, the analysis requires a deeper understanding of how fragments of the equation are changed during the algorithm and how they depend one on another.

Theorem 2 ([37]). *A variant of recompression based algorithm which encodes the equation using Huffman coding (nondeterministically) decides word equations problem in* $\mathcal{O}(m)$ *bit-space; where* m *is the bit-size encoding of the input using any prefix-free code.*

Note that we allow some bit-optimization in the size of the input problem.

As a reminder: a PSPACE algorithm for this problem was already known [65]. Its memory consumption is not stated explicitly in that work, however, it is much larger than $\mathcal{O}(n \log n)$: the stored equations are of length $\mathcal{O}(n^3)$ and during the transformations the algorithm uses essentially more memory.

3   Extensions of the Algorithm for Word Equations

3.1 $\mathcal{O}(n \log n)$ Space

In order to improve the space consumption from quadratic to $\mathcal{O}(n \log n)$ we want to perform several compressions in parallel. To make it more precise, observe that

- All block compressions (also for different letters) can be performed in parallel, as such blocks do not overlap. Moreover, uncrossing different letters can also be done in parallel: if a is the first letter of $S(X)$ and b the last, then we pop from X the a-prefix and b-suffix.
- If Σ_ℓ and Σ_r are disjoint, then the pair compressions for ab with $a \in \Sigma_\ell$ and $b \in \Sigma_r$ can be done in parallel. Similarly as in the previous case, uncrossing can be done in parallel, by popping first letter if it is from Σ_r and last if it is from Σ_ℓ.
- We do not compress all pairs, only those from $\mathcal{O}(1)$ partitions Σ_ℓ, Σ_r that cover 'many' occurrences of pairs in the equation and in the solution.

The crucial things is the choice of partitions. It turns out that choosing a random partition reduces the length of the solution by a constant fraction: consider two consecutive letters ab in $S(X)$. If $a = b$ then they will be compressed as part of the maximal block. If $a \neq b$ then there is $1/4$ chance that $ab \in \Sigma_\ell \Sigma_r$. Thus, in expectation, the length of the word shortens by one fourth of its length.

A similar argument also shows that the number of letters in the equation remains linear, when a random partition is chosen. Thus, the equation will be of linear size (though each letter may need $\mathcal{O}(\log n)$ bits for the encoding).

3.2 Equations with Regular Constraints and Inversion; Equations in Free Groups

As already mentioned, it is natural and important to extend the word equations by regular constraints and inversion, in particular this leads to an algorithm for equations in free groups [13] (the reduction between those two problems is fully syntactical and does not depend on the particular algorithm for solving word equations). Note that it is not known, whether the algorithm generating a representation of all solutions can be also extended by regular constraints and inversion. Thus the only previously known algorithm for representation of all solutions of an equation in a free group was due to Razborov [68], and it was based on Makanin's algorithm for word equations in free groups.

Adding the regular constraints to the recompression based algorithm Word-EqSAT is fairly standard: We can encode all constraints using one non-deterministic finite automaton (the constraints for particular variables differ only in the set of accepting states). For each letter c we store its *transition function*, i.e. a function $f_c : Q \to 2^Q$, which says that the automaton in state q after reading a letter c reaches a state in $f_c(q)$. This function naturally extends to words: it still defines which states can be reached from q after reading w. Formally $f_{wa} = (f_w \circ f_a)(q) = \{p \mid \exists q' \in f_w(q) \text{ i } p \in f_a(q')\}$ for a letter a. If we introduce a new letter c (which replaces a word w) then we naturally define the transition function $f_c \leftarrow f_w$. We can express the regular constraints in terms of this function: saying that $S(X)$ is accepted by an automaton means that $f_{S(X)}(q_0)$ is one of the accepting states. So it is enough to guess the value of $f_{S(X)}$ which satisfies this condition; in this way we can talk about the value f_X for a variable X. Popping letters from a variable means that we need to adjust the transition function, i.e. when we replace X by aX then $f_X = f_a \circ f_{X'}$, we similarly define f_X when we pop letters to the right.

More problems are caused by the *inversion*: intuitively it corresponds to taking the inverse element in the group and on the semigroup level we this is simulated by requiring that $\overline{\overline{a}} = a$ for each letter a and $\overline{a_1 a_2 \ldots a_m} = \overline{a_m} \ldots \overline{a_2} \overline{a_1}$. This has an impact on the compression: when we compress a pair ab to c, then we should also replace $\overline{ab} = \overline{b}\overline{a}$ by a letter $\overline{c}$. At the first sight this looks easy, but becomes problematic, when those two pairs are not disjoint, i.e. when $\overline{a} = a$ (or $\overline{b} = b$); in general we cannot exclude such a case and if it happens, in a sequence $ba\overline{b}$ during the pair compression for ba we want to simultaneously replace ba and $a\overline{b}$, which is not possible. Instead, we replace maximal fragments that can be fully covered with pairs ab or $\overline{b}\overline{a}$, in this case this: the whole triple $ba\overline{b}$. In the worst case (when $a = \overline{a}$ and $b = \overline{b}$) we need to replace whole sequences of the form $(ab)^n$, which is a common generalisation of both pairs and blocks compression.

Theorem 3 ([6,14]). *A recompression based algorithm generates in polynomial space the description of all solutions of a word equation in free semigroups with inversion and regular constraints.*

3.3   Context Unification

Recall that the context unification is a generalisation of word equations to the case of terms (Fig. 2). What type of equations we would like to consider? Clearly we consider terms over a fixed signature (which is usually part of the input), and allow occurrences of constants and variables. If we allow only that the variables represent full terms, then the satisfiability of such equations is decidable in polynomial time [69] and so probably does not generalise the word equations (which are NP-hard). This is also easy to observe when we look closer at a word equation: the words represented by the variables can be concatenated at both ends, i.e. they represent terms with a missing argument.

We arrive at a conclusion that our generalisation should use variables *with arguments*, i.e. the (second-order) variables take an argument that is a full term and can use it, perhaps several times. Such a definition leads to a *second-order unification*, which is known to be undecidable even in very restricted subcases [16, 26,47,49].

Thus we would like to have a subclass of second order unification that still generalises word equations. In order to do that we put additional restriction on the solutions: each argument can be used by the term *exactly once*. Observe that this still generalises the word equations: using the argument exactly once naturally corresponds to concatenation (Fig. 1).

Formally, in the context unification problem [7,8,74], we consider an equation $u = v$ in which we use term variables (representing closed terms), which we denote by letters x, y, as well as context variables (representing terms with one 'hole' for the argument, they are usually called *contexts*), which we denote by letters X, Y. Syntactically, u and v are terms that use letters from signature Σ

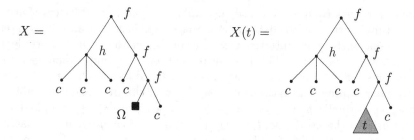

Fig. 1. A context and the same context applied on an argument.

(which is part of the input), term variables and context variables, the former are treated as symbols of arity 0, while the latter as symbols of arity 1. A *substitution* S assigns to each variable a closed term over Σ and to each context variable it assigns a *context*, i.e. a term over $\Sigma \cup \{\Omega\}$ in which the special symbol Ω has arity 0 and is used exactly once. (Intuitively it corresponds to a place in which we later substitute the argument). S is extended to u, v in a natural way, note that for a context variable X the term $S(X(t))$ is obtained by replacing in $S(X)$ the unique symbol Ω by $S(t)$. A *solution* is a substitution satisfying $S(u) = S(v)$.

Example 2. Consider a signature $\{f, c, c'\}$, where f has arity 2 while c, c' have arity 0 and consider an equation $X(c) = Y(c')$, where X and Y are context variables. The equation has a solution $S(X) = f(\Omega, c'), S(Y) = f(c, \Omega)$ and then $S(X(c)) = f(c, c') = S(Y(c'))$.

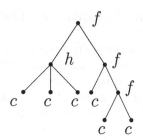

Fig. 2. Term $f(h(c, c, c), f(c, f(c, c)))$ viewed as a tree, f is of arity 2, h: 3 and c: 0.

We try to apply the main idea of the recompression also in the case of terms: we iterate local compression operations and we guarantee that the word (term) equation is polynomial size. Since several term problems were solved using compression-based methods [9,17–19,48], there is a reasonable hope that our approach may succeed.

Pair and block compression easily generalise to sequences of letters of arity 1 (we can think of them as words), unfortunately, there is no guarantee that a term has even one such letter. Intuitively, we rather expect that it has mostly leaves and symbols of larger arity. This leads us to another local compression operation: *leaf compression*. Consider a node labelled with f and its i-th child that is a leaf. We want to compress f with this child, leaving other children (and their subtrees) unchanged. Formally, given f of arity at least 1, position $1 \leq i \leq \operatorname{ar}(f)$ and a letter c of arity 0 the $\mathsf{LeafComp}(f, i, c, t)$ operation (*leaf compression*) replaces in term t nodes labelled with f and subterms $t_1, \ldots, t_{i-1}, c, t_{i+1}, \ldots, t_{\operatorname{ar}(f)}$ (where c and position i are fixed, while other terms $t_1, \ldots, t_{i-1}, t_{i+1}, \ldots, t_{\operatorname{ar}(f)}$—varying) by a term labelled with f' and subterms $t'_1, \ldots, t'_{i-1}, t'_{i+1}, \ldots, t'_{\operatorname{ar}(f)}$ that are obtained by applying recursively $\mathsf{LeafComp}$ to terms $t_1, \ldots, t_{i-1}, t_{i+1}, \ldots, t_{\operatorname{ar}(f)}$; in other words, we first change the label from f to f' and then remove the i-th child, which has a label c and we apply such a compression to all occurrences of f and c in parallel.

The notion of crossing pair generalizes to this case in a natural way and the uncrossing replaces a term variable with a constant or replaces $X(t)$ with $X(f(x_1, \ldots, x_i, t, x_{i+1}, \ldots, x_\ell))$. Note that this introduces new variables.

Now the whole algorithm looks similar as in the case of word equations, we simply use additional compression operation. However, the analysis is much more involved, as the new uncrossing introduces fresh term variables. However, their number at any point can be linearly bounded and the polynomial upper-bound follows.

Theorem 4 ([31]). *Recompression based algorithm solves context unification in nondeterministic polynomial space.*

4   Recompression and Compressed Data

The recompression technique is (partially) inspired by methods coming from the algorithm's design [1,58]. In this section we show that it is able to contribute back to algorithmics: some algorithmic questions for compressed data can be solved using a recompression technique. The obtained solutions are as good and sometimes better than the known ones, which is surprising taking into the account the robustness of the method.

4.1   Straight Line Programs and Recompression

Recall that the *Straight Line Programme (SLP)* was defined as a context-free grammar whose each nonterminal generates exactly one word. We employ the following naming conventions for SLPs: its nonterminals are ordered (without loss of generality: $X_1, X_2, \ldots, X_m$), each nonterminal has exactly one production and if X_j occurs in the production for X_i then $j < i$; we will use symbols $\mathcal{A}$, $\mathcal{B}$, etc. to denote an SLP. The unique word generated by a nonterminal X_i is denoted by $\operatorname{val}(X_i)$, while the whole SLP $\mathcal{A}$ defines a word $\operatorname{val}(\mathcal{A}) = \operatorname{val}(X_m)$.

We can treat SLP as a system of word equations (in variables $X_1, \ldots, X_m$): production $X_i \rightarrow \alpha_i$ corresponds to an equation $X_i = \alpha_i$; observe that such an equality is meaningful as $\text{val}(X) = \text{val}(\alpha)$ (where val is naturally extended to strings of letters and nonterminals), moreover, this is the unique solution of this equation. Thus the recompression technique can be applied to SLPs as well (so far we used recompression only to one equation but it easily generalises also to a system of equations).

However, there are two issues that need to be solved: non-determinism and efficiency: the recompression for word equations is highly non-deterministic while algorithms for SLPs should, if possible, be deterministic and we usually want them to be efficient, i.e. we want as small polynomial degree as possible.

Let us inspect the source of non-determinism of recompression-based approach, it is needed to:

1. establish, whether $\text{val}(X_i) = \epsilon$;
2. establish the first (and last) letter of $\text{val}(X_i)$;
3. establish the length of a-prefix and suffix of $\text{val}(X_i)$;
4. the choice of the partition to compress.

The first three question ask about some basic properties of the solution and can be easily answered in case of SLPs: assuming that we already know the answers for X_j for $j < i$: let $X_i \rightarrow \alpha_i$, then we first remove from α_i all nonterminals X_j, for which $\text{val}(X_j) = \epsilon$, and then

1. $\text{val}(X_i) = \epsilon$ if and only if $\alpha_i = \epsilon$;
2. the first letter of $\text{val}(X_i)$ is the first letter of α_i or the first letter of $\text{val}(X_j)$, if the first symbol of α_i is X_j;
3. the length of the a-prefix depends only on the letters a in α_i and the lengths of a-prefixes in nonterminals in α_i.

All those conditions can be verified in linear time. The last question is of different nature. However, the argument used to show that a good choice of a partition exists actually shown that in expectation the choice is a good one and this approach can be easily derandomised using conditional expectation approach. In particular, this subprocedure can be implemented in linear time.

Concerning the running time, the generalisations of Pop, PairComp, CutPref-Suff and BlockComp can be implemented in linear time, thus the recompression for SLPs runs in polynomial (in SLP's size) time, so polynomial in total.

Lemma 8. *The recompression for SLPs runs in $\mathcal{O}(n \log N) \leq \mathcal{O}(n^2)$ time, where n is the size of the input SLP and N is the length of the defined word.*

4.2   SLP Equality and Fully Compressed Pattern Matching

One of the first (and most important) problems considered for SLPs is the equality testing, i.e. for two SLPs we want to decide if they define the same word. The first polynomial algorithm for this problem was given in 1994 by Plandowski [63], to be more precise, his algorithm run in $\mathcal{O}(n^4)$ time. Afterwards research was mostly focused on the more general problem of *fully compressed pattern matching*: for given SLPs $\mathcal{A}$ and $\mathcal{B}$ we want to decide, whether val($\mathcal{A}$) occurs in val($\mathcal{B}$) (as a subword). The first solution to this problem was given by Karpiński et al. [40] in 1995. Gasieniec et al. [21] gave a faster randomised algorithm. In 1997 Miyazaki et al. [59] constructed an $\mathcal{O}(n^4)$ algorithm. Finally, Lifshits gave an $\mathcal{O}(n^3)$ algorithm for this problem [52]. All of the mentioned papers were based on the same original idea as Plandowski's algorithm.

Recompression can be naturally applied to equality testing of SLPs: given two SLPs $\mathcal{A}$ and $\mathcal{B}$ we add an equation $X_{m_A} = Y_{m_A}$ and ask about the satisfiability of the whole system. As already observed, the recompression based algorithm will work in polynomial time. It turns out that the proper implementation (using many nontrivial algorithmic techniques) runs in time $\mathcal{O}(n \log N)$, where $N = |\text{val}(\mathcal{A})| = |\text{val}(\mathcal{B})|$ (if $|\text{val}(\mathcal{A})| \neq |\text{val}(\mathcal{B})|$ then clearly $\mathcal{A}$ and $\mathcal{B}$ are not equal) and n the sum of sizes of SLPs $\mathcal{A}$ and $\mathcal{B}$. In order to obtain such a running time, we need several optimisations.

Theorem 5 ([33]). *The recompression based algorithm for equality testing for SLPs runs in $\mathcal{O}(n \log N)$ time, where n is the sum of SLPs' sizes while N the size of the defined (decompressed) words.*

In order to use the recompression technique for the fully compressed pattern matching problem, we need some essential modifications: consider *ba*-pair compression on a pattern ab and text bab. We obtain the same pattern ab and text cb, loosing the only occurrence of the pattern in the text. This happens because the compression (on the text) is done partially on the pattern occurrence and partially outside it. To remedy this, we perform the compression operations in a particular order, which takes into the account what are the first and last letters of pattern and text. (In the considered example, we make the ab-pair compression first and this preserves the occurrences of the pattern.) Similar approach works also for block compression.

Theorem 6 ([33]). *The recompression based algorithm for fully compressed pattern matching runs in $\mathcal{O}(n \log M)$ time, where n is the sum of SLPs' sizes while M the length of the (uncompressed) pattern.*

References

1. Alstrup, S., Brodal, G.S., Rauhe, T.: Pattern matching in dynamic texts. In: Shmoys, D.B. (ed.) SODA, pp. 819–828. ACM/SIAM (2000). https://doi.org/10.1145/338219.338645, http://dl.acm.org/citation.cfm?id=338219.338645
2. Busatto, G., Lohrey, M., Maneth, S.: Efficient memory representation of XML document trees. Inf. Syst. 33(4–5), 456–474 (2008)
3. Büchi, J.R., Senger, S.: Definability in the existential theory of concatenation and undecidable extensions of this theory. Math. Log. Q. 34(4), 337–342 (1988). https://doi.org/10.1002/malq.19880340410

4. Charatonik, W., Pacholski, L.: Word equations with two variables. In: IWWERT, pp. 43–56 (1991). https://doi.org/10.1007/3-540-56730-5_30
5. Charikar, M., et al.: The smallest grammar problem. IEEE Trans. Inf. Theory **51**(7), 2554–2576 (2005). https://doi.org/10.1109/TIT.2005.850116
6. Ciobanu, L., Diekert, V., Elder, M.: Solution sets for equations over free groups are EDT0L languages. IJAC **26**(5), 843–886 (2016). https://doi.org/10.1142/S0218196716500363
7. Comon, H.: Completion of rewrite systems with membership constraints. Part I: deduction rules. J. Symb. Comput. **25**(4), 397–419 (1998). https://doi.org/10.1006/jsco.1997.0185
8. Comon, H.: Completion of rewrite systems with membership constraints. Part II: constraint solving. J. Symb. Comput. **25**(4), 421–453 (1998). https://doi.org/10.1006/jsco.1997.0186
9. Creus, C., Gascón, A., Godoy, G.: One-context unification with STG-compressed terms is in NP. In: Tiwari, A. (ed.) 23rd International Conference on Rewriting Techniques and Applications (RTA 2012). LIPIcs, vol. 15, pp. 149–164. Schloss Dagstuhl – Leibniz Zentrum fuer Informatik, Dagstuhl, Germany (2012). https://doi.org/10.4230/LIPIcs.RTA.2012.149, http://drops.dagstuhl.de/opus/volltexte/2012/3490
10. Dąbrowski, R., Plandowski, W.: Solving two-variable word equations. In: Díaz, J., Karhumäki, J., Lepistö, A., Sannella, D. (eds.) ICALP 2004. LNCS, vol. 3142, pp. 408–419. Springer, Heidelberg (2004). https://doi.org/10.1007/978-3-540-27836-8_36
11. Dąbrowski, R., Plandowski, W.: On word equations in one variable. Algorithmica **60**(4), 819–828 (2011). https://doi.org/10.1007/s00453-009-9375-3
12. Diekert, V., Elder, M.: Solutions of twisted word equations, EDT0L languages, and context-free groups. In: Chatzigiannakis, I., Indyk, P., Kuhn, F., Muscholl, A. (eds.) ICALP. LIPIcs, vol. 80, pp. 96:1–96:14. Schloss Dagstuhl - Leibniz-Zentrum fuer Informatik (2017). https://doi.org/10.4230/LIPIcs.ICALP.2017.96
13. Diekert, V., Gutiérrez, C., Hagenah, C.: The existential theory of equations with rational constraints in free groups is PSPACE-complete. Inf. Comput. **202**(2), 105–140 (2005). http://dx.doi.org/10.1016/j.ic.2005.04.002
14. Diekert, V., Jeż, A., Plandowski, W.: Finding all solutions of equations in free groups and monoids with involution. Inf. Comput. **251**, 263–286 (2016). https://doi.org/10.1016/j.ic.2016.09.009
15. Diekert, V., Muscholl, A.: Solvability of equations in free partially commutative groups is decidable. Int. J. Algebr. Comput. **16**, 1047–1070 (2006). https://doi.org/10.1142/S0218196706003372. Conference version in Proceedings of ICALP 2001, pp. 543-554, LNCS 2076
16. Farmer, W.M.: Simple second-order languages for which unification is undecidable. Theor. Comput. Sci. **87**(1), 25–41 (1991). https://doi.org/10.1016/S0304-3975(06)80003-4
17. Gascón, A., Godoy, G., Schmidt-Schauß, M.: Context matching for compressed terms. In: Proceedings of the Twenty-Third Annual IEEE Symposium on Logic in Computer Science, LICS 2008, 24–27 June 2008, Pittsburgh, PA, USA, pp. 93–102. IEEE Computer Society (2008). https://doi.org/10.1109/LICS.2008.17
18. Gascón, A., Godoy, G., Schmidt-Schauß, M.: Unification and matching on compressed terms. ACM Trans. Comput. Log. **12**(4), 26 (2011). https://doi.org/10.1145/1970398.1970402

19. Gascón, A., Godoy, G., Schmidt-Schauß, M., Tiwari, A.: Context unification with one context variable. J. Symb. Comput. **45**(2), 173–193 (2010). https://doi.org/10.1016/j.jsc.2008.10.005

20. Gasieniec, L., Karpiński, M., Plandowski, W., Rytter, W.: Efficient algorithms for Lempel-Ziv encoding. In: SWAT, pp. 392–403 (1996). https://doi.org/10.1007/3-540-61422-2_148

21. Gasieniec, L., Karpiński, M., Plandowski, W., Rytter, W.: Randomized efficient algorithms for compressed strings: the finger-print approach. In: CPM, pp. 39–49 (1996). https://doi.org/10.1007/3-540-61258-0_3

22. Gasieniec, L., Rytter, W.: Almost optimal fully LZW-compressed pattern matching. In: DCC, pp. 316–325. IEEE Computer Society (1999)

23. Gawrychowski, P.: Pattern matching in Lempel-Ziv compressed strings: fast, simple, and deterministic. In: Demetrescu, C., Halldórsson, M.M. (eds.) ESA 2011. LNCS, vol. 6942, pp. 421–432. Springer, Heidelberg (2011). https://doi.org/10.1007/978-3-642-23719-5_36

24. Gawrychowski, P.: Tying up the loose ends in fully LZW-compressed pattern matching. In: Dürr, C., Wilke, T. (eds.) STACS. LIPIcs, vol. 14, pp. 624–635. Schloss Dagstuhl – Leibniz-Zentrum für Informatik (2012). https://doi.org/10.4230/LIPIcs.STACS.2012.624

25. Gawrychowski, P.: Optimal pattern matching in LZW compressed strings. ACM Trans. Algorithms **9**(3), 25 (2013). https://doi.org/10.1145/2483699.2483705

26. Goldfarb, W.D.: The undecidability of the second-order unification problem. Theor. Comput. Sci. **13**, 225–230 (1981). https://doi.org/10.1016/0304-3975(81)90040-2

27. Gutiérrez, C.: Satisfiability of word equations with constants is in exponential space. In: FOCS, pp. 112–119 (1998). https://doi.org/10.1109/SFCS.1998.743434

28. Ilie, L., Plandowski, W.: Two-variable word equations. ITA **34**(6), 467–501 (2000). https://doi.org/10.1051/ita:2000126

29. Jaffar, J.: Minimal and complete word unification. J. ACM **37**(1), 47–85 (1990)

30. Jeż, A.: The complexity of compressed membership problems for finite automata. Theory Comput. Syst. **55**, 685–718 (2014). https://doi.org/10.1007/s00224-013-9443-6

31. Jeż, A.: Context unification is in PSPACE. In: Koutsoupias, E., Esparza, J., Fraigniaud, P. (eds.) ICALP. LNCS, vol. 8573, pp. 244–255. Springer (2014). https://doi.org/10.1007/978-3-662-43951-7_21, full version at http://arxiv.org/abs/1310.4367

32. Jeż, A.: Approximation of grammar-based compression via recompression. Theor. Comput. Sci. **592**, 115–134 (2015). https://doi.org/10.1016/j.tcs.2015.05.027

33. Jeż, A.: Faster fully compressed pattern matching by recompression. ACM Trans. Algorithms **11**(3), 20:1–20:43 (2015). https://doi.org/10.1145/2631920

34. Jeż, A.: A really simple approximation of smallest grammar. Theor. Comput. Sci. **616**, 141–150 (2016). https://doi.org/10.1016/j.tcs.2015.12.032

35. Jeż, A.: One-variable word equations in linear time. Algorithmica **74**, 1–48 (2016). https://doi.org/10.1007/s00453-014-9931-3

36. Jeż, A.: Recompression: a simple and powerful technique for word equations. J. ACM **63**(1), 4:1–4:51 (2016). https://doi.org/10.1145/2743014

37. Jeż, A.: Word equations in nondeterministic linear space. In: Chatzigiannakis, I., Indyk, P., Kuhn, F., Muscholl, A. (eds.) ICALP. LIPIcs, vol. 80, pp. 95:1–95:13. Schloss Dagstuhl–Leibniz-Zentrum fuer Informatik (2017). https://doi.org/10.4230/LIPIcs.ICALP.2017.95

38. Jeż, A., Lohrey, M.: Approximation of smallest linear tree grammar. Inf. Comput. **251**, 215–251 (2016). https://doi.org/10.1016/j.ic.2016.09.007

39. Kärkkäinen, J., Mikkola, P., Kempa, D.: Grammar precompression speeds up Burrows–Wheeler compression. In: Calderón-Benavides, L., González-Caro, C., Chávez, E., Ziviani, N. (eds.) SPIRE 2012. LNCS, vol. 7608, pp. 330–335. Springer, Heidelberg (2012). https://doi.org/10.1007/978-3-642-34109-0_34

40. Karpinski, M., Rytter, W., Shinohara, A.: Pattern-matching for strings with short descriptions. In: Galil, Z., Ukkonen, E. (eds.) CPM 1995. LNCS, vol. 937, pp. 205–214. Springer, Heidelberg (1995). https://doi.org/10.1007/3-540-60044-2_44

41. Kharlampovich, O., Myasnikov, A.: Irreducible affine varieties over a free group. II: systems in triangular quasi-quadratic form and description of residually free groups. J. Algebra **200**, 517–570 (1998)

42. Kharlampovich, O., Myasnikov, A.: Elementary theory of free non-abelian groups. J. Algebra **302**, 451–552 (2006)

43. Kościelski, A., Pacholski, L.: Complexity of Makanin's algorithm. J. ACM **43**(4), 670–684 (1996). https://doi.org/10.1145/234533.234543

44. Kościelski, A., Pacholski, L.: Makanin's algorithm is not primitive recursive. Theor. Comput. Sci. **191**(1–2), 145–156 (1998). https://doi.org/10.1016/S0304-3975(96)00321-0

45. Laine, M., Plandowski, W.: Word equations with one unknown. Int. J. Found. Comput. Sci. **22**(2), 345–375 (2011). https://doi.org/10.1142/S0129054111008088

46. Larsson, N.J., Moffat, A.: Offline dictionary-based compression. In: Data Compression Conference, pp. 296–305 (1999). https://doi.org/10.1109/DCC.1999.755679

47. Levy, J.: Linear second-order unification. In: Ganzinger, H. (ed.) RTA 1996. LNCS, vol. 1103, pp. 332–346. Springer, Heidelberg (1996). https://doi.org/10.1007/3-540-61464-8_63

48. Levy, J., Schmidt-Schauß, M., Villaret, M.: On the complexity of bounded second-order unification and stratified context unification. Log. J. IGPL **19**(6), 763–789 (2011). https://doi.org/10.1093/jigpal/jzq010

49. Levy, J., Veanes, M.: On the undecidability of second-order unification. Inf. Comput. **159**(1–2), 125–150 (2000). https://doi.org/10.1006/inco.2000.2877

50. Levy, J., Villaret, M.: Linear second-order unification and context unification with tree-regular constraints. In: Bachmair, L. (ed.) RTA 2000. LNCS, vol. 1833, pp. 156–171. Springer, Heidelberg (2000). https://doi.org/10.1007/10721975_11

51. Levy, J., Villaret, M.: Currying second-order unification problems. In: Tison, S. (ed.) RTA 2002. LNCS, vol. 2378, pp. 326–339. Springer, Heidelberg (2002). https://doi.org/10.1007/3-540-45610-4_23

52. Lifshits, Y.: Processing compressed texts: a tractability border. In: Ma, B., Zhang, K. (eds.) CPM 2007. LNCS, vol. 4580, pp. 228–240. Springer, Heidelberg (2007). https://doi.org/10.1007/978-3-540-73437-6_24

53. Lohrey, M.: Algorithmics on SLP-compressed strings: a survey. Groups Complex. Cryptol. **4**(2), 241–299 (2012)

54. Makanin, G.: The problem of solvability of equations in a free semigroup. Matematicheskii Sbornik **2**(103), 147–236 (1977). (in Russian)

55. Makanin, G.: Equations in a free group. Izv. Akad. Nauk SSR Ser. Math. **46**, 1199–1273 (1983). English translation in Math. USSR Izv. 21 (1983)

56. Makanin, G.: Decidability of the universal and positive theories of a free group. Izv. Akad. Nauk SSSR Ser. Mat. 48, 735–749 (1984). in Russian. English translation. In: Math. USSR Izvestija **25**(75–88) (1985)

57. Matiyasevich, Y.: Some decision problems for traces. In: Adian, S., Nerode, A. (eds.) LFCS 1997. LNCS, vol. 1234, pp. 248–257. Springer, Heidelberg (1997). https://doi.org/10.1007/3-540-63045-7_25

58. Mehlhorn, K., Sundar, R., Uhrig, C.: Maintaining dynamic sequences under equality tests in polylogarithmic time. Algorithmica **17**(2), 183–198 (1997). https://doi.org/10.1007/BF02522825

59. Miyazaki, M., Shinohara, A., Takeda, M.: An improved pattern matching algorithm for strings in terms of straight-line programs. In: Apostolico, A., Hein, J. (eds.) CPM 1997. LNCS, vol. 1264, pp. 1–11. Springer, Heidelberg (1997). https://doi.org/10.1007/3-540-63220-4_45

60. Nevill-Manning, C.G., Witten, I.H.: Identifying hierarchical structure in sequences: a linear-time algorithm. J. Artif. Intell. Res. (JAIR) **7**, 67–82 (1997). https://doi.org/10.1613/jair.374

61. Niehren, J., Pinkal, M., Ruhrberg, P.: On equality up-to constraints over finite trees, context unification, and one-step rewriting. In: McCune, W. (ed.) CADE 1997. LNCS, vol. 1249, pp. 34–48. Springer, Heidelberg (1997). https://doi.org/10.1007/3-540-63104-6_4

62. Niehren, J., Pinkal, M., Ruhrberg, P.: A uniform approach to under specification and parallelism. In: Cohen, P.R., Wahlster, W. (eds.) ACL, pp. 410–417. Morgan Kaufmann Publishers/ACL (1997). https://doi.org/10.3115/979617.979670

63. Plandowski, W.: Testing equivalence of morphisms on context-free languages. In: van Leeuwen, J. (ed.) ESA 1994. LNCS, vol. 855, pp. 460–470. Springer, Heidelberg (1994). https://doi.org/10.1007/BFb0049431

64. Plandowski, W.: Satisfiability of word equations with constants is in NEXPTIME. In: STOC, pp. 721–725. ACM (1999). https://doi.org/10.1145/301250.301443

65. Plandowski, W.: Satisfiability of word equations with constants is in PSPACE. J. ACM **51**(3), 483–496 (2004). https://doi.org/10.1145/990308.990312

66. Plandowski, W.: An efficient algorithm for solving word equations. In: Kleinberg, J.M. (ed.) STOC, pp. 467–476. ACM (2006). https://doi.org/10.1145/1132516.1132584

67. Plandowski, W., Rytter, W.: Application of Lempel-Ziv encodings to the solution of word equations. In: Larsen, K.G., Skyum, S., Winskel, G. (eds.) ICALP 1998. LNCS, vol. 1443, pp. 731–742. Springer, Heidelberg (1998). https://doi.org/10.1007/BFb0055097

68. Razborov, A.A.: On systems of equations in free groups. Ph.D. thesis, Steklov Institute of Mathematics (1987). (in Russian)

69. Robinson, J.A.: A machine-oriented logic based on the resolution principle. J. ACM **12**(1), 23–41 (1965)

70. Rytter, W.: Application of Lempel-Ziv factorization to the approximation of grammar-based compression. Theor. Comput. Sci. **302**(1–3), 211–222 (2003). https://doi.org/10.1016/S0304-3975(02)00777-6

71. Saarela, A.: On the complexity of Hmelevskii's theorem and satisfiability of three unknown equations. In: Diekert, V., Nowotka, D. (eds.) DLT 2009. LNCS, vol. 5583, pp. 443–453. Springer, Heidelberg (2009). https://doi.org/10.1007/978-3-642-02737-6_36

72. Sahinalp, S.C., Vishkin, U.: Symmetry breaking for suffix tree construction. In: Leighton, F.T., Goodrich, M.T. (eds.) SODA, pp. 300–309. ACM (1994). https://doi.org/10.1145/195058.195164

73. Sakamoto, H.: A fully linear-time approximation algorithm for grammar-based compression. J. Discrete Algorithms **3**(2–4), 416–430 (2005). https://doi.org/10.1016/j.jda.2004.08.016

74. Schmidt-Schauß, M.: Unification of stratified second-order terms (1994). Internal Report 12/94, Johann-Wolfgang-Goethe-Universität

75. Schmidt-Schauß, M.: A decision algorithm for stratified context unification. J. Log. Comput. **12**(6), 929–953 (2002). https://doi.org/10.1093/logcom/12.6.929

76. Schmidt-Schauß, M.: Decidability of bounded second order unification. Inf. Comput. **188**(2), 143–178 (2004). https://doi.org/10.1016/j.ic.2003.08.002

77. Schmidt-Schauß, M., Schulz, K.U.: On the exponent of periodicity of minimal solutions of context equations. In: Nipkow, T. (ed.) RTA 1998. LNCS, vol. 1379, pp. 61–75. Springer, Heidelberg (1998). https://doi.org/10.1007/BFb0052361

78. Schmidt-Schauß, M., Schulz, K.U.: Solvability of context equations with two context variables is decidable. J. Symb. Comput. **33**(1), 77–122 (2002). https://doi.org/10.1006/jsco.2001.0438

79. Schulz, K.U.: Makanin's algorithm for word equations-two improvements and a generalization. In: Schulz, K.U. (ed.) IWWERT 1990. LNCS, vol. 572, pp. 85–150. Springer, Heidelberg (1992). https://doi.org/10.1007/3-540-55124-7_4

80. Storer, J.A., Szymanski, T.G.: The macro model for data compression. In: STOC, pp. 30–39 (1978)

How to Prove that a Language Is Regular or Star-Free?

Jean-Éric Pin[(✉)]

IRIF, CNRS and Université Paris-Diderot, Case 7014, 75205 Paris Cedex 13, France
Jean-Eric.Pin@irif.fr

Abstract. This survey article presents some standard and less standard methods used to prove that a language is regular or star-free.

Most books of automata theory [9, 23, 29, 45, 49] offer exercises on regular languages, including some difficult ones. Further examples can be found on the web sites math.stackexchange.com and cs.stackexchange.com. Another good source of tough questions is the recent book *200 Problems in Formal Languages and Automata Theory* [36]. Surprisingly, there are very few exercises related to star-free languages. In this paper, we present various methods to prove that a language is regular or star-free.

1 Background

1.1 Regular and Star-Free Languages

Let's start by reminding us what a regular language and a star-free language are.

Definition 1. *The class of* regular languages *is the smallest class of languages containing the finite languages that is closed under finite union, finite product and star.*

The definition of star-free languages follows the same pattern, with the difference that the star operation is replaced by the complement:

Definition 2. *The class of* star-free languages *is the smallest class of languages containing the finite languages that is closed under finite union, finite product and complement.*

For instance, the language A^* is star-free, since $A^* = \emptyset^c$. More generally, if B is a subset of A, then B^* is star-free since

$$B^* = A^* - \sum_{a \in A-B} A^* a A^* = \left(\sum_{a \in A-B} \emptyset^c a \emptyset^c \right)^c$$

J.-É. Pin—Work supported by the DeLTA project (ANR-16-CE40-0007).

A. Leporati et al. (Eds.): LATA 2020, LNCS 12038, pp. 68–88, 2020.
https://doi.org/10.1007/978-3-030-40608-0_5

On the alphabet $\{a, b\}$, the language $(ab)^*$ is star-free since

$$(ab)^* = (b\emptyset^c + \emptyset^c a + \emptyset^c aa\emptyset^c + \emptyset^c bb\emptyset^c)^c.$$

Since regular languages are closed under complement, every star-free language is regular, but the converse is not true: one can show that the language $(aa)^*$ is not star-free.

1.2 Early Results and Their Consequences

Kleene's theorem [26] states that regular languages are accepted by finite automata.

Theorem 1. *Let L be a language. The following conditions are equivalent:*

(1) L is regular,
(2) L is accepted by a finite deterministic automaton,
(3) L is accepted by a finite non-deterministic automaton.

Given a language L and a word u, the *left [right] quotient* of L by u are defined by $u^{-1}L = \{v \mid uv \in L\}$ and $Lu^{-1} = \{v \mid vu \in L\}$, respectively. The quotients of a regular [star-free] language are also regular [star-free].

Here is another standard result, due to Nerode.

Theorem 2. *A language is regular if and only if it has finitely many left (respectively right) quotients.*

Example 1. Nerode's theorem suffices to show that if L_1 and L_2 are regular [star-free], then the language

$$L = \{uw \mid \text{there exists } v \text{ such that } uv \in L_1 \text{ and } vw \in L_2\}$$

is also regular [star-free]. Indeed $L = \bigcup_{v \in A^*} (L_1 v^{-1})(v^{-1}L_2)$ and since L_1 and L_2 are regular [star-free], this apparently infinite union can be rewritten as a finite union. Thus L is regular [star-free].

1.3 Recognition by a Monoid and Syntactic Monoid

It is often useful to have a more algebraic definition of regular languages, based on the following result.

Proposition 1. *Let L be a language. The following conditions are equivalent:*

(1) L is regular,
(2) L is recognised by a finite monoid,
(3) the syntactic monoid of L is finite.

For readers who may have forgotten the definitions used in this proposition, here are some reminders. A language L of A^* is *recognised by a monoid* M if there is a surjective monoid morphism $f : A^* \to M$ and a subset P of M such that $f^{-1}(P) = L$.

The *syntactic congruence* of a language L of A^* is the equivalence relation $\sim_L$ on A^* defined as follows: $u \sim_L v$ if and only if, for every $x, y \in A^*$, xuy and xvy are either both in L or both outside of L. The *syntactic monoid* of L is the quotient monoid $A^*/\sim_L$.

Moreover, the syntactic monoid of a regular language is the transition monoid of its minimal automaton, which gives a convenient algorithm to compute it. It is also the minimal monoid (in size, but also for the division ordering[1]) that recognises the language.

Syntactic monoids are particularly useful to show that a language is star-free. Recall that a finite monoid M is *aperiodic* if, for every $x \in M$, there exists $n \geqslant 0$ such that $x^{n+1} = x^n$.

Theorem 3 (Schützenberger [46]). *For a language L, the following conditions are equivalent:*

(1) L is star-free,
(2) L is recognised by a finite aperiodic monoid,
(3) the syntactic monoid of L a finite aperiodic monoid.

Schützenberger's theorem is considered, right after Kleene's theorem, as the most important result of the algebraic theory of automata.

Example 2. The languages $(ab + ba)^*$ and $(a(ab)^*b)^*$ are star-free, but the languages $(aa)^*$ and $(a + bab)^*$ are not. This is easy to prove by computing the syntactic monoid of these languages.

The following classic example is a good example of the usefulness of the monoid approach. For each language L, let $\sqrt{L} = \{u \mid uu \in L\}$.

Proposition 2. *If L is regular [star-free], then so is $\sqrt{L}$.*

Proof. Let $h : A^* \to M$ be the syntactic morphism of L, let $P = h(L)$ and let $Q = \{x \in M \mid x^2 \in P\}$. Then

$$h^{-1}(Q) = \{u \in A^* \mid h(u) \in Q\} = \{u \in A^* \mid h(u)^2 \in P\}$$
$$= \{u \in A^* \mid h(u^2) \in P\} = \{u \in A^* \mid u^2 \in L\} = \sqrt{L}.$$

Thus M recognises $\sqrt{L}$ and the result follows.

Although the star operation is prohibited in the definition of a star-free language, some languages of the form L^* are star-free. A submonoid M of A^* is *pure* if, for all $u \in A^*$ and $n > 0$, the condition $u^n \in M$ implies $u \in M$. The following result is due to Restivo [43] for finite languages and to Straubing [52] for the general case.

---

[1] Let M and N be monoids. We say that M *divides* N if there is a submonoid R of N and a monoid morphism that maps R onto M.

Theorem 4. *If L is star-free and L^* is pure, then L^* is star-free.*

Here is another example, based on [51, Theorem 5]. For each language L, let

$$f_W(L) = \{u \in A^* \mid \text{there exists } x, z \in A^* \text{ and } y \in W \text{ with } u = xz \text{ and } xyz \in L\}$$

Proposition 3. *If L is regular [star-free], then so is $f_W(L)$.*

Proof. Let $h: A^* \to M$ be the syntactic morphism of L and let $P = h(L)$. Note that the conditions $x^{-1}Lz^{-1} \cap W \neq \emptyset$ and $P \cap h(x)h(W)h(z) \neq \emptyset$ are equivalent, for any $x, z \in A^*$. Setting $R = h(W)$ and $T = \{(u, v) \in M \times M \mid uRv \cap P \neq \emptyset\}$ one gets

$$f_W(L) = \bigcup_{(u,v)\in T} h^{-1}(u)h^{-1}(v).$$

and the result now follows easily.

2   Iteration Properties

The bible on this topic is the book of de Luca and Varricchio [13]. I only present here a selection of their numerous results.

2.1   Pumping

The standard pumping lemma is designed to prove that a language is *non-regular*, although some students try to use it to prove the opposite. In a commendable effort to comfort these poor students, several authors have proposed extensions of the pumping lemma that *characterise* regular languages. The first is due to Jaffe [24]:

Theorem 5. *A language L is regular if and only if there is an integer m such that every word x of length $\geqslant m$ can be written as $x = uvw$, with $v \neq 1$, and for all words z and for all $k \geqslant 0$, $xz \in L$ if and only if $uv^k wz \in L$.*

Stronger versions were proposed by Stanat and Weiss [50] and Ehrenfeucht, Parikh and Rozenberg [15], but the most powerful version was given by Varricchio [54].

Theorem 6. *A language L is regular if and only if there is an integer $m > 0$ such that, for all words x, $u_1, \ldots, u_m$ and y, there exist i, j with $1 \leqslant i < j \leqslant m$ such that for all $k > 0$,*

$$x u_1 \cdots u_{i-1}(u_i \cdots u_j)^k u_{j+1} \cdots u_m y \in L \iff x u_1 \cdots u_m y \in L$$

2.2   Periodicity and Permutation

Definition 3. *Let L be a language of A^*.*

(1) L is periodic if, for any $u \in A^*$, there exist integers $n, k > 0$ such that, for all $x, y \in A^*$, $xu^n y \in L \iff xu^{n+k}y \in L$.

(2) L is n-permutable if, for any sequence $u_1, \ldots, u_n$ of n words of A^*, there exists a nontrivial permutation σ of $\{1, \ldots, n\}$ such that, for all $x, y \in A^*$, $xu_1 \cdots u_n y \in L \iff xu_{\sigma(1)} \cdots u_{\sigma(n)} y \in L$.

(3) L is permutable if it is permutable for some $n > 1$.

These definitions were introduced by Restivo and Reutenauer [44], who proved the following result.

Proposition 4. *A language is regular if and only if it is periodic and permutable.*

2.3   Iteration Properties

The book of de Luca and Varricchio [13] also contains many results about iterations properties. Here is an example of this type of results.

Proposition 5. *A language L is regular if and only if there exist integers m and s such that for any $z_1, \ldots, z_m \in A^*$, there exist integers h, k with $1 \leqslant h \leqslant k \leqslant m$, such that for all for all $u, v \in A^*$,*

$$uz_1 \cdots z_m v \in L \iff uz_1 \cdots z_{h-1}(z_h \cdots z_k)^n z_{k+1} \cdots z_m v \in L, \tag{1}$$

for all $n \geqslant s$.

3   Rewriting Systems and Well Quasi-orders

Rewriting systems and well quasi-orders are two powerful methods to prove the regularity of a language. We follow the terminology of Otto's survey [37].

3.1   Rewriting Systems

A *rewriting system* is a binary relation R on A^*. A pair (ℓ, r) from R is usually referred to as the *rewrite rule* or simply the *rule* $\ell \to r$. A rule is *special* if $r = 1$, *context-free* if $|\ell| \leqslant 1$, *inverse context-free* if $|r| \leqslant 1$, *length-reducing* if $|r| < |\ell|$. It is *monadic* if it is length-reducing and inverse context-free. A rewriting system is special (context-free, inverse context-free, length-reducing, monadic) if its rules have the corresponding properties.

The *reduction relation* $\xrightarrow{*}_R$ the reflexive and transitive closure of the *single-step reduction relation* $\to_R$ defined as follows: $u \to_R v$ if $u = x\ell y$ and $v = xry$ for some $(\ell, r) \in R$ and some $x, y \in A^*$. For each language L, we set

$$[L]_{\xrightarrow{*}_R} = \{v \in A^* \mid \text{ there exists } u \in L \text{ such that } u \xrightarrow{*}_R v\}$$

A rewriting system R is said to *preserve regularity* if, for each regular language L, the language $[L]_{\xrightarrow{*}_R}$ is regular. The following result is well-known.

Theorem 7. *Inverse context-free rewriting systems preserve regularity.*

Proof. Let R be an inverse context-free rewriting system and let L be a regular language. Starting from the minimal deterministic automaton of L, construct an automaton with the same set of states, but with 1-transitions, by iterating the following process: for each rule $u \to 1$ and for each path $p \overset{u}{\leadsto} q$, create a new transition $p \overset{1}{\to} q$; for each rule $v \to a$ with $a \in A$ and for each path $p \overset{v}{\leadsto} q$, create a new transition $p \overset{a}{\to} q$. The automaton obtained at the end of the iteration process will accept $[L]_{\overset{*}{\to}_R}$.

A similar technique can be used to prove the following result [38]. If K is a regular language, then the smallest language L containing K and such that $xu^+y \subseteq L \implies xy \in L$ is regular.

3.2 Suffix Rewriting Systems

A *suffix rewriting system* is a binary relation S on A^*. Its elements are called *suffix rules*. The *suffix-reduction* relation $\overset{*}{\to}_S$ defined by S is the reflexive transitive closure of the *single-step suffix-reduction* relation defined as follows: $u \to_S v$ if $u = x\ell$ and $v = xr$ for some $(\ell, r) \in S$ and some $x \in A^*$. *Prefix rewriting systems* are defined symmetrically. For each language L, we set

$$[L]_{\overset{*}{\to}_S} = \{v \in A^* \mid \text{there exists } u \in L \text{ such that } u \overset{*}{\to}_S v\}$$

The following early result is due to Büchi [8].

Theorem 8. *Suffix (prefix) rewriting systems preserve regularity.*

3.3 Deleting Rewriting Systems

We follow Hofbauer and Waldmann [22] for the definition of deleting systems. If u is a word, the *content* of u is the set $c(u)$ of all letters of u occurring in u. A *precedence relation* is an irreflexive and transitive binary relation. A precedence relation $<$ on an alphabet A can be extended to a precedence relation on A^*, by setting $u < v$ if $c(u) \neq c(v)$ and, for each $a \in c(u)$, there exists $b \in c(v)$ such that $a < b$. A rewriting system R is $<$-*deleting* if for each rule $\ell \to r$ of R, $\ell < r$.
Hofbauer and Waldmann [22] proved the following result.

Theorem 9. *Every deleting string rewriting system preserves regularity.*

3.4 Rules of the Form $u^n \to u^m$

Rules of the form $u^n \to u^m$ were studied in several papers, for instance [5,16,34]. The following result is due to Bovet and Varricchio [5].

Proposition 6. *The rewriting systems $\{(u \to uu) \mid u \in \{a,b\}^*\}$ and $\{(u \to uu) \mid u \in \{a,b\}^*, |u| \leqslant 2\}$ both preserve regularity.*

This result can be used to solve the following exercise. Let L be a language such that, for all $x, y \in A^*$, $x^{-1}Ly^{-1}$ is a semigroup. Prove that L is regular. Indeed, this condition implies that $xuy \in L$ implies $xu^2y \in L$.

Several results were obtained by Leupold [33,34]. Let us say that a rewriting system is k-*period-expanding* [k-*period-reducing*] if its rules are of the form $u^n \to u^m$, with $n < m$ [$m < n$] and $|u| = k$. Any union of finitely many k-period-expanding and k-period reducing SRSs is called a k-*periodic rewriting system*.

Proposition 7 (Leupold).

(1) Every k-periodic rewriting system preserves regularity.

(2) For each $k \leqslant 3$, the rewriting system $\{(u \to uu) \mid |u| \leqslant k\}$ preserves regularity.

(3) For each k and for $m \geqslant n$, the rewriting system $\{u^n \to u^m \mid |u| \leqslant k\}$ preserves regularity.

3.5   Well Quasi-orders

A *quasi-order* (or *preorder*) on A^* is a reflexive and transitive relation. A quasi-order $\leqslant$ is *stable* (or *monotone*) if, for all words u, v, x, y, the condition $u \leqslant v$ implies $xuy \leqslant xvy$. A language U is an *upper set* with respect to a quasi-order $\leqslant$ is the conditions $u \in U$ and $u \leqslant v$ imply $v \in U$. The *upper set generated by a language* L is the language $\uparrow L = \{u \in A^* \mid \text{there exists } v \in L \text{ such that } v \leqslant u\}$.

A quasi-order $\leqslant$ on A^* is a *well quasi-order* (*wqo*) if every upper set is generated by some finite language. The connection with regular languages was first established in [14] (see also [13, Theorem 6.3.1, p. 203] and [12]).

Theorem 10. *A language is regular if and only if it is an upper set with respect to some stable well quasi-order on A^*.*

It follows that if the reduction relation defined by a rewriting system is a well quasi-order, then this rewriting system preserves regularity. Actually, a stronger property holds. Following Conway [11], let us say that a rewriting system R is a *total regulator* if for any language L, the language $[L]_{\xrightarrow{*}_R}$ is regular.

Theorem 11. *Any rewriting system whose reduction relation is a well quasi-order is a total regulator.*

The most famous example is the rewriting system $\{1 \to a \mid a \in A\}$, which defines the subword ordering. A word $u = a_1 \cdots a_n$ is a *subword* of a word v if $v \in A^*a_1A^* \cdots A^*a_nA^*$. Higman's theorem states that if A is finite, the subword relation is a well quasi-order on A^*. It follows that for any language L (regular or not), the shuffle product $L \shuffle A^*$ is regular.

The following result extends Higman's theorem on the subword order. Let us say that a set H of words of A^* is *unavoidable* if the language $A^* - A^*HA^*$ is finite.

Theorem 12 (Ehrenfeucht, Haussler, Rozenberg [14, Theorem 4.8]). *If H is a unavoidable finite set of words of A^*, then the reduction relation of the rewriting system $\{1 \to u \mid u \in H\}$ is a well quasi-order on A^*.*

A similar result holds for rewriting systems with rules of the form $a \to u$, where a is a letter.

Theorem 13 (Bucher, Ehrenfeucht and Haussler [6, Theorem 2.3]). *Let R be a finite rewriting system with rules of the form $a \to x$ with $a \in A$ and $x \in A^*$. The following conditions are equivalent:*

(1) the relation $\xrightarrow{*}_R$ is a well quasi-order,

(2) The set $\{ax \mid x \in A^* \text{ and } a \xrightarrow{*}_R ax\} \cup \{xa \mid x \in A^* \text{ and } a \xrightarrow{*}_R xa\}$ is unavoidable,

(3) The set $\{axa \mid x \in A^* \text{ and } a \xrightarrow{*}_R axa\}$ is unavoidable.

It follows for instance that the following rewriting systems are total regulators:

$$R_1 = \{a \to aa, a \to aba, b \to bb, b \to bab\}$$
$$R_2 = \{a \to b, b \to a, b \to bb\}$$

Bucher, Ehrenfeucht and Haussler [6] considered context-free rewriting systems related to semigroup morphims. Recall that an *ordered semigroup* is a semigroup equipped with a stable partial order. Let $(S, \leqslant)$ be a finite ordered semigroup and let $\sigma \colon A^+ \to S$ be a semigroup morphism. Consider the rewriting system

$$R_\sigma = \{a \to u \mid a \in A, u \in A^+ \text{ and } \sigma(a) \leqslant \sigma(u)\}.$$

Let $\mathcal{L}$ be a finite set of languages of A^+. Consider a (possibly infinite) system of inequations of the form

$$P_i(X_1, \ldots, X_n) \subseteq E_i(X_1, \ldots, X_n) \quad (i \in I) \tag{2}$$

where each $P_i(X_1, \ldots, X_n)$ is a product built from the variables $X_1, \ldots, X_n$ and arbitrary constant languages and each $E_i(X_1, \ldots, X_n)$ is an expression built from the variables $X_1, \ldots, X_n$ and constant languages belonging to the set $\mathcal{L} \cup \{1\}$, using concatenation, possibly infinite union and possibly infinite intersection. Note that the expressions E_i can also use Kleene star, since it can be rewritten as an infinite union of products.

Theorem 14 (Kunc [30]). *Let $\sigma \colon A^+ \to S$ be a semigroup morphism that recognises all languages in $\mathcal{L}$. If $\xrightarrow{*}_{R_\sigma}$ is a well quasi-order on A^*, then the components of every maximal solution of (2) is regular and they are star-free is S is aperiodic.*

Characterising the semigroup morphisms for which $\xrightarrow{*}_{R_\sigma}$ is a well quasi-order, is an open problem. However, Kunc found a complete answer for finite semigroups $(S, =)$ ordered by the equality relation.

Theorem 15 (Kunc [30]). *Let $(S, =)$ be a finite ordered semigroup ordered by the equality relation and let $\sigma\colon A^+ \to S$ be a surjective semigroup morphism. Then the relation $\xrightarrow{*}_{R_\sigma}$ is a well quasi-order on A^* if and only if S is a chain of simple semigroups.*

In particular any finite group is a simple semigroup. It follows that if L is a language recognised by a finite group, then, for any subset S of $\mathbb{N}$, the language $\bigcup_{n \in S} L^n$ is regular.

Example 3. The following example is given by Kunc [30, Example 19]. Let L be the language consisting of those words $u \in A^+$ which contain some occurrence of b and where the difference between the length of u and the number of blocks of occurrences of b in u is even. Here is the minimal automaton of this language.

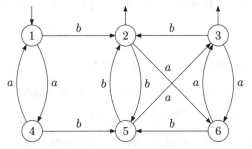

The syntactic semigroup of L is defined by the relations $a^3 = a$, $b^3 = b$, $ab^2 = a^2b$, $ba^2 = b^2a$ and $bab = b^2$. It is a chain of two simple semigroups whose elements are represented by the words a, a^2 and b, b^2, ab, ab^2, ba, b^2a, aba, ab^2a, respectively.

Let us consider the inequality $aXaXa \subseteq LXL$ with one variable X. It is easy to verify that this inequality has a largest solution, namely the regular language $(a^2)^*ab^2a(a^2)^* \cup A^*bA^+bA^*$.

3.6   Equations and Inequalities

Inequations in languages in which the right hand side is a constant language were first considered by Conway [11], see also Bala [1]. In Chap. 21 of the forthcoming Handbook of Automata Theory, Kunc and Okhotin [32] give the following remarkable result. Consider a finite system of inequations of the form

$$\bigcup_{j \in J_i} P_{i,j}(X_1, \ldots, X_n) \subseteq C_i \quad (1 \leqslant i \leqslant k) \tag{3}$$

where each $P_{i,j}(X_1, \ldots, X_n)$ is a product of arbitrary constant languages and variables, each C_i is a constant regular language and each index set J_i is possibly infinite.

Theorem 16 (Kunc and Okhotin [32]). *Every system of the form (3) has only finitely many maximal solutions and every maximal solution has all components regular. If all C_i are star-free, then the maximal solutions are star-free. Furthermore, the result still holds if any inequalities are replaced by equations.*

Proof. Let $h: A^* \to M$ be the simultaneous syntactic monoid of the languages C_i. If $(L_1, \ldots, L_n)$ is a solution, then so is $(h^{-1}h(L_1), \ldots, h^{-1}h(L_n))$. It follows that every solution is contained in a solution in which all components are recognised by h and the result follows.

Inequations of the form $XK \subseteq LX$ were considered by Kunc [30].

Theorem 17 (Kunc [30]). *Let K be an arbitrary language and let L be a regular language. Then the greatest solution of the inequality $XK \subseteq LX$ is regular.*

The situation is totally different for equations of the type $XK = LX$. Indeed Kunc [31] has shown that there exists a finite language L such that the greatest solution of the equation $XL = LX$ is co-recursively enumerable complete.

4 Logic

Logic can be used in various ways to characterise regular languages. We consider successively logic on words, linear temporal logic and logic on trees.

4.1 Logic on Words

Let $u = a_1 \ldots a_n$ be a nonempty word on the alphabet A. The *domain* of u, denoted by $\mathrm{Dom}(u)$, is the set $\mathrm{Dom}(u) = \{1, \ldots, n\}$. For each letter $a \in A$, let **a** be a unary predicate symbol, where **a**x is interpreted as "the letter in position x is an a". We also use the binary predicate symbols $<$ and S, interpreted as the usual order relation and the successor relation on $\mathrm{Dom}(u)$, respectively. The language defined by a sentence φ is the set

$$L(\varphi) = \{u \in A^+ \mid u \text{ satisfies } \varphi\}.$$

We let **FO**$[<]$ and **MSO**$[<]$ denote the set of *first-order* and *monadic second-order* formulas of signature $\{<, (\mathbf{a})_{a \in A}\}$, respectively. Similarly, we let **FO**$[S]$ and **MSO**$[S]$ denote the same sets of formulas of signature $\{S, (\mathbf{a})_{a \in A}\}$.

Let us say that a syntactic fragment of logic F *captures* a class of languages $\mathcal{C}$ if every sentence of the fragment F defines a language of $\mathcal{C}$ and every language of $\mathcal{C}$ can be defined by a sentence of F.

Two famous results are a natural ingredient of this survey. The first one is due to Buchi [7] and was independently obtained by Elgot [20] and Trakhtenbrot [53].

Theorem 18 (Buchi [7]). **MSO**$[S]$ *captures the class of regular languages.*

The second one relates first order logic and star-free languages.

Theorem 19 (McNaughton [35]). **FO**$[<]$ *captures the class of star-free languages.*

Second order logic **SO** is much more expressive than monadic second order, but two successive results led to a complete characterisation of the syntactic fragments of **SO** — in the signature $\{S, (\mathbf{a})_{a \in A}\}$ — that capture the regular languages.

A *quantifier prefix* is any word on the alphabet $\{\exists, \forall\}$. A *quantifier prefix class* is any set of quantifier prefixes. For any quantifier prefix Q, let $\Sigma_0^1(Q)$ (resp. $\Pi_0^1(Q)$) be the set of all formulas of the shape $\exists \mathbf{R}\ Q\varphi$ (resp. $\forall \mathbf{R}\ Q\varphi$) where $\mathbf{R}$ is a list of relations and φ is quantifier free. For every $k \geqslant 0$, let $\Sigma_{k+1}^1(Q)$ (resp., $\Pi_{k+1}^1(Q)$) be the set of all formulas of the form $\exists \mathbf{R}\ \Phi$ (resp. $\forall \mathbf{R}\ \Phi$) where Φ is a $\Pi_k^1(Q)$ (resp. $\Sigma_k^1(Q)$) formula. Finally, for every quantifier prefix class $\mathcal{Q}$, let $\Sigma_k^1(\mathcal{Q}) = \bigcup_{Q \in \mathcal{Q}} \Sigma_k^1(Q)$.

The fragment Σ_1^1, also known as *existential second order* and frequently denoted by **ESO**, was first explored by Eiter, Gottlob and Gurevich [17].

Theorem 20 (Eiter, Gottlob and Gurevich [17]). *A syntactic fragment* **ESO**$(\mathcal{Q})$ *captures the regular languages if and only if $\mathcal{Q}$ is a quantifier prefix class contained in $\exists^* \forall (\forall \cup \exists^*)$ whose intersection with $\exists^* \forall \{\exists, \forall\}^+$ is nonempty.*

The proof of this result is very difficult. It relies on combinatorial methods related to hypergraph transversals for the fragment $\exists^* \forall \exists^*$ and on more logical techniques for the fragment $\exists^* \forall \forall$. Eiter, Gottlob and Gurevich further proved the following dichotomy theorem: a class **ESO**$[\mathcal{Q}]$ either expresses only regular languages or it expresses some NP-complete languages.

The fragments $\Sigma_k^1(\mathcal{Q})$, with $k \geqslant 2$, were explored by Eiter, Gottlob and Schwentick [18].

Theorem 21 (Eiter, Gottlob and Schwentick [18]). *The fragments $\Sigma_2^1(\forall \forall)$ and $\Sigma_2^1(\forall \exists)$ capture the class of regular languages. Furthermore, for each $k \geqslant 0$, the fragments $\Sigma_k^1(\forall)$ and $\Sigma_k^1(\exists)$ only define regular languages.*

For more information on this topic, the reader is invited to read the beautiful survey of Eiter, Gottlob and Schwentick [19].

4.2   Linear Temporal Logic

Linear temporal logic (LTL for short) on an alphabet A is defined as follows. The vocabulary consists of an atomic proposition p_a (for each letter $a \in A$), the usual connectives $\vee$, $\wedge$ and $\neg$ and the temporal operators $\mathbf{X}$ (*next*), $\mathbf{F}$ (*eventually*) and $\mathbf{U}$ (*until*). The formulas are constructed according to the following rules:

(1) for every $a \in A$, p_a is a formula,
(2) if φ and ψ are formulas, so are $\varphi \vee \psi$, $\varphi \wedge \psi$, $\neg \varphi$, $\mathbf{X}\varphi$, $\mathbf{F}\varphi$ and $\varphi \mathbf{U} \psi$.

Semantics are defined by induction on the formation rules. Given a word $w \in A^+$, and $n \in \{1, 2, ..., |w|\}$, we define the expression "w satisfies φ at the instant n" (denoted $(w, n) \models \varphi$) as follows:

(1) $(w, n) \models p_a$ if the n-th letter of w is an a.
(2) $(w, n) \models \varphi \vee \psi$ (resp. $\varphi \wedge \psi$, $\neg\varphi$) if $(w, n) \models \varphi$ or $(w, n) \models \psi$ (resp. if $(w, n) \models \varphi$ and $(w, n) \models \psi$, if (w, n) does not satisfy φ).
(3) $(w, n) \models \mathbf{X}\varphi$ if $(w, n + 1)$ satisfies φ.
(4) $(w, n) \models \mathbf{F}\varphi$ if there exists m such that $n \leqslant m \leqslant |w|$ and $(w, m) \models \varphi$.
(5) $(w, n) \models \varphi\mathbf{U}\psi$ if there exists m such that $n \leqslant m \leqslant |w|$, $(w, m) \models \psi$ and, for every k such that $n \leqslant k < m$, $(w, k) \models \varphi$.

Note that, if $w = w_1 w_2 \cdots w_{|w|}$, $(w, n) \models \varphi$ only depends on the word $w = w_n w_{n+1} \cdots w_{|w|}$.

Example 4. Let $w = abbababcba$. Then $(w, 4) \models p_a$ since the fourth letter of w is an a, $(w, 4) \models \mathbf{X}p_b$ since the fifth letter of w is a b and $(w, 4) \models \mathbf{F}(p_c \wedge \mathbf{X}p_b)$ since cb is a factor of $babcba$.

If φ is a temporal formula, we say that w satisfies φ if $(w, 1) \models \varphi$. The language defined by a LTL formula φ is the set $L(\varphi)$ of all words of A^+ that satisfy φ.

A famous result of Kamp [25] states that LTL is equivalent to the first-order logic of order. As a consequence, one gets the following result.

Theorem 22. *A language of A^+ is star-free if and only if it is LTL-definable.*

We just defined *future* temporal formulas but one can define in the same way *past* temporal formulas by reversing time: it suffices to replace *next* by *previous*, *eventually* by *sometimes* and *until* by *since*. The expressive power of this extended temporal logic remains the same: it still captures the class of star-free languages.

4.3 Rabin's Tree Theorem

We now consider the structure $(A^*, (S_a)_{a \in A})$, where each S_a is a binary relation symbol, interpreted on A^* as follows: $S_a(u, v)$ if and only if $v = ua$. Let $\varphi(X)$ be a monadic second order formula with a free set-variable X. We write $\exists! X \; \varphi(X)$ as a short hand for the formula $\exists X \Big(\varphi(X) \wedge \big(\forall Y \; [\varphi(Y) \rightarrow (Y = X)] \big) \Big)$. A language L is said to be definable in $\mathbf{MSO}[(S_a)_{a \in A}]$ if there exists a monadic second order formula $\varphi(X)$ such that L satisfies $\exists! X \; \varphi(X)$.

The following result is a consequence of Rabin's tree theorem [42].

Theorem 23. *A language of A^* is regular if and only if it is definable in $\mathbf{MSO}[(S_a)_{a \in A}]$.*

5 Transductions

Transductions proved to be a powerful tool to study regular languages. Let us first recall some useful facts about rational and recognisable sets.

5.1   Rational and Recognisable Sets

Let M be a monoid. A subset P of M is *recognisable* if there exists a finite monoid F, and a monoid morphism $\varphi \colon M \to F$ such that $P = \varphi^{-1}(\varphi(P))$. It is well known that the class $\mathrm{Rec}(M)$ of recognisable subsets of M is closed under Boolean operations, left and right quotients and under inverses of monoid morphisms. The recognisable subsets of a product of monoids were described by Mezei (unpublished).

Theorem 24. *Let $M_1, \ldots, M_n$ be monoids. A subset of $M_1 \times \cdots \times M_n$ is recognisable if and only if it is a finite union of subsets of the form $R_1 \times \cdots \times R_n$, where $R_i \in \mathrm{Rec}(M_i)$.*

Furthermore, the following property holds:

Proposition 8. *Let $A_1, \ldots, A_n$ be finite alphabets. Then $\mathrm{Rec}(A_1^* \times \cdots \times A_n^*)$ is closed under product.*

The class $\mathrm{Rat}(M)$ of *rational* subsets of M is the smallest set $\mathcal{R}$ of subsets of M containing the finite subsets and closed under finite union, product and star (where X^* is the submonoid of M generated by X). Rational sets are closed under monoid morphisms. Kleene's theorem shows that $\mathrm{Rec}(A^*) = \mathrm{Rat}(A^*)$, but this result does not extend to arbitrary monoids.

5.2   Matrix Representations of Transductions

Let M be a monoid. We denote by $\mathcal{P}(M)$ the semiring of subsets of M with union as addition and the usual product of subsets as multiplication. Note that both $\mathrm{Rat}(M)$ and $\mathrm{Rec}(M)$ are subsemirings of $\mathcal{P}(M)$. Let also $\mathcal{P}(M)^{n \times n}$ denote the semiring of $n \times n$-matrices with entries in $\mathcal{P}(M)$.

Let M and N be two monoids. A *transduction* $\tau \colon M \to N$ is a relation on M and N, viewed as a function from M to $\mathcal{P}(N)$. One extends τ to a function $\mathcal{P}(M) \to \mathcal{P}(N)$ by setting $\tau(P) = \bigcup_{m \in P} \tau(m)$. The inverse transduction $\tau^{-1} \colon N \to M$ is defined by $\tau^{-1}(Q) = \{ m \in M \mid \tau(m) \cap Q \neq \emptyset \}$. The transduction is *rational* if the set $\{ (m, n) \in M \times N \mid n \in \tau(m) \}$ is a rational subset of $M \times N$.

A transduction $\tau \colon A^* \to M$ admits a *linear matrix representation* (λ, μ, ν) *of degree* n if there exist $n > 0$, a monoid morphism $\mu \colon A^* \to \mathcal{P}(M)^{n \times n}$, a row vector $\lambda \in \mathcal{P}(M)^{1 \times n}$ and a column vector $\nu \in \mathcal{P}(M)^{n \times 1}$ such that, for all $u \in A^*$, $\tau(u) = \lambda \mu(u) \nu$.

A *substitution* from A^* to a monoid M is a monoid morphism from A^* to $\mathcal{P}(M)$. Thus a substitution has linear matrix representation of degree 1.

Kleene-Schützenberger's theorem (see [2]) states that a transduction $\tau \colon A^* \to M$ is rational if and only if it admits a linear matrix representation with entries in $\mathrm{Rat}(M)$.

The following result already suffices for most of the applications we have in mind. It relies on the fact that every monoid morphism $M \to N$ can be extended to a semiring morphism $\mathcal{P}(M) \to \mathcal{P}(N)$ and, for each $n > 0$, to a semiring morphism $\mathcal{P}(M)^{n \times n} \to \mathcal{P}(N)^{n \times n}$.

Theorem 25. *Let $\tau\colon A^* \to M$ be a transduction that admits a linear matrix representation (λ, μ, ν) of degree n and let P be a subset of M recognised by a morphism $\eta\colon M \to N$. Then the language $\tau^{-1}(P)$ is recognised by the submonoid $\eta\mu(A^*)$ of the monoid of matrices $\mathcal{P}(N)^{n \times n}$.*

This result was generalised in [39, 40]. Let us say that a transduction $\tau\colon A^* \to M$ admits a *matrix representation* (S, μ) of degree n if there exist a morphism $\mu\colon A^* \to \mathcal{P}(M)^{n \times n}$ and an expression $S(X_{1,1}, \ldots, X_{n,n})$, where S is a possibly infinite union of products involving arbitrary languages and the variables $(X_{i,j})_{1 \leqslant i,j \leqslant n}$, such that, for all $u \in A^*$, $\tau(u) = S[\mu_{1,1}(u), \ldots, \mu_{n,n}(u)]$. Theorem 25 can now be generalized as follows.

Theorem 26. *Let $\tau\colon A^* \to M$ be a transduction that admits a matrix representation (S, μ) of degree n and let P be a subset of M recognised by a morphism $\eta\colon M \to N$. Then the language $\tau^{-1}(P)$ is recognised by the submonoid $\eta\mu(A^*)$ of the monoid of matrices $\mathcal{P}(N)^{n \times n}$.*

Example 5. Let us come back to the example $\sqrt{L} = \{u \in A^* \mid u^2 \in L\}$. Observe that $\sqrt{L} = \tau^{-1}(L)$ where $\tau(u) = u^2$. Clearly τ admits the matrix representation (S, μ) where $\mu(u) = u$ and $S = X^2$.

Example 6. Let us show that if L is a regular language and S is a subset of $\mathbb{N}^2$ then the language

$$L_S = \{u \in A^* \mid \text{there exist } (x, y) \in A^* \text{ and } (p, q) \in S$$
$$\text{such that } |x| = p|u|, |y| = q|u| \text{ and } xuy \in L\}$$

is also regular. It suffices to observe that $L_S = \tau^{-1}(L)$ where the transduction $\tau(u) = \bigcup_{(p,q) \in S} A^{p|u|} u A^{q|u|}$ admits the matrix representation (S, μ), where

$$\mu(u) = \begin{pmatrix} A^{|u|} & \emptyset & \emptyset \\ \emptyset & u & \emptyset \\ \emptyset & \emptyset & A^{|u|} \end{pmatrix} \quad \text{and} \quad S(X_{1,1}, \ldots, X_{3,3}) = \bigcup_{(p,q) \in S} X_{1,1}^p X_{2,2} X_{3,3}^q$$

Example 7. Finally the reader who likes more complicated examples may prove by the same method that if $L \subseteq \{a, b\}^*$ is regular, then the following language is also regular (D^* is the Dyck language):

$$L' = \bigcup_{n \text{ square-free}} \{u \in A^* \mid D^* u^{\lfloor \sqrt{n} \rfloor} a^n u^{n!} b \cap L \neq \emptyset\}$$

Many more examples can be found in [39, 40].

5.3   Decompositions of Languages

For each $n > 0$, consider the transduction $\tau_n\colon A^* \to (A^*)^n$ defined by

$$\tau_n(u) = \{(u_1, \ldots, u_n) \mid u_1 \cdots u_n = u\}$$

Theorem 27. *Let L be a language of A^*. The following conditions are equivalent:*

(1) L is rational,
(2) for some $n > 0$, $\tau_n(L)$ is a recognisable subset of $(A^*)^n$,
(3) for all $n > 0$, $\tau_n(L)$ is a recognisable subset of $(A^*)^n$.

Proof. (1) implies (3). Let $\mathcal{A} = (Q, A, \cdot, i, F)$ be the minimal automaton of L. For each state p, q of $\mathcal{A}$, let $L_{p,q}$ be the language accepted by $\mathcal{A}$ with p as initial state and q as unique final state. Let $S = \{i\} \times Q^{n-2} \times F$. We claim that

$$\tau_n(L) = \bigcup_{(q_0,\dots,q_n) \in S} L_{q_0,q_1} \times L_{q_1,q_2} \times \cdots \times L_{q_{n-1},q_n} \qquad (4)$$

Let R be the right hand side of (4). Let $(u_1, \dots, u_n) \in \tau_n(L)$. Let $q_0 = i$, $q_1 = q_0 \cdot u_1$, ..., $q_n = q_{n-1} \cdot u_n$. Since $u_1 \cdots u_n \in L$, one has $q_n \in F$ and hence $(q_0, \dots, q_n) \in S$. Moreover, by construction, $u_1 \in L_{q_0,q_1}, \dots, u_n \in L_{q_{n-1},q_n}$ and hence $(u_1, \dots, u_n) \in R$.

Let now $(u_1, \dots, u_n) \in R$. Then, for some $(q_0, \dots, q_n) \in S$, one has $u_1 \in L_{q_0,q_1}$, ..., $u_n \in L_{q_{n-1},q_n}$. It follows that $q_1 = q_0 \cdot u_1$, ..., $q_n = q_{n-1} \cdot u_n$ and thus $i \cdot u_1 \cdots u_n = q_n \in F$ and hence $u \in L$.

6   Profinite Topology

Let M be a monoid. A monoid morphism $\varphi : M \to N$ *separates* two elements u and v of M if $\varphi(u) \neq \varphi(v)$. By extension, we say that a monoid N *separates* two elements of M if there exists a morphism $\varphi : M \to N$ which separates them. A monoid is *residually finite* if any pair of distinct elements of M can be separated by a finite monoid.

Let us consider the class $\mathcal{M}$ of monoids that are finitely generated and residually finite. This class include finite monoids, free monoids, free groups, free commutative monoids and many others. It is closed under direct products and thus monoids of the form $A_1^* \times A_2^* \times \cdots \times A_n^*$ are also in $\mathcal{M}$.

Each monoid M of $\mathcal{M}$ can be equipped with the *profinite metric*, defined as follows. Let, for each $(u, v) \in M^2$,

$$r(u, v) = \min\{\operatorname{Card}(N) \mid N \text{ separates } u \text{ and } v\}$$

Then we set $d(u, v) = 2^{-r(u,v)}$, with the usual conventions $\min \emptyset = +\infty$ and $2^{-\infty} = 0$. One can show that d is an ultrametric and that the product on M is uniformly continuous for this metric.

6.1   Uniformly Continuous Functions and Recognisable sets

The connection with recognisable sets is given by the following result:

Proposition 9. *Let $M, N \in \mathcal{M}$ and let $f : M \to N$ be a function. Then the following conditions are equivalent:*

(1) for every $L \in \mathrm{Rec}(N)$, one has $f^{-1}(L) \in \mathrm{Rec}(M)$,
(2) the function f is uniformly continuous for the profinite metric.

Here is an interesting example [41].

Proposition 10. *The function $g \colon A^* \times \mathbb{N} \to A^*$ defined by $g(x, n) = x^n$ is uniformly continuous.*

Example 8. As an application, let us show that if L is a regular language of A^*, then the language

$$K = \{u \in A^* \mid u^{|u|} \in L\}$$

is also regular. Indeed, $K = h^{-1}(L)$, where h is the function defined by $h(u) = u^{|u|}$. Observe that $h = g \circ f$, where $f : A^* \to A^* \times \mathbb{N}$ is the monoid morphism defined by $f(u) = (u, |u|)$ and g is the function defined in Proposition 10. Now since $L \in \mathrm{Rec}(A^*)$, one gets $g^{-1}(L) \in \mathrm{Rec}(A^* \times \mathbb{N})$ by Proposition 10 and $f^{-1}(g^{-1}(L)) \in \mathrm{Rec}(A^*)$ since f is a monoid morphism. Thus K is regular.

Uniformly continuous functions from $\mathbb{N}$ to $\mathbb{N}$ are of special interest. A function $f \colon \mathbb{N} \to \mathbb{N}$ is *residually ultimately periodic* (rup) if, for each monoid morphism h from $\mathbb{N}$ to a finite monoid F, the sequence $h(f(n))$ is ultimately periodic. It is *cyclically ultimately periodic* if, for every $p > 0$, there exist two integers $m \geqslant 0$ and $r > 0$ such that, for each $n \geqslant m$, $f(n) \equiv f(n + r) \pmod{p}$. It is *ultimately periodic threshold t* if the function $\min(f(n), t)$ is ultimately periodic.

For instance, the functions n^2 and $n!$ are residually ultimately periodic. The function $\binom{2n}{n}$ is not cyclically ultimately periodic. Indeed, it is known that $\binom{2n}{n} \equiv 2 \bmod 4$ if and only if n is a power of 2. It is shown in [48] that the sequence $\lfloor \sqrt{n} \rfloor$ is not cyclically ultimately periodic.

Let us mention a last example, first given in [10]. Let b_n be a non-ultimately periodic sequence of 0 and 1. The function $f(n) = (\sum_{0 \leqslant i \leqslant n} b_i)!$ is residually ultimately periodic. It follows that the function $\Delta f(n) = f(n+1) - f(n)$ is not residually ultimately periodic since $\min(\Delta f(n), 1) = b_n$.

The following result was proved in [3].

Proposition 11. *For a function $f \colon \mathbb{N} \to \mathbb{N}$, the following conditions are equivalent:*

(1) f is uniformly continuous,
(2) f is residually ultimately periodic,
(3) f is cyclically ultimately periodic and ultimately periodic threshold t for all $t \geqslant 0$.

The class of cyclically ultimately periodic functions has been studied by Siefkes [48], who gave in particular a recursion scheme for producing such functions. The class of residually ultimately periodic sequences was also thoroughly studied in [10,55] (see also [27,28,47]). Their properties are summarized in the next proposition.

Theorem 28. *Let g and g be rup functions. Then the following functions are also rup: $f \circ g$, $f + g$, fg, f^g, $\sum_{0 \leqslant i \leqslant g(n)} f(i)$, $\prod_{0 \leqslant i \leqslant g(n)} f(i)$. Furthermore, if $f(n) \geqslant g(n)$ for all n and $\lim_{n \to \infty} (f - g)(n) = +\infty$, then $f - g$ is also rup.*

In particular, the functions f^k and $n \to k^{f(n)}$ (for a fixed k), are rup. The *tetration function* $^n2$ (exponential stack of 2's of height n), considered in [47], is also rup, according to the following result: if k is a positive integer, then the function $f(n)$ defined by $f(0) = 1$ and $f(n+1) = k^{f(n)}$ is rup.

The existence of non-recursive rup functions was established in [47]: if f is a strictly increasing, non-recursive function, then the function $g(n) = n!f(n)$ is non-recursive but is rup.

Coming back to regular languages, Seiferas and McNaughton [47] proved the following result.

Theorem 29. *Let $f \colon \mathbb{N} \to \mathbb{N}$ be a rup function. If L is regular, then so is the language*

$$P(f, L) = \{x \in A^* \mid \text{there exists } y \in A^* \text{ such that } |y| = f(|x|) \text{ and } xy \in L\}.$$

Here is another application of rup functions. A *filter* is a strictly increasing function $f \colon \mathbb{N} \to \mathbb{N}$. *Filtering a word* $a_0a_1 \cdots a_n$ by f consists in deleting the letters a_i such that i is not in the range of f. For each language L, let $L[f]$ denote the set of all words of L filtered by f. A filter is said to *preserve regular languages* if, for every regular language L, the language $L[f]$ is also regular. The following result was proved in [3].

Theorem 30. *A filter f preserves regular languages if and only if the function Δf defined by $\Delta f(n) = f(n+1) - f(n)$ is rup.*

6.2   Transductions and Recognisable Sets

Some further topological results are required to extend Proposition 9 to transductions.

The completion of the metric space (M, d), denoted by $(\widehat{M}, d)$, is called the *profinite completion* of M. Since multiplication on M is uniformly continuous, it extends, in a unique way, to a multiplication on $\widehat{M}$, which is again uniformly continuous. One can show that $\widehat{M}$ is a metric compact monoid.

Let $\mathcal{K}(\widehat{M})$ be the monoid of compact subsets of $\widehat{M}$. The *Hausdorff metric* on $\mathcal{K}(\widehat{M})$ is defined as follows. For $K, K' \in \mathcal{K}(\widehat{M})$, let

$$\delta(K, K') = \sup_{x \in K} \inf_{x' \in K'} d(x, x')$$

$$h(K, K') = \begin{cases} \max(\delta(K, K'), \delta(K', K)) & \text{if } K \text{ and } K' \text{ are } nonempty, \\ 0 & \text{if } K \text{ and } K' \text{ are empty}, \\ 1 & \text{otherwise.} \end{cases}$$

By a standard result of topology, $\mathcal{K}(\widehat{M})$, equipped with this metric, is compact.

Let now $\tau \colon M \to N$ be a transduction. Define a map $\widehat{\tau} \colon M \to \mathcal{K}(\widehat{N})$ by setting, for each $x \in M$, $\widehat{\tau}(x) = \overline{\tau(x)}$, the topological closure of $\tau(x)$. The following extension of Proposition 9 was proved in [41].

Theorem 31. *Let $M, N \in \mathcal{M}$ and let $\tau \colon M \to N$ be a transduction. Then the following conditions are equivalent:*

(1) for every $L \in \mathrm{Rec}(N)$, one has $\tau^{-1}(L) \in \mathrm{Rec}(M)$,
(2) the function $\widehat{\tau} \colon M \to \mathcal{K}(\widehat{N})$ is uniformly continuous.

Let us say that a transduction τ is uniformly continuous, if $\widehat{\tau}$ is uniformly continuous. Uniformly continuous transductions are closed under composition and they are also closed under direct product.

Proposition 12. *Let $\tau_1 \colon M \to N_1$ and $\tau_2 \colon M \to N_2$ be uniformly continuous transductions. Then the transduction $\tau \colon M \to N_1 \times N_2$ defined by $\tau(x) = \tau_1(x) \times \tau_2(x)$ is uniformly continuous.*

Proposition 13. *For every $M \in \mathcal{M}$, the transduction $\sigma \colon M \to M$ defined by $\sigma(x) = x^*$ is uniformly continuous.*

7 Further Examples and Conclusion

Here are a few results relating regular languages and Turing machines.

Theorem 32 ([9, Theorem 3.84, p. 185]). *The language accepted by a one-tape Turing machine that never writes on its input is regular.*

Theorem 33 (Hartmanis [21]). *The language accepted by a one-tape Turing machine that works in time $o(n \log n)$ is regular.*

The following result is proposed as an exercise in [9, Exercise 4.16, p. 243].

Theorem 34. *The language accepted by a Turing machine that works in space $o(\log \log n)$ is regular.*

Let me also mention a result related to formal power series.

Theorem 35 (Restivo and Reutenauer [44]). *If a language and its complement are support of a rational series, then it is a regular language.*

Many other examples could not be included in this survey, notably the work of Bertoni, Mereghetti and Palano [4, Theorem 3, p. 8] on 1-way quantum automata and the large literature on splicing systems.

I would be very grateful to any reader providing me new interesting examples to enrich this survey.

86   J.-É. Pin

Acknowledgements. I would like to thank Olivier Carton for his useful suggestions.

References

1. Bala, S.: Complexity of regular language matching and other decidable cases of the satisfiability problem for constraints between regular open terms. Theory Comput. Syst. **39**(1), 137–163 (2006)
2. Berstel, J.: Transductions and Context-Free Languages. Teubner (1979)
3. Berstel, J., Boasson, L., Carton, O., Petazzoni, B., Pin, J.-É.: Operations preserving recognizable languages. Theor. Comput. Sci. **354**, 405–420 (2006)
4. Bertoni, A., Mereghetti, C., Palano, B.: Quantum computing: 1-way quantum automata. In: Ésik, Z., Fülöp, Z. (eds.) DLT 2003. LNCS, vol. 2710, pp. 1–20. Springer, Heidelberg (2003). https://doi.org/10.1007/3-540-45007-6_1
5. Bovet, D.P., Varricchio, S.: On the regularity of languages on a binary alphabet generated by copying systems. Inform. Process. Lett. **44**(3), 119–123 (1992)
6. Bucher, W., Ehrenfeucht, A., Haussler, D.: On total regulators generated by derivation relations. Theor. Comput. Sci. **40**(2–3), 131–148 (1985)
7. Büchi, J.R.: Weak second-order arithmetic and finite automata. Z. Math. Logik und Grundl. Math. **6**, 66–92 (1960)
8. Büchi, J.R.: Regular canonical systems. Arch. Math. Logik Grundlagenforsch. **6**, 91–111 (1964) (1964)
9. Carton, O.: Langages formels, calculabilité et complexité. Vuibert (2008)
10. Carton, O., Thomas, W.: The monadic theory of morphic infinite words and generalizations. Inform. Comput. **176**, 51–76 (2002)
11. Conway, J.H.: Regular Algebra and Finite Machines. Chapman and Hall, London (1971)
12. D'Alessandro, F., Varricchio, S.: Well quasi-orders in formal language theory. In: Ito, M., Toyama, M. (eds.) DLT 2008. LNCS, vol. 5257, pp. 84–95. Springer, Heidelberg (2008). https://doi.org/10.1007/978-3-540-85780-8_6
13. De Luca, A., Varricchio, S.: Finiteness and Regularity in Semigroups and Formal Languages. Monographs in Theoretical Computer Science. An EATCS Series. Springer, Heidelberg (1999). https://doi.org/10.1007/978-3-642-59849-4
14. Ehrenfeucht, A., Haussler, D., Rozenberg, G.: On regularity of context-free languages. Theor. Comput. Sci. **27**(3), 311–332 (1983)
15. Ehrenfeucht, A., Parikh, R., Rozenberg, G.: Pumping lemmas for regular sets. SIAM J. Comput. **10**(3), 536–541 (1981)
16. Ehrenfeucht, A., Rozenberg, G.: On regularity of languages generated by copying systems. Discrete Appl. Math. **8**(3), 313–317 (1984)
17. Eiter, T., Gottlob, G., Gurevich, Y.: Existential second-order logic over strings. J. ACM **47**(1), 77–131 (2000)
18. Eiter, T., Gottlob, G., Schwentick, T.: Second-order logic over strings: regular and non-regular fragments. In: Kuich, W., Rozenberg, G., Salomaa, A. (eds.) DLT 2001. LNCS, vol. 2295, pp. 37–56. Springer, Heidelberg (2002). https://doi.org/10.1007/3-540-46011-X_4
19. Eiter, T., Gottlob, G., Schwentick, T.: The model checking problem for prefix classes of second-order logic: a survey. In: Blass, A., Dershowitz, N., Reisig, W. (eds.) Fields of Logic and Computation. LNCS, vol. 6300, pp. 227–250. Springer, Heidelberg (2010). https://doi.org/10.1007/978-3-642-15025-8_13
20. Elgot, C.C.: Decision problems of finite automata design and related arithmetics. Trans. Am. Math. Soc. **98**, 21–51 (1961)

21. Hartmanis, J.: Computational complexity of one-tape Turing machine computations. J. Assoc. Comput. Mach. **15**, 325–339 (1968)
22. Hofbauer, D., Waldmann, J.: Deleting string rewriting systems preserve regularity. Theor. Comput. Sci. **327**(3), 301–317 (2004)
23. Hopcroft, J.E., Ullman, J.D.: Introduction To Automata Theory, Languages, And Computation. Addison-Wesley Publishing Co., Reading (1979). Addison-Wesley Series in Computer Science
24. Jaffe, J.: A necessary and sufficient pumping lemma for regular languages. SIGACT News **10**(2), 48–49 (1978)
25. Kamp, J.: Tense Logic and the Theory of Linear Order. Ph.D. thesis, University of California, Los Angeles (1968)
26. Kleene, S.C.: Representation of events in nerve nets and finite automata. In: Automata Studies, pp. 3–41. Princeton University Press, Princeton (1956). Ann. Math. Stud. **34**
27. Kosaraju, S.R.: Regularity preserving functions. SIGACT News **6**(2), 16–17 (1974). Correction to "Regularity preserving functions", SIGACT News 6(3), (1974), p. 22
28. Kozen, D.: On regularity-preserving functions. Bull. Europ. Assoc. Theor. Comput. Sci. **58**, 131–138 (1996). Erratum: on regularity-preserving functions. Bull. Europ. Assoc. Theor. Comput. Sci. **59**, 455 (1996)
29. Kozen, D.C.: Automata and computability. Undergraduate Texts in Computer Science. Springer, New York (1997). https://doi.org/10.1007/978-3-642-85706-5
30. Kunc, M.: Regular solutions of language inequalities and well quasi-orders. Theor. Comput. Sci. **348**(2–3), 277–293 (2005)
31. Kunc, M.: The power of commuting with finite sets of words. Theory Comput. Syst. **40**(4), 521–551 (2007)
32. Kunc, M., Okhotin, A.: Language equations. In: Pin, J.E. (ed.) Handbook of Automata Theory, vol. II, chap. 21. European Mathematical Society, Zürich (2020, To appear)
33. Leupold, P.: Languages generated by iterated idempotency. Theor. Comput. Sci. **370**(1–3), 170–185 (2007)
34. Leupold, P.: On regularity-preservation by string-rewriting systems. In: Martín-Vide, C., Otto, F., Fernau, H. (eds.) LATA 2008. LNCS, vol. 5196, pp. 345–356. Springer, Heidelberg (2008). https://doi.org/10.1007/978-3-540-88282-4_32
35. McNaughton, R., Papert, S.: Counter-Free Automata. The M.I.T. Press, Cambridge (1971). With an appendix by William Henneman, M.I.T. ResearchMonograph, No. 65
36. Niwiński, D., Rytter, W.: 200 Problems in Formal Languages and Automata Theory. University of Warsaw (2017)
37. Otto, F.: On the connections between rewriting and formal language theory. In: Narendran, P., Rusinowitch, M. (eds.) RTA 1999. LNCS, vol. 1631, pp. 332–355. Springer, Heidelberg (1999). https://doi.org/10.1007/3-540-48685-2_27
38. Pin, J.-É.: Topologies for the free monoid. J. Algebra **137**, 297–337 (1991)
39. Pin, J.-É., Sakarovitch, J.: Some operations and transductions that preserve rationality. In: Cremers, A.B., Kriegel, H.-P. (eds.) GI-TCS 1983. LNCS, vol. 145, pp. 277–288. Springer, Heidelberg (1982). https://doi.org/10.1007/BFb0036488
40. Pin, J.-É., Sakarovitch, J.: Une application de la représentation matricielle des transductions. Theor. Comput. Sci. **35**, 271–293 (1985)
41. Pin, J.-É., Silva, P.V.: A topological approach to transductions. Theor. Comput. Sci. **340**, 443–456 (2005)
42. Rabin, M.O.: Decidability of second-order theories and automata on infinite trees. Trans. Am. Math. Soc. **141**, 1–35 (1969)

43. Restivo, A.: Codes and aperiodic languages. In: Erste Fachtagung der Gesellschaft für Informatik über Automatentheorie und Formale Sprachen (Bonn, 1973), LNCS, vol. 2, pp. 175–181. Springer, Berlin (1973)
44. Restivo, A., Reutenauer, C.: On cancellation properties of languages which are supports of rational power series. J. Comput. Syst. Sci. **29**(2), 153–159 (1984)
45. Sakarovitch, J.: Elements of Automata Theory. Cambridge University Press, Cambridge (2009). Translated from the 2003 French original by Reuben Thomas
46. Schützenberger, M.P.: On finite monoids having only trivial subgroups. Inf. Control **8**, 190–194 (1965)
47. Seiferas, J.I., McNaughton, R.: Regularity-preserving relations. Theor. Comput. Sci. **2**(2), 147–154 (1976)
48. Siefkes, D.: Decidable extensions of monadic second order successor arithmetic. In: Automatentheorie und formale Sprachen (Tagung, Math. Forschungsinst., Oberwolfach, 1969), pp. 441–472. Bibliographisches Inst., Mannheim (1970)
49. Sipser, M.: Introduction to the Theory of Computation. 3rd edn. Cengage Learning (2012)
50. Stanat, D.F., Weiss, S.F.: A pumping theorem for regular languages. SIGACT News **14**(1), 36–37 (1982)
51. Stearns, R.E., Hartmanis, J.: Regularity preserving modifications of regular expressions. Inf. Control **6**, 55–69 (1963)
52. Straubing, H.: Relational morphisms and operations on recognizable sets. RAIRO Inf. Theor. **15**, 149–159 (1981)
53. Trakhtenbrot, B.A.: Barzdin′, Y.M.: Finite Automata, Behavior and Synthesis. North-Holland Publishing Co., Amsterdam (1973). Translated from the Russian by D. Louvish, English translation edited by E. Shamir and L. H. Landweber, Fundamental Studies in Computer Science, vol. 1
54. Varricchio, S.: A pumping condition for regular sets. SIAM J. Comput. **26**(3), 764–771 (1997)
55. Zhang, G.Q.: Automata, boolean matrices, and ultimate periodicity. Inform. Comput. **152**(1), 138–154 (1999)

Deciding Classes of Regular Languages: The Covering Approach

Thomas Place$^{(\boxtimes)}$

LaBRI, Université de Bordeaux, Institut Universitaire de France, Talence, France
tplace@labri.fr

Abstract. We investigate the *membership problem* that one may associate to every class of languages C. The problem takes a regular language as input and asks whether it belongs to C. In practice, finding an algorithm provides a deep insight on the class C. While this problem has a long history, many famous open questions in automata theory are tied to membership. Recently, a breakthrough was made on several of these open questions. This was achieved by considering a more general decision problem than membership: *covering*. In the paper, we investigate how the new ideas and techniques brought about by the introduction of this problem can be applied to get new insight on earlier results. In particular, we use them to give new proofs for two of the most famous membership results: Schützenberger's theorem and Simon's theorem.

Keywords: Regular languages · Automata · Covering · Membership · Star-free languages · Piecewise testable languages

1 Introduction

Historical Context. A prominent question in formal languages theory is to solve the membership problem for classes of regular languages. Given a fixed class C, one must find an algorithm which decides whether an input regular language belongs to C. Such a procedure is called a C-*membership algorithm*. What motivates this question is the deep insight on the class C that is usually provided by a solution. Intuitively, being able to formulate an algorithm requires a *solid understanding* of all languages contained in the class C. In other words, membership is used as a mathematical tool whose purpose is to analyze classes.

This research effort started with a famous theorem of Schützenberger [36] which describes the class of *star-free languages* (SF). These are the languages that can be expressed by a regular expression using union, concatenation and *complement*, but *not Kleene star*. This is a prominent class which admits natural alternate definitions. For example, the star-free languages are those which can be defined in first-order logic [15] or equivalently in linear temporal logic [11]. Schützenberger's theorem yields an algorithm which decides whether an input regular language is star-free (*i.e.* an SF-membership algorithm). This provides

© Springer Nature Switzerland AG 2020
A. Leporati et al. (Eds.): LATA 2020, LNCS 12038, pp. 89–112, 2020.
https://doi.org/10.1007/978-3-030-40608-0_6

insight on SF not because of the algorithm itself, but rather because of its proof. Indeed, it includes a generic construction which builds an expression witnessing membership in SF for every input language on which the algorithm answers positively. This result was highly influential and pioneered a very successful line of research. The theorem itself was often revisited [5, 7, 8, 10, 14, 16, 17, 21, 23, 41] and researchers successfully obtained similar results for other prominent classes of languages. Famous examples include the locally testable languages [4, 42] or the piecewise testable languages [38]. However, membership is a difficult question and despite years of investigation, there are still many open problems.

Among these open problems, a famous one is the *dot-depth problem*. Brzozowski and Cohen [2] defined a natural classification of the star-free languages: the *dot-depth hierarchy*. Each star-free language is assigned a "complexity level" (called dot-depth) according to the number of alternations between concatenations and complements that are required to define it with an expression. It is known that this hierarchy is strict [3]. Hence, a natural question is whether membership is decidable for each level. This has been a very active research topic since the 70s (see [20, 28, 32] for surveys). Yet, only the first two levels are known to be decidable so far. An algorithm for dot-depth one was published by Knast in 1983 [13]. Despite a lot of partial results along the way, it took thirty more years to solve the next level: the decidability of dot-depth two was shown in 2014 [26, 33]. This situation is easily explained: in practice, getting new membership results always required new conceptual ideas and techniques. In the paper, we are interested in the ideas that led to a solution for dot-depth two. The key ingredient was a new more general decision problem called *covering*.

Covering. The problem was first considered implicitly in [26] and properly defined later in [31]. Given a class $\mathcal{C}$, the $\mathcal{C}$-covering problem is as follows. The input consists in two objects: a regular language L and a finite set of regular languages $\mathbf{L}$. One must decide whether there exists a $\mathcal{C}$-cover $\mathbf{K}$ of L (a finite set of languages in $\mathcal{C}$ whose union includes L) such that no language in $\mathbf{K}$ intersects all languages in $\mathbf{L}$. Naturally, this definition is more involved than the one of membership and it is more difficult to find an algorithm for $\mathcal{C}$-covering than for $\mathcal{C}$-membership. Yet, covering was recently shown to be decidable for many natural classes (see for example [6, 24, 25, 30, 34, 35]) including the star-free languages [29].

At the time of its introduction, there were two motivations for investigating this new question. First, while harder, covering is also more rewarding than membership: it yields a more robust understanding of the classes. Indeed, a $\mathcal{C}$-membership algorithm only yields benefits for the languages of $\mathcal{C}$: we manage to detect them and to build a description witnessing this membership. On the other hand, a $\mathcal{C}$-covering algorithm applies to *arbitrary* languages. One may view $\mathcal{C}$-covering as an approximation problem: on inputs L and $\mathbf{L}$, we want to over-approximate L with a $\mathcal{C}$-cover while $\mathbf{L}$ specifies what an acceptable approximation is. A second key motivation was the application to the dot-depth hierarchy. It turns out that all recent membership results for this hierarchy rely heavily on covering arguments. More precisely, they are based on techniques that allow to lift covering results for a level in the hierarchy as membership results for a higher level (see [32] for a detailed explanation).

Contribution. In the paper, we are not looking to provide new covering algorithms. Instead, we look at a slightly different question. As we explained, finding an algorithm for C-covering is even harder than for C-membership. Consequently, the recent breakthroughs that were made on this question required developing new ideas, new techniques and new ways to formulate intricate proof arguments. In the paper, we look back at the original membership problem and investigate how these new developments can be applied to get new insight on earlier results. We prove that even if one is only interested in membership, reasoning in terms of "covers" is quite natural and rather intuitive when presenting proof arguments. In particular, C-covers are a very powerful tool for presenting generic constructions which build descriptions of languages in the class C. We illustrate this point by using covers to give new intuitive proofs for two of the most important membership results in the literature: Schützenberger theorem [36] for the star-free languages and Simon's theorem [38] for the piecewise testable languages.

Organization of the Paper. We first recall standard terminology about regular languages and define membership in Sect. 2. We introduce covering in Sect. 3 and explain why reasoning in terms of covers is intuitive and relevant even if one is only interested in membership. We illustrate this point in Sect. 4 with a new proof of Schützenberger's theorem. Finally, we present a second example in Sect. 5 with a new proof of Simon's theorem.

2 Preliminaries

In this section, we briefly recall standard terminology about finite words and classes regular languages. Moreover, we introduce the membership problem.

Regular Languages. An alphabet is a finite set A. As usual, A^* denotes the set of all words over A, including the empty word ε. For $w \in A^*$, we write $|w| \in \mathbb{N}$ for the *length* of w (*i.e.* the number of letters in w). Moreover, for $u, v \in A^*$, we denote by uv the word obtained by concatenating u and v.

Given an alphabet A, a *language* (over A) is a subset of A^*. Abusing terminology, we shall often denote by u the singleton language $\{u\}$. We lift concatenation to languages: for $K, L \subseteq A^*$, we let $KL = \{uv \mid u \in K \text{ and } v \in L\}$. Finally, we use Kleene star: if $K \subseteq A^*$, K^+ denotes the union of all languages K^n for $n \geq 1$ and $K^* = K^+ \cup \{\varepsilon\}$. In the paper, we only consider *regular languages*. These are the languages that can be equivalently defined by regular expressions, monadic second-order logic, finite automata or finite monoids. We shall use the definition based on monoids which we briefly recall now (see [21] for details).

A *monoid* is a set M endowed with an associative multiplication $(s, t) \mapsto s \cdot t$ (also denoted by st) having a neutral element 1_M. An *idempotent* of a monoid M is an element $e \in M$ such that $ee = e$. It is folklore that for any *finite* monoid M, there exists a natural number $\omega(M)$ (denoted by ω when M is understood) such that s^ω is an idempotent for every $s \in M$. Observe that A^* is a monoid whose multiplication is concatenation (the neutral element is ε). Thus, we may consider monoid morphisms $\alpha : A^* \to M$ where M is an arbitrary monoid. Given such a morphism and $L \subseteq A^*$, we say that L is *recognized* by α when there exists a set $F \subseteq M$ such that $L = \alpha^{-1}(F)$. A language L is *regular* if and only if it is recognized by a morphism into a *finite* monoid.

Classes. We investigate classes of languages. Mathematically speaking, a *class of languages* $\mathcal{C}$ is a correspondence $A \mapsto \mathcal{C}(A)$ which associates a (possibly infinite) set of languages $\mathcal{C}(A)$ over A to every alphabet A. For the sake of avoiding clutter, we shall often abuse terminology and omit the alphabet when manipulating classes. That is, whenever A is fixed and understood, we directly write $L \in \mathcal{C}$ to indicate that some language $L \subseteq A^*$ belongs to $\mathcal{C}(A)$.

While this is the mathematical definition, in practice, the term "class" is used to indicate that $\mathcal{C}$ is presented in a specific way. Typically, classes are tied to a particular *syntax* used to describe all the languages they contain. For example, the regular languages are tied to regular expressions and monadic second-order logic. Consequently, the classes that we consider in practice are natural and have robust properties that we present now.

A *lattice* is a class $\mathcal{C}$ which is closed under finite union and intersection: for every alphabet A, we have $\emptyset, A^* \in \mathcal{C}(A)$ and for every $K, L \in \mathcal{C}(A)$, we have $H \cup L, H \cap L \in \mathcal{C}(A)$. Moreover, a *Boolean algebra* is a lattice $\mathcal{C}$ which is additionally closed under complement: for every alphabet A and $K \in \mathcal{C}(A)$, we have $A^* \setminus K \in \mathcal{C}(A)$. Finally, we say that a class $\mathcal{C}$ is *quotient-closed* when for every alphabet A, every $L \in \mathcal{C}(A)$ and every $w \in A^*$, the following two languages belong to $\mathcal{C}(A)$ as well:

$$w^{-1}L \stackrel{\text{def}}{=} \{u \in A^* \mid wu \in L\},$$
$$Lw^{-1} \stackrel{\text{def}}{=} \{u \in A^* \mid uw \in L\}.$$

The techniques that we discuss in the paper are meant to be applied for classes that are quotient-closed lattices and contain *only regular languages*. The two examples that we detail are quotient-closed Boolean algebras of regular languages.

Membership. When encountering a new class $\mathcal{C}$, a natural objective is to precisely understand the languages it contains. In other words, we want to understand what properties can be expressed with the syntax defining $\mathcal{C}$. Of course, this is an informal objective. In practice, we rely on a decision problem called membership which we use as a mathematical tool to approach this question.

The problem is parameterized by an arbitrary class of languages $\mathcal{C}$: we speak of $\mathcal{C}$-*membership*. It takes as input a regular language L and asks whether L belongs to $\mathcal{C}$. The key idea is that obtaining an algorithm for $\mathcal{C}$-membership is not possible without a solid understanding of $\mathcal{C}$. In the literature, such an algorithm is also called a *decidable characterization of* $\mathcal{C}$.

Remark 1. We are not only interested in $\mathcal{C}$-membership algorithms themselves but also in their correctness proofs. In practice, the deep insight that we obtain on the class $\mathcal{C}$ comes from these proofs. Typically, the difficult part in such an argument is to prove that a membership is sound: when it answers positively, prove that the input language does belong to $\mathcal{C}$. Typically, this requires a generic construction for building a syntactic description of the language witnessing its membership in $\mathcal{C}$.   □

Finding membership algorithms has been an important quest for a long time in formal languages theory. The solutions that were obtained for important classes are milestones in the theory of regular languages [13,22,33,36,38,40]. In the paper, we prove two of them: Schützenberger's theorem [36] and Simon's theorem [38]. We frame these proofs using a new formalism based on a more general problem which was recently introduced [31]: *covering*.

3   The Covering Problem

The covering problem generalizes membership. It was first considered implicitly in [26,27] and was later formalized in [31] (along with a detailed framework designed for handling it). At the time, its introduction was motivated by two reasons. First, an algorithm for covering is usually more rewarding than an algorithm for membership as the former provides more insight on the investigated class of languages. Second, covering was introduced as a key ingredient for handling difficult membership questions. For several important classes, membership is effectively reducible to covering for another simpler class. Recently, this idea was applied to prominent hierarchies of classes called "concatenation hierarchies" (see the surveys [28,32] for details on these results).

In the paper, we are interested in covering for a slightly different reason. In particular, we do not present any covering algorithm. Instead, we look at how the new ideas that were recently introduced with covering in mind can be applied in the simpler membership setting. It turns out that even for the early membership results, reasoning in terms of covers is quite natural and allows to present arguments in a very intuitive way. We manage to formulate new proof arguments for two famous membership algorithms.

We first define covering and explain why it generalizes membership as a decision problem. Then, we come back to membership and briefly recall the general approach that is usually followed in order to handle it. We show that this approach can actually be formulated in a convenient and natural way with covering. For the sake of avoiding clutter, we fix an arbitrary alphabet A for the presentation: all languages that we consider are over A.

3.1   Definition

Similarly to membership, covering is parameterized by an arbitrary class of languages $\mathcal{C}$: we speak of $\mathcal{C}$-*covering*. It is designed with the same objective in mind: it serves as a mathematical tool for investigating the class $\mathcal{C}$.

For a class $\mathcal{C}$, the $\mathcal{C}$-covering takes a language L and a *finite set* of languages **L** as input. It asks whether there exists a $\mathcal{C}$-*cover of* L which is *separating for* **L**. Let us first define these two notions.

Given a language L, a *cover of* L is a **finite** set of languages **K** such that $L \subseteq \bigcup_{K \in \mathbf{K}} K$. Additionally, given some class $\mathcal{C}$, a $\mathcal{C}$-*cover of* L is a cover **K** of L such that every $K \in \mathbf{K}$ belongs to $\mathcal{C}$.

Moreover, given two finite sets of languages **K** and **L**, we say that **K** is *separating for* **L** if for every $K \in \mathbf{K}$, there exists $L \in \mathbf{L}$ which satisfies $K \cap L = \emptyset$. In other words, there exists no language in **K** which intersects all languages in **L**. Given a class $\mathcal{C}$, the $\mathcal{C}$-covering problem is now defined as follows:

INPUT: A regular language L and a finite set of regular languages **L**.

OUTPUT: Does there exist a $\mathcal{C}$-cover of L which is separating for **L**?

A simple observation is that covering generalizes another well-known decision problem called *separation*. Given a class $\mathcal{C}$ and two languages L_1 and L_2, we say that L_1 is $\mathcal{C}$-*separable* from L_2 when there exists a third language $K \in \mathcal{C}$ such that $L_1 \subseteq K$ and $K \cap L_2 = \emptyset$. We have the following lemma (see [31] for a proof).

Lemma 2. *Let $\mathcal{C}$ be a lattice and L_1, L_2 two languages. Then L_1 is $\mathcal{C}$-separable from L_2, if and only if there exist a $\mathcal{C}$-cover of L_1 which is separating for $\{L_2\}$.*

Lemma 2 proves that $\mathcal{C}$-covering generalizes $\mathcal{C}$-membership as a decision problem. Indeed, given as input a regular language L, it is immediate that L belongs to $\mathcal{C}$ if and only if L is $\mathcal{C}$-separable from $A^* \setminus L$ (which is also regular). Thus, there exists an effective reduction from $\mathcal{C}$-membership to $\mathcal{C}$-covering.

Yet, this not the only connection between membership and covering. More importantly, this is not how we use covering in the paper. While each membership algorithm existing in the literature is based on unique ideas (specific to the class under investigation), most of them are formulated and proved within a standard common framework. It turns out that this framework boils down to a particular kind of covering question: this is the property that we shall exploit in the paper.

3.2   Application to Membership

We first summarize the standard general approach that is commonly used to handle membership questions and formulate solutions. Historically, this approach was initiated by Schützenberger who applied it to obtain the first known membership algorithm [36] (for the class of star-free languages). We shall detail and prove this result in Sect. 4.

The syntactic approach. Obtaining a membership algorithm for a given class $\mathcal{C}$ is intuitively hard, as it requires to decide a semantic property which may not be apparent on the piece of syntax that defines the input regular language L (be it a regular expression, an automaton or a monoid morphism). To palliate this issue, the syntactic approach relies on the existence of a *canonical recognizer* for any given regular language. The idea is that while belonging to $\mathcal{C}$ may not be apparent on an arbitrary syntax for L, it should be apparent on a canonical representation of L. Typically, the *syntactic morphism* of L serves as this canonical representation. As the name suggests, this object is a canonical morphism into a finite monoid which recognizes L (and can be computed from any representation of L).

Let us first define the syntactic morphism properly. Consider a language L. One may associate a canonical equivalence relation $\equiv_L$ over A^* to L. Given two words $u, v \in A^*$, we write,

$$u \equiv_L v \qquad \text{if and only if} \qquad \text{for every } x, y \in A^*, \ xuy \in L \Leftrightarrow xvy \in L$$

Clearly, $\equiv_L$ is an equivalence relation and one may verify that it is a *congruence for word concatenation*: for every $u, v, u', v' \in A^*$, if $u \equiv_L v$ and $u' \equiv_L v'$, then $uu' \equiv_L vv'$. Consequently, the quotient set $A^*/\equiv_L$ is a monoid called the *syntactic monoid of L*. Moreover, the map $\alpha : A^* \to A^*/\equiv_L$ which maps each word to its $\equiv_L$-class is a monoid morphism called the *syntactic morphism* of L. In particular, this morphism recognizes the language L: $L = \alpha^{-1}(F)$ where F is the set of all $\equiv_L$-classes which intersect L. It is well-known and simple to verify that L is regular if and only if its syntactic monoid is *finite*. Moreover, in that case, one may compute the syntactic morphism of L from any representation of L (such as an automaton or an arbitrary monoid morphism recognizing L).

We are ready to present the key result behind the syntactic approach: for every quotient-closed Boolean algebra $\mathcal{C}$, membership of an arbitrary regular language in $\mathcal{C}$ depends only on its syntactic morphism. This claim is formalized with the following standard result.

Proposition 3. *Let $\mathcal{C}$ be a quotient-closed Boolean algebra, L a regular language and α its syntactic morphism. Then L belongs to $\mathcal{C}$ if and only if every language recognized by α belongs to $\mathcal{C}$.*

Proof. The right to left implication is immediate since L is recognized by its syntactic morphism. We concentrate on the converse one. Assume that $L \in \mathcal{C}$. We show that every language recognized by α belongs to $\mathcal{C}$ as well. By definition, these languages are exactly the unions of $\equiv_L$-classes. Thus, since $\mathcal{C}$ is closed under union, it suffices to show that every $\equiv_L$-class belongs to $\mathcal{C}$. Observe that the definition of $\equiv_L$ can be reformulated as follows. Given $u, v \in A^*$, we have,

$$u \equiv_L v \quad \text{if and only if} \quad u \in x^{-1}Ly^{-1} \Leftrightarrow v \in x^{-1}Ly^{-1} \text{ for every } x, y \in A^*.$$

Let $x, y \in A^*$. Since L is recognized by α, it is clear that whether some word $w \in A^*$ belongs to $x^{-1}Ly^{-1}$ depends only on its image $\alpha(w)$. In other words, $x^{-1}Ly^{-1}$ is recognized by α. Moreover, since L is regular, its syntactic monoid is finite which implies that α recognizes finitely many languages. Thus, while there are infinitely many words $x, y \in A^*$, there are finitely many languages $x^{-1}Ly^{-1}$.

Altogether, we obtain that every $\equiv_L$-class is a *finite* Boolean combination of languages $x^{-1}Ly^{-1}$ where $x, y \in A^*$. Since $L \in \mathcal{C}$ and $\mathcal{C}$ is quotient-closed, every such language belongs to $\mathcal{C}$. Hence, since $\mathcal{C}$ is a Boolean algebra, we conclude that every $\equiv_L$-class belongs to $\mathcal{C}$, completing the proof. $\square$

Proposition 3 implies that membership of a regular language L in some fixed quotient-closed Boolean algebra is equivalent to some property of an algebraic abstraction of L: its syntactic morphism. In particular, this is independent from the accepting set $F = \alpha(L)$. By itself, this is a simple result. Yet, it captures the gist of the syntactic approach.

Naturally, the proposition tells nothing about the actual the property on the syntactic morphism that one should look for. This question is specific to each particular class $\mathcal{C}$: one has to find the right decidable property characterizing $\mathcal{C}$.

Remark 4. This may seem counterintuitive. We replaced the question of deciding whether a *single language* belongs to the class $\mathcal{C}$ by an intuitively harder one: deciding whether *all languages* recognized by a given monoid morphism belong to $\mathcal{C}$. The idea is that the set of languages recognized by a morphism has a structure which can be exploited in membership arguments.   □

Remark 5. Proposition 3 is restricted quotient-closed Boolean algebras. This excludes quotient-closed lattices that are not closed under complement. One may generalize the syntactic approach to such classes (as done by Pin [19]). We do not discuss this as our two examples are quotient-closed Boolean algebras. □

Back to Covering. We proved that for every quotient-closed Boolean algebra $\mathcal{C}$, the associated membership problem boils down to deciding whether *all languages* recognized by an input morphism belong to $\mathcal{C}$. It turns out that this new question is a particular instance of $\mathcal{C}$-covering. In order to explain this properly, we require a last definition.

Consider a morphism $\alpha : A^* \to M$ into a finite monoid M and a finite set of languages **K**. We say that **K** is *confined* by α if it is separating for the set $\{\alpha^{-1}(M \setminus \{s\}) \mid s \in M\}$. The following fact can be verified from the definitions and reformulates this property in a way that is easier to manipulate.

Fact 6. *Let $\alpha : A^* \to M$ be a morphism into a finite monoid and **K** a finite set of languages. Then **K** is confined by α if and only if for every $K \in$ **K**, there exists $s \in M$ such that $K \subseteq \alpha^{-1}(s)$.*

Proof. By definition **K** is confined by α if and only if for every $K \in$ **K**, there exists $s \in M$ such that $K \cap \alpha^{-1}(M \setminus \{s\}) = \emptyset$. Since $\alpha^{-1}(M \setminus \{s\}) = A^* \setminus \alpha^{-1}(s)$, the fact follows.   □

We show that given a lattice $\mathcal{C}$ and a morphism $\alpha : A^* \to M$ into a finite monoid, all languages recognized by α belong to $\mathcal{C}$ if and only if there exists a $\mathcal{C}$-cover of A^* which is confined by α. The latter question is a particular case of $\mathcal{C}$-covering. In fact, we prove a slightly more general result that we shall need later when dealing with our two examples.

Proposition 7 *Let $\mathcal{C}$ be a lattice, $\alpha : A^* \to M$ a morphism into a finite monoid and $H \in \mathcal{C}$ a language. The two following properties are equivalent:*

1. *For every language L recognized by α, we have $L \cap H \in \mathcal{C}$.*
2. *There exists a $\mathcal{C}$-cover of H which is confined by α.*

Proof. Assume first that $L \cap H \in \mathcal{C}$ for every language L recognized by α. We define $\mathbf{K} = \{\alpha^{-1}(s) \cap H \mid s \in M\}$. Clearly, $\mathbf{K}$ is a cover of H and it is a $\mathcal{C}$-cover by hypothesis. Moreover, it is clear from Fact 6 that $\mathbf{K}$ is confined by α.

For the converse direction, assume that there exists a $\mathcal{C}$-cover $\mathbf{K}$ of H which is confined by α. Let L be a language recognized by α, we show that,

$$L \cap H = \left(\bigcup_{\{K \in \mathbf{K} \mid K \cap L \neq \emptyset\}} K \right) \cap H$$

This implies that $L \cap H \in \mathcal{C}$ since $H \in \mathcal{C}$, every language in $\mathbf{K}$ belongs to $\mathcal{C}$ and $\mathcal{C}$ is a lattice. The left to right inclusion is immediate since $\mathbf{K}$ is a cover of H. We prove the converse one. Let $K \in \mathbf{K}$ such that $K \cap L \neq \emptyset$, we show that $K \cap H \subseteq L \cap H$. Let $u \in K \cap H$. Consider $v \in K \cap L$ (which is nonempty by definition of K). Since $u, v \in K$ and $\mathbf{K}$ is confined by α, we have $\alpha(u) = \alpha(v)$ by Fact 6. Thus, since $v \in L$ and L is recognized by α, it follows that $u \in L$, concluding the proof: we obtain $K \cap H \subseteq L \cap H$. $\square$

Let us combine Propositions 3 and 7. When put together, they imply that for every quotient-closed Boolean algebra $\mathcal{C}$, a regular language L belongs to $\mathcal{C}$ if and only if there exists a $\mathcal{C}$-cover of A^* which is confined by the syntactic morphism of L.

The key point is that this formulation is very convenient when writing proof arguments. As we explained in Remark 1, the technical core of membership proofs consists in generic constructions which build descriptions of languages in $\mathcal{C}$. It turns out that building a $\mathcal{C}$-cover which is confined by some input morphism is an objective that is much easier to manipulate than directly proving that all languages recognized by the morphism belong to $\mathcal{C}$. We illustrate this point in the next section with new proofs for two well-known membership algorithms: the star-free languages and the piecewise testable languages.

4   Star-Free Languages and Schützenberger's Theorem

We now illustrate the discussion of the previous section with a first example: Schützenberger's theorem [36]. This result is important as it started the quest for membership algorithms. It provides such an algorithm for a very famous class: the *star-free languages* (SF). Informally, these are the languages which can be defined by a regular expression in which the Kleene star is disallowed (hence the name "star-free") but a new operator for the complement operation is allowed instead. This class is important as it admits several natural alternate definitions. For example, the star-free languages are those which can be defined in first-order logic [15] or equivalently in linear temporal logic [11].

Schützenberger's theorem states an algebraic characterization of SF: a regular language is star-free if and only if its syntactic monoid is *aperiodic*. This yields an algorithm for SF-membership as aperiodicity is a decidable property of finite monoids. Historically, Schützenberger's theorem was the first result of its kind. It motivated the systematic investigation of the membership problem for important classes of languages. It is often viewed as one of the most important results of automata theory. This claim is supported by the number of times this theorem has been revisited over the years and the wealth of existing proofs [5,7,8,10,14, 16,17,21,23,41].

In this section, we present our own proof, based on SF-covers. Let us point out that while the formulation is new, the original ideas behind the argument can be traced back to the proof of Wilke [41]. We first recall the definition of the star-free languages. Then, we state the theorem properly and present the proof.

4.1 Definition

Let us define the class of star-free languages (SF). For every alphabet A, $SF(A)$ is the least set containing $\emptyset$ and all singletons $\{a\}$ for $a \in A$, which is closed under union, complement and concatenation. That is, for every $K, L \in SF(A)$, the languages $K \cup L$, $A^* \setminus K$ and KL belong to $SF(A)$ as well.

Example 8. For every sub-alphabet $B \subseteq A$, we have $B^* \in SF(A)$. Indeed, by closure under complement, $A^* = A^* \setminus \emptyset \in SF(A)$. We then get $A^* a A^* \in SF(A)$ by closure under concatenation. Finally, this yields,

$$B^* = A^* \setminus \left(\bigcup_{a \in A \setminus B} A^* a A^* \right) \in SF(A)$$

Another standard example is $(ab)^*$ (where a, b are two *distinct* letters of A). Indeed, $(ab)^*$ is the complement of $bA^* \cup A^* aaA^* \cup A^* bbA^* \cup A^* a$ (provided that $A = \{a, b\}$) which is clearly star-free. □

By definition, SF is a Boolean algebra and one may verify that it is quotient-closed (the details are left to the reader). We complete the definition with a standard property that we require to prove the "easy" direction of Schützenberger's theorem (every star-free language has an aperiodic syntactic monoid). Another typical application of this property is to show that examples of languages are *not* star-free. For example, $(AA)^*$ (words with even length) is not star-free since since it does not satisfy the following lemma.

Lemma 9 *Let A be an alphabet and $L \in SF(A)$. There exists a number $k \geq 1$ such that for every $\ell \geq k$ and $w \in A^*$, we have $w^\ell \equiv_L w^{\ell+1}$.*

Proof. We proceed by structural induction on the definition of L as a star-free language. When $L = \emptyset$, it is clear that the lemma holds for $k = 1$. When $L = \{a\}$ for $a \in A$, one may verify that the lemma holds for $k = 2$. We turn to the inductive cases. Assume first that $L = L_1 \cup L_2$ where $L_1, L_2 \in SF$ are simpler languages. Induction yields $k_1, k_2 \geq 1$ such that for $i = 1, 2$, if $\ell \geq k_i$ and $w \in A^*$, we have $w^\ell \equiv_{L_i} w^{\ell+1}$. Hence, the lemma holds for $k = \max(k_1, k_2)$ in that case. We turn to complement: $L = A^* \setminus H$ where $H \in SF$ is a simpler language. By induction, we get $h \geq 1$ such that for every $w \in A^*$ and $\ell \geq h$, we have $w^\ell \equiv_H w^{\ell+1}$. Clearly, the lemma holds for $k = h$.

We now consider concatenation: $L = L_1 L_2$ where $L_1, L_2 \in$ SF are simpler languages. Induction yields $k_1, k_2 \geq 1$ such that for $i = 1, 2$, if $\ell \geq k_i$ and $w \in A^*$, we have $w^\ell \equiv_{L_i} w^{\ell+1}$. Let m be the maximum between k_1 and k_2. We prove that the lemma holds for $k = 2m + 1$. Let $w \in A^*$ and $\ell \geq k$, we have to show that $w^\ell \equiv_L w^{\ell+1}$, i.e. $xu^\ell y \in L \Leftrightarrow xu^{\ell+1}y \in L$ for every $x, y \in A^*$. We concentrate on the right to left implication (the converse one is symmetrical). Assume that $xu^{\ell+1}y \in L$. Since $L = L_1 L_2$, we get $w_1 \in L_1$ and $w_2 \in L_2$ such that $xu^{k+1}y = w_1 w_2$. Since $k \geq 2m + 1$, it follows that either xu^{m+1} is a prefix of w_1 or $u^{m+1}y$ is a suffix of w_2. By symmetry, we assume that the former property holds: we have $w_1 = xu^{m+1}z$ for some $z \in A^*$. Observe that since $xu^{k+1}y = w_1 w_2$, it follows that $zw_2 = u^{k-m}y$. Moreover, we have $m \geq k_1$ by definition of m. Since $xu^{m+1}z = w_1 \in L_1$, we know therefore that $xu^m z \in L_1$ by definition of k_1. Thus, $xu^m zw_2 \in L_1 L_2 = L$. Since $zw_2 = u^{k-m}y$, this yields $xu^k y \in L$, concluding the proof. □

4.2 Schützenberger's Theorem

We may now present and prove Schützenberger's theorem. Let us first define aperiodic monoids. There are several equivalent definitions in the literature. We use an equational one based on the idempotent power ω available in finite monoids. A *finite* monoid M is aperiodic when it satisfies the following property:

$$\text{for every } s \in M, \quad s^\omega = s^{\omega+1} \tag{1}$$

We are ready to state Schützenberger's theorem.

Theorem 10 (Schützenberger [36]). *A regular language is star-free if and only if its syntactic monoid is aperiodic.*

Theorem 10 illustrates of the syntactic approach presented in Sect. 3. It validates Proposition 3: the star-free languages are characterized by a property of their syntactic morphism. In fact, for this particular class, one does not even need the full morphism, the syntactic monoid suffices.

The main application is a membership algorithm for the class of star-free languages. Given as input a regular language L, one may compute its syntactic monoid and check whether it satisfies Eq. (1): this boils down to testing all elements in the monoid. By Theorem 10, this decides whether L is star-free. However, as we explained in Remark 1 when we first introduced membership, this theorem is also important for the arguments that are required to prove it. Indeed, providing these arguments requires a deep insight on SF. The right to left implication is of particular interest: "given a regular language whose syntactic monoid is aperiodic, prove that it is star-free". This involves devising a generic way to construct a star-free description for *every* regular language recognized by a monoid satisfying a *syntactic* property. This is the implication that we handle with covers. On the other hand, the converse implication is simple and standard (essentially, we already proved it with Lemma 9).

Proof. We fix an alphabet A and a regular language $L \subseteq A^*$ for the proof. Let $\alpha : A^* \to M$ be the syntactic morphism of L. We prove that $L \in \mathrm{SF}(A)$ if and only if M is aperiodic. Let us first handle the left to right implication.

From star-free languages to aperiodicity. Assume that $L \in \mathrm{SF}(A)$. We prove that M is aperiodic, *i.e.* that (1) is satisfied. Let $s \in M$, we have to show that $s^\omega = s^{\omega+1}$.

Since α is a syntactic morphism, it is surjective and there exists $w \in A^*$ such that $\alpha(w) = s$. Moreover, since $L \in \mathrm{SF}(A)$, Lemma 9 yields $k \geq 1$ such that $w^{k\omega} \equiv_L w^{k\omega+1}$. By definition of the syntactic morphism, this implies that $\alpha(w^{k\omega}) = \alpha(w^{k\omega+1})$. Since $\alpha(w) = s$, this yields $s^\omega = s^{\omega+1}$ as desired.

From aperiodicity to star-free languages. Assume that M is aperiodic. We show that L is star-free. We rely on the notions introduced in the Sect. 3 and directly prove that *every* language recognized by α is star-free.

Remark 11. Intuitively, this property is stronger than L being star-free. Yet, since SF is a quotient-closed Boolean algebra, it is equivalent by Proposition 3.   □

The argument is based on Proposition 7: we use induction to construct an SF-cover $\mathbf{K}$ of A^* which is confined by α. By the proposition, this implies that every language recognized by α belongs to $\mathrm{SF}(A)$. We start with a preliminary definition that we require to formulate the induction.

Let B be an arbitrary alphabet, $\beta : B^* \to M$ a morphism and $s \in M$. We say that a finite set of languages $\mathbf{K}$ (over B) is (s, β)-*safe* if for every $K \in \mathbf{K}$ and every $w, w' \in K$, we have $s\beta(w) = s\beta(w')$.

Lemma 12. *Let B be an alphabet. Consider a morphism $\beta : B^* \to M$, $C \subseteq B$ and $s \in M$. There exists an SF-cover of C^* which is (s, β)-safe.*

We first use Lemma 12 to conclude the main argument. We apply the lemma for $B = A$, $\beta = \alpha$ and $s = 1_M$. This yields an SF-cover $\mathbf{K}$ of A^* which is $(1_M, \alpha)$-safe. By definition, it follows that for every $K \in \mathbf{K}$, we have $\alpha(w) = \alpha(w')$ for all $K \in \mathbf{K}$. By Fact 6, this implies that $\mathbf{K}$ is confined by α, completing the main argument.

It remains to prove Lemma 12. Let B be an alphabet, $\beta : B^* \to M$ a morphism, $C \subseteq B$ and $s \in M$. We build an SF-cover $\mathbf{K}$ of C^* which is (s, β)-safe using induction on the three following parameters listed by order of importance:

1. The size of $\beta(C^+) \subseteq M$.
2. The size of C.
3. The size of $s\beta(C^*) \subseteq M$.

Remark 13. The aperiodic monoid M remains fixed throughout the whole proof. On the other hand, the alphabets B and C, the morphism $\beta : B^* \to M$ and $s \in M$ may change when applying induction.   □

We distinguish two cases depending on the following property of β, C and s. We say that s is (β, C)-*stable* when the following holds:

$$\text{for every } c \in C, \quad s\beta(C^*) = s\beta(C^*c). \tag{2}$$

We first consider the case when s is (β, C)-stable. This is the base case which we handle using the hypothesis that M is aperiodic.

Base case: s is (β, C)-stable. In that case, we define $\mathbf{K} = \{C^*\}$ which is clearly an SF-cover of C^* (we have $C^* \in \mathrm{SF}(B)$ as seen in Example 8). It remains to show that $\mathbf{K}$ is (s, β)-safe. For $w, w' \in C^*$, we have to show that $s\beta(w) = s\beta(w')$. We actually prove that $s\beta(w) = s$ for every $w \in C^*$ which implies the desired result. Since s is (β, C)-stable, we have the following fact.

Fact 14. *For every $u \in C^*$, there exists $t \in \beta(C^*)$ such that $st\beta(u) = s$.*

Proof. We use induction on the length of $u \in C^*$. If $u = \varepsilon$, the fact holds for $t = 1_M$. Assume now that $u \in C^+$. We have $u = cu'$ for $u' \in C^*$ and $c \in C$. Induction yields $t' \in \beta(C^*)$ such that $st'\beta(u') = s$. Moreover, since s is (β, C)-stable, (2) yields $t \in \beta(C^*)$ such that $st\beta(c) = st'$. Altogether, we obtain that $st\beta(u) = st\beta(c)\beta(u') = st'\beta(u') = s$ which concludes the proof. □

Consider the word $w^\omega \in C^*$ (with ω as the idempotent power of M). We apply Fact 14 for $u = w^\omega$. This yields $t \in \beta(C^*)$ such that $s = st(\beta(w))^\omega$. Since M is aperiodic, we have $(\beta(w))^\omega = (\beta(w))^{\omega+1}$ by Eq. (1). This yields $s\beta(w) = st(\beta(w))^{\omega+1} = st(\beta(w))^\omega = s$, concluding the base case.

Inductive case: s is not (β, C)-stable. By hypothesis, there exists a letter $c \in C$ such that the following *strict* inclusion holds $s\beta(C^*c) \subsetneq s\beta(C^*)$. We fix $c \in C$ for the remainder of the argument.

Let D be the sub-alphabet $D = C \setminus \{c\}$. By definition, $|D| < |C|$. Hence, induction on our second parameter in Lemma 12 (*i.e.*, the size of C) yields an SF-cover $\mathbf{H}$ of D^* which is $(1_M, \beta)$-safe. Note that it is clear that our first induction parameter (the size of $\alpha(C^+)$) has not increased since $D \subseteq C$.

We distinguish two independent sub-cases. Clearly, we have $\beta(C^*c) \subseteq \beta(C^+)$. The argument differs depending on whether this inclusion is strict or not.

Sub-case 1: $\beta(C^*c) = \beta(C^+)$. Consider a language $H \in \mathbf{H}$. Since $\mathbf{H}$ is a cover of D^* which is $(1_M, \beta)$-safe by definition, there exists some element $t_H \in \beta(D^*)$ such that $\beta(w) = t_H$ for every $w \in H$. The construction of the desired SF-cover $\mathbf{K}$ of C^* is based on the following fact which we prove using induction on our third parameter (the size of $s\beta(C^*)$).

Fact 15. *For every language $H \in \mathbf{H}$, there exists an SF-cover $\mathbf{U}_H$ of C^* which is $(st_H\beta(c), \beta)$-safe.*

Proof. Since $t_H \in \beta(D^*)$, it is immediate that $st_H\beta(c) \in s\beta(D^*c)$. Hence, $st_H\beta(c)\beta(C^*) \subseteq s\beta(C^+)$. Moreover, $\beta(C^*c) = \beta(C^+)$ by hypothesis in Sub-case 1. Thus, $st_H\beta(c)\beta(C^*) \subseteq s\beta(C^*c)$. Finally, recall that the letter c satisfies

$s\beta(C^*c) \subsetneq s\beta(C^*)$ by definition. Consequently, we have the **strict** inclusion $st_H\beta(c)\beta(C^*) \subsetneq s\beta(C^*)$. Hence, we may apply induction on our third parameter in Lemma 12 (*i.e.* the size of $s\beta(C^*)$) to obtain the desiredn SF-cover $\mathbf{U}_H$ of C^* which is $(st_H\beta(c), \beta)$-safe. Note that here, our first two parameters have not increased (they only depend on β and C which remain unchanged).   □

We may now use Fact 15 to build the desired cover $\mathbf{K}$ of C^*. We define $\mathbf{K} = \mathbf{H} \cup \{HcU \mid H \in \mathbf{H} \text{ and } U \in \mathbf{U}_H\}$. Clearly, $\mathbf{K}$ is an SF-cover of C^* by hypothesis on $\mathbf{H}$ and $\mathbf{U}_H$ since $D = C\backslash\{c\}$ and SF is closed under concatenation. We need to show that $\mathbf{K}$ is (s, β)-safe. Let $K \in \mathbf{K}$ and $w, w' \in K$, we need to show that $s\beta(w) = s\beta(w')$. By definition of $\mathbf{K}$, there are two cases. When $K \in \mathbf{H}$, the result is immediate since $\mathbf{H}$ is $(1_M, \beta)$-safe by definition. Otherwise, $K = HcU$ for $H \in \mathbf{H}$ and $U \in \mathbf{U}_H$. Thus, we get $x, x' \in H$ and $u, u' \in U$ such that $w = xcu$ and $w' = x'cu'$. By definition, $\beta(x) = \beta(x') = t_H$. Moreover, since $\mathbf{U}_H$ is $(st_H\beta(c), \beta)$-safe by definition in Fact 15, we have $st_H\beta(cu) = st_H\beta(cu')$. Altogether, this yields $s\beta(xcu) = s\beta(x'cu')$, *i.e.* $s\beta(w) = s\beta(w')$ as desired.

Sub-case 2: $\beta(C^*c) \subsetneq \beta(C^+)$. Let us first explain informally how the cover $\mathbf{K}$ of C^* is built in this case. Let $w \in C^*$. Since $D = C \setminus \{c\}$, w admits a unique decomposition $w = uv$ such that $u \in (D^*c)^*$ and $v \in D^*$ (*i.e.*, v is the largest suffix of w in D^* and u is the corresponding prefix). Using induction, we construct SF-covers of the possible prefixes and suffixes. Then, we combine them to construct a cover of the whole set C^*. Actually, we already covered the suffixes: we have an SF-cover $\mathbf{H}$ of C^* which is $(1_M, \beta)$-safe. It remains to cover the prefixes. We do so this in the following lemma which we prove using induction on our first parameter (the size of $\beta(C^+)$).

Lemma 16. *There exists an SF-cover $\mathbf{V}$ of $(D^*c)^*$ which is $(1_M, \beta)$-safe.*

Proof. Let $E = \beta(D^*c)$. Using E as a new alphabet, we apply induction on the first parameter in Lemma 12 (*i.e.*, the size of $\beta(C^+)$) to build an auxiliary SF-cover of E^* which we then use to construct $\mathbf{V}$.

Since $E = \beta(D^*c) \subseteq M$, there exists a natural morphism $\gamma : E^* \to M$ defined by $\gamma(e) = e$ for every $e \in E$. Clearly, $\gamma(E^+) \subseteq \beta(C^*c)$. Since $\beta(C^*c) \subsetneq \beta(C^+)$ by hypothesis of Sub-case 2, this implies $\gamma(E^+) \subsetneq \beta(C^+)$ and induction on the first parameter in Lemma 12 yields an SF-cover $\mathbf{W}$ of E^* which is $(1_M, \gamma)$-safe. We use $\mathbf{W}$ to construct $\mathbf{V}$. First, we define a map $\mu : (D^*c)^* \to E^*$.

We let $\mu(\varepsilon) = \varepsilon$. Otherwise, let $w \in (D^*c)^+$ be a nonempty word. Since $c \notin D$, w admits a **unique** decomposition $w = w_1 \cdots w_n$ with $w_1, \ldots, w_n \in D^*c$. Hence, we may define $\mu(w_1 \cdots w_n) = e_1 \cdots e_n$ with $e_i = \beta(w_i)$ for every $i \leq n$ (recall that $E = \beta(D^*c)$ by definition). We are ready to define $\mathbf{W}$. We let,

$$\mathbf{V} = \{\mu^{-1}(W) \mid W \in \mathbf{W}\}$$

It remains to show that $\mathbf{V}$ is an SF-cover of $(D^*c)^*$ which is $(1_M, \beta)$-safe. It is immediate that $\mathbf{V}$ is a cover of $(D^*c)^*$ since $\mathbf{W}$ was a cover of E^*.

Let us prove that $\mathbf{V}$ is $(1_M, \beta)$-safe. Let $V \in \mathbf{V}$ and $v, v' \in V$. We prove that $\beta(v) = \beta(v')$. By definition, there exists $w \in \mathbf{W}$ such that $V = \mu^{-1}(W)$. Thus,

$\mu(v), \mu(v') \in W$ which implies that $\gamma(\mu(v)) = \gamma(\mu(v'))$ since $\mathbf{W}$ is $(1_M, \gamma)$-safe by definition. One may now verify from the definitions that $\gamma(\mu(v)) = \beta(v)$ and $\gamma(\mu(v')) = \beta(v')$. Thus, we obtain $\beta(v) = \beta(v')$ as desired.

It remains to show that every $V \in \mathbf{V}$ is star-free. By definition of $\mathbf{V}$, it suffices to show that for every $W \in \mathrm{SF}(E)$, we have $\mu^{-1}(W) \in \mathrm{SF}(B)$. We proceed by induction on the definition of W as a star-free language. When $W = \emptyset$, it is clear that $\mu^{-1}(W) = \emptyset \in \mathrm{SF}(B)$. Assume now that $W = \{e\}$ for some $e \in E$. By definition, $\mu^{-1}(e) = \{w \in D^*c \mid \beta(w) = e\}$. This may be reformulated as follows: $\mu^{-1}(e) = Uc$ with $U = \{u \in D^* \mid \beta(uc) = e\}$. Clearly, U is the intersection of D^* with a language recognized by β. Recall that we have an SF-cover $\mathbf{H}$ of D^* which is $(1_M, \beta)$-safe (and therefore confined by β). Hence, Proposition 7 implies that $U \in \mathrm{SF}(B)$. It follows that $\mu^{-1}(e) = Uc \in \mathrm{SF}(B)$ as desired. We turn to the inductive cases.

First, assume that there are simpler languages $W_1, W_2 \in \mathrm{SF}(E)$ such that either $W = W_1 W_2$ or $W = W_1 \cup W_2$. By induction, $\mu^{-1}(W_i) \in \mathrm{SF}(B)$ for $i = 1, 2$. Moreover, the definition of μ implies that $\mu^{-1}(W_1 W_2) = \mu^{-1}(W_1)\mu^{-1}(W_2)$ and $\mu^{-1}(W_1 \cup W_2) = \mu^{-1}(W_1) \cup \mu^{-1}(W_2)$. Hence, we obtain $\mu^{-1}(W) \in \mathrm{SF}(B)$. Finally, assume that $W = E^* \setminus W'$ for a simpler language $W' \in \mathrm{SF}(E)$. By induction, $\mu^{-1}(W') \in \mathrm{SF}(E)$. Moreover, $\mu^{-1}(W) = (D^*c)^* \setminus \mu^{-1}(W')$. Clearly, $(D^*c)^* = C^* \setminus (C^*D) \in \mathrm{SF}(B)$. Thus, we get $\mu^{-1}(W) \in \mathrm{SF}(B)$ as desired. □

We are ready to construct the desired SF-cover $\mathbf{K}$ of C^*. Let $\mathbf{V}$ be the $(1_M, \beta)$-safe SF-cover of $(D^*c)^*$ given by Lemma 16 and consider our $(1_M, \beta)$-safe SF-cover $\mathbf{H}$ of D^*. We define $\mathbf{K} = \{VH \mid V \in \mathbf{V} \text{ and } H \in \mathbf{H}\}$. It is immediate by definition that $\mathbf{K}$ is an SF-cover of C^* since $D = C \setminus \{c\}$ and SF is closed under concatenation. It remains to verify that $\mathbf{K}$ is (s, β)-safe (it is in fact $(1_M, \beta)$-safe). Let $K \in \mathbf{K}$ and $w, w' \in K$, we show that $\beta(w) = \beta(w')$ (which implies $s\beta(w) = s\beta(w')$). By definition, $K = VU$ with $V \in \mathbf{V}$ and $U \in \mathbf{U}$. Therefore, $w = vu$ and $w' = v'u'$ with $u, u' \in U$ and $v, v' \in V$. Since U and V are both $(1_M, \beta)$-safe by definition, we have $\beta(u) = \beta(u')$ and $\beta(v) = \beta(v')$. It follows that $\beta(w) = \beta(w')$. This concludes the proof of Lemma 12. □

5   Piecewise Testable Languages and Simon's Theorem

We turn to our second example: Simon's theorem [38]. This results states an algebraic characterization of another prominent class of regular languages: the *piecewise testable languages* (PT). It is quite important in the literature as it was among the first results of this kind after Schützenberger's theorem (which we proved in Sect. 4). Over the years, many different proofs have been found (examples include [1,9,12,18,38,39]). We present a new proof, based on PT-covers and entirely independent from previously known arguments. It relies on a concatenation principle for the piecewise testable languages that can only be formulated with PT-covers.

We first recall the definition of piecewise testable languages. Then, we state the theorem properly and present the proof.

5.1 Definition

Let us define the class of piecewise testable languages (PT). Given an alphabet A and $u, v \in A^*$, we say that u is a *piece* of v and write $u \preceq v$ when u can be obtained from v by removing letters and gluing the remaining ones together. More precisely, $u \preceq v$ when there exist $a_1, \ldots, a_n \in A$ and $v_0, \ldots, v_n \in A^*$ such that,

$$u = a_1 a_2 \cdots a_n \quad \text{and} \quad v = v_0 a_1 v_1 a_2 v_2 \cdots v_{n-1} a_n v_n.$$

For instance, acb is a piece of $bb\underline{a}b\underline{cb}cbba$. Note that by definition, the empty word "ε" is a piece of every word (this is the case $n = 0$). Furthermore, it is clear that the relation $\preceq$ is a preorder on A^*.

For every word $u \in A^*$, we write $\uparrow u \subseteq A^*$ for the language consisting of all words v such that u is a piece of v. If $u = a_1 \cdots a_n$, we have by definition:

$$\uparrow u = \{ v \in A^* \mid u \preceq v \} = A^* a_1 A^* a_2 A^* \cdots a_{n-1} A^* a_n A^*.$$

We may now define PT. A language $L \subseteq A^*$ is *piecewise testable* (*i.e.* $L \in \mathrm{PT}(A)$) when L is a (finite) Boolean combination of languages $\uparrow w$ for $w \in A^*$.

Example 17. We let $A = \{a, b\}$ as the alphabet. Then $a^+ b^+ \in \mathrm{PT}(A)$. Indeed, $a^+ b^+ = A^* a A^* b A^* \setminus A^* b A^* a A^*$. Moreover, observe that every finite language is piecewise testable. Since PT is closed under union, it suffices to show that every singleton is piecewise testable. Consider a word $w = a_1 \cdots a_n$. By definition, w is the only word belonging to $A^* a_1 A^* a_2 A^* \cdots a_{n-1} A^* a_n A^*$ but not to $A^* b_1 A^* b_2 A^* \cdots b_n A^* b_{n+1} A^*$, where $b_1, \ldots, b_{n+1}$ denotes any sequence of $n + 1$ letters. Hence, $\{w\}$ is piecewise testable.   □

Clearly PT is a Boolean algebra and one may verify that it is quotient-closed (the details are left to the reader). We complete the definition with two properties of PT. The first one is standard and we shall need it to prove that "easy" direction of Simon's theorem (every piecewise testable language satisfies the characterization).

Lemma 18. *Let A be an alphabet and $L \in \mathrm{PT}(A)$. There exists $k \geq 1$ such that for every $\ell \geq k$ and $u, v \in A^*$, we have $(uv)^\ell u \equiv_L (uv)^\ell \equiv_L v(uv)^\ell$.*

Proof. Since $L \in \mathrm{PT}$, there exists $k \geq 1$ such that L is a Boolean combinations of language $\uparrow w$ with $w \in A^*$ such that $|w| \leq k$ (*i.e.* w has length at most k). We prove that the lemma holds for this number k. Let $u, v \in A^*$ and $\ell \geq k$. We show that $(uv)^\ell u \equiv_L (uv)^\ell \equiv_L v(uv)^\ell$. By symmetry, we concentrate on $(uv)^\ell u \equiv_L (uv)^\ell$: given $x, y \in A^*$, we show that $x(uv)^\ell u y \in L \Leftrightarrow x(uv)^\ell y \in L$. Since $\ell \geq k$, one may verify that for every $w \in A^*$ such that $|w| \leq k$, we have $w \preceq x(uv)^\ell u y \Leftrightarrow w \preceq x(uv)^\ell y$. In other words, $x(uv)^\ell u y \in \uparrow w \Leftrightarrow x(uv)^\ell y \in \uparrow w$. Since L is a Boolean combination of such languages, this implies the equivalence $x(uv)^\ell u y \in L \Leftrightarrow x(uv)^\ell y \in L$ as desired.   □

The second result is specific to our covering-based approach for proving Simon's theorem. It turns out that elegant proof arguments for membership algorithms often apply to classes that are closed under concatenation (or some weak variant thereof). As seen in the previous section, the star-free languages are an example. Unfortunately, PT is *not* closed under concatenation. For example, consider the alphabet $A = \{a, b\}$. We have $A^* \in$ PT and $\{a\} \in$ PT as seen in Example 17. Yet, one may verify with Lemma 18 that $A^*a \notin$ PT.

We solve this issue with a "weak concatenation principle" for piecewise testable languages. This result can only be formulated using PT-covers. While its proof is rather technical, an interesting observation is that it characterizes the piecewise testable languages. In the proof of Simon's theorem, we only use this concatenation principle and the hypothesis that PT is a Boolean algebra (we never come back to the original definition of PT).

Proposition 19. *Let $u, v \in A^*$ and $a \in A$. Moreover, let $\mathbf{K}_u$ and $\mathbf{K}_v$ be PT-covers of $\uparrow u$ and $\uparrow v$ respectively. There exists a PT-cover $\mathbf{K}$ of $\uparrow(uav)$ such that for every $K \in \mathbf{K}$ we have $K_u \in \mathbf{K}_u$ and $K_v \in \mathbf{K}_v$ satisfying $K \subseteq K_u a K_v$.*

Proof. We start with standard definitions that we need to describe $\mathbf{K}$. For every $k \in \mathbb{N}$, we associate a preorder $\preceq_k$ over A^*. For $w, w' \in A^*$, we write $w \preceq_k w'$ to indicate that for every $x \in A^*$ such that $|x| \leq k$, we have $x \preceq w \Rightarrow x \preceq w'$. Clearly, $\preceq_k$ is a preorder which is coarser than $\preceq$: for every w, w' such that $w \preceq w'$, we have $w \preceq_k w'$. Moreover, we write $\sim_k$ for the equivalence generated by this preorder: $w \sim_k w'$ if and only if $x \preceq w \Leftrightarrow x \preceq w'$ for every $x \in A^*$ such that $|x| \leq k$. Clearly, $\sim_k$ has finite index.

Since $\mathbf{K}_u$ and $\mathbf{K}_v$ are PT-covers, there exists some number $k \in \mathbb{N}$ every language $K \in \mathbf{K}_u \cup \mathbf{K}_v$ is a finite Boolean combination of languages $\uparrow x$ for $x \in A^*$ such that $|x| \leq k$. In other words, every such language K is a union of $\sim_k$-classes. Moreover, we may choose k so that $|u| \leq k$ and $|v| \leq k$. We shall define the cover $\mathbf{K}$ as a set of $\sim_h$-classes for an appropriate number h that we choose using the following technical lemma.

Lemma 20. *Let $h \geq 2|A|^{k+1}+1$, $a \in A$ and $u', v', w \in A^*$ such that $u'av' \preceq_h w$. There exist $u'', v'' \in A^*$ such that $w = u''av''$, $u' \preceq_k u''$ and $v' \preceq_k v''$.*

Proof. We claim that there exist $y, z \in A^*$ with length at most $|A|^{k+1}$ such that $y \preceq u' \preceq_k y$ and $z \preceq v' \preceq_k z$. We first use this claim to prove the lemma. Clearly, $|yaz| \leq 2|A|^{k+1} + 1 \leq h$ and $yaz \preceq u'av'$. Therefore, since $u'av' \preceq_h w$, it follows that $yaz \preceq w$. This yields a decomposition $w = u''av''$ such that $y \preceq u''$ and $z \preceq v''$. Since $u' \preceq_k y$ and $v' \preceq_k z$, this implies $u' \preceq_k u''$ and $v' \preceq_k v''$ as desired.

It remains to prove the claim. We only construct a piece $y \in A^*$ such that $|y| \leq |A|^{k+1}$ and $y \preceq u' \preceq_k y$, as the construction of z is analogous. Let F be the set of all pieces of u' of size at most k, that is,

$$F = \{u'' \in A^* \mid u'' \preceq u' \text{ and } |u''| \leq k\}.$$

Clearly, $|F| \leq |A|^{k+1}$. For $x \in A^*$, let $L_F(x)$ be the set of words of F that are pieces of x. Let $u' = u_1 a u_2$ be some decomposition of u'. Note that $L_F(u_1) \subseteq L_F(u_1 a)$.

We say that the occurrence of a given by the decomposition $u' = u_1au_2$ is *bad* if $L_F(u_1) = L_F(u_1a)$. Let y be the word obtained from u' by deleting all bad letters (and keeping the other ones). By construction, $y \preceq u'$ and $L_F(y) = L_F(u')$. The latter property implies that $u' \preceq y$ for every $u' \in F$. By definition of F, this means that $u' \preceq_k y$. Furthermore, letters of y are not bad, and one may verify that there are at most $|L_F(u')| = |F|$ such letters. Therefore, $|y| \leq |F| \leq |A|^{k+1}$, which concludes the proof.   □

We define $h = 2|A|^{k+1} + 1$. It is immediate that every $\sim_h$-class is a language of PT (it is a Boolean combination of languages $\uparrow x$ for $x \in A^*$ such that $|x| \leq h$). Hence, the set $\mathbf{K}$ containing all $\sim_h$-classes which intersect $\uparrow(uav)$ is a PT-cover of $\uparrow(uav)$. It remains to show that for every $K \in \mathbf{K}$, there exist $K_u \in \mathbf{K}_u$ and $K_v \in \mathbf{K}_v$ such that $K \subseteq K_uaK_v$. We fix the language $K \in \mathbf{K}$ for the proof. We need the following result.

Lemma 21. *Let $H \subseteq K$ be a finite language. There exist $K' \in \mathbf{K}_u$ and $K'' \in \mathbf{K}_v$ such that $H \subseteq K'aK''$.*

Proof. Let $w_1, \ldots, w_n \in A^*$ be the words in H, i.e., $H = \{w_1, \ldots, w_n\}$. Our goal is to find $K' \in \mathbf{K}_u$ and $K'' \in \mathbf{K}_v$ such that $w_i \in K'aK''$ for all $i = 1, \ldots, n$. Therefore, we first have to find a suitable decomposition of each word w_i as u_iav_i, and then to show that all u_i's belong to some $K' \in \mathbf{K}_u$ and all v_i's belong to some $K'' \in \mathbf{K}_v$.

By definition, K is a $\sim_h$-class and it intersects $\uparrow(uav)$. This yields a word $x \in \uparrow(uav)$ such that $x \sim_h w_1 \sim_h \cdots \sim_h w_n$. Since $x \in \uparrow(uav)$, there exist $u' \in \uparrow u$ and $v' \in \uparrow v$ such that $x = u'av'$. Let $\ell = |w_1| + 1$. We may write the relations $x \sim_h w_1 \sim_h \cdots \sim_h w_n$ as follows:

$$u'av' \preceq_h \underbrace{w_1 \preceq_h \cdots \preceq_h w_n}_{\text{block 1}} \preceq_h \underbrace{w_1 \preceq_h \cdots \preceq_h w_n}_{\text{block 2}} \preceq_h \cdots \preceq_h \underbrace{w_1 \preceq_h \cdots \preceq_h w_n}_{\text{block } \ell}.$$

$$\underbrace{}_{n\ell \text{ words}}$$

Since $h \geq 2|A|^{k+1} + 1$ by definition, may apply Lemma 20 $n\ell$ times to get $u_{1,1}, \ldots, u_{n,1}, \ldots, u_{1,\ell}, \ldots, u_{n,\ell} \in A^*$ and $v_{1,1}, \ldots, v_{n,1}, \ldots, v_{1,\ell}, \ldots, v_{n,\ell} \in A^*$ such that,

- for every $i \leq n$ and $j \leq \ell$, we have $w_i = u_{i,j}av_{i,j}$, and,
- $u' \preceq_k u_{1,1} \preceq_k \cdots \preceq_k u_{n,1} \preceq_k \cdots \preceq_k u_{1,\ell} \preceq_k \cdots \preceq_k u_{n,\ell}$, and,
- $v' \preceq_k v_{1,1} \preceq_k \cdots \preceq_k v_{n,1} \preceq_k \cdots \preceq_k v_{1,\ell} \preceq_k \cdots \preceq_k v_{n,\ell}$.

Since $\ell = |w_1|+1$, the first property and the pigeonhole principle yield $j_1 < j_2 \leq \ell$ such that $u_{1,j_1} = u_{1,j_2}$ and $v_{1,j_1} = v_{1,j_2}$. For every $i \leq n$, we let $u_i = u_{i,j_1}$ and $v_i = v_{i,j_1}$. Therefore, for all $i = 1, \ldots, n$, we have $w_i = u_iav_i$.

The second and third properties now yield $u' \preceq_k u_1 \preceq_k \cdots \preceq_k u_n \preceq_k u_1$ and $v' \preceq_k v_1 \preceq_k \cdots \preceq_k v_n \preceq_k v_1$, whence:

$$u' \preceq_k u_1 \sim_k \cdots \sim_k u_n \quad \text{and} \quad v' \preceq_k v_1 \sim_k \cdots \sim_k v_n.$$

Recall that $|u| \leq k$ by definition of k. Since $u' \in \uparrow u$ and $u' \preceq_k u_1$, it follows that $u_1 \in \uparrow u$. Since $\mathbf{K}_u$ is a cover of $\uparrow u$, this yields $K' \in \mathbf{K}_u$ such that $u_1 \in K'$.

Since K' is a union of $\sim_k$-classes by choice of k and since $u_1 \sim_k \cdots \sim_k u_n$, we deduce that $u_1, \ldots, u_n \in K'$. Symmetrically, we obtain $K'' \in \mathbf{K}_v$ such that $v_1, \ldots, v_n \in K''$. Finally, since $w_i = u_i a v_i$ for every $i \leq n$, this yields $H = \{w_1, \ldots, w_n\} \subseteq K'aK''$, as desired. $\qquad\square$

We may now finish the proof. For every $n \in \mathbb{N}$, we let $H_n \subseteq K$ be the (finite) language containing all words of length at most n in K. Clearly, $K = \bigcup_{n \in \mathbb{N}} H_n$ and $H_n \subseteq H_{n+1}$ for every $n \in \mathbb{N}$. Moreover, Lemma 21 implies that for every $n \in \mathbb{N}$, we have $K'_n \in \mathbf{K}_u$ and $K''_n \in \mathbf{K}_v$ such that $H_n \subseteq K'_n a K''_n$. Since $\mathbf{K}_u$ and $\mathbf{K}_v$ are finite sets, there exist $K_u \in \mathbf{K}_u$ and $K_v \in \mathbf{K}_v$ such that $K'_n = K_u$ and $K''_n = K_v$ for infinitely many n. Since $H_n \subseteq H_{n+1}$ for every $n \in \mathbb{N}$, it then follows that $H_n \subseteq K_u a K_v$ for every $n \in \mathbb{N}$. Finally, since $K = \bigcup_{n \in \mathbb{N}} H_n$, this implies $K \subseteq K_u a K_v$ which concludes the proof. $\qquad\square$

5.2   Simon's Theorem

We may now present and prove Simon's theorem. It characterizes the star-free languages as those whose syntactic monoid is $\mathcal{J}$-*trivial*. The original definition of this notion is based on the Green relation $\mathcal{J}$ defined on every finite monoid. Here, we do not consider this relation. Instead, we use an equational definition. A *finite* monoid M is $\mathcal{J}$-trivial when it satisfies the following property:

$$\text{for every } s, t \in M \quad (st)^\omega s = (st)^\omega = t(st)^\omega. \tag{3}$$

Theorem 22 (Simon [38]). *A regular language is piecewise testable if and only if its syntactic monoid is $\mathcal{J}$-trivial.*

As expected, the main application of Simon's theorem is the decidability of PT-membership. Given a regular language L as input, one may compute its syntactic monoid and check whether it satisfies Eq. (3) by testing all possible combinations. By Theorem 22, this decides whether L is piecewise testable. Yet, as for the star-free languages in Sect. 4, this theorem is also important for the arguments that are required to prove it. We present such a proof now.

Proof. We fix an alphabet A and a regular language $L \subseteq A^*$ for the proof. Let $\alpha : A^* \to M$ be the syntactic morphism of L. We prove that $L \in \mathrm{PT}(A)$ if and only if M is $\mathcal{J}$-trivial. We start with the left to right implication which is essentially immediate from Lemma 18. As expected, the difficult and most interesting part of the proof is the converse implication.

From piecewise testable languages to $\mathcal{J}$-triviality. Assume that we have $L \in \mathrm{PT}(A)$. We prove that M is $\mathcal{J}$-trivial: (3) holds. Let $s, t \in M$, we have to show that $(st)^\omega s = (st)^\omega = t(st)^\omega$.

Since α is a syntactic morphism, it is surjective and there exists $u, v \in A^*$ such that $\alpha(u) = s$ and $\alpha(v) = t$. Moreover, since $L \in \mathrm{SF}(A)$, Lemma 18 yields $k \geq 1$ such that $(uv)^{k\omega} u \equiv_L (uv)^{k\omega} \equiv_L v(uv)^{k\omega}$. By definition of the syntactic morphism, this implies that $\alpha((uv)^{k\omega} u) = \alpha((uv)^{k\omega}) = \alpha(v(uv)^{k\omega})$. Since $\alpha(u) = s$ and $\alpha(v) = t$, this yields $(st)^\omega s = (st)^\omega = t(st)^\omega$ as desired.

From $\mathcal{J}$-triviality to piecewise testable languages. Assume that M is $\mathcal{J}$-trivial. We show that L is piecewise testable. We rely on the notions introduced in the Sect. 3 and directly prove that *every* language recognized by α is piecewise testable. The argument is based on Proposition 7: we use induction to construct a PT-cover $\mathbf{K}$ of A^* which is confined by α. By the proposition, this implies that every language recognized by α belongs to PT(A). We start with a preliminary definition that we require to formulate the induction.

Given a finite set of languages $\mathbf{K}$, and $s, t \in M$, we say that $\mathbf{K}$ is (s,t)-*safe* if for every $K \in \mathbf{K}$ and $w, w' \in K$, we have $s\alpha(w)t = s\alpha(w')t$. The argument is based on the following lemma.

Lemma 23. *Let $s, t \in M$ and $w \in A^*$. There exists a PT-cover of $\uparrow w$ which is (s,t)-safe.*

We first use Lemma 23 to complete the main argument. We apply the lemma for $s = t = 1_M$ and $w = \varepsilon$. Since $\uparrow\varepsilon = A^*$, this yields a PT-cover $\mathbf{K}$ of A^* which is $(1_M, 1_M)$-safe. Thus, for every $K \in \mathbf{K}$ and $w, w' \in A^*$, we have $\alpha(w) = \alpha(w')$. By Fact 6, this implies that $\mathbf{K}$ is confined by α, concluding the proof.

It remains to prove Lemma 23. Let $s, t \in M$ and $w \in A^*$. We construct a PT-cover $\mathbf{K}$ of $\uparrow w$ which is (s,t)-safe. We write $P[s, w, t] \subseteq M \times M$ for the following set:

$$P[s, w, t] = \{(s\alpha(x), \alpha(y)t) \mid x, y \in A^* \text{ and } xy \in \uparrow w\}.$$

We proceed by induction on the two following parameters, listed by order of importance:

1. The size of $P[s, w, t]$.
2. The length of w.

We consider two cases depending on whether w is empty or not. We first assume that this property holds.

First case: $w = \varepsilon$. We handle this case using induction on our first parameter. Let $H \subseteq A^*$ be the language of all words $v \in A^*$ such that $(s, t) \notin P[s, v, t]$. We use induction to build a PT-cover of H (note that it may happen that H is empty in which case we do not need induction).

Fact 24. *There exists a PT-cover $\mathbf{K}_H$ of H which is (s,t)-safe.*

Proof. One may verify with a pumping argument that there exists a *finite* set $F \subseteq H$ such that $H \subseteq \bigcup_{v \in F} (\uparrow v)$ (this is also an immediate consequence of Higman's lemma). Hence, it suffices to prove that for every $v \in H$, there exists a PT-cover $\mathbf{K}_v$ of $\uparrow v$ which is (s,t)-safe. Indeed, one may then choose $\mathbf{K}_H$ to be the union of all covers $\mathbf{K}_v$ for $v \in F$. We fix $v \in H$ for the proof.

Since $w = \varepsilon$, we have $\uparrow w = A^*$. Since α is surjective (it is a syntactic morphism), it follows that $P[s, w, t] = \{(sq, rt) \mid q, r \in M\}$. Therefore, we have $P[s, v, t] \subseteq P[s, w, t]$ and $(s, t) \in P[s, w, t]$. Since $(s, t) \notin P[s, v, t]$ by definition of H, we get $|P[s, v, t]| < |P[s, w, t]|$. Hence, induction on the first parameter in Lemma 23 (the size of $P[s, w, t]$) yields a PT-cover $\mathbf{K}_v$ of $\uparrow v$ which is (s,t)-safe, as desired. $\square$

We let $\mathbf{K}_H$ be the PT-cover $\mathbf{K}_H$ of H given by Fact 24. We define,

$$K_\perp = A^* \setminus \left(\bigcup_{K \in \mathbf{K}_H} K \right).$$

Finally, we let $\mathbf{K} = \{K_\perp\} \cup \mathbf{K}_H$. It is immediate that $\mathbf{K}$ is a PT-cover of $A^* = \uparrow\varepsilon$ since PT is a Boolean algebra. It remains to verify that $\mathbf{K}$ is (s,t)-safe. Consider $K \in \mathbf{K}$ and let $u, u' \in K$. We prove that $s\alpha(u)t = s\alpha(u')t$. If $K \in \mathbf{K}_H$, this is immediate since $\mathbf{K}_H$ is (s,t)-safe by construction. Hence, it suffices to show that $K_\perp$ is (s,t)-safe. This is a direct consequence of the following fact. Note that this is the only place in the proof where we use the hypothesis that M satisfies (3).

Fact 25. *For every word $v \in K_\perp$, we have $s\alpha(v)t = st$.*

Proof. Let $v \in K_\perp$. By definition of $K_\perp$, $v \notin K'$ for every $K' \in \mathbf{K}_H$. Since $\mathbf{K}_H$ is a cover of H, it follows that $v \notin H$. By definition of H, it follows that $(s,t) \in P[s,v,t]$. By definition, this yields $x, y \in A^*$ such that $s\alpha(x) = s$, $t = \alpha(y)t$ and $xy \in \uparrow v$. The latter property yields $x', y' \in A^*$ such that $v = x'y'$, $x \in \uparrow x'$ and $y \in \uparrow y'$. We prove that $s\alpha(x') = s$ and $t = \alpha(y')t$, which yields as desired that $s\alpha(v)t = s\alpha(x'y')t = st$. By symmetry, we only show that $s = s\alpha(x')$.

Since $s = s\alpha(x)$, we have $s = s(\alpha(x))^\omega$. Moreover, since $x \in \uparrow x'$, we have $x_0, \ldots, x_n \in A^*$ and $a_1, \ldots, a_n \in A$ such that $x' = a_1 \cdots a_n$ and $x = x_0 a_1 x_1 \cdots a_n x_n$. It follows from (3) that for every $1 \le i \le n$, we have:

$$(\alpha(x))^\omega = (\alpha(x))^\omega \alpha(x_0 a_1 x_1 \cdots x_{i-1}) = (\alpha(x))^\omega \alpha(x_0 a_1 x_1 \cdots x_{i-1} a_i).$$

This yields $(\alpha(x))^\omega = (\alpha(x))^\omega \alpha(a_i)$. Therefore, since we know that $s = s(\alpha(x))^\omega$, we obtain $s\alpha(a_i) = s(\alpha(x))^\omega \alpha(a_i) = s(\alpha(x))^\omega = s$. Finally, this yields,

$$s = s\alpha(a_n) = s\alpha(a_{n-1}a_n) = \cdots = s\alpha(a_1 \cdots a_{n-1}a_n) = s\alpha(x').$$

This concludes the proof.   □

Second case: $w \in A^+$. In that case, we have $u, v \in A^*$ and $a \in A$ such that $w = uav$ (the choice of u, v and a is arbitrary). Consider the two following subsets of M:

$$M_u = \{\alpha(xa) \mid x \in \uparrow u\} \quad \text{and} \quad M_v = \{\alpha(ay) \mid y \in \uparrow v\}.$$

Moreover, we say that a cover $\mathbf{K}$ of some language H is *tight* when $K \subseteq H$ for every $K \in \mathbf{K}$. We use induction to prove the following fact.

Fact 26. *There exist tight PT-covers $\mathbf{K}_u$ and $\mathbf{K}_v$ of $\uparrow u$ and $\uparrow v$ which satisfy the following properties:*

- *for every $r \in M_u$, the cover $\mathbf{K}_v$ of $\uparrow v$ is (sr, t)-safe.*
- *for every $r \in M_v$, the cover $\mathbf{K}_u$ of $\uparrow u$ is (s, rt)-safe.*

Proof. We construct $\mathbf{K}_v$ (the construction of $\mathbf{K}_u$ is symmetrical). Let $M_u = \{r_1, \ldots, r_n\}$. For every $i \leq n$, assume that we already have a PT-cover $\mathbf{H}_i$ of $\uparrow v$ which is (sr_i, t)-safe. We define,

$$\mathbf{K}_v = \{\uparrow v \cap H_1 \cap \cdots \cap H_n \mid H_i \in \mathbf{H}_i \text{ for every } i \leq n\}.$$

Since PT is a Boolean algebra, it is immediate that $\mathbf{K}_v$ is a tight PT-cover of $\uparrow v$ which is (sr, t)-safe for every $r \in M_u$. Thus, it remains to build for every $i \leq n$ such a PT-cover $\mathbf{H}_i$.

We fix $i \leq n$ for the proof. By definition of M_u, we have $r_i = \alpha(u_i a)$ for some word $u_i \in \uparrow u$. Observe that since $w = uav$, we have $P[sr_i, v, t] \subseteq P[s, w, t]$ by definition: our first induction parameter (*i.e.*, the size of $P[s, w, t]$) has **not** increased. Hence, since $|v| < |w|$, it follows by induction on our second parameter in Lemma 23 (the length of w) that there exists a PT-cover $\mathbf{H}_i$ of $\uparrow v$ which is (sr_i, t)-safe. This concludes the proof.   □

We are ready to construct the desired PT-cover $\mathbf{K}$ of $\uparrow w$. Consider the tight PT-covers $\mathbf{K}_u$ and $\mathbf{K}_v$ of $\uparrow u$ and $\uparrow v$ described in Fact 26. Since $w = uav$, Proposition 19 yields a PT-cover $\mathbf{K}$ of $\uparrow w$ such that for every $K \in \mathbf{K}$, there exist $K_u \in \mathbf{K}_u$ and $K_v \in \mathbf{K}_v$ satisfying $K \subseteq K_u a K_v$. It remains to prove that $\mathbf{K}$ is (s, t)-safe. Let $K \in \mathbf{K}$ and $x, x' \in K$. We prove that $s\alpha(x)t = s\alpha(x')t$.

By definition, $K \subseteq K_u a K_v$ for $K_u \in \mathbf{K}_u$ and $K_v \in \mathbf{K}_v$. Hence, there exist $y, y' \in K_u$ and $z, z' \in K_v$ such that $x = yaz$ and $x' = y'az'$. Since $\mathbf{K}_u$ is a tight cover of $\uparrow u$, we know that $y \in \uparrow u$, which implies that $\alpha(ya) \in M_u$ by definition. It follows that $\mathbf{K}_v$ is $(s\alpha(ya), t)$-safe by Fact 26. Therefore, since $z, z' \in K_v$ and $K_v \in \mathbf{K}_v$, we obtain $s\alpha(yaz)t = s\alpha(yaz')t$. Symmetrically, one may verify that $s\alpha(yaz')t = s\alpha(y'az')t$. Altogether, it follows that $s\alpha(yaz)t = s\alpha(y'az')t$, meaning that $s\alpha(x)t = s\alpha(x')t$. This concludes the proof of Lemma 23.   □

6   Conclusion

We explained how covering provides a natural and convenient framework for handling membership questions. We illustrated this point by using covers to formulate new proofs for Schützenberger's theorem and Simon's theorem. We chose these two examples as they are arguably the two most famous characterization theorems of this kind. However, this approach is also relevant for other prominent characterization theorems. A first promising example is the class of *unambiguous languages*. It was also characterized by Schützenberger [37] and it also famous as the class of languages that can be define in two-variable first-order logic (this was shown by Thérien and Wilke [40]). Another interesting example is Knast's theorem [13] which characterizes the languages of dot-depth one. This class is natural generalization of the piecewise testable languages.

References

1. Almeida, J.: Implicit operations on finite j-trivial semigroups and a conjecture of I. Simon. J. Pure Appl. Algebra **69**, 205–218 (1990)
2. Brzozowski, J.A., Cohen, R.S.: Dot-depth of star-free events. J. Comput. Syst. Sci. **5**(1), 1–16 (1971)
3. Brzozowski, J.A., Knast, R.: The dot-depth hierarchy of star-free languages is infinite. J. Comput. Syst. Sci. **16**(1), 37–55 (1978)
4. Brzozowski, J.A., Simon, I.: Characterizations of locally testable events. Discrete Math. **4**(3), 243–271 (1973)
5. Colcombet, T.: Green's relations and their use in automata theory. In: Dediu, A.-H., Inenaga, S., Martín-Vide, C. (eds.) LATA 2011. LNCS, vol. 6638, pp. 1–21. Springer, Heidelberg (2011). https://doi.org/10.1007/978-3-642-21254-3_1
6. Czerwiński, W., Martens, W., Masopust, T.: Efficient separability of regular languages by subsequences and suffixes. In: Fomin, F.V., Freivalds, R., Kwiatkowska, M., Peleg, D. (eds.) ICALP 2013. LNCS, vol. 7966, pp. 150–161. Springer, Heidelberg (2013). https://doi.org/10.1007/978-3-642-39212-2_16
7. Diekert, V., Gastin, P.: First-order definable languages. In: Flum, J., Grädel, E., Wilke, T. (eds.) Logic and Automata: History and Perspectives, Texts in Logic and Games, vol. 2, pp. 261–306. Amsterdam University Press, Amsterdam (2008)
8. Eilenberg, S.: Automata, Languages, and Machines, vol. B. Academic Press Inc., Orlando (1976)
9. Higgins, P.: A proof of simon's theorem on piecewise testable languages. Theor. Comput. Sci. **178**(1), 257–264 (1997)
10. Higgins, P.M.: A new proof of Schützenberger's theorem. Int. J. Algebra Comput. **10**(02), 217–220 (2000)
11. Kamp, H.W.: Tense logic and the theory of linear order. Ph.D. thesis, Computer Science Department, University of California at Los Angeles, USA (1968)
12. Klima, O.: Piecewise testable languages via combinatorics on words. Discrete Math. **311**(20), 2124–2127 (2011)
13. Knast, R.: A semigroup characterization of dot-depth one languages. RAIRO - Theor. Inform. Appl. **17**(4), 321–330 (1983)
14. Lucchesi, C.L., Simon, I., Simon, I., Simon, J., Kowaltowski, T.: Aspectos teóricos da computação. IMPA, Sao Paulo (1979)
15. McNaughton, R., Papert, S.A.: Counter-Free Automata. MIT Press, Cambridge (1971)
16. Meyer, A.R.: A note on star-free events. J. ACM **16**(2), 220–225 (1969)
17. Perrin, D.: Finite automata. In: Formal Models and Semantics. Elsevier (1990)
18. Pin, J.E.: Varieties of Formal Languages. Plenum Publishing Co., New York (1986)
19. Pin, J.E.: A variety theorem without complementation. Russ. Math. (Izvestija vuzov.Matematika) **39**, 80–90 (1995)
20. Pin, J.E.: The dot-depth hierarchy, 45 years later, pp. 177–202. World Scientific (2017). (chap. 8)
21. Pin, J.E.: Mathematical foundations of automata theory (2019, in preparation). https://www.irif.fr/~jep/PDF/MPRI/MPRI.pdf
22. Pin, J.E., Weil, P.: Polynomial closure and unambiguous product. Theory Comput. Syst. **30**(4), 383–422 (1997)
23. Pippenger, N.: Theories of Computability. Cambridge University Press, Cambridge (1997)

24. Place, T.: Separating regular languages with two quantifier alternations. Log. Methods Comput. Sci. **14**(4) (2018)
25. Place, T., van Rooijen, L., Zeitoun, M.: Separating regular languages by piecewise testable and unambiguous languages. In: Chatterjee, K., Sgall, J. (eds.) MFCS 2013. LNCS, vol. 8087, pp. 729–740. Springer, Heidelberg (2013). https://doi.org/10.1007/978-3-642-40313-2_64
26. Place, T., Zeitoun, M.: Going higher in the first-order quantifier alternation hierarchy on words. In: Esparza, J., Fraigniaud, P., Husfeldt, T., Koutsoupias, E. (eds.) ICALP 2014. LNCS, vol. 8573, pp. 342–353. Springer, Heidelberg (2014). https://doi.org/10.1007/978-3-662-43951-7_29
27. Place, T., Zeitoun, M.: Separating regular languages with first-order logic. In: Proceedings of the Joint Meeting of the 23rd EACSL Annual Conference on Computer Science Logic (CSL 2014) and the 29th Annual ACM/IEEE Symposium on Logic in Computer Science (LICS 2014), pp. 75:1–75:10. ACM, New York (2014)
28. Place, T., Zeitoun, M.: The tale of the quantifier alternation hierarchy of first-order logic over words. SIGLOG News **2**(3), 4–17 (2015)
29. Place, T., Zeitoun, M.: Separating regular languages with first-order logic. Log. Methods Comput. Sci. **12**(1) (2016)
30. Place, T., Zeitoun, M.: Separation for dot-depth two. In: Proceedings of the 32th Annual ACM/IEEE Symposium on Logic in Computer Science (LICS 2017), pp. 202–213. IEEE Computer Society (2017)
31. Place, T., Zeitoun, M.: The covering problem. Log. Methods Comput. Sci. **14**(3) (2018)
32. Place, T., Zeitoun, M.: Generic results for concatenation hierarchies. Theory Comput. Syst. (ToCS) **63**(4), 849–901 (2019). Selected papers from CSR 2017
33. Place, T., Zeitoun, M.: Going higher in first-order quantifier alternation hierarchies on words. J. ACM **66**(2), 12:1–12:65 (2019)
34. Place, T., Zeitoun, M.: On all things star-free. In: Proceedings of the 46th International Colloquium on Automata, Languages, and Programming (ICALP 2019), pp. 126:1–126:14 (2019)
35. Place, T., Zeitoun, M.: Separation and covering for group based concatenation hierarchies. In: Proceedings of the 34th Annual ACM/IEEE Symposium on Logic in Computer Science (LICS 2019), pp. 1–13 (2019)
36. Schützenberger, M.P.: On finite monoids having only trivial subgroups. Inf. Control **8**(2), 190–194 (1965)
37. Schützenberger, M.P.: Sur le produit de concaténation non ambigu. Semigroup Forum **13**, 47–75 (1976)
38. Simon, I.: Piecewise testable events. In: Brakhage, H. (ed.) GI-Fachtagung 1975. LNCS, vol. 33, pp. 214–222. Springer, Heidelberg (1975). https://doi.org/10.1007/3-540-07407-4_23
39. Straubing, H., Thérien, D.: Partially ordered finite monoids and a theorem of I. Simon. J. Algebra **119**(2), 393–399 (1988)
40. Thérien, D., Wilke, T.: Over words, two variables are as powerful as one quantifier alternation. In: Proceedings of the 30th Annual ACM Symposium on Theory of Computing (STOC 1998), pp. 234–240. ACM, New York (1998)
41. Wilke, T.: Classifying discrete temporal properties. In: Meinel, C., Tison, S. (eds.) STACS 1999. LNCS, vol. 1563, pp. 32–46. Springer, Heidelberg (1999). https://doi.org/10.1007/3-540-49116-3_3
42. Zalcstein, Y.: Locally testable languages. J. Comput. Syst. Sci. **6**(2), 151–167 (1972)

Algebraic Structures

Nonstandard Cayley Automatic Representations for Fundamental Groups of Torus Bundles over the Circle

Dmitry Berdinsky[1,2]([✉]) and Prohrak Kruengthomya[1,2]

[1] Department of Mathematics, Faculty of Science, Mahidol University,
Bangkok, Thailand
berdinsky@gmail.com
[2] Centre of Excellence in Mathematics, Commission on Higher Education,
Bangkok, Thailand
prohrakju@gmail.com

Abstract. We construct a new family of Cayley automatic representations of semidirect products $\mathbb{Z}^n \rtimes_A \mathbb{Z}$ for which none of the projections of the normal subgroup $\mathbb{Z}^n$ onto each of its cyclic components is finite automaton recognizable. For $n = 2$ we describe a family of matrices from $GL(2, \mathbb{Z})$ corresponding to these representations. We are motivated by a problem of characterization of all possible Cayley automatic representations of these groups.

Keywords: FA–presentable structure · Cayley automatic representation · Semidirect product · Pell's equation

1 Introduction and Preliminaries

Thurston and Epstein showed that a fundamental group of a closed 3–manifold is automatic if and only if none of its prime factors is a closed manifold modelled on nilgeometry or solvgeometry [9, Chapter 12]. A fundamental group of a closed manifold modelled on nilgeometry or solvgeometry has a finite index subgroup isomorphic to $\mathbb{Z}^2 \rtimes_A \mathbb{Z}$, where A is unipotent or Anosov, respectively. These groups are not automatic due to [9, Theorems 8.2.8 and 8.1.3]. To include all fundamental groups of closed 3–manifolds, the class of automatic groups had been extended by Bridson and Gilman [5], Baumslag, Shapiro and Short [1]; see also autostackable groups proposed by Brittenham, Hermiller and Holt [7]. In this paper we use the concept of Cayley automatic groups, extending the class of automatic groups, proposed by Kharlampovich, Khoussainov and Miasnikov [11].

All semidirect products of the form $\mathbb{Z}^n \rtimes_A \mathbb{Z}$ are Cayley automatic [11, Proposition 13.5]. These groups are the fundamental groups of torus bundles over the circle and they play important role in group theory. Bridson and Gersten studied the Dehn function for this family groups [6]. In this paper we construct a new family of Cayley automatic representations for semidirect products $\mathbb{Z}^n \rtimes_A \mathbb{Z}$.

A. Leporati et al. (Eds.): LATA 2020, LNCS 12038, pp. 115–127, 2020.
https://doi.org/10.1007/978-3-030-40608-0_7

These representations demonstrate unforeseen behaviour violating a basic property, to be explained below in this section, known for representations described in [11, Proposition 10.5]. They also reveal an unexpected connection with Pell's equation. The results of this paper are based on the original construction of FA–presentation for $(\mathbb{Z}^2, +)$ found by Nies and Semukhin [13].

In general, we are interested in the following question: Given a Cayley automatic group, is there any way to characterize all of its Cayley automatic representations in terms of some numerical characteristics or by any other means? Despite the generality of the notion of Cayley automatic groups which retains only computational mechanism of automatic groups, it is possible to partly answer this question for some Cayley automatic groups in terms of a certain numerical characteristic which is intimately related to the Dehn function. We discuss it in more details in the end of this section. In the following few paragraphs we briefly recall the notion of Cayley automatic groups and representations, and a standard way to construct such representations for semidirect products $\mathbb{Z}^n \rtimes_A \mathbb{Z}$.

Let Σ be a finite alphabet. We denote by $\Sigma_\diamond$ the alpahbet $\Sigma \cup \{\diamond\}$, where $\diamond \notin \Sigma$ is called a padding symbol. The convolution $w_1 \otimes \cdots \otimes w_m \in \Sigma_\diamond^m$ of strings $w_1, \ldots, w_m \in \Sigma^*$ is the string of length $\max\{|w_1|, \ldots, |w_m|\}$ obtained by placing $w_1, \ldots, w_m$ one under another and adding the padding symbol $\diamond$ at the end of each string to make their lengths equal. More formally, the kth symbol of $w_1 \otimes \cdots \otimes w_m$ is $(\sigma_1, \ldots, \sigma_m)^\top$, where σ_i, $i = 1, \ldots, m$ is the kth symbol of w_i if $k \leqslant |w_i|$ and $\diamond$ otherwise. The convolution $\otimes R$ of a m–ary relation $R \subseteq \Sigma^{*m}$ is defined as $\otimes R = \{w_1 \otimes \cdots \otimes w_m \mid (w_1, \ldots, w_m) \in R\}$. The relation R is called FA–recognizable if $\otimes R$ is recognized by a finite automaton.

Let $\mathcal{A} = (A; R_1^{m_1}, \ldots, R_\ell^{m_\ell}, f_1^{k_1}, \ldots, f_r^{k_r})$ be a structure, where A is the domain, $R_i^{m_i} \subseteq A^{m_i}$, $i = 1, \ldots, \ell$ is a m_i–ary relation over A and $f_j^{k_j} : A^{k_j} \to A$, $j = 1, \ldots, r$ is a k_j–ary operation on A. Assume that there exist a regular language $L \subseteq \Sigma^*$ and a bijection $\psi : L \to A$ such that all relations $\psi^{-1}(R_i^{m_i}) = \{(w_1, \ldots, w_{m_i}) \in \Sigma^{*m_i} \mid (\psi(w_1), \ldots, \psi(w_{m_i})) \in R_i^{m_i}\}$, $i = 1, \ldots, \ell$ and $\psi^{-1}(\mathrm{Graph}(f_j)) = \{(w_1, \ldots, w_{k_j}, w_{k_j+1}) \in \Sigma^{*(k_j+1)} \mid f_j(\psi(w_1), \ldots, \psi(w_{k_j})) = \psi(w_{k_j+1})\}$, $j = 1, \ldots, r$ are FA–recognizable. In this case the structure $\mathcal{A}$ is called FA–presentable and the bijection $\psi : L \to A$ is called FA–presentation of $\mathcal{A}$ [12]. For a recent survey of the theory of FA–presentable structures we refer the reader to [16]. A finitely generated group G is called Cayley automatic if the labelled directed Cayley graph $\Gamma(G, S)$ is a FA–presentable structure for some generating set $S \subseteq G$ [11]. Cayley automatic groups form a special class of FA–presentable structures and they naturally generalize automatic groups retaining its basic algorithmic properties. We call a FA–presentation $\psi : L \to G$ of $\Gamma(G, S)$ a Cayley automatic representation of the group G.

We recall that every element of a group $\mathbb{Z}^n \rtimes_A \mathbb{Z}$, where $A \in \mathrm{GL}(n, \mathbb{Z})$, is given as a pair (b, h), where $b \in \mathbb{Z}$ and $h \in \mathbb{Z}^n$. The group multiplication is given by $(b_1, h_1) \cdot (b_2, h_2) = (b_1 + b_2, A^{b_2} h_1 + h_2)$. The maps $b \mapsto (b, \mathbf{0})$ and $h \mapsto (0, h)$ give the natural embeddings of $\mathbb{Z}$ and $\mathbb{Z}^n$ into $\mathbb{Z}^n \rtimes_A \mathbb{Z}$, respectively, where 0 and $\mathbf{0}$ denote the identities of the groups $\mathbb{Z}$ and $\mathbb{Z}^n$, respectively. Let $g_0 = (1, \mathbf{0})$ and

$g_i = (0, e_i)$, where $e_i = (0, \ldots, 0, \underset{i}{1}, 0, \ldots, 0)^t \in \mathbb{Z}^n$. The elements $g_0, g_1, \ldots, g_n$ generate the group $\mathbb{Z}^n \rtimes_A \mathbb{Z}$. The right multiplication by $g_i, i = 0, 1, \ldots, n$ is as follows: for a given $g = (b, h) \in \mathbb{Z}^n \rtimes_A \mathbb{Z}$, $gg_0 = (b+1, Ah)$ and $gg_i = (b, h + e_i)$.

Let $\psi_1 : L_1 \to \mathbb{Z}$ be a Cayley automatic representation of $\mathbb{Z}$ and $\psi_2 : L_2 \to \mathbb{Z}^n$ be a Cayley automatic representations of $\mathbb{Z}^n$ such that the automorphism of $\mathbb{Z}^n$ given by the matrix A is FA–recognizable. Then, due to [11, Theorem 10.3], one gets a Cayley automatic representation $\psi : L \to \mathbb{Z}^n \rtimes_A \mathbb{Z}$ as follows: $L = L_1 L_2$ (we may assume that $L_1 \subset \Sigma_1$, $L_2 \subset \Sigma_2$ and $\Sigma_1 \cap \Sigma_2 = \varnothing$) and for given $u \in L_1$ and $v \in L_2$, $\psi(uv) = (\psi_1(u), \psi_2(v))$. A standard way to construct $\psi_2 : L_2 \to \mathbb{Z}^n$ is to take a FA–presentation $\varphi : L_0 \to \mathbb{Z}$ of the structure $(\mathbb{Z}, +)$, for example a binary representation, and define L_2 as $L_2 = \{w_1 \otimes \cdots \otimes w_n \mid w_i \in L_0, i = 1, \ldots, n\}$ and ψ_2 as $\psi_2(w_1 \otimes \cdots \otimes w_n) = (\varphi(w_1), \ldots, \varphi(w_n))$ for every $w_1, \ldots, w_n \in L_0$. Clearly, for such a representation ψ_2 every automorphism of $\mathbb{Z}^n$ is FA–recognizable. Therefore, ψ_1 and φ as above give a Cayley automatic representation of $\mathbb{Z}^n \rtimes_A \mathbb{Z}$. We call such a representation standard. Every standard Cayley automatic representation $\psi : L \to \mathbb{Z}^n \rtimes_A \mathbb{Z}$ satisfies the following basic properties:

(a) The language $L_{\mathbb{Z}^n} = \psi^{-1}(\mathbb{Z}^n)$ of the strings representing elements in the subgroup $\mathbb{Z}^n \trianglelefteq \mathbb{Z}^n \rtimes_A \mathbb{Z}$ is regular and the relation $R_A = \{(u, v) \in L_{\mathbb{Z}^n} \times L_{\mathbb{Z}^n} \mid A\psi(u) = \psi(v)\}$ is FA–recognizable.
(b) For each projection $p_i : \mathbb{Z}^n \to \mathbb{Z}^n$, $i = 1, \ldots, n$, on the ith component given by $p_i((z_1, \ldots, z_n)) = (0, \ldots, 0, z_i, 0, \ldots, 0)$ the relation $P_i = \{(u, v) \in L_{\mathbb{Z}^n} \times L_{\mathbb{Z}^n} \mid p_i\psi(u) = \psi(v)\}$ is FA–recognizable.

In this paper we construct Cayley automatic representations of groups $\mathbb{Z}^n \rtimes_A \mathbb{Z}$ for which the property (a) holds but the property (b) does not hold – in other words, these representations are nonstandard. Namely, in Sect. 2 we construct Cayley automatic representations of $\mathbb{Z}^n$ for which every projection $p_i : \mathbb{Z}^n \to \mathbb{Z}^n$, $i = 1, \ldots, n$ is not FA–recognizable while some nontrivial automorphisms $A \in \mathrm{GL}(n, \mathbb{Z})$ are FA–recognizable. A family of these automorphisms for the case $n = 2$ is described in Sect. 3. Taking such a representation as ψ_2 and an arbitrary Cayley automatic representation $\psi_1 : L_1 \to \mathbb{Z}$ one obtains a Cayley automatic representation of $\mathbb{Z}^n \rtimes_A \mathbb{Z}$ as described above. Clearly, for this representation the property (a) holds while the property (b) does not hold. In this paper we primarily focus on the case $n = 2$ briefly discussing the case $n > 2$. Section 4 concludes the paper.

Apart from the importance of semidirect products $\mathbb{Z}^n \rtimes_A \mathbb{Z}$, let us explain another reason motivated us to study Cayley automatic representations of this family of groups violating at least one of the properties (a) or (b). We first briefly recall some notation and results. For a given f.g. group G with some finite set of generators $A \subseteq G$, we denote by A^{-1} the set of inverses of the elements of A in G and by d_A the word metric in G with respect to A. We denote by $\pi : \left(A \cup A^{-1}\right)^* \to G$ the canonical map sending a word $w \in (A \cup A^{-1})^*$ to the corresponding group element $\pi(w)$. For the rest of the section we assume that $L \subseteq (A \cup A^{-1})^*$. We denote by $L^{\leqslant n}$ the language $L^{\leqslant n} = \{w \in L \mid |w| \leqslant n\}$. For a Cayley automatic representation $\psi : L \to G$ we denote by h the function: $h(n) = \max\{d_A(\psi(w), \pi(w)) \mid w \in L^{\leqslant n}\}$.

The function h had been introduced in [3] as a measure of deviation of Cayley automatic representation ψ from π, i.e., from being automatic in the classical sense of Thurston. For two nondecreasing functions $h : [Q_1, +\infty) \to \mathbb{R}^+$ and $f : [Q_2, +\infty) \to \mathbb{R}^+$, where $[Q_1, +\infty), [Q_2, +\infty) \subseteq \mathbb{N}$, we say that $h \preceq f$ if there exist positive integer constants K, M and N such that for all $n \geqslant N$: $h(n) \leqslant Kf(Mn)$. A f.g. group is said to be in $\mathcal{B}_f$ if there exists a Cayley automatic representation ψ for which the function $h \preceq f$. It was shown that the identity function $\mathrm{i}(n) = n$ is the sharp lower bound of the function h (in the sense of $\preceq$) for all Cayley automatic representations of the Baumslag–Solitar groups $BS(p, q), 1 \leqslant p < q$ [3, Theorem 11] and the wreath products $G \wr H$, if H is virtually cyclic and G is in the class $\mathcal{B}_{\mathrm{i}}$ [2].

We recall that the Heisenberg group $\mathcal{H}_3(\mathbb{Z})$ is isomorphic to $\mathbb{Z}^2 \rtimes_T \mathbb{Z}$ for some lower triangular matrix T, see Remark 12. The result of [4, Theorem 5.1] shows that if a Cayley automatic representation of the Heisenberg group $\psi : L \to \mathcal{H}_3(\mathbb{Z})$ satisfies certain conditions, then the function h is bounded from below by the exponential function $\mathfrak{e}(n) = \exp(n)$. In particular, for every Cayley automatic representation $\psi : L \to \mathcal{H}_3(\mathbb{Z})$ satisfying the properties (a) and (b) the function h has the exponential lower bound: $\mathfrak{e} \preceq h$. The lower bounds for all possible Cayley automatic representations of the Heisenberg group and the groups $\mathbb{Z}^2 \rtimes_A \mathbb{Z}$, if $A \in \mathrm{GL}(2, \mathbb{Z})$ is a matrix with two real eigenvalues not equal to ± 1, known to us are given by the functions $\sqrt[3]{n}$ and i, respectively, see [4, Corollary 2.4]. However, it is not known whether or not these lower bounds are sharp. These observations motivated us to seek nonstandard Cayley automatic representations for a whole family of groups $\mathbb{Z}^n \rtimes_A \mathbb{Z}$, $A \in \mathrm{GL}(n, \mathbb{Z})$. While we construct nonstandard representations for a large family of groups $\mathbb{Z}^n \rtimes_A \mathbb{Z}$, see Theorem 8 for the case $n = 2$, it does not contain nilpotent groups including the Heisenberg group $\mathcal{H}_3(\mathbb{Z})$. This leads us to think that the case of nilpotent groups is special.

2   Nies–Semukhin FA–Presentations of $(\mathbb{Z}^n, +)$

Nies and Semukhin constructed a FA–presentation of $(\mathbb{Z}^2, +)$ for which no nontrivial cyclic subgroup is FA–recognizable [13, § 6]. Let us briefly recall their construction. The group $\mathbb{Z}^2$ is identified with the additive group of the quotient ring $\mathbb{Z}[x]/\langle p_3 \rangle$, where $p_3(x) = x^2 + x - 3^1$. A polynomial $a_n x^n + \cdots + a_0 \in \mathbb{Z}[x]$ is called reduced if $|a_i| \leqslant 2$ for all $i = 0, \ldots, n$. For given $f, g \in \mathbb{Z}[x]$, it is said that $f \sim g$ if p_3 divides $f - g$. In [13, Proposition 6.2] it is then shown that every $f(x) \in \mathbb{Z}[x]$ is equivalent to a reduced polynomial $\widetilde{f}(x)$. Let $\Sigma = \{-2, -1, 0, 1, 2\}$. Each reduced polynomial $a_n x^n + \cdots + a_0$ is represented by a string $a_0 \ldots a_n$ over the alphabet Σ. Two strings $u = a_0 \ldots a_n$ and $v = b_0 \ldots b_m$ from Σ^* are said to be equivalent $(u \sim v)$ if $a_n x^n + \cdots + a_0 \sim b_m x^m + \cdots + b_0$. It is then shown that this equivalence relation defined on Σ^* is FA–recognizable. Let $llex$ be the length–lexicographical

---

[1] In [13, Remark 6.1] it is said that one can use a polynomial $x^2 + x - q$ for a prime $q \geqslant 3$.

order on Σ^* with respect to the ordering $-2 < -1 < 0 < 1 < 2$. A regular domain for a presentation of $\mathbb{Z}^2$ is defined as $\mathrm{Dom} = \{w \in \Sigma^* : (\forall u <_{llex} w)\, u \not\sim w\}$. Then a FA–recognizable relation $R(x_1, x_2, x_3) \subset \Sigma^{*3}$ is defined such that for every pair $x_1, x_2 \in \Sigma^*$ there exists a unique $x_3 \in \Sigma^*$ for which $(x_1, x_2, x_3) \in R$ and if $(x_1, x_2, x_3) \in R$, then for the corresponding polynomials f_1, f_2 and f_3: $f_1 + f_2 \sim f_3$. It enables to define a FA–recognizable relation $\mathrm{Add}(x, y, z)$ on Dom as follows: $\mathrm{Add} = \{(x, y, z) : x, y, z \in \mathrm{Dom} \wedge \exists w (R(x, y, w) \wedge (w \sim z))\}$. Clearly, the structure $(\mathrm{Dom}, \mathrm{Add})$ is isomorphic to $(\mathbb{Z}^2, +)$.

Now we notice that the Nies–Semukhin construction can be generalized for a given polynomial $t(x) = x^2 + px - q \in \mathbb{Z}[x]$ for which $1 + |p| < |q|$. Again, we identify $\mathbb{Z}^2$ with the additive group of the quotient ring $\mathbb{Z}[x]/\langle t \rangle$. The inequality $1 + |p| < |q|$ implies that $|q| \geqslant 2$. We say that a polynomial $a_n x^n + \cdots + a_0 \in \mathbb{Z}[x]$ is reduced if $|a_i| < |q|$ for all $i = 0, \ldots, n$ and two polynomials $f, g \in \mathbb{Z}[x]$ are equivalent $f \sim g$ if t divides $f - g$. For a given real r we denote by $[r]$ the integral part of r: $[r] = \max\{m \in \mathbb{Z} \mid m \leqslant r\}$ if $r \geqslant 0$ and $[r] = \min\{m \in \mathbb{Z} \mid m \geqslant r\}$ if $r < 0$.

Proposition 1. *Every polynomial $f(x) \in \mathbb{Z}[x]$ is equivalent to a reduced polynomial $\widetilde{f}(x)$.*

Proof. Let $f(x) = a_n x^n + \cdots + a_0$ and $k_0 = \left[\frac{a_0}{q}\right]$. Since $x^2 + px \sim q$, $f(x) \sim f_1(x) = b_n x^n + \cdots + b_0$, where $b_0 = a_0 - k_0 q$, $b_1 = a_1 + k_0 p$, $b_2 = a_2 + k_0$ and $b_i = a_i$ for $i > 2$. If $|a_0| < |q|$, then $f_1(x) = f_0(x)$. Otherwise, we get that $\sum_{i=0}^{n} |a_i| > \sum_{i=0}^{n} |b_i|$. Let $k_1 = \left[\frac{b_1}{q}\right]$. Since $x^3 + px^2 \sim qx$, $f_1(x) \sim f_2(x) = c_n x^n + \cdots + c_0$, where $c_0 = b_0$, $c_1 = b_1 - k_1 q$, $c_2 = b_2 + k_1 p$, $c_3 = b_3 + k_1$ and $c_i = b_i$ for $i > 3$. If $|b_1| < |q|$, then $f_2(x) = f_1(x)$. Otherwise, we get that $\sum_{i=0}^{n} |b_i| > \sum_{i=0}^{n} |c_i|$. We have: $|c_0| = |b_0| < |q|$ and $|c_1| < |q|$. If we continue in this way, the process will terminate after a finite number of iterations producing a reduced polynomial $\widetilde{f}(x)$ at the last iteration. $\square$

Remark 2. It can be seen that if the inequality $1 + |p| < |q|$ is not satisfied, then the procedure described in Proposition 1 fails to produce a reduced polynomial for some input polynomials $f(x)$. For example, let $t(x) = x^2 + 2x - 3$ and $f(x) = 2x + 6$. Applying the procedure from Proposition 1 one gets an infinite sequence of polynomials $f_i(x) = 2x^{i+1} + 6x^i$ which never terminates.

Let $\Sigma_q = \{-(|q|-1), \ldots, |q|-1\}$. We represent a reduced polynomial $a_n x^n + \cdots + a_0$ by a string $a_0 \ldots a_n$ over the alphabet Σ_q. Similarly, we say that two strings $a_0 \ldots a_n$ and $b_0 \ldots b_m$ over Σ_q are equivalent if the polynomials $a_n x_n + \cdots + a_0$ and $b_m x^m + \cdots + b_0$ are equivalent. An algorithm checking whether two given reduced polynomials $f(x) = a_n x^n + \cdots + a_0$ and $g(x) = b_m x^m + \cdots + b_0$ are equivalent is the same, up to minor changes, as it is described by Nies and Semukhin for the case $t(x) = x^2 + x - 3$, see [13, § 6]. We first check if q divides $a_0 - b_0$; if not, $f \not\sim g$. We remember two carries $r_0 = p \frac{a_0 - b_0}{q}$ and $r_1 = \frac{a_0 - b_0}{q}$, and then verify whether q divides $r_0 + a_1 - b_1$; if not, $f \not\sim g$. Otherwise, we update the carries: $r_0 \to r_1 + p\frac{r_0+a_1-b_1}{q}$ and $r_1 \to \frac{r_0+a_1-b_1}{q}$, and then verify whether q divides $r_0 + a_2 - b_2$. Proceeding in this way we check if $f \sim g$ or not. Initially, $|r_1| \leqslant 1 \leqslant |q| - 1$ and $|r_0| \leqslant |p| < (|q| - 1)^2$. Since q divides $r_0 + a_i - b_i$ at every step of our process unless $f \not\sim g$, we can change the formulas for updating carries as follows: $r_0 \to r_1 + p\left[\frac{r_0+a_i-b_i}{q}\right]$ and $r_1 \to \left[\frac{r_0+a_i-b_i}{q}\right]$. Now, if $|r_1| \leqslant |q| - 1$ and $|r_0| \leqslant (|q| - 1)^2$, then $\left|\left[\frac{r_0+a_i-b_i}{q}\right]\right| \leqslant \left[\frac{(|q|-1)^2+2(|q|-1)}{|q|}\right] = |q| - 1$ and $\left|r_1 + p\left[\frac{r_0+a_i-b_i}{q}\right]\right| \leqslant (|q|-1) + |p|\left|\left[\frac{r_0+a_i-b_i}{q}\right]\right| \leqslant (|q|-1) + (|q|-2)(|q|-1) = (|q|-1)^2$. This shows that $|r_1|$ and $|r_0|$ are always bounded by $|q|-1$ and $(|q|-1)^2$. This algorithm requires only a finite amount of memory, so the equivalence relation $\sim$ is FA–recognizable.

Similarly, one can construct a FA–recognizable relation $R(u, v, w) \subset \Sigma_q^*$ such that for every pair $(u, v) \in \Sigma_q^*$ there exists a unique $w \in \Sigma_q^*$ for which $(u, v, w) \in R$ and if $(u, v, w) \in R$ then for the corresponding polynomials f_u, f_v and f_w: $f_u + f_v \sim f_w$. Again, the construction of such a relation R is the same, up to minor changes, as it is described by Nies and Semukhin for the case $t(x) = x^2 + x - 3$. Let $u = a_0 \dots a_n$ and $v = b_0 \dots b_m$. Then a string $w = c_0 \dots c_k$ for which $(u, v, w) \in R$ is obtained as follows. Let c_0 be an integer such that $|c_0| < |q| - 1$, c_0 has the same sign as $a_0 + b_0$ and $c_0 \equiv a_0 + b_0 \pmod{q}$. We remember two carries $r_0 = p\left[\frac{a_0+b_0}{q}\right]$ and $r_1 = \left[\frac{a_0+b_0}{q}\right]$. We put c_1 to be an integer such that $|c_1| \leqslant |q| - 1$, c_1 has the same sign as $r_0 + a_1 + b_1$ and $c_1 \equiv r_0 + a_1 + b_1 \pmod{q}$, and update the carries as $r_0 \to r_1 + p\left[\frac{r_0+a_1+b_1}{q}\right]$ and $r_1 \to \left[\frac{r_0+a_1+b_1}{q}\right]$. This process is continued until the string w is generated. The formulas for updating carries are $r_0 \to r_1 + p\left[\frac{r_0+a_i+b_i}{q}\right]$ and $r_1 \to \left[\frac{r_0+a_i+b_i}{q}\right]$. The proof that $|r_1|$ and $|r_0|$ are bounded by $(|q| - 1)$ and $(|q| - 1)^2$, respectively, is the same as in the paragraph above, so the relation R is FA–recognizable.

Fixing the ordering $-(|q|-1) < \cdots < (|q|-1)$ on Σ_q, the domain Dom and the relation Add are then defined in exactly the same way as by Nies and Semuhkhin, see the first paragraph of this section. So, for every pair of integers p and q, for which $1 + |p| < |q|$, we obtain a regular domain $\mathrm{Dom}_{p,q}$ and a FA–recognizable relation $\mathrm{Add}_{p,q}$ for which $(\mathrm{Dom}_{p,q}, \mathrm{Add}_{p,q})$ is isomorphic to $(\mathbb{Z}^2, +)$. For given p and q satisfying the inequality $1 + |p| < |q|$, we denote by $\psi_{p,q} : \mathrm{Dom}_{p,q} \to \mathbb{Z}^2$ the representation of $(\mathbb{Z}^2, +)$ described above. Let $g \in \mathbb{Z}[x]$ be some fixed polynomial. Clearly, if $f_1 \sim f_2$, then $f_1 g \sim f_2 g$. Therefore, multiplication by g induces a map from $\mathbb{Z}[x]/\langle t \rangle$ to $\mathbb{Z}[x]/\langle t \rangle$ which sends an equivalence class $[f]_\sim$ to the equivalence class $[fg]_\sim$. So, by Proposition 1, multiplication by g induces a map $\varphi_g : \mathrm{Dom}_{p,q} \to \mathrm{Dom}_{p,q}$.

Proposition 3. *For every representation $\psi_{p,q}$ the function $\varphi_g : \mathrm{Dom}_{p,q} \to \mathrm{Dom}_{p,q}$ is FA–recognizable.*

Proof. Since the equivalence relation $\sim$ and Add are FA–recognizable, it is enough only to show that multiplication by a monomial x is FA–recognizable.

It is true because for a string $u = a_0 \ldots a_n \in \mathrm{Dom}_{p,q}$ the string $\varphi_x(u)$ is equivalent to the shifted string $0a_0 \ldots a_n$. Clearly, such shifting of strings is FA–recognizable. $\qquad\square$

Nies and Semukhin showed that every nontrivial cyclic subgroup $\langle z \rangle$ of $\mathbb{Z}^2$ is not FA–recognizable for the representation $\psi_{1,3}$ [13, § 6]. We will show that each of the two cyclic components of $\mathbb{Z}^2$ is not FA–recognizable for every representation $\psi_{p,q}$, if $\gcd(p,q) = 1$. Let $\xi = [1]_\sim$, where 1 is the polynomial $f(x) = 1$; also, ξ corresponds to the single–letter string $1 \in \mathrm{Dom}_{p,q}$: $\psi_{p,q}(1) = \xi$. Let us show that the cyclic subgroup generated by ξ is not FA–recognizable with respect to $\psi_{p,q}$, if $\gcd(p,q) = 1$. We will use arguments analogous to the ones in [13, § 6] with relevant modifications. It is straightforward that [13, Lemma 6.3] claiming that for given two equivalent reduced polynomials $f(x)$ and $g(x)$, $x^k | f$ implies $x^k | g$, holds valid. It is said that $f(x) \in \mathbb{Z}[x]$ starts with k zeros in reduced form if there exists a reduced polynomial $g(x)$ for which $f \sim g$ and $x^k | g(x)$: in this case the string representing $g(x)$ starts with k zeros. For a given $k > 0$, the polynomial q^k starts with at least k zeros in reduced form because $q^k \sim x^k(x+p)^k$.

Assume now that $L_\xi = \psi_{p,q}^{-1}(\langle \xi \rangle)$ is regular and recognized by a finite automaton with k_0 states. The string $\psi_{p,q}^{-1}([q^{k_0}]_\sim) \in L_\xi$ starts with at least k_0 zeros, i.e., $\psi_{p,q}^{-1}([q^{k_0}]_\sim) = 0^k u$ for $k \geqslant k_0$ and some $u \in \Sigma_q^*$, which does not have 0 as the first symbol. By pumping lemma, there exist k_1, k_2 and $0 < d \leqslant k_0$, for which $k_1 + d + k_2 = k$, such that $s_i = 0^{k_1 + di + k_2} u \in L_\xi$ for all $i \geqslant 0$. Since $s_i \in L_\xi$, we have a sequence of integers n_i, $i \geqslant 0$ for which $\psi_{p,q}(s_i) = [n_i]_\sim$, so n_i starts with $k_1 + di + k_2$ zeros in reduced form. For a given integer n, if it starts with at least one zero in reduced form, then $q \mid n$: it is because $n = q\ell + r$ for some ℓ and $r \in \{0, \ldots, |q| - 1\}$, so if $r \neq 0$ then $n \sim x(x+p)\ell + r$ starts with no zeros in reduced form.

Proposition 4. *Assume that $\gcd(p,q) = 1$. If $n = q\ell$ starts with $m > 0$ zeros in reduced form, then ℓ starts with $m - 1$ zeros in reduced form.*

Proof. Let $f(x) = x^i(b_j x^{j-i} + \cdots + b_i)$ be a reduced polynomial equivalent to ℓ, where $b_i \neq 0$. We have $n = q\ell \sim x^{i+1}(x+p)(b_j x^{j-i} + \cdots + b_i)$. Since $\gcd(p,q) = 1$ and $|b_i| < |q|$, $q \nmid pb_i$. Therefore, n starts with $i + 1$ zeros in reduced form, so $i = m - 1$. Therefore, ℓ starts with $m - 1$ zeros in reduced form. $\qquad\square$

Thus, if $\gcd(p,q) = 1$, by Proposition 4, we obtain that $q^{k_1 + di + k_2} | n_i$, so $n_i = q^{k_1 + di + k_2} m_i$ for some nonzero integer m_i. Let α and β be the roots of the polynomial $t(x) = x^2 + px - q$. We have $\alpha\beta = -q$, so $|\alpha\beta| = |q|$. Therefore, either $|\alpha|$ or $|\beta|$ must be less or equal than $\sqrt{|q|}$. So, let us assume that $|\alpha| \leqslant \sqrt{|q|}$. For every two equivalent polynomials $f \sim g$: $f(\alpha) = g(\alpha)$. Let f_i be the reduced polynomials corresponding to the strings s_i. If $|\alpha| > 1$, then $|f_i(\alpha)|$ is bounded from above by $(|q| - 1)|u||\alpha|^{|s_i| - 1}$, where $|s_i| = k_1 + di + k_2 + |u|$ is the length of the string s_i; it is because there are only at most $|u|$ nonzero coefficients of the polynomial f_i and the absolute value of each of which is less than or equal to $|q| - 1$. Therefore, $|f_i(\alpha)| \leqslant C_1 |\alpha|^{di}$, where $C_1 = (|q| - 1)|u||\alpha|^{k_1+k_2+|u|-1}$. If $|\alpha| \leqslant 1$, then $|f_i(\alpha)| \leqslant C_2$, where $C_2 = (|q| - 1)|u|$. In both cases we obtain that $|f_i(\alpha)| \leqslant C\sqrt{|q|}^{di}$ for some constant C. On the other hand, since $f_i \sim n_i$, $f_i(\alpha) = n_i = q^{k_1+di+k_2}m_i$. Therefore, $|f_i(\alpha)| = |q|^{k_1+di+k_2}|m_i| \geqslant |q|^{di}$. Thus, we obtain that $|q|^{di} \leqslant C\sqrt{|q|}^{di}$ for all $i \geqslant 0$, which apparently leads to a contradiction since $|q| > 1$. Thus, L_ξ is not regular.

Let $\eta = [x]_\sim$, where x is the polynomial $f(x) = x$; also, η corresponds to the string $01 \in \mathrm{Dom}_{p,q}$: $\psi_{p,q}(01) = \eta$. Clearly, $\mathbb{Z}^2$ is the direct sum of its cyclic subgroups $\langle \xi \rangle$ and $\langle \eta \rangle$. Let $L_\eta = \psi_{p,q}^{-1}(\langle \eta \rangle)$. We notice that $L_\xi = \{w \in \mathrm{Dom}_{p,q} \mid \varphi_x(w) \in L_\eta\}$. The inclusion $L_\xi \subseteq \{w \in \mathrm{Dom}_{p,q} \mid \varphi_x(w) \in L_\eta\}$ is straightforward. For the inclusion $\{w \in \mathrm{Dom}_{p,q} \mid \varphi_x(w) \in L_\eta\} \subseteq L_\xi$ it is enough to notice that if $\psi_{p,q}(w) = [sx + r]_\sim$, then $\varphi_x(w) = [x(sx + r)]_\sim = [s(-px + q) + rx]_\sim = [(r - sp)x + sq]_\sim$ which is equal to $[kx]_\sim$ for some $k \in \mathbb{Z}$ only if $sq = 0$. The map $\varphi_x : \mathrm{Dom}_{p,q} \to \mathrm{Dom}_{p,q}$ is FA–recognizable, by Proposition 3. So, the regularity of L_η implies the regularity of L_ξ. Therefore, L_η is not regular. Clearly, the fact that L_ξ and L_η are not regular implies that the projections of $\mathbb{Z}^2$ onto its cyclic components $\langle \xi \rangle$ and $\langle \eta \rangle$ are not FA–recognizable. Let us summarize the results we obtained in the following theorem.

Theorem 5. *For every pair of integers p and q for which $1 + |p| < |q|$ the map $\psi_{p,q} : \mathrm{Dom}_{p,q} \to \mathbb{Z}^2$ gives a FA–presentation of $(\mathbb{Z}^2, +)$. Moreover, if $\gcd(p, q) = 1$, then none of the two cyclic components of $\mathbb{Z}^2$ and the projections onto theses components is FA–recognizable with respect to $\psi_{p,q}$.*

Remark 6. In order to guarantee that all nontrivial cyclic subgroups of $\mathbb{Z}^2$ are not FA–recognizable with respect to $\psi_{p,q}$, one should additionally require that the polynomial $t(x) = x^2 + px - q$ is irreducible in $\mathbb{Z}[x]$. Let $\gamma = [g]_\sim$ for some $g \in \mathbb{Z}[x]$, $g \not\sim 0$, and $L_\gamma = \psi_{p,q}^{-1}(\langle \gamma \rangle)$. We have: $L_\xi = \{w \in \mathrm{Dom}_{p,q} \mid \varphi_g(w) \in L_\gamma\}$. To prove the inclusion $\{w \in \mathrm{Dom}_{p,q} \mid \varphi_g(w) \in L_\gamma\} \subseteq L_\xi$ we notice that if $\psi_{p,q}(w) = [sx + r]_\sim$, then $\varphi_g(w) = [g(sx + r)]_\sim$ which is equal to $[gk]_\sim$ for some $k \in \mathbb{Z}$ iff the polynomial t divides $g(sx + r - k)$. Since t is irreducible and t does not divide g, then $s = 0$ and $r = k$. Therefore, by Proposition 3, if L_γ is regular, then L_ξ is regular. So, L_γ is not regular. Also, if t is irreducible, every nonzero endomorphism of $\mathbb{Z}^2$ with nontrivial kernel is not FA–recognizable.

Now, let $n > 2$ and $t(x) = x^n + p_{n-1}x + \cdots + p_1 x - q$ be a polynomial with integers coefficients for which $1 + |p_{n-1}| + \cdots + |p_1| < |q|$. We identify the group $\mathbb{Z}^n$ with the additive group of the ring $\mathbb{Z}[x]/\langle t \rangle$. We denote by $\bar{p}$ a tuple $\bar{p} = \langle p_1, \ldots, p_{n-1} \rangle$. Clearly, one gets a representation $\psi_{\bar{p},q} : \mathrm{Dom}_{\bar{p},q} \to \mathbb{Z}^n$, in exactly the same way as it is described for the case $n = 2$. It can be seen that all arguments presented in this section hold valid up to the following minor modifications. For an algorithm recognizing the equivalence $\sim$, one should use n carries $r_0, r_1, \ldots, r_{n-1}$ updated as follows: $r_0 \to r_1 + p_1[\frac{r_0+a_i-b_i}{q}]$, $r_1 \to r_2 + p_2[\frac{r_0+a_i-b_i}{q}], \ldots, r_{n-2} \to r_{n-1} + p_{n-1}[\frac{r_0+a_i-b_i}{q}], r_{n-1} \to [\frac{r_0+a_i-b_i}{q}]$. It can be directly verified that $r_0 \leqslant (|q| - 1)^2, r_1 \leqslant (|q| - 1)(1 + |p_{n-1}| + |p_{n-2}| + \cdots + |p_2|)), \ldots, |r_{n-2}| \leqslant (|q| - 1)(1 + |p_{n-1}|)$ and $|r_{n-1}| \leqslant |q| - 1$. So, the algorithm requires only a finite amount of memory. The same remains true for an algorithm recognizing the addition. In Proposition 4 one should change p to p_1. Also, clearly, there is a root α of polynomial $t(x)$ for which $|\alpha| \leqslant \sqrt[n]{|q|}$. We call all presentations $\psi_{\bar{p},q}$ satisfying the conditions $1 + |p_{n-1}| + \cdots + |p_1| < |q|$ and $\gcd(p_1, q) = 1$ Nies–Semukhin FA–presentations. The following theorem generalizes Theorem 5 for the case $n > 2$.

Theorem 7. *For every tuple $\bar{p} = \langle p_1, \ldots, p_{n-1} \rangle$ and an integer q for which $1 + |p_{n-1}| + \cdots + |p_1| < |q|$ the map $\psi_{\bar{p},q} : \mathrm{Dom}_{\bar{p},q} \to \mathbb{Z}^n$ gives a FA–presentation of $(\mathbb{Z}^n, +)$. If $\gcd(p_1, q) = 1$, then none of the cyclic components of $\mathbb{Z}^n$ and the projections onto these components is FA–recognizable with respect to $\psi_{\bar{p},q}$.*

3   FA–Recognizable Automorphisms of $\mathbb{Z}^n$

In this section until the last paragraph we discuss the case $n = 2$. By Proposition 3, for a polynomial $g \in \mathbb{Z}[x]$, multiplication by g induces a FA–recognizable map $\varphi_g : \mathrm{Dom}_{p,q} \to \mathrm{Dom}_{p,q}$. Clearly, if $f \sim g$, then $\varphi_g = \varphi_f$. Therefore, since every polynomial from $\mathbb{Z}[x]$ is equivalent to a polynomial of degree at most one, we may assume that $g(x) = ax + b$ for $a, b \in \mathbb{Z}$. Let $h(x) = h_1 x + h_2$, for $h_1, h_2 \in \mathbb{Z}$. The equivalence class $[h]_\sim$ is identified with $(h_1, h_2) \in \mathbb{Z}^2$. We have: $g(x)h(x) = (ax + b)(h_1 x + h_2) = ah_1 x^2 + (ah_2 + bh_1)x + bh_2 \sim ah_1(-px + q) + (ah_2 + bh_1)x + bh_2 = ((b - ap)h_1 + ah_2)x + aqh_1 + bh_2$. Clearly, $\xi = [1]_\sim$ and $\eta = [x]_\sim$, already defined in Section 2, generate the group $\mathbb{Z}^2$. We denote by H_1 and H_2 the cyclic subgroups of $\mathbb{Z}^2$ generated by η and ξ, respectively. Thus, multiplication by g induces an endomorphism of $\mathbb{Z}^2 = H_1 \oplus H_2$ given by a matrix $A = \begin{pmatrix} b - ap & a \\ aq & b \end{pmatrix}$. The condition that $A \in \mathrm{GL}(2, \mathbb{Z})$ yields the equations $b^2 - abp - a^2 q = \pm 1$. The latter is equivalent to $(2b - ap)^2 - (p^2 + 4q)a^2 = \pm 4$. Let $c = 2b - ap$. Then we have:

$$A = \begin{pmatrix} \frac{c - ap}{2} & a \\ aq & \frac{c + ap}{2} \end{pmatrix}, \tag{1}$$

where p, q, a and c satisfy one of the following two equations:

$$c^2 - (p^2 + 4q)a^2 = \pm 4. \tag{2}$$

For given p and q, the trivial solutions of (1), $a = 0$ and $c = \pm 2$, correspond to the matrices $A = \pm I$. We will assume that $a \neq 0$. Let $n = p^2 + 4q$. Clearly, nontrivial solutions of (2) exist only if $n \geqslant -4$. The following theorem can be verified by direct calculations.

Theorem 8. *For a given $n \geqslant -4$, the matrices A defined by (1) together with the coefficients p and q for which p, q, a and c satisfy: $1 + |p| < |q|$, $\gcd(p, q) = 1$, $n = p^2 + 4q$, $a \neq 0$ and the equation $c^2 - na^2 = \pm 4$ are as follows:*

- For $n = -4$, $A = \pm \begin{pmatrix} -r & 1 \\ -(r^2+1) & r \end{pmatrix}$, $p = 2r$ and $q = -(r^2+1)$, where $r \in (-\infty, -4] \cup [4, +\infty)$ and $r \equiv 0 \pmod 2$.

- For $n = -3$, $A = \pm \begin{pmatrix} -r & 1 \\ -(r^2+r+1) & (r+1) \end{pmatrix}$ or $A = \pm \begin{pmatrix} -(r+1) & 1 \\ -(r^2+r+1) & r \end{pmatrix}$, $p = 2r+1$ and $q = -(r^2+r+1)$, where $r \in (-\infty, -3] \cup [2, +\infty)$ and either $r \equiv 0 \pmod 3$ or $r \equiv 2 \pmod 3$.

- For $n = 0$, $n = -1$ and $n = -2$, there exist no nontrivial solutions.

- For $n = m^2 > 0$, nontrivial solutions exist only if $n = 1$ or $n = 4$. For $n = 1$, $A = \pm \begin{pmatrix} -(2r+1) & 2 \\ -2(r^2+r) & (2r+1) \end{pmatrix}$, $p = 2r+1$ and $q = -(r^2+r)$, where $r \in (-\infty, -4] \cup [3, +\infty)$. For $n = 4$, $A = \pm \begin{pmatrix} -r & 1 \\ 1-r^2 & r \end{pmatrix}$, $p = 2r$ and $q = 1-r^2$, where $r \in (-\infty, -4] \cup [4, +\infty)$ and $r \equiv 0 \pmod 2$.

- For a positive nonsquare integer n, the equality $n = p^2 + 4q$ implies that either $n \equiv 0 \pmod 4$ or $n \equiv 1 \pmod 4$. For these two cases we have:

  - For $n = 4s$, $A = \pm \begin{pmatrix} x-ra & a \\ a(s-r^2) & x+ra \end{pmatrix}$ or $A = \pm \begin{pmatrix} -x-ra & a \\ a(s-r^2) & -x+ra \end{pmatrix}$, $p = 2r$ and $q = s-r^2$, where $x > 0$ and $a > 0$ give a solution of Pell's equation or negative Pell's equation:

    $$x^2 - sa^2 = \pm 1,$$

    and r either satisfies the inequality $|r| < \sqrt{s} - 1$ or the inequality $|r| > \sqrt{s+2} + 1$. Also, it is required that $\gcd(r, s) = 1$ and $r \not\equiv s \pmod 2$.

  - For $n \equiv 1 \pmod 4$, $A = \pm \begin{pmatrix} \frac{c-pa}{2} & a \\ a\frac{n-p^2}{4} & \frac{c+pa}{2} \end{pmatrix}$ or $A = \pm \begin{pmatrix} \frac{-c-pa}{2} & a \\ a\frac{n-p^2}{4} & \frac{-c+pa}{2} \end{pmatrix}$, $p \equiv 1 \pmod 2$ and $q = \frac{n-p^2}{4}$, where $c > 0$ and $a > 0$ give a solution of one of the following Pell–type equations:

    $$c^2 - na^2 = \pm 4,$$

    and p either satisfies the inequality $|p| < \sqrt{n} - 2$ or the inequality $|p| > \sqrt{n+8} + 2$. Also, it is required that $\gcd(p, n) = 1$.

Remark 9. We recall that for a nonsquare integer $n > 0$ Pell's equation $x^2 - ny^2 = 1$ has infinitely many solutions which are recursively generated, using Brahmagupta's identity: $(x_1^2 - ny_1^2)(x_2^2 - ny_2^2) = (x_1x_2 + ny_1y_2)^2 - n(x_1y_2 + y_1x_2)^2$, from the fundamental solution – the one for which positive x and y are minimal. The fundamental solution can be found, for example, using continued fraction of $\sqrt{n}$. All solutions of negative Pell's equation $x^2 - ny^2 = -1$ are also generated from its fundamental solution. However, solutions of negative Pell's equation do not always exist. The first 54 numbers for which solutions exist are given by the sequence A031396 in OEIS [15]. Similarly, for the Pell–type equations $c^2 - na^2 = 4$ and $c^2 - na^2 = -4$, all solutions are recursively generated from the fundamental solutions. For the latter equation solutions exist if and only if they exist for the equation $x^2 - ny^2 = -1$. Furthermore, by Cayley's theorem, if the fundamental solution (u, v) of the equation $c^2 - na^2 = 4$ is odd (i.e., both u and v are odd), then $((u^2 - 3)u/2, (u^2 - 1)v/2)$ gives the fundamental solution of the equation $x^2 - ny^2 = 1$. Similarly, the odd fundamental solution (u, v) of the equation $c^2 - na^2 = -4$ leads to the fundamental solution $((u^2 + 3)u)/2, ((u^2 + 1)v))/2)$ of the equation $x^2 - ny^2 = -1$ [14]. If the fundamental solution is even then it is obtained from the fundamental solution of the corresponding Pell's equation by multiplication by 2.

Remark 10. For a fixed pair p and q, the matrices (1) with coefficients satisfying (2) form a submonoid $\mathcal{S}_{p,q}$ in $\mathrm{GL}(2, \mathbb{Z})$. Let $\mathcal{P}$ be the set of all pairs (p, q) for which $1 + |p| < |q|$, $\gcd(p, q) = 1$ and $n = p^2 + 4q$ is equal to either $-4, -3, 1, 4$ or a nonsquare positive integer. Then a set of all matrices given by Theorem 8 is the union $\mathcal{S} = \bigcup_{(p,q) \in \mathcal{P}} \mathcal{S}_{p,q}$. For different pairs $(p, q)(p', q') \in \mathcal{P}$ we clearly have $\mathcal{S}_{p,q} \cap \mathcal{S}_{p',q'} = \{\pm I\}$. Moreover, it can be verified that each of these submonoids $\mathcal{S}_{p,q}$ is isomorphic to one of the groups: $\mathbb{Z}_4$, $\mathbb{Z}_6$, $\mathbb{Z}_2 \times \mathbb{Z}_2$ and $\mathbb{Z} \times \mathbb{Z}_2$. Namely, from Theorem 8 we obtain the following. For $n = -4$, $n = -3$ and $n = 1, 4$, $\mathcal{S}_{p,q}$ is a finite group isomorphic to $\mathbb{Z}_4$, $\mathbb{Z}_6$ and $\mathbb{Z}_2 \times \mathbb{Z}_2$, respectively. For a positive nonsquare integer n, $\mathcal{S}_{p,q} \cong \mathbb{Z} \times \mathbb{Z}_2$.

Remark 11. Let $(p, q) \in \mathcal{P}$ such that the polynomial $t(x) = x^2 + px - q$ is irreducible in $\mathbb{Z}[x]$. One can easily construct an infinite family of not FA–recognizable automorphisms of $\mathbb{Z}^2$ with respect to the representation $\psi_{p,q}$. Let $A = \begin{pmatrix} a_{11} & a_{12} \\ a_{21} & a_{22} \end{pmatrix} \in \mathcal{S}_{p,q}$. For a matrix $A' = A + D$, where $D = \begin{pmatrix} k\ell & kn \\ m\ell & mn \end{pmatrix}$ is a nonzero singular matrix, $\det A' = \det A$ iff $m(a_{11}n + a_{12}\ell) + k(a_{21}n + a_{22}\ell) = 0$. The latter equation admits infinitely many solutions for k, l, m and n. Since A is FA–recognizable with respect to $\psi_{p,q}$, assuming that A' is FA–recognizable with respect to $\psi_{p,q}$, we get that $D = A' - A$ must be FA–recognizable with respect to $\psi_{p,q}$. But D is not FA–recognizable (see Remark 6), so A' is not FA–recognizable.

Remark 12. There exist automorphisms of $\mathbb{Z}^2$ which are not FA–recognizable with respect to every representation $\psi_{p,q}$, $(p, q) \in \mathcal{P}$. For example, all automorphisms of $\mathbb{Z}^2$ given by the matrices $T_n = \begin{pmatrix} 1 & 0 \\ n & 1 \end{pmatrix}$ for nonzero integer n are not FA–recognizable. This follows from the fact that I is FA–recognizable but the endomorphisms $T_n - I$ for $n \neq 0$ are not FA–recognizable. In particular, none of the representations $\psi_{p,q}$, $(p, q) \in \mathcal{P}$ can be used to construct a Cayley automatic representation for the Heisenberg group $\mathcal{H}_3(\mathbb{Z}) \cong \mathbb{Z}^2 \rtimes_{T_1} \mathbb{Z}$.

Remark 13. We note that for two conjugate matrices A and $B = TAT^{-1}$ in $\mathrm{GL}(2, \mathbb{Z})$ the groups $\mathbb{Z}^2 \rtimes_A \mathbb{Z}$ and $\mathbb{Z}^2 \rtimes_B \mathbb{Z}$ are isomorphic. An algorithm for solving conjugacy problem in $\mathrm{GL}(2, \mathbb{Z})$ is described in [8]; see also an algorithm for solving conjugacy problem in $\mathrm{SL}(2, \mathbb{Z})$ using continued fractions [10, § 7.2]. It can be verified that for the cases $n = -4, -3, 1, 4$ each of the matrices from Theorem 8 is conjugate to one of the following matrices in $\mathrm{GL}(2, \mathbb{Z})$:

$\begin{pmatrix} 0 & -1 \\ 1 & 0 \end{pmatrix}, \begin{pmatrix} 1 & 1 \\ -1 & 0 \end{pmatrix}, \begin{pmatrix} 0 & 1 \\ -1 & -1 \end{pmatrix}, \begin{pmatrix} 1 & 0 \\ 0 & -1 \end{pmatrix}$ and $\begin{pmatrix} 0 & 1 \\ 1 & 0 \end{pmatrix}$. If n is a positive non-square integer, every matrix from Theorem 8, which is in $\mathrm{SL}(2, \mathbb{Z})$, is Anosov. Moreover, in this case, for a pair $(p, q) \in \mathcal{P}$ satisfying $n = p^2 + 4q$ the matrices from $\mathcal{S}_{p,q}$ generate infinitely many conjugacy classes in $\mathrm{GL}(2, \mathbb{Z})$. The latter immediately follows from the observation that for different values of c, which is the trace of the matrix (1), we have different conjugacy classes.

Similarly to the case $n = 2$, one gets a family of FA–recognizable automorphisms $A \in \mathrm{GL}(n, \mathbb{Z})$ with respect to the Nies–Semukhin FA–presentations $\psi_{\bar{p},q}$ of $\mathbb{Z}^n$. We postpone a careful analysis of this family for future work.

4   Conclusion and Open Questions

In this paper we generalize the Nies–Semukhin FA–presentation of $(\mathbb{Z}^2, +)$, originally constructed for the polynomial $x^2 + x - 3$, to a polynomial $x^2 + px - q$ such that $1 + |p| < |q|$ and $\gcd(p, q) = 1$. We also show how this construction is generalized for $(\mathbb{Z}^n, +), n > 2$. Based on this, we construct a new family of Cayley automatic representations of groups $\mathbb{Z}^n \rtimes_A \mathbb{Z}, A \in \mathrm{GL}(n, \mathbb{Z})$ that violate the basic property known for standard representations – projections $p_i : \mathbb{Z}^n \to \mathbb{Z}^n, i = 1, \ldots, n$ are FA–recognizable, i.e., the property (b) in Sect. 1. For $n = 2$ we describe the set of matrices $\mathcal{S} \subseteq \mathrm{GL}(2, \mathbb{Z})$ corresponding to this family of nonstandard representations and show its connection with Pell's equation. Let us pose the following questions that are apparent from the results of this paper.

- Is there a nonstandard representation, e.g., preserving the property (a) and violating the property (b), for the Heisenberg group $\mathcal{H}_3(\mathbb{Z})$?
- What is the set of conjugacy classes of the set of matrices $\mathcal{S}$ in $\mathrm{GL}(2, \mathbb{Z})$?

References

1. Baumslag, G., Shapiro, M., Short, H.: Parallel poly-pushdown groups. J. Pure Appl. Algebra **140**, 209–227 (1999)
2. Berdinsky, D., Elder, M., Taback, J.: Separating automatic from Cayley automatic groups, in preparation
3. Berdinsky, D., Trakuldit, P.: Measuring closeness between Cayley automatic groups and automatic groups. In: Klein, S.T., Martín-Vide, C., Shapira, D. (eds.) LATA 2018. LNCS, vol. 10792, pp. 245–257. Springer, Cham (2018). https://doi.org/10.1007/978-3-319-77313-1_19
4. Berdinsky, D., Trakuldit, P.: Towards quantitative classification of Cayley automatic groups. East-West J. Math. **20**(2), 107–124 (2018)
5. Bridson, M.R., Gilman, R.H.: Formal language theory and the geometry of 3-manifolds. Commentarii Mathematici Helvetici **71**(1), 525–555 (1996)
6. Bridson, M., Gersten, S.: The optimal isoperimetric inequality for torus bundles over the circle. Q. J. Math. **47**(1), 1–23 (1996)

7. Brittenham, M., Hermiller, S., Holt, D.: Algorithms and topology of Cayley graphs for groups. J. Algebra **415**, 112–136 (2014)
8. Campbell, J.T., Trouy, E.C.: When are two elements of GL(2, ℤ) similar? Linear Algebra Its Appl. **157**, 175–184 (1991)
9. Epstein, D.B.A., Cannon, J.W., Holt, D.F., Levy, S.V.F., Paterson, M.S., Thurston, W.P.: Word Processing in Groups. Jones and Barlett Publishers, Boston (1992)
10. Karpenkov, O.: Geometry of Continued Fractions. Springer, Heidelberg (2013)
11. Kharlampovich, O., Khoussainov, B., Miasnikov, A.: From automatic structures to automatic groups. Groups Geom. Dyn. **8**(1), 157–198 (2014)
12. Khoussainov, B., Nerode, A.: Automatic presentations of structures. In: Leivant, D. (ed.) Logic and Computational Complexity. Lecture Notes in Computer Science, vol. 960, pp. 367–392. Springer, Heidelberg (1995). https://doi.org/10.1007/3-540-60178-3_93
13. Nies, A., Semukhin, P.: Finite automata presentable Abelian groups. Ann. Pure Appl. Logic **161**(3), 458–467 (2009)
14. Piezas III, T.: A collection of algebraic identities. https://sites.google.com/site/tpiezas/008
15. Sloane, N.J.A.: On-Line Encyclopedia of Integer Sequences. https://oeis.org/A031396
16. Stephan, F.: Automatic structures—recent results and open questions. J. Phys.: Conf. Ser. **622**, 012013 (2015)

⟨ℝ, +, <, 1⟩ Is Decidable in ⟨ℝ, +, <, ℤ⟩

Alexis Bès[1](✉) and Christian Choffrut[2]

[1] Université Paris Est Creteil, LACL 94000, Creteil, France
bes@u-pec.fr
[2] IRIF, CNRS and Université Paris 7 Denis Diderot, Paris, France

Abstract. We show that it is decidable whether or not a relation on the reals definable in the structure ⟨ℝ, +, <, ℤ⟩ can be defined in the structure ⟨ℝ, +, <, 1⟩. This result is achieved by obtaining a topological characterization of ⟨ℝ, +, <, 1⟩-definable relations in the family of ⟨ℝ, +, <, ℤ⟩-definable relations and then by following Muchnik's approach of showing that this characterization can be expressed in the logic of ⟨ℝ, +, <, 1⟩.

1 Introduction

Consider the structure ⟨ℝ, +, <, 1⟩ of the additive ordered group of reals along with the constant 1. It is well-known that the subgroup ℤ of integers is not first-order-definable. Add the predicate $x \in \mathbb{Z}$ resulting in the structure ⟨ℝ, +, <, ℤ⟩. Our main result shows that given a ⟨ℝ, +, <, ℤ⟩-definable relation it is decidable whether or not it is ⟨ℝ, +, <, 1⟩-definable.

The structure ⟨ℝ, +, <, ℤ⟩ is a privileged area of application of algorithmic verification of properties of reactive and hybrid systems, where logical formalisms involving reals and arithmetic naturally appear, see e.g [1,4,13]. It admits quantifier elimination and is decidable as proved independently by Miller [16] and Weisfpfenning [20]. The latter's proof uses reduction to the theories of ⟨ℤ, +, <⟩ and ⟨ℝ, +, <, 1⟩.

There are many ways to come across the structure ⟨ℝ, +, <, ℤ⟩, which highlights its significance. One approach is through automata. Cobham considers a fixed base r and represents integers as finite strings of r digits. A subset X of integers is r−recognizable if there exists a finite automaton accepting precisely the representations in base r of its elements. Cobham's theorem says that if X is r- and s-recognizable for two multiplicatively independent values r and s (i.e., for all $i, j > 0$ it holds $r^i \neq s^j$) then X is definable in Presburger arithmetic, i.e., in ⟨ℕ, +⟩ [11,18]. Conversely, each Presburger-definable subset of ℕ is r-recognizable for every r. This result was extended to integer relations of arbitrary arity by Semënov [19].

Consider now recognizability of sets of reals. As early as in 1962 Büchi interprets subsets of integers as characteristic functions of reals in their binary representations and shows the decidability of a structure which is essentially an extension of ⟨ℝ, +, <, ℤ⟩, namely ⟨ℝ₊, <, P, ℕ⟩ where P if the set of positive powers of 2

© Springer Nature Switzerland AG 2020
A. Leporati et al. (Eds.): LATA 2020, LNCS 12038, pp. 128–140, 2020.
https://doi.org/10.1007/978-3-030-40608-0_8

and $\mathbb{N}$ the set of natural numbers [9, Thm 4]. Going one step further Boigelot et al. [7] consider reals as infinite strings of digits and use Muller automata to speak of r-recognizable subsets and more generally of r-recognizable relations of reals. In the papers [3, 5, 6] the equivalence was proved between (1) $\langle \mathbb{R}, +, <, \mathbb{Z} \rangle$-definability, (2) r- and s-recognizability where the two bases have distinct primes in their factorization [6, Thm 5] and (3) r- and s-weakly recognizability for two independently multiplicative bases, [6, Thm 6] (a relation is r-weakly recognizable if it is recognized by some deterministic Muller automaton in which all states in the same strongly connected component are either final or nonfinal). Consequently, as far as reals are concerned, definability in $\langle \mathbb{R}, +, <, \mathbb{Z} \rangle$ compared to recognizability or weak recognizability by automata on infinite strings can be seen as the analog of Presburger arithmetic for integers compared to recognizability by automata on finite strings.

A natural issue is to find effective characterizations of subclasses of $r-$recognizable relations. In the case of relations over integers, Muchnik proved that for every base $r \geq 2$ and arity $k \geq 1$, it is decidable whether a r-recognizable relation $X \subseteq \mathbb{N}^k$ is Presburger-definable [17] (see a different approach in [14] which provides a polynomial time algorithm). For relations over reals, up to our knowledge, the only known result is due to Milchior who proved that it is decidable (in linear time) whether a weakly $r-$recognizable subset of $\mathbb{R}$ is definable in $\langle \mathbb{R}, +, <, 1 \rangle$ [15]. Our result provides an effective characterization of $\langle \mathbb{R}, +, <, 1 \rangle$-definable relations within $\langle \mathbb{R}, +, <, \mathbb{Z} \rangle$-definable relations. Our approach is inspired by Muchnik's one, which consists of giving a combinatorical characterization of $\langle \mathbb{N}, + \rangle$-definable relations that can be expressed in $\langle \mathbb{N}, + \rangle$ itself.

Now we give a short outline of our paper. Section 2 gathers all the basic on the two specific structures $\langle \mathbb{R}, +, <, \mathbb{Z} \rangle$ and $\langle \mathbb{R}, +, <, 1 \rangle$, taking advantage of the existence of quantifier elimination which allows us to work with simpler formulas. Section 3 introduces topological notions. In particular we say that the neighborhood of a point $x \in \mathbb{R}^n$ relative to a relation $X \subseteq \mathbb{R}^n$ has <u>strata</u> if there exists a direction such that the intersection of all sufficiently small neighborhoods around x with X is the trace of a union of lines parallel to the given direction. This reflects the fact that the relations we work with are defined by finite unions of regions of the spaces delimited by hyperplanes of arbitrary dimension. In Sect. 5 we show that when X is $\langle \mathbb{R}, +, <, 1 \rangle$-definable all points (except finitely many which we call singular) have at least one direction which is a stratum. In Sect. 6 we give a necessary and sufficient condition for a $\langle \mathbb{R}, +, <, \mathbb{Z} \rangle$-definable relation to be $\langle \mathbb{R}, +, <, 1 \rangle$-definable, namely (1) it has finitely many singular points and (2) all intersections of X with arbitrary hyperplanes parallel to $n - 1$ axes and having rational components on the remaining axis are $\langle \mathbb{R}, +, <, 1 \rangle$-definable. Then we show that these properties are expressible in $\langle \mathbb{R}, +, <, 1, X \rangle$.

2   Preliminaries

Throughout this work we assume the vector space $\mathbb{R}^n$ is provided with the metric L_∞ (i.e., $|x| = \max_{1 \leq i \leq n} |x_i|$). The open ball centered at $x \in \mathbb{R}^n$ and of radius

$r > 0$ is denoted by $B(x, r)$. Given $x, y \in \mathbb{R}^n$ we denote by $[x, y]$ (resp. (x, y)) the closed segment (resp. open segment) with extremities x, y. We use also notations such as $[x, y)$ or $(x, y]$ for half-open segments.

Let us specify our logical conventions and notations. We work within first-order predicate calculus with equality. We confuse formal symbols and their interpretations, except in Sect. 6.2 where the distinction is needed. We are mainly concerned with the structures $\langle \mathbb{R}, +, <, 1 \rangle$ and $\langle \mathbb{R}, +, <, \mathbb{Z} \rangle$. In the latter structure, $\mathbb{Z}$ should be understood as a unary predicate which is satisfied only by elements of $\mathbb{Z}$ - in other words, we deal only with one-sorted structures. Given a structure $\mathcal{M}$ with domain D and $X \subseteq D^n$, we say that X is definable in $\mathcal{M}$, or $\mathcal{M}$-definable, if there exists a formula $\varphi(x_1, \ldots, x_n)$ in the signature of $\mathcal{M}$ such that $\varphi(a_1, \ldots, a_n)$ holds in $\mathcal{M}$ if and only if $(a_1, \ldots, a_n) \in X$.

The $\langle \mathbb{R}, +, <, 1 \rangle$-theory admits quantifier elimination in the following way, which can be interpreted geometrically as saying that a $\langle \mathbb{R}, +, <, 1 \rangle$-definable relation is a finite union of closed and open polyhedra.

Theorem 1 *[12, Thm 1]. Every formula in $\langle \mathbb{R}, +, <, 1 \rangle$ is equivalent to a Boolean combination of inequalities between linear combinations of variables with coefficients in $\mathbb{Z}$ (or, equivalently, in $\mathbb{Q}$).*

In particular in the unary case, the definable subsets are finite unions of intervals whose endpoints are rational numbers, which shows that $\mathbb{Z}$ is not $\langle \mathbb{R}, +, <, 1 \rangle$-definable.

In the larger structure $\langle \mathbb{R}, +, <, \mathbb{Z} \rangle$ it is possible to separate the integer (superscript 'I') and fractional (superscript 'F') parts of the reals as follows.

Theorem 2 *[8],[6, p. 7]. Let $X \subseteq \mathbb{R}^n$ be definable in $\langle \mathbb{R}, +, <, \mathbb{Z} \rangle$. Then there exists a unique finite union*

$$X = \bigcup_{k=1}^{K} (X_k^{(I)} + X_k^{(F)}) \tag{1}$$

where

- *the relations $X_k^{(I)}$ are pairwise disjoint subsets of $\mathbb{Z}^n$ and are $\langle \mathbb{Z}, +, < \rangle$-definable*
- *the relations $X_k^{(F)}$ are distinct subsets of $[0, 1)^n$ and are $\langle \mathbb{R}, +, <, 1 \rangle$-definable*

There is again a geometric interpretation of $\langle \mathbb{R}, +, <, \mathbb{Z} \rangle$-definable relations as a regular (in a precise technical way) tiling of the space by a finite number of tiles which are themselves finite unions of polyhedra. As a consequence, the restriction of a $\langle \mathbb{R}, +, <, \mathbb{Z} \rangle$-definable relation to a bounded subset is $\langle \mathbb{R}, +, <, 1 \rangle$-definable as stated in the following lemma.

Lemma 1. *For every $\langle \mathbb{R}, +, <, \mathbb{Z} \rangle$-definable relation $X \subseteq \mathbb{R}^n$, its restriction to a bounded domain $[a_1, b_1] \times \cdots \times [a_n, b_n]$ where the a_i's and the b_i's are rationals, is $\langle \mathbb{R}, +, <, 1 \rangle$-definable.*

By considering the restriction of the $\langle \mathbb{R}, +, <, \mathbb{Z} \rangle$-relation to a ball containing all possible tiles with their closest neighbors, we get that the neighborhoods of $\langle \mathbb{R}, +, <, \mathbb{Z} \rangle$- and $\langle \mathbb{R}, +, <, 1 \rangle$-definable relations are indistinguishable.

Lemma 2. *For every $\langle \mathbb{R}, +, <, \mathbb{Z} \rangle$-definable relation $X \subseteq \mathbb{R}^n$ there exists a $\langle \mathbb{R}, +, <, 1 \rangle$-definable relation $Y \subseteq \mathbb{R}^n$ such that for all $x \in \mathbb{R}^n$ there exists $y \in \mathbb{R}^n$ and a real $r > 0$ such that the translation $u \mapsto u + y - x$ is a one-to-one mapping between $B(x, r) \cap X$ and $B(y, r) \cap Y$.*

3 Strata

The aim is to decide, given $n \geq 1$ and a $\langle \mathbb{R}, +, <, \mathbb{Z} \rangle$-definable relation $X \subseteq \mathbb{R}^n$, whether X is $\langle \mathbb{R}, +, <, 1 \rangle$-definable. Though the relations defined in the two structures have very specific properties we define properties that make sense in a setting as general as possible. The following clearly defines an equivalence relation.

Definition 1. *Given $x, y \in \mathbb{R}^n$ we write $x \underset{X}{\sim} y$ or simply $x \sim y$ when X is understood, if there exists a real $r > 0$ such that the translation $w \mapsto w + y - x$ is a one-to-one mapping from $B(x, r) \cap X$ onto $B(y, r) \cap X$.*

Example 1. Consider a closed subset of the plane delimited by a square. There are 10 equivalence classes: the set of points interior to the square, the set of points interior to its complement, the four vertices and the four open edges.

Definition 2. *1. Given a non-zero vector $v \in \mathbb{R}^n$ and a point $y \in \mathbb{R}^n$ we denote by $L_v(y)$ the line passing through y in the direction v. More generally, if $X \subseteq \mathbb{R}^n$ we denote by $L_v(X)$ the set $\bigcup_{x \in X} L_v(x)$.*
2. A non-zero vector $v \in \mathbb{R}^n$ is an X-stratum at x (or simply a stratum when X is understood) if there exists a real $r > 0$ such that

$$B(x, r) \cap X = B(x, r) \cap L_v(X) \tag{2}$$

This can be seen as saying that inside the ball $B(x, r)$, the relation X is a union of lines parallel to v.
3. The set of X-strata at x is denoted by $Str_X(x)$, or simply $Str(x)$.

Proposition 1. *For all $X \subseteq \mathbb{R}^n$ and $x \in \mathbb{R}^n$ the set $Str(x)$ is either empty or a (vector) subspace of $\mathbb{R}^n$.*

Definition 3. *The dimension $dim(x)$ of a point $x \in \mathbb{R}^n$ is the dimension of the subspace $Str(x)$ if $Str(x)$ is nonempty or 0 otherwise.*

Definition 4. *Given a relation $X \subseteq \mathbb{R}^n$, a point $x \in \mathbb{R}^n$ is X-singular, or simply singular, if $Str(x)$ is empty, otherwise it is nonsingular.*

Note that non-$\langle \mathbb{R}, +, <, \mathbb{Z} \rangle$-definable relations may have no singular points: consider in the plane the collection of vertical lines at abscissa $\frac{1}{n}$ for all positive integers n. In this case any vertical vector is a stratum.

Now it can be shown that all strata at x can be defined by a common value r in expression (2).

Proposition 2. *If $\underline{Str}(x) \neq \emptyset$ then there exists a real $r > 0$ such that for every $v \in \underline{Str}(x)$ we have*

$$B(x, r) \cap X = B(x, r) \cap L_v(X).$$

Definition 5. *A $\underline{safe\ radius}$ (for x) is a real $r > 0$ satisfying the condition of Proposition 2. Clearly if r is safe then so are all $0 < s \leq r$. By convention every real is a safe radius if $Str(x) = \emptyset$.*

Example 2 (Example 1 continued). For an element x of the interior of the square or the interior of its complement, let r be the (minimal) distance from x to the edges of the square. Then r is safe for x. If x is a vertex then $\mathrm{Str}(x)$ is empty and every $r > 0$ is safe for x. In all other cases r is the minimal distance of x to a vertex.

Lemma 3. *If $x \sim y$ then $\underline{Str}(x) = \underline{Str}(y)$.*

The converse of Lemma 3 is false in general. Indeed consider e.g. $X = \{(x, y) \mid y \leq 0\} \cup \{(x, y) \mid y = 1\}$ in $\mathbb{R}^2$. The points $(0, 0)$ and $(0, 1)$ have the same subspace of strata, namely that generated by $(1, 0)$, but $x \not\sim y$.

Now we combine the notions of strata and of safe radius.

Lemma 4. *Let $X \subseteq \mathbb{R}^n$, $x \in \mathbb{R}^n$ and r be a safe radius for x. Then for all $y \in B(x, r)$ we have $\underline{Str}(x) \subseteq \underline{Str}(y)$.*

Example 3 (Example 1 continued). Consider a point x on an (open) edge of the square and a safe radius r. For every point y in $B(x, r)$ which is not on the edge we have $\mathrm{Str}(x) \subset \mathrm{Str}(y) = \mathbb{R}^2$. For all other points we have $\mathrm{Str}(x) = \mathrm{Str}(y)$.

We relativize the notion of singularity and strata to an affine subspace $P \subseteq \mathbb{R}^n$. The next definition should come as no surprise.

Definition 6. *Given an affine subspace $P \subseteq \mathbb{R}^n$, a subset $X \subseteq P$ and a point $x \in P$, we say that a vector v parallel to P is an (X, P)-$\underline{stratum\ for\ the\ point\ }x$ if for all sufficiently small $r > 0$ it holds*

$$P \cap X \cap B(x, r) = P \cap L_v(X) \cap B(x, r)$$

A point $x \in P$ is (X, P)-$\underline{singular}$ if it has no (X, P)-stratum. For simplicity when P is the space $\mathbb{R}^n$ we will still stick to the previous terminology and speak of X-strata and X-singular points.

Singularity and nonsingularity do not go through restriction to affine subpaces.

Example 4. In the real plane, let $X = \{(x, y) \mid y < 0\}$ and P be the line $x = 0$. Then the origin is not X–singular but it is $(X \cap P, P)$–singular. All other elements of P admit $(0, 1)$ as an $(X \cap P, P)$–stratum thus they are not $(X \cap P, P)$–singular. The opposite situation may occur. In the real plane, let $X = \{(x, y) \mid y < 0\} \cup P$ where $P = \{(x, y) \mid x = 0\}$. Then the origin is X–singular but it is not $(X \cap P, P)$–singular.

4   Local Properties

4.1   Local Neighborhoods

In this section we recall that if $X \subseteq \mathbb{R}^n$ is $\langle \mathbb{R}, +, <, 1 \rangle$-definable then the equivalence relation $\sim$ (introduced in Definition 1) has finite index. This extends easily to the case where X is $\langle \mathbb{R}, +, <, \mathbb{Z} \rangle$-definable.

We modify the usual notion of cones so that it suits better our purposes.

Definition 7. *A <u>cone</u> is an intersection of finitely many halfspaces defined by a condition of the form $u(x) < 0$ or $u(x) \leq 0$ where u is a linear expression having rational coefficients. The origin of the space is thus an <u>apex</u> of the cone.*

In particular a point, the empty set and the whole space are specific cones in our sense (on the real line they can be described respectively by $x \leq 0 \wedge -x \leq 0$, $x < 0 \wedge -x < 0$ and $x \leq 0 \vee -x \leq 0$). By convention, the origin is an apex of the empty set.

By paraphrasing [2, Thm 1] where "face" means "$\sim$-equivalence class" in our terminology we have.

Proposition 3. *Consider an $\langle \mathbb{R}, +, <, 1 \rangle$-definable relation X. There exists a finite collection Θ of $\langle \mathbb{R}, +, <, 1 \rangle$-formulas defining finite unions of cones such that for all $\xi \in \mathbb{R}^n$ there exist some θ in Θ and some real $s > 0$ such that for all $t \leq s$ we have*

$$\theta(t) \wedge |t| < s \leftrightarrow \phi(\xi + t) \wedge |t| < s \tag{3}$$

Corollary 1. *Let $X \subseteq \mathbb{R}^n$ be $\langle \mathbb{R}, +, <, 1 \rangle$-definable.*

1. *The equivalence relation $\sim$ has finite index.*
2. *The set $\underline{Str}(x)$ is finite when x runs over $\mathbb{R}^n$.*
3. *There exists a fixed finite collection $\mathcal{C}$ of cones (in the sense of Definition 7) such that for each $\sim$-class E there exists a subset $\mathcal{C}' \subseteq \mathcal{C}$ such that for every $x \in E$ there exists $r > 0$ such that*

$$(x + t \in X) \wedge |t| < r \quad \leftrightarrow \quad \left(t \in \bigcup_{C \in \mathcal{C}'} C \right) \wedge |t| < r$$

Because of Lemma 2 we have

Corollary 2. *The statements of Corollary 1 extend to the case where X is $\langle \mathbb{R}, +, <, \mathbb{Z} \rangle$-definable.*

Combining Corollaries 1 and 2 allows us to specify properties of singular points for $\langle \mathbb{R}, +, <, 1 \rangle$- and $\langle \mathbb{R}, +, <, \mathbb{Z} \rangle$-definable relations.

Proposition 4. *Let $X \subseteq \mathbb{R}^n$. If X is $\langle \mathbb{R}, +, <, 1 \rangle$-definable then it has finitely many singular points and their components are rational numbers. If X is $\langle \mathbb{R}, +, <, \mathbb{Z} \rangle$-definable then it has a countable number of singular points and their components are rational numbers.*

4.2   Application: Expressing the Singularity of a Point in a $\langle \mathbb{R}, +, <, \mathbb{Z} \rangle$-Definable Relation

The singularity of a point x is defined as the property that no intersection of X with a ball centered at x is a union of lines parallel with a given direction. This property is not directly expressible within $\langle \mathbb{R}, +, <, \mathbb{Z} \rangle$ since the natural way would be to use multiplication on reals, which is not $\langle \mathbb{R}, +, <, \mathbb{Z} \rangle$-definable. In order to be able to express the property, we give an alternative characterization of singularity which relies on the assumption that X is $\langle \mathbb{R}, +, <, \mathbb{Z} \rangle$-definable.

Lemma 5. *Given an $\langle \mathbb{R}, +, <, \mathbb{Z} \rangle$-definable relation $X \subseteq \mathbb{R}^n$ and $x \in \mathbb{R}^n$ the following two conditions are equivalent:*

1. *x is singular.*
2. *for all $r > 0$, there exists $s > 0$ such that for all vectors v of norm less than s, there exist two points $y, z \in B(x, r)$ such that $y = z + v$ and $y \in X \Leftrightarrow z \notin X$.*

Observe that when X is not $\langle \mathbb{R}, +, <, \mathbb{Z} \rangle$-definable, then the two assertions are no longer equivalent. E.g., $\mathbb{Q}$ has only singular points but condition 2 holds for no point in $\mathbb{R}$.

5   Relations Between Neighborhoods

We illustrate the purpose of this section with a very simple example. We start with a cube sitting in the horizontal plane with only one face visible. The rules of the game is that we are given a finite collection of vectors such that for all 6 faces and all 12 edges it is possible to choose vectors that generate the vectorial subspace of the smallest affine subspace in which they live. Let the point at the center of the upper face move towards the observer (assuming that this direction belongs to the initial collection). It will eventually hit the upper edge of the visible face. Now let the point move to the left along the edge (this direction necessarily exists because of the assumption on the collection). The point will hit the upper left vertex. Consequently, in the trajectory the point visits three different $\sim$-classes: that of the points on the open upper face, that of the points on the open edge and that of the upper left vertex. Here we investigate the adjacency of such equivalence classes having decreasing dimensions. Observe that another finite collection of vectors may have moved the point from the center of the upper face directly to the upper left vertex.

Since two $\sim$-equivalent points either have no stratum or the same subspace of strata, given a $\sim$-class E it makes sense to denote by $\mathrm{Str}(E)$ the empty set in the first case and the common subspace of all points in E in the latter case. Similarly, $\dim(E)$ is the common dimension of the points in E.

5.1   Compatibility

The above explanation should help the reader understand the following definition by considering the backwards trajectory: the point passes from an $\sim$-equivalence class of low dimension into an $\sim$-equivalence class of higher dimension along a direction that is proper to this latter class. This leads to the notion of compatibility. For technical reasons we allow a class to be compatible with itself.

Definition 8. *Let E be a nonsingular $\sim$-class and let v be one of its strata. Given a $\sim$-class F, a point $y \in F$ is v-compatible with E if there exists $\epsilon > 0$ such that for all $0 < \alpha \le \epsilon$ we have $y + \alpha v \in E$.*

A $\sim$-class F is v-compatible with E if there exists a point $y \in F$ which is v-compatible with E.

Lemma 6. *Given a $\sim$-class F and a vector $v \in \mathbb{R}^n$ there exists at most one $\sim$-class E such that F is v-compatible with E. If F is v-compatible with E, all elements of F are v-compatible with E.*

Observe that for any nonsingular $\sim$-class E and one of its strata v there always exists a $\sim$-class v-compatible with E, namely E itself, but also that conversely there might be different classes v-compatible with E.

Example 5. Let X be the union of the two axes of the 2-dimensional plane and $v = (1,1)$. The different classes are: the complement of X, the origin $\{0\}$ which is a singular point, the horizontal axis deprived of the origin, and the vertical axis deprived of the origin. The two latter $\sim$-classes are both v-compatible with the class $\mathbb{R}^2 \setminus X$.

5.2   Intersection of a Line and Equivalence Classes

In this section we describe the intersection of a $\sim$-class E with a line parallel to some $v \in \mathrm{Str}(E)$.

With the above example of the cube, a line passing through a point x on the upper face along any of the directions of $\mathrm{Str}(x)$ of dimension 2 intersects an open edge or a vertex at point y. In the former case $\dim(y) = 1$ and in the latter $\dim(y) = 0$, and in both cases $\mathrm{Str}(y) \subset \mathrm{Str}(x)$.

Lemma 7. *Let $X \subseteq \mathbb{R}^n$, F, G be two $\sim$-classes, and $v \in \underline{Str}(F)$. Let y be an element of G which is adherent to $L_y(v) \cap F$. Then $\underline{Str}(G) \subseteq \underline{Str}(F)$.*

If F, G are different, then $\underline{Str}(G) \subseteq \underline{Str}(F) \setminus \{v\}$ and therefore $\dim(G) < \dim(F)$.

With the above example of the cube, every point x of a face (which is an open subset on the delimiting affine space supporting the face) is interior to some open segment passing through x, parallel to any direction of the subspace $Str(x)$ and included in the face. The same observation holds for a point on an open edge of the cube.

Lemma 8. *Let $X \subseteq \mathbb{R}^n$, $x \in \mathbb{R}^n$ a nonsingular point and $v \in \underline{Str}(x)$. There exist $y, z \in L_v(x)$ such that $x \in (y, z)$ and every element w of (y, z) satisfies $w \sim x$.*

Consequently, via Lemmas 7 and 8 we get the following.

Corollary 3. *Let $X \subseteq \mathbb{R}^n$, $x \in \mathbb{R}^n$, E its $\sim$-class and let $v \in Str(x)$. The set $L_v(x) \cap E$ is a union of disjoint open segments (possibly infinite in one or two directions) of $L_v(x)$, i.e., of the form $(y - \alpha v, y + \beta v)$ with $0 < \alpha, \beta \leq \infty$ and $y \in E$.*

If $\alpha < \infty$ (resp. $\beta < \infty$) then the point $y - \alpha v$ (resp. $y + \beta v$) belongs to a $\sim$-class $F \neq E$ where F is v-compatible (resp. $(-v)$-compatible) with E, and $dim(F) < dim(E)$.

Corollary 4. *Given a nonsingular $\sim$-class E, a point $x \in E$ and $v \in \underline{Str}(x)$, the intersection of E with the line $L_v(x)$ is a union of open segments whose endpoints have dimension (cf. Definition 3) less than that of E.*

6   Characterization and Effectivity

6.1   Characterization of $\langle \mathbb{R}, +, <, 1 \rangle$ in $\langle \mathbb{R}, +, <, \mathbb{Z} \rangle$

In this section we give the characterization of $\langle \mathbb{R}, +, <, \mathbb{Z} \rangle$-definable relations which are $\langle \mathbb{R}, +, <, 1 \rangle$-definable. A <u>rational section</u> of a relation $X \subseteq \mathbb{R}^n$ is a relation of the form

$$X_c^{(i)} = X \cap (\mathbb{R}^i \times \{c\} \times \mathbb{R}^{n-i-1}) \quad \text{for some } c \in \mathbb{Q}, \ 0 \leq i < n$$

Theorem 3. *Let $n \geq 1$ and let $X \subseteq \mathbb{R}^n$ be $\langle \mathbb{R}, +, <, \mathbb{Z} \rangle$-definable. Then X is $\langle \mathbb{R}, +, <, 1 \rangle$-definable if and only if the following two conditions hold*

1. *There exist finitely many X − singular points.*
2. *Every rational section of X is $\langle \mathbb{R}, +, <, 1 \rangle$-definable.*

Observe that both conditions (1) and (2) are needed. Indeed, the relation $X = \mathbb{R} \times \mathbb{Z}$ is $\langle \mathbb{R}, +, <, \mathbb{Z} \rangle$-definable. It has no singular point thus it satisfies condition (1), but does not satisfy (2) since, e.g., the rational section $X_0^{(0)} = \{0\} \times \mathbb{Z}$ is not $\langle \mathbb{R}, +, <, 1 \rangle$-definable. Now, consider the relation $X = \{(x, x) \mid x \in \mathbb{Z}\}$ which is $\langle \mathbb{R}, +, <, \mathbb{Z} \rangle$-definable. It does not satisfy condition (1) since every element of X is singular, but it satisfies (2) because every rational section of X is either empty or equal to the singleton $\{(x, x)\}$ for some $x \in \mathbb{Z}$, thus is $\langle \mathbb{R}, +, <, 1 \rangle$-definable.

Now we give an idea of the proof since it cannot fit in the space allowed. The necessity of point 1 follows from Proposition 4. That of point 2 results from the fact that all rational constants are $\langle \mathbb{R}, +, <, 1 \rangle$-definable by Theorem 1, and moreover that $\langle \mathbb{R}, +, <, 1 \rangle$-definable relations are closed under direct product and intersection.

Now the sufficiency. Corollary 4 suggests that we proceed by induction on the dimension of the $\sim$-classes. There are finitely many classes of dimension 0 since there are finitely many singular points so the base of the induction is guaranteed. Now the intersection of a nonsingular class E with a line passing through a point x in the class and parallel to a direction of the class is a finite union of open segments, see Lemma 6. If the segment containing x is closed or half-closed then one of its adherent point belongs to a class F of lower dimension and we can define E relatively to F via the notion of compatibility. However the line may not intersect any other equivalence class. So we consider the canonical subspaces, see below, since every line has an intersection with one of these.

$$H_i = \{(x_1, \ldots, x_n) \in \mathbb{R}^n \mid x_i = 0\} \quad i \in \{1, \ldots, n\}$$
$$Q_I = \bigcap_{i \in I} H_i, \quad Q_I' = (Q_I \setminus \bigcup_{i \in \{1, \ldots, n\} \setminus I} H_i) \text{ for all } \emptyset \subset I \subseteq \{1, \ldots, n\} \quad (4)$$

In particular $Q_{\{1, \ldots, n\}} = \{0\}$ and by convention $Q_\emptyset = \mathbb{R}^n$. The Q_i's are the canonical subspaces. The Q_i''s are not vectorial subspaces but with some abuse of language we will write $\dim(Q_I')$ to mean $\dim(Q_I) = n - |I|$. Observe that point 2 of the theorem implies that for every I the intersection $X \cap Q_I$ (resp. $X \cap Q_I'$) is $\langle \mathbb{R}, +, <, 1 \rangle$-definable.

We consider the finite decomposition of the space consisting of all subsets $E \cap Q_I'$ where E is a $\sim$ −class and Q_I' is as in 4. We associate to each subset $E \cap Q_I'$ the pair of integers $(\dim(\mathrm{Str}(E) \cap Q_I), \dim(Q_I'))$ equipped with the product ordering, and we proceed by induction. The result follows from the fact that X is a union of finitely many $\sim$-classes, since if $x \sim y$ then both x and y belong to X or both belong to its complement.

The proof can be seen as describing a trajectory starting from a point x in a $\sim$-class E, traveling along a stratum of E until it reaches a class of lower dimension F (by Corollary 4) or some canonical subspace. In the first case it resumes the journey from the new class F on. In the second case it is trapped in the canonical subspace: it resumes the journey by choosing one direction of the subspace until it reaches a new $\sim$-class or a point belonging to a proper canonical subspace. Along the journey, either the dimension of the new class or the dimension of the canonical subspace decreases. The journey stops when the point reaches a (X, Q_I)−singular point, or the origin which is the least canonical subspace.

6.2 Decidability

So far we did not distinguish between formal symbols and their interpretations but here we must do it if we want to avoid any confusion. Let $X_n \subseteq \mathbb{R}^n$ be a relation defined by a $\langle \mathbb{R}, +, <, \mathbb{Z} \rangle$-formula ϕ. In order to express that X_n is actually $\langle \mathbb{R}, +, <, 1 \rangle$-definable we proceed as follows. Let $\{ \mathcal{X}_n(x_1, \ldots, x_n) \mid n \geq 1 \}$ be a collection of relational symbols. We construct a $\{ +, <, 1, \mathcal{X}_n \}$−sentence $\psi_n(\mathcal{X}_n)$ such that $\psi_n(X_n)$ holds if and only X_n is $\langle \mathbb{R}, +, <, 1 \rangle$-definable.

Proposition 5. *Let $\{ \mathcal{X}_n(x_1, \ldots, x_n) \mid n \geq 1 \}$ denote a set of relational symbols. For every $n \geq 1$ there exists a $\{ +, <, 1, \mathcal{X}_n \}$−sentence ψ_n such that for every $\{ +, <, 1, \mathcal{X}_n \}$− structure $\mathcal{M} = (\mathbb{R}, +, <, 1, X_n)$, if X_n is $\langle \mathbb{R}, +, <, \mathbb{Z} \rangle$-definable then we have $\mathcal{M} \models \psi_n$ if and only if X_n is $\langle \mathbb{R}, +, <, 1 \rangle$-definable.*

Sketch. The formula is of the form

$$\sigma_n(\mathcal{X}_n) \wedge \bigwedge_{1 \leq i \leq n} \forall y \; \psi_{n-1}^{(i)}(y, \mathcal{X}_{n-1}) \tag{5}$$

where each $\psi_{n-1}^{(i)}(y, \mathcal{X}_{n-1})$ is obtained from $\psi_{n-1}(\mathcal{X}_{n-1})$ by inserting y at position i in the sequence of variables of the interpretation X_n. The conjunct $\sigma_n(\mathcal{X}_n)$ expresses the fact that X_n has finitely many singular points (point 1 of Theorem 3) and each conjunct $\psi_{n-1}^{(i)}(y, \mathcal{X}_{n-1})$ expresses the fact that, interpreting y as a parameter, the section is $\langle \mathbb{R}, +, <, \mathbb{Z} \rangle$-definable (point 2 of Theorem 3). As an example $\sigma_1(\mathcal{X}_1)$ is as follows (the formula is correct only when $\mathcal{X}_1$ is interpreted as a $\langle \mathbb{R}, +, <, \mathbb{Z} \rangle$-definable relation)

$$\exists r \forall x \in \mathbb{R} \; (\forall t > 0$$
$$((\exists y \in \mathcal{X}_1 \wedge |y - x| < t) \wedge (\exists y \notin \mathcal{X}_1 \wedge |y - x| < t))) \to |x| \leq r)$$

Theorem 4. *For every $n \geq 1$ and every $\langle \mathbb{R}, +, <, \mathbb{Z} \rangle$-definable relation $X \subseteq \mathbb{R}^n$, it is decidable whether X is $\langle \mathbb{R}, +, <, 1 \rangle$-definable.*

Proof. In Proposition 5, if we substitute the predicate $\phi(x)$ for every occurrence of $x \in \mathcal{X}_n$ in ψ_n, then ψ_n can be interpreted in the structure $\langle \mathbb{R}, +, <, \mathbb{Z} \rangle$ and the decidability of its truth value results from the decidability of $\langle \mathbb{R}, +, <, \mathbb{Z} \rangle$ [20].

7   Conclusion

We discuss some extensions and open problems. Is it possible to remove our assumption that X is $\langle \mathbb{R}, +, <, \mathbb{Z} \rangle$-definable in Theorem 3? We believe that the answer is positive and it can be formally proven in dimension 2. Note that even if one proves such a result, the question of providing an effective characterization is more complex. Indeed the sentence ψ_n of Proposition 5 expresses a variant of the criterion of Theorem 3, and we use heavily the fact that we work within $\langle \mathbb{R}, +, <, \mathbb{Z} \rangle$ to ensure that this variant is actually equivalent to the criterion. In particular the construction of ψ_n relies on Lemma 5 to express that a point is X−singular. However if we consider e.g. $X = \mathbb{Q}$ then every element x of X is singular while no element x of X satisfies the condition stated in Lemma 5.

Another question is the following. In Presburger arithmetic it is decidable whether or not a formula is equivalent to a formula in the structure without $<$, cf. [10]. What about the case where the structure is $\langle \mathbb{R}, +, <, \mathbb{Z} \rangle$?

References

1. Becker, B., Dax, C., Eisinger, J., Klaedtke, F.: LIRA: handling constraints of linear arithmetics over the integers and the reals. In: Damm, W., Hermanns, H. (eds.) CAV 2007. LNCS, vol. 4590, pp. 307–310. Springer, Heidelberg (2007). https://doi.org/10.1007/978-3-540-73368-3_36
2. Bieri, H., Nef, W.: Elementary set operations with d-dimensional polyhedra. In: Noltemeier, H. (ed.) CG 1988. LNCS, vol. 333, pp. 97–112. Springer, Heidelberg (1988). https://doi.org/10.1007/3-540-50335-8_28
3. Boigelot, B., Brusten, J., Bruyère., V.: On the sets of real numbers recognized by finite automata in multiple bases. LMCS **6**(1), 1–17 (2010)
4. Boigelot, B.: The Liege automata-based symbolic handler (LASH). http://www.montefiore.ulg.ac.be/boigelot/research/lash/
5. Boigelot, B., Brusten, J.: A generalization of Cobham's theorem to automata over real numbers. Theor. Comput. Sci. **410**(18), 1694–1703 (2009)
6. Boigelot, B., Brusten, J., Leroux, J.: A generalization of Semenov's theorem to automata over real numbers. In: Schmidt, R.A. (ed.) CADE 2009. LNCS (LNAI), vol. 5663, pp. 469–484. Springer, Heidelberg (2009). https://doi.org/10.1007/978-3-642-02959-2_34
7. Boigelot, B., Rassart, S., Wolper, P.: On the expressiveness of real and integer arithmetic automata. In: Larsen, K.G., Skyum, S., Winskel, G. (eds.) ICALP 1998. LNCS, vol. 1443, pp. 152–163. Springer, Heidelberg (1998). https://doi.org/10.1007/BFb0055049
8. Bouchy, F., Finkel, A., Leroux, J.: Decomposition of decidable first-order logics over integers and reals. In: 2008 15th International Symposium on Temporal Representation and Reasoning, pp. 147–155. IEEE (2008)
9. Büchi, J.R.: On a decision method in the restricted second-order arithmetic. In: Proceedings International Congress Logic, Methodology and Philosophy of Science, Berkeley 1960, pp. 1–11. Stanford University Press (1962)
10. Choffrut, C., Frigeri, A.: Deciding whether the ordering is necessary in a Presburger formula. DMTCS **12**(1), 20–38 (2010)
11. Cobham, A.: On the base-dependence of sets of numbers recognizable by finite automata. Math. Syst. Theor. **3**(2), 186–192 (1969)
12. Ferrante, J., Rackoff, C.: A decision procedure for the first order theory of real addition with order. SIAM J. Comput. **4**(1), 69–76 (1975)
13. Fränzle, M., Quaas, K., Shirmohammadi, M., Worrell, J.: Effective definability of the reachability relation in timed automata. Inf. Proc. Lett. **153**, 105871 (2020)
14. Leroux, J.: A polynomial time Presburger criterion and synthesis for number decision diagrams. In: Proceedings of LICS 2005, pp. 147–156. IEEE (2005)
15. Milchior, A.: Büchi automata recognizing sets of reals definable in first-order logic with addition and order. In: Gopal, T.V., Jäger, G., Steila, S. (eds.) TAMC 2017. LNCS, vol. 10185, pp. 440–454. Springer, Cham (2017). https://doi.org/10.1007/978-3-319-55911-7_32
16. Miller, C.: Expansions of dense linear orders with the intermediate value property. J. Symb. Logic **66**(4), 1783–1790 (2001)
17. Muchnik, A.A.: The definable criterion for definability in Presburger arithmetic and its applications. Theor. Comput. Sci. **290**(3), 1433–1444 (2003)
18. Presburger, M.: Uber die vollstandigkeit eines gewissen systems der arithmetic ganzer zahlen, in welchem die addition als einzige operation hervortritt. In: du Premier Congrès des Mathématiciens des Pays Slaves, Warsaw, vol. 395, pp. 92–101 (1927)

19. Semenov, A.L.: Presburgerness of predicates regular in two number systems. Siberian Math. J. **18**(2), 289–300 (1977)
20. Weispfenning, V.: Mixed real-integer linear quantifier elimination. In: Proceedings of the 1999 International Symposium on Symbolic and Algebraic Computation, ISSAC 1999, pp. 129–136. ACM, New York (1999)

Ordered Semiautomatic Rings
with Applications to Geometry

Ziyuan Gao[1(✉)], Sanjay Jain[2], Ji Qi[1], Philipp Schlicht[3], Frank Stephan[1,2],
and Jacob Tarr[4]

[1] Department of Mathematics, National University of Singapore,
10 Lower Kent Ridge Road, S17, Singapore 119076, Republic of Singapore
ziyuan84@yahoo.com
[2] Department of Computer Science, National University of Singapore,
13 Computing Drive, COM1, Singapore 117417, Republic of Singapore
{sanjay,fstephan}@comp.nus.edu.sg
[3] School of Mathematics, University of Bristol,
Fry Building, Woodland Road, Bristol BS8 1UG, UK
philipp.schlicht@bristol.ac.uk
[4] University of British Columbia, Vancouver, Canada
jacobdtarr@gmail.com

Abstract. The present work looks at semiautomatic rings with automatic addition and comparisons which are dense subrings of the real numbers and asks how these can be used to represent geometric objects such that certain operations and transformations are automatic. The underlying ring has always to be a countable dense subring of the real numbers and additions and comparisons and multiplications with constants need to be automatic. It is shown that the ring can be selected such that equilateral triangles can be represented and rotations by 30° are possible, while the standard representation of the b-adic rationals does not allow this.

1 Introduction

Hodgson [6,7] as well as Khoussainov and Nerode [11] and Blumensath and Grädel [1] initiated the study of automatic structures. A structure, say the ordered semigroup of natural numbers $(\mathbb{N}, \circ, \leq)$ is then automatic iff there is an isomorphic structure $(A, \circ, \leq)$ where A is regular and $\circ, \leq, =$ are automatic in the following sense: A finite automaton reads all tuples of possible inputs and outputs with the same speed in a synchronised way and accepts these tuples which are valid tuples in the relations $\leq$ and $=$ or which are valid combinations

S. Jain and F. Stephan are supported in part by Singapore Ministry of Education Tier 2 AcRF MOE2016-T2-1-019 / R146-000-234-112. S. Jain was also supported in part by NUS grant C252-000-087-001. P. Schlicht is supported by the European Union under the Marie Skłodowska-Curie grant 794020 (IMIC). J. Qi and J. Tarr worked on this paper as UROPS projects at NUS. The authors would like to thank Bakhadyr Khoussainov and Sasha Rubin for correspondence.

© Springer Nature Switzerland AG 2020
A. Leporati et al. (Eds.): LATA 2020, LNCS 12038, pp. 141–153, 2020.
https://doi.org/10.1007/978-3-030-40608-0_9

(x, y, z) with $x \circ y = z$ in the case of the semigroup operation (function) $\circ$. For this, one assumes that the inputs and outputs of relations and functions are aligned with each other, like decimal numbers in addition, and for this alignment – which has to be the same for all operations – one fills the gaps with a special character. So words are functions with some domain $\{-m, -m+1, \ldots, n-1, n\}$ and some fixed range Σ and the finite automaton reads, when processing a pair (x, y) of inputs, in each round the symbols $(x(k), y(k))$ where the special symbol $\# \notin \Sigma$ replaces $x(k)$ or $y(k)$ in the case that these are not defined. See Example 3 below for an example of a finite automaton checking whether $x + y = z$ for numbers x, y, z; here a finite automaton computes a function by checking whether the output matches the inputs. Automatic functions are characterised as those computed by a position-faithful one-tape Turing machine in linear time [3].

The reader should note, that after Hodgson's pioneering work [6,7], Epstein, Cannon, Holt, Levy, Paterson and Thurston [5] argued that in the above formalisation, automaticity is, at least from the viewpoint of finitely generated groups, too restrictive. They furthermore wanted that the representatives of the group elements are given as words over the generators, leading to more meaningful representatives than arbitrary strings. Their concept of automatic groups led, for finitely generated groups, to a larger class of groups, though, by definition, of course it does not include groups which require infinitely many generators; groups with infinitely many generators, to some extent, were covered in the notion of automaticity by Hodgson, Khoussainov and Nerode. Nies, Oliver and Thomas provide in several papers [14,15] results which contrast and compare these two notions of automaticity and give an overview on results for groups which are automatic in the sense of Hodgson, Khoussainov and Nerode.

Jain, Khoussainov, Stephan, Teng and Zou [8] investigated the general approach where, in a structure for some relations and functions, it is only required that the versions of the functions or relations with all but one variable fixed to constants is automatic. Here the convention is to put the automatic domains, functions and relations before a semicolon and the semiautomatic relations after the semicolon. The present work will focus more on structures like rings than groups, although the field of automatic and semiautomatic structures has a strong group theoretic component. The construction of these semiautomatic rings is similar to that of Nies and Semukhin [13] for a presentation of $\mathbb{Z}^2$ where no 1-dimensional subgroup is a regular subset.

The interested reader finds information about automatic structures in the surveys of Khoussainov and Minnes [10] and Rubin [16]. Related but different links between automata theory and geometry have been studied previously like, for example, the usage of weighted automata and transducers to generate fractals [4], ω-automata to represent geometric objects in the reals [2,9] and the field of reals not being ω-automatic [19]. The last section of the present work applies the results and methods of the current work to ω-automatic structures.

The present work looks at semiautomatic rings which can be used to represent selected points in the real plane. Addition and subtraction and comparisons as well as multiplication with constants have to be automatic; however, the full multiplication is not automatic. It depends on the structures which geometric objects and operations with such object can be represented.

Definition 1. The *convolution* of two words v, w is a mapping from the union of their domains to $(\Sigma \cup \{\#\}) \times (\Sigma \cup \{\#\})$ such that first one extends v, w to v', w', each having the domain $dom(v) \cup dom(w)$, by assigning $\#$ whenever v or w are undefined and then letting the convolution u map every $h \in dom(v) \cup dom(w)$ to the new symbol $(v'(h), w'(h))$. Similarly one defines the convolutions of three, four or more words.

A h-ary relation R is *automatic* [1,6,7,11] iff the set of all convolutions of $(x_1, \ldots, x_h) \in R$ is regular; a h-ary function f is automatic iff the set of all convolutions of $(x_1, \ldots, x_h, y)$ with $f(x_1, \ldots, x_h) = y$ is regular. A h-ary relation P is *semiautomatic* [8] iff for all indices $i \in \{1, \ldots, h\}$ and for all possible fixed values x_j with $j \neq i$ the resulting set $\{x_i : (x_1, \ldots, x_h) \in P\}$ is regular. A h-ary function g is semiautomatic iff for all indices $i \in \{1, \ldots, h\}$ and all possible values x_j with $j \neq i$ the function $x_i \mapsto g(x_1, \ldots, x_h)$ is automatic.

A structure $(A, f_1, \ldots, f_k, R_1, \ldots, R_\ell; g_1, \ldots, g_i, P_1, \ldots, P_j)$ is *semiautomatic* [8] iff (i) A is a regular set of words where each word maps a finite subset of $\mathbb{Z}$ to a fixed alphabet, (ii) each f_h is automatic, (iii) each R_h is automatic, (iv) each g_h is semiautomatic and (v) each P_h is semiautomatic. The semicolon separates the automatic components of the structure from those which are only semiautomatic. Structures without semiautomatic items are just called automatic.

An *automatic family* $\{L_d : d \in E\}$ is a collection of sets such that their index set E and the set of all convolutions of (d, x) with $x \in L_d$ and $d \in E$ are regular.

Definition 2. A *semiautomatic grid* or, in this paper, just grid, is a semiautomatic ring $(A, +, =, <; \cdot)$ where the multiplication is only semiautomatic and the addition and comparisons are automatic such that A forms a dense subring of the reals, that is, whenever p, r are real numbers with $p < r$ then there is an $q \in A$ with $p < q \wedge q < r$ and furthermore, all elements of A represent real numbers.

It makes sense to define density as a property of an ordered ring that is embeddable into the reals, since the embedding is unique. A necessary and sufficient criterion for the ring to be dense is that it has an element strictly between 0 and 1.

Example 3. The ring $(\mathbb{D}_b, +, =, <; \cdot)$ of the rational numbers in base b with only finitely many nonzero digits is a grid. Here $\mathbb{D}_b = \{n/b^m : n, m \in \mathbb{Z}\}$. Addition and comparison follow the school algorithm as in the following example of Stephan [17]. In $\mathbb{D}_{10}$, given three numbers x, y, z, an automaton to check whether $x + y = z$ would process from the back to the front and the states would be "correct and carry to next digit (c)", "correct and no carry to next digit (n)" and "incorrect (i)". In the following three examples, x stands on the top, y in the second and z in the last row. The states of the automaton are for starting from the end of the string to the beginning after having processed the digits after them but not those before them. The filling symbol $\#$ is identified with 0.

The decimal dot is not there physically, it just indicates the position between digit a_0 and digit a_{-1}. The domain of each string is an interval from a negative to a positive number plus an entry for the sign $-$ if needed.

Correct Addition	Incorrect Addition	Incomplete Addition
# 2 3 5 8. 2 2 5	3 3 3 3. 3 3 #	9 9 1 2 3. 4 5 6
# 9 1 1 2. # # #	# # 2 2. 2 2 2	# # 9 8 7. 6 5 4
1 1 4 7 0. 2 2 5	# 1 5 5. 5 5 2	0 0 1 1 1. 1 1 #
n c n n c n n n n	i i n n n n n n	c c c c c c c c n

The difference $x - y = z$ is checked by checking whether $x = y + z$ and then one can compare the outcome of additions of possibly negative numbers by going to $-$ when the signs of the numbers require this. Furthermore, $x < y$ iff $y - x$ is positive and $x = y$ if the two numbers are equal as strings.

For checking whether $x \cdot i/j = y$ for given rational constant i/j, one just checks whether $i \cdot x = j \cdot y$ which, as i, j are constants, can be done by i times adding x to itself and j time adding y to itself and then comparing the results. So $x \cdot 3/2 = y$ is equivalent to $x + x + x = y + y$ and the latter check is automatic. Also the set of all $x \in \mathbb{D}_{10}$ so that x is a multiple of 3 is regular, as it is first-order definable as $\{x : \exists y \in \mathbb{D}_{10} \, [x = y + y + y]\}$ and 1.2 would be in this set and 1.01 not. This works for all multiples of fixed rational numbers in $\mathbb{D}_b$.

2   Grids with Special Properties

Jain, Khoussainov, Stephan, Teng and Zou [8] showed that for every natural number c which is not a square there is a grid containing $\sqrt{c}$. Though these grids are dense subsets of the real numbers, they do not have the property that one can divide by any natural number, that is, for each $b \geq 2$ there is a ring element x such that x/b is not in the ring. The reason is that most of the rings considered by Jain, Khoussainov, Stephan, Teng and Zou are of the form $\mathbb{Z} \oplus \sqrt{c} \cdot \mathbb{Z}$. The following result will produce grids for which one can always divide by some number $b \geq 2$, if this number is composite, it might allow division by finitely many primes. Note that the number of primes cannot be infinite by a result of Tsankov [18].

Theorem 4. *Assume that $b \in \{2, 3, 4, \ldots\}$ and c is some root of an integer and let $u > 1$ be a real number chosen such that the following four polynomials p_1, p_2, p_3, p_4 in a variable x and constants $\ell, \hat{c}$ exist, where all polynomials have only finitely many nonzero coefficients and all coefficients are integers:*

1. *$p_1(u) = \sum_{k \in \mathbb{Z}} b_k u^k = 1/b$;*
2. *$p_2(u) = \sum_{k \in \mathbb{Z}} c_k u^k = c$;*
3. *$p_3(u) = \sum_{k=0,-1,-2,\ldots,-h+1} d_k u^k = 0$ with $d_0 = 1$;*
4. *$p_4(u) = \sum_{k \in \mathbb{Z}} e_k u^k = 0$ with $e_\ell > \sum_{k \neq \ell} |e_k|$ and $|e_k|$ being the absolute value of e_k.*

Furthermore, the choice of the above has to be such that $\hat{c} > 3|e_\ell|$ and one can run for every polynomial $p = \sum_{k=-m,\dots,n} a_k x^k$ with every a_k being an integer satisfying $|a_k| \leq 3|e_\ell|$ the following algorithm C satisfying the below termination condition:

> Let $k = n + h$.
> While $k > -m$ and $|a_{k'}| \leq \hat{c}$ for $k' = k, k-1, \dots, k-h+1$
> Do Begin $p = p - a_k \cdot p_3(u) \cdot u^k$ and update the coefficients of the polynomial
> p accordingly; Let $k = k - 1$ End.

The termination condition on C is that whenever the algorithm terminates at some $k > -m$ with some $|a_{k'}| > \hat{c}$ then

$$|\textstyle\sum_{k'=k,k-1,\dots,k-h+1} u^{k'} a_{k'}| > u^{k-h}/(1 - u^{-1}) \cdot 3|e_\ell|.$$

If all these assumptions are satisfied then one can use the representation

$$S = \{ \sum_{k=-m,\dots,n} a_k u^k : m, n \in \mathbb{N}, \ a_k \in \mathbb{Z} \text{ and } |a_k| < |e_\ell|\}$$

to represent every member of $\mathbb{D}_b[c]$ and the ring $(S, +, <, =; \cdot)$ has automatic addition and comparisons and semiautomatic multiplication. Furthermore, as $1/b$ is in the ring, it is a dense subset of the reals, thus the ring forms a semiautomatic grid.

Proof. When not giving $-m, n$ explicitly in the sum, sums like $\sum_{k \in \mathbb{Z}} a_k u^k$ use the assumption that almost all a_k are 0. For ease of notation, let S' be the set

$$S' = \{\sum_{k \in \mathbb{Z}} a_k x^k : \text{ almost all } a_k \text{ are 0 and all } a_k \in \mathbb{Z}\}$$

so that $S \subseteq S'$. On members $p, q \in S'$, one defines that $p \leq q$ iff $p(u) \leq q(u)$ when the polynomial is evaluated at the real number u. Furthermore, $p = q$ iff $p \leq q$ and $q \leq p$. Addition and subtraction in S' is defined using componentwise addition of coefficients.

Now one shows that for every $p \in S'$ there is a $q \in S$ with $p = q$. For this one lets initially $h = 0$ and $q_h = p$ and whenever there is a coefficient a_k of q_h with $|a_k| \geq |e_\ell|$ then one either lets $q_{h+1} = q_h - x^{k-\ell} \cdot p_4$ (in the case that $a_k > 0$) or lets $q_{h+1} = q_h + x^{k-\ell} \cdot p_4$ (in the case that $a_k < 0$). Now let $||q_h||$ be the sum of the absolute values of the coefficients; note that

$$||q_{h+1}|| \leq ||q_h|| - e_\ell + \sum_{k \neq \ell} |e_k| < ||q_h||$$

and as there is no infinite strictly decreasing sequence of positive integers, there is a h where q_h is defined but q_{h+1} not, as this update can no longer be made. Thus all coefficients of q_h are between $-|e_\ell|$ and $+|e_\ell|$ and furthermore, as each polynomial $p_4(u) \cdot u^{k-\ell}$ added or subtracted has the value 0, $q_h = p$. Now let $q = q_h$ and note that q is a member of S with the same value at u as p, so $p(u) = q(u)$.

Now let p, q, r be members of S. In order to see what the sign of $p + q - r$ is, that is, whether $p(u) + q(u) < r(u)$, $p(u) + q(u) = r(u)$ or $p(u) + q(u) > r(u)$, one adds the coefficients pointwise and to check the expression $p + q - r$ at u, one then runs the algorithm C. If C terminates with some $|a_{k'}| > \hat{c}$, then the sign of the current value of

$$\tilde{a} = \sum_{k' = k, k-1, \ldots, k-h+1} u^{k'} a_{k'}$$

gives the sign of $p + q - r$, as the not yet processed tail-sum of $p + q - r$ is bounded by $u^{k-h}/(1 - u^{-1}) \cdot 3|e_\ell|$. In the case that C terminates with all $|a_{k'}| \leq \hat{c}$ and $k = -m$, then only the coefficients at $k' = k, k-1, \ldots, k - h + 1$ are not zero and again the sign of $\tilde{a}$ is the sign of the original polynomial $p + q - r$.

Note that the algorithm C can be carried out by a finite automaton, as it only needs to memorise the current values of $(a_k, a_{k-1}, \ldots, a_{k-h+1})$ which are $(0, 0, \ldots, 0)$ at the start and which are updated in each step by reading a_{k-h} for $k = n+h, n+h-1, \ldots, -m$; the update is just subtracting $a_{k'} = a_{k'} - a_k \cdot d_{k'-k}$ for $k' = k, k-1, \ldots, k - h + 1$ and then updating $k = k - 1$ which basically requires to read a_{k-h} into the window and shift the window by one character; note that the first member, which goes out of the window, is 0. Furthermore, during the whole runtime of the algorithm, all values in the window have at most the values $(1 + \max\{|d_{k''}| : 0 \geq k'' \geq -h + 1\}) \cdot \hat{c}$ and thus there are only finitely many choices for $(a_k, a_{k-1}, \ldots, a_{k-h+1})$, and thus the determination of the sign of $\sum_{k' = k, k-1, \ldots, k-h+1} u^{k'} a_{k'}$ can be done by looking up a finite table. Early termination of the finite automaton can be handled by not changing the state on reading new symbols, once it has gone to a state with some $|a_{k'}| > \hat{c}$. Thus comparisons and addition are automatic; note that for automatic functions, the automaton checks whether the tuple (inputs, output) is correct, it does not compute output from inputs.

For the multiplication with constants, note that multiplication with u or u^{-1} is just shifting the coefficients in the representation by one position; multiplication with -1 can be carried out componentwise on all coefficients; multiplication with integers is repeated addition with itself. This also then applies to polynomials put together from these ground operations, so $p \cdot (u^2 - 2 + u^{-1})$ can be put together as the sum of $p \cdot u \cdot u$, $-p$, $-p$, $p \cdot u^{-1}$. All four terms of the sum can be computed by concatenated automatic functions, thus there is an automatic function which also computes the sum of these terms from a single input p. □

Example 5. There is a semiautomatic grid containing $\sqrt{2}$ and $1/2$.

Proof. For $c = \sqrt{2}$ and $b = 2$, one chooses

1. $u^{-1} = 1 - c/2$ (note that $u = 1/(1 - \sqrt{1/2}) = 2/(2 - \sqrt{2}) > 1$),
2. $p_1(u) = 2u^{-1} - u^{-2} = 1/2$,
3. $p_2(u) = 2 - 2u^{-1} = c$,
4. $p_3(u) = 1 - 4u^{-1} + 2u^{-2} = 0$,
5. $p_4(u) = -u + 4 - 2u^{-1} = 0$ with $\ell = 0$ and $e_\ell = 4$,
6. $\hat{c} = 100$ (or any larger value).

While all operations above come from straight-forward manipulations of the choice of u^{-1}, one has to show the termination condition of the algorithm.

For this one uses that $u \geq 3.41$ and $1/(1 - 1/u) = \sum_{k \leq 0} u^k = \sqrt{2} \leq 1.4143$. Assume that the algorithm satisfies before doing the step for k that all $|a_{k'}| \leq \hat{c}$ and does not satisfy this after updating a_k, a_{k-1}, a_{k-2} respectively to 0, $a' = a_{k-1} + 4a_k$ and $a'' = a_{k-2} - 2a_k$; in the following, a_k, a_{k-1}, a_{k-2} refer to the values before the update. Without loss of generality assume that $a_k > 0$, the case $a_k < 0$ is symmetric, the case $a_k = 0$ does not make the coefficients go beyond $\hat{c}$. If $a'' < -\hat{c}$ — it can only go out of the range to the negative side — then $2a_k \geq \hat{c} - 3(e_\ell - 1)$ and $p(u)$ is at least $a_k \cdot (4 - 2/u) \cdot u^{k-1} - \hat{c} \cdot u^{k-1}/(1 - 1/u) \geq ((2 - 1/u) \cdot (\hat{c} - 9) - 1.4143\hat{c})u^{k-1} \geq (1.7 \cdot (\hat{c} \cdot 0.9) - 1.4143\hat{c})u^{k-1} \geq 0.1 \cdot \hat{c} \cdot u^{k-1} > 0$. If $a'' \geq -\hat{c}$ and $a' > \hat{c}$ then $p(u) \geq (\hat{c} \cdot u - 1/(1 - 1/u)\hat{c}) \cdot u^{k-2} \geq \hat{c} \cdot u^{k-2} > 0$. So in both cases, one can conclude that $p(u)$ is positive. Similarly, when $a_k < 0$ and the bound $\hat{c}$ becomes violated in the updating process then $p(u) < 0$. □

Example 6. There is a grid which contains $\sqrt{3}$ and $1/2$ or, more generally, any c of the form $c = \sqrt{b^2 - 1}$ and $1/b$ for some fixed integer $b \geq 2$.

Proof. One chooses

1. $u^{-1} = 1 - c/b$ (note that $u = b/(b - c) > 1$),
2. $p_1(u) = 2bu^{-1} - bu^{-2} = 1/b$,
3. $p_2(u) = b - bu^{-1} = c$,
4. $p_3(u) = 1 - 2b^2u^{-1} + b^2u^{-2} = 0$,
5. $p_4(u) = -u + 2b^2 - b^2u^{-1} = 0$ with $\ell = 0$ and $e_\ell = 2b^2$,
6. $\hat{c} = 1000 \cdot b^5$ (or any larger value).

While all operations above come from straight-forward manipulations of the equations, the termination condition of the algorithm needs some additional work. Note that $u > b$, as $b - c < 1$. Indeed, by $u \geq 1$ and $p_3(u) = 0$ and $b \geq 2$, one has $1 - b^2u^{-1} \geq 0$ and $u \geq b^2$ and $\sum_{k \leq 0} u^k \leq 2$. For the algorithm, one now notes that if after an update at k where, without loss of generality, $a_k > 0$, it happens that either (a) $a'' = a_{k-2} - b^2a_k < -\hat{c}$ or (b) $a'' \geq -\hat{c}$ and $a' = a_{k-1} + 2b^2a_k > \hat{c}$ then the following holds: In the case (a), $a_k \geq 1000b^3 - 6b^2$ and the value of the sum is at least

$$(a_k \cdot (2b^2u - b^2) - \hat{c} \cdot u - 12b^4) \cdot u^{k-2} >$$
$$((20000b^5u - 6b^4) - 1000b^5 \cdot u - 12b^4) \cdot u^{k-2} >$$
$$(1000b^5 - 18b^4) \cdot u^{k-1} > 0$$

where the tail sum $12b^4$ estimates that all digits $a_{k'}$ with $k' \leq k - 2$ are at least $-6b^2$ in the expression and the a_{k-1} is at least $-\hat{c}$ by assumption. In case (b), one just uses that the first coefficient in the sum is greater than $\hat{c}$ while all other coefficients are of absolute value below $\hat{c}$, in particular as $\hat{c} \geq 6b^2$, so that, since $u \geq 2$,

$$\hat{c} \cdot u^{k-1} > \sum_{k' < k-1} \hat{c}u^{k'} \text{ and } \hat{c} \cdot u^{k-1} > 2 \cdot \hat{c} \cdot u^{k-2}.$$

Thus the algorithm terminates as required. □

3 Applications to Geometry

One can use the grid to represent the coordinates of geometric objects. For this, one uses in the field of automatic structures the concept of convolution which uses the overlay of constantly many words into one word. One introduces a new symbol, #, which is there to pad words onto the same length. Now, for example, if in the grid of decimal numbers, one wants to describe a point of coordinates $(1.112, 22.2895)$, this would be done with the convolution $(\#, 2)(1, 2).(1, 2)(1, 8)(2, 9)(\#, 5)$ where these six characters are the overlay of two characters and the dot is virtual and only marking the position where the numbers have to be aligned, that means, the position between the symbols at location 0 and location -1. Instead of combining two numbers, one can also combine five numbers or any other arity.

An automatic family is a family of sets L_e with the indices e from some regular set D such that the set $\{conv(e, x) : x \in L_e\}$ is regular. Given a grid G, the set of all lines parallel to the x-axis in $G \times G$ is an automatic family: Now $D = G$ and $L_y = \{conv(x, y) : x \in G\}$. The next example shows that one cannot have an automatic family of all lines.

Example 7. The set of all lines (with arbitrary slope) is not an automatic family, independent of the definition of the semiautomatic grid. Given a grid G and assuming that $\{L_e : e \in D\}$ is the automatic family of all lines, one can first-order define the multiplication using this automatic family:

> $x \cdot y = z$ if either at least one of x, y and also z are 0 or $x = 1$ and $y = z$ or $y = 1$ and $x = z$ or all are nonzero and neither x nor y is 1 and there exists an $e \in D$ such that $conv(0, 0), conv(1, y), conv(x, z)$ are all three in L_e.

As the grid G has to be dense and is a ring with automatic addition and comparison and as $G \subset \mathbb{R}$, the ring G is an integral domain and furthermore, G has an automatic multiplication by the above first-order definition. Khoussainov, Nies, Rubin and Stephan [12] showed that no integral domain is automatic, hence the collection of all lines cannot be an automatic family, independent of the choice of the grid.

Similarly one can consider the family of all triangles.

Theorem 8. *Independently of the choice of the semiautomatic grid G, the family of all triangles in the plane is not an automatic family. However, every triangle with corner points in $G \times G$ is a regular set.*

Proof. For the first result, assume that $\{L_e : e \in D\}$ is a family of all triangles – when viewed as closed subsets of $G \times G$ – which are represented in the grid and that this family contains at least all triangles with corner points in $G \times G$. Now one can define for $x, y, z > 0$ the multiplication-relation $z = x \cdot y$ using this family as follows:

$z = x \cdot y \Leftrightarrow$ some $e \in D$ satisfies the following conditions:
$\forall v, w \in G$ with $v \leq 0 \, [(v, w) \in L_e \Leftrightarrow (v, w) = (0, 0)]$,
$\forall w \in G \, [(1, w) \in L_e \Leftrightarrow 0 \leq w \wedge w \leq y]$,
$\forall w \in G \, [(x, w) \in L_e \Leftrightarrow 0 \leq w \wedge w \leq z]$.

This definition can be extended to a definition for the multiplication on full G with a straightforward case-distinction. Again this cannot happen as then the grid would form an infinite automatic integral domain which does not exist.

However, given a triangle with corner points $(x, y), (x', y'), (x'', y'')$, note that one can find that linear functions from $G \times G$ into G which are nonnegative iff the input point is on the right side of the line through (x, y) and (x', y'). So one would require that the function

$$f(v, w) = (w - y) \cdot (x' - x) - (v - x) \cdot (y' - y)$$

is either always nonpositive or always nonnegative, depending on which side of the line the triangle lies; by multiplying f with -1, one can enforce nonnegativeness. Note here that $x' - x$ and $y' - y$ are constants and multiplying with constants is automatic, as the ring has a semiautomatic multiplication. Thus a point is in the triangle or on its border iff all three automatic functions associated with the three border-lines of the triangle do not have negative values. This allows to show that every triangle with corner points in $G \times G$ is regular.   □

Note that this also implies that polygons with all corner points being in $G \times G$ are regular subsets of the plane $G \times G$.

Proposition 9. *Moving a polygon by a distance (v, w) can be done in any grid, as it only requires adding (v, w) to the coordinates of each points. However, rotating by $30°$ or $45°$ is possible in some but not all grids.*

Proof. Note that the formula for rotating around $30°$, one needs to map each point (x, y) by the mapping $(x, y) \mapsto (\cos(30°)x - \sin(30°)y, \sin(30°)x + \cos(30°)y)$ and similarly for $45°$ and $60°$. For $30°$, as $\sin(30°) = 1/2$ and $\cos(30°) = \sqrt{3}/2$, one needs a grid which allows to divide by 2 and multiply by $\sqrt{3}$, an example is given by the grid of Example 6. For rotating by $60°$, as it is twice doing a rotation by $30°$, the same requirements on the grid need to be there. For rotating by $45°$, the grid from Example 5 can be used. However, these operations cannot be done with grids which do not have the corresponding roots and also do not have the possibility to divide by 2. In particular, the grids $\mathbb{D}_b$ do not allow to multiply by roots and those grids of the form $\mathbb{Z} \cup \sqrt{c} \cdot \mathbb{Z}$ in prior work [8] do not allow to divide by 2. Furthermore, the authors are not aware of any grid which has both, $\sqrt{2}$ and $\sqrt{3}$ and thus allow to rotate by both, $30°$ and $45°$.   □

Remark 10. A grid allows to represent all equilateral triangles with side-length in G iff $\sqrt{3}$ and $1/2$ are both in G.

Remark 11. Note that one can represent a word $a_5 a_4 \ldots a_1 a_0 . a_{-1} a_{-2} \ldots a_{-7}$ also by starting with a_0 and then putting alternatingly the digits of even and odd indices given and one can show that in this representation, the same semi-automaticity properties are valid as in the previously considered representation. However, one gets one additional relation: One can recognise whether two digits a_{-m} and a_n satisfy that $n = m + c$ for a given integer constant c. This is used in the following example.

Example 12. The family $\{E_d : d \in D\}$ of all axis-parallel rectangles is an automatic family in all grids. Furthermore, let $d \equiv d'$ denote that E_d and $E_{d'}$ have the same area. In no grid, this relation $\equiv$ is automatic, as otherwise one could reconstruct the multiplication.

For p being a prime power, in the grid $(\mathbb{D}_p, +, =, <; \cdot)$ from Example 3, the relation $\equiv$ is semiautomatic using the representation given in Remark 11. To see this, for a given area $\ell \cdot p^k$, (i) one can disjunct over all factorisations $\ell_1 \cdot \ell_2$ of ℓ which are pairs of natural numbers not divisible by p, then (ii) check whether the length of the sides of a given rectangle are of the form $\ell_1 \cdot p^i$ and $\ell_2 \cdot p^j$ with $i + j = k$, where i, j are the positions of the last nonzero digits in the p-adic representation of the lengths and (iii) check, by Remark 11, whether $i + j$ are the given constant k. Note that representations using prime powers can be translated into representations based on the corresponding primes.

However, for grids such as $(\mathbb{D}_6, +, =, <; \cdot)$, where b is a composite number other than a prime power, this method does not work. This is mainly because one needs to use base 6 for the comparison $<$ and then a finite automaton cannot see whether the two sides are, for example, of lengths 2^k and 2^{-k} when recognising squares of area 1. Knowing that this method does not work, however, does not say that no other method works. It is an open problem whether one can find a semiautomatic grid which allows to divide by 6 and to represent axis-parallel rectangles in a way such that checking whether two rectangles have same area is semiautomatic. The same applies to the grids of Examples 5 and 6.

4   Cube Roots

Jain, Khoussainov, Stephan, Teng and Zou [8] did not find any example of other roots than square roots to be represented in a semiautomatic ordered ring. The following example represents a cube root.

Example 13. There is a grid which contains $\sqrt[3]{7}$. Furthermore, there is a grid which contains $\sqrt[3]{65}$ and $1/2$.

For the first, as one does not want to represent a proper rational, p_1 is not needed. For this, one chooses

1. $u^{-1} = 2 - \sqrt[3]{7}$,
2. $p_2(u) = 2 - u^{-1} = \sqrt[3]{7}$,
3. $p_3(u) = 1 - 12u^{-1} + 6u^{-2} - u^{-3} = 0$ and $p_4(u) = -p_3(u)$ with $\ell = -1$,
4. Instead of a flat $\hat{c}$, one uses a bit different bound for the algorithm, namely $|a_k| \le 16\hat{c}$, $|a_{k-1}| \le 4\hat{c}$ and $|a_{k-2}| \le \hat{c}$ for $\hat{c} = 360$.

The equations for p_3, p_4 follow from $p_3(u) = (p_2(u))^3 - 7$. Note that $11 < u < 12$ and $u^{-1} + u^{-2} + \dots \le 1/10$. Furthermore, the coefficients in the normal form are between -12 and $+12$ and, when three numbers are added coefficientwise, between -36 and $+36$. Let $p = \sum_k a_k \cdot u^k$ be such a sum of three numbers whose sign has to be determined; all the coefficients have absolute values up to 36.

The main thing is that the algorithm can detect the sign of the number whenever the first three coefficients overshoot for the first time. Note that they start with $(0, 0, 0)$ and so one runs the updates $a_{k-k'} = a_{k-k'} - a_k \cdot d_{-k'}$ simultaneously for $k' = 1, 2, 3$ and then sets $a_k = 0$ and $k = k - 1$. Here $d.$ are coefficients of p_3. Assume that the update would make the coefficients to overshoot for the first time and let $k, a_k, a_{k-1}, a_{k-2}, a_{k-3}$ and $p = \sum_{k'} a_{k'} u^{k'}$ denote the values just before the update.

Without loss of generality, assume that $a_k > 0$ and it will be shown that this implies that the polynomial p would be positive. Note that before the update, for all $k' < k$, $|a_{k'}| \le 4\hat{c}$ and $|\sum_{k' < k} a_{k'} u^{k'}| \le 0.4 \cdot \hat{c} \cdot u^k$.

If a_{k-3} grows above $\hat{c}$ at the update then $a_k \ge \hat{c} \cdot 9/10$ and $p > (0.9 \cdot \hat{c} - \sum_{k' \le -1} a_{k+k'} \cdot u^{k'}) \cdot u^k \ge (0.9 - 0.4) \cdot \hat{c} \cdot u^k > 0$.

If a_{k-2} grows below $-4\hat{c}$ at the update but a_{k-3} stays inside the bound then $a_k \ge \hat{c} \cdot 3 \cdot 1/6$ and $p > (0.5 - 0.4) \cdot \hat{c} \cdot u^k > 0$.

If a_{k-1} grows beyond $16\hat{c}$ at the update but a_{k-2} and a_{k-3} stay inside their bounds then $a_k \ge \hat{c} \cdot 12 \cdot 1/12$ and $p > (1 - 0.4) \cdot \hat{c} \cdot u^k > 0$.

Thus there is a semiautomatic grid containing $\sqrt[3]{7}$. One similarly proves the second item that there is a semiautomatic grid containing $\sqrt[3]{65}$ and $1/2$.

5   Representing All Reals

Now a comment on the ω-automatic approach [2,4,9]. The reals with addition and multiplication and infinite integral domains in general are not ω-automatic [19]. It is also clear that $(\mathbb{R}, +; \cdot)$ is not ω-semiautomatic, as one otherwise would need uncountably many different ω-automata for recognising the uncountably many functions $x \mapsto r \cdot x$ for constants $r \in \mathbb{R}$. So the best what one can expect is that $(\mathbb{R}, +, <, =)$ is ω-automatic and that there are countably many functions $f_r : x \mapsto r \cdot x$ which are ω-automatic as well. These functions certainly include, independent of the ring representation, all f_r with $r \in \mathbb{Q}$, as one only verifies the relation $x \cdot r = y$ and for $r = i/j$ this is equivalent with verifying $x \cdot i = y \cdot j$ with i, j are integers and multiplication with integers can be realised by repeated self-addition. The following result shows that one can carry over ideas of Theorem 4 to ω-automatic structures in order to get that multiplication with all constants from $\mathbb{Q}[\sqrt{b}]$ are ω-automatic where $b \ge 2$ is given. As all reals are represented and multiplication by rational constants comes for free, one can can use ω-versions of the previously known representations [8, Theorem 26].

Theorem 14. *There is an ω-automatic representation of the reals where addition, subtraction and comparisons are ω-automatic and furthermore the multiplication with any constant from $\mathbb{Q}[\sqrt{b}]$ is also an ω-automatic unary function.*

References

1. Blumensath, A., Grädel, E.: Automatic structures. In: Fifteenth Annual IEEE Symposium on Logic in Computer Science, LICS 2000, pp. 51–62 (2000)
2. Boigelot, B., Jodogne, S., Wolper, P.: An effective decision procedure for linear arithmetic over the integers and reals. ACM Trans. Comput. Logic **6**(3), 614–633 (2005)
3. Case, J., Jain, S., Seah, S., Stephan, F.: Automatic functions, linear time and learning. Logical Methods Comput. Sci. **9**(3) (2013)
4. Culik II, K., Kari, J.: Computational fractal geometry with WFA. Acta Informatica **34**, 151–166 (1997)
5. Epstein, D.B.A., Cannon, J.W., Holt, D.F., Levy, S.V.F., Paterson, M.S., Thurston, W.P.: Word Processing in Groups. Jones and Bartlett Publishers, Boston (1992)
6. Hodgson, B.R.: Théories décidables par automate fini. Ph.D. thesis, Département de mathématiques et de statistique, Université de Montréal (1976)
7. Hodgson, B.R.: Décidabilité par automate fini. Annales des sciences mathématiques du Québec **7**(1), 39–57 (1983)
8. Jain, S., Khoussainov, B., Stephan, F., Teng, D., Zou, S.: Semiautomatic structures. Theory Comput. Syst. **61**(4), 1254–1287 (2017)
9. Jürgensen, H., Staiger, L., Yamasaki, H.: Finite automata encoding geometric figures. Theor. Comput. Sci. **381**(2–3), 20–30 (2007)
10. Khoussainov, B., Minnes, M.: Three lectures on automatic structures. In: Proceedings of the Logic Colloquium 2007. Lecture Notes in Logic, vol. 35, pp. 132–176 (2010)
11. Khoussainov, B., Nerode, A.: Automatic presentations of structures. In: Leivant, D. (ed.) LCC 1994. LNCS, vol. 960, pp. 367–392. Springer, Heidelberg (1995). https://doi.org/10.1007/3-540-60178-3_93
12. Khoussainov, B., Nies, A., Rubin, S., Stephan, F.: Automatic structures: richness and limitations. Logical Methods Comput. Sci. **3**(2) (2007)
13. Nies, A., Semukhin, P.: Finite automata presentable Abelian groups. Ann. Pure Appl. Logic **161**, 458–467 (2009)
14. Nies, A., Thomas, R.: FA-presentable groups and rings. J. Algebra **320**, 569–585 (2008)
15. Oliver, G.P., Thomas, R.M.: Automatic presentations for finitely generated groups. In: Diekert, V., Durand, B. (eds.) STACS 2005. LNCS, vol. 3404, pp. 693–704. Springer, Heidelberg (2005). https://doi.org/10.1007/978-3-540-31856-9_57
16. Rubin, S.: Automata presenting structures: a survey of the finite string case. Bull. Symb. Logic **14**, 169–209 (2008)
17. Stephan, F.: Automatic structures - recent results and open questions. In: Third International Conference on Science and Engineering in Mathematics, Chemistry and Physics, ScieTech 2015, Journal of Physics: Conference Series, vol. 622, isssue no. 1742/6596/622/1 (2015). https://iopscience.iop.org/issue/1742-6596/622/1, 10 pages, Paper No. 012013

18. Tsankov, T.: The additive group of the rationals does not have an automatic presentation. J. Symb. Logic **76**(4), 1341–1351 (2011)
19. Zaid, F.A., Grädel, E., Kaiser, L., Pakusa, W.: Model-theoretic properties of ω-automatic structures. Theory Comput. Syst. **55**, 856–880 (2014)

Automata

Boolean Monadic Recursive Schemes as a Logical Characterization of the Subsequential Functions

Siddharth Bhaskar[1(⊠)], Jane Chandlee[2], Adam Jardine[3],
and Christopher Oakden[3]

[1] DIKU, Københavns Universitet, 2100 Copenhagen, Denmark
sbhaskar@di.ku.dk
[2] Haverford College, Haverford, PA, USA
jchandlee@haverford.edu
[3] Rutgers University, New Brunswick, NJ, USA
{adam.jardine,chris.oakden}@rutgers.edu

Abstract. This paper defines boolean monadic recursive schemes (BMRSs), a restriction on recursive programs, and shows that when interpreted as transductions on strings they describe exactly the subsequential functions. We discuss how this new result furthers the study of the connections between logic, formal languages and functions, and automata.

Keywords: Subsequential functions · Logic · Recursive program schemes · Finite automata

1 Introduction

A fundamental result in the connection between automata and logic is that of Elgot [7], Büchi [1], and Trakhtenbrot [21], which states that sentences in monadic second-order (MSO) logic describe exactly the same class of formal languages as finite-state acceptors (FSAs); namely, the regular class of languages. Further work established many connections between restrictions on MSO, restrictions on FSAs, and sub-classes of the regular languages [14,20].

More recently, a major result of Engelfriet and Hoogeboom shows the relationship between MSO and regular *functions* on strings—that is, exactly those functions described by two-way finite state transducers [9]. Essentially, string functions can be described by a MSO *interpretation* in which the binary successor relation and alphabet labels of the output string are defined by a series of binary and unary predicates in the MSO logic of the input strings, relativized over a *copy set* which allows the output string to be larger than the input string. Each element in the output string is thus a copy of an index in the input string, and the character it receives and where it is in the order is determined by which predicates are satisfied by the input string at that index. This technique has

© Springer Nature Switzerland AG 2020
A. Leporati et al. (Eds.): LATA 2020, LNCS 12038, pp. 157–169, 2020.
https://doi.org/10.1007/978-3-030-40608-0_10

allowed a rich study of the relationship between sub-MSO logics and restrictions on finite-state transducers [10,11] parallel to the earlier work on logic and finite-state automata and languages.

However, there remain some interesting classes for which no logical characterization has been previously established. In this paper, we investigate the *subsequential* functions, a strict sub-class of the *rational* functions, or those that are describable by one-way finite-state transducers.[1] While a weak class, there are a number of reasons why the subsequential class is a worthy object of study. From a theoretical perspective, the subsequential functions admit an abstract characterization that generalizes the Myhill-Nerode equivalence classes of regular languages [19]. This property makes the subsequential functions learnable from a sample of positive data [18]. In terms of practical applications, the subsequential functions have applications to speech and language processing [16], and form a hypothesis for the computational upper bound of functions in certain domains of natural language phonology [12,13].

In this paper, we define *boolean monadic recursive schemes* (BMRSs), a restriction on the general notion of a recursive program scheme in the sense of Moschovakis [17]. As indicated by the name, these schemes recursively define a series of unary functions that take as inputs indices from a string and return a boolean value. A system of BMRS functions can be used to express a logical transduction in the sense of Engelfriet and Hoogeboom by assigning these functions to symbols in an output alphabet. An output string then consists of the characters whose functions are true at each index in the input string. We show that string transductions defined by BMRS transductions with predecessor or successor describe exactly the left- and right-subsequential functions, respectively. This is an entirely novel result; the closest result in the literature is that of [6], who give a fragment of least-fixed point logic that captures strict subsets of the left- and right-subsequential functions. As we discuss at the end of the paper, the current result allows for further study of the connections among subclasses of the subsequential functions and of rational functions in general.

This paper is structured as follows. Sections 2 and 3 establish the notation and definitions for strings, subsequential functions, and subsequential transducers. Section 4 establishes BMRSs and BMRS transductions, and Sect. 5 shows the equivalence between BMRS transductions and subsequential functions. Sections 6 and 7 discuss the implications of this result and conclude the paper.

2   Preliminaries

An alphabet Σ is a finite set of symbols; let Σ^* be all strings over Σ, including λ, the empty string. We will frequently make use of special left and right string boundary symbols $\rtimes, \ltimes \notin \Sigma$. We denote by $\rtimes\Sigma^*\ltimes$ the set $\{\rtimes w \ltimes \mid w \in \Sigma^*\}$. Let $\Sigma_\rtimes = \Sigma \cup \{\rtimes\}$, likewise $\Sigma_\ltimes = \Sigma \cup \{\ltimes\}$ and $\Sigma_\bowtie = \Sigma \cup \{\rtimes, \ltimes\}$. For a string w, $|w|$ indicates the length of w. We write w^r for the reversal of w.

---

[1] We mean *subsequential* in the sense of Schützenberger and Mohri; other authors (e.g. [11]) use the term *sequential* for the same class.

A string u is a *prefix* of w, written $u \sqsubseteq w$, iff $w = uv$ for some string v. For a set $L \subseteq \Sigma^*$ of strings let the *common prefixes* be $\mathtt{comprefs}(L) = \bigcap_{w \in L}\{u \mid u \sqsubseteq w\}$. The *longest common prefix* of L is the maximum element in $\mathtt{comprefs}(L)$: $\mathtt{lcp}(L) = w \in \mathtt{comprefs}(L)$ s.t. for all $v \in \mathtt{comprefs}(L), |v| \le |w|$.

3 Subsequential Functions and Transducers

3.1 Abstract Definition

We first define the subsequential functions based on the notion of *tails* [16,19]. Let $f : \Sigma^* \to \Gamma^*$ be an arbitrary function and $f^p(x) = \mathtt{lcp}(\{f(xu) \mid u \in \Sigma^*\})$. Then of course, for every u, $f^p(x) \sqsubseteq f(xu)$. Now let the *tail function* $f_x(u)$ be defined as v such that $f^p(x)v = f(xu)$. This function represents the *tails* of x. This allows us to define the subsequential functions as follows.

Definition 1 (Left-subsequential). *A function f is* left-subsequential *iff the set $\{f_x \mid x \in \Sigma^*\}$ is finite.*

Example 1. For input alphabet $\Sigma = \{a\}$, the function f defined as

$$f(a^n) = \begin{array}{ll} (abb)^{n/2}c & \text{if } n \text{ is even;} \\ (abb)^{(n-1)/2}ad & \text{if } n \text{ is odd,} \end{array}$$

is left-subsequential. Note that for any $x = a^n$ for an even n, $f^p(x) = (abb)^{n/2}$, and so $f_x = f$. For any $y = a^n$ for an odd n, then $f^p(y) = (abb)^{(n-1)/2}a$, and so f_y is the function $f_y(a^m) = d$ if $m = 0$; $bb \cdot f(a^{m-1})$ otherwise. Then f is describable by these two tail functions $\{f_x, f_y\}$.

Conversely, the function g defined as

$$g(a^n) = \begin{array}{ll} ca^{n-1} & \text{if } n \text{ is even;} \\ da^{n-1} & \text{if } n \text{ is odd,} \end{array}$$

is not left-subsequential. Note that for any $x = a^n$, $g^p(x) = \lambda$. This is because $\{g(xu) \mid u \in \Sigma^*\}$ includes both ca^i and da^j for some i and j. Because $g_x(u)$ is defined as v such that $g^p(x)v = g(xu)$, and because $g^p(x) = \lambda$, $g_x(u) = g(xu)$. The consequence of this is that for any $x = a^n$ and $y = a^m$ for a distinct $m \ne n$, for any u, $g_x(u) \ne g_y(u)$. Thus the set of tails functions for g is an infinite set $\{g_{x_1}, g_{x_2}, \ldots\}$ of distinct functions for each $x_i = a^i$.

The right-subsequential functions are those that are the mirror image of some left-subsequential function.

Definition 2 (Right-subsequential). *A function f is* right-subsequential *iff there is some left-subsequential function f_ℓ such that for any string in the domain of f, $f(w) = (f_\ell(w^r))^r$.*

We leave it to the reader to show that g is right-subsequential. Thus, the subsequential functions are those functions that are either left- or right-subsequential.

3.2   Subsequential Finite-State Transducers

A (left-)subsequential finite-state transducer (SFST) for an input alphabet Σ and an output alphabet Γ is a tuple $\mathcal{T} = \langle Q, q_0, Q_f, \delta, o, \omega \rangle$, where Q is the set of states, $q_0 \in Q$ is the (unique) start state, $Q_f \subseteq Q$ is the set of final states, $\delta : Q \times \Sigma \to Q$ is the transition function, $o : Q \times \Sigma \to \Gamma^*$ is the output function, and $\omega : Q_f \to \Gamma^*$ is the final function. We define the reflexive, transitive closure of δ and o as $\delta^* : Q \times \Sigma^* \to Q$ and $o^* : Q \times \Sigma^* \to \Gamma^*$ in the usual way.

The semantics of a SFST is a transduction $t(\mathcal{T})$ defined as follows; let $t = t(\mathcal{T})$. For $w \in \Sigma^*$, $t(w) = uv$ where $o^*(q_0, w) = u$, and $\omega(q_f) = v$ if $\delta^*(q_0, w) = q_f$ for some $q_f \in Q_f$; $t(w)$ undefined otherwise.

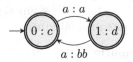

Fig. 1. A graph representation of the SFST for the function f from Example 1.

Theorem 1 ([16,19]). *The left-subsequential functions are exactly those describable by a SFST reading a string left-to-right. The right-subsequential functions are exactly those describable by a SFST reading a string right-to-left and reversing the output.*

Theorem 2 ([16]). *Both the left- and right-subsequential functions are a strict subset of the rational functions.*

For more properties of the subsequential functions and their application to speech and language processing see [16].

4   Boolean Monadic Recursive Schemes

4.1   Syntax and Semantics

We identify strings in Σ^* with structures of the form $\mathbf{S} = \langle D; \sigma_1, \sigma_2, ..., \sigma_n, p, s \rangle$ where the *domain* D is the set of indices; for each character $\sigma \in \Sigma_{\bowtie}$, we also write σ_i for the unary relation $\sigma_i \subseteq D$ selecting the indices of that character (and we assume that the least and greatest indices contain the characters $\rtimes$ and $\ltimes$, respectively); p is the predecessor function on indices (fixing the least index); and s is the successor function on indices (fixing the greatest index). As an abbreviatory convention we use $\mathbf{x} - i$ for i applications of p to $\mathbf{x}$, and likewise $\mathbf{x} + i$ for i applications of s. (E.g. $\mathbf{x} - 2$ is the same as $p(p(\mathbf{x}))$).

Boolean monadic recursive schemes are simple programs that operate over such string structures. They are a particular case of the *recursive programs* of Moschovakis [17]. We briefly review the syntax and semantics of such recursive programs in this particular signature, then impose (Definition 3) the pertinent syntactic restriction to obtain BMRSs.

Data and Variables. We have two types of data: boolean values and string indices. We have two countably infinite set of variables: *(index) variables* X, which range over string indices, and *recursive function names* F. Each recursive function name $f \in F$ comes with an *arity* $n \in \mathbb{N}$ and an *output type*, either "index" or "boolean". Function names f of arity n and type s range over n-ary functions from string indices to s.

Terms. Terms are given by the following grammar

$$T \rightarrow x \mid T_1 = T_2 \mid \top \mid \bot \mid f(T_1, \ldots, T_k) \mid$$
$$s(T_1) \mid p(T_1) \mid \sigma(T_1) \ (\sigma \in \Sigma_{\bowtie}) \mid \text{if } T_1 \text{ then } T_2 \text{ else } T_3$$

Terms inherit "boolean" or "index" types inductively from their variables and function names, and term formation is subject to the usual typing rules: for $f(T_1, \ldots, T_k)$, $\sigma(T_1)$, $s(T_1)$ or $p(T_1)$, the type of each T_I must be "index"; for $T_1 = T_2$, the types of T_1 and T_2 must be the same; for and "if T_1 then T_2 else T_3," then the type of T_1 must be "boolean," and the types of T_2 and T_3 must agree.

Programs. A *program* consists of a tuple $(f_1, \ldots, f_k)$ of function names, plus k lines of the form $f_i(x_{1_i}, \ldots, x_{n_i}) = T_i$, where T_i is a term whose type agrees with the output type of f_i, every variable that occurs in T_i is some x_{i_j}, and every function name that occurs in T_i is some f_j. Syntactically, we will write

$$f_1(\vec{x}_1) = T_1(\vec{f}, \vec{x}_1)$$
$$\vdots$$
$$f_k(\vec{x}_k) = T_k(\vec{f}, \vec{x}_k)$$

to indicate that the above properties hold.

Semantics. We impose the usual least fixed-point semantics on recursive programs. Briefly; over a given string, terms denote functionals which are monotone relative to extension relation on partial functions. We define the semantics of a program to be the first coordinate $\bar{f}_1$ of the least fixed-point $(\bar{f}_1, \ldots, \bar{f}_k)$ of the monotone operator $(f, \ldots, f_k) \mapsto (T_1(\vec{f}), \ldots, T_k(\vec{f}))$ [17].

Definition 3. *A* boolean monadic recursive scheme (BMRS) *is a program in which the arity of every function name in the program is one, and the output type of every function name in the program is "boolean."*

Boolean monadic recursive schemes compute (partial) functions from string indices to booleans, or equivalently (partial) subsets of indices. For example, the following scheme detects exactly those indices with some preceding b.

$$f(x) = \text{if } \rtimes (p(x)) \text{ then } \bot \text{ else if } b(p(x)) \text{ then } \top \text{ else } f(p(x)) \qquad (1)$$

4.2   Schemes as Definitions of String Transductions

We can define a string transduction $t : \Sigma^* \to \Gamma^*$ via a BMRS interpretation as follows. Fix a *copy set* $C = \{1, \ldots, m\}$ and for $n = |\Gamma|$ consider a system T of equations with a set of recursive functions $\vec{\mathbf{f}} = (\gamma_1^1, \ldots, \gamma_1^m, \gamma_2^1, \ldots, \gamma_n^m, \mathbf{f}_1, \ldots, \mathbf{f}_k)$; that is, with a function γ^c for each $\gamma \in \Gamma$ and $c \in C$.

Following the definition of logical string transductions [9,10], the semantics of T given an input model $\mathbf{S}$ with a universe D as follows. For each $d \in D$, we output a copy d^c of d if and only if there is exactly one $\gamma \in \Gamma$ for $c \in C$ such that $\gamma^c(\mathbf{x}) \in T$ evaluates to $\top$ when $\mathbf{x}$ is mapped to d. We fix the order of these output copies to be derived from C and the order on D induced by the predecessor function p: for any two copies d^c and d^e of a single index d, $d^c < d^e$ iff $c < e$ in the order on C, and for any copies d_i^c and d_j^e for distinct input indices d_i, d_j, $d_i^c < d_j^e$ iff $d_i < d_j$ in the order on the indices in $\mathbf{S}$. We fix the order due to the relation between order-preserving logical transductions and one-tape finite-state transducers [10].

This semantics of T thus defines a string transduction $t = t(T)$ where for a string $w \in \Sigma^*$ of length ℓ, $t(w) = u_0 u_1 \ldots u_\ell u_{\ell+1}$, where each $u_i = \gamma_1 \ldots \gamma_r$ if and only if for each γ_j, $1 \le j \le r$, γ_j is the unique symbol in Γ for $j \in C$ such that $\gamma_j^j(\mathbf{x})$ evaluates to $\top$ when $\mathbf{x}$ is assigned to i in the structure of $\rtimes w \ltimes$. An example is given in Example 2.

To describe partial functions we can add to $\vec{\mathbf{f}}$ a special function $\mathtt{def}(\mathbf{x})$ and specify the semantics of t to state that $t(w)$ is defined iff $\mathtt{def}(\mathbf{x})$ evaluates to $\top$ for element ℓ in w.

Example 2. The following is a BMRS definition of f from Example 1 using strings models from $\rtimes \Sigma^* \ltimes$. The copy set is $C = \{1, 2\}$.

$a^1(\mathbf{x}) =$ if $a(\mathbf{x})$ then
    if $\rtimes (p(\mathbf{x}))$ then $\top$ else $b^1(p(\mathbf{x}))$
    else $\perp$
$a^2(\mathbf{x}) = \perp$
$b^1(\mathbf{x}) =$ if $a(\mathbf{x})$ then $a^1(p(x))$ else $\perp$
$b^2(\mathbf{x}) =$ if $a(\mathbf{x})$ then $a^1(p(x))$ else $\perp$

$c^1(\mathbf{x}) =$ if $\ltimes (\mathbf{x})$ then $b^1(p(\mathbf{x}))$ else $\perp$
$c^2(\mathbf{x}) = \perp$
$d^1(\mathbf{x}) =$ if $\ltimes (\mathbf{x})$ then $a^1(p(\mathbf{x}))$ else $\perp$
$d^2(\mathbf{x}) = \perp$

The following shows how this maps $aaaaa$ to $abbabbad$:

	0	1	2	3	4	5	6
Input:	$\rtimes$	a	a	a	a	a	$\ltimes$
Copy 1:		a	b	a	b	a	d
Copy 2:			b		b		

We define two important variants of BMRS logic. For BMRS systems of equations over a set of recursive function symbols $\mathbf{f}$, we say a system of equations $T \in \mathrm{BMRS}^p$ iff it contains no terms of the form $s(T_1)$ for any term T_1, and likewise $T \in \mathrm{BMRS}^s$ iff it contains no terms of the form $p(T_1)$ for any term T_1. We define these as they fix the 'direction' of the recursion, which will be important in connecting them to the left- and right-subsequential functions.

4.3   Convergence and Well-Definedness

We only want to consider BMRS that compute well-defined transductions. Therefore, we require that for each string $w \in \Sigma^*$, each index i of w, and each $c \in C$ and $\gamma \in \Gamma$, every function $\gamma^c(i)$ converges, and furthermore for each c, there is a unique γ such that $\gamma^c(i) = \top$.

This is of course a semantic property, which is not an issue as far as the following proofs of extensional equivalence are concerned. However, there is an effective way of transforming a BMRS T into a BMRS T' such that T' computes a well-defined transduction, and agrees with T on inputs where T is well-defined.[2] Therefore, considering partially-defined schemata do not increase the computational power in any appreciable way.

5   Equivalence

5.1   Subsequential Functions Are BMRS-Definable

For a left-subsequential function $f : \Sigma^* \to \Gamma^*$, we can define an equivalent function in BMRS^p over models of strings in $\ltimes \Sigma^* \rtimes$. We do this by giving a construction of its SFST.

For an SFST $T = \langle Q, q_0, Q_f, \delta, o, \omega \rangle$, where Q is the set of k states, we construct a BMRS^p system of equations T over the set of recursive functions $\vec{f} = (\gamma_1^1, ..., \gamma_1^m, \gamma_2^1, ..., \gamma_n^m, q_0, ..., q_{k-1})$, where $n = |\Gamma|$ and m is the maximum length of any output of o or ω. The definitions in T are fixed as follows. First, we define $q_0, ..., q_{k-1}$ to parallel the transition function δ. For each state $q \in Q$ we define its corresponding recursive function symbol q as

$$q(x) = \quad \text{if } q_1(p(x)) \text{ then } \sigma_1(x) \qquad\qquad (2)$$
$$\text{else} \quad \text{if } q_2(p(x)) \text{ then } \sigma_2(x)$$
$$\text{else} \quad ...$$
$$\text{else} \quad \text{if } q_\ell(p(x)) \text{ then } \sigma_\ell(x)$$
$$\text{else} \quad \bot$$

where $q_1, ..., q_\ell$ is the set of states reaching q; that is, the set of states such that for each q_i, $\delta(q_i, \sigma_i) = q$. For the start state we instead set the final 'else' statement to x is the minimum element in the string; i.e. that $\ltimes(p(x))$.

We then define the set of functions $\gamma_1^1, ..., \gamma_1^m, \gamma_2^1, ..., \gamma_n^m$ representing the symbols in the output strings to parallel the output and final functions o and ω:

$$\gamma^c(x) = \quad \text{if } q_1(x) \text{ then } \sigma_1(x) \qquad\qquad (3)$$
$$\text{else} \quad \text{if } q_2(x) \text{ then } \sigma_2(x)$$
$$\text{else} \quad ...$$
$$\text{else} \quad \text{if } q_\ell(x) \text{ then } \sigma_n(x) \text{ else } \bot$$

---

[2] For example, we can augment a boolean monadic recursive scheme with a "clock" that returns some default value if the program does not terminate within a given polynomial number of steps. (For each BMRS, there is some polynomial which bounds the number of steps in each terminating computation). Using a large "switch statement," we can ensure that exactly one character gets printed.

for all states q_i whose output on σ_i has γ as the cth symbol. That is, for each q_i either $o(q_i, \sigma_i) = u_1 \gamma u_2$ or, if $\sigma_i = \ltimes$, that $\omega(q_i) = u_1 \gamma u_2$, where $|u_1| = c - 1$. If there are no such states we set $\gamma^c(\mathbf{x}) = \bot$.

Finally, in cases when $Q_f \subsetneq Q$ we can, via the definition of the semantics of BMRS transductions for partial functions, we set the equation for the special function $\mathtt{def}(\mathbf{x})$ determining when the function is defined as

$$
\mathtt{def}(\mathbf{x}) = \quad \text{if } \mathtt{q_1}(\mathbf{x}) \text{ then } \top \qquad\qquad (4)
$$
$$
\text{else} \quad \text{if } \mathtt{q_2}(\mathbf{x}) \text{ then } \top
$$
$$
\text{else} \quad \ldots
$$
$$
\text{else} \quad \text{if } \mathtt{q_\ell}(\mathbf{x}) \text{ then } \top \text{ else } \bot
$$

for $q_i \in Q_f$. When $Q_f = Q$, we set $\mathtt{def}(\mathbf{x}) = \top$.

An example definition modeling the SFST in Fig. 1, and an example computation for an input string $aaaa$ is given in Table 1.

Table 1. A BMRS transduction for the SFST in Fig. 1 (left) and an example derivation (right). The rows for $\mathtt{a^2}(\mathbf{x})$, $\mathtt{c^2}(\mathbf{x})$, and $\mathtt{d^2}(\mathbf{x})$ have been omitted.

			Input:	$\ltimes$ a a a a $\ltimes$
$\mathtt{def}(\mathbf{x}) = \top$				0 1 2 3 4 5
$\mathtt{q_0}(\mathbf{x})$	$=$	if $\mathtt{q_1}(p(\mathbf{x}))$ then $a(\mathbf{x})$ else $\rtimes (p(\mathbf{x}))$	$\mathtt{q_0}(\mathbf{x})$	$\bot$ $\top$ $\bot$ $\top$ $\bot$ $\top$
$\mathtt{q_1}(\mathbf{x})$	$=$	if $\mathtt{q_0}(p(\mathbf{x}))$ then $a(\mathbf{x})$ else $\bot$	$\mathtt{q_1}(\mathbf{x})$	$\bot$ $\bot$ $\top$ $\bot$ $\top$ $\bot$
$\mathtt{a^1}(\mathbf{x})$	$=$	if $\mathtt{q_0}(\mathbf{x})$ then $a(\mathbf{x})$ else $\bot$	$\mathtt{a^1}(\mathbf{x})$	$\bot$ $\top$ $\bot$ $\top$ $\bot$ $\bot$
$\mathtt{a^2}(\mathbf{x})$	$= \bot$		$\mathtt{b^1}(\mathbf{x})$	$\bot$ $\bot$ $\top$ $\bot$ $\top$ $\bot$
$\mathtt{b^1}(\mathbf{x})$	$=$	if $\mathtt{q_1}(\mathbf{x})$ then $a(\mathbf{x})$ else $\bot$	$\mathtt{b^2}(\mathbf{x})$	$\bot$ $\bot$ $\top$ $\bot$ $\top$ $\bot$
$\mathtt{b^2}(\mathbf{x})$	$=$	if $\mathtt{q_1}(\mathbf{x})$ then $a(\mathbf{x})$ else $\bot$	$\mathtt{c^1}(\mathbf{x})$	$\bot$ $\bot$ $\bot$ $\bot$ $\bot$ $\top$
$\mathtt{c^1}(\mathbf{x})$	$=$	if $\mathtt{q_0}(\mathbf{x})$ then $\ltimes (\mathbf{x})$ else $\bot$	$\mathtt{d^1}(\mathbf{x})$	$\bot$ $\bot$ $\bot$ $\bot$ $\bot$ $\bot$
$\mathtt{c^2}(\mathbf{x})$	$= \bot$		Output:	
$\mathtt{d^1}(\mathbf{x})$	$=$	if $\mathtt{q_1}(\mathbf{x})$ then $\ltimes (\mathbf{x})$ else $\bot$	Copy 1 :	a b a b c
$\mathtt{d^2}(\mathbf{x})$	$= \bot$		Copy 2 :	b b

Lemma 1. *Any left-subsequential function has some BMRS^p definition.*

Proof. It is sufficient to show that the above construction creates from any SFST $\mathcal{T}$ a BMRS^p system of equations T whose transduction $t(T) = t(\mathcal{T})$.

Consider any string in $w = \sigma_1 \ldots \sigma_n \in \Sigma^*$ of length n; we refer to the positions in $\ltimes w \ltimes$ as their indices $0, 1, \ldots, n+1$. From the construction $\mathtt{q_0}(\mathbf{x})$ is always true of position 1; likewise by definition $\mathcal{T}$ is in state q_0 at position 1. By definition (2) for T, whenever $\mathcal{T}$ is in state q_i, reads position i, and $\delta(q_i, \sigma_i) = q_j$, then $\mathtt{q_j}(\mathbf{x})$ in T evaluates to $\top$ for $i+1$, because 'if $\mathtt{q_i}(\mathbf{x})$ then $\sigma_i(\mathbf{x})$' is in the definition for $\mathtt{q_j}(\mathbf{x})$. By induction on δ^* it is thus the case that whenever $\mathcal{T}$ is in state q_i at position i, position i satisfies $\mathtt{q_i}(\mathbf{x})$ in T.

Let $o(q_i, \sigma_i) = u = \gamma_1...\gamma_m$ for any position i in w. By (3), for each γ_j there is a function $\gamma_j^j(\mathbf{x})$ whose definition includes 'if $\mathbf{q_i}(\mathbf{x})$ then $\sigma_i(x)$'. Because i satisfies $\mathbf{q_i}(\mathbf{x})$ in T, then each jth copy of i will be γ_j, and so the output of i under T will also be $\gamma_1...\gamma_j = u$. This also holds for the output function ω.

Thus for any w, $t(T)(w) = w'$ implies that $t(T)(w) = w'$, and it is not hard to show that the reverse holds. $\qquad\square$

The following lemma shows that the same is true for right-subsequential functions and BMRS^s, which follows by the same logic as for Lemma 1.

Lemma 2. *Any right-subsequential function has some BMRS^s definition.*

5.2   BMRS^p and BMRS^s-Definable String Functions Are Subsequential

To show the converse, we show that for any well-defined BMRS^p transduction T, for $f = t(T)$, the sets $\{f_x \mid x \in \Sigma^*\}$ are finite. For a copy set $C = \{1, ..., m\}$ and for $n = |\Gamma|$ consider a system T of equations with a set of recursive functions

$$\vec{f} = (\gamma_1^1, ..., \gamma_1^m, \gamma_2^1, ..., \gamma_n^m, \mathbf{f}_1, ..., \mathbf{f}_k);$$

let F be the set of function names appearing in $\vec{f}$, and let ℓ be the maximum number such that $\mathbf{x} - \ell$ appears as a term in T.

First, define $\mathtt{sats}(w, i) = \{\mathbf{f} \in T \mid \mathbf{f}(i) = \top \text{ in } w\}$ to identify the functions in T true in w at index i. The following fact will be used throughout this proof.

Remark 1. For any $\mathbf{f} \in F$ and string $w \in \ltimes \Sigma^* \rtimes$, the value of $\mathbf{f}(i)$ can be calculated from the sets $F_\ell, F_{\ell-1}, ..., F_1$, where for each $1 \le j \le \ell$, $F_j = \mathtt{sats}(w, i-j)$.

Proof. Let $\mathbf{f}(\mathbf{x}) = T_{\mathbf{f}}$ be the equation for $\mathbf{f}$ in T. By the definition of T, ℓ is the maximum number of times the p function can be applied to a variable in any term in T. Thus, for any function $\mathbf{g} \in F$, $T_{\mathbf{f}}$ can only contain $\mathbf{g}(\mathbf{x} - h)$ for at most some $h \le \ell$. Thus, in terms of the semantics of $\mathbf{f}(i)$ for some index i in w, the value of $\mathbf{g}(i - h)$ can be determined by whether $\mathbf{g}$ is in F_h. The remainder of the semantics $\mathbf{f}(i)$ then follows from the definition of the semantics of BMRSs. $\square$

The following states that $\mathtt{sats}(w, i)$ holds no matter how w is extended. This follows directly from Remark 1.

Remark 2. For any $w, v \in \ltimes \Sigma^* \rtimes$, $\mathtt{sats}(w, i) = \mathtt{sats}(wv, i)$.

Recall that among the functions in F there is a function $\gamma^c \in F$ for each $\gamma \in \Gamma$ and $c \in C$. Recall also that the semantics of BMRS transductions produces an output string u_i at each input index i such that γ is the cth position in u_i if and only if $\gamma^c(i)$ evaluates to $\top$. (The stipulation that there is only one such γ^c ensures that only a single output string is produced for each index). To refer to this string we define $\mathtt{out}(w, i) = \gamma_1\gamma_2...\gamma_h$ where each $\gamma_j \in \mathtt{sats}(w, i)$.

Then let $\text{out}_T(w) = \text{out}(w,1)\cdot\text{out}(w,2)\cdot...\cdot\text{out}(w,\text{last}(w))$, where $\text{last}(w)$ indicates the final index in w.

We can now connect these facts to the string function $f = t(T)$ described by T. Recall the technicality that the domain of f is Σ^* but T is defined over string models of the form $\ltimes \Sigma^* \ltimes$. First, the above allows us to make the following assertion about the relationship between out_T and f^p.

Remark 3. $\text{out}_T(\ltimes w) \sqsubseteq f^p(w)$.

Proof. This follows directly from Remark 2: the output at each index at w will be constant no matter how w is extended. Thus, $f^p(w)$ at least includes $\text{out}_T(\ltimes w)$.

The final piece is to define when two strings w and v are equivalent with respect to T, which we then show that they are equivalent with respect to f; that is, that $f_w = f_v$. Intuitively, w and v are equivalent if their final ℓ indices satisfy exactly the same functions in F. Formally,

$$w \equiv_T v \text{ iff for all } 0 \le i < \ell, \text{sats}(\ltimes w, \text{last}(\ltimes w) - i) = \text{sats}(\ltimes v, \text{last}(\ltimes v) - i)$$

Remark 4. The partition on Σ^* induced by $\equiv_T$ is finite.

Proof. For any sequence of ℓ indices, there are at most $(2^{|F|})^\ell$ possible sequences of subsets of F that they satisfy.

The following states the key implication that equivalence with respect to T implies equivalence with respect to f.

Lemma 3. *For any two strings* $w, v \in \Sigma^*$, $w \equiv_T v$ *implies* $f_w = f_v$.

Proof. First, for any $\sigma \in \Sigma_\ltimes$, $\text{out}(\ltimes w\sigma, \text{last}(\ltimes w\sigma)) = \text{out}(\ltimes v\sigma, \text{last}(\ltimes v\sigma))$. In other words, the string output at any additional σ following w and v is the same. This follows from Remark 1 and the fact that the final ℓ indices in $\ltimes w$ and $\ltimes v$ satisfy the same sets of functions in F.

For any string $u \in \Sigma^*$, then, by induction on the length of $u\ltimes$ it is clear that $f(wu) = \text{out}_T(\ltimes w)u'$ and $f(vu) = \text{out}_T(\ltimes v)u'$ for the same $u' \in \Gamma^*$. From this and Remark 3, we know that $f^p(w) = \text{out}_T(\ltimes w)u_1$ and $f^p(v) = \text{out}_T(\ltimes v)u_1$ for the same $u_1 \in \Gamma^*$. Clearly then for any $u \in \Sigma^*$, $f(wu) = f^p(w)u'$ and $f(vu) = f^p(v)u'$ and so by the definition of f_w and f_v, $f_w = f_v$.

Lemma 4. *For any BMRS^p transduction T, the function $f = t(T)$ is a left-subsequential function.*

Proof. The set $\{f_x \mid x \in \Sigma^*\}$ is finite: from Remark 4, $\equiv_T$ induces a finite partition on Σ^*, and by Lemma 3, for any two strings w, v in the same block in this partition, $f_w = f_v$. Thus there can only be finitely many such functions f_x.

We omit the proof for the following parallel lemma for BMRS^s.

Lemma 5. *For any BMRS^s transduction T, the function $f = t(T)$ is a right-subsequential function.*

5.3   Main Theorem

We now can give the central result of the paper.

Theorem 3. *BMRS^p (respectively, BMRS^s) transductions are equivalent to the left-subsequential (resp., right-subsequential) functions.*

Proof. From Lemmas 1, 2, 4, and 5.

6   Discussion

The above result provides the first logical characterization of the subsequential functions. A consequence of this is we can get a better understanding of subclasses of the subsequential functions. We sketch two here.

First, the *input strictly local* (ISL) functions are a strict subset of the subsequential class for which the output string is computed by referencing a bounded window in the *input* string only [2,3]. Briefly, a function is ISL iff there is some number k such that for any two strings w and v that share a $k - 1$ suffix, $f_w = f_v$. This class has attractive learnability properties [3] and empirically is relevant to processes in natural language phonology [5]. We omit a proof, but it is almost certainly the case that a BMRS system of equations T corresponds to an ISL function iff for each function symbol $f \in \vec{f}$, the definition of f contains no recursive function calls. This is further interesting in that it suggests that any left-subsequential function f has a ISL counterpart whose input alphabet subsumes the recursive function symbols in the BMRS^p definition of f.[3] This is strongly reminiscent of the old result that any regular language is the homomorphism of a strictly 2-local language [15].

A sister class to the ISL functions is the *output strictly local* (OSL) functions, which are those subsequential functions which compute the output string by referencing the current input and a bounded window in the output [2,4]. They are divided into two classes the left- and right-OSL functions depending on whether the string is read from the left or right. We conjecture that a BMRS system of equations T corresponds to an OSL function iff for each function $f_i \in f$ corresponding to $\gamma^c \in \Gamma$, for any non recursively-defined $\sigma(t)$ ($\sigma \in \Sigma$), then $t = x$. BMRS^p systems of equations of this type correspond to left-OSL functions, while BMRS^s systems of this type correspond to right-OSL functions.

Finally, this paper has limited its discussion to BMRS transductions restricted to either p or s, so an obvious open question is to what functions are described by BMRS transductions without this restriction. As any rational function is the composition of a right- and left-subsequential function [8], it is clear that BMRS transductions in general are strictly more expressive than either the BMRS^p and BMRS^s transductions. Based on this, we tentatively conjecture that the BMRS transductions in general are equivalent to the rational functions, but this claim requires more rigorous investigation than can be done here.

---

[3] We thank Jeff Heinz for pointing this out.

7   Conclusion

This paper has given the first logical characterization of the subsequential functions. As with previous work connecting logical, language-theoretic, and automata-theoretic characterizations of formal languages and functions, we are confident this will further study of the connections between subclasses of the subsequential functions, and subclasses of the rational functions in general.

References

1. Büchi, J.R.: Weak second-order arithmetic and finite automata. Z. Math. Log. Grundl. Mathmatik **6**, 66–92 (1960)
2. Chandlee, J.: Strictly Local Phonological Processes. Ph.D. thesis, University of Delaware (2014)
3. Chandlee, J., Eyraud, R., Heinz, J.: Learning strictly local subsequential functions. Trans. Assoc. Comput. Linguist. **2**, 491–503 (2014)
4. Chandlee, J., Eyraud, R., Heinz, J.: Output strictly local functions. In: Kornai, A., Kuhlmann, M. (eds.) Proceedings of the 14th Meeting on the Mathematics of Language (MoL 2014), Chicago, IL, pp. 52–63, July 2015
5. Chandlee, J., Heinz, J.: Strictly locality and phonological maps. Linguist. Inq. **49**, 23–60 (2018)
6. Chandlee, J., Jardine, A.: Autosegmental input-strictly local functions. Trans. Assoc. Comput. Linguist. **7**, 157–168 (2019)
7. Elgot, C.C.: Decision problems of finite automata design and related arithmetics. Trans. Am. Math. Soc. **98**(1), 21–51 (1961)
8. Elgot, C.C., Mezei, J.E.: On relations defined by generalized finite automata. IBM J. Res. Dev. **9**, 47–68 (1965)
9. Engelfriet, J., Hoogeboom, H.J.: MSO definable string transductions and two-way finite-state transducers. ACM Trans. Comput. Log. **2**, 216–254 (2001)
10. Filiot, E.: Logic-automata connections for transformations. In: Banerjee, M., Krishna, S.N. (eds.) ICLA 2015. LNCS, vol. 8923, pp. 30–57. Springer, Heidelberg (2015). https://doi.org/10.1007/978-3-662-45824-2_3
11. Filiot, E., Reynier, P.: Transducers, logic, and algebra for functions of finite words. ACM SIGLOG News **3**(3), 4–19 (2016)
12. Heinz, J.: The computational nature of phonological generalizations. In: Hyman, L., Plank, F. (eds.) Phonological Typology. Phonetics and Phonology, pp. 126–195. De Gruyter Mouton, Berlin (2018). Chapter 5
13. Heinz, J., Lai, R.: Vowel harmony and subsequentiality. In: Kornai, A., Kuhlmann, M. (eds.) Proceedings of the 13th Meeting on Mathematics of Language, Sofia, Bulgaria, pp. 52–63 (2013)
14. McNaughton, R., Papert, S.: Counter-Free Automata. MIT Press, Cambridge (1971)
15. Medvedev, Y.T.: On the class of events representable in a finite automaton. In: Moore, E.F. (ed.) Sequential Machines - Selected Papers, pp. 215–227. Addison-Wesley, New York (1964)
16. Mohri, M.: Finite-state transducers in language and speech processing. Comput. Linguist. **23**(2), 269–311 (1997)
17. Moschovakis, Y.N.: Abstract Recursion and Intrinsic Complexity. Lecture Notes in Logic, vol. 48. Cambridge University Press, Cambridge (2019)

18. Oncina, J., García, P., Vidal, E.: Learning subsequential transducers for pattern recognition tasks. IEEE Trans. Pattern Anal. Mach. Intell. **15**, 448–458 (1993)
19. Schützenberger, M.P.: Sur une variante des fonctions séquentielles. Theor. Comput. Sci. **4**, 47–57 (1977)
20. Thomas, W.: Classifying regular events in symbolic logic. J. Comput. Syst. Sci. **25**, 360–376 (1982)
21. Trakhtenbrot, B.A.: Finite automata and logic of monadic predicates. Dokl. Akad. Nauk SSSR **140**, 326–329 (1961)

Expressiveness and Conciseness of Timed Automata for the Verification of Stochastic Models

Susanna Donatelli[1]([⊠])[iD] and Serge Haddad[2][iD]

[1] Dipartimento di Informatica, Università di Torino, Turin, Italy
donatelli@di.unito.it
[2] LSV, ENS Paris-Saclay, CNRS, Inria, Université Paris-Saclay, Cachan, France
haddad@lsv.fr

Abstract. Timed Automata are a well-known formalism for specifying timed behaviours. In this paper we are concerned with Timed Automata for the specification of timed behaviour of Continuous Time Markov Chains (CTMC), as used in the stochastic temporal logic CSL^{TA}. A timed path formula of CSL^{TA} is specified by a Deterministic Timed Automaton (DTA) that features two kinds of transitions: *synchronizing* transitions (triggered by CTMC transitions) and *autonomous* transitions (triggered when a clock reaches a given threshold). Other definitions of CSL^{TA} are based on DTAs that do not include autonomous transitions. This raises the natural question: do autonomous transitions enhance expressiveness and/or conciseness of DTAs? We prove that this is the case and we provide a syntactical characterization of DTAs for which autonomous transitions do not add expressive power, but allow one to define exponentially more concise DTAs.

1 Introduction

Stochastic logics like CSL [5] allow one to express assertions about the probability of timed executions of Continuous Time Markov Chains (CTMC). In CSL, model executions (typically called "paths") are specified by two operators: timed neXt and timed Until. CSL has been extended in several ways to include action names (name of the events in the paths) and path properties specified using regular expressions leading to asCSL [6], or rewards, leading to CSRL [7]. Note that asCSL can specify rather complex path behaviour, expressed by regular expressions, but the timing requirements cannot be mixed within these expressions. GCSRL [14] is an extension of CSRL for model checking of CTMC generated by Generalized Stochastic Petri nets (GSPN) [1] taking into account both stochastic and immediate events.

Automata with time constraints have been used to specify path-based performance indices [16] for Stochastic Activity Networks [15], while hybrid automata have been used to define rather complex forms of passage of time [2] for GSPN, as well as generic performance properties [9] that are estimated using simulation. The use of a Deterministic Timed Automaton (DTA) in the stochastic

© Springer Nature Switzerland AG 2020
A. Leporati et al. (Eds.): LATA 2020, LNCS 12038, pp. 170–183, 2020.
https://doi.org/10.1007/978-3-030-40608-0_11

logic CSL^{TA} [12] allows to specify paths in terms of state propositions and action names associated to CTMC states and transitions (respectively) and in terms of the timed behaviour of *portions of the paths*. The CTMC actions are the input symbols for the DTA, and two types of transitions are distinguished: *synchronizing* transitions that read the input symbols of the CTMC, and *autonomous* transitions, that are taken by the DTA when the clock reaches some threshold, with priority over synchronizing ones. The determinism requirement ensures that the synchronized product of the DTA and the CTMC is still a stochastic process as all sources of non-determinism are eliminated. CSL^{TA} strictly includes [12] CSL and asCSL. Various extensions of CSL^{TA} have been presented in the literature. DTA with multiple clocks have been used for defining an extension of CSL^{TA} [10,13] but autonomous transitions are not allowed. In this paper we concentrate on single-clock CSL^{TA} with autonomous transitions, as in the original definition of CSL^{TA}. Indeed the single-clock limitation is a necessary requirement to reduce the CSL^{TA} model-checking problem to the (steady-state) solution of a Markov Regenerative Process, which is the largest class of stochastic processes for which we can compute an exact numerical solution, supported by efficient solution tools [3,4]. The single-clock setting allows also to investigate whether the definition of CSL^{TA} in [10,13], once limited to a single clock, is equivalent to the original definition of CSL^{TA} (introduced in [12]).

Paper Contributions. This paper addresses two research questions. The first one (Sect. 3) is *whether the presence of autonomous transitions enhances the expressiveness of DTAs* both in terms of timed languages (qualitative comparison) and in terms of probability of accepting the random path of a CTMC (quantitative comparison). We establish that autonomous transitions do enhance expressiveness. Given that eliminating autonomous transitions from a DTA is not always feasible, the second question (Sect. 4) is *which are the uses of autonomous transitions that can be emulated by DTA w/o autonomous transitions*. We have identified a hierarchy of subclasses of DTA in which the presence of autonomous transitions does not extend expressiveness (and autonomous transitions can therefore be eliminated), but that exponentially improves the DTA size. Only the most interesting proofs and properties have been included in this paper. Missing proofs and the full set of properties can be found in [11].

2   Context and Definitions

Although our motivations rely on the acceptance of paths of CTMCs featuring atomic propositions that label states and actions that label transitions, we set our work in the general context of acceptance of timed paths, where the $i + 1$-th state of a timed path is identified by v_i (we count indices from 0), the boolean evaluation of the atomic propositions in that state. δ_i indicates a delay, or a sojourn time in state i, and τ_i indicates the time elapsed until exiting state i. A timed path leaves state v_i with action a_i after a sojourn time in the state equal to δ_i. The elapsed time can be computed as: $\tau_i = \delta_i + \tau_{i-1}$, with $\tau_{-1} = 0$.

Definition 1 (Timed Path). *Given a set AP of atomic propositions and a set Act of actions, a timed (infinite) path is a sequence* $(v_0, \delta_0) \xrightarrow{a_0} (v_1, \delta_1) \xrightarrow{a_1}$ $\cdots (v_i, \delta_i) \xrightarrow{a_i} \cdots$ *such that for all* $i \in \mathbb{N} : v_i \in \{\top, \bot\}^{AP}, a_i \in Act, \delta_i \in \mathbb{R}_{\geqslant 0}$.

Example 1 (Timed Path). In writing timed paths we indicate functions v_i as the set of elements in AP that evaluate to $\top$. Given $AP = \{p, q\}$ and $Act = \{a, b, c\}$, a timed path $(\{p, q\}, 0.5) \xrightarrow{a} (\{q\}, 1.3) \xrightarrow{b} \cdots$, is interpreted as the system staying in a state that satisfies $p \wedge q$ in the time interval $[0, 0.5[$, at time 0.5 action a takes place and the system moves to a state that satisfies $\neg p \wedge q$, stays there for 1.3 time units and then action b takes place (at the global time $\tau = 1.8$).

DTA definition includes a clock x and two types of constraints: boundary ones, $\mathsf{BoundC} = \{x = \alpha, \alpha \in \mathbb{N}\}$ and inner ones, $\mathsf{InC} = \{\alpha \bowtie x \bowtie' \beta\}$, with $\bowtie, \bowtie' \in \{<, \leqslant, \}, \alpha \in \mathbb{N}$, and $\beta \in \mathbb{N} \cup \{\infty\}$. In the sequel, C is the largest time constant occurring in a DTA. Before formally defining the syntax and semantic of a DTA (Definitions 2, 3 and 4), let us introduce its main ingredients. During the execution of a stochastic discrete event system (e.g. a Markov chain) that can be represented by a timed path, one manages (1) an index i of the timed path (2) a location, say ℓ, is matched with the current state of the path indexed by i, and (3) a delay $\delta \leqslant \delta_i$ until the next state change from i to $i + 1$. The function Λ mapping the set of locations to the set of boolean expressions over atomic propositions, $\mathcal{B}_{AP}$, restricts the possible matchings since the valuation v_i must satisfy the formula $\Lambda(\ell)$. This matching evolves in three ways depending on the delay δ, elapsed until the next transition $(v_i, \delta_i) \xrightarrow{a_i} (v_{i+1}, \delta_{i+1})$ of the path.

- Either after some delay $\delta' \leqslant \delta$, there is an outgoing *autonomous transition* from ℓ whose boundary condition (say $x = \alpha$) is satisfied and such that v_i fulfills $\Lambda(\ell')$ where ℓ' is the target location of the transition. Then ℓ' is matched with i, delay δ becomes $\delta - \delta'$, the clock x is increased by δ' and the index i is unchanged.
- Else if there is a *synchronizing transition* outgoing from ℓ such that (1) after time δ has elapsed its inner condition (say $\alpha \bowtie x \bowtie' \beta$) is satisfied, (2) the action a_i belongs to the subset of actions associated with the synchronizing transition, and (3) v_{i+1} satisfies $\Lambda(\ell')$ where ℓ' is the target location of the transition. Then ℓ' is matched with $i + 1$, the new delay δ is set to δ_{i+1}, the clock x is either increased by δ or reset depending on the transition, and the index becomes $i + 1$.
- Otherwise there is no possible matching and the timed path is rejected by the DTA.

In the first two cases above, when $\ell' = \ell_f$, the *final location*, the timed path is accepted by the DTA whatever its future. This is ensured due to $\Lambda(\ell_f) = \top$ and the existence of the unique (looping) synchronizing transition from ℓ_f with no timing and action conditions. Observe that the synchronization may last forever without visiting ℓ_f: in this case the timed path is rejected.

Furthermore the synchronization of the stochastic system with the DTA should not introduce non determinism. So (1) the formulas associated with the *initial locations* are mutually exclusive, (2) synchronizing transitions outgoing from the same location are never simultaneously enabled, (3) autonomous transitions outgoing from the same location are never simultaneously enabled, and (4) autonomous transitions have priority over synchronizing transitions.

Definition 2 (DTA). *A single-clock Deterministic Timed Automaton with autonomous transitions is defined by a tuple* $\mathcal{A} = \langle L, \Lambda, L_0, \ell_f, AP, Synch, Aut \rangle$ *where L is a finite set of* locations, *$L_0 \subseteq L$ is the set of* initial locations, *$\ell_f \in L$ is the* final location, *$\Lambda : L \to \mathcal{B}_{AP}$ is a function that assigns to each location a boolean expression over the set of propositions AP, $Synch \subseteq L \times \mathsf{InC} \times 2^{Act} \times \{\varnothing, \downarrow\} \times L$ is the set of* synchronizing transitions, *and $Aut \subseteq L \times \mathsf{BoundC} \times \sharp \times \{\varnothing, \downarrow\} \times L$ is the set of* autonomous transitions, *with $E = Synch \cup Aut$. $\ell \xrightarrow{\gamma, B, r} \ell'$ denotes the transition $(\ell, \gamma, B, r, \ell')$.*
Furthermore $\mathcal{A}$ fulfills the following conditions.

- **Initial determinism.** $\forall \ell, \ell' \in L_0, \Lambda(l) \wedge \Lambda(l') \Leftrightarrow \bot$.
- **Determinism on actions.** $\forall B, B' \subseteq Act$ s.t. $B \cap B' \neq \varnothing, \forall \ell, \ell', \ell'' \in L$,
  if $\ell \xrightarrow{\gamma, B, r} \ell'$ and $\ell \xrightarrow{\gamma', B', r'} \ell''$ then $\Lambda(\ell') \wedge \Lambda(\ell'') \Leftrightarrow \bot$ or $\gamma \wedge \gamma' \Leftrightarrow \bot$.
- **Determinism on autonomous transitions.** $\forall \ell, \ell', \ell'' \in L$,
  if $\ell \xrightarrow{x=\alpha, \sharp, r} \ell'$ and $\ell \xrightarrow{x=\alpha', \sharp, r'} \ell''$ then $\Lambda(\ell') \wedge \Lambda(\ell'') \Leftrightarrow \bot$ or $\alpha \neq \alpha'$.
- **Conditions on the final location ℓ_f.** $\Lambda(\ell_f) = \top$ and $(\ell_f, \top, Act, \varnothing, \ell_f) \in Synch$.

Given a clock constraint γ and a clock valuation $\bar{x}$, $\bar{x} \models \gamma$ denotes the satisfaction of γ by $\bar{x}$. Similarly given a boolean formula φ and a valuation of atomic propositions v, $v \models \varphi$ denotes the satisfaction of φ by v.

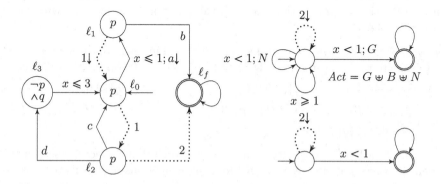

Fig. 1. Some examples of DTA.

Example 2 (DTA). Figure 1, left, shows a DTA with five locations: $\ell_0, \ell_1, \ell_2, \ell_3$ and ℓ_f. There is a single initial location, ℓ_0. Autonomous transitions are depicted as dotted arcs, while synchronizing are depicted as solid arcs. For readability we omit: (1) the symbol $\sharp$ on autonomous transitions; (2) the set r when there is no reset; (3) *Act* if a transition accepts all actions; (4) trivially true guards (like $x \geqslant 0$) and boolean conditions; (5) the name x of the clock in $x = \alpha$ guards. As a result an autonomous transition is depicted as either $l \xrightarrow{\alpha,\downarrow} l'$, as between ℓ_1 and ℓ_0, or as $l \xrightarrow{\alpha} l'$, as between ℓ_0 and ℓ_2. We informally write "a transition with reset" or "a transition without reset" to indicate the condition $r = \downarrow$ and $r = \varnothing$ respectively. The arc from ℓ_0 to ℓ_1 represents a synchronizing transition with a clock reset. The arc from ℓ_0 to ℓ_2 represents an autonomous transition to be taken when the clock is equal to 1, with no clock reset. Boolean expression of locations are: p, associated with ℓ_0, ℓ_1, ℓ_2 and $(\neg p \wedge q)$, associated with ℓ_3.

Let us describe a possible run of this DTA. At time 0.5, it goes from ℓ_0 to ℓ_1 by performing action a and resets x. Then at time 1.5, it autonomously comes back to location ℓ_0 and clock x is again reset. Then it autonomously goes to ℓ_2 at time 2.5 and later to ℓ_f at time 3.5. While irrelevant, x has current value 2.

Definition 3 (Run of $\mathcal{A}$). *A run of a DTA $\mathcal{A}$ is a sequence:* $(\ell_0, v_0, \bar{x}_0, \delta_0)$ $\xrightarrow{\gamma_0, B_0, r_0} (\ell_1, v_1, \bar{x}_1, \delta_1) \cdots (\ell_i, v_i, \bar{x}_i, \delta_i) \xrightarrow{\gamma_i, B_i, r_i} \cdots$ *such that for all* $i \in \mathbb{N}$: $\ell_i \in L, l_0 \in L_0, v_i \in \{\top, \bot\}^{AP}, \delta_i \in \mathbb{R}_{\geqslant 0}$:

$$\ell_i \xrightarrow{\gamma_i, B_i, r_i} \ell_{i+1} \in E, \quad v_i \models \Lambda(\ell_i), \quad \bar{x}_i + \delta_i \models \gamma_i, \quad \bar{x}_{i+1} = \begin{cases} 0 & \text{if } r = \downarrow \\ \bar{x}_i + \delta_i & \text{otherwise} \end{cases}$$

To enforce priority of autonomous transitions,

$$\text{let } \bar{x}_\sharp = min\{\alpha \mid \exists \ell_i \xrightarrow{x=\alpha, \sharp, r} \ell \in E \wedge \bar{x}_i \leqslant \alpha \wedge v_i \models \Lambda(\ell)\} \ (min(\varnothing) = \infty)$$
$$\text{If } B_i = \sharp \text{ then } \bar{x}_i + \delta_i = \bar{x}_\sharp \text{ and } v_{i+1} = v_i \text{ else } \bar{x}_i + \delta_i < x_\sharp.$$

A run is therefore a path in the DTA where the visited locations are coupled with a valuation of propositions, a clock value and a delay in a consistent way w.r.t. the DTA.

Example 3 (DTA run). Given that v is described in terms of the subset of *AP* that evaluate to $\top$, a run for the DTA of Fig. 1, left, is: $0:(\ell_0, \{p\}, \bar{x}_0 = 0.0, \delta_0 = 0.2)$ $\xrightarrow{x \leqslant 1, \{a\}, \downarrow}$ $1:(\ell_1, \{p, q\}, 0.0, 1.0)$ $\xrightarrow{x=1, \sharp, \downarrow}$ $2:(\ell_0, \{p, q\}, 0.0, 1.0)$ $\xrightarrow{x=1, \sharp, \varnothing}$ $3:(\ell_2, \{p\}, 1.0, 1.0)$ $\xrightarrow{x=2, \sharp, \varnothing}$ $4:(\ell_f, \{p\}, 2.0, 3.1)$ $\xrightarrow{x \geqslant 0, Act, \varnothing}$ $5:(\ell_f, \{q\}, 5.1, 0.5)$ $\xrightarrow{x \geqslant 0, Act, \varnothing}$ $6:(\ell_f, \{q\}, 5.6, \delta) \cdots$

A timed path σ is recognized by a run ρ of $\mathcal{A}$ such that the occurrences of the actions in σ are matched by the synchronizing transitions in ρ. This requires to define a mapping to match the points in the paths in which synchronizing transitions take place. This can be done by identifying a strictly increasing mapping for the indices of the timed path σ to the subset of the indices of the run ρ that correspond to a synchronizing transition. Note that, due to determinism, if such a run exists, it is unique.

Definition 4 (Path recognized by $\mathcal{A}$ and $\mathcal{L}(\mathcal{A})$). *Let* $\sigma = (v_0, \delta_0) \xrightarrow{a_0}$ $(v_1, \delta_1) \xrightarrow{a_1} \cdots (v_i, \delta_i) \xrightarrow{a_i} \cdots$ *be a timed path and* $\rho = (\ell_0, v_0', \bar{x}_0, \delta_0') \xrightarrow{\gamma_0, B_0, r_0}$ $\cdots (\ell_i, v_i', \bar{x}_i, \delta_i') \xrightarrow{\gamma_i, B_i, r_i} \cdots$ *be a run of a DTA $\mathcal{A}$. Then σ is recognized by ρ if there is a strictly increasing mapping $\kappa : \mathbb{N} \to \mathbb{N}$ (extended to $\kappa(-1) = -1$), such that for all $i \in \mathbb{N}$*

- $a_i \in B_{\kappa(i)}$ *and* $\delta_i = \sum_{\kappa(i-1) < h \leqslant \kappa(i)} \delta_h'$
- $\forall h,\ \kappa(i-1) < h \leqslant \kappa(i) \Rightarrow v_h' = v_i$ *and* $h \notin \kappa(\mathbb{N}) \Rightarrow B_h = \sharp$

A timed path σ is accepted by $\mathcal{A}$ if σ is recognized by a run ρ and ρ visits ℓ_f. The language $\mathcal{L}(\mathcal{A})$ of $\mathcal{A}$ is the set of the timed paths σ accepted by $\mathcal{A}$.

*Example 4 **(Path recognized by a run).** A timed path $\sigma = 0 : (p, 0.2) \xrightarrow{a} 1 :$ $(\{p, q\}, 6.1) \xrightarrow{b} 2 : (q, 0.5) \xrightarrow{d} 3 : (p, \delta) \cdots$ is recognized by the run of Example 3 with mapping κ: $\kappa(0) = 0, \kappa(1) = 4,\ \kappa(2) = 5, \kappa(3) = 6, \ldots$. The run visits ℓ_f and the path is accepted.*

We consider timed paths generated by a CTMC with state properties and actions.

Definition 5 (CTMC representation). *A continuous time Markov chain with state and action labels is represented by a tuple $\mathcal{M} = \langle S, s_0, Act, AP, lab, \boldsymbol{R} \rangle$, where S is a finite set of states, $s_0 \in S$ the initial state, Act is a finite set of action names, AP is a finite set of atomic propositions, $lab : S \to \{\top, \bot\}^{AP}$ is a state-labeling function that assigns to each state s a valuation of the atomic propositions, $\boldsymbol{R} \subseteq S \times Act \times S \to \mathbb{R}_{\geqslant 0}$ is a rate function. If $\lambda = \boldsymbol{R}(s, a, s') \wedge \lambda > 0$, we write $s \xrightarrow{a, \lambda} s'$.*

We assume that each state has at least one successor: for all $s \in S$, exists $a \in Act$, $s' \in S$ such that $\boldsymbol{R}(s, a, s') > 0$. CTMC executions lead to timed paths, and a CTMC is a generator of a random path. We define by $\mathbf{Pr}_{\mathcal{M}}(\mathcal{A})$ the probability that the random path of $\mathcal{M}$ is accepted by $\mathcal{A}$ (probability measure of all paths accepted by $\mathcal{A}$ as in [8]).

3 Autonomous Transitions and Expressiveness

We indicate with $\mathbb{A}$ the whole family of automata of Definition 2 and with $\mathbb{A}^{na}$ the subclass of automata with no autonomous transitions: $\mathbb{A}^{na} = \{\mathcal{A} \in \mathbb{A} \mid Aut(\mathcal{A}) = \varnothing\}$ The comparison of the expressive power of $\mathbb{A}$ and $\mathbb{A}^{na}$ is both qualitative (based on the timed path language) and quantitative (based on accepting probabilities).

Definition 6. *Let $\mathbb{A}_1$ and $\mathbb{A}_2$ be families of DTA. Then:*

- $\mathbb{A}_2$ *is at least as expressive as $\mathbb{A}_1$ w.r.t. language, denoted $\mathbb{A}_1 <_{\mathcal{L}} \mathbb{A}_2$, if for all $\mathcal{A}_1 \in \mathbb{A}_1$ there exists $\mathcal{A}_2 \in \mathbb{A}_2$ such that $\mathcal{L}(\mathcal{A}_2) = \mathcal{L}(\mathcal{A}_1)$;*

- $\mathbb{A}_2$ *is at least as expressive as* $\mathbb{A}_1$ *w.r.t. Markov chains, denoted* $\mathbb{A}_1 <_{\mathcal{M}} \mathbb{A}_2$, *if for all* $\mathcal{A}_1 \in \mathbb{A}_1$ *there exists* $\mathcal{A}_2 \in \mathbb{A}_2$ *such that for all Markov chains* $\mathcal{M}$, $\mathbf{Pr}_{\mathcal{M}}(\mathcal{A}_2) = \mathbf{Pr}_{\mathcal{M}}(\mathcal{A}_1)$.

As usual, we derive other relations between such families. $\mathbb{A}_1$ and $\mathbb{A}_2$ are *equally expressive* w.r.t. language (resp. Markov chains), denoted $\mathbb{A}_1 \sim_{\mathcal{L}} \mathbb{A}_2$ (resp. $\mathbb{A}_1 \sim_{\mathcal{M}} \mathbb{A}_2$) if $\mathbb{A}_1 <_{\mathcal{L}} \mathbb{A}_2$ and $\mathbb{A}_2 <_{\mathcal{L}} \mathbb{A}_1$ (resp. $\mathbb{A}_1 <_{\mathcal{M}} \mathbb{A}_2$ and $\mathbb{A}_2 <_{\mathcal{M}} \mathbb{A}_1$). $\mathbb{A}_2$ is *strictly more expressive than* $\mathbb{A}_1$ w.r.t. language (resp. Markov chains), denoted $\mathbb{A}_1 \precsim_{\mathcal{L}} \mathbb{A}_2$ (resp. $\mathbb{A}_1 \precsim_{\mathcal{M}} \mathbb{A}_2$) if $\mathbb{A}_1 <_{\mathcal{L}} \mathbb{A}_2$ and not $\mathbb{A}_2 <_{\mathcal{L}} \mathbb{A}_1$ (resp. $\mathbb{A}_1 <_{\mathcal{M}} \mathbb{A}_2$ and not $\mathbb{A}_2 <_{\mathcal{M}} \mathbb{A}_1$).

Observe that by definition $\mathbb{A}_1 <_{\mathcal{L}} \mathbb{A}_2$ implies $\mathbb{A}_1 <_{\mathcal{M}} \mathbb{A}_2$. We now establish that autonomous *resetting* transitions extend the expressive power of DTA w.r.t. Markov chains ($\mathbb{A}^{na} \precsim_{\mathcal{M}} \mathbb{A}$). The weaker result w.r.t. language ($\mathbb{A}^{na} \precsim_{\mathcal{L}} \mathbb{A}$) is shown in [11].

Theorem 1. *There exists* $\mathcal{A} \in \mathbb{A}$ *such that for all* $\mathcal{A}' \in \mathbb{A}^{na}$ *there exists a Markov chain* $\mathcal{M}$ *with* $\mathbf{Pr}_{\mathcal{M}}(\mathcal{A}') \neq \mathbf{Pr}_{\mathcal{M}}(\mathcal{A})$.

Before proving this theorem, we prove some intermediate properties. We first establish a kind of 0-1 law for DTA in $\mathbb{A}^{na}$ and Markov chains. In order to obtain this intermediate result, we introduce some objects. *Simple chains* are Markov chains with a single action, no atomic proposition (or equivalently with the same valuation for all states) and such that each state s has a single successor state $sc(s)$ reached with rate λ_s. W.r.t. the acceptance probability of simple chains, we can consider DTAs without actions and atomic propositions. Moreover we add to each DTA an additional garbage location and we split the transitions, so that, w.l.o.g. one can assume that for each location ℓ of a DTA in $\mathbb{A}^{na}$, there are $C+1$ outgoing transitions: $\{\ell \xrightarrow{i-1 \leqslant x < i, r_i} sc_i(\ell) \mid 1 \leqslant i \leqslant C\} \cup \{\ell \xrightarrow{x \geqslant C, r_{C+1}} sc_{C+1}(\ell)\}$ where C is the maximal constant occurring in the DTA. The shape of the guards is not a restriction in the context of Markov chains. For all clock valuations $\bar{x}$, the clock valuation $sc(\ell, \bar{x})$ is defined by:

- Let $i = \min(j \mid j \in \{1, \ldots, C\} \wedge \bar{x} < j)$ with $\min(\varnothing) = C + 1$;
- If $r_i = \downarrow$ then $sc(\ell, \bar{x}) = 0$ else $sc(\ell, \bar{x}) = \bar{x}$.

Observe the difference between sc_i, defined at the syntactical level, which maps a location to its ith successor and sc, defined at the semantical level, which maps a pair consisting in a location and a clock valuation to the new clock valuation obtained by firing the single transition enabled w.r.t. the clock valuation.

We also define the region (multi-)graph $G_{\mathcal{A}} = (V, E)$ of such a DTA $\mathcal{A}$ as follows.

- V, the set of vertices, is defined by $V = \{(\ell, i) \mid \ell \in L \wedge 0 \leqslant i \leqslant C + 1\}$;
- Let (ℓ, i) be a vertex, then for all j s.t. $\max(i, 1) \leqslant j \leqslant C + 1$, there is a transition from (ℓ, i) to $(sc_j(\ell), j')$ labelled by j with $j' = 0$ if $r_j = \downarrow$ and $j' = j$ otherwise.

One interprets G_A as follows. The vertex $(\ell, 0)$ corresponds to the region defined by location ℓ with clock valuation 0. The vertex $(\ell, 1)$ corresponds to the region defined by location ℓ with clock valuation in $]0, 1[$. The vertex (ℓ, i) for $1 < i \leqslant C$ corresponds to the region defined by location ℓ with clock valuation in $[i-1, i[$. The vertex $(\ell, C+1)$ corresponds to the region defined by location ℓ with clock valuation in $[C, \infty[$. The transition outgoing from (ℓ, i) labelled by j corresponds to the combination of time elapsing to enter the region (ℓ, j) followed by an action of the Markov chain, leading to either (ℓ', j) or to $(\ell', 0)$, in case of reset.

Given s a state of a Markov chain, ℓ a location of DTA, and $\bar{x}$ a clock valuation, $p(s, \ell, \bar{x})$ denotes the probability of acceptance when the Markov chain starts in s and the DTA starts in ℓ with clock valuation $\bar{x}$. In particular for a DTA $\mathcal{A}$ applied to a Markov chain $\mathcal{M}$, $\mathbf{Pr}_{\mathcal{M}}(\mathcal{A}) = p(s_0, \ell_0, 0)$ where s_0 is the initial state of $\mathcal{M}$ and ℓ_0 is the initial location of $\mathcal{A}$ such that $lab(s_0) \models \Lambda(\ell_0)$.

Lemma 1. *Let s be a state of a simple Markov chain $\mathcal{M}$ and ℓ be a location of a DTA in $\mathbb{A}^{na}$. Then the function that maps t to $p(s, \ell, t)$ is continuous and for $i - 1 \leqslant t \leqslant i \leqslant C$ it is equal to:*

$$\int_t^i \lambda_s e^{-\lambda_s(\tau-t)} p(sc(s), sc_i(\ell), sc(\ell, \tau)) d\tau + \int_C^\infty \lambda_s e^{-\lambda_s(\tau-t)} p(sc(s), sc_{C+1}(\ell), sc(\ell, \tau)) d\tau$$
$$+ \sum_{i < j \leqslant C} \int_{j-1}^j \lambda_s e^{-\lambda_s(\tau-t)} p(sc(s), sc_j(\ell), sc(\ell, \tau)) d\tau \tag{1}$$

The above formula represents the probability of acceptance when the Markov chain starts in s and the DTA starts in ℓ with clock valuation t, with $i - 1 \leqslant t \leqslant i \leqslant C$, therefore within the region (l, i). This probability is computed in terms of the probability of having the next CTMC transition within the region (l, i) itself, or any later region (l, j), multiplied by the probability of acceptance from the state reached by accepting the CTMC transition.

Proof. Define $p_n(s, \ell, t)$ as the probability that the run associated with a random timed path of $\mathcal{M}$ starting in s when the DTA starts in ℓ with clock valuation t reaches location ℓ_f after performing n actions. Then for $\ell \neq \ell_f$, $p_0(s, \ell, t) = 0$ and $p_0(s, \ell_f, t) = 1$. Assume that $p_n(s, \ell, t)$ is continuous (and so measurable) for all s and ℓ. Then the following equation holds for $i - 1 \leqslant t \leqslant i \leqslant C$:

$$p_{n+1}(s, \ell, t) = \int_t^i \lambda_q e^{-\lambda_s(\tau-t)} p_n(sc(s), sc_i(\ell), sc(\ell, \tau)) d\tau$$
$$+ \sum_{i < j \leqslant C} \int_{j-1}^j \lambda_s e^{-\lambda_q(\tau-t)} p_n(sc(s), sc_j(\ell), sc(\ell, \tau)) d\tau$$
$$+ \int_C^\infty \lambda_s e^{-\lambda_s(\tau-t)} p_n(sc(s), sc_{C+1}(\ell), sc(\ell, \tau)) d\tau$$

Observe that for $\tau > C$, $p_n(sc(s), sc_{C+1}(\ell), sc(\ell, \tau))$ is constant since if there is a reset then $sc(\ell, \tau) = 0$ and if there is no reset then $sc(\ell, \tau) = \tau > C$ and so the valuation of the clock is irrelevant. Thus the equation can be rewritten as follows.

$$p_{n+1}(s, \ell, t) = \int_t^i \lambda_s e^{-\lambda_s(\tau - t)} p_n(sc(s), sc_i(\ell), sc(\ell, \tau)) d\tau$$

$$+ \sum_{i < j \leqslant C} \int_{j-1}^j \lambda_s e^{-\lambda_s(\tau - t)} p_n(sc(s), sc_j(\ell), sc(\ell, \tau)) d\tau$$

$$+ e^{-\lambda_s(C-t)} p_n(sc(s), sc_{C+1}(\ell), sc(\ell, C+1))$$

Observe that $\max(1, \lambda_s) e^{-\lambda_s \tau}$ is uniformly continuous. So pick $\eta' > 0$ such that for all $\tau < \tau' \leqslant \tau + \eta'$ $\max(1, \lambda_s) |e^{-\lambda_s \tau} - e^{-\lambda_s \tau'}| \leqslant \frac{\varepsilon}{3C}$. Let $\eta = \min(\eta', \frac{\varepsilon}{3\lambda_s})$. Then for all $t < t' \leqslant t + \eta$, one bounds $|p_{n+1}(s, \ell, t) - p_{n+1}(s, \ell, t')|$ by the sum of three terms using the above equation to establish that $|p_{n+1}(s, \ell, t) - p_{n+1}(s, \ell, t')| \leqslant \varepsilon$. Thus $p_{n+1}(s, \ell, t)$ is continuous. When $t > C$, $p_{n+1}(s, \ell, t)$ is constant and so continuous.

Observe that $p(s, \ell, t) = \lim_{n \to \infty} p_n(s, \ell, t)$. So the mapping $p(s, \ell, t)$ is measurable as a limit of continuous mappings. Thus Eq. 1 holds for $i - 1 \leqslant t \leqslant i \leqslant C$: Repeating the same argument as the one for the inductive case yields the result. When $t > C$, $p(s, \ell, t)$ is constant and so continuous.

Proposition 1. *Let $\mathcal{A} \in \mathbb{A}^{na}$ and $z \in [0, 1]$ such that for all Markov chains $\mathcal{M}$, $\mathbf{Pr}_{\mathcal{M}}(\mathcal{A}) = z$, then $z \in \{0, 1\}$.*

Proof. We will even prove this result when restricting the quantification to Markov chains with a single action and a single valuation of propositions for all states and a single successor for all states. Thus we can omit propositions and actions in the DTA and only consider simple chains.

Let $\mathcal{A}$ be an automaton that satisfies the hypothesis. We want to establish that *for all configurations (ℓ, t) in some region of G_A reachable from $(\ell_0, 0)$, and for all states s of a simple Markov chain, $p(s, \ell, t) = z$.* We do this by induction on the distance from the initial region in the region graph and then we prove that z is either 0 or 1. The basis case of the induction corresponds to the assumption $\mathbf{Pr}_{\mathcal{M}}(\mathcal{A}) = z$, for all $\mathcal{M}$.

For the inductive step we assume that for a given (ℓ, t), and for all states s of a simple chain, $p(s, \ell, t) = z$ and we prove that the $p(s', \ell', t') = z$, for all (s', ℓ', t') reachable in one step from (s, ℓ, t).

Let $\mathcal{M}$ be an arbitrary simple chain and define $\mathcal{M}_\lambda$ as the simple chain with a single transition outgoing from its initial state to the initial state of $\mathcal{M}$ whose rate is λ. Let s be the initial state of $\mathcal{M}_\lambda$.

By assumption, $p(s, \ell, t) = z$. Define $f(\tau)$ by $p(sc(s), sc_j(\ell), sc(\ell, t + \tau))$ when $j - 1 < t + \tau \leqslant j \leqslant C$ and by $p(sc(s), sc_{C+1}(\ell), sc(\ell, t + \tau))$ when $t + \tau > C$. Equation 1 can be rewritten as $p(s, \ell, t) = \int_{\tau \geqslant 0} \lambda e^{-\lambda \tau} f(\tau) d\tau$. Since for all λ,

$\mathbf{Pr}_{\mathcal{M}_\lambda}(\mathcal{A}) = z$, the Laplace transform of $f(\tau)$ is equal to $\frac{z}{\lambda}$, i.e. the Laplace transform of the constant function z. By the theorem of unicity of Laplace transforms, this entails that $f(\tau) = z$ except for a set of null measure. However, consider a successor region (ℓ', i) of location ℓ with clock valuation t'.

- Either $i = 0$ (meaning that there has been a reset) and the region has a single point reached with non null probability. So $p(sc(s), \ell', 0) = z$.
- Or $i > 0$, so by Lemma 1, $p(sc(s), \ell', t')$ is continuous inside the region w.r.t. t' and thus everywhere equal to z.

So the induction is established. So if a region of ℓ_f is reachable in the region graph, then $z = 1$. Otherwise ℓ_f is not reachable implying that no run is accepting, and thus $z = 0$.

We can now prove Theorem 1 ($\mathbb{A}^{na} \lesssim_{\mathcal{M}} \mathbb{A}$).
Proof of Theorem 1. The DTA $\mathcal{A}$ in Fig. 1 (lower right) has an action set reduced to a singleton $\{a\}$ (omitted in the figure) and an empty set of propositions. The language of $\mathcal{A}$ is the set of timed paths whose first action occurs at time $\tau \in [2i, 2i+1[$ for some $i \in \mathbb{N}$. Assume by contradiction that there exists $\mathcal{A}' \in \mathbb{A}^{na}$ such that for all Markov chain $\mathcal{M}$, $\mathbf{Pr}_{\mathcal{M}}(\mathcal{A}') = \mathbf{Pr}_{\mathcal{M}}(\mathcal{A})$. Pick an arbitrary Markov chain $\mathcal{M}$ and define $\mathcal{M}_\lambda$ as the Markov chain which has a single transition from its initial state to the initial state of $\mathcal{M}$ with rate λ. It is routine to check that $\mathbf{Pr}_{\mathcal{M}_\lambda}(\mathcal{A}) = \frac{1-e^{-\lambda}}{1-e^{-2\lambda}}$ (as only the first transition of $\mathcal{M}_\lambda$ is relevant) and, consequently, $\lim_{\lambda \to 0} \mathbf{Pr}_{\mathcal{M}_\lambda}(\mathcal{A}) = \frac{1}{2}$ and, given the hypothesis, also $\lim_{\lambda \to 0} \mathbf{Pr}_{\mathcal{M}_\lambda}(\mathcal{A}') = \frac{1}{2}$.
$\mathbf{Pr}_{\mathcal{M}_\lambda}(\mathcal{A}')$ can be decomposed as $p_{1,\lambda} + p_{2,\lambda}$ where $p_{1,\lambda}$ is the probability to accept the random timed path and that the first action takes place at most at time C and $p_{2,\lambda}$ is the probability to accept the random timed path and that the first action takes place after C, where C is the maximal constant of $\mathcal{A}'$. But $\lim_{\lambda \to 0} p_{1,\lambda} = 0$ and therefore $\lim_{\lambda \to 0} p_{2,\lambda} = \frac{1}{2}$.
On the other hand, let ℓ_1 be the location of $\mathcal{A}'$ reached from its initial location when the value of the clock is greater than C, its maximal constant. There must be one, if not $\lim_{\lambda \to 0} p_{2,\lambda} = 0$, which contradicts what derived above. We want to design an automaton $\mathcal{A}''$ equivalent to $\mathcal{A}'$ when reaching ℓ_1 with clock value greater than C: any timed path is accepted by $\mathcal{A}''$ iff it is accepted by $\mathcal{A}'$ when starting in ℓ_1 with clock valuation greater than C. For the construction we duplicate the automaton and merge the final location, the initial location is location ℓ_1 of the first copy, and in the first copy we add to the guard of all transitions the formula $x > C$ and redirect the transitions that reset the clock to the corresponding location of the second copy.
But then $\lim_{\lambda \to 0} p_{2,\lambda} = \mathbf{Pr}_{\mathcal{M}}(\mathcal{A}'')$. Since $\lim_{\lambda \to 0} p_{2,\lambda} = \frac{1}{2}$ and $\mathcal{M}$ is arbitrary, this contradicts Proposition 1 applied to $\mathcal{A}''$.
The DTA in Fig. 1 (upper right) shows that the above counter-example is of practical interest. Consider a periodic system that cycles over phases of duration 2, each split in two sub-phases of duration 1 (for example a running and a reset phase) and that can experience good (G), bad (B), and neutral (N) actions,

generated from a CTMC of arbitrary complexity. The depicted DTA allows one to compute the probability of the CTMC behaviours characterized by a good action in the running sub-phase, given that in the preceding phases no bad action has happened in the running phase. Any action is instead allowed during the reset phase.

4   Autonomous Transitions and Conciseness

We have established that there exists DTAs that cannot be translated into DTAs without autonomous transitions ($\mathbb{A}^{na} \lesssim_M \mathbb{A}$). We now investigate whether restricted forms of use of autonomous transitions are as expressive as $\mathbb{A}^{na}$. To this goal we identify two additional subclasses of $\mathbb{A}$, namely $\mathbb{A}^{nra}$ and $\mathbb{A}^{rc}$, characterized by a limited presence of autonomous transitions and that are in the following subset relationship: $\mathbb{A}^{na} \subseteq \mathbb{A}^{nra} \subseteq \mathbb{A}^{rc} \subseteq \mathbb{A}$.

Restricted cycles. $\mathbb{A}^{rc}$ is the subclass of automata $\mathcal{A} \in \mathbb{A}$ in which all cycles of $\mathcal{A}$ including an autonomous transition with a reset also include a synchronizing transition $(\ell, \gamma, B, r, \ell')$ with $r = \downarrow$ or $\gamma = (x > C)$.

No reset on autonomous transitions. $\mathbb{A}^{nra}$ is the subclass of automata $\mathcal{A} \in \mathbb{A}^{rc}$ in which there is no autonomous transition that resets the clock: $\mathbb{A}^{nra} = \{\mathcal{A} \in \mathbb{A} \mid (\ell, \gamma, \sharp, r, \ell') \in Aut(\mathcal{A}) \Rightarrow r = \varnothing\}$.

The DTA on the left of Fig. 1 belongs to $\mathbb{A}^{rc} \setminus \mathbb{A}^{nra}$: indeed there is an autonomous transition with reset (from ℓ_1 to ℓ_0), therefore it is not in $\mathbb{A}^{nra}$, but although the transition is part of a cycle, that cycle also includes a synchronizing transition with reset (from ℓ_0 to ℓ_1). Any DTA with no reset on autonomous transitions is an example of $\mathbb{A}^{nra}$. The family $\mathbb{A}^{rc}$ has been introduced to provide an accurate syntactical characterization of DTA for which the autonomous transitions do not add expressive power. In some sense, the DTA of Theorem 1 emphasizes the interest of $\mathbb{A}^{rc}$ since the cycle performed by the autonomous resetting transition points out what increases the expressive power. $\mathbb{A}^{nra}$, which forbids clock resets on autonomous transitions, removes from CSL^{TA} the capacity of combining time constants depending on the time elapsed during (a portion of) an execution. As observed in [12](section 4), clock resets on autonomous transitions are what makes CSL^{TA} more expressive than asCSL [6].

The following frame summarizes the results for $\mathbb{A}$ subclasses.

$$\mathbb{A}^{na} \sim_{\mathcal{L}} \mathbb{A}^{nra} \sim_{\mathcal{L}} \mathbb{A}^{rc} \lesssim_M \mathbb{A}$$
with $\mathbb{A}^{rc}$ ($\mathbb{A}^{nra}$) exponentially more concise than $\mathbb{A}^{nra}$ ($\mathbb{A}^{na}$, respectively)

We first establish that in $\mathbb{A}^{rc}$ the autonomous resetting transitions can be mimicked in $\mathbb{A}^{nra}$ using additional finite memory, but with exponential cost.

Proposition 2. *There exists an algorithm operating in exponential time that takes as input $\mathcal{A} \in \mathbb{A}^{rc}$ and outputs $\mathcal{A}' \in \mathbb{A}^{nra}$ with $\mathcal{L}(\mathcal{A}') = \mathcal{L}(\mathcal{A})$.*

Sketch of Proof. The construction (1) duplicates locations by memorizing in the location an integer value, (2) take into account this value for modifying the guard and the destination of the outgoing transitions, and (3) deletes the reset of autonomous transitions. This value corresponds to the accumulated value of constants in the guards of resetting autonomous transitions since the last visit of a synchronizing transition with a reset or a guard $x > C$. The restriction over $\mathbb{A}^{rc}$ ensures that this value is bounded by some finite integer K. However K may be exponential in the size of $\mathcal{A}$ and thus this transformation is exponential.

The exponential blowup due to the duplication of locations is unavoidable:

Proposition 3. *There exists a family $\{\mathcal{A}_n\}_{n \in \mathbb{N}}$ in $\mathbb{A}^{rc}$ such that the size of $\mathcal{A}_n$ is $O(n^2)$ and for all $\mathcal{A} \in \mathbb{A}^{nra}$ with $\mathcal{L}(\mathcal{A}) = \mathcal{L}(\mathcal{A}_n)$, $(|Aut| + 1)|Synch| \geqslant 2^n$.*

We now prove that autonomous transitions in $\mathbb{A}^{nra}$ can be eliminated, also at an exponential cost.

Proposition 4. *There exists an algorithm operating in exponential time that takes as input $\mathcal{A} \in \mathbb{A}^{nra}$ and outputs $\mathcal{A}' \in \mathbb{A}^{na}$ with $\mathcal{L}(\mathcal{A}') = \mathcal{L}(\mathcal{A})$.*

Sketch of Proof. The construction proceeds in two steps: at first, cycles of autonomous transitions are eliminated, then all (linear) paths of autonomous transitions are eliminated. The first construction is quadratic, as we duplicate each location to store in the location the information on the number of autonomous transitions visited since the last visit of a synchronized transition. The idea of this construction is that if a path exceeds the number of autonomous transitions it must visit twice the same autonomous transition without visiting a synchronized transition and so diverges. In words: in the resulting DTA, divergence has been transformed into deadlock. This finite memory has a linear size w.r.t. the size of the original DTA.

The second step consists in eliminating autonomous transitions when there are no such cycles. The key point is to select a location ℓ which is the source of the last autonomous transition of a maximal path of such transitions. Thus every autonomous transition outgoing from ℓ reaches some location ℓ_u where only synchronized transitions are possible. Roughly speaking, the construction builds a synchronized transition corresponding to a sequence of an autonomous transition followed by a synchronized transition. However the construction is more involved since ℓ has to be duplicated in order to check which autonomous transition can be triggered (or if no autonomous transition can be triggered). This duplication also has an impact on the incoming transitions of ℓ. Repeating (at most $|L|$ times) this transformation eliminates all autonomous transitions. The exponential blowup due to the repetition of duplication of locations is unavoidable:

Proposition 5. *There exists a family of automata $\{\mathcal{A}_n\}_{n \in \mathbb{N}}$ in $\mathbb{A}^{nra}$ such that the size of $\mathcal{A}_n$ belongs to $O(n \log(n))$ and for all $\mathcal{A} \in \mathbb{A}^{na}$ with $\mathcal{L}(\mathcal{A}) = \mathcal{L}(\mathcal{A}_n)$ the number of its locations is at least 2^n.*

5 Conclusion and Future Work

We have established that autonomous transitions do enhance expressiveness of single clock DTAs, and more precisely for the less discriminating case of the probability of the random paths of a CTMC accepted by the DTA. This is the most relevant one for comparing some variations of (1-clock) CSL^{TA} defined in the literature. This enhanced expressiveness is due to the possibility of associating clock resets with autonomous transitions that occur in a cycle. The small counterexample of Proposition 1 can be seen as the basic construct to study systems with periodic behaviours or periodic phases, with clear practical implications. Even in DTA subclasses for which the autonomous transitions do not enhance expressiveness, they do play a role in defining concise DTAs: removing autonomous transitions may lead to an exponential blow up of the DTA.

We plan to investigate whether the precise identification of the characteristics that enhance expressiveness and conciseness can help the identification of the best algorithms for CSL^{TA} model-checking, in particular for the component-based method [4]. Moreover, following the suggestion by an anonymous reviewer, we intend to investigate further consequences of Proposition 1, for example to study systems that include probabilistic choices of autonomous transitions.

References

1. Ajmone-Marsan, M., Balbo, G., Conte, G., Donatelli, S., Franceschinis, G.: Modelling with Generalized Stochastic Petri Nets. Wiley, Hoboken (1995)
2. Amparore, E.G., Ballarini, P., Beccuti, M., Donatelli, S., Franceschinis, G.: Expressing and computing passage time measures of GSPN models with HASL. In: Colom, J.-M., Desel, J. (eds.) PETRI NETS 2013. LNCS, vol. 7927, pp. 110–129. Springer, Heidelberg (2013). https://doi.org/10.1007/978-3-642-38697-8_7
3. Amparore, E.G., Donatelli, S.: MC4CSL^{TA}: an efficient model checking tool for CSL^{TA}. In: QEST 2010, pp. 153–154. IEEE Computer Society (2010)
4. Amparore, E.G., Donatelli, S.: Efficient model checking of the stochastic logic CSLTA. Perform. Eval. **123–124**, 1–34 (2018)
5. Aziz, A., Sanwal, K., Singhal, V., Brayton, R.: Model-checking continuous-time Markov chains. ACM Trans. Comput. Log. **1**(1), 162–170 (2000)
6. Baier, C., Cloth, L., Haverkort, B.R., Kuntz, M., Siegle, M.: Model checking Markov chains with actions and state labels. IEEE TSE **33**, 209–224 (2007)
7. Baier, C., Haverkort, B., Hermanns, H., Katoen, J.-P.: On the logical characterisation of performability properties. In: Montanari, U., Rolim, J.D.P., Welzl, E. (eds.) ICALP 2000. LNCS, vol. 1853, pp. 780–792. Springer, Heidelberg (2000). https://doi.org/10.1007/3-540-45022-X_65
8. Baier, C., Haverkort, B., Hermanns, H., Katoen, J.-P.: Model-checking algorithms for continuous-time Markov chains. IEEE TSE **29**(6), 524–541 (2003)
9. Ballarini, P., Barbot, B., Duflot, M., Haddad, S., Pekergin, N.: HASL: a new approach for performance evaluation and model checking from concepts to experimentation. Perform. Eval. **90**, 53–77 (2015)
10. TChen, T., Han, T., Katoen, J.-P., Mereacre, A.: Model checking of continuous-time Markov chains against timed automata specifications. Log. Methods Comput. Sci. **7**(1:12), 1–34 (2011)

11. Donatelli, S., Haddad, S.: Autonomous Transitions Enhance CSA^{TA} Expressiveness and Conciseness. Research report, Inria Saclay Ile de France, LSV, ENS Cachan, CNRS, INRIA, Université Paris-Saclay, Cachan, France, Universita degli Studi di Torino, October 2019. https://hal.inria.fr/hal-02306021
12. Donatelli, S., Haddad, S., Sproston, J.: Model checking timed and stochastic properties with CSL^{TA}. IEEE TSE **35**(2), 224–240 (2009)
13. Feng, Y., Katoen, J.-P., Li, H., Xia, B., Zhan, N.: Monitoring CTMCs by multiclock timed automata. In: Chockler, H., Weissenbacher, G. (eds.) CAV 2018. LNCS, vol. 10981, pp. 507–526. Springer, Cham (2018). https://doi.org/10.1007/978-3-319-96145-3_27
14. Kuntz, M., Haverkort, B.R.: GCSRL-a logic for stochastic reward models with timed and untimed behaviour. In: 8th PMCCS, pp. 50–56 (2007)
15. Meyer, J.F., Movaghar, A., Sanders, W.H.: Stochastic activity networks: structure, behavior, and application. In: International Workshop on Timed Petri Nets, pp. 106–115. IEEE CS (1985)
16. Obal II, W.D., Sanders, W.H.: State-space support for path-based reward variables. Perform. Eval. **35**, 233–251 (1999)

Windable Heads and Recognizing NL with Constant Randomness

Mehmet Utkan Gezer$^{(\boxtimes)}$ (iD)

Boğaziçi University, Bebek, Istanbul, Turkey
utkan.gezer@boun.edu.tr

Abstract. Every language in NL has a k-head two-way nondeterministic finite automaton (2nfa(k)) recognizing it. It is known how to build a constant-space verifier algorithm from a 2nfa(k) for the same language with constant-randomness, but with error probability $(k^2 - 1)/2k^2$ that can not be reduced further by repetition. We have defined the unpleasant characteristic of the heads that causes the high error as the property of being "windable". With a tweak on the previous verification algorithm, the error is improved to $(k_W^2 - 1)/2k_W^2$, where $k_W \leq k$ is the number of windable heads. Using this new algorithm, a subset of languages in NL that have a 2nfa(k) recognizer with $k_W \leq 1$ can be verified with arbitrarily reducible error using constant space and randomness.

Keywords: Interactive proof systems · Multi-head finite automata · Probabilistic finite automata

1 Introduction

Probabilistic Turing machines (PTM) are classical Turing machines with randomness as a resource. These machines alone can be recognizers of a language, or be verifiers for the proofs of membership in an interactive proof system (IPS). In either scenario, a noticeable error might be incurred in machines' decisions due to randomness involved in their execution. This error can usually be reduced via repeated execution in PTM's control.

The class of languages verifiable by the constant-randomness two-way probabilistic finite automata (2pfa) is the same as NL, the class of languages recognizable by the nondeterministic sub-linear space Turing Machines. Curiously, however, the error of these verifiers in recognizing languages of this class seems to be irreducible beyond a certain threshold [6].

In this paper, we introduce a characteristic for the languages in NL. Based on this characteristic, we lower the error threshold established in [6] for almost all languages in NL. Finally, we delineate a subset of NL in which each language is verifiable by a constant-randomness 2pfa with arbitrarily low error.

The remaining of the paper is structured as follows: Sects. 2 and 3 provides the necessary background as well as our terminology in the domain. A key property of the multi-head finite automata is identified in Sect. 4. Our verification

© Springer Nature Switzerland AG 2020
A. Leporati et al. (Eds.): LATA 2020, LNCS 12038, pp. 184–195, 2020.
https://doi.org/10.1007/978-3-030-40608-0_12

algorithm, which improves on Say and Yakaryılmaz algorithm, and a subset of NL on which this algorithm excels are described in Sect. 5.

The following notation will be common throughout this paper:

- $\mathcal{L}(M)$ denotes the language recognized by the machine M.
- $\mathcal{L}(\mathsf{X}) = \{\,\mathcal{L}(M) \mid M \in \mathsf{X}\,\}$ for a class of machines X.
- $S_{\backslash q}$ denotes the set S without its element q.
- σ_i denotes the ith element of the sequence σ.
- $w^\times$ denotes the substring of w without its last character.
- $\sigma \circ \tau$ denotes the sequence σ concatenated with the element or sequence τ.

2   Finite Automata with k Heads

Finite automata are the Turing machines with read-only tape heads on a single tape. A finite automata with only one head is equivalent to a DFA (deterministic finite automaton) in terms of language recognition [3], hence recognizes a regular language. Finite automata with $k > 1$ heads can recognize more than just regular languages. Their formal definition may be given as follows:

Definition 1 (Multi-head nondeterministic finite automata). *A 2nfa(k) is a 5-tuple, $M = (Q, \Sigma, \delta, q_0, q_f)$, where;*

1. *Q is the finite set of states,*
2. *Σ is the finite set of input symbols,*
   (a) $\triangleright, \triangleleft$ are the left and right end-markers for the input on the tape,
   (b) $\Gamma = \Sigma \cup \{\triangleright, \triangleleft\}$ is the tape alphabet,
3. *$\delta \colon Q \times \Gamma^k \to \mathcal{P}(Q_{\backslash q_0} \times \Delta^k)$ is the transition function, where;*
   (a) $\Delta = \{-1, 0, 1\}$ is the set of head movements,
4. *$q_0 \in Q$ is the unique initial state,*
5. *$q_f \in Q$ is the unique accepting state.*

Machine M is said to execute on a string $w \in \Sigma^*$, when $\triangleright w \triangleleft$ is written onto M's tape, all of its heads rewound to the cell with $\triangleright$, its state is reset to q_0, and then it executes in steps by the rules of δ. At each step, inputs to δ are the state of M and the symbols read by respective heads of M.

When $|\delta| = 1$ with the only member $(q', (d_1, \ldots, d_k)) \in Q_{\backslash q_0} \times \Delta^k$, the next state of M becomes q', and M moves its ith head by d_i. Whenever $|\delta| > 1$, the execution branches, and each branch runs in parallel. A branch is said to reject w, if $|\delta| = 0$, or if all of its branches reject. A branch accepts w, if its state is at q_f, or if any one of its branches accepts. A branch may also do neither, in which case the branch is said to loop.

A string w is in $\mathcal{L}(M)$, if the root of M's execution on w is an accepting branch. Otherwise, $w \notin \mathcal{L}(M)$, and the root of M's execution is either a rejecting or a looping branch.

Restricting δ to not have transitions inbound to q_0 does not detriment the language recognition of a 2nfa(k) in terms of its language recognition: Any 2nfa(k) with such transitions can be converted into one without, by adding a new initial state q_0' and setting $\delta(q_0', \triangleright, \ldots, \triangleright) = \{(q_0, 0, \ldots, 0)\}$.

Lemma 1. *The containment* $\mathcal{L}(2nfa(k)) \subsetneq \mathcal{L}(2nfa(k+1))$ *is proper [4, 5].*

Lemma 2. *Given a 2nfa(k), one can construct a 2nfa(2k) recognizing the same language, which is guaranteed to halt.*

Proof. A k-headed automaton running on an input w of length n has n^k distinct configurations. Additional k heads can count up to $n^k = (nnn \ldots n)_n$, and halt the machine with a rejection.

Lemma 3. *Every 2nfa(k) can be converted into an equivalent 2nfa(k) which does not move its heads beyond the end markers.*

Conversion in Lemma 3 is done via trivial modifications on the transition function.

Definition 2 (Multi-head deterministic finite automata). *A 2dfa(k) is a 2nfa(k) that is restricted to satisfy $|\delta| \leq 1$, where δ is its transition function.*

Lemma 4. *The following are shown in [2]:*

$$\cup_{k=1}^{\infty} \mathcal{L}(2nfa(k)) = NL \tag{1}$$
$$\cup_{k=1}^{\infty} \mathcal{L}(2dfa(k)) = L \tag{2}$$

Definition 3 (Multi-head one-way finite automata). *A 1nfa(k) is a restricted 2nfa(k) that does not move its heads backwards on the tape. In its definition, $\Delta = \{0, 1\}$. A 1dfa(k) is similarly a restriction of 2dfa(k).*

Definition 4 (Multi-head probabilistic finite automata). *A 2pfa(k) M is a PTM defined similar to a 2nfa(k) with the following modifications on Definition 1:*

1.' $Q = Q_D \cup Q_P$, where Q_D and Q_P are disjoint.
3.' *Transition function δ is overloaded as follows:*
 – $\delta \colon Q_D \times \Gamma^k \to \mathcal{P}(Q_{\backslash q_0} \times \Delta^k)$
 – $\delta \colon Q_P \times \Gamma^k \times \{0, 1\} \to \mathcal{P}(Q_{\backslash q_0} \times \Delta^k)$
 The output of δ may at most have 1 element.

States Q_D are called deterministic, and Q_P probabilistic. Depending on the state of the machine, δ receives a third parameter, where a 0 or 1 is provided by a random bit-stream. We write 2pfa instead of 2pfa(1).

A string w is in $\mathcal{L}(M)$, iff M accepts w with a probability greater than $1/2$.

Due to the probabilistic nature of a given 2pfa(k) M, the following three types of error in the language recognition are inherent to it. For $w \in \mathcal{L}(M)$:

$$\varepsilon_{\text{fail-to-accept}}(M) = \Pr[M \text{ does not accept } w] \qquad \text{(Failure to accept)}$$

And for $w \notin \mathcal{L}(M)$:

$$\varepsilon_{\text{fail-to-reject}}(M) = \Pr[M \text{ does not reject } w] \qquad \text{(Failure to reject)}$$

$$\varepsilon_{\text{false-accept}}(M) = \Pr[M \text{ accepts } w] \qquad \text{(False acceptance)}$$

The overall weak and strong errors of a probabilistic machine M are defined as follows [1]:

$$\varepsilon_{\text{weak}}(M) = \max(\varepsilon_{\text{fail-to-accept}}(M), \varepsilon_{\text{false-accept}}(M)) \qquad \text{(Weak error)}$$

$$\varepsilon_{\text{strong}}(M) = \max(\varepsilon_{\text{fail-to-accept}}(M), \varepsilon_{\text{fail-to-reject}}(M)) \qquad \text{(Strong error)}$$

Note that a 2pfa(k) M can fail to reject a string w, by either accepting it, or going into an infinite loop. Consequently, $\varepsilon_{\text{fail-to-reject}} \geq \varepsilon_{\text{false-accept}}$ and $\varepsilon_{\text{strong}} \geq \varepsilon_{\text{weak}}$ are always true.

Given a k and $\varepsilon < 1/2$, let

$$\mathcal{L}_{\text{weak},\varepsilon}\left(2\text{pfa}(k)\right) = \{\, \mathcal{L}(M) \mid M \in 2\text{pfa}(k), \varepsilon_{\text{weak}}(M) \leq \varepsilon \,\}$$

be the class of languages recognized by a 2pfa(k) with a weak error at most ε. Class $\mathcal{L}_{\text{strong},\varepsilon}\left(2\text{pfa}(k)\right)$ is defined similarly.

3   Interactive Proof Systems

An interactive proof system (IPS) models the verification process of proofs. Of the two components in an IPS, the *prover* produces the purported proof of membership for a given input string, while the *verifier* either accepts or rejects the string, alongside its proof. The catch is that the prover is assumed to advocate for the input string's membership without regards to truth, and the verifier is expected to be accurate in its decision, holding a healthy level of skepticism against the proof.

The verifier is any Turing machine with capabilities to interact with the prover via a shared communication cell. The prover can be seen as an infinite state transducer that has access to both an original copy of the input string and the communication cell. Prover never halts, and its output is to the communication cell.

Our focus will be on the one-way IPS, which restricts the interaction to be a monologue from the prover to the verifier. Since there is no influx of information to the prover, prover's output will be dependent on the input string only. Consequently, a one-way IPS can also be modeled as a verifier paired with a certificate function, $c\colon \Sigma^* \to \Lambda^\infty$, where Λ is the communication alphabet. A formal definition follows:

Definition 5 (One-way interactive proof systems). *An* IP(*restriction-list*) *is defined with a tuple of a verifier and a certificate function, $S = (V, c)$. The verifier V is a Turing machine of type specified by the* restriction-list*. The certificate function c outputs the claimed proof of membership $c(w) \in \Lambda^\infty$ for a given input string w.*

The verifier's access to the certificate is only in the forward direction. The qualifier "one-way", however, specifies that the interaction in the IPS is a monologue from the prover to the verifier, not the aforementioned fact, which is true for all IPS.

The language recognized by S can be denoted with $\mathcal{L}(S)$, as well as $\mathcal{L}(V)$. A string w is in $\mathcal{L}(S)$ *iff* the interaction results in an acceptance of w by V.

If the verifier of the IPS is probabilistic, its error becomes the error of the IPS. The notation $\mathcal{L}_{\text{weak},\varepsilon}(\text{IP}(\text{restriction-list}))$ and $\mathcal{L}_{\text{strong},\varepsilon}(\text{IP}(\text{restriction-list}))$ is also adopted.

Say and Yakaryılmaz proved that [6]:

$$\text{NL} \subseteq \mathcal{L}_{\text{weak},\varepsilon}(\text{IP}(\text{2pfa}, \text{constant-randomness})) \quad \text{for } \varepsilon > 0 \text{ arbitrarily small, (3)}$$

$$\text{NL} \subseteq \mathcal{L}_{\text{strong},\varepsilon}(\text{IP}(\text{2pfa}, \text{constant-randomness})) \quad \text{for } \varepsilon = \frac{1}{2} - \frac{1}{2k^2}, k \to \infty. \quad (4)$$

For the latter proposition, the research proves that any language $L \in \text{NL}$ can be recognized by a one-way IPS $S \in \text{IP}(\text{2pfa}, \text{constant-randomness})$, which satisfies $\varepsilon_{\text{strong}}(S) \leq 1/2 - 1/2k$, and where k is the minimum number of heads among the $\text{2nfa}(k)$ recognizing L that also halts on every input. Existence of such a $\text{2nfa}(k)$ is guaranteed by Lemmas 2 and 4.

This work improves on the findings of [6]. For their pertinence, an outline of the algorithms attaining the errors in Eqs. (3) and (4) is provided in the following sections.

3.1   Reducing Weak Error Arbitrarily Using Constant-Randomness Verifier

Given a language $L \in \text{NL}$ with a halting $\text{2nfa}(k)$ recognizer M, verifier $V_1 \in \text{2pfa}$ expects a certificate to report (i) the k symbols read, and (ii) the nondeterministic branch taken for each transition made by M on the course of accepting w. Such a report necessarily contains a lie, if $w \notin \mathcal{L}(M) = L$.

Verifier V_1 has an internal representation of M's control. Then, the algorithm for the verifier is as follows:

1. Repeat m times:
    (a) Move head left, until ▷ is read.
    (b) Reset M's state in the internal representation, denoted q_m.
    (c) Randomly choose a head of M by flipping $\lceil \log k \rceil$ coins.
    (d) Repeat until q_m becomes the accepting state of M:
        i. Read k symbols and the nondeterministic branch taken by M from the certificate.
        ii. *Reject* if the reading from V_1's head disagrees with the corresponding symbol on the certificate.
        iii. Make the transition in the internal representation if it is valid, and move the chosen head as dictated by the nondeterministic branch. *Reject* otherwise.
2. *Accept*.

For the worst case errors, it is assumed that there is a lie for the certificate to tell about each one of the heads alone and in any single one of the transitions, which causes V_1 to fail to reject a string $w \notin L$. Similar lies are assumed to exist for the false acceptances. The following are then the (upper bounds of) errors for V_1:

$$\varepsilon_{\text{fail-to-accept}}(V_1) = 0 \quad \varepsilon_{\text{fail-to-reject}}(V_1) \leq \frac{k-1}{k} \quad \varepsilon_{\text{false-accept}}(V_1) \leq \frac{1}{k^m}$$

A discrepancy between $\varepsilon_{\text{false-accept}}$ and $\varepsilon_{\text{fail-to-reject}}$ is observed, because an adversarial certificate may wind V_1 up in an infinite loop on its first round of m repetitions. This is possible despite M being a halting machine. The lie in the certificate can present an infinite and even changing input string from the perspective of the head being lied about.

Being wound up counts as a failure to reject, but does not yield a false acceptance. The resulting weak error is $\varepsilon_{\text{strong}} = k^{-m}$, which can be made arbitrarily small.

3.2 Bringing Strong Error Below 1/2 Using Constant-Randomness Verifier

Presented first in [6], verifier V_1' with the following algorithm manages to achieve $\varepsilon_{\text{strong}}(V_1') < 1/2$, outlined as follows:

1. Randomly *reject* with $(k-1)/2k$ probability by flipping $\lceil \log k \rceil + 1$ coins.
2. Continue as V_1.

This algorithm then has the following upper bounds for the errors:

$$\varepsilon_{\text{fail-to-accept}}(V_1') = \frac{k-1}{2k} \quad \varepsilon_{\text{fail-to-reject}}(V_1') \leq \frac{k^2-1}{2k^2} \quad \varepsilon_{\text{false-accept}}(V_1') \leq \frac{k+1}{2k^{m+1}}$$

Since $\varepsilon_{\text{fail-to-reject}}(V_1')$ is potentially greater than $\varepsilon_{\text{fail-to-accept}}(V_1')$, the strong error is bounded by $(k^2-1)/2k^2$.

4 Windable Heads

This section will introduce a property of the heads of a 2nfa(k). It leads to a characterization of the 2nfa(k) by the number of heads with this property. A subset rNL of the class NL will be defined, which will also be a subset of $\mathcal{L}_{\text{strong},\varepsilon}(\text{IP}(2\text{pfa}, \text{constant-randomness}))$ for $\varepsilon > 0$ approaching zero.

A head of a 2nfa(k) M is said to be *windable*, if these three conditions hold:

– There is a cycle on the graph of M's transition diagram, and a path from q_0 to a node on the cycle.
– The movements of the head-in-question add up to zero in a full round of that cycle.
– The readings of the head is consistent along the said path and cycle.

The definition of a head being windable completely disregards the readings of the other heads, hence the witness path and the cycle need not be a part of a realistic execution of the machine M.

We will define the windable heads formally to clarify its distinguishing points. Some preliminary definitions will be needed.

Definition 6 (Multi-step transition function).

$$\delta^t \colon Q \times (\Gamma^t)^k \to \mathcal{P}\left(Q_{\backslash q_0} \times (\Delta^t)^k\right)$$

is the t-step extension of the transition function δ of a 2nfa(k) M. It is defined recursively, as follows:

$$\delta^1 = \delta$$

$$\delta^t(q, g_1, \dots, g_k) = \left\{ (r, D_1 \circ d_1, \dots, D_k \circ d_k) \;\middle|\; \begin{array}{l} (r, d_1, \dots, d_k) \in \delta(s, g_{1t}, \dots, g_{kt}) \\ (s, D_1, \dots, D_k) \in \delta^{t-1}(q, g_1^\times, \dots, g_k^\times) \end{array} \right\}$$

The set $\delta^t(q, g_1, \dots, g_k)$ contains a $(k+1)$-tuple for each nondeterministic computation to be performed by M, as it starts from the state q and reads g_i with its ith head. These tuples, each referred to as a *computation log*, consist of the state reached, and the movement histories of the k heads during that computation.

The constraint of a constant and persistent tape contents that is present in an execution of a 2nfa(k) is blurred in the definition for multi-step transition function. This closely resembles the verifier's perspective of the remaining heads that it does not verify in the previous section. There, however, the verifier's readings were consistent in itself. This slight will be accounted for with the next pair of definitions.

Definition 7 (Relative head position during ith transition). *Let M be a 2nfa(k) that does not attempt to move its heads beyond the end markers on the input tape, and δ be its transition function. Let H be a head of M, and D be any t-step movement history in the output of δ^t of that head. The relative position of H while making the ith transition of D since before making the first movement in that history is given by the function $\rho_D(i) \colon \mathbb{N}_1^{\le t} \to (-t, t)$ defined as*

$$\rho_D(i) = \mathrm{sum}(D_{1:i-1}).$$

By Lemmas 3 and 4, given any language in NL there is a 2nfa(k) recognizing it, which also does not attempt to move its heads beyond the end markers.

Definition 8 (1-head consistent δ^t). $\delta_1^t \colon Q \times (\Gamma^t)^k \to \mathcal{P}\left(Q_{\backslash q_0} \times (\Delta^t)^k\right)$ *is the ith-head consistent subset of δ^t of a 2nfa(k) M. It filters out the first-head inconsistent computation logs by scrutinizing the purportedly read characters by examining the movement histories against the readings. The formal definition assumes that M does not attempt to move its heads beyond the end markers, and is as follows:*

$$\delta_1^t(q, g_1, \dots, g_k) = \left\{ (r, D_1, \dots, D_k) \in \delta^t(q, g_1, \dots, g_k) \;\middle|\; \right.$$
$$\left. \forall p \in (-t, t), \; \forall x, y \in \rho_{D_i}^{-1}(p) \; [g_{i_x} = g_{i_y}] \right\}$$

For each pair of transitions departing from the same tape cell, it is checked whether the same symbol is read while being performed. This check is needed to be done only for $p \in (-t, t)$, since in t steps, a head may at most travel t cells afar, and the last cell it can read from will then be the previous one. This is also consistent with the definition of ρ_D.

This last definition is the exact analogue of the verifiers' perspective in the algorithms proposed by [6]. It can be used directly in our next definition, that will lead us to a characterization of the 2nfa(k).

Definition 9 (Windable heads). *The ith head of a 2nfa(k) M is windable iff there exists;*

1. $g_1, \ldots, g_k \in \Gamma^t$ and $g'_1, \ldots, g'_k \in \Gamma^l$, for t and l positive,
2. $(q, D_1, \ldots, D_k) \in \delta_i^t(q_0, g_1, \ldots, g_k)$,
3. $(q, D_1 \circ D'_1, \ldots, D_k \circ D'_k) \in \delta_i^{t+l}(q_0, g_1 \circ g'_1, \ldots, g_k \circ g'_k)$ *where* sum$(D'_i) = 0$.

When these conditions hold, $g_1, \ldots, g_k$ can be viewed as the sequences of characters that can be fed to δ to bring M from q_0 to q, crucially without breaking consistency among the ith head's readings. This ensures reachability to state q. Then, the sequences $g'_1, \ldots, g'_k$ wind the ith head into a loop; bringing M back to state q and the first head back to where it started the loop, all while keeping the ith head's readings consistent. The readings from the other heads are allowed to be inconsistent, and their position can change with every such loop.

A head is *reliable* iff the head is not windable.

It is important to note that a winding is not based on a realistic execution of a 2nfa(k). A head of a 2nfa(k) M might be windable, even if it is guaranteed to halt on every input. This is because the property of being windable allows other heads to have *unrealistic*, inconsistent readings that may be never realized with any input string.

5 Recognizing Some Languages in **NL** with Constant-Randomness and Reducible-Error Verifiers

Consider a language $L \in$ NL with a 2nfa(k) recognizer M that halts on every input. In designing the randomness-restricted 2pfa(1) verifier V_2, the following three cases will be considered:

All Heads Are Reliable. In this case, V_1 suffices by itself to attain reducible error. Without any windable heads in the underlying 2nfa(k), each round of V_1 will terminate. The certificate can only make V_1 falsely accept, and the chances for that can be reduced arbitrarily by increasing m.

All Heads Are Windable. In this case, unless the worst-case assumptions are alleviated, any verification algorithm using a simulation principle similar to V_1 will be wound up on the first round. The head with the minimum probability of getting chosen will be the weakest link of V_2, thus the head the certificate will be lying about. The failure to reject rate is equal 1 minus that probability. This rate is the lowest when the probabilities are equal, and is then $(k-1)/k$.

It Is a Mix. Let k_W, k_R denote the windable and reliable head counts, respectively. Thus $k_W + k_R = k$. The new verifier algorithm V_2 is similar to V_1, but instead of choosing a head to simulate with equal probability, it will do a *biased branching*. With biased branching, V_2 favors the reliable heads over the windable heads while choosing a head to verify.

Let P_W, P_R denote the desired probability of choosing a windable and reliable head, respectively. Note that $P_W + P_R = 1$. The probabilities of choosing a head within types (windable or reliable) are kept equal. Denote the probability of choosing a particular windable head as $p_W = P_W/k_W$, and similarly $p_r = P_R/k_R$. Assume P_W, P_R are finitely representable in binary, and with b digits after the decimal point. Then, the algorithm of V_2 is the same as V_1, with the only difference at step 1c:

1c.' Randomly choose a head of M by biased branching:

- Instead of flipping $\lceil \log k \rceil$ coins, flip $b + \lceil \log(\max(k_W, k_R)) \rceil$ coins. Let $z_1, z_2, \ldots, z_b$ be the outcomes of the first b coins.
- If $\sum_{i=1}^{b} 2^{-i} z_i < P_W$, choose one of the windable heads depending on the outcomes of the next $\lceil \log k_W \rceil$ coins. Otherwise, similarly choose a reliable head via $\lceil \log k_R \rceil$ coins.

For an Input String $w \in L$. Verifier V_2 is still perfectly accurate. Certificate may provide any route that leads M to acceptance. Repeating this for m-many times, V_2 will accept after m rounds of validation.

For an Input String $w \notin L$. To keep V_2 from rejecting, the certificate will need to lie about at least one of the heads. Switching the head to lie about in between rounds cannot be of any benefit to the certificate on its mission, since the rounds are identical both from V_2's and the certificate's points of view. Hence, it is reasonable to assume that the certificate repeats itself in each round, and simplify our analysis.

The worst-case assumption is that the certificate can lie about a single (arbitrary) head alone and deceive V_2 in the worst means possible, depending on the head it chooses:

- If it chooses the head being lied about, V_2 detects the lie rather than being deceived.
- Otherwise, if a windable head was chosen, V_2 loops indefinitely.
- Otherwise (i.e. a reliable head was chosen), V_2 runs for another round or accepts w.

The head which the certificate fixes to lie about is either a windable head or a reliable one. Given a V_2 algorithm with its parameter P_W set, let $F_W(P_R)$ be the probability of V_2 failing to reject against a certificate that lies about any one windable head. Failure to reject would either be a result of up to $m - 1$ rounds of false-acceptance followed by getting wound up in an infinite loop, or by m rounds of false-acceptance.

$$F_W(P_R) = \sum_{i=0}^{m-1} P_R^i (P_W - p_W) + P_R^m$$

$$= (1 - P_R^m) \cdot \left(1 - \frac{1}{k_W}\right) + P_R^m$$

$$= 1 - \frac{1 - P_R^m}{k_W}$$

Let $F_R(P_R)$ similarly be the probability for the reliable counterpart.

$$F_R(P_R) = \sum_{i=0}^{m-1} (P_R - p_R)^i P_W + (P_R - p_R)^m$$

$$= \frac{1 - (P_R - p_R)^m}{1 - (P_R - p_R)} \cdot P_W + (P_R - p_R)^m$$

$$= \frac{P_W}{P_W + p_R} + \left(1 - \frac{P_W}{P_W + p_R}\right)(P_R - p_R)^m$$

The most evil certificate would lie about the head that yields a higher error. Thus, the worst-case failure to reject probability is given by

$$F(P_R) = \max(F_W(P_R), F_R(P_R)).$$

The objective is to find the optimum P_R, denoted P_R^*, minimizing the error $F(P_R)$. We note that $F(1)$ is 1. Hence, $P_R^* < 1$.

Constant m may be chosen arbitrarily large. For $P_R < 1$, and m very large, approximations of F_W and F_R are, respectively, given as

$$F_W^*(P_R) = 1 - \frac{1}{k_W} \qquad\qquad F_R^*(P_R) = \frac{P_W}{P_W + p_R}.$$

Error F_W^* is a constant between 0 and 1. For $0 \le P_R \le 1$, error F_R^* decreases from 1 to 0, and in a strictly monotonous fashion:

$$\frac{dF_R^*}{dP_R} = \frac{-p_R - P_W/k_W}{(P_W + p_R)^2} < 0$$

These indicate that $F_W^*(P_R)$ and $F_R^*(P_R)$ are equal for a unique $P_R = P_R^*$. The optimality of P_R^* will be proved shortly. It is easy to verify that

$$P_R^* = \frac{k_R}{k - 1}. \tag{5}$$

Using P_R^* we can define F^* as the following partial function:

$$F^*(P_R) = \begin{cases} F_R^*(P_R) & \text{for } P_R \le P_R^* \\ F_W^*(P_R) & \text{for } P_R \ge P_R^* \end{cases}$$

Since F_R^* is a decreasing function, $F(P_R) > F(P_R^*)$ for any $P_R < P_R^*$. The approximation F_W^* is a constant function. Function F_W, however, is actually an increasing one. Therefore, given m large, probability P_R^* approximates the optimum for V_2 choosing a reliable head among the k heads of the M, while verifying for the language $\mathcal{L}(M) \in$ NL. Consequently the optimum error for V_2 is

$$F(P_R^*) = 1 - \frac{1}{k_W}. \tag{6}$$

This points to some important facts.

Theorem 1. *The minimum error for V_2 depends only on the number of windable heads of the 2nfa(k) M recognizing $L \in$ NL.*

Definition 10 (Reducible strong error subset of NL). *For $\varepsilon > 0$ approaching zero, the reducible strong error subset of NL is defined as*

$$rNL = NL \cap \mathcal{L}_{strong,\varepsilon}\left(IP(2pfa, constant\text{-}randomness)\right).$$

Theorem 2. *For $k_W \leq 1$ and k_R arbitrary,*

$$\mathcal{L}(2nfa(k_W + k_R)) \subseteq rNL.$$

Equations (5) and (6), and their consequent Theorems 1 and 2, constitute the main results of this study.

Similar to how V_1' was obtained, the algorithm for V_2' is as follows:

1. Randomly *reject* with $(k_W - 1)/2k_W$ probability by flipping $\lceil \log k_W \rceil + 1$ coins.
2. Continue as V_2.

The strong error of V_2' is then given by $\varepsilon_{strong}(V_2') \leq 1/2 - 1/2k_W$.

5.1   Example Languages from rNL and Potential Outsiders

Let w_a denote the amount of symbols a in a string w.

The following two are some example languages with 2nfa($k_W + k_R$) recognizers, where $k_W = 0$:

$$A_1 = \{\, a^n b^n c^n d^n \mid n \geq 0 \,\}$$
$$A_2 = \{\, w \in \{a, b, c\} \mid w_a = w_b = w_c \,\}$$

An example language with a $k_W \leq 1$ recognizer is the following:

$$A_3 = \{\, a_1 a_2 \cdots a_n \# a_1^+ a_2^+ \cdots a_n^+ \mid n \geq 0 \,\}$$

Lastly, it is an open question whether the following language is inside or outside rNL:

$$A_4 = \{\, w \in \{a, b, c\} \mid w_a \cdot w_b = w_c \,\}$$

6   Open Questions

It is curious to us whether $\mathcal{L}\left(2\mathsf{nfa}(k_W + k_R)\right)$ coincides with any known class of languages for $k_W = 0$ or 1, or $k_W \leq 1$. The minimum number or windable heads required for a language in NL to be recognized by a halting $2\mathsf{nfa}(k)$, could establish a complexity class. Conversely, one might be able to discover yet another infinite hierarchy of languages based on the number of windable heads, alongside the hierarchy in Lemma 1. For some $c > 0$ and $k'_W = k_W + c$, this hierarchy might be of the form

$$\mathcal{L}\left(2\mathsf{nfa}(k = k_W + k_R)\right) \subsetneq \mathcal{L}\left(2\mathsf{nfa}(k' = k'_W + k'_R)\right)$$

for $k = k'$, $k_R = k'_R$, or without any further restriction.

References

1. Condon, A.: The complexity of space bounded interactive proof systems. In: Ambos-Spies, A., et al. (eds.) Complexity Theory: Current Research, pp. 147–189. Cambridge University Press, Cambridge (1992). https://www.cs.ubc.ca/~condon/papers/ips-survey.pdf
2. Hartmanis, J.: On non-determinancy in simple computing devices. Acta Informatica **1**(4), 336–344 (1972). https://doi.org/10.1007/BF00289513
3. Holzer, M., Kutrib, M., Malcher, A.: Complexity of multi-head finite automata: origins and directions. Theoret. Comput. Sci. **412**(1–2), 83–96 (2011). https://doi.org/10.1016/j.tcs.2010.08.024
4. Monien, B.: Transformational methods and their application to complexity problems. Acta Informatica **6**(1), 95–108 (1976). https://doi.org/10.1007/BF00263746
5. Monien, B.: Two-way multihead automata over a one-letter alphabet. RAIRO Informatique Théorique **14**(1), 67–82 (1980). https://doi.org/10.1051/ita/1980140100671
6. Say, C., Yakaryılmaz, A.: Finite state verifiers with constant randomness. Log. Methods Comput. Sci. **10**(3) (2014). https://doi.org/10.2168/LMCS-10(3:6)2014. arXiv:1102.2719

Alternating Finite Automata
with Limited Universal Branching

Chris Keeler[✉] and Kai Salomaa

School of Computing, Queen's University, Kingston, ON K7L 2N8, Canada
{keeler,ksalomaa}@cs.queensu.ca

Abstract. We consider measures that limit universal parallelism in computations of an alternating finite automaton (AFA). *Maximum pared tree width* counts the largest number of universal branches in any computation and *acceptance width* counts the number of universal branches in the best accepting computation, i.e., in the accepting computation with least universal parallelism. We give algorithms to decide whether the maximum pared tree width or the acceptance width of an AFA are bounded by an integer k. For a constant k the algorithm for maximum pared tree width operates in polynomial time. An AFA with m states and acceptance width k can be converted to an NFA with $(m + 1)^k$ states. We consider corresponding lower bounds for the transformation. The *tree width* of an AFA counts the number of all (existential and universal) branches of the computation. We give upper and lower bounds for converting an AFA of bounded tree width to a DFA.

1 Introduction

Deterministic and nondeterministic finite automata (DFA and NFA) are well understood models for which a significant number of results are known. As a generalization of nondeterminism, *alternation* was introduced in [1], and has since been studied extensively for Turing machines [5,6,23], and pushdown automata [1,20].

The power of alternation in finite automata (AFAs) was first studied by Chandra, Kozen, and Stockmeyer [1], later by King [15] and Hromkovič [10], and state complexity trade-offs with NFAs and DFAs were given by Fellah et al. [3]. However, results on alternating finite automata remain relatively sparse compared to alternating pushdown automata and alternating (infinite) automata, and little effort has been made towards examining restricted computations within the context of alternation.

Restricted amounts of nondeterminism have been measured in various ways, including but not limited to *ambiguity* [19], *tree width* [11,22], and *string path width* [13]. These so-called "measures of nondeterminism" examine some aspect of an automaton's computations. For example, the number of partial, or accepting computations on a given string. For a particular regular language and model, the *state complexity* is a measure of how complicated it is for that model to capture that language. The state complexity is combined with these measures of

© Springer Nature Switzerland AG 2020
A. Leporati et al. (Eds.): LATA 2020, LNCS 12038, pp. 196–207, 2020.
https://doi.org/10.1007/978-3-030-40608-0_13

restricted nondeterminism, yielding tradeoffs between the amount of nondeterminism and the number of states required.

An automaton is said to *alternate* when it switches from an existential state to a universal state (or vice versa) [1]. There exists an exponential state complexity blow-up between two-way AFAs with at most k alternations and two-way AFAs with at most $k + 1$ alternations, and in general this hierarchy is infinite [7]. The emptiness problem for AFAs was shown to be PSPACE-Complete for general alphabets [8,12]. More recently, the state complexity of various operations on AFAs has also been studied [9].

In this paper, we focus on the original model of AFAs (introduced by Chandra, Kozen, and Stockmeyer) where the states are either *existential* or *universal* [1,7,10,12,15,23], rather than the one where states are labeled with boolean functions [18]. However, both of these models recognize exactly the regular languages. We also do not consider states or transitions with negation, though there is only a linear blow-up between our model and the one which can perform negation [3].

This paper is organized as follows. Section 2 recalls several definitions, and fixes our model for alternating finite automata. Section 2.1 introduces the notions of acceptance width and maximal pared tree width, and provides several initial results and bounds for these new metrics. Section 3 gives a polynomial transformation for an NFA to simulate an AFA with bounded parallelism, shows that the decidability of several decision problems for AFAs with finite acceptance width, and gives algorithms to decide whether an AFA's maximal pared tree width or acceptance width is bounded by a given constant. Section 4 presents unary witness languages with finite acceptance width (with respect to the number of states) which require only a small number of states to be recognized by an AFA, but require an exponential number of states to be recognized by an NFA or DFA. Finally, Sect. 4.1 introduces a non-unary witness language, and provides another exponential state complexity blow-up; this time between AFAs with bounded tree width (with respect to the number of states), and NFAs and DFAs.

2 Preliminaries

An AFA is a 6-tuple, $A = (Q_e, Q_u, \Sigma, \delta, q_0, F)$ where Q_e (the existential state set) and Q_u (the universal state set) are finite sets of states such that $Q_e \cap Q_u = \emptyset$, Σ is the input alphabet, $\delta : (Q_e \cup Q_u) \times \Sigma \to 2^{Q_e \cup Q_u}$ is the transition function, $q_0 \in Q_e \cup Q_u$ is the initial state, and $F \subseteq Q_e \cup Q_u$ is the set of final states. We use ε to mean the empty string, and A_q to mean A with a different specified starting state, $q \in Q_e \cup Q_u$. Note that the standard NFA model can be seen as an AFA where Q_e contains all of the states, and Q_u is empty. We must further specify the *language* of an AFA, to account for the differences caused by universal states. We do this by defining them bottom-up with respect to their states.

Definition 1. *Let $A = (Q_e, Q_u, \Sigma, \delta, q_0, F)$ be an AFA, and A_q be a copy of the AFA with $q \in Q_e \cup Q_u$ as the initial state. We point out that $\varepsilon \in L(A_q)$ if $q \in F$.*

Consider $q \in Q_e \cup Q_u, a \in \Sigma$ where $\delta(q,a) = \{p_1,\ldots,p_n\}$. Then for $x \in \Sigma^*$, define:

- *If $q \in Q_u$, then $ax \in L(A_q)$ if and only if $x \in L(A_{p_i})$ for all $1 \leq i \leq n$.*
- *If $q \in Q_e$, then $ax \in L(A_q)$ if and only if $x \in L(A_{p_i})$ for some $1 \leq i \leq n$.*

The language of A is defined as $L(A) = L(A_{q_0})$.

The *computation tree* of an AFA A on ε from $q \in Q_e \cup Q_u$, denoted $T_{A,q,\varepsilon}$ is the singleton node (q,ε). The *computation tree* of an AFA A on cv from q, denoted $T_{A,q,cv}$, such that $q \in Q_e \cup Q_u, c \in \Sigma, v \in \Sigma^*$ is defined inductively as the tree:

- whose internal nodes are labeled by a tuple (p,a), for $p \in Q, a \in \Sigma$ (i.e., each internal node is labeled by a state and character)
- which is rooted by a node (q,c)
- where the trees rooted at the children of (q,c) are
  - the computation trees $(T_{A,p_1,v},\ldots,T_{A,p_n,v})$ if $\delta(q,c) = \{p_1,\ldots,p_n\}$, and
  - the failure node $\perp$ if $\delta(q,c) = \emptyset$ (that is, if $\delta(q,c)$ is undefined).

If a computation tree of an AFA A on a string x starts on the initial state of A, then we omit the state label, denoting it as $T_{A,x}$. We use the notation leaves(T) to mean the (depth-first) ordered tuple of leaves in the computation tree T. The computation tree of an NFA is defined similarly, except its nodes are always labeled by existential states [11].

We define the *paring* of a computation tree, which serves as the transformation around which our new measures are defined. For an AFA $A = (Q_e, Q_u, \Sigma, \delta, q_0, F)$ and a string $x \in \Sigma^*$, a *pared computation tree* of $T_{A,x}$ is defined as a tree where for each node $(q,a) \in T_{A,x}$:

- if $q \in Q_e$ then keep only one child node, and
- if $q \in Q_u$ then keep all child nodes.

Since there is a choice made on each of the existential nodes, the same computation tree can result in many different pared computation trees. A pared tree represents a possible computation of the AFA A. At nodes labeled by existential states, the pared tree follows one (nondeterministically chosen) way to continue the computation. The nodes labeled by universal states have children labeled by all states reachable from that state in the next computation step. Note that every pared tree of an NFA will only have one leaf, since all of its states are existential. We denote the set of all pared computation trees on a tree T as $\succ\!\!\prec(T)$. A pared computation tree is *accepting* if all of its leaves are labeled by accepting states (implying that no leaf is the failure node), and a string x is accepted by an AFA if and only if A has an accepting pared computation tree in $\succ\!\!\prec(T_{A,x})$.

Without loss of generality, we assume that all of an AFA's universal states are reachable. However, since emptiness for AFAs is PSPACE-Complete, we cannot assume that all of an AFA's states are useful in the sense that they can be used in an accepting computation. Since a universal state with at most one outgoing transition per character is no different than using an existential state, we also assume that every universal state has multiple outgoing transitions on at least one character.

For a regular language L, $\mathrm{sc}(L)$, (respectively, $\mathrm{nsc}(L), \mathrm{asc}(L)$), is the *state complexity*, (respectively, nondeterministic and alternating state complexity) of L.

2.1   Tree Width of Alternating Machines

The *tree width* [11] of an AFA A on a string x, denoted $\mathrm{tw}(A, x)$, is the number of leaves in the computation tree of A on x. That is, $\mathrm{tw}(A, x) = |leaves(T_{A,x})|$.

Since the notion of tree width is originally based on the computation tree of an NFA, and our AFA definition extends the original notion of computation trees, it seems natural to look at "alternating tree widths".

Definition 2. *Let $A = (Q_e, Q_u, \Sigma, \delta, q_0, F)$ be an AFA. Then the* acceptance width *of A on a string $x \in \Sigma^*$, denoted $\mathrm{aw}(A, x)$, is the minimum number of leaves of any accepting pared computation tree of $T_{A,x}$. The* maximum pared tree width *of A on a string $x \in \Sigma^*$, denoted $\mathrm{mptw}(A, x)$, is the maximum number of leaves of any pared computation tree of $T_{A,x}$. Formally, these are:*

$$\mathrm{aw}(A, x) = \min\{|leaves(T)| \mid T \in {\prec}(T_{A,x}), \ leaves(T) \subseteq F\}$$

$$\mathrm{mptw}(A, x) = \max\{|leaves(T)| \mid T \in {\prec}(T_{A,x})\}$$

Since the (original) tree width does not perform the paring operation, we get that for any AFA A and string x, $\mathrm{aw}(A, x) \le \mathrm{mptw}(A, x) \le \mathrm{tw}(A, x)$. We also get the following condition for equality between the measures, which occurs when the paring operation does not change the computation tree.

Remark 1. Let A be an AFA, and x a string. Then $\mathrm{mptw}(A, x) = \mathrm{tw}(A, x)$ if and only if each node in $T_{A,x}$ with more than one child is labeled by some universal state in A.

We extend the acceptance width and maximum pared tree width functions as functions on integers in the normal manner:

$$\mathrm{aw}(A, \ell) = \max\{\mathrm{aw}(A, x) \mid x \in \Sigma^\ell\},$$

$$\mathrm{mptw}(A, \ell) = \max\{\mathrm{mptw}(A, x) \mid x \in \Sigma^\ell\}.$$

$$\mathrm{aw}(A) = \sup_{\ell \in \mathbb{N}}\{\mathrm{aw}(A, \ell)\}, \text{ and } \mathrm{mptw}(A) = \sup_{\ell \in \mathbb{N}}\{\mathrm{mptw}(A, \ell)\}.$$

If, for a string x, there are no accepting computation trees, then $\mathrm{aw}(A, x) = 0$. Since the emptiness problem is PSPACE-complete for AFAs [8], and these results hold even for unary languages, then we get the following equivalence.

Remark 2 ([8]). Let A be an AFA. Then it is PSPACE-complete to decide whether or not $\mathrm{aw}(A) = 0$.

If an m-state AFA has finite tree width, then its tree width is at most 2^{m-2} [22]. Since, on any string, the acceptance width and maximal pared tree width of an AFA are upper-bounded by the tree width, we get the following conditional upper bound.

Corollary 1 ([22]). *Let A be an m-state AFA with finite tree width. Then $\mathrm{aw}(A) \leq \mathrm{mptw}(A) \leq 2^{m-2}$.*

Alternatively, we could replace the computation trees by directed acyclic graphs by merging any nodes on the same state on the same level. However, in this case, the acceptance width and maximal pared tree width of an m-state AFA would be at most m.

3   Decision Problems for Pared Tree Width and Acceptance Width

Normally, an NFA may require an exponential state blow-up to simulate an AFA [3]. However, an NFA can simulate any finite acceptance width AFA with at most a polynomial blow-up in the number of states. An m-state AFA A with acceptance width k can be simulated by an NFA where the states are k-tuples of states of A and transitions of the NFA simulate at most k parallel computations of A.

Lemma 1. *Let A be an m-state AFA, such that $\mathrm{aw}(A) \leq k$, for some constant k. Then $(m+1)^k$ states are sufficient for an NFA to simulate A.*

It is known that the emptiness problem for NFAs can be solved in linear time, with respect to the number of states, using a breadth first search [4]. The transformation from Lemma 1 then yields a polynomial-time algorithm to decide emptiness for a finite acceptance width AFA.

Corollary 2. *Let A be an m-state AFA with finite acceptance width k, for some constant k. Then in $O(m^k)$ time we can decide whether $L(A) = \emptyset$.*

Using the transformation from Lemma 1, but modifying which states of the NFA are accepting, we can also decide whether the maximal pared tree width of an AFA is bounded.

Theorem 1. *Let A be an m-state AFA and k a constant. Then we can decide whether or not the maximal pared tree width of A is at most k in $O(m^k)$ time.*

Using similar ideas from the characterization of NFAs with finite tree width [22], we are able to characterize AFAs with finite maximal pared tree width.

Corollary 3. *Let $A = (Q_u, Q_e, \Sigma, \delta, q_0, F)$ be an AFA. Then $\mathrm{mptw}(A) > 2^{m-2}$ if and only if there exists some state $q \in Q_u$ and character $c \in \Sigma$ such that $|\delta(q, c)| \geq 2$ and q is involved in a cycle.*

Modifying existing algorithms for deciding finiteness of an NFA's tree width [14], we are also able to decide finiteness of an AFA's maximal pared tree width in polynomial time.

Corollary 4 ([14]). *Let $A = (Q_u, Q_e, \Sigma, \delta, q_0, F)$ be an m-state AFA. Then we can decide whether or not the maximal pared tree width of A is bounded by some constant k in $O(m^3 \cdot |\Sigma|)$ time[1].*

The general membership problem is P-complete for AFAs [12], and this holds even for finite unary languages. In fact, this P-completeness is even stronger, as it holds for all cycle-free AFAs.

Since an m-state cycle-free AFA has at most $m - 1$ states being evaluated in parallel, then the membership problem for AFAs with bounded parallel computations is also P-complete.

Corollary 5 ([12]). *Let A be a finite maximal pared tree width AFA. Then for a string x, it is P-complete to decide whether $x \in L(A)$.*

We can also decide whether the pared acceptance width of an AFA is finitely bounded by some number.

Theorem 2. *Let A be an AFA, and $k \in \mathbb{N}$. Then it is decidable whether the acceptance width of A is bounded by k.*

While it is decidable whether the acceptance width of an AFA is bounded by an integer k, the algorithm presented in Theorem 2 is not an efficient one and we cannot expect to have an efficient algorithm for this problem[2]. For a given AFA A and $k \in \mathbb{N}$ we can construct an AFA A' that begins the computation by a universal step with $k+1$ choices, where the first computation simulates A and the remaining k computations always accept deterministically. Then $aw(A') \leq k$ if and only if $L(A) = \emptyset$ and deciding the emptiness of an AFA is PSPACE-complete [8].

For any AFA A with finite tree width, the acceptance width of A must also be finite. Under this restriction, we can decide whether the acceptance width of A is finite using the construction from Theorem 2.

Corollary 6. *Let A be an m-state AFA with finite tree width. By Corollary 1, the acceptance width is then at most 2^{m-2}. Since the acceptance width of A is finite if and only if it is at most 2^{m-2}, then it is decidable whether the acceptance width of A is finite. We do this by using Theorem 2 with an input value of 2^{m-2}.*

Since the acceptance width of an AFA is only upper bounded by its tree width, it is possible that an AFA has infinite tree width and finite acceptance width. In this case, we do not have an upper bound for the acceptance width.

---

[1] The DCFS proceedings has a slightly worse bound of $O(m^4 \cdot |\Sigma|)$, and the specifics of the improved version will appear in a future paper.

[2] This observation, with a justification different from the below one, was suggested by an anonymous referee.

Question 1. *Let A be an m-state AFA with infinite tree width and finite acceptance width k. Is there any expression in m which bounds k?*

As a result, it is not immediately obvious whether the finiteness of an AFA's acceptance width is decidable in general.

Question 2. *For an AFA A such that* $\mathrm{tw}(A) \notin O(1)$, *does there exist an algorithm to decide whether or not* $\mathrm{aw}(A) \in O(1)$?

4   State Complexity

Let $\mathcal{I}$ be a set of integers, and $LCM(\mathcal{I})$ be the least common multiple of all elements in $\mathcal{I}$. We define $L_{\forall \mathcal{I}}$ as the set of all unary strings whose lengths are the product of all integers in $\mathcal{I}$.

$$L_{\forall \mathcal{I}} = \{a^y \mid (\forall i \in \mathcal{I})\ y \equiv 0 \ (\mathrm{mod}\ i)\} \tag{1}$$

Equivalently, we have $L_{\forall \mathcal{I}} = \{a^{y \cdot z} \mid z \geq 0, y = LCM(\mathcal{I})\}$.

Lemma 2. *Let $\mathcal{I}$ be a set of integers. Then* $\mathrm{sc}(L_{\forall \mathcal{I}}) = \mathrm{nsc}(L_{\forall \mathcal{I}}) = LCM(\mathcal{I})$.

The state complexity is, of course, maximal with respect to the size of the input set when its elements are pairwise coprime.

Lemma 3. *Let $\mathcal{I} = \{p_1, \ldots, p_n\}$ be a set of n integers. If the elements of $\mathcal{I}$ are pairwise coprime, then there exists an AFA A recognizing $L_{\forall \mathcal{I}}$ with* $1 + \sum_{i=1}^{n} p_i$ *states and tree width n such that* $\mathrm{sc}(L(A)) = \mathrm{nsc}(L(A)) = \prod_{i=1}^{n} p_i$.

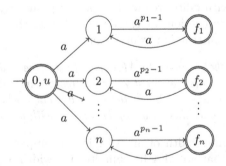

Fig. 1. AFA for $L_{\forall \mathcal{P}}$ where $\mathcal{P} = \{p_1, \ldots, p_n\}$. Universal states are marked with an additional label 'u', and existential states are given as normal.

Proof. Let $\mathcal{I} = \{p_1, \ldots, p_n\}$ be a set of integers whose elements are pairwise coprime. We give the AFA recognizing $L_{\forall \mathcal{I}}$ in Fig. 1, whose tree width and number of states matches the claim. Since $\mathcal{I}$'s elements are pairwise coprime, $LCM(\mathcal{I}) = \prod_{i=1}^{n} p_i$. And by Lemma 2, $sc(L_{\forall \mathcal{I}}) = nsc(L_{\forall \mathcal{I}}) = LCM(\mathcal{I})$. $\qquad\square$

Recognizing that the state complexity blow-up in Lemma 3 is exactly Landau's function [2,21], we get the following exponential state complexity trade-off between AFAs with finite tree width (and therefore also finite acceptance width) and NFAs. A similar idea and result was also given by Kupferman et al. [17], though it was formulated to capture the unary language a^{n+i}, for $i \geq 0$.

Theorem 3 ([2,17,21]). *Let $\mathcal{I}$ be a set of pairwise coprime integers, and A be an $(m-1)$-state AFA recognizing $L_{\forall \mathcal{I}}$ with tree width $|\mathcal{I}|$. Then any NFA equivalent to A will require at least $e^{(1+o(1)) \cdot \sqrt{m \ln m}}$ states.*

While Landau's function gives a lower bound for the state complexity blow-up of simulating a restricted tree width AFA with an NFA, it is only given in terms of the number of states.

Lemma 4. *Let $\mathcal{I} = \{p_1, \ldots, p_n\}$ be a set of pairwise coprime integers, for some $n \in \mathbb{N}$. Let A be an m-state AFA such that A has acceptance width n and recognizes $L_{\forall \mathcal{I}}$. Then any NFA equivalent to A will require at least $(\frac{m}{n \cdot p_n})^n$ states.*

In the general case, for every m, there exists an m-state AFA which cannot be simulated by any NFA with fewer than 2^m states [3], and any equivalent DFA needs 2^{2^m} states [1]. However, to get this double-exponential state complexity blow-up, the m-state AFA needs a tree width much larger than m.

Let $\mathcal{P} = \{p_1, \ldots, p_n\}$ be a set of n prime numbers. We define $L_{2\mathcal{P}}$, the set of all unary strings whose lengths are a product of *at least two* distinct primes from $\mathcal{P}$.

$$L_{2\mathcal{P}} = \{a^x \mid (\exists i, j)\ 1 \leq i < j \leq n,\ \text{such that } p_i \text{ and } p_j \text{ divide } x\} \qquad (2)$$

Lemma 5. *There exists an AFA A recognizing $L_{2\mathcal{P}}$ with $1 + \frac{n(n-1)}{2} + \sum_{i=1}^{n}(p_i - 1)$ states[3] and a maximal pared tree width of 2.*

We extend $L_{2\mathcal{P}}$, defining $L_{k\mathcal{P}}$ as the set of all unary strings whose lengths are a product of *at least k* distinct primes from $\mathcal{P}$, for some constant k.

$$L_{k\mathcal{P}} = \{a^y \mid (\exists r_1, \ldots, r_k)\ \{r_1, \ldots, r_k\} \subseteq \mathcal{P}, \qquad\qquad (3)$$
$$\text{such that } (\forall i)\ 1 \leq i \leq k, y \equiv 0 \pmod{r_i}$$

Using similar ideas as the proof from Lemma 5 but operating on an arbitrary number of elements instead of only two, we get the following result.

Lemma 6. *For every $k \geq 2$, there exists an AFA A recognizing $L_{k\mathcal{P}}$ with $1 + \binom{n}{k} + \sum_{i=1}^{n}(p_i - 1)$ states and a maximal pared tree width of k.*

---

[3] We need one extra state each if 2 or $3 \in \mathcal{P}$.

4.1   Universal Infix Language

For two strings $v, v' \in \Sigma^*$, we say that v and v' are *disjoint* if they do not share any symbols. We extend this notion to tuples of strings, such that a tuple of strings $\mathcal{W}$ is disjoint if and only if all pairs of strings $x, x' \in \mathcal{W}$ are disjoint.

A bitstring $b_1 \cdots b_n \in \{0,1\}^n$ is a string for representing some boolean value across a set of n elements. We define the cardinality of a bistring as the number of 1s appearing in that bitstring.

The *universal infix language* of an ordered string tuple $\mathcal{W}$ consists of strings that contain each $x \in \mathcal{W}$ as an infix. We define a labeling function $h_{\mathcal{W}} : \Sigma^* \rightarrow \{0,1\}^n$ which takes as input a string $s \in \Sigma^*$ and an n-tuple $\mathcal{W}$, and produces the bitstring $b_1 \cdots b_n$, where $b_i = 1$ if and only if the ith element of $\mathcal{W}$ is an infix of s, for $1 \leq i \leq n$. More formally, the universal infix language over a tuple of strings $\mathcal{W}$ and an alphabet Σ is defined as:

$$L_{\alpha\mathcal{W}} = \{s \in \Sigma^* \mid (\forall x \in \mathcal{W}) \ x \text{ is a substring of } s\} \tag{4}$$

An AFA with small amounts of alternation can recognize this language with relatively few states, and limited universal branching.

Lemma 7. *Let $\mathcal{W} = (x_1, \ldots, x_n)$ be an ordered, disjoint tuple of strings. Then there exists an AFA recognizing $L_{\alpha\mathcal{W}}$ with $2 + \sum_{i=1}^{n} |x_i|$ states and tree width n.*

Proof. Let $\mathcal{W} = (x_1, \ldots, x_n)$ be an ordered, disjoint tuple of strings, and let $x_i[j]$ be the jth character of the ith string. We give the general structure for an AFA in Fig. 2, which recognizes $L_{\alpha\mathcal{W}}$ with 1 universal and $1 + \sum_{i=1}^{n} |x_i|$ existential states. This AFA has tree width n, and only alternates between universal and existential states once. The only final state is the one at the end of all the branches. And, excepting the initial state, we define the transition function deterministically. If the machine is reading x_i, has read up to $x_i[j]$, and then encounters some mismatched symbol, then the computation path currently in state $i.j$ will return to state i, indicating that the infix must be restarted.   □

However, a DFA for $L_{\forall\mathcal{W}}$ needs exponentially more states than an AFA.

Lemma 8. *Let $\mathcal{W} = (x_1, \ldots, x_n)$ be a disjoint tuple of strings. Then*

$$\text{sc}(L_{\alpha\mathcal{W}}) = 2^n + 2^{n-1} \cdot \sum_{i=1}^{n} (|x_i| - 1).$$

Furthermore, the addition of nondeterminism does not improve this bound.

Lemma 9. *Let $\mathcal{W} = (x_1, \ldots, x_n)$ be a disjoint tuple of strings. Then*

$$\text{nsc}(L_{\alpha\mathcal{W}}) = 2^n + 2^{n-1} \cdot \sum_{i=1}^{n} (|x_i| - 1).$$

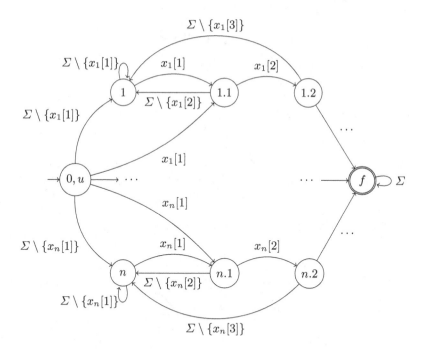

Fig. 2. AFA for a universal infix language over $(x_1, \ldots, x_n)$

Combining Lemmas 7, 8, and 9, we get the following theorem.

Theorem 4. *There exists an m-state AFA A (where m can be arbitrarily large) with tree width n such that any equivalent NFA needs $(m - n) \cdot 2^{n-1}$ states. The AFA A can be chosen to alternate only once between universal and existential states. We note that the alphabet size of A depends on n.*

We give the following constructive example to help clarify the state blow-up from Theorem 4.

Example 1. Let $\mathcal{W} = (aa, b, c)$, and $A = (Q, \{a, b, c\}, \delta, q_0, \{111\})$ be the DFA given in Fig. 3, which recognizes $L_{\alpha(aa,b,c)}$.

To make counting of states easier, below we assume that an AFA computation step always has at most two choices (i.e. computation step is either undefined, is deterministic, or has exactly two existential or universal choices). This assumption can be made with only a constant factor blow-up of the automaton's state complexity [16].

Lemma 10. *Let A be an m-state AFA with tree width n. Then A has an equivalent DFA B with at most $(m + 1)^n \cdot (2^n - 1)$ states.*

Combining the upper and lower bounds from Lemmas 8, 9 and 10, we get the following state complexity range for simulating a finite tree width AFA with a DFA.

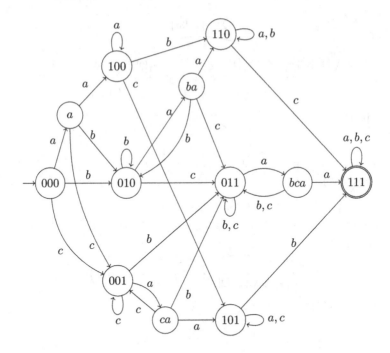

Fig. 3. 12-State DFA for $L_{\alpha(aa,b,c)}$

Corollary 7. *Let A be an m-state AFA with tree width n. Then*

$$2^{n-1} \cdot (m - n) \leq \text{sc}(L(A)) \leq (2^n - 1) \cdot (m + 1)^n.$$

Acknowledgments. Research supported by NSERC grant OGP0147224.

We thank the referees for their helpful and thoughtful comments. But, due to the short deadline for submitting the proceedings version, we will try to implement some revisions for a later journal version.

References

1. Chandra, A.K., Kozen, D.C., Stockmeyer, L.J.: Alternation. J. ACM **28**(1), 114–133 (1981)
2. Chrobak, M.: Finite automata and unary languages. Theoret. Comput. Sci. **47**, 149–158 (1986)
3. Fellah, A., Jürgensen, H., Yu, S.: Constructions for alternating finite automata. Int. J. Comput. Math. **35**(1–4), 117–132 (1990)
4. Fernau, H., Krebs, A.: Problems on finite automata and the exponential time hypothesis. Algorithms **10**(1), 24 (2017)
5. Fijalkow, N.: The state complexity of alternating automata. In: Proceedings of the 33rd Annual ACM/IEEE Symposium on Logic in Computer Science, LICS 2018, Oxford, UK, 09–12 July 2018, pp. 414–421 (2018)

6. Finkbeiner, B., Sipma, H.: Checking finite traces using alternating automata. Formal Methods Syst. Des. **24**(2), 101–127 (2004)
7. Geffert, V.: An alternating hierarchy for finite automata. Theor. Comput. Sci. **445**, 1–24 (2012)
8. Holzer, M.: On emptiness and counting for alternating finite automata. In: Developments in Language Theory II, At the Crossroads of Mathematics, Computer Science and Biology, Magdeburg, Germany, 17–21 July 1995, pp. 88–97 (1995)
9. Hospodár, M., Jirásková, G., Krajňáková, I.: Operations on boolean and alternating finite automata. In: Fomin, F.V., Podolskii, V.V. (eds.) CSR 2018. LNCS, vol. 10846, pp. 181–193. Springer, Cham (2018). https://doi.org/10.1007/978-3-319-90530-3_16
10. Hromkovič, J.: On the power of alternation in automata theory. J. Comput. Syst. Sci. **31**(1), 28–39 (1985)
11. Hromkovič, J., Seibert, S., Karhumäki, J., Klauck, H., Schnitger, G.: Communication complexity method for measuring nondeterminism in finite automata. Inform. Comput. **172**(2), 202–217 (2002)
12. Jiang, T., Ravikumar, B.: A note on the space complexity of some decision problems for finite automata. Inf. Process. Lett. **40**(1), 25–31 (1991)
13. Keeler, C., Salomaa, K.: Branching measures and nearly acyclic NFAs. In: Pighizzini, G., Câmpeanu, C. (eds.) DCFS 2017. LNCS, vol. 10316, pp. 202–213. Springer, Cham (2017). https://doi.org/10.1007/978-3-319-60252-3_16
14. Keeler, C., Salomaa, K.: Nondeterminism growth and state complexity. In: Hospodár, M., Jirásková, G., Konstantinidis, S. (eds.) DCFS 2019. LNCS, vol. 11612, pp. 210–222. Springer, Cham (2019). https://doi.org/10.1007/978-3-030-23247-4_16
15. King, K.N.: Alternating multihead finite automata (extended abstract). In: Even, S., Kariv, O. (eds.) ICALP 1981. LNCS, vol. 115, pp. 506–520. Springer, Heidelberg (1981). https://doi.org/10.1007/3-540-10843-2_40
16. King, K.N.: Measures of parallelism in alternating computation trees (extended abstract). In: Proceedings of the 13th Annual ACM Symposium on Theory of Computing, 11–13 May 1981, Milwaukee, Wisconsin, USA, pp. 189–201 (1981)
17. Kupferman, O., Ta-Shma, A., Vardi, M.Y.: Counting with automata. Short Paper Presented at the 15th Annual IEEE Symposium on Logic in Computer Science (LICS 2000) (2000)
18. Leiss, E.L.: Succinct representation of regular languages by boolean automata. Theor. Comput. Sci. **13**, 323–330 (1981)
19. Leung, H.: Descriptional complexity of nfa of different ambiguity. Int. J. Found. Comput. Sci. **16**(5), 975–984 (2005)
20. Moriya, E.: A grammatical characterization of alternating pushdown automata. Theor. Comput. Sci. **67**(1), 75–85 (1989)
21. Okhotin, A.: Unambiguous finite automata over a unary alphabet. Inf. Comput. **212**, 15–36 (2012)
22. Palioudakis, A., Salomaa, K., Akl, S.G.: State complexity of finite tree width nfas. J. Autom. Lang. Comb. **17**(2–4), 245–264 (2012)
23. Ruzzo, W.L.: Tree-size bounded alternation. J. Comput. Syst. Sci. **21**(2), 218–235 (1980)

Pebble-Intervals Automata
and FO² with Two Orders

Nadia Labai[✉], Tomer Kotek, Magdalena Ortiz, and Helmut Veith

TU Wien, Vienna, Austria
labai@dbai.tuwien.ac.at

Abstract. We introduce a novel automata model, which we call *pebble-intervals automata (PIA)*, and study its power and closure properties. PIAs are tailored for a decidable fragment of FO that is important for reasoning about structures that use data values from infinite domains: the two-variable fragment with one total preorder and its induced successor relation, one linear order, and an arbitrary number of unary relations. We prove that the string projection of every language of data words definable in the logic is accepted by a pebble-intervals automaton $\mathcal{A}$, and obtain as a corollary an automata-theoretic proof of the ExpSpace upper bound for finite satisfiability due to Schwentick and Zeume.

Keywords: Automata and logic · Pebble-intervals automata · Emptiness testing · Decidability · Two-variable fragment · Data words

1 Introduction

Finding decidable fragments of First Order Logic (FO) that are expressive enough for reasoning in different applications is a major line of research. A prominent such fragment is *the two-variable fragment* FO^2 *of FO*, which has a decidable finite satisfiability problem [13,21] and is well-suited for handling graph-like structures. It captures many *description logics*, which are prominent formalisms for knowledge representation, and several authors have recently applied fragments based on FO^2 to verification of programs [1,7,8,16,26]. Unfortunately, FO^2 has severe limitations, e.g., it cannot express transitivity, and in the applications to verification above, it cannot reason about programs whose variables range over data values from infinite domains. This has motivated the exploration of decidable extensions of FO^2 with special relations which are not axiomatizable in FO^2. For example, finite satisfiability of FO^2 with a linear order was shown to be NExpTime-complete in [24], even in the presence of the induced successor relation [12], and equivalence relations have been used to

N. Labai—This work was supported by the Austrian Science Fund (FWF) projects P30360, P30873, and W1255.

This article is dedicated to the memory of Helmut Veith, who passed away tragically while this manuscript was being prepared.

© Springer Nature Switzerland AG 2020
A. Leporati et al. (Eds.): LATA 2020, LNCS 12038, pp. 208–221, 2020.
https://doi.org/10.1007/978-3-030-40608-0_14

model data values which can be tested for equality [3,4,10,23]. However, related extensions of FO^2 with preorders easily become undecidable [3,19]. Recently the logic FO$^2(\leq_1, \precsim_2, S_2)$, that is FO^2 with a linear order $\leq_1$, a total preorder $\precsim_2$ and its induced successor S_2, and any number of unary relations from a finite alphabet, was shown to have an ExpSpace-complete satisfiability problem [27]. This logic can compare data values in terms of which is smaller than which and whether they are consecutive in $\precsim_2$, making it suitable to model linearly ordered data domains, and a good candidate for extending existing verification methods which use two-variable logics. We continue the study of FO$^2(\leq_1, \precsim_2, S_2)$, and in particular, focus on a suitable automata model for it. Establishing a connection to suitable automata for fragments of FO that can talk about values from infinite domains is an active area of research. Automata are also important in automated verification, where they are used, for example, to reason about temporal properties of program traces [9,30]. We make the following contributions:

- As an automata model for FO$^2(\leq_1, \precsim_2, S_2)$ we propose *pebble-intervals automata* (PIAs). Similarly to classical finite-state automata, PIAs are read-once automata for strings. However, they read the input in varying order. Using a fixed set of pebbles $[m] = \{1, \ldots, m\}$, a PIA reads a position p by choosing three pebbles $i, j, k \in [m]$ and non-deterministically moving k to position p between the positions of i and j.
- We study the computational power and closure properties of PIAs. We describe a restricted class of PIAs that accept exactly the regular languages, and show that some context-free languages, and even languages which are not context-free, are accepted by PIAs. We prove that PIAs are effectively closed under union, concatenation, Kleene star, shuffle, and iterated shuffle, but not effectively closed under intersection, even with regular languages, nor under complement.
- We show that the emptiness problem for PIA is NL-complete if the number of pebbles is logarithmic in the size of the automaton, and is PSpace in general.
- We show that PIAs contain FO$^2(\leq_1, \precsim_2, S_2)$ in the following sense: for each sentence ψ, there is a PIA whose language coincides with the *projection language* of ψ, obtained by omitting $\precsim_2$ and S_2 from the structures satisfying ψ.
- As a corollary, we get an automata-theoretic proof for ExpSpace membership of finite satisfiability for FO$^2(\leq_1, \precsim_2, S_2)$ that was established in [27].

Due to space limitations, we have omitted the proofs from the body of the paper. They can be found in the extended version.

2   Pebble-Intervals Automata

In this section, we introduce pebble-intervals automata (PIA). We study their emptiness problem, their expressive power, and closure properties of the languages they accept.

Let $[n] = \{1,\ldots,n\}$. A *string* of length $n \geq 0$ over alphabet Σ is a mapping $w : [n] \to \Sigma$, written also $w = w(1)\cdots w(n)$. Note that $[0] = \emptyset$ and $w : [0] \to \Sigma$ is the empty string ε. We often use s, u, v, and w for strings, and $|w|$ for the length of w.

A PIA is equipped with a finite number m of pebbles. It begins its computation with no pebbles on the input w, and uses MOVE transitions to place and replace pebbles. In a k-MOVE$_{i,j}$ transition, the pebble k (which may or may not have been previously placed on w) is non-deterministically placed on a previously unread position in the interval between pebbles i and j. The input boundaries can be used as interval boundaries, e.g., a k-MOVE$_{i,\lhd}$ transition places pebble k to the right of pebble i. For convenience we allow *silent* transitions that go to a new state without moving any pebbles. As pebbles can only be placed on unread positions, each position of w is read at most once. In an accepting run all positions must be read, and the run must end at an accepting state.

Definition 1 (Pebble-intervals automata). *A PIA $\mathcal{A}$ is a tuple $(\Sigma, m, Q, q_{\text{init}}, F, \delta)$, where Σ is the (finite) alphabet, $m \in \mathbb{N}$, Q is the finite set of states, $q_{\text{init}} \in Q$ is the initial state, $F \subseteq Q$ are the accepting states, and $\delta \subseteq (Q \times Q) \cup (Q \times \text{MOVE}_m \times \Sigma \times Q)$ is the transition relation with* $\text{MOVE}_m = \{k\text{-MOVE}_{i,j} \mid i \in [m] \cup \{\rhd\}, j \in [m] \cup \{\lhd\}, k \in [m], i \neq j\}$. *We may omit m when it is clear from the context. Transitions in $Q \times \text{MOVE} \times \Sigma \times Q$ are MOVE transitions, and transitions in $Q \times Q$ are silent transitions. The size of $\mathcal{A}$ is $|\delta| + |\Sigma| + |Q|$.*

The positions of m pebbles on a string of length n during a run of a PIA are described by an (m, n)-*pebble assignment*, which is a function $\tau : [m] \to [n] \cup \{\bot\}$ with either $\tau(i) \neq \tau(j)$ or $\tau(i) = \tau(j) = \bot$ for each $1 \leq i < j \leq m$; the pebbles j with $\tau(j) = \bot$ are unassigned. We define $\rho_\bot$ as $\rho_\bot(i) = \bot$ for every $i \in [m]$. By $\hat{\tau} : [m] \cup \{\rhd, \lhd\} \to \{0\} \cup [n+1]$ we denote the extension of τ with $\hat{\tau}(\rhd) = 0$ and $\hat{\tau}(\lhd) = n+1$.

Definition 2 (Semantics of PIAs). *Consider a PIA $\mathcal{A} = (\Sigma, m, Q, q_{\text{init}}, F, \delta)$. A configuration of $\mathcal{A}$ on string $u \in \Sigma^\star$ is a triple (q, ρ, N) where $q \in Q$ is the current state, $\rho : [m] \to [|u|] \cup \{\bot\}$ is the current pebble assignment, and $N \subseteq [|u|]$ is the set of already-read positions. The initial configuration π_{init} is $(q_{\text{init}}, \rho_\bot, \emptyset)$. A configuration (q, ρ, N) is accepting if $q \in F$ and $N = [|u|]$. Let $\pi = (q, \rho, N)$ and $\pi' = (q', \rho', N')$ be configurations on u. We call them consecutive and write $\pi \overset{t}{\leadsto} \pi'$ if there exists a transition t in δ such that either:*

1. *t is a silent transition of the form (q, q'), $N = N'$, and $\rho = \rho'$; or*
2. *t is a MOVE transition $(q, k\text{-MOVE}_{i,j}, u(\ell), q')$ with $\hat{\rho}(i) < \ell < \hat{\rho}(j)$ and $\ell \in [|u|] - N$, and additionally $\rho' = \rho[k \mapsto \ell]$ and $N' = N \cup \{\ell\}$. That is, pebble k is placed on position ℓ in the open interval between i and j, reading the letter $u(\ell)$.*

Let $\bar{t} = (t_1, \ldots, t_r)$ and $\bar{\pi} = (\pi_0, \ldots, \pi_r)$ be sequences of transitions and configurations. We call $(\bar{t}, \bar{\pi})$ a computation of $\mathcal{A}$ on u if $\pi_0 = \pi_{\text{init}}$ and $\pi_{i-1} \overset{t_i}{\leadsto}$

π_i for every $i \in [r]$, and write $\pi_0 \overset{\bar{t}}{\leadsto} \pi_r$. We call $(\bar{t}, \bar{\pi})$ accepting if π_r is accepting. We write $\pi \overset{\star}{\leadsto} \pi'$ if $\pi \overset{\bar{t}}{\leadsto} \pi'$ for some $\bar{t}$. The automaton $\mathcal{A}$ accepts u if there is an accepting computation of $\mathcal{A}$ on u. The set of all u accepted by $\mathcal{A}$ is denoted $L(\mathcal{A})$, and called a PI language.

Computational Power of Pebble-Intervals Automata. PIAs generalize standard non-deterministic finite-state automata. A PIA $\mathcal{A} = (\Sigma, 1, Q, q_{\text{init}}, F, \delta)$ with one pebble is *unidirectional* if q_{init} has no incoming transitions, and the MOVE transitions from other states use 1-MOVE$_{1,\lhd}$ only.

Proposition 1. *A language L is accepted by a standard non-deterministic finite-state automaton iff $L = L(\mathcal{A})$ for a unidirectional PIA $\mathcal{A}$ with the same number of states.*

PI languages also contain non-regular languages, and even some non-context-free ones.

Examples 1. *The following are examples of PI languages:*

1. *There is a PIA $\mathcal{A}_{Dyck}$ with one pebble that accepts the Dyck language L_{Dyck} of well-nested brackets, which is context-free but not regular. The alphabet has two letters $[$ and $]$, and the states are $q_[$ and $q_]$. The initial and only accepting state is $q_]$. The transition relation contains $(q_], 1\text{-MOVE}_{\rhd,\lhd}, [, q_[)$ and $(q_[, 1\text{-MOVE}_{1,\lhd},], q_])$. $\mathcal{A}_{Dyck}$ accepts a string iff there are as many left as right brackets, and no prefix has more right than left brackets.*

2. *A similar one pebble PIA accepts the language L_{two} of all strings of two types of parentheses, where each type is well-nested with respect to itself, but not necessarily to the other type. E.g., $([)] \in L_{two}$, but $(] \notin L_{two}$. L_{two} is not context-free.*

3. *$\{a^n\$b^n\#c^n \mid n \geq 0\}$, which is not context-free, is accepted by a PIA with 3 pebbles. Pebbles 1 and 2 read the $\$$ and the $\#$, and then the PIA keeps doing the following: pebble 3 reads an a to the left of pebble 1, a b between pebbles $1, 2$, and a c to the right of pebble 2.*

4. *$\{w\$w \mid w \in \{0,1\}^+\}$ is not context-free, and is accepted by a PIA with 3 pebbles. Pebble 1 reads the $\$$, pebble 2 reads a letter σ to the left of pebble 1, and pebble 3 also reads σ to the right of pebble 1. Then the PIA repeats: (i) a letter σ is non-deterministically chosen, (ii) pebble 2 reads σ between its current position and pebble 1, and (iii) pebble 3 reads σ to the right of its current position. Similar languages are PI languages, e.g., $\{ww^Rww \mid w \in \Sigma^\star\}$, where w^R is w in reverse.*

We conjecture that not all context-free language are PI languages; e.g, the Dyck language of two types of well-nested parentheses seems not to be PI.

Closure Properties. We provide a construction of suitable PIAs in the appendix to show the following.

Theorem 1. *The class of PI languages is effectively closed under union, concatenation, Kleene-$\star$, shuffle, and iterated shuffle. It is not effectively closed under intersection, even with regular languages, nor under complement.*

From the construction used in the proof of the above theorem, we also obtain:

Corollary 1. *The universality and inclusion problems for PIAs are undecidable.*

Emptiness. For deciding whether $L(\mathcal{A}) \neq \emptyset$ for a given PIA, we use *feasible sequences of transitions*, which are those that correspond to an actual computation of a PIA. One can show that for a given PIA with m pebbles, $L(\mathcal{A}) \neq \emptyset$ iff there is a feasible sequence of transitions $\bar{t}$ of length at most $|\mathcal{A}| \cdot 2^{O(m \log m)}$, and that the existence of the latter can be guessed and verified using a bounded amount of information (roughly a counter, two transitions, and two pebble assignments). This gives us the upper bounds below, which hold also if $\mathcal{A}$ is not given explicitly, as long as δ can be computed non-deterministically in $\log(|\mathcal{A}|)$ space. For the case where $\mathcal{A}$ has $O(\log|\mathcal{A}|)$ pebbles, NL-hardness follows from the same result for standard finite state automata and Proposition 1.

Theorem 2. *If a PIA $\mathcal{A}$ has $O(\log|\mathcal{A}|)$ pebbles, its emptiness problem is NL-complete. In general, the emptiness problem for PIA is in* PSPACE.

Related Automata Models. *Jumping finite automata* [20] are probably the closest to PIAs: they are essentially PIAs with one pebble, which is placed on an arbitrary unvisited position without specifying an interval. In the context of languages with infinite alphabets, various automata models have been proposed that run on *data words*: string words where values from an infinite domain are attached to each position. Register automata are finite-state machines on data words which use registers to compare whether data values are equal [6,17,22]; their string projection languages are regular. Pebble automata [22] use pebbles in a stack discipline to test for equality of data values. Data automata [3–5] are an extension of register automata introduced to prove the decidability of satisfiability of FO^2 on words with a linear order, a successor relation, and an equivalence relation. Their projection languages are accepted by multicounter automata, which are finite automata on strings extended with counters, that are equivalent to Vector Addition Systems or Petri Nets [11]. Class Memory Automata [2] have the same expressive power as data automata. Variable Finite Automata [15] extend finite state automata with variables from an infinite alphabet. Many works have studied these automata models and their variations, see [28] and [18, Chapter 4] for surveys.

3   PIAs and $FO^2(\leq_1, \precsim_2, S_2)$

To establish the relation between $FO^2(\leq_1, \precsim_2, S_2)$ and PIAs, we need some preliminaries. Recall that a total preorder $\precsim$ is a transitive total relation which can be seen as an equivalence relation whose equivalence classes are linearly ordered. We use $x \sim_2 y$ as shorthand for $(x \precsim_2 y) \wedge (y \precsim_2 x)$. The induced successor relation S of a total preorder $\precsim$ is such that $S(x, y)$ if $x \precsim y$ and there is no z such that $x \precnsim z \precnsim y$.

Two-variable logic (FO^2) is the restriction of FO to formulas that only use two variables x and y, and FO$^2(\leq_1, \precsim_2, S_2)$ is FO^2 with a linear order $\leq_1$, a total preorder $\precsim_2$ and its induced successor S_2, and any number of unary relations from a finite alphabet.

All structures and strings in this paper are finite. For a structure $\mathcal{A}$, we denote its universe by A and its size by $|A|$. The *empty structure* has $A = \emptyset$ and is denoted $\emptyset_{\text{voc}}$.

Data Words. Let Σ a finite alphabet. Its *extension for data words* is $\text{voc}_{\text{DW}}(\Sigma) = \langle \leq_1, \precsim_2, S_2, \sigma : \sigma \in \Sigma \rangle$. A *data word* over Σ is a finite $\text{voc}_{\text{DW}}(\Sigma)$-structure $\mathcal{D}$ with universe D where $\sigma : \sigma \in \Sigma$ are interpreted as unary relations that partition D. We use $\mathcal{D}$, $\mathcal{D}'$, etc. to denote data words. The empty word is denoted by $\emptyset_{\text{DW}(\Sigma)}$, and the class of all data words over Σ by $\text{DW}(\Sigma)$. A set of data words is called a *data language*.

Let φ_1, φ_2 be FO$^2(\text{voc}_{\text{DW}}(\Sigma))$ formulas. We write $\varphi_1 \models_{\text{DW}(\Sigma)} \varphi_2$ if $\mathcal{D} \models \varphi_1$ implies $\mathcal{D} \models \varphi_2$ for every $\mathcal{D} \in \text{DW}(\Sigma)$, and define equivalence $\equiv_{\text{DW}(\Sigma)}$ analogously. We may omit Σ if clear from context. The *data value value*$_\mathcal{D}(d)$ of an element $d \in D$ is the number of equivalence classes E of $\sim_2$ whose elements $d' \in E$ satisfy $d' \precsim_2 d$, and $maxval_\mathcal{D} = \max_{d \in D} value_\mathcal{D}(d)$. The *string projection* of $\mathcal{D}$, denoted $string(\mathcal{D})$, is the string w of length $|w| = |D|$ where for all $\ell \in [\|w\|]$, $w(\ell) = \sigma$ if and only if $\mathcal{D} \models \sigma(d)$ where d is the unique element of $\mathcal{D}$ such that $\ell = |\{d' \in D \mid \mathcal{D} \models d' \leq_1 d\}|$. The projection of the empty structure $\emptyset_{\text{voc}_{\text{DW}}(\Sigma)}$, and only of $\emptyset_{\text{voc}_{\text{DW}}(\Sigma)}$, is ε. The *projection language* of a data language Δ is the string language $L(\Delta) = \{w \mid w = string(\mathcal{D}) \text{ for some } \mathcal{D} \in \Delta\}$. If a formula ψ defines Δ, we write $L(\psi)$ for $L(\Delta)$.

Example 1. To avoid ambiguity, in our running examples we use underlined symbols. Let $\underline{\Xi} = \{\underline{\xi}_1, \underline{\xi}_2\}$ be a set of unary relations and let $\underline{\mathcal{D}}$ be the data word with universe $\underline{D} = \{\underline{a}, \underline{b}, \underline{c}, \underline{d}, \underline{e}, \underline{f}\}$ where $\leq_1$ is the lexicographic order, the interpretation of $\underline{\xi}_1$ is $\{\underline{a}, \underline{b}, \underline{c}, \underline{e}\}$, the interpretation of $\underline{\xi}_2$ is $\{\underline{d}, \underline{f}\}$, and $\underline{b} \precnsim_2 \underline{a} \precnsim_2 \underline{e} \precnsim_2 \underline{c} \precnsim_2 \underline{d} \sim_2 \underline{f}$. Note e.g. that $\underline{\mathcal{D}} \models S_2(\underline{a}, \underline{e})$ and $\underline{\mathcal{D}} \models \neg S_2(\underline{b}, \underline{e}) \wedge (\underline{b} \precsim_2 \underline{e})$. The string projection of $\underline{\mathcal{D}}$ is $string(\underline{\mathcal{D}}) = \underline{\xi}_1 \underline{\xi}_1 \underline{\xi}_1 \underline{\xi}_2 \underline{\xi}_1 \underline{\xi}_2$.

The goal of this section is to prove the following theorem.

Theorem 3. *If ψ is a FO$^2(\leq_1, \precsim_2, S_2)$ sentence, there is a PIA $\mathcal{A}$ with $L(\psi) = L(\mathcal{A})$.*

To prove this, we rely on the normal form defined next. A *1-type* $\nu(x)$ over a vocabulary $\text{voc}_{\text{DW}}(\Sigma)$ is a maximal consistent conjunction of atomic and negated atomic formulas with the free variable x. A *2-type* $\theta(x, y)$ is defined similarly. Given a FO$^2(\text{voc}_{\text{DW}}(\Sigma))$ formula ψ, we obtain a φ in normal form by taking the Scott Normal Form [14, Theorem 2.1] of ψ, and expanding the quantifier-free formulas to Disjunctive Normal Form, and in fact to disjunctions of 2-types θ.

The Scott Normal Form of ψ introduces linearly many new symbols, resulting in an extended Σ'. We let $\Xi = \{\xi_a \mid a \in [A]\}$ be an alphabet containing a symbol for every 1-type over Σ'.

Theorem 4 (Normal Form). *Let* $\psi \in \mathrm{FO}^2(\mathrm{voc}_{\mathrm{DW}}(\Sigma))$. *Then there exist* $A, B, C \in \mathbb{N}$, *an alphabet* $\Xi = \{\xi_a \mid a \in [A]\}$, *a formula* $\varphi \in \mathrm{FO}^2(\mathrm{voc}_{\mathrm{DW}}(\Xi))$ *of the form* $\varphi = \varphi_\forall \wedge \varphi_\exists$ *and a letter-to-letter substitution* $h : \Xi \to \Sigma$ *such that* $L(\psi) = h(L(\varphi))$,

$$\varphi_\forall = \forall x \forall y \bigvee_{\theta \in \Theta_\forall} \theta(x,y) \qquad\qquad \varphi_\exists = \varphi_\epsilon \wedge \forall x \bigwedge_{a \in [A]} \xi_a(x) \to \bigwedge_{b \in [B]} \exists y \bigvee_{c \in [C]} \theta_{abc}(x,y)$$

with θ *and* θ_{abc} *2-types over* $\mathrm{voc}_{\mathrm{DW}}(\Xi)$, *and* $\varphi_\epsilon = True$ *if* $\emptyset_{\mathrm{voc}_{\mathrm{DW}}(\Sigma)} \models_{\mathrm{DW}(\Sigma)} \psi$ *and* $\varphi_\epsilon = \exists x \, (True)$ *if* $\emptyset_{\mathrm{voc}_{\mathrm{DW}}(\Sigma)} \not\models_{\mathrm{DW}(\Sigma)} \psi$. *Moreover,* φ *is computable in* ExpSpace *and is of length exponential in* $|\psi|$.

We let $\Theta_\exists = \{\theta_{abc} \mid a \in [A], b \in [B], c \in [C]\}$ and $\Theta = \Theta_\forall \cup \Theta_\exists$. Given $a \in [A]$, a *witness type set for* a is a choice of 2-types satisfying the right-hand side of the implication for ξ_a. That is, a set of 2-types $\omega \subseteq \Theta_\exists$ that contains one θ_{abc} for every $b \in [B]$, representing a choice of the existential constraints an element needs to fulfill. Denote by Ω_a the set of witness type sets for a and let $\Omega = \bigcup_{a \in [A]} \Omega_a$. For a witness type set $\omega \in \Omega$, let $\omega(x) = \bigwedge_{\theta \in \omega} \exists y \, \theta(x,y)$ be its *existential constraints*. Note that $\omega(x)$ is always satisfiable and that there is a unique letter $\xi^\omega \in \Xi$ such that $\omega(x) \models_{\mathrm{DW}(\Xi)} \xi^\omega(x)$.

Example 2. Consider the following formula φ given in normal form

$$\forall x \forall y \, \underline{\chi}(x,y) \wedge \forall x \left(\underline{\xi}_1(x) \to \exists y \, (\underline{\theta}_1(x,y) \vee \underline{\theta}_3(x,y)) \wedge \underline{\xi}_2(x) \to \exists y \, (\underline{\theta}_2(x,y) \vee \underline{\theta}_4(x,y)) \right)$$

where $\underline{\chi}(x,y)$ is the disjunction of 2-types equivalent to $(\underline{\xi}_2(x) \wedge \underline{\xi}_2(y)) \to x \sim_2 y$, and the $\underline{\theta}_i$ are given as the following 2-types (omitted clauses are negated):

$$\underline{\theta}_1 = x <_1 y \wedge S_2(x,y) \wedge \underline{\xi}_1(x) \wedge \underline{\xi}_2(y) \quad \underline{\theta}_3 = x <_1 y \wedge \neg S_2(x,y) \wedge x \napprox_2 y \wedge \underline{\xi}_1(x) \wedge \underline{\xi}_2(y)$$

$$\underline{\theta}_2 = y <_1 x \wedge S_2(y,x) \wedge \underline{\xi}_2(x) \wedge \underline{\xi}_1(y) \quad \underline{\theta}_4 = y <_1 x \wedge \neg S_2(y,x) \wedge y \napprox_2 x \wedge \underline{\xi}_2(x) \wedge \underline{\xi}_1(y)$$

A data word satisfies φ iff it is the empty structure, or *(a)* the largest element of $\leq_1$ has letter $\underline{\xi}_2$, *(b)* the smallest element of $\leq_1$ has letter $\underline{\xi}_1$, *(c)* all elements with $\underline{\xi}_2$ have maximal value, and *(d)* no element with $\underline{\xi}_1$ has maximal value.

Note that $\mathcal{D} \models \varphi$. The projection language $L(\varphi)$ is the regular language with regular expression $\underline{\xi}_1(\underline{\xi}_1 + \underline{\xi}_2)^* \underline{\xi}_2 + \varepsilon$. We have $\Theta_\exists = \{\underline{\theta}_1, \underline{\theta}_2, \underline{\theta}_3, \underline{\theta}_4\}$. For φ, we have $A = 2$, $B = 1$, and $C = 2$. The witness type sets of φ are $\{\theta_{111}\}$, $\{\theta_{112}\}$, $\{\theta_{211}\}$, and $\{\theta_{212}\}$, where $\theta_{111} = \underline{\theta}_1$, $\theta_{112} = \underline{\theta}_3$, $\theta_{211} = \underline{\theta}_2$, and $\theta_{212} = \underline{\theta}_4$. Hence, we have $\Omega = \{\{\underline{\theta}_1\}, \{\underline{\theta}_2\}, \{\underline{\theta}_3\}, \{\underline{\theta}_4\}\}$, and $\xi^{\{\underline{\theta}_1\}} = \xi^{\{\underline{\theta}_3\}} = \underline{\xi}_1$, and $\xi^{\{\underline{\theta}_2\}} = \xi^{\{\underline{\theta}_4\}} = \underline{\xi}_2$.

We construct a PIA $\mathcal{A}^\varphi$ that accepts a string w iff it can be extended into a data word $\mathcal{D}$ that satisfies the normal form φ of a given sentence ψ. Note that ψ and φ have different alphabets, but since there is a letter-to-letter substitution h such that $L(\psi) = h(L(\mathcal{A}^\varphi))$, and PIAs are closed under letter-to-letter substitutions, this proves Theorem 3.

For constructing our PIA, we first focus on the existential part, i.e., whether w can be extended into a $\mathcal{D}$ that satisfies $\varphi_\exists$. This is achieved in two steps: **(S1)** We reduce the existence of $\mathcal{D}$ to the existence of a sequence of *consecutive task words*, data words that store additional information of already satisfied vs. 'promised' subformulas; the sequence should lead to a *completed* task word where all promises are fulfilled. **(S2)** We do not have a bound on the length of task words and their data values, so we use *extremal strings* to decide the existence of the desired sequence with the limited memory of PIAs. After these two steps, we introduce *perfect* extremal strings to guarantee the satisfaction of $\varphi_\forall$. Our PIA will then decide if a sequence of perfect extremal strings exists.

Task Words for $\varphi_\exists$. We start by defining *task words*, which are like data words but do more book-keeping. Additionally to data values, elements in task words are assigned *tasks*, which are witness type sets where each 2-type may be marked as *completed* if its satisfaction has already been established, or as *promised* otherwise. We reduce the satisfaction of $\varphi_\exists$ to the existence of a sequence of $\mathcal{T}_1, \ldots, \mathcal{T}_n$ of *consecutive* task words, where we keep assigning new data values and promised into completed tasks, until we reached a *completed* task word $\mathcal{T}_n$.

Definition 3 (Tasks). *For $\theta \in \Theta_\exists$, we call C_θ a completed task and P_θ a promised task. Let* $\text{Tasks}_C = \{C_\theta \mid \theta \in \Theta_\exists\}$, $\text{Tasks}_P = \{P_\theta \mid \theta \in \Theta_\exists\}$ *and* $\text{Tasks} = \text{Tasks}_C \cup \text{Tasks}_P$.

For each task set $ts \subseteq \text{Tasks}$, there is at most one witness type set $\omega \in \Omega$ that ts *realizes*, which means that for every $\theta \in \Theta_\exists$, **(1)** $|\{P_\theta, C_\theta\} \cap ts| \leq 1$, and **(2)** $|\{P_\theta, C_\theta\} \cap ts| = 1$ if and only if $\theta \in \omega$. If there is such an ω, we denote it $\omega(ts)$, and call ts an Ω-*realization*. The set of all Ω-realizations is 2_Ω^{Tasks}, and $2_\Omega^{\text{Tasks}_C} = 2_\Omega^{\text{Tasks}} \cap 2^{\text{Tasks}_C}$ and $2_\Omega^{\text{Tasks}_P} = 2_\Omega^{\text{Tasks}} \cap 2^{\text{Tasks}_P}$.

Example 3. Since the witness type sets in $\underline{\Omega}$ are singletons, so are the $ts \in 2_{\underline{\Omega}}^{\text{Tasks}}$. Let $\underline{ts}_i^C = \{C_{\underline{\theta}_i}\}$ and $\underline{ts}_i^P = \{P_{\underline{\theta}_i}\}$ for $i \in [4]$. Then we have $2_{\underline{\Omega}}^{\text{Tasks}} = \{\underline{ts}_i^C \mid i \in [4]\} \cup \{\underline{ts}_i^P \mid i \in [4]\}$, and $\{C_{\underline{\theta}_i}\}$ and $\{P_{\underline{\theta}_i}\}$ are $\{\underline{\theta}_i\}$-realizations for $i \in [4]$.

$\mathcal{D}$-*task words* are data words that assign tasks to the elements of $\mathcal{D}$. More precisely, each $d \in D$ is assigned, instead of a letter ξ_a, a task set ts that realizes a witness type set ω which contains C_θ for each $\theta \in \omega$ that d satisfies, and P_θ for the remaining $\theta \in \omega$.

Definition 4 (Task word). *Let $\mathcal{D}$ be a data word over Ξ. A $\mathcal{D}$-task word is a data word $\mathcal{T}$ over 2_Ω^{Tasks} that has the same universe and order relations as $\mathcal{D}$, and for every $d \in D$ with $\mathcal{T} \models ts(d)$, **(1)** $\mathcal{D} \models \xi^{\omega(ts)}(d)$, and **(2)** for every $\theta \in \omega(ts)$, $C_\theta \in ts$ iff $\mathcal{D} \models \exists y\, \theta(d,y)$. A task word $\mathcal{T}$ is a $\mathcal{D}$-task word for some $\mathcal{D}$, and it is completed if $\mathcal{T} \models \varphi_\varepsilon \wedge \forall x \bigvee_{ts \in 2_\Omega^{\text{Tasks}_C}} ts(x)$.*

Example 4. We define a $\underline{\mathcal{D}}$-task word $\underline{\mathcal{T}}$; its vocabulary is $2_{\underline{\Omega}}^{\text{Tasks}}$, its universe is $\{\underline{a}, \underline{b}, \underline{c}, \underline{d}, \underline{e}, \underline{f}\}$, and $\leq_1$, $\precsim_2$, and S_2 are the same as in $\underline{\mathcal{D}}$. The interpretation of the letter $\underline{ts}_1^C$ is $\{\underline{c}\}$, that of $\underline{ts}_2^C$ is $\{\underline{d}\}$, that of $\underline{ts}_3^C$ is $\{\underline{a}, \underline{b}, \underline{e}\}$, and that of

ts_4^C is $\{\underline{f}\}$; the other letters are empty. As $\underline{\mathcal{D}} \models \underline{\varphi}$, all existential constraints are satisfied and $\underline{\mathcal{I}}$ is completed.

The satisfaction of $\varphi_\exists$ coincides with the existence of a completed task word.

Lemma 1. *Let $\mathcal{D} \in \mathrm{DW}(\Xi)$. There exists a completed $\mathcal{D}$-task word iff $\mathcal{D} \models \varphi_\exists$.*

We now characterize the notion of *consecutive* task words using *trimmings*.

Definition 5 (Trimming, consecutiveness). *The trimming of a data word $\mathcal{D}$, denoted $\mathcal{D}^{\backslash 1}$, is the substructure of $\mathcal{D}$ induced by removing the elements with the maximal data value. For task words, trimmings are obtained by removing the elements with the largest data value and updating the tasks of the remaining elements correctly. That is, a trimming of a $\mathcal{D}$-task word $\mathcal{T}$ is a $\mathcal{D}^{\backslash 1}$-task word $\mathcal{T}_1$ such that $\omega(ts) = \omega(ts_1)$ for every d and every $ts, ts_1 \in 2_\Omega^{\mathrm{Tasks}}$ with $\mathcal{T} \models ts(d)$ and $\mathcal{T}_1 \models ts_1(d)$. We say that $\mathcal{T}_1, \mathcal{T}$ are consecutive if $\mathcal{T}_1$ is a trimming of $\mathcal{T}$.*

The trimming of a task word is unique, and we denote it $\mathcal{T}^{\backslash 1}$.

Example 5. $\underline{\mathcal{D}}^{\backslash 1}$ is obtained from $\underline{\mathcal{D}}$ by removing $\underline{d}$ and $\underline{f}$. The $\underline{\mathcal{D}}^{\backslash 1}$-task word $\underline{\mathcal{T}}^{\backslash 1}$ has universe $\{\underline{a}, \underline{b}, \underline{c}, \underline{e}\}$ and order relations as in $\underline{\mathcal{D}}^{\backslash 1}$. Note that $\underline{d}$ and $\underline{f}$ contributed in $\underline{\mathcal{D}}$ to the satisfaction of $\underline{\varphi_\exists}$, so $\underline{\mathcal{T}}^{\backslash 1}$ has promised tasks and is no longer completed, with interpretations $\underline{ts}_1^P = \{\underline{c}\}$, $\underline{ts}_3^P = \{\underline{a}, \underline{b}, \underline{e}\}$, and the remaining letters empty. Note that the tasks for the shared elements of $\underline{\mathcal{I}}$ and $\underline{\mathcal{T}}^{\backslash 1}$ realize the same witness type sets.

We have achieved **(S1)**: reducing satisfaction of $\varphi_\exists$ to finding a sequence of task words.

Proposition 2. *There exists a data word $\mathcal{D} \models \varphi_\exists$ if and only if there is a sequence $\mathcal{T}_1 \ldots, \mathcal{T}_n$ of consecutive task words, where $\mathcal{T}_n$ is a completed $\mathcal{D}$-task word.*

Now to **(S2)**: as the limited memory of PIAs hinders the manipulation of task words with unbounded length and data values, we operate on their *extremal strings* instead.

First, in *data abstractions* of task words, we do not distinguish all data values, but only the *top layer* elements with maximal value, the *second to top layer*, and the rest. We let Layers $= \{1\mathrm{top}, 2\mathrm{top}, \mathrm{rest}\}$, and define the alphabet $\Gamma = \mathrm{Layers} \times 2_\Omega^{\mathrm{Tasks}}$. We also define its restrictions to completed and promised tasks as $\Gamma_C = \mathrm{Layers} \times 2_\Omega^{\mathrm{Tasks}_C}$ and $\Gamma_P = \mathrm{Layers} \times 2_\Omega^{\mathrm{Tasks}_P}$, while $\Gamma_h = \{h\} \times 2_\Omega^{\mathrm{Tasks}}$ is the restriction of Γ to some specific $h \in \mathrm{Layers}$. For a symbol $\gamma = (h, ts)$ in Γ, we denote $ts(\gamma) = ts$ and $\omega(\gamma) = \omega(ts)$.

Definition 6 (Data abstraction). *Let $\mathcal{T}$ be a $\mathcal{D}$-task word. For every $d \in D$, let ts_d be such that $\mathcal{T} \models ts_d(d)$, and let $\mathcal{A}$ be the data word over Γ with same universe and order relations as $\mathcal{T}$, and with $\mathcal{A} \models \gamma_h(d)$ where $\gamma_h = (h, ts_d)$ iff (a) $h = 1\mathrm{top}$ and $value_\mathcal{D}(d) = maxval_\mathcal{D}$, (b) $h = 2\mathrm{top}$ and $value_\mathcal{D}(d) = maxval_\mathcal{D} - 1$, or (c) $h = \mathrm{rest}$ and $value_\mathcal{D}(d) \in [maxval_\mathcal{D} - 2]$. The data abstraction $\mathrm{abst}(\mathcal{T})$ of $\mathcal{T}$ is the string projection $\mathrm{string}(\mathcal{A})$.*

Extremal strings are obtained from data abstractions by keeping only the maximal and minimal positions in each layer with respect to the tasks. We extend to them the notions of *consecutive* and *completed*.

Definition 7 (extremal strings). *For $w \in \Gamma^*$, define its extremal positions* extPos(w):

$$\text{pos}_{h,\theta}(w) = \{\ell \in [|w|] \mid w(\ell) = (h, ts), \ \theta \in \omega(ts)\}$$
$$\text{pos}_{\text{rest}, P_\theta}(w) = \{\ell \in [|w|] \mid w(\ell) = (\text{rest}, ts), \ P_\theta \in ts\}$$
$$\text{extPos}_{h,\theta}(w) = \{\ell \mid \ell = \max(\text{pos}_{h,\theta}(w)) \ \text{ or } \ \ell = \min(\text{pos}_{h,\theta}(w))\}$$

$\text{If } \theta \models x \leq_1 y, \quad \text{extPos}_\theta(w) = \{\ell \mid \ell = \max(\text{pos}_{\text{rest}, P_\theta}(w))\}$

$\text{If } \theta \models y <_1 x, \quad \text{extPos}_\theta(w) = \{\ell \mid \ell = \min(\text{pos}_{\text{rest}, P_\theta}(w))\}$

$$\text{extPos}(w) = \bigcup_{\theta \in \Theta_\exists} \left(\text{extPos}_\theta(w) \bigcup_{h \in \text{Layers}} \text{extPos}_{h,\theta}(w) \right)$$

If extPos(w) $= \{\ell_1, \ldots, \ell_r\}$ *and* $\ell_1 < \cdots < \ell_r$, *then the extremal string of* w *is* ext(w) $= w(\ell_1) \cdots w(\ell_r)$. EXT($\Gamma$) $= \{\text{ext}(w) \mid w \in \Gamma^*\}$ *denotes the set of extremal strings. Note that* $s = \text{ext}(w)$ *implies* ext(s) $= s$ *and* ext(ε) $= \varepsilon$. *An extremal string* s *is completed if* $s \in \Gamma_C^+$, *or if* $s = \varepsilon$ *and* $\emptyset_{\text{DW}(\Sigma)} \models_{\text{DW}(\Sigma)} \psi$. *We occasionally write* ext($\mathcal{T}$) *to mean* ext(abst($\mathcal{T}$)).

A pair s', s *of extremal strings is consecutive if* $s' = \text{ext}(\mathcal{T}^{\backslash 1})$ *and* $s = \text{ext}(\mathcal{T})$ *for some task word* $\mathcal{T}$.

For an extremal string s and $\ell \in [|s|]$, the set of letters that can augment s at position ℓ without being extremal is $\Gamma^{\text{not ext}}(s, \ell) = \{\gamma \in \Gamma \mid \text{ext}(s) = \text{ext}(s(1) \cdots s(\ell-1) \gamma s(\ell) \cdots s(|s|))\}$, and we define $\Gamma_h^{\text{not ext}}(s, \ell) = \Gamma_h \cap \Gamma^{\text{not ext}}(s, \ell)$ for $h \in$ Layers.

Example 6. Let $\underline{w}$ be the following 6-letter string over $\underline{\Gamma} = \text{Layers} \times 2_\Omega^{\text{Tasks}}$:
$(\text{rest}, \underline{ts}_3^C)(\text{rest}, \underline{ts}_3^C)(2\text{top}, \underline{ts}_1^C)(1\text{top}, \underline{ts}_2^C)(\text{rest}, \underline{ts}_3^C)(1\text{top}, \underline{ts}_4^C)$.
Then extPos($\underline{w}$) $= \{1, 3, 4, 5, 6\}$, since the letter at position 2 appears both to the left, at position 1, and to the right, at position 5, and $\underline{s} = \text{ext}(\underline{w})$ is the substring obtained from $\underline{w}$ by removing the non-extremal position 2.

The concludes **(S2)**, reducing the existence of $\mathcal{D}$ to a sequence of extremal strings.

Corollary 2. *There is a data word* $\mathcal{D} \models \varphi_\exists$ *if and only if there is a sequence of consecutive extremal strings where the last one is completed.*

Perfect Extremal Strings for $\varphi_\forall$. We define in the appendix a formula which intuitively 'extracts' the 2-type of elements in a data word. Let $\alpha = (h_\alpha, ts_\alpha)$ and $\beta = (h_\beta, ts_\beta)$ in Γ with at least one of them in $\Gamma_{1\text{top}}$. The formula perf$_{\alpha,\beta}(x,y)$ implies for every atomic formula either itself or its negation. For example, if $h_\alpha = h_\beta = 1\text{top}$, then perf$_{\alpha,\beta,\precsim_2}(x,y)$ implies $x \precsim_2 y$, $y \precsim_2 x$, $\neg S_2(x,y)$, and $\neg S_2(y,x)$. Hence for all $\alpha, \beta \in \Gamma$ with at least one of them in $\Gamma_{1\text{top}}$, there exists a 2-type $\theta(x,y)$ such that perf$_{\alpha,\beta}(x,y) \equiv_{\text{DW}(\Xi)} \theta(x,y)$. This allows us to describe the 2-type of elements in task words via perf$_{\alpha,\beta}$ formulas. For any two elements of the data word, there is a (possibly iterated) trimming in which both appear and one of them has the maximal data value, and their perfect formula, which is equivalent to their 2-type, determines whether they satisfy the universal constraint χ. Thus we can ensure satisfaction of χ using $\mathrm{perf}_{\alpha,\beta}(x,y)$ formulas from all the trimmings.

Definition 8 (Perfect string, perfect task word). *Let $w \in \Gamma^*$. We say w is a* perfect string *if for every two positions $\ell_1 < \ell_2$ in w such that $\{w(\ell_1), w(\ell_2)\} \cap \Gamma_{1\mathrm{top}} \neq \emptyset$ we have $\mathrm{perf}_{w(\ell_1),w(\ell_2)}(x,y) \models_{\mathrm{DW}(\Xi)} \chi(x,y) \wedge \chi(y,x)$. Note that the empty string ε is perfect. A task word $\mathcal{T}$ is* perfect *if it is empty, or if $\mathrm{ext}(\mathcal{T})$ and $\mathrm{ext}(\mathcal{T}^{\backslash\backslash 1})$ are perfect.*

Example 7. Let $\underline{\alpha} = (2\mathrm{top}, \underline{ts}_1^C)$ and $\underline{\beta} = (1\mathrm{top}, \underline{ts}_2^C)$. Then $\mathrm{perf}_{\underline{\alpha},\underline{\beta}}(x,y)$ is given by: $\mathrm{perf}_{\underline{\alpha},\underline{\beta}}(x,y) = \underline{\xi}_1(x) \wedge \underline{\xi}_2(y) \wedge (x <_1 y) \wedge (x \not\sim_2 y) \wedge S_2(x,y)$.
The 2-type θ to which $\mathrm{perf}_{\underline{\alpha},\underline{\beta}}(x,y)$ is equivalent over $\mathrm{DW}(\Xi)$ is given by the conjunction of $\mathrm{perf}_{\underline{\alpha},\underline{\beta}}(x,y)$ with $\neg\underline{\xi}_2(x) \wedge \neg\underline{\xi}_1(y) \wedge (y \not<_1 x) \wedge (y \not\sim_2 x) \wedge \neg S_2(y,x)$. We have that $\underline{w}$ is a perfect string, and $\mathrm{perf}_{\underline{\alpha},\underline{\beta}}(x,y) \models_{\mathrm{DW}(\Xi)} \underline{\chi}(x,y) \wedge \underline{\chi}(y,x)$.

We characterize satisfiability in terms of perfect completed task words.

Lemma 2. *Let $\mathcal{T}$ be a $\mathcal{D}$-task word. $\mathcal{T}$ is perfect if and only if $\mathcal{D} \models \varphi_\forall$.*

As a corollary of Lemma 2 and Lemma 1, we get:

Proposition 3. *For every data word $\mathcal{D} \in \mathrm{DW}(\Xi)$, $\mathcal{D} \models \varphi$ if and only if there exists a perfect completed $\mathcal{D}$-task word. There is $\mathcal{D} \models \varphi$ if and only if there is a sequence of consecutive perfect extremal strings where the last one is completed.*

We are almost ready to define $\mathcal{A}^\varphi$. Intuitively, it will guess a sequence of extremal strings as in Proposition 3, placing pebbles from an extremal string to a consecutive one. This requires the automaton to verify consecutiveness, and to know which positions in consecutive extremal strings correspond to the same position in the input. This is easy if we have the underlying task word; indeed, given a task word $\mathcal{T}$ and an extremal string $s' = \mathrm{ext}(\mathcal{T})$, there is a bijective mapping from the *extremal elements* of $\mathcal{T}$ that s' stores, to their positions in s'. The same holds for $\mathcal{T}^{\backslash\backslash 1}$ and $s = \mathrm{ext}(\mathcal{T}^{\backslash\backslash 1})$. By composing these mappings after inverting the latter, and restricting its domain to positions that remain extremal after updating the abstracted data values (that is, shifting the top layer to second top, and the second top into the remaining layer), we obtain a *partial embedding from s to s' via $\mathcal{T}$* that keeps track of the matching positions; the precise definition is in the appendix. But one major hurdle remains: these notions are defined in terms of a task word $\mathcal{T}$, and our PIA cannot store task words, only their extremal strings. We overcome this through a merely syntactic characterization of consecutiveness, which can be verified without a concrete task word. This rather technical step relies on the fact that if s, s' are consecutive, then s' can be obtained by guessing a substring r that will get new data values, interleaving it into the proper positions g of s, which can also be guessed, and updating the abstracted data values. Also the partial embedding that keeps track of matching the positions can be obtained without a concrete $\mathcal{T}$, using r and g.

Lemma 3. *We can decide whether two given extremal strings s, s' are consecutive in* EXPSPACE. *If they are, then we can also obtain in* EXPSPACE *a partial embedding* $\mathsf{PEmb}_{s \hookrightarrow s'}$ *from positions in s to positions in s' that coincides with the partial embedding from s to s' via T for every task word T such that $s' = \mathsf{ext}(T)$ and $s = \mathsf{ext}(T^{\backslash\!\backslash 1})$.*

The Automaton. We give a high-level description of $\mathcal{A}^\varphi = (\Xi, m + 1, Q, q_{\mathrm{init}}, F, \delta)$, and refer to the extended version for a full definition. We have $m = 7 \cdot |\Theta_\exists|$: there is one pebble for each existential constraint in $\Theta_\exists$ and each layer in Γ, plus an additional pebble per constraint, and one designated pebble $m + 1$ to read non-extremal positions. $Q = Q_e \cup Q_p$ has two types of states:

- Q_e contains states (s, τ) with s a perfect extremal string and τ an $(m+1, |s|)$-pebble assignment, which intuitively describes the assignment after reading s.
- Q_p contains states of the forms $(s, \tilde{s}, \tau, 0)$ and $(s, \tilde{s}, \tau, 1)$ for every perfect extremal string s, non-empty prefix $\tilde{s}$ of s, and $(m+1, |s|)$-pebble assignment τ that satisfies certain conditions that hold when only the prefix $\tilde{s}$ has been read.

The initial state is $q_{\mathrm{init}} = (\varepsilon, \rho_\perp) \in Q_e$ and the final states are $F = \{(s, \tau) \in Q_e \mid s \text{ is completed}\}$. The transition δ is roughly as follows. $\mathcal{A}^\varphi$ should transition from $(s, \tau) \in Q_e$ to $(s', \tau') \in Q_e$ for consecutive s, s', but since it can only move one pebble at a time, we have intermediate states in Q_p which allow it to read s' from left to right by iterating over all its prefixes. We start reading s' by moving to $(s', s'(1), \tau'_{q'}, 0) \in Q_p$, where $\tau'_{q'}$ stores the pebble assignment induced by $\mathsf{PEmb}_{s' \hookrightarrow s}$. Once the whole extremal string s' has been read, we move to the next extremal state.

This finishes the construction of the automaton $\mathcal{A}^\varphi$ with $L(\mathcal{A}^\varphi) = L(\varphi)$, and thus the proof of Theorem 3. Concerning the upper bound on finite satisfiability, by Theorem 4 and $\mathsf{EXT}(\Gamma) \subseteq \Gamma^{7|\Theta_\exists|}$, we get that $\mathcal{A}^\varphi$ has size at most double exponential in $|\psi|$. For the EXPSPACE upper bound, we need to show that the transition relation of $\mathcal{A}^\varphi$ is EXPSPACE-computable (Lemma 3 in the appendix). This with Theorem 2 gives an alternative proof of the upper bound in [27]:

Corollary 3. *Finite satisfiability of* FO$^2(\leq_1, \precsim_2, S_2)$ *is in* EXPSPACE.

Relation to the Proof of Schwentick and Zeume [27]. Naturally, there are similarities between the techniques; our extremal strings and tasks are similar to their profiles and directional constraints. However, a key difference is that in their 'geometric' view, elements of the data word are assigned points (a, b) in the plane with a a position in $\leq_1$, and b a data value. Existential constraints are indicated by marking the witnesses with the letters they should have, and many profiles in a consistent sequence can contain points with the same a value. In contrast, our 'temporal' view arises from the computation of the PIA. We mark elements with existential constraints they need to satisfy and that they have satisfied, which is compatible with the read-once nature of PIA. It does not seem possible to use their proof techniques without modifying PIA to allow multiple readings of the input. The modified model would work for the logic-to-automata relation established here, but we suspect it would be too strong for the other direction.

4   Discussion and Conclusion

We introduced pebble-intervals automata (PIA) and studied their computational power. We proved that the projections of data languages definable in $FO^2(\leq_1, \precsim_2, S_2)$ are PI languages, and as a by-product, obtained an alternative proof that finite satisfiability is in ExpSpace. The main question that remains is the converse of our main result: whether every PI language is the projection of an $FO^2(\leq_1, \precsim_2, S_2)$ definable data language. We believe this is the case. Our work also gives rise to other questions. We suspect that our results can be extended to ω-languages, and we would like to adapt them to C^2, which extends FO^2 with counting quantifiers [25,29]. We also plan to explore further the computational power of our automata model, for instance, to establish a pumping lemma that allows us to prove that some context-free languages are not PI languages.

Acknowledgments. We thank the anonymous reviewers for their helpful remarks.

References

1. Ahmetaj, S., Calvanese, D., Ortiz, M., Simkus, M.: Managing change in graph-structured data using description logics. ACM Trans. Comput. Logic **18**(4), 27:1–27:35 (2017)
2. Björklund, H., Schwentick, T.: On notions of regularity for data languages. Theor. Comput. Sci. **411**(4–5), 702–715 (2010)
3. Bojańczyk, M., David, C., Muscholl, A., Schwentick, T., Segoufin, L.: Two-variable logic on data trees and XML reasoning. In: PODS, pp. 10–19. ACM (2006)
4. Bojańczyk, M., David, C., Muscholl, A., Schwentick, T., Segoufin, L.: Two-variable logic on data words. TOCL **12**(4), 27 (2011)
5. Bojańczyk, M., Muscholl, A., Schwentick, T., Segoufin, L., David, C.: Two-variable logic on words with data. In: LICS, pp. 7–16. IEEE (2006)
6. Bouyer, P., Petit, A., Thérien, D.: An algebraic approach to data languages and timed languages. Inf. Comput. **182**(2), 137–162 (2003)
7. Calvanese, D., Kotek, T., Šimkus, M., Veith, H., Zuleger, F.: Shape and content. In: Albert, E., Sekerinski, E. (eds.) IFM 2014. LNCS, vol. 8739, pp. 3–17. Springer, Cham (2014). https://doi.org/10.1007/978-3-319-10181-1_1
8. Calvanese, D., Ortiz, M., Simkus, M.: Verification of evolving graph-structured data under expressive path constraints. In: ICDT, pp. 15:1–15:19 (2016)
9. Clarke, E., Henzinger, T.A., Veith, H., Bloem, R. (eds.): Handbook of Model Checking. Springer, Cham (2018). https://doi.org/10.1007/978-3-319-10575-8
10. David, C., Libkin, L., Tan, T.: On the satisfiability of two-variable logic over data words. In: Fermüller, C.G., Voronkov, A. (eds.) LPAR 2010. LNCS, vol. 6397, pp. 248–262. Springer, Heidelberg (2010). https://doi.org/10.1007/978-3-642-16242-8_18

11. Esparza, J.: Decidability and complexity of Petri net problems — an introduction. In: Reisig, W., Rozenberg, G. (eds.) ACPN 1996. LNCS, vol. 1491, pp. 374–428. Springer, Heidelberg (1998). https://doi.org/10.1007/3-540-65306-6_20

12. Etessami, K., Vardi, M., Wilke, T.: First-order logic with two variables and unary temporal logic. Inform. Comput. **179**(2), 279–295 (2002)

13. Grädel, E., Kolaitis, P., Vardi, M.: On the decision problem for two-variable first-order logic. Bull. Symb. Log. **3**(01), 53–69 (1997)

14. Grädel, E., Otto, M.: On logics with two variables. Theor. Comput. Sci. **224**(1), 73–113 (1999)

15. Grumberg, O., Kupferman, O., Sheinvald, S.: Variable automata over infinite alphabets. In: Dediu, A.-H., Fernau, H., Martín-Vide, C. (eds.) LATA 2010. LNCS, vol. 6031, pp. 561–572. Springer, Heidelberg (2010). https://doi.org/10.1007/978-3-642-13089-2_47

16. Itzhaky, S., et al.: On the automated verification of web applications with embedded SQL. In: ICDT. LIPIcs, vol. 68, pp. 16:1–16:18 (2017)

17. Kaminski, M., Francez, N.: Finite-memory automata. Theor. Comput. Sci. **134**(2), 329–363 (1994)

18. Kara, A.: Logics on data words. Ph.D. thesis, Technical University of Dortmund (2016)

19. Manuel, A., Zeume, T.: Two-variable logic on 2-dimensional structures. In: CSL, pp. 484–499 (2013)

20. Meduna, A., Zemek, P.: Jumping finite automata. Int. J. Found. Comput. Sci. **23**(7), 1555–1578 (2012)

21. Mortimer, M.: On languages with two variables. Math. Log. Q. **21**(1), 135–140 (1975)

22. Neven, F., Schwentick, T., Vianu, V.: Finite state machines for strings over infinite alphabets. TOCL **5**(3), 403–435 (2004)

23. Niewerth, M., Schwentick, T.: Two-variable logic and key constraints on data words. In: ICDT, pp. 138–149. ACM (2011)

24. Otto, M.: Two variable first-order logic over ordered domains. J. Symb. Logic **66**(2), 685–702 (2001)

25. Pratt-Hartmann, I.: Logics with counting and equivalence. In: CSL-LICS, pp. 76:1–76:10. ACM (2014)

26. Rensink, A.: Canonical graph shapes. In: Schmidt, D. (ed.) ESOP 2004. LNCS, vol. 2986, pp. 401–415. Springer, Heidelberg (2004). https://doi.org/10.1007/978-3-540-24725-8_28

27. Schwentick, T., Zeume, T.: Two-variable logic with two order relations. Log. Meth. Comput. Sci. **8**(1) (2012)

28. Segoufin, L.: Automata and logics for words and trees over an infinite alphabet. In: Ésik, Z. (ed.) CSL 2006. LNCS, vol. 4207, pp. 41–57. Springer, Heidelberg (2006). https://doi.org/10.1007/11874683_3

29. Tan, T.: Extending two-variable logic on data trees with order on data values and its automata. ACM Trans. Comput. Log. **15**(1), 8:1–8:39 (2014)

30. Vardi, M., Wolper, P.: An automata-theoretic approach to automatic program verification (preliminary report). In: LICS, pp. 332–344. IEEE (1986)

Limited Two-Way Deterministic Finite Automata with Advice

Ahmet Bilal Uçan[✉] [iD]

Bogazici University, Istanbul, Turkey
ahmet.ucan@boun.edu.tr

Abstract. External assistance in the form of strings called advice is given to an automaton in order to make it a non-uniform model of computation. Automata with advice are then examined to better understand the limitations imposed by uniformity, which is a typical property shared by all feasible computational models. The main contribution of this paper is to introduce and investigate an extension of the model introduced by Küçük et al. [6]. The model is called *circular deterministic finite automaton with advice tape (cdfat)*. In this model the input head is allowed to pass over input multiple times. The number of allowed passes over the input, which is typically a function of input length, is considered as a resource besides the advice amount. The results proved for the model include a hierarchy for cdfat with real-time heads, simulation of 1w/1w cdfat by 1w/rt cdfat, lower bounds of resources provided to a cdfat in order to make it powerful enough to recognize any language, utilizable advice limit regardless of the allowed pass limit, a relation between utilizable pass limit and advice limit, and some closure properties.

Keywords: Formal languages · Automata theory · Advised computation

1 Introduction

Advised computation, where external trusted assistance is provided to a machine to help it for computational tasks, was introduced by Karp and Lipton [4] in 1982. Damm and Holzer [1] considered giving advice to restricted versions of Turing machines. Recent work on finite automata with advice include the papers of Yamakami [8–11], Tadaki et al. [7], Freivalds et al. [3], Küçük et al. [6] and Ďuriš et al. [2]. Today, there are many different models in literature, partly because of the several options available for a machine to access its advice. However, all such models share some common properties. There is an advice function, which maps input lengths to advice strings and not needed to be computable. Advice strings are composed of characters from an advice alphabet. The machine has to use the same advice string when operating on inputs of the same length. We investigate the class of languages recognized by a machine when it consults some advice function having some bounded growing rate. We then play with that upper bound

© Springer Nature Switzerland AG 2020
A. Leporati et al. (Eds.): LATA 2020, LNCS 12038, pp. 222–232, 2020.
https://doi.org/10.1007/978-3-030-40608-0_15

to see what happens to the aforementioned class. An advised automaton takes advantage of an advice string by reading the character under the advice head and choosing appropriate transition from its transition function accordingly. So the same machine may recognize different languages using different advice functions.

We focus on the advice tape model introduced by Küçük et al. in [6]. Since that model becomes extremely powerful (able to recognize all languages) when allowed to use a 2-way input head, and is remarkably limited for the 1-way head case, [2, Theorem 2], [6, Theorem 13], we examine a limited version of two-way input access.

Some common terminology to be used in this paper are as follows: n denotes input length, M denotes an automaton, L denotes a language, h denotes an advice function, w denotes a string, Σ denotes input alphabet, Γ denotes advice alphabet, $\star$ means any, ALL denotes the set of all languages, and $|w|_c$ denotes the number of occurrences of character c in string w.

Here are some definitions of concepts that will be used in our discussion,

Definition 1 [6]. $w_1 \equiv_{L,n,k} w_2 \iff w_1, w_2 \in \Sigma^k \land \forall z \in \Sigma^{n-k}[w_1 z \in L \iff w_2 z \in L]$.

Definition 2 [2, Definition 5]. Let $\{R_n\}_{n=1}^{\infty}$ be a family of relations $R_n \subseteq \Sigma^n \times \Sigma^{f(n)}$ for some $f : \mathbb{N} \to \mathbb{N}$ such that $\forall x_0, x_1 \in \Sigma^n, x_0 \neq x_1$, there is a $y \in \Sigma^{f(n)}$ such that $R_n(x_i, y)$ and $\neg R_n(x_{1-i}, y)$ for some $i \in \{0, 1\}$. Let L_R be the language $L_R := \{xy | x \in \Sigma^\star, |y| = f(|x|), R_{|x|}(x, y)\}$. We call L_R a prefix-sensitive language for relation family R.

Definition 3. We call L a prefix-sensitive language iff there exists a relation family R such that L_R is a prefix-sensitive language for relation family R.

2   Our Model

We defined this model and decided to work on it because the model seems to provide a smooth passage from one-way input head to two-way input head. The name of the new model is *circular deterministic finite automaton with advice tape* (cdfat) which may have real-time or 1-way input and advice heads (4 possible versions). Circular machines read their input circularly, that is, when the input endmarker has seen and the next transition dictates machine to move its input head to right, the input head immediately returns to the beginning position. Advice head is not allowed to perform such a move.

Note that when restricted to a single pass on input, this model is exactly the same with the standard *deterministic finite automaton with advice tapes* model (except the two-way input head version) introduced by Küçük et al. [6].

2.1   Definition

A circular deterministic finite automaton is a 9-tuple $(Q, \Sigma, \Gamma, T_I, T_A, \delta, q_0, q_{acc}, q_{rej})$ where

(i) Q is a finite set of internal states,

(ii) Σ is a finite set of symbols called the input alphabet that does not contain the endmarker symbol, \$, such that \$ $\notin \Sigma$ and $\Sigma' = \Sigma \cup \{\$\}$,

(iii) Γ is a finite set of symbols called advice alphabet that does not contain the endmarker symbol, \$, such that \$ $\notin \Gamma$ and $\Gamma' = \Gamma \cup \{\$\}$,

(iv) $T_I \in \{\{S, R\}, \{R\}\}$ represents the set of allowed input head movements where S and R means *stay-put* and *right* respectively,

(v) $T_A \in \{\{S, R\}, \{R\}\}$ represents the set of allowed advice head movements where S and R means *stay-put* and *right* respectively,

(vi) $q_0 \in Q$ is the initial state on which the execution begins,

(vii) $q_{acc} \in Q$ is the accept state on which the execution halts and accepts,

(viii) $q_{rej} \in Q$ is the reject state on which the execution halts and rejects,

(ix) $\delta : Q \times \Sigma \times \Gamma \to Q \times T_I \times T_A$ is the transition function such that, $\delta(q_1, \sigma, \gamma) = (q_2, t_I, t_A)$ implies that when the automaton is in state $q_1 \in Q$ and it scans $\sigma \in \Sigma'$ on its input tape and $\gamma \in \Gamma'$ on its advice tape, a transition occurs which changes the state of the automaton to $q_2 \in Q$, meanwhile moving the input and advice tape heads in the directions specified respectively by $t_I \in T_I$ and $t_A \in T_A$,

A cdfat $M = (Q, \Sigma, \Gamma, T_I, T_A, \delta, q_0, q_{acc}, q_{rej})$ is said to accept (reject) a string $x \in \Sigma^*$ with the help of an advice string $a \in \Gamma^*$ if and only if M, when started at its initial state q_0 with $x\$$ on the input tape and $a\$$ on the advice tape and while the tape heads scan the first symbols, reaches the accepting (rejecting) state, q_{acc} (q_{rej}), by changing states and moving the input and advice tape heads as specified by its transition function, δ.

A language L defined on the alphabet Σ, is said to be recognized by such a cdfat M with the help of an advice function $h : \mathbb{N} \to \Gamma^*$ if and only if

- $L = \{x \mid M$ accepts x with the help of $h(|x|)\}$, and
- $\bar{L} = \{x \mid M$ rejects x with the help of $h(|x|)\}$.

A language L is said to be recognized by a cdfat, M, using $O(g(n))$-length advice if there exists an advice function h with the following properties:

- $|h(n)| \in O(g(n))$, and
- M recognizes L with the help of $h(n)$.

A language L is said to be recognized by a cdfat, M, using $f(n)$ passes over the input if and only if during the execution of any input of length n, transitions of the form $\delta(\_, \$, \_) = (\_, R, \_)$ are used at most $f(n)$ times in total.

Note that it is not allowed for a cdfat to have a transition of the form $\delta(\_, \_, \$) = (\_, \_, R)$, however, there can be transitions $\delta(\_, \$, \_) = (\_, R, \_)$. The endmarker of the input is for informing the machine. It may be a different model if we omit it, for the sake of backward compatibility we continue to use it.

For the notational purposes, $\mathcal{L}\{rt - f(n)\}$ denotes the set of languages recognized by cdfat with real-time heads, $(n + 1)f(n)$ length advice and $f(n)$ passes. When a head is allowed to stay-put on its tape, we use a different notation. For instance $\mathcal{L}\{1 - [f(n)]/g(n)\}$ denotes the set of languages recognized by cdfat with 1-way input head and real-time advice head, using $g(n)$ length advice and $f(n)$ passes.

2.2   Results

Theorem 1. *A language L is prefix-sensitive if and only if for all $k \in \mathbb{N}$, there exists $n \in \mathbb{N}$ such that $\equiv_{L,n,k}$ has $|\Sigma|^k$ equivalence classes.*

Proof. Assume that for some language L it holds that for all $k \in \mathbb{N}$, there exists $n \in \mathbb{N}$ such that $\equiv_{L,n,k}$ has $|\Sigma|^k$ equivalence classes. Let f be a function which maps any $k \in \mathbb{N}$ to an n so that $\equiv_{L,n,k}$ has $|\Sigma|^k$ equivalence classes. Define an infinite family of relations $\{R_k\}_{k=1}^{\infty}$ such that $R_k \subseteq \Sigma^k \times \Sigma^{f(k)-k}$ and for all $x \in \Sigma^k$ and all $y \in \Sigma^{f(k)-k}$, $xy \in L \iff R_k(x,y)$. It holds that $\forall x_0, x_1 \in \Sigma^k, x_0 \neq x_1$, there is a $y \in \Sigma^{f(k)-k}$ such that $R_k(x_i, y)$ and $\neg R_k(x_{1-i}, y)$ for some $i \in \{0,1\}$. Because if there were no such y for some x_0 and x_1, then $x_0 \equiv_{L,f(k),k} x_1$ would be true and the number of equivalence classes would not be $|\Sigma|^k$. According to the Definition 2, we concluded that L is prefix-sensitive.

For the other direction, let L be a prefix-sensitive language. According to the Definition 2, $L = \{xy | x \in \Sigma^*, R_{|x|}(x,y)\}$ where $f : \mathbb{N} \to \mathbb{N}$ is a function and $\{R_k\}_{k=1}^{\infty}$ is an infinite sequence of relations such that $R_k \subseteq \Sigma^k \times \Sigma^{f(k)}$ and $\forall x_0, x_1 \in \Sigma^k, x_0 \neq x_1$, there is a $y \in \Sigma^{f(k)}$ such that $R_k(x_i, y)$ and $\neg R_k(x_{1-i}, y)$ for some $i \in \{0,1\}$. It holds that for all $k \in \mathbb{N}$, $\equiv_{L,k+f(k),k}$ has $|\Sigma|^k$ equivalence classes. Because if the number of equivalence classes of $\equiv_{L,k+f(k),k}$ is less than $|\Sigma|^k$ for some k, then there would be two strings x_0 and x_1 such that $x_0 \equiv_{L,k+f(k),k} x_1$ and that would imply that there is no y of length $f(k)$ such that $R_k(x_i, y)$ and $\neg R_k(x_{1-i}, y)$ for some $i \in \{0,1\}$. □

Theorem 2. $\mathcal{L}\{rt - 2^{O(n)}\} = ALL.$

Proof. Let $h(n) = w_1 c_1 w_2 c_2 \ldots w_{|\Sigma|^n} c_{\Sigma^n}$ where each w_i is a distinct input word of length n and each $c_i \notin \Sigma$ is either the accept or the reject symbol. Devise a machine M such that, it tries to match the input word and advice character by character in real-time execution. If a mismatch occurs while trying to match the input word, machine M will advance its input head until it is at the beginning position again. Note that the advice head will be at the first character of the next word on advice at the end of this process. Then it tries to match the next word and so on. At some point matching ends with success, that is, machine M will see the endmarker of input while trying to match the characters. At that point it will accept or reject the string depending on which c_i character it is seeing on the advice. □

Theorem 3. *For any function $f : \mathbb{N} \to \mathbb{N}$, $\mathcal{L}\{rt - f(n)\} = \mathcal{L}\{rt - O(f(n))\}$.*

Proof. The idea is that for any given machine M, one can devise a new machine M' such that M' uses k times less passes than M for all n and for an arbitrary $k \in \mathbb{N}$, and still recognizes the same language with the help of some other advice function. Let us group the passes of machine M so that i^{th} group consists of passes from $(i-1)k+1$ to ik. With a single pass, machine M' simulates a group of k passes of M. First pass simulates the first group and second pass simulates the second group and so on. Since M' does not know which state to begin with a pass without knowing the result of the previous one, it simulates all possibilities and remembers the final state of the previous group of passes using again its states. Therefore the size of the state set of M' is s^{ks+1} where s is the number of states of M.

The new advice function h' is a compressed version of the old one. Let Γ' be the new advice alphabet whose symbols represent the k permutations of the symbols of Γ. $|\Gamma'| = |\Gamma|^k$ holds. Let $|h'(n)| = |h(n)|/k$ for all $n > 0$. Note that without loss of generality we assume that $|h(n)|$ is an integer multiple of k. We prepare the new advice strings so that $h'(1)$ represents all strings from $h(1)$ to $h(k)$, $h'(2)$ represents all strings from $h(k+1)$ to $h(2k)$ and so on.   □

Theorem 4. *For any function $f : \mathbb{N} \to \mathbb{N}$, $L_1, L_2 \in \mathcal{L}\{rt - f(n)\} \implies L_1 L_2 \in \mathcal{L}\{rt - nf(n)\}$.*

Proof. Let M_1, M_2 be machines recognizing L_1, L_2 with the help of advice functions h_1, h_2 respectively. Let M_3 be the machine which is claimed to recognize the concatenation language $L_1 L_2$ with the help of advice function h_3. The idea is to predict the words $w_1 \in L_1$ and $w_2 \in L_2$ such that $w_1 w_2$ is the input word. Machine M_3 doesn't know from where to divide the input, so it just tries all the possibilities. We replace the advice characters whose locations correspond to the last character of the first portion of the input with their marked versions in order to inform the machine M_3.

In the first pass over the input, machine M_3 first simulates M_1 on the first portion of the input and stores the last internal state of that execution. Then it simulates M_2 on the rest of the input and stores the last state of that execution too. Then it begins the second pass simulating M_1 again but this time starting from the last saved state of that thread and when it completes, M_3 will update the last state of the thread and so on. Throughout the execution of M_3, two separate threads of execution are simulated at the same time. At the end of at most $f(n)$ passes, if both threads end with accepting their respective sub-inputs, M_3 accepts the input. Otherwise, M_3 continues the computation with a different division of the input. Note that, given an input word of length n, there are $n+1$ different pairs of words such that their concatenation is the input word. At the end of at most $(n+1)f(n)$ passes, if no division works, M_3 rejects the input. According to the Theorem 3, asymptotic rate of the passes is the important part so $nf(n)$ passes can do the same job.

Note that we should double the old advice alphabet size and introduce marked versions of the old symbols in order to mark the position of input separation on the advice h_3. Also note that advice string $h_3(n)$ will be an interleaved version of the $h_1(k)$ and $h_2(n - k)$ concatenated for all $k \in [0, n]_{\mathbb{Z}}$.   □

Corollary 1. $\mathcal{L}\{rt - poly\}$ *is closed under concatenation.*

Lemma 1. *Let $L \in \mathcal{L}\{rt - f(n)\}$. Then for all n and for all k smaller than n, $\equiv_{L,n,k}$ has $2^{O(f(n))}$ equivalence classes.*

Proof. Let $s = |Q|$ and let $Q' = \{q_1, q_2, \ldots q_{s-2}\}$ be the set of all states except the accept and reject states. Let $\alpha_{w,i} : Q' \to Q'$ be a mapping which maps the internal state of machine when input head is for the first time on the first character of w and advice head is at the ith position to the internal state of machine when input head is for the first time on the first character right after the w. Besides its parameters w and i, this mapping depends on the content of the advice and transition function of the machine. Here we consider a single machine working on inputs of the same length n therefore the mapping depends only on its parameters.

Consider execution of a real-time circular machine on two different inputs of length n, namely $w_1 z$ and $w_2 z$. If we can find two words w_1 and w_2 such that $\alpha_{w_1,i} = \alpha_{w_2,i}$ for all $i \in \{1, 1 + (n+1), \ldots 1 + (f(n) - 1)(n+1)\}$ then the two inputs must have the same fate for all z.

Given a single i, there are less than s^s distinct functions $\alpha_{w,i}$. Considering all $f(n)$ functions mentioned above for a word w, there are less than $(s^s)^{f(n)}$ different permutations. Assuming that the number of equivalence classes of relation $\equiv_{L,n,k}$ is greater than $(s^s)^{f(n)}$ for some k and n, there would be two words w_1 and w_2 such that they are in different equivalence classes and have all the same mappings. This is a contradiction. $\square$

Theorem 5. *Let* $f(n), g(n) \in O(n)$ *and* $f(n) \in o(g(n))$. *Then* $\mathcal{L}\{rt - f(n)\} \subsetneq \mathcal{L}\{rt - g(n)\}$.

Proof. Consider the language family $L_\rho = \{w^{\rho(|w|)} \mid w \in \Sigma^*, \rho : \mathbb{N} \to \mathbb{N}\}$. Note that ρ is assumed to be a non-decreasing function and the input length $n = |w|\rho(|w|)$. Inputs consist of repetitions of a substring w. Define $\phi(m\rho(m)) = m$ for all $m \in \mathbb{N}^+$. Depending on the choice of ρ, $\phi(n) \in \omega(1) \cap O(n)$. We will give three lemmas. Two of them show a hierarchy for the range $\omega(1) \cap O(n)$ and the last one is to put the $\Theta(1)$ in.

Lemma 2. $L_\rho \in \mathcal{L}\{rt - \phi(n)\}$.

Since given the input length n and the function ρ we can deduct the period of input, we can check a position of the repeating substring w for each pass. Therefore our machine will need $|w| = \phi(n)$ many passes.

The advice strings are of the form (parentheses are meta-characters),

$$h(n) = (10^{|w|-1})^{\rho(|w|)} \#(010^{|w|-2})^{\rho(|w|)} \ldots \#(0^{|w|-1}1)^{\rho(|w|)}$$

Our machine will first search for the first 1 on advice tape and when it has been found, the machine saves the corresponding input character in its states and continue searching for the next 1. When it sees the next 1 it checks the corresponding input character with the one it saved before. If they mismatch input is rejected. The machine then continue searching for 1s and do the same checking till the end of the first pass. It then start with the second pass and do the same procedure again, checking the equality of next character position in substring w. If the endmarker of advice is reached, input is accepted.

Lemma 3. $L_\rho \notin \mathcal{L}\{rt - o(\phi(n))\}$.

Observe that any L_ρ is prefix-sensitive. Thinking each word as concatenation of first period w and the rest, in other words selecting k to be $\phi(n)$ for all n, $\equiv_{L_\rho,n,k}$ has $|\Sigma|^{\phi(n)}$ equivalence classes. According to the Lemma 1, $L_\rho \notin \mathcal{L}\{rt - o(\phi(n))\}$.

Lemma 4. *No prefix-sensitive language is in $\mathcal{L}\{rt - O(1)\}$.*

According to the Lemma 1, for any language $L \in \mathcal{L}\{rt - O(1)\}$, $\equiv_{L,n,k}$ has $2^{O(1)} = O(1)$ equivalence classes. Therefore according to Theorem 1, L is not prefix sensitive.   □

Theorem 6. *Let $L_1 \in \mathcal{L}\{1 - [f(n)]/1 - [g(n)]\}$ and $L_2 \in \mathcal{L}\{1 - [f'(n)]/1 - [g'(n)]\}$. Then $L_1 \cup L_2 \in \mathcal{L}\{1 - [f(n) + f'(n)]/1 - [g(n) + g'(n)]\}$.*

Proof. Let M_1, M_2 be machines recognizing languages L_1, L_2 with the help of advice functions h_1 and h_2 respectively. Devise a new advice function,

$$h_3(n) = h_1(n)\#h_2(n)$$

for all n where $\#$ is a brand new advice character that occurs nowhere else. Let M_3 be the machine recognizing the union language with the help of h_3. Machine M_3 first simulates the M_1 and during this simulation it treats the $\#$ character in advice as an endmarker. When this simulation ends, which may take at most $f(n)$ passes over the input, M_3 stores the result in its states and start simulating M_2 after adjusting its heads to proper positions, that is input head to the beginning and advice head to the next character after $\#$. After at most $f'(n)$ passes over the input, it completes the execution and store the result in its states. In this way it may end up in 4 different states for 4 possible acceptance status of M_1 and M_2. Via combining some of those states into the accept state and the rest into the reject state; union, intersection or difference of L_1 and L_2 are all recognizable.   □

Corollary 2. $\mathcal{L}\{1 - [O(f(n))]/1 - [O(g(n))]\}$ *is closed under union and intersection.*

Theorem 7. *For any function $f : \mathbb{N} \to \mathbb{N}$, $\mathcal{L}\{1 - [f(n)]/1 - [\star]\} = \mathcal{L}\{1 - [f(n)]/1 - [2^{O(n)}]\}$.*

Proof. The proof is an easy modification of the proof given by Ďuriš et al. for [2, Theorem 3].   □

Theorem 8. *For any function $g : \mathbb{N} \to \mathbb{N}$, $\mathcal{L}\{1 - [\star]/1 - [g(n)]\} = \mathcal{L}\{1 - [O(g(n))]/1 - [g(n)]\}$.*

Proof. Consider the execution of an s-state cdfat with one-way heads. Pausing the advice head, passing on the input more than s times forces the machine to enter an infinite loop. Thus, a machine must advance its advice head before that threshold. Therefore at most $sg(n)$ passes are possible for an execution which eventually halts.   □

Theorem 9. *For any functions $f, g : \mathbb{N} \to \mathbb{N}$, $\mathcal{L}\{1 - [f(n)]/1 - [g(n)]\} \subseteq \mathcal{L}\{1 - [f(n)]/O(nf(n)g(n))\}$.*

Proof. It is possible to simulate the one-way advice head with real-time advice head using additional advice. The idea is to replicate each advice character $(n+1)f(n)$ times and use separator characters # to mark the transition locations. That is, for all n,

$$h(n) = c_1 c_2 \dots c_k \implies h'(n) = c_1^{(n+1)f(n)} \# c_2^{(n+1)f(n)} \# \dots c_k^{(n+1)f(n)} \# c_\$^{(n+1)f(n)}$$

where $c_i \in \Gamma$ for all $i \in \{1, 2 \dots k\}$ and the $c_\$$ is a new advice character which is for repeating the endmarker (it is not allowed to have more than one real endmarker character). When the new machine reads $c_\$$ on h', it behaves exactly like the old machine seeing endmarker on h.

Instead of stay-putting advice head in old machine, let it move right one step in new machine. Instead of moving advice head one step in old machine, enter a subprogram which takes advice head to the next # character in new machine.

This trick works because a cdfat with one-way heads must forward its advice head within $(n + 1)f(n)$ computational steps. This is because without loss of generality we can assume at least one head is moving in each step and of course input head can move at most $(n + 1)f(n)$ times in an execution.   □

Corollary 3. *For any function $f : \mathbb{N} \to \mathbb{N}$, $\mathcal{L}\{1 - [f(n)]/1 - [poly]\} = \mathcal{L}\{1 - [f(n)]/poly\}$.*

It is already known that dfat with 2-way input head is equal in power with the prefix advice model when provided with constant advice [5, Theorem 3.8]. Since our model is sandwiched in between the 2-way input model and advice prefix model when it comes to power, we deduce that $\mathcal{L}\{1 - [i]/1 - [k]\} = \mathcal{L}\{1 - [i + 1]/1 - [k]\}$ for all $i \in \mathbb{N}$. Therefore an interesting question to ask is what is the minimum advice for which more passes over input enlarges the class of languages recognized. Küçük and others showed that when provided with polynomial advice, 2-way input head is more powerful than 1-way head [6, Theorem 14]. We proved a stronger result and gave an ultimate answer to the aforementioned question. It turns out that even 2 passes over input is more powerful than a single pass when the machine is provided with an increasing advice.

Theorem 10. *Let $f : \mathbb{N} \to \mathbb{N}$ be any function in $\omega(1)$. Then $\mathcal{L}\{1 - [1]/1 - [f(n)]\} \subsetneq \mathcal{L}\{1 - [2]/1 - [f(n)]\}$.*

Proof. Consider the language family $L_\rho = \{w | w \in \{1, 2, 3\}^*, |w|_1 = |w|_2 = \rho(|w|)\}$. The following two lemmas establish the proof.

Lemma 5. *$L_\rho \notin \mathcal{L}\{1 - [1]/1 - [O(\rho(n))]\}$.*

Proof. Küçük et al. proved that for any advice length function f, if $L \in \mathcal{L}\{1 - [1]/1 - [f(n)]\}$, then for all n and all $k \leq n$, $\equiv_{L,n,k}$ has $O(f(n))$ equivalence classes, [6, Lemma 6]. It can be shown that for all n, there exists $k \leq n$ such that $\equiv_{L_\rho,n,k}$ has $\Theta(\rho^2(n))$ equivalence classes. Since $\rho(n) \in \omega(1) \implies \rho(n) \in o(\rho^2(n))$, we conclude that $L_\rho \notin \mathcal{L}\{1 - [1]/1 - [O(\rho(n))]\}$.

Lemma 6. $L_\rho \in \mathcal{L}\{1 - [2]/1 - [O(\rho(n))]\}$.

Proof. The idea is to devise a machine which in first pass counts the character 1 and in second pass counts the character 2. Let $L_1 = \{w|w \in \{1,2,3\}^*, |w|_1 = \rho(|w|)\}$ and $L_2 = \{w|w \in \{1,2,3\}^*, |w|_2 = \rho(|w|)\}$. Observe that L_1 or L_2 can easily be recognized by a cdfat with a single pass. In order to recognize L_1 for instance, let $h(n) = 1^{\rho(n)}$ be the advice function, then consider a machine which stay-puts its advice head when it sees a character other than 1 on its input and advances its advice head when it sees 1 on input. It will accept a string iff both endmarkers are read at the same time. L_2 can be recognized similarly. Since $L_1, L_2 \in \mathcal{L}\{1 - [1]/1 - [O(\rho(n))]\}$, according to Theorem 6, $L_1 \cap L_2 = L_\rho \in \mathcal{L}\{1 - [2]/1 - [O(\rho(n))]\}$. □

Lemma 7. *Let $L \in \mathcal{L}\{1-[f(n)]/1-[g(n)]\}$. Then for all n and for all k smaller than n, $\equiv_{L,n,k}$ has $2^{O(g(n)\log g(n))}$ equivalence classes.*

Proof. Define a configuration c_i of a machine to be the pair of internal state and advice position. Define a non-stopping configuration $c = (q, m)$ of a machine to be any configuration where q is a state other than accept and reject states. Let $C = \{c_1, c_2, \ldots, c_{(s-2)(g(n)+1)}\}$ be the set of all non-stopping configurations for a machine and for input length n ($s = |Q|$). Without loss of generality assume our machines always end their execution when input head is on the endmarker. Let w be a substring of input (not containing the endmarker) and let $\alpha_w : C \to C$ be a mapping which maps the configuration of machine when the first character of word w is read first time on input tape to the configuration of machine when the character right after the word w is read first time on input tape. Function α depends on transition function of the machine, the specific word w being processed and the advice content. We focus on a single machine and inputs of the same length n, therefore in our case α depends only on w.

Consider execution of a circular machine on two different inputs of length n, namely $w_1 z$ and $w_2 z$. Both inputs start execution at the initial configuration and after each pass they start with a new configuration. If we can find two words w_1 and w_2 such that $\alpha_{w_1} = \alpha_{w_2}$ then the two inputs $w_1 z$ and $w_2 z$ must have the same fate for all z.

There are less than $2sg(n)^{2sg(n)}$ distinct functions α. Assuming that the number of equivalence classes of $\equiv_{L,n,k}$ is greater than $2sg(n)^{2sg(n)}$ for some k and n, there would be two words w_1, w_2 in two different equivalence classes such that they have the same mapping. This is a contradiction. □

Theorem 11. *Let $f(n) \in \omega(1) \cap o(\log n)$. Then the classes $\mathcal{L}\{rt - f(n)\}$ and $\mathcal{L}\{1 - [1]/1 - [\star]\}$ are incomparable.*

Proof. Recall that $\mathcal{L}\{1-[1]/1-[\star]\}$ is nothing but our way of notating the class of languages recognized by the model introduced by Küçük et al. in [6] given access to unlimited advice. According to Theorem 5, a prefix-sensitive language is in $\mathcal{L}\{rt - f(n)\}$ no matter how slow $f(n)$ grows. However we know from Ďuriš et al. [2, Theorem 2] that no prefix-sensitive language is in $\mathcal{L}\{1 - [1]/1 - [\star]\}$. Therefore $\mathcal{L}\{rt - f(n)\} \nsubseteq \mathcal{L}\{1 - [1]/1 - [\star]\}$.

On the other hand, as stated in proof of Lemma 6, the language $L = \{w | w \in \{1, 2, 3\}^*, |w|_1 = \rho(|w|)\}$ can be easily recognized by a machine with one-way heads, given access to $\Theta(\rho(n))$ length advice. It is easy to see that for all n, there exists k such that $\equiv_{L_\rho, n, k}$ has $\Theta(\rho(n))$ equivalence classes. When the $\rho(n)$ is selected to be linear in n, according to Lemma 1, $L \notin \mathcal{L}\{rt - f(n)\}$. Therefore $\mathcal{L}\{1 - [1]/1 - [\star]\} \nsubseteq \mathcal{L}\{rt - f(n)\}$. □

An interesting question to ask is what is the minimum advice or pass needed in order for a model to recognize any language. We can show some lower bounds using Lemmas 1 and 7. PAL is the language of even palindromes.

Corollary 4. $g(n) \log g(n) \in o(n) \implies PAL \notin \mathcal{L}\{1 - [f(n)]/1 - [g(n)]\}$.

Corollary 5. $f(n) \in o(n) \implies PAL \notin \mathcal{L}\{rt - f(n)\}$.

3   Conclusions and Open Questions

We showed that cdfat with real-time heads can utilize up to linearly many passes over input. We showed that with exponential pass, the real-time machine can recognize any language. However we do not know if the machine can utilize more than linear passes. There may be a clever algorithm for recognizing any language with linear passes.

We showed that even the most powerful version of the cdfat, that is the one having one-way input and advice heads, cannot recognize some languages when there is not enough advice (a nearly linear bound). However we are not aware of an algorithm for this machine which uses less than exponential resources to recognize any language. It would be nice to know the minimum amount of resources needed to recognize any language.

We compared the class of languages recognized by single pass deterministic finite automaton with one-way heads and unlimited advice with the growing class of languages recognized by a real-time cdfat as we allow more passes over input. Since we know that the former class is bigger than the latter when we allow only constant amount of pass over input and the reverse is true when we allow exponential passes over input, we wonder how that growing takes place and is there any pass limit for which the two classes are equal. It turned out that this is not the case. As long as the allowed pass limit is not constant and sub-logarithmic, two classes are not subsets of each other. However we do not know exactly when the latter class encompasses the former one.

Acknowledgements. Thanks to Prof. Cem Say who have helped editing the paper and correcting my mistakes and to my family for their constant support and love.

References

1. Damm, C., Holzer, M.: Automata that take advice. In: Wiedermann, J., Hájek, P. (eds.) MFCS 1995. LNCS, vol. 969, pp. 149–158. Springer, Heidelberg (1995). https://doi.org/10.1007/3-540-60246-1_121
2. Ďuriš, P., Korbaš, R., Královič, R., Královič, R.: Determinism and nondeterminism in finite automata with advice. In: Böckenhauer, H.-J., Komm, D., Unger, W. (eds.) Adventures Between Lower Bounds and Higher Altitudes. LNCS, vol. 11011, pp. 3–16. Springer, Cham (2018). https://doi.org/10.1007/978-3-319-98355-4_1
3. Freivalds, R.: Amount of nonconstructivity in deterministic finite automata. Theoret. Comput. Sci. 411(38–39), 3436–3443 (2010). https://doi.org/10.1016/j.tcs.2010.05.038
4. Karp, R., Lipton, R.: Turing machines that take advice. Enseign. Math. 28, 191–209 (1982)
5. Küçük, U.: Finite and small-space automata with advice. Ph.D. thesis, Boğaziçi University (2018)
6. Küçük, U., Say, A.C.C., Yakaryılmaz, A.: Finite automata with advice tapes. In: Béal, M.-P., Carton, O. (eds.) DLT 2013. LNCS, vol. 7907, pp. 301–312. Springer, Heidelberg (2013). https://doi.org/10.1007/978-3-642-38771-5_27
7. Tadaki, K., Yamakami, T., Lin, J.C.H.: Theory of one-tape linear-time turing machines. Theoret. Comput. Sci. 411(1), 22–43 (2010). https://doi.org/10.1016/j.tcs.2009.08.031
8. Yamakami, T.: Swapping lemmas for regular and context-free languages with advice. CoRR abs/0808.4122 (2008). http://arxiv.org/abs/0808.4122
9. Yamakami, T.: The roles of advice to one-tape linear-time turing machines and finite automata. Int. J. Found. Comput. Sci. 21(6), 941–962 (2010). https://doi.org/10.1142/S0129054110007659
10. Yamakami, T.: Immunity and pseudorandomness of context-free languages. Theoret. Comput. Sci. 412(45), 6432–6450 (2011). https://doi.org/10.1016/j.tcs.2011.07.013
11. Yamakami, T.: One-way reversible and quantum finite automata with advice. In: Dediu, A.-H., Martín-Vide, C. (eds.) LATA 2012. LNCS, vol. 7183, pp. 526–537. Springer, Heidelberg (2012). https://doi.org/10.1007/978-3-642-28332-1_45

Complexity

On the Size of Depth-Two Threshold Circuits for the Inner Product Mod 2 Function

Kazuyuki Amano[✉][ID]

Department of Computer Science, Gunma University,
1-5-1 Tenjin, Kiryu, Gunma 376-8515, Japan
amano@gunma-u.ac.jp

Abstract. In this paper, we study the size of depth-two threshold circuits computing the inner product mod 2 function $IP2_n(x_1, \ldots, x_n, y_1, \ldots, y_n) := \sum_i x_i y_i$ (mod 2). First, we reveal that $IP2_n$ can be computed by a depth-two threshold circuit of size significantly smaller than a folklore construction of size $O(2^n)$. Namely, we give a construction of such a circuit (denoted by THR ∘ THR circuit) of size $O(1.682^n)$. We also give an upper bound of $O(1.899^n)$ for the case that the weights of the top threshold gate are polynomially bounded (denoted by MAJ ∘ THR circuit). Second, we give new lower bounds on the size of depth-two circuits of some special form; the top gate is an unbounded weight threshold gate and the bottom gates are symmetric gates (denoted by THR ∘ SYM circuit). We show that any such circuit computing $IP2_n$ has size $\Omega((1.5 - \epsilon)^n)$ for every constant $\epsilon > 0$. This improves the previous bound of $\Omega(\sqrt{2^n}/n)$ based on the sign-rank method due to Forster et al. [JCSS '02, FSTTCS '01]. Our technique has a unique feature that the lower bound is obtained by giving an explicit feasible solution to (the dual of) a certain linear programming problem. In fact, the problem itself was presented by the author over a decade ago [MFCS '05], and finding a good solution is an actual contribution of this work.

Keywords: Circuit complexity · Threshold circuits · Linear programming · Upper bounds · Lower bounds

1 Introduction

The problem of proving strong lower bounds on the size (i.e., the number of gates) of depth-two threshold circuits computing an explicit Boolean function is a big challenge in complexity theory. Currently, we cannot refute that every function in the class NEXP (non-deterministic exponential time) can be computed by a polynomial-size depth-two circuit consisting of threshold gates with unbounded weights (denoted by THR ∘ THR circuit). There is a long line of research aiming for understanding the computational power and the limitation of depth-two threshold circuits (e.g, [5, 9, 10, 13, 14] or see an excellent book [12, Chapter 11.10]). The strongest known lower bound on the size of THR ∘ THR circuits for a function in NP is $\Omega(n^{3/2})$ due to Kane and Williams [13].

© Springer Nature Switzerland AG 2020
A. Leporati et al. (Eds.): LATA 2020, LNCS 12038, pp. 235–247, 2020.
https://doi.org/10.1007/978-3-030-40608-0_16

In this paper, we focus on the size complexity of depth-two threshold circuits for the *inner product mod 2* function:

$$\text{IP2}_n(x_1, \ldots, x_n, y_1, \ldots, y_n) = \sum_{i=1}^{n} (x_i \wedge y_i) \qquad (\text{mod } 2).$$

The inner product mod 2 function IP2_n has been widely studied in the context of depth-two threshold circuits (e.g., [7, 10, 13]).

It is a long standing open question whether IP2_n has a polynomial size depth-two threshold circuit with unbounded weights threshold gates in both layers. If we restrict the weights of threshold gates in one of two layers to be polynomial, then strong lower bounds are known. Let MAJ denote the class of threshold functions whose weights are bounded to be $\mathbb{Z} \cap [-\text{poly}(n), \text{poly}(n)]$. Hajnal et al. [10] proved that every MAJ ∘ THR circuit computing IP2_n has size $\Omega(2^{(1/3-\epsilon)n})$ using the discriminator method. An exponential lower bound were also shown by Nisan [16] using a communication complexity argument. Forster et al. [7, 8] proved that every THR ∘ MAJ circuit computing IP2_n has size $\Omega(\sqrt{2}^n/\text{poly}(n))$ by lowerbounding the sign-rank of the communication matrix of IP2_n.

Note that IP2_n has an $O(n)$ size threshold circuit of *depth-three*; in the first layer, we use n gates to compute $x_i \wedge y_i$ for each i, and then in the second and third layer, we use $O(n)$ gates to compute the parity of the outputs of them. If the gates at the bottom layer are restricted to be And, Exclusive-or or Symmetric gates, stronger lower bounds for IP2_n are known (see Table 1). Remark that, in recent years, several results providing the separation between depth-two and depth-three threshold circuits were given for *real-valued* functions (e.g., [6, 18]). However, to the best of our knowledge, the arguments used in these works can not directly be applied for Boolean functions.

Table 1. Known upper and lower bounds on the size of depth-two circuits using threshold gates that computes IP2_n. Entries marked with (*) are shown in this paper. Unmarked results are folklore.

Circuit type	Lower bound	Upper bound
THR ∘ AND	2^n [3]	2^n
THR ∘ XOR	2^n [4]	$O(2.966^n)$ [2, 19]
THR ∘ SYM	$\Omega((1.5 - \epsilon)^n)$ (*)	2^n
THR ∘ MAJ	$\Omega((\sqrt{2}^n/\text{poly}(n))$ [7, 8]	2^n
THR ∘ THR	$\Omega(n)$ [17]	$O(1.682^n)$ (*)
MAJ ∘ THR	$\Omega(2^{(1/3-\epsilon)n})$ [10]	$O(1.899^n)$ (*)

1.1 Our Contributions

The contribution of this work is twofold.

First, we consider *upper bounds* on the size of depth-two threshold circuits for $\mathsf{IP2}_n$. Although we know that lower bounds are more preferable, we pursuit upper bounds because we think that the lack of knowledge on good upper bounds for the problem is one of the reasons why we could not obtain a good lower bound.

It is folklore that $\mathsf{IP2}_n$ can be computed by a $\mathsf{THR} \circ \mathsf{AND}$ circuit (hence also by a $\mathsf{THR} \circ \mathsf{THR}$ circuit) of size 2^n by applying the inclusion-exclusion formula. Namely,

$$\mathsf{IP2}_n(x_1, \ldots, x_n, y_1, \ldots, y_n) = \sum_{\emptyset \neq S \subseteq \{1,\ldots,n\}} (-2)^{|S|-1} \prod_{i \in S} x_i y_i.$$

To the best of our knowledge, no asymptotically better bound has not been published. Note that $\mathsf{IP2}_n$ has $2n$ input variables and the construction via the DNF representation of $\mathsf{IP2}_n$ needs $\sim 3^n$ gates.

In this work, we show that $\mathsf{IP2}_n$ has a depth-two threshold circuit of size significantly smaller than 2^n. Namely, we give an explicit construction of a $\mathsf{THR} \circ \mathsf{THR}$ circuit of size $O(1.682^n)$ as well as a $\mathsf{MAJ} \circ \mathsf{THR}$ circuit of size $O(1.899^n)$ computing $\mathsf{IP2}_n$.

The second contribution of this work is to give a new lower bound on the size of depth-two threshold circuits with some special restriction on the bottom gates. A *symmetric gate* is a gate that takes Boolean inputs whose output is depending only on the number of one's in inputs. Let $\mathsf{THR} \circ \mathsf{SYM}$ denote depth-two circuits consisting of a threshold gate with unbounded weights at the top and symmetric gates at the bottom.

In [7], Forster established a breakthrough result that the sign-rank of the $2^n \times 2^n$ Hadamard matrix is $\Omega(\sqrt{2}^n)$. Here the sign-rank of a matrix $M = (M_{i,j})$ with nonzero entries is the least rank of a matrix $A = (A_{i,j})$ with $M_{i,j} A_{i,j} > 0$ for all i and j. By combining this result and a simple fact that the communication matrix of any symmetric function has rank at most $n + 1$, Forster et al. [8] established an $\Omega(\sqrt{2}^n/n)$ lower bound on the size of $\mathsf{THR} \circ \mathsf{SYM}$ circuits for $\mathsf{IP2}_n$.

In this paper, we improve their bound to $\Omega((1.5 - \epsilon)^n)$. Although the improvement is somewhat limited, our method has a unique feature; the lower bound is obtained by giving an explicit feasible solution to a certain linear programming problem.

Over a decade ago, building on the work of Basu et al. [3], the author developed an LP-based method to obtain a lower bound on the size of $\mathsf{THR} \circ \mathsf{SYM}$ circuits for $\mathsf{IP2}_n$ [1]. In [1], we showed that the problem of obtaining a lower bound on the size of such circuits can be reduced to the problem of solving a certain linear programming problem. Then we solved an obtained linear programming problem over 2^{16} variables using an LP solver to establish a lower bound of $\Omega(1.3638^n)$ on the size of $\mathsf{THR} \circ \mathsf{SYM}$ circuits for $\mathsf{IP2}_n$. However, the problem of determining a highest lower bound that can be obtained by our LP-based method was left as an open problem in [1].

In this work, we show that this limit is in fact $\Omega((1.5-\epsilon)^n)$, surpassing the $\Omega(\sqrt{2}^n/n)$ bounds obtained by the sign-rank method. We achieve this by giving an explicit feasible solution to the *dual* of the linear programming problem presented in [1] and estimating the value of the objective function. Showing this is an actual contribution of the second part of this work.

The rest of the paper is organized as follows. In Sect. 2, we introduce some notations. In Sect. 3, we give new upper bounds on the size of depth-two threshold circuits for $\mathsf{IP2}_n$. Then in Sect. 4, we review an LP-based lower bounds method presented in our previous work [1], and establish a new lower bound on the size of $\mathsf{THR} \circ \mathsf{SYM}$ circuits for $\mathsf{IP2}_n$.

2   Preliminaries

For an integer $n \geq 1$, $[n]$ denotes the set $\{1, 2, \ldots, n\}$. The *inner product mod 2 function* $\mathsf{IP2}_n$ is a Boolean function over $2n$ variables defined by

$$\mathsf{IP2}_n(x_1, \ldots, x_n, y_1, \ldots, y_n) = \sum_{i=1}^{n} (x_i \wedge y_i) \quad (\mathrm{mod}\ 2).$$

For a Boolean predicate P, let $[\![P]\!]$ denote the Iverson bracket function defined as $[\![P]\!] = 1$ if P is true and $[\![P]\!] = 0$ if P is false.

Let $x_1, \ldots, x_n \in \{0, 1\}$ be Boolean variables. A *linear threshold function* is a Boolean function of the form

$$[\![w_1 x_1 + \cdots + w_n x_n \geq t]\!],$$

for some $w_1, \ldots, w_n, t \in \mathbb{R}$. Similarly, an *exact threshold function* is a Boolean function of the form

$$[\![w_1 x_1 + \cdots + w_n x_n = t]\!].$$

We call $w_1, \ldots, w_n$ the *weights* and t the *threshold*. It is well known that, without loss of generality, we can assume that the weights and the threshold are integers of absolute value $2^{O(n \log n)}$ [15]. Hence, hereafter, we assume that the weights and the threshold are all integers. A gate that computes a linear threshold function is called a *threshold gate*. The class of all linear threshold functions (exact threshold functions, respectively) is denoted by THR (ETHR, respectively).

As usual, a depth-two circuit such that the top gate computes a function in C, and every bottom gate computes a function in $\mathcal{D}$ is called a $C \circ \mathcal{D}$ *circuit*. For example, a $\mathsf{THR} \circ \mathsf{THR}$ circuit is a depth-two circuit with threshold gates of unbounded weights in both layers. The *size* of a depth-two circuit is defined to be the number of gates in the bottom layer. The *size complexity* of a Boolean function f for $C \circ \mathcal{D}$ circuits is the minimum size of a $C \circ \mathcal{D}$ circuit computing f.

A *majority gate* is a gate computing a linear threshold function with additional restriction that $w_i \in \{-1, 1\}$ for all i. Here the threshold t can be an arbitrary value, i.e., is not restricted to be the half of the number of input variables. The class of functions computed by a majority gate is denoted by MAJ. In our definition, a majority gate is allowed to read a variable multiple times. For example, we can say that the function

$$[\![x_1 - 2x_2 + 3x_3 \geq 2]\!]$$

is computed by a majority gate of fan-in $1 + 2 + 3 = 6$. Remark that a majority gate is often defined as a gate that computes a linear threshold function with polynomially bounded weights. If we adapt this definition of majority gates, the size complexity may be reduced by at most a polynomial factor. However, such a difference will not affect all the results described in this paper.

A function $f : \{0, 1\}^n \to \mathbb{R}$ is called *symmetric* if the value of f depends only on the number of ones in the input. A gate that computes a symmetric function is called a *symmetric gate* and the class of all symmetric functions is denoted by SYM. Note that a symmetric gate is usually defined as a Boolean gate, i.e., it outputs a binary value. In this paper, we extend the domain from $\{0, 1\}$ to $\mathbb{R}$. By this extension, the set of symmetric functions turns out to be closed under linear combinations. This property is useful when we view a threshold-of-symmetric circuit as (the sign of) a real polynomial (see Sect. 4.1). Note also that a symmetric gate can simulate all of AND, OR, the modulo gate. It can also simulate a restrict version of the majority gate where the gate reads each variable at most once and all the weights are restricted to be 1.

3 Upper Bounds

In this section, we give upper bounds on the size of depth-two threshold circuits for $IP2_n$, which is significantly smaller than a folklore bound of $O(2^n)$.

We begin with two simple lemmas about exact threshold functions. Both lemmas were appeared in [11].

Lemma 1 [11]. *Suppose that a Boolean function f can be computed by a THR∘ETHR circuit of size s. Then, f can be computed by a THR ∘ THR circuit of size at most $2s$. The same relationship holds for MAJ ∘ ETHR and MAJ ∘ THR circuits.*

Lemma 2 [11]. *The AND of an arbitrary number of exact threshold functions is also an exact threshold function. In other words, the class of exact threshold functions is closed under the AND operation.*

Before stating our upper bounds, we describe an idea of our construction. Consider the function $IP2_2(x_1, x_2, y_1, y_2)$. Define two exact threshold functions g_1 and g_2 as follows.

$$g_1(x_1, x_2, y_1, y_2) = [\![x_1 + x_2 + y_1 + y_2 = 1]\!],$$
$$g_2(x_1, x_2, y_1, y_2) = [\![x_1 - x_2 + y_1 - y_2 = 0]\!].$$

It is easy to verify that

$$IP2_2(x_1, x_2, y_1, y_2) = \text{sgn}(2 \cdot g_1(x_1, x_2, y_1, y_2) + 2 \cdot g_2(x_1, x_2, y_1, y_2) - 1),$$

where $\text{sgn}(v)$ is defined to be 0 if $v > 0$ and is 1 if $v < 0$.

Then, when n is even, $IP2_n(x_1, \ldots, x_n, y_1, \ldots, y_n)$ is given by

$$\text{sgn}\left(\prod_{i \in [\frac{n}{2}]} (2 \cdot g_1(x_{2i-1}, x_{2i}, y_{2i-1}, y_{2i}) + 2 \cdot g_2(x_{2i-1}, x_{2i}, y_{2i-1}, y_{2i}) - 1)\right). \qquad (1)$$

By expanding the product in Eq. (1), we can obtain a polynomial of $3^{n/2}$ terms in which each term is an AND of exact threshold functions. By Lemma 2, we can express each term by a single ETHR gate. Therefore, we have a THR∘ETHR circuit of size $O(3^{n/2}) = O(1.733^n)$ for $IP2_n$, and also have a THR ∘ THR circuit of the same order by Lemma 1.

It is natural to expect that we can obtain a better bound by considering $IP2_k$ for $k > 2$ as a base case. These ideas can be summarized as the following theorem.

Theorem 3. *Let k be a positive integer. We write $x = (x_1, \ldots, x_k) \in \{0, 1\}^k$ and $y = (y_1, \ldots, y_k) \in \{0, 1\}^k$. Suppose that $IP2_k$ can be represented by the sign of the linear combination of ℓ exact threshold functions where all weights are integers, i.e.,*

$$IP2_k(x, y) = sgn\left(\sum_{i \in [\ell]} w_i C_i(x, y)\right),$$

where $w_i \in \mathbb{Z}$ and $C_i \in$ ETHR for $i \in [\ell]$. Then,

1. *The size complexity of $IP2_n$ for THR ∘ ETHR circuits as well as THR ∘ THR circuits is $O((\ell^{1/k})^n)$,*
2. *The size complexity of $IP2_n$ for MAJ ∘ THR circuits is $O((\sum_{i \in [\ell]} |w_i|)^{n/k})$.*

Proof (Sketch). First, observe that $IP2_n$ is just a PARITY of n/k copies of $IP2_k$. Replace each $IP2_k$ with a constructed ℓ-gate THR ∘ ETHR circuit. The PARITY of n/k THR of ℓ ETHRs can be written as the sign of the *product* of n/k sums of ℓ ETHRs. Applying distributivity to the product of sums, we get a sum of $\ell^{n/k}$ products of ETHRs. But the product of a bunch of ETHRs can be written as one ETHR, so we get a THR of $\ell^{n/k}$ ETHRs, completing the proof of Statement 1 of the theorem. The proof for Statement 2 is similar. □

With the aid of computers, we found a formula of length 8 for $IP2_4$ as well as a formula of total weight 13 for $IP2_4$ that lead us to the following theorems.

Theorem 4. *The size complexity of $IP2_n$ for THR ∘ ETHR circuits (and also for THR ∘ THR circuits) is $O(8^{n/4}) = O(1.682^n)$.*

Theorem 5. *The size complexity of $IP2_n$ for MAJ ∘ THR circuits is $O(13^{n/4}) = O(1.899^n)$.*

Proof of Theorem 4. Let $\{x_1, \ldots, x_4, y_1, \ldots, y_4\}$ denote the input variables for $IP2_4$. For $i \in [4]$, we write $z_i := x_i + y_i$. We introduce the following seven exact threshold functions and write them as $g_1, \ldots, g_7$.

$$\begin{array}{ll} [\![-z_1 + z_2 + z_3 + z_4 = 1]\!], & [\![z_1 - z_2 + z_3 + z_4 = 1]\!], \\ [\![z_1 + z_2 - z_3 + z_4 = 1]\!], & [\![z_1 + z_2 + z_3 - z_4 = 1]\!], \\ [\![z_1 - z_2 - z_3 + z_4 = 0]\!], & [\![z_1 - z_2 + z_3 - z_4 = 0]\!], \\ [\![z_1 + z_2 - z_3 - z_4 = 0]\!]. & \end{array}$$

It is elementary to verify that

$$IP2_4(x_1, \ldots, x_4, y_1, \ldots, y_4) = sgn\left(-3 + 2\sum_{i \in [7]} g_i(z_1, z_2, z_3, z_4)\right).$$

This gives a desired bound by Theorem 3.   □

Proof of Theorem 5. Let $\{x_1, \ldots, x_4, y_1, \ldots, y_4\}$ denote the input variables for $\mathsf{IP2}_4$. For $i \in [4]$, we write $z_i := x_i + y_i$. We introduce the following twelve exact threshold functions and write them as $g_1, \ldots, g_{12}$.

$$
\begin{array}{ll}
[\![3z_1 - 3z_2 + 2z_3 + 4z_4 = 8]\!], & [\![3z_1 - 3z_2 + 4z_3 + 2z_4 = 8]\!], \\
[\![-3z_1 + 3z_2 + 2z_3 + 4z_4 = 8]\!], & [\![-3z_1 + 3z_2 + 4z_3 + 2z_4 = 8]\!], \\
[\![2z_1 + 4z_2 + 3z_3 - 3z_4 = 8]\!], & [\![4z_1 + 2z_2 + 3z_3 - 3z_4 = 8]\!], \\
[\![2z_1 + 4z_2 - 3z_3 + 3z_4 = 8]\!], & [\![4z_1 + 2z_2 - 3z_3 + 3z_4 = 8]\!], \\
[\![3z_1 + 3z_2 + 2z_3 + 4z_4 = 11]\!], & [\![3z_1 + 3z_2 + 4z_3 + 2z_4 = 11]\!], \\
[\![2z_1 + 4z_2 + 3z_3 + 3z_4 = 11]\!]. & [\![4z_1 + 2z_2 + 3z_3 + 3z_4 = 11]\!].
\end{array}
$$

It is elementary to verify that

$$
\mathsf{IP2}_4(x_1, \ldots, x_4, y_1, \ldots, y_4) = \mathrm{sgn}\left(-1 + \sum_{i \in [12]} g_i(z_1, z_2, z_3, z_4)\right).
$$

This gives a desired bound by Theorem 3.   □

It is plausible that our bounds can further be improved by considering $\mathsf{IP2}_k$ for $k \geq 5$ as a base case. We remark that, for the case of $\mathsf{MAJ} \circ \mathsf{THR}$ circuits, the following argument says that there is a barrier at $O(\sqrt{2^n})$: The proof of Theorem 5 actually gives a construction of $\mathsf{MAJ} \circ \mathsf{ETHR}$ circuits for $\mathsf{IP2}_n$. By applying the "discriminator lemma" developed in [10] carefully, we can prove an $\Omega(2^{(1/2-\epsilon)n})$ lower bound on the size complexity of $\mathsf{IP2}_n$ for $\mathsf{MAJ} \circ \mathsf{ETHR}$ circuits. Currently, we do not know such a barrier for $\mathsf{THR} \circ \mathsf{THR}$ circuits.

4 Lower Bounds for THR ∘ SYM Circuits

In this section, we show $\Omega((1.5 - \epsilon)^n)$ lower bounds on the size of depth-two circuits for $\mathsf{IP2}_n$ where the top gate is a threshold gate and the bottom gates are symmetric gates. In Sect. 4.1, we review our LP-based method presented in our previous work [1], and then we establish the lower bound in Sect. 4.2.

Throughout this section, we label the input variables of $\mathsf{IP2}_n$ as $\{x_1, \ldots, x_{2n}\}$ and define $\mathsf{IP2}_n(x_1, \ldots, x_{2n}) := \sum_{i \in [n]} x_{2i-1} x_{2i} \pmod 2$. This indexing is different from the one used in the previous section, but will be convenient for a later discussion.

4.1 LP-Based Method for Lower Bounds on Circuit Size

As defined before, we call a depth-two circuit with unbounded weights threshold gate at the top and symmetric gates at the bottom as a THR ∘ SYM circuit. For a Boolean function f, the size complexity of $\mathsf{IP2}_n$ for THR ∘ SYM circuits is simply denoted by $s(f)$. Throughout of this section, we treat a THR ∘ SYM circuit as the sign of a real polynomial.

Definition 6. *We say that a real polynomial $P(x_1, \ldots, x_n)$ sign represents a Boolean function f on n variables if, for every $(x_1, \ldots, x_n) \in \{0, 1\}^n$,*

$$f(x_1, \ldots, x_n) = 0 \implies P(x_1, \ldots, x_n) > 0,$$
$$f(x_1, \ldots, x_n) = 1 \implies P(x_1, \ldots, x_n) < 0.$$

$\square$

We consider a polynomial $P : \{0, 1\}^X \to \mathbb{R}$

$$P(X) = \sum_{S \subseteq X} w_S h_S(X), \tag{2}$$

where $w_S \in \mathbb{R}$ and h_S is a symmetric function over the set of variables S. The *support* of P is defined by $\text{supp}(P) := \{S \subseteq X \mid w_S \neq 0\}$. Obviously, $s(f)$ is equal to the minimum size of the support of a polynomial P of the form (2) that sign represents f.

A point of our method is to define the parameter z_k, which gives a lower bound on $s(f)$, by introducing a certain linear programming problem.

Recall that the input variables of $\mathsf{IP2}_n$ is $X := \{x_1, \ldots, x_{2n}\}$.

Let $z_0 = z_1 = 1$. For $k \geq 2$, the parameter z_k is defined inductively (on k) such that z_k is the minimum value of the objective function of the following linear programming problem. Let $X_k = \{x_1, x_2, \ldots, x_{2k}\}$ be the first $2k$ variables of X. The program has 2^{2k} real-valued variables $\{q_T\}_{T \subseteq X_k}$ and $2k + 4\binom{k}{2}$ constraints.

$$
\begin{aligned}
\text{Minimize} \quad & \sum_{T \subseteq X_k} q_T, \\
\text{Subject to} \quad & \sum_{T : v \in T} q_T \;\geq z_{k-1} \; (v \in X_k), \\
& \sum_{T : |\{u,v\} \cap T| = 1} q_T \geq z_{k-2} \begin{pmatrix} i, j \in [k], i \neq j \\ u \in \{x_{2i-1}, x_{2i}\}, v \in \{x_{2j-1}, x_{2j}\} \end{pmatrix}, \\
& q_T \quad\;\; \geq 0 \quad (T \subseteq X_k).
\end{aligned}
\tag{3}
$$

The key observation is the following.

Fact 7 ([1]). *Suppose that $k \geq 2$. Let z_{k-1} and z_{k-2} be real numbers such that $s(\mathsf{IP2}_n) \geq z_{k-1} \cdot s(\mathsf{IP2}_{n-(k-1)})$ and $s(\mathsf{IP2}_n) \geq z_{k-2} \cdot s(\mathsf{IP2}_{n-(k-2)})$ for every n. Let z_k be the minimum value of the objective function of the LP problem (3). Then $s(\mathsf{IP2}_n) \geq z_k \cdot (\mathsf{IP2}_{n-k})$*

The following corollary is immediate from Fact 7.

Corollary 8 ([1]). *For every $k \geq 1$, $s(\mathsf{IP2}_n) \geq (z_k^{1/k})^n$.* $\square$

In the following, we give a sketch of the proof of Fact 7 for completeness.

Let $f : \{0, 1\}^X \to \mathbb{R}$ be a real function and $\rho : X \to \{0, 1, *\}$ be a partial assignment to X. Let $\text{res}(\rho)$ denote the set of variables that assigned a constant by ρ, i.e., $\text{res}(\rho) := \{v \in X \mid \rho(v) \neq *\}$. The restriction of f by ρ, denoted by $f|_\rho$, is the function obtained by setting x_i to $\rho(x_i)$ if $x_i \in \text{res}(\rho)$ and leaving x_i as a variable otherwise.

The restriction of a polynomial P of the form (2), denoted by $P|_\rho$, is defined similarly. First, replace each h_S in P by $h_S|_\rho$, which is a symmetric function over the set of variables $S - \text{res}(\rho)$. Then, if there are two (or more) functions $h_{S_1}|_\rho$ and $h_{S_2}|_\rho$ such that $S_1 \backslash \text{res}(\rho) = S_2 \backslash \text{res}(\rho)$, then they are merged into a single symmetric function. This is possible by the fact that the linear combination of two (or more) symmetric functions over the same set of variables is also a symmetric function.

For a polynomial P of the form (2), we decompose P into P_T's for $T \subseteq X_k$ in such a way that

$$P_T(X) := \sum_{\substack{S \in \text{supp}(P) \\ S \cap X_k = T}} w_S h_S(X).$$

Let $\tilde{q}_T$ be the number of terms in P_T. Note that

$$P(X) = \sum_{T \subseteq X_k} P_T(X),$$

and

$$|\text{supp}(P)| = \sum_{T \subseteq X_k} \tilde{q}_T.$$

We use the following fact that is easy to verify but useful.

Fact 9 ([1]). *Let ρ_1 and ρ_2 be two partial assignments such that $\text{res}(\rho_1) = \text{res}(\rho_2)$. Then, $\sum_{v \in T \cap \text{res}(\rho_1)} \rho_1(v) = \sum_{v \in T \cap \text{res}(\rho_2)} \rho_2(v)$ implies $P_T|_{\rho_1} - P_T|_{\rho_2} \equiv 0$.* □

Proof of Fact 7 (sketch). Suppose that a polynomial P of the form (2) sign-represents IP2_n. In what follows, we consider two types of pairs of partial assignments.

Type 1. Choose $i \in [k]$ and then choose $u \in \{x_{2i-1}, x_{2i}\}$. The unchosen variable in $\{x_{2i-1}, x_{2i}\}$ is denoted by v. Let ρ_1 and ρ_2 be two partial assignments such that $\text{res}(\rho_1) = \text{res}(\rho_2) = \{x_{2i-1}, x_{2i}\}$, $(\rho_1(v), \rho_1(u)) = (0, 1)$ and $(\rho_2(v), \rho_2(u)) = (1, 1)$.

A key observation is that for every such pair of partial assignments (ρ_1, ρ_2), we have $\text{IP2}_n|_{\rho_1} \equiv \text{IP2}_{n-1}$ and $\text{IP2}_n|_{\rho_2} \equiv \overline{\text{IP2}_{n-1}}$. This implies that the polynomial $P|_{\rho_1} - P|_{\rho_2}$ sign represents IP2_{n-1}. Fact 9 says that $P_T|_{\rho_1} - P_T|_{\rho_2}$ is vanished if $v \notin T$. Hence, we have

$$\sum_{T:v \in T} \tilde{q}_T \geq |\text{supp}(P|_{\rho_1} - P|_{\rho_2})| \geq s(\text{IP2}_{n-1}) \geq z_{k-1} \cdot s(\text{IP2}_{n-k}), \tag{4}$$

where the last inequality follows from the assumption in the statement of Fact 7. Let $q_T := \tilde{q}_T / s(\text{IP2}_{n-k})$ for $T \subseteq X_k$. By dividing both side of (4) by $s(\text{IP2}_{n-k})$, we have

$$\sum_{T:v \in T} q_T \geq z_{k-1},$$

which is the first constraint in the LP problem (3).

We also consider another type of partial assignments.

Type 2. Choose $i, j \in [k]$ such that $i \neq j$, and then choose $v \in \{x_{2i-1}, x_{2i}\}$ and $u \in \{x_{2j-1}, x_{2j}\}$. Let v' and u' be the unchosen variables in $\{x_{2i-1}, x_{2i}\}$ and $\{x_{2j-1}, x_{2j}\}$, respectively. Let ρ_1 and ρ_2 be two partial assignments such that

$res(\rho_1) = res(\rho_2) = \{x_{2i-1}, x_{2i}, x_{2j-1}, x_{2j}\}$, $(\rho_1(v), \rho_1(v'), \rho_1(u), \rho_1(u')) = (0, 1, 1, 0)$ and $(\rho_2(v), \rho_2(v'), \rho_2(u), \rho_2(u')) = (1, 1, 0, 0)$.

Similar to the case of Type 1, we have $\mathsf{IP2}_n|_{\rho_1} \equiv \mathsf{IP2}_{n-2}$ and $\mathsf{IP2}_n|_{\rho_2} \equiv \overline{\mathsf{IP2}_{n-2}}$, and hence $P|_{\rho_1} - P|_{\rho_2}$ sign represents $\mathsf{IP2}_{n-2}$. In addition, $P_T|_{\rho_1} - P_T|_{\rho_2}$ is vanished if $|T \cap \{u, v\}|$ is zero or two. Hence, we have

$$\sum_{T:|\{u,v\}\cap T|=1} \tilde{q}_T \geq |\mathrm{supp}(P|_{\rho_1} - P|_{\rho_2})| \geq s(\mathsf{IP2}_{n-2}) \geq z_{k-2} \cdot s(\mathsf{IP2}_{n-k}), \tag{5}$$

where the last inequality follows from the assumption of the statement in Fact 7. This inequality is equivalent to

$$\sum_{T:|\{u,v\}\cap T|=1} q_T \geq z_{k-2},$$

which is the second constraint in the LP problem (3).

If P is an optimal polynomial for $\mathsf{IP2}_n$, then

$$s(\mathsf{IP2}_n) = \sum_{T \subseteq X_k} \tilde{q}_T,$$

which is equivalent to

$$s(\mathsf{IP2}_n) = \sum_{T \subseteq X_k} q_T \cdot s(\mathsf{IP2}_{n-k}).$$

Therefore, the minimum value z_k of the objective function of the LP program (3) satisfies $s(\mathsf{IP2}_n) \geq z_k \cdot s(\mathsf{IP2}_{n-k})$. This completes the proof of Fact 7.   □

The LP problem (3) can easily be generated and solved by using a computer when k is small. In our previous work [1], we have succeeded to solve these problems by an LP solver for $k \leq 8$ (see Table 2). During this work, we could extend the table up to $k = 10$. The best lower bound obtained in this way is $\Omega(1.3808^n)$, but still weaker than a bound of $s(\mathsf{IP2}_n) = \Omega(\sqrt{2^n}/n)$ due to Forster et al. [7,8].

Obviously, the best possible lower bound that could be obtained by our approach is $s(\mathsf{IP2}_n) \geq z_\infty^n$ where $z_\infty := \lim_{k \to \infty}(z_k)^{1/k}$. However, finding the value of z_∞ was left as an open problem in [1].

Table 2. The values of z_k and $z_k^{1/k}$ for $k \leq 10$. The numbers shown in the table are truncated (not rounded) at the third or fourth decimal places.

n	2	3	4	5	6	7	8	9	10
z_k	1.5	2	2.833	4.027	5.750	8.254	11.970	17.335	25.207
$z_k^{1/k}$	1.2247	1.2599	1.2974	1.3213	1.3384	1.3519	1.3638	1.3729	1.3808

4.2 New Lower Bounds on THR ∘ SYM Circuits

In this section, we show that $z_\infty \geq 1.5$ establishing a new lower bound on the size complexity of $\mathsf{IP2}_n$ for THR ∘ SYM circuits.

Theorem 10. *For every $k \geq 1$,*

$$z_k \geq 1.5^k \left(1 - \frac{1}{\sqrt{k}}\right)^k.$$

Hence, $s(\mathsf{IP2}_n) = \Omega((1.5 - \epsilon)^n)$ for every $\epsilon > 0$.

Although we only prove the lower bound, we strongly believe that our bound on z_∞ is tight, i.e., $z_\infty = 1.5$. Note that $s(\mathsf{IP2}_n) \leq 2^n$ by the construction described in Introduction and the fact that AND is contained in SYM. To the best of our knowledge, this is the best known upper bound on $s(\mathsf{IP2}_n)$[1].

Proof of Theorem 10. The proof is done by giving a feasible solution to the dual of the LP problem (3), and then estimating the value of the objective function.

We define Z_k to be

$$Z_k := \{\{2i + a, 2j + b\} \mid i, j \in [k], i \neq j \text{ and } a, b \in \{0, 1\}\}.$$

For $x \in \{0, 1\}^{2k}$ and $v \in [2k]$, let x_v denote the v's bit of x.

The dual of (3) is given by

$$
\begin{aligned}
\text{Maximize } & z_{k-1} \sum_{v \in [2k]} s_v + z_{k-2} \sum_{\{u,v\} \in Z_k} t_{u,v}, \\
\text{Subject to } & \sum_{v \in [2k]: x_v = 1} s_v + \sum_{\{u,v\} \in Z_k : x_u \neq x_v} t_{u,v} \leq 1 \& (x \in \{0, 1\}^{2k}), \\
& s_v \geq 0 && (v \in [2k]), \\
& t_{u,v} \geq 0 && (\{u, v\} \in Z_k).
\end{aligned}
\tag{6}
$$

The LP duality theorem guarantees that the maximum value of the objective function in this dual program (6) equals to z_k. Since LP (6) is a maximization problem, any feasible solution gives a lower bound on z_k.

Here we present a feasible solution to LP (6) that will be analyzed in the proof. Define

$$\boldsymbol{s} \circ \boldsymbol{t} = (s_v)_{v \in [2k]} \circ (t_{u,v})_{\{u,v\} \in Z_k} \in \mathbb{R}^{2k + 4\binom{k}{2}}$$

as follows: For $v = 1, \ldots, 2k$, let $s_v = \frac{3}{4k}$ if v is odd and $s_v = 0$ if v is even. For $\{u, v\} \in Z_k$, let $t_{u,v} = \frac{9}{4k^2}$ if both of u and v are odd and $t_{u,v} = 0$ otherwise. Note that we inspired this solution through actually solving LP (6) using an LP solver.

In order to show the feasibility of $\boldsymbol{s} \circ \boldsymbol{t}$, it is enough to verify that the first constraint in LP (6) is satisfied. For $x \in \{0, 1\}^{2k}$, let

$$\alpha_x = \frac{|\{v \mid v \in \{1, 3, 5, \ldots, 2k - 1\} \text{ and } x_v = 1\}|}{k}.$$

---

[1] Actually, this is true only in an asymptotic sense. For example, an exhaustive computation shows $s(\mathsf{IP2}_2) = 2$, $s(\mathsf{IP2}_3) \leq 4$, $s(\mathsf{IP2}_4) \leq 7$ and $s(\mathsf{IP2}_5) \leq 14$.

Then, for $x \in \{0, 1\}^{2k}$, the first constraint in LP (6) can be written as

$$\frac{3}{4k}\alpha_x k + \frac{9}{4k^2}\alpha_x k(1 - \alpha_x)k - 1 \leq 0.$$

This can easily be verified by observing that the LHS of this equation is equal to $-\left(\frac{3}{2}\alpha_x - 1\right)^2$, completing the proof of the feasibility of $s \circ t$.

We proceed to the estimation of the value of the objective function.

The proof is by the induction on k. For $k \leq 10$, we can verify the theorem by a direct calculation (see Table 2). Suppose that $k \geq 11$. By the definition of $s \circ t$ and the inductive assumption, we have

$$z_k \geq z_{k-1}\frac{3}{4k}k + z_{k-2}\frac{9}{4k^2}\binom{k}{2}$$

$$\geq \frac{3}{4} \cdot 1.5^{k-1}\left(1 - \frac{1}{\sqrt{k-1}}\right)^{k-1} + \frac{9}{8} \cdot 1.5^{k-2}\left(1 - \frac{1}{\sqrt{k-2}}\right)^{k-2}\left(1 - \frac{1}{k}\right)$$

$$= \frac{1}{2} \cdot 1.5^k\left\{\left(1 - \frac{1}{\sqrt{k-1}}\right)^{k-1} + \left(1 - \frac{1}{\sqrt{k-2}}\right)^{k-2}\left(1 - \frac{1}{k}\right)\right\}. \qquad (7)$$

By an elementary but somewhat lengthy calculation, we can show that

$$z_k \geq 1.5^k\left(1 - \frac{1}{\sqrt{k}}\right)^k$$

as desired. The detailed calculations are omitted due to the page restriction and will appear in the full version of the paper.   □

Acknowledgement. The author would like to thank anonymous referees for their helpful comments and suggestions. This work is supported in part by JSPS Kakenhi 18K11152 and 18H04090.

References

1. Amano, K., Maruoka, A.: On the complexity of depth-2 circuits with threshold gates. In: Jędrzejowicz, J., Szepietowski, A. (eds.) MFCS 2005. LNCS, vol. 3618, pp. 107–118. Springer, Heidelberg (2005). https://doi.org/10.1007/11549345_11
2. Amano, K., Tate, S.: On XOR lemmas for the weight of polynomial threshold functions. Inf. Comput. **269**, 104439 (2019)
3. Basu, S., Bhatnagar, N., Gopalan, P., Lipton, R.: Polynomials that sign represent parity and descartes' rule of signs. Comput. Complex. **17**(3), 377–406 (2008). (Conference version in CCC '04)
4. Bruck, J.: Harmonic analysis of polynomial threshold functions. SIAM J. Discrete Math. **3**(2), 168–177 (1990)
5. Chattopadhyay, A., Mande, N.: A short list of equalities induces large sign rank. In: Proceedings of FOCS 2018, pp. 47–58 (2018)
6. Eldan, R., Shamir, O.: The power of depth for feedforward neural networks. In: Proceedings of COLT 2016, pp. 907–940 (2016)

7. Forster, J.: A linear lower bound on the unbounded error probabilistic communication complexity. J. Comput. Syst. Sci. **65**(4), 612–625 (2002)
8. Forster, J., Krause, M., Lokam, S.V., Mubarakzjanov, R., Schmitt, N., Simon, H.U.: Relations between communication complexity, linear arrangements, and computational complexity. In: Hariharan, R., Vinay, V., Mukund, M. (eds.) FSTTCS 2001. LNCS, vol. 2245, pp. 171–182. Springer, Heidelberg (2001). https://doi.org/10.1007/3-540-45294-X_15
9. Goldmann, M., Håstad, J., Razborov, A.: Majority gates vs. general weighted threshold gates. Comput. Complex. **2**, 277–300 (1992)
10. Hajnal, A., Maass, W., Pudlák, P., Szegedy, M., Turán, G.: Threshold circuits of bounded depth. J. Comput. Syst. Sci. **46**(2), 129–154 (1993)
11. Hansen, K., Podolskii, V.: Exact threshold circuits. In: Proceedings of CCC 2010, pp. 270–279 (2010)
12. Jukna, S.: Boolean Function Complexity, Advances and Frontiers. Algorithms and Combinatorics, vol. 27. Springer, Heidelberg (2012). https://doi.org/10.1007/978-3-642-24508-4
13. Kane, D., Williams, R.: Super-linear gate and super-quadratic wire lower bounds for depth-two and depth-three threshold circuits. In: Proceedings of STOC 2016, pp. 633–643 (2016)
14. Krause, M., Pudlák, P.: On the computational power of depth-2 circuits with threshold and modulo gates. Theor. Comput. Sci. **174**(1–2), 137–156 (1997)
15. Muroga, S.: Threshold Logic and Its Applications. Wiley, Hoboken (1971)
16. Nisan, N.: The communication complexity of threshold gates. In: Proceedings of "Combinatorics, Paul Erdős is Eighty", pp. 301–315 (1994)
17. Roychowdhury, V., Orlitsky, A., Siu, K.Y.: Lower bounds on threshold and related circuits via communication complexity. IEEE Trans. Inf. Theory **40**(2), 467–474 (1994)
18. Safran, I., Eldan, R., Shamir, O.: Depth separations in neural networks: what is actually being separated?. In: Proceedings of COLT 2019, pp. 2664–2666 (2019). (full version at Arxiv:1904.06984)
19. Sezener, C., Oztop, E.: Minimal sign representation of boolean functions: algorithms and exact results for low dimensions. Neural Comput. **27**(8), 1796–1823 (2015)

Complexity Issues of String to Graph Approximate Matching

Riccardo Dondi[1]([✉]), Giancarlo Mauri[2], and Italo Zoppis[2]

[1] Università degli Studi di Bergamo, Bergamo, Italy
riccardo.dondi@unibg.it
[2] Università degli Studi di Milano-Bicocca, Milan, Italy
{mauri,zoppis}@disco.unimib.it

Abstract. The problem of matching a query string to a directed graph, whose vertices are labeled by strings, has application in different fields, from data mining to computational biology. Several variants of the problem have been considered, depending on the fact that the match is exact or approximate and, in this latter case, which edit operations are considered and where are allowed. In this paper we present results on the complexity of the approximate matching problem, where edit operations are symbol substitutions and are allowed only on the graph labels or both on the graph labels and the query string. We introduce a variant of the problem that asks whether there exists a path in a graph that represents a query string with any number of edit operations and we show that is NP-complete, even when labels have length one and in the case the alphabet is binary. Moreover, when it is parameterized by the length of the input string and graph labels have length one, we show that the problem is fixed-parameter tractable and it is unlikely to admit a polynomial kernel. The NP-completeness of this problem leads to the inapproximability (within any factor) of the approximate matching when edit operations are allowed only on the graph labels. Moreover, we show that the variants of approximate string matching to graph we consider are not fixed-parameter tractable, when the parameter is the number of edit operations, even for graphs that have distance one from a DAG. The reduction for this latter result allows us to prove the inapproximability of the variant where edit operations can be applied both on the query string and on graph labels.

Keywords: Algorithms on strings · Computational complexity · Graph query · Parameterized complexity · Patterns · String to graph matching

1 Introduction

Given a query string s and a directed graph G whose vertices are labeled with strings (referred as labeled graph), the matching and the approximate matching

---

Riccardo Dondi dedicates the paper to the memory of his beloved father, Gilberto, who passed away on November 26, 2019.

A. Leporati et al. (Eds.): LATA 2020, LNCS 12038, pp. 248–259, 2020.
https://doi.org/10.1007/978-3-030-40608-0_17

of s to G ask for a path (not necessarily simple) in G that represents s, that is by concatenating the labels of the vertices on the path we obtain s or an approximate occurrence of s.

The matching and the approximate matching of a query string to a labeled graph have applications in different areas, from graph databases and data mining to genome research. The problems have been introduced in the context of pattern matching in hypertext [1,3,10,15], but have found recently new applications. Indeed in computational biology a representation of variants of related sequences is often provided by a labeled graph [11,17] and the query of a string in a labeled graph has found application in computational pan-genomics [13,18].

The exact matching problem is known to be in P [1,3,15]. Furthermore, conditional lower bounds for this problem has been recently given in [7].

The approximate string to graph matching problem, referred to String to Graph Approximate Matching, has the goal of minimizing the number of edit operations (of the query string or of the labels of the graph) such that there exists a path p in G whose labels match the query string. String to Graph Restricted Approximate Matching denotes the variant where edit operations are allowed only on the graph labels. String to Graph Approximate Matching and String to Graph Restricted Approximate Matching are known to be NP-hard [12], even for binary alphabet [9]. When the edit operations are allowed only on the query string, then String to Graph Approximate Matching is polynomial-time solvable [9]. Moreover, when the input graph is a Directed Acyclic Graph (DAG), String to Graph Approximate Matching and String to Graph Restricted Approximate Matching are polynomial-time solvable [10].

In this contribution, we consider the String to Graph Approximate Matching problem and the String to Graph Restricted Approximate Matching problem, with the goal of deepening the understanding of their complexity. Notice that the edit operations we consider are symbol substitutions of the graph labels or of the query string. Other variants with different edit operations have been considered in literature [3,9].

We introduce a variant of String to Graph Restricted Approximate Matching, called String to Graph Compatibility Matching, that asks whether it is possible to find an occurrence of a query string in a graph with any number of edit operations of the graph labels. This decision problem is helpful to characterize whether a feasible solution of String to Graph Restricted Approximate Matching exists or not. We show in Sect. 3 that String to Graph Compatibility Matching is NP-complete, even when the labels of the graph have length one or when the alphabet is binary. The reduction shows also that String to Graph Compatibility Matching when parameterized by the length of the query string is unlikely to have a polynomial kernel[1] (for details on kernelization we refer to [6,14]). A consequence of the intractability of String to Graph Compatibility Matching is that String to Graph Restricted Approximate Matching cannot be approximated

---

[1] A problem parameterized by parameter t admits a polynomial kernel if there exists a polynomial-time algorithm that reduces the instance of the problem so that it has a size which is a polynomial in t.

within any factor in polynomial time. Notice that if we allow edit operations of the query string, then the existence of a path that represents an approximate matching of the query string can be decided in polynomial time. Indeed, it is enough to check whether the input graph contains a (non necessarily simple) path p in G that represents a string of length $|s|$.

We consider in Sect. 4 the parameterized complexity of String to Graph Restricted Approximate Matching and of String to Graph Approximate Matching and we show that they are W[2]-hard when parameterized by the number of edit operations, even for a labeled graph having distance one from a DAG. This result shows that, while String to Graph Restricted Approximate Matching and String to Graph Approximate Matching are solvable in polynomial time when the labeled graph is a DAG [10], even for graphs that are very close to DAG they become hard. The reduction designed to prove this latter result allows us to show that String to Graph Approximate Matching is not approximable within factor $\Omega(\log(|V|))$ and $\Omega(\log(|s|))$, for a labeled graph $G = (V, E)$ and a query string s.

In Sect. 5, we provide a fixed-parameter tractable algorithm for String to Graph Compatibility Matching, when parameterized by size of the query string and when the graph labels have length one. We conclude the paper in Sect. 6 with some open problems, while in Sect. 2 we introduce some definitions and the problems we are interested in. Some of the proofs are not included due to page limit.

2   Definitions

Given an alphabet Σ and a string s over Σ, we denote by $|s|$ the length of s, by $s[i]$, with $1 \leq i \leq |s|$, the i-th symbol of s and by $s[i, j]$, with $1 \leq i \leq j \leq |s|$, the substring of s that starts at position i and ends at position j.

Every graph we consider in this paper is *directed*. Given a graph $G = (V, E)$ and a vertex $v \in V$, we define $N^+(v) = \{u \in V : (v, u) \in E\}$ and $N^-(v) = \{w \in V : (w, v) \in E\}$.

A labeled graph $G = (V, E, \sigma)$ is a graph whose vertices are labeled with strings, formally assigned by a labeled function $\sigma : V \to \Sigma^*$, where Σ is an alphabet of symbols. Notice that $\sigma(v)$, with $v \in V$, denotes the string associated by σ to vertex v. Let $p = v_1 v_2 \ldots v_z$ be a path (non necessarily simple) in G, the set of vertices that induces p is denoted by $V(p)$ and the string associated with p is defined as $\sigma(p) = \sigma(v_1)\sigma(v_2) \ldots \sigma(v_z)$, that is $\sigma(p)$ is obtained by concatenating the strings that label the vertices of path p.

Consider a string s on alphabet Σ and a labeled graph $G = (V, E, \sigma)$. We say that a path p in G is an occurrence of s if $\sigma(p) = s$; in this case we call $\sigma(p)$ an exact matching of s and we say that p matches s.

An edit operation of a string s is a substitution of the symbol in a position i, with $1 \leq i \leq |s|$, of s with a different symbol in Σ. An edit operation of $G = (V, E, \sigma)$ is an edit operation of a string $\sigma(v)$, with $v \in V$. A path p in G is an *approximate matching* of s if, after $k_1 \geq 0$ edit operations of labels of G,

$\sigma(p) = s'$, where s' is a string obtained with $k_2 \geq 0$ edit operations of s. In this case, we say that the approximate matching requires $k = k_1 + k_2$ edit operations. We say that p in G is a *restricted approximate matching* of s, if, after after $k \geq 0$ edit operations to labels of G, $s = \sigma(p)$ (that is the edit operations are allowed only on the labels of G).

Consider a path p that matches (exactly, approximately or restricted approximately) the query string s. If position i, $1 \leq i \leq |s|$, in s and the j-th position, $1 \leq j \leq |\sigma(u)|$, of the label of vertex u in p match (possibly after an edit operation), we say that position i is mapped in $\sigma(u)[j]$; if $|\sigma(u)| = 1$, by slightly abusing the notation, we say that position i is mapped in u.

Next, we define the first combinatorial problem we are interested in.

Problem 1. **String to Graph Approximate Matching**
Input: A labeled graph $G = (V, E, \sigma)$ and a query string s, both on alphabet Σ.
Output: An approximate matching p of s that requires the minimum number of edit operations.

We define now the variant of the problem, called String to Graph Restricted Approximate Matching, where edit operations are allowed only on the labels of the labeled graph.

Problem 2. **String to Graph Restricted Approximate Matching**
Input: A labeled graph $G = (V, E, \sigma)$ and a query string s, both on alphabet Σ.
Output: A restricted approximate matching p of s that requires the minimum number of edit operations.

Consider a labeled graph $G = (V, E, \sigma)$ and a query string s over Σ. If there exists a path p in G which is a restricted approximate matching of s, we say that p is *compatible* with s. Notice that the definition of compatibility does not put any bound on the number of edit operations of graph labels and that no edit operation is allowed on the query string. In this paper, we introduce a decision problem, called String to Graph Compatibility Matching, related to String to Graph Restricted Approximate Matching, that asks whether there exists a path in $G = (V, E, \sigma)$ compatible with s.

Problem 3. **String to Graph Compatibility Matching**
Input: A labeled graph $G = (V, E, \sigma)$, a query string s, both on alphabet Σ.
Output: Does there exist a path in G that is compatible with s?

3   Hardness of String to Graph Compatibility Matching

In this section we consider the computational complexity of String to Graph Compatibility Matching and we prove that the problem is indeed NP-complete and it is unlikely to admit a polynomial kernel. This result, as discussed in Theorem 3, is not only interesting to characterize the complexity of String to Graph Compatibility Matching, but also to give insights into the approximation complexity of String to Graph Restricted Approximate Matching.

We start by proving that String to Graph Compatibility Matching is NP-complete when the labels of the graph have length one, via a reduction from the h-Path problem. The reduction is inspired by that in [3] to prove the NP-hardness of String to Graph Restricted Approximate Matching. Then we modify the reduction so that it holds also for binary alphabet. We recall the definition of h-Path, which is known to be NP-complete [8].

Problem 4. h-Path
Input: A directed graph $G = (V_L, E_L)$.
Output: Does there exist a simple path in G_L of length h?

3.1 Graph Labels of Length One

Consider a graph $G_L = (V_L, E_L)$, with $V_L = \{v_1^l, \ldots, v_n^l\}$, which is an instance of h-Path, we define an instance of String to Graph Compatibility Matching consisting of a labeled graph $G = (V, E, \sigma)$ and a query string s.

First, define the alphabet Σ as follows: $\Sigma = \{x_i : 1 \le i \le n\} \cup \{y_i : 1 \le i \le h\}$. The labeled graph $G = (V, E, \sigma)$ is defined as follows:

$$V = \{v_i : v_i^l \in V, 1 \le i \le n\}, \qquad E = \{(v_i, v_j) : (v_i^l, v_j^l) \in E_L\}.$$

The labelling function $\sigma : V \to \Sigma^*$ of the graph vertices is defined as follows: $\sigma(v_i) = x_i$, for each i with $1 \le i \le n$.

Finally, we define the query string $s = y_1 y_2 \cdots y_h$.

The following lemma allows us to prove the hardness of String to Graph Compatibility Matching.

Lemma 1. *Let $G_L = (V_L, E_L)$ be a graph instance of h-Path and let $(G = (V, E, \sigma), s)$ be the corresponding instance of* String to Graph Compatibility Matching. *There exists a simple path of length h in G_L if and only if there exists a path in G compatible with s.*

Proof. Consider a simple path $v_{i_1}^l v_{i_2}^l \cdots v_{i_h}^l$ in G_L. Then consider the corresponding path $v_{i_1} v_{i_2} \cdots v_{i_h}$ in G and edit the symbol of each vertex v_{i_j}, with $1 \le j \le h$, so that it is associated with symbol y_i. It follows that p matches s. Then $v_{i_1} v_{i_2} \cdots v_{i_h}$ is a path of G compatible with s.

Consider a path $p = v_{i_1} v_{i_2} \cdots v_{i_h}$ in G_L compatible with s. Notice that p must be a simple path, since s consists of h distinct symbols. As a consequence, the corresponding path $v_{i_1}^l v_{i_2}^l \cdots v_{i_h}^l$ in G_L is a simple path of length h. $\qquad\square$

Lemma 1 and the NP-completeness of h-Path [8] allow to prove the following result.

Theorem 1. String to Graph Compatibility Matching *is NP-complete even when the labels of the graph have length one.*

Notice that the reduction we have described is also a Polynomial Parameter Transformation [5] from h-Path parameterized by h to String to Graph Compatibility Matching parameterized by $|s|$, as $|s| = h$. Since h-Path when parameterized by h does not admit a polynomial kernel unless $NP \subseteq coNP/Poly$ [4], the reduction leads to the following result.

Corollary 1. *The* String to Graph Compatibility Matching *problem parameterized by $|s|$ does not admit a polynomial kernel unless $NP \subseteq coNP/Poly$ even when the labels of the graph have length one.*

3.2 Binary Alphabet

Next, we show that the String to Graph Compatibility Matching problem is NP-complete even on binary alphabet. The reduction is similar to the reduction of the Sect. 3.1, except for the definition of the query string s and the labeling $\sigma : V \to \Sigma^*$ of the labeled graph.

Consider a graph $G_L = (V_L, E_L)$, with $V_L = \{v_1^l, \dots, v_n^l\}$, that is an instance of h-Path, we define a corresponding instance $(G = (V, E, \sigma), s)$ of String to Graph Compatibility Matching. The alphabet is binary, hence $\Sigma = \{0, 1\}$. Next, we define the labeled graph $G = (V, E, \sigma)$. The sets V of vertices and E of edges are defined as in Sect. 3.1. For each $v_i \in V$, with $1 \leq i \leq h$, $\sigma(v_i) = 0^h$, namely it is a string consisting of h occurrences of symbol 0.

The construction of the query string s requires the introduction of strings s_i, with $1 \leq i \leq h$, having length h and defined as follows:

$$s_i[i] = 1; \qquad s_i[j] = 0, \text{ with } 1 \leq j \leq h \text{ and } j \neq i.$$

Finally, s is defined as the concatenation of s_1, s_2, $\dots s_n$, that is $s = s_1 \, s_2 \, \dots s_n$.

Next, we prove the correctness of the reduction.

Lemma 2. *Let $G_L = (V_L, E_L)$ be a graph instance of h-Path and let $(G = (V, E, \sigma), s)$ be the corresponding instance of* String to Graph Compatibility Matching *on binary alphabet. There exists a simple path of length h in G_L if and only if there exists a path compatible with s in G.*

Proof. Consider a simple path $v_{i_1}^l v_{i_2}^l \dots v_{i_h}^l$ in G_L. Then consider the corresponding path $v_{i_1} v_{i_2} \dots v_{i_h}$ in G and edit the label of each vertex v_{i_j}, with $1 \leq j \leq h$, such that is associated with string s_j. Then the resulting string is an exact match of s, hence $v_{i_1} v_{i_2} \dots v_{i_h}$ is a path compatible with s.

Consider a path $p = v_{i_1} v_{i_2} \dots v_{i_h}$ in G that is compatible with s. Since $\sigma(p)$ must match s after some symbol substitutions and, by construction, $|\sigma(v_j)| = |s_l|$, for each $1 \leq j \leq n$ and $1 \leq l \leq h$, it follows that the positions of s_l, $1 \leq l \leq h$, are mapped to the positions of $\sigma(v_{i_t})$, for some t with $1 \leq t \leq h$. Moreover, since $s_l \neq s_q$, with $t \neq q$, all the vertices in p are distinct and p is a simple path in G of length h. As a consequence the corresponding path $v_{i_1}^l v_{i_2}^l \dots v_{i_h}^l$ in G_L is a simple path of length h, thus concluding the proof.   □

Thus, based on Lemma 2, we can prove the following result.

Theorem 2. String to Graph Compatibility Matching *is NP-complete even on binary alphabet.*

The results of Theorems 1 and 2 have a consequence not only on the complexity of String to Graph Compatibility Matching, but also on the approximation of String to Graph Restricted Approximate Matching.

Theorem 3. *The* String to Graph Restricted Approximate Matching *problem cannot be approximated within any factor in polynomial time, unless $P = NP$, even when the labels of the graph have length one or when the alphabet is binary.*

Proof. The NP-completeness of String to Graph Compatibility Matching implies that, given an instance $(G = (V, E, \sigma), s)$, even deciding whether there exists a feasible solution of String to Graph Restricted Approximate Matching, with any number of edit operations in G, is NP-complete. Hence if there exists a polynomial-time approximation algorithm $\mathcal{A}$ for String to Graph Restricted Approximate Matching, with some approximation factor α, it follows that $\mathcal{A}$ can be used to decide the String to Graph Compatibility Matching problem: if $\mathcal{A}$ returns an approximated solution for String to Graph Restricted Approximate Matching with input (G, s), then it follows that there exists a path in G compatible with s, if $\mathcal{A}$ does not return an approximated solution for String to Graph Restricted Approximate Matching with input (G, s), then there is no path in G compatible with s. Since String to Graph Compatibility Matching is NP-complete, when the labels of the graph have length one (by Theorem 1) and on binary alphabet (by Theorem 2), then there does not exist a polynomial-time approximation algorithm with any approximation factor for String to Graph Restricted Approximate Matching when the graph labels have length one or when the alphabet is binary, unless $P = NP$. □

4   Hardness of Parameterization

In this section, we consider the parameterized complexity of String to Graph Restricted Approximate Matching and String to Graph Approximate Matching. The reduction we present allows us to prove that String to Graph Restricted Approximate Matching and String to Graph Approximate Matching, when parameterized by the number of edit operations, are W[2]-hard for a labeled graph having distance one from a DAG. Moreover, the same reduction will allow us to prove that String to Graph Approximate Matching is not approximable within factor $\Omega(\log(|V|))$ and $\Omega(\log(|s|))$.

We prove these results by presenting a reduction, that is parameterized [6,14] and approximate preserving [19], from the Minimum Set Cover problem. We recall here the definition of Minimum Set Cover.

Problem 5. Minimum Set Cover
Input: A collection $C = \{S_1, \ldots, S_m\}$ of sets over a universe $U = \{u_1, \ldots, u_n\}$.

Output: A subcollection C' of C of minimum cardinality such that for each $u_i \in U$, with $1 \leq i \leq n$, there exists a set in C' containing u_i.

First, we focus on String to Graph Restricted Approximate Matching, then we show that the same reduction can be applied to String to Graph Approximate Matching.

Given an instance (U, C) of Minimum Set Cover, in the following we define an instance $(G = (V, E, \sigma), s)$ of String to Graph Restricted Approximate Matching (see Fig. 1 for an example). We start by defining the alphabet Σ:

$$\Sigma = \{x_i : 0 \leq i \leq m\} \cup \{y_i : 1 \leq i \leq n\} \cup \{z\}.$$

Then, we define the labeled graph $G = (V, E, \sigma)$:

$$V = \{v_i : 0 \leq i \leq m\} \cup \{v_{i,j} : 1 \leq i \leq m, 1 \leq j \leq |S_i|\}$$

$$E = \{(v_0, v_i) : 1 \leq i \leq m\} \cup \{(v_i, v_{i,j}) : 1 \leq i \leq m, 1 \leq j \leq |S_i|\}$$
$$\cup \{(v_{i,j}, v_0) : 1 \leq i \leq m, 1 \leq j \leq |S_i|\}.$$

Now, we define the labeling σ of the vertices of G:

- $\sigma(v_i) = x_i, \ 0 \leq i \leq m$
- $\sigma(v_{i,l}) = y_j, \ 1 \leq i \leq m, \ 1 \leq l \leq |S_i|$ and $1 \leq j \leq n$, where the l-th element of S_i is u_j (based on some ordering of the elements in S_i)

The query string s is defined as follows: $s = x_0 \ z \ y_1 \ x_0 \ z \ y_2 \ldots x_0 \ z \ y_n$.

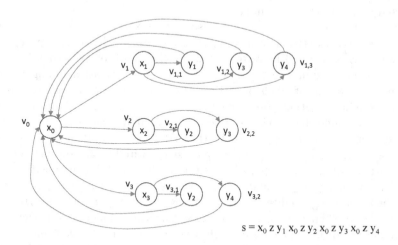

$$s = x_0 \ z \ y_1 \ x_0 \ z \ y_2 \ x_0 \ z \ y_3 \ x_0 \ z \ y_4$$

Fig. 1. A labeled graph G and a query string s associated with the following instance of Minimum Set Cover: $U = \{u_1, u_2, u_3, u_4\}$; $S_1 = \{u_1, u_3, u_4\}$, $S_2 = \{u_2, u_3\}$, $S_3 = \{u_2, u_4\}$. Inside each vertex we represent its label.

First, we prove that the labeled graph G, has distance one from a DAG, that is by removing a vertex of G (namely, v_0), we obtain a DAG.

Lemma 3. *Let (C, U) be an instance of* Minimum Set Cover *and let $(G = (V, E, \sigma), s)$ be the corresponding instance of* String to Graph Restricted Approximate Matching. *Then, G has distance one from a DAG.*

Next, we present the main result to prove the correctness of the reduction.

Lemma 4. *Let (C, U) be an instance of* Minimum Set Cover *and let $(G = (V, E, \sigma), s)$ be the corresponding instance of* String to Graph Restricted Approximate Matching. *There exists a cover C' of U of cardinality $h < n$ if and only if there exists a solution of* String to Graph Restricted Approximate Matching *that requires h edit operations.*

Proof. We present only one direction of the proof. Consider a path p in G such that p is a restricted approximate matching of s requiring at most h edit operations of the labels of vertices in p. First, we prove some properties of G. If v_0 is removed from G, then the resulting graph G' contains paths consisting of at most 2 vertices. Since $|s| = 3n$, there is no path in G' that can be a restricted approximate matching of s. This implies that at least one position of s is mapped in v_0.

Now, assume that the first vertex of p is not v_0. Assume that the first position of s is mapped in v_i, for some i with $1 \le i \le m$. By construction, $p = v_i \, v_{i,j} \, v_0 \, v_l \, v_{l,t} \, v_0 \ldots$, since $N^+(v_i) = \{v_{i,j} : 1 \le j \le |S_j|\}$, $N^+(v_{i,j}) = \{v_0\}$ and $N^+(v_0) = \{v_i : 1 \le i \le m\}$. Then each occurrence of a symbol y_q, $1 \le q \le n$, in s is mapped in v_0, while the symbol associated with v_0 can be at most one of $y_1, \ldots, y_n$, thus there is no path in G that starts with a vertex v_i and that is a restricted approximate matching of s.

Assume that the first vertex of p is some vertex $v_{i,j}$, with $1 \le i \le m$ and $1 \le j \le |S_i|$. By construction, $p = v_{i,j} \, v_0 \, v_l \, v_{l,t} \, v_0 \ldots$. Hence each position of s containing z is mapped in vertex v_0, while each position of s containing y_t, $1 \le t \le n$, is mapped in a vertex v_q, with $1 \le q \le m$. This last mapping requires $n > h$ edit operations of labels of vertices of G, violating the hypothesis that at most $h < n$ edit operations are applied.

We can conclude that if p is a restricted approximate matching of s requiring $h < n$ edit operations, then v_0 must be the first vertex of p. It follows that each label of a vertex v_i, $1 \le i \le n$, in path p must be edited to z. Consider the case that position t of s, $1 \le t \le |s|$, where $s[t] = y_q$, $1 \le q \le n$, is mapped to some vertex $v_{i,j}$, with $1 \le i \le m$ and $1 \le j \le |S_i|$, such that $\sigma(v_{i,j}) \ne y_q$, and that hence the label of $v_{i,j}$ is edited to y_q. Let v_a, with $1 \le a \le m$, be the vertex that precedes $v_{i,j}$ in p. Then, we can modify p, so that the number of edit operations are not increased, by replacing v_a with a vertex v_b, with $1 \le b \le m$, and $v_{i,j}$ with $v_{b,l}$, with $1 \le l \le |S_b|$, so that $\sigma(v_{b,l}) = y_q$, and by editing the label of v_b (if it is no already edited) to z. This implies that the only vertices of p whose labels are edited are vertices v_i, $1 \le i \le m$.

Now, we can define a solution C' of Minimum Set Cover consisting of h sets as follows: $C' = \{S_i : \text{the label of vertex } v_i \text{ in } p \text{ is edited to } z, 1 \le i \le m\}$. Since at most h labels of vertices of p are edited (to z), it follows that at most h sets belong to C'. Furthermore, since each vertex with label y_j, $1 \le j \le n$, is connected to a vertex v_i in p, $1 \le i \le m$, by construction it follows that each element of U belongs to some set in C'.   □

Based on Lemma 3 and on Lemma 4, we can prove the following result.

Theorem 4. *The* String to Graph Restricted Approximate Matching *problem is W[2]-hard when parameterized by the number of edit operations, even when the input graph has distance one from a DAG.*

Proof. Notice that, by Lemma 3, G has distance one from a DAG. The W[2]-hardness of String to Graph Approximate Matching follows from Lemma 4 and from the W[2]-hardness of Minimum Set Cover [16].   □

Next, we show that the same reduction allows us to prove the W[2]-hardness and the inapproximability of String to Graph Approximate Matching. Essentially, we will prove that we can avoid edit operations of the query string.

Theorem 5. *The* String to Graph Approximate Matching *problem is W[2]-hard when parameterized by the number of edit operations, even when the input graph has distance one from a DAG. Moreover,* String to Graph Approximate Matching *cannot be approximated within factor $\Omega(\log(|V|))$ and $\Omega(\log(|s|))$, unless $P = NP$, even when the input graph has distance one from a DAG.*

5   String to Graph Compatibility Matching **Parameterized by $|s|$**

We present a fixed-parameter algorithm for String to Graph Compatibility Matching when parameterized by $|s|$. We consider the case where each vertex of G is labeled with exactly one symbol (notice that in this case, by Theorem 1, String to Graph Compatibility Matching is NP-complete and, by Corollary 1, String to Graph Compatibility Matching parameterized by $|s|$ does not admit a polynomial kernel unless $NP \subseteq coNP/Poly$).

We start by proving an easy property of an instance of String to Graph Compatibility Matching.

Lemma 5. $|\Sigma| \le |s|$.

The fixed-parameter algorithm is based on the color-coding technique [2] and on dynamic programming. Consider a path p in G that is compatible with s and the set $V(p)$ of vertices that induces p, where $|V(p)| = k$. It holds $k \le |s|$, since each position of s is mapped in at least one vertex of p.

We consider a coloring of V with a set of colors $\{c_1, \dots, c_k\}$, where, given a vertex $v \in V$, we denote by $c(v)$ the color assigned to v. Based on color-coding (see Definition 1), we assume that the coloring is *colorful*, that is each vertex of $V(p)$ is assigned a distinct color in $\{c_1, \dots, c_k\}$.

Now, each color c_i, with $1 \le i \le k$, is associated by a function r: $\{c_1, \dots, c_k\} \to \Sigma$, with a symbol in Σ, that represents the fact that the vertices of p that are colored by c_i, with $1 \le i \le k$, must match a position of s

containing symbol $r(c_i)$. In this case we say that p *satisfies* r. The algorithm iterates over the possible colorings of graph G based on a family of perfect hash functions and over the possible functions r.

Now, given a coloring of G and a function r, define a function $M_r[i, v]$, with $1 \leq i \leq |s|$ and $v \in V$, as follows. $M_r[i, v]$ is equal to 1 if there exists a path p of G that is compatible with $s[1, i]$ and such that (1) position i of s is mapped in v, and (2) p satisfies r; else $M_r[i, v] = 0$. Notice that, since $s[1, i]$ is mapped in v, it follows that v is the last vertex of p. Next, we describe the recurrence to compute $M_r[i, v]$. For $i \geq 2$, if $r(c(v)) \neq s[i]$, then $M_r[i, v] = 0$; if $r(c(v)) = s[i]$, then:

$$M_r[i, v] = \bigvee_{u \in V : (u,v) \in E} M_r[i - 1, u]$$

In the base case, it holds $M_r[1, v] = 1$ if and only if $r(c(v)) = s[1]$, else $M_r[1, v] = 0$. Next, we prove the correctness of the recurrence.

Lemma 6. *$M_r[i, v]$ is equal to 1 if and only if there exists a path p of G that is compatible with $s[1, i]$ and such that (1) position i of s is mapped in v, and (2) p satisfies r.*

In order to compute a colorful coloring of G, we consider a perfect family of hash functions for the set of vertices of G.

Definition 1. *Let $G = (V, E, \sigma)$ be a labeled graph and let $C = \{c_1, \ldots, c_k\}$ be a set of colors. A family F of hash functions from V to C is called* perfect *if for each subset $V' \subseteq V$, with $|V'| = k$, there exists a function $f \in F$ such that for each $x, y \in V'$, with $x \neq y$, $f(x) = c_i$, $f(y) = c_j$, with $1 \leq i, j \leq k$ and $i \neq j$.*

It has been shown in [2] that a perfect family F of hash functions from V to C, having size $2^{O(k)} O(\log |V|)$, can be computed in time $2^{O(k)} O(|V| \log |V|)$. From Lemma 6 and by using a perfect family of hash functions to color the vertices in G, we can prove the main result of this section.

Theorem 6. *The* String to Graph Compatibility Matching *problem can be decided in time $2^{O(|s|)} O(|s|^{|s|+1} |V|^2 \log |V|)$.*

6   Conclusion

In this contribution we have presented results on the tractability of the approximate matching of a query string to a labeled graph. There are several open questions related to variants of this problem. It will be interesting to further investigate the approximability of String to Graph Approximate Matching, since it can be trivially approximated within factor $|s|$ in polynomial time, while it cannot be approximated within factor $\Omega(\log(|s|))$, unless P = NP. Another interesting open question is to investigate the parameterized complexity of String to Graph Approximate Matching when the edit operations are not restricted to symbol substitutions, but include symbol insertions and deletions.

References

1. Akutsu, T.: A linear time pattern matching algorithm between a string and a tree. In: 4th Annual Symposium on Combinatorial Pattern Matching, CPM 93, Padova, Italy, 2–4 June 1993, Proceedings, pp. 1–10 (1993)
2. Alon, N., Yuster, R., Zwick, U.: Color-coding. J. ACM **42**(4), 844–856 (1995)
3. Amir, A., Lewenstein, M., Lewenstein, N.: Pattern matching in hypertext. J. Algorithms **35**(1), 82–99 (2000)
4. Bodlaender, H.L., Downey, R.G., Fellows, M.R., Hermelin, D.: On problems without polynomial kernels. J. Comput. Syst. Sci. **75**(8), 423–434 (2009)
5. Bodlaender, H.L., Jansen, B.M.P., Kratsch, S.: Kernel bounds for path and cycle problems. Theor. Comput. Sci. **511**, 117–136 (2013)
6. Downey, R.G., Fellows, M.R.: Fundamentals of Parameterized Complexity. In: Gries, D., Hazzan, O. (eds.) TCS. Springer, London (2013). https://doi.org/10.1007/978-1-4471-5559-1
7. Equi, M., Grossi, R., Mäkinen, V., Tomescu, A.I.: On the complexity of string matching for graphs. In: Baier, C., Chatzigiannakis, I., Flocchini, P., Leonardi, S. (eds.) 46th International Colloquium on Automata, Languages, and Programming, ICALP 2019, Patras, Greece, 9–12 July 2019. LIPIcs, vol. 132, pp. 55:1–55:15. Schloss Dagstuhl - Leibniz-Zentrum fuer Informatik (2019)
8. Garey, M.R., Johnson, D.S.: Computers and Intractability: A Guide to the Theory of NP-Completeness. WH Freeman & Co., New York (1979)
9. Jain, C., Zhang, H., Gao, Y., Aluru, S.: On the complexity of sequence to graph alignment. In: Cowen, L.J. (ed.) RECOMB 2019. LNCS, vol. 11467, pp. 85–100. Springer, Cham (2019). https://doi.org/10.1007/978-3-030-17083-7_6
10. Manber, U., Wu, S.: Approximate string matching with arbitrary cost for text and hypertext. In: Advances in Structural and Syntactic Pattern Recognition, pp. 22–33 (1992)
11. Myers, E.W.: The fragment assembly string graph. Bioinformatics **21**(suppl_2), ii79–ii85 (2005)
12. Navarro, G.: Improved approximate pattern matching on hypertext. Theor. Comput. Sci. **237**(1–2), 455–463 (2000)
13. Nguyen, N., et al.: Building a pan-genome reference for a population. J. Comput. Biol. **22**(5), 387–401 (2015)
14. Niedermeier, R.: Invitation to Fixed-Parameter Algorithms. Oxford University Press, Oxford (2006)
15. Park, K., Kim, D.K.: String matching in hypertext. In: Galil, Z., Ukkonen, E. (eds.) CPM 1995. LNCS, vol. 937, pp. 318–329. Springer, Heidelberg (1995). https://doi.org/10.1007/3-540-60044-2_51
16. Paz, A., Moran, S.: Non deterministic polynomial optimization problems and their approximations. Theor. Comput. Sci. **15**, 251–277 (1981)
17. Pevzner, P., Tang, H., Waterman, M.S.: An Eulerian path approach to DNA fragment assembly. Proc. Nat. Acad. Sci. **98**(17), 9748–97533 (2001)
18. The Computational Pan-Genomics Consortium: Computational pan-genomics: status, promises and challenges. Brief. Bioinform. **19**(1), 118–135 (2018)
19. Williamson, D.P., Shmoys, D.B.: The Design of Approximation Algorithms. Cambridge University Press, New York (2011)

Complexity of Automatic Sequences

Hans Zantema[1,2(✉)]

[1] Department of Computer Science, TU Eindhoven, P.O. Box 513,
5600 MB, Eindhoven, The Netherlands
h.zantema@tue.nl
[2] Radboud University Nijmegen, P.O. Box 9010,
6500 GL, Nijmegen, The Netherlands

Abstract. Automatic sequences can be defined by DFAs with output (DFAO) in two natural ways. We propose to consider the minimal size of a corresponding DFAO as the complexity measure of the automatic sequence, for both variants. This paper compares these complexity measures and investigates their properties like the relationships with kernel and morphic sequences. There exist automatic sequences for which the one complexity is exponentially greater than the other one, in both directions. For both complexity measures we investigate the effect of taking basic operations on sequences like removing or adding an element in front, and observe that these operations may increase the complexity by at most a quadratic factor.

1 Introduction

Automatic sequences form an important class of infinite sequences over a finite alphabet; roughly speaking it is a first regular class going beyond ultimately periodic sequences. They have been extensively studied, in particular in the book [1] that serves as the main reference for research in this area. More recent references on the topic include [5,9].

Automatic sequences depend on a base $k > 1$, with special interest for $k = 2$. Two well-known 2-automatic sequences are the Thue-Morse sequence and the regular paper folding sequence, to be defined in Sect. 2. Automatic sequences admit several equivalent characterizations, many of which are closely related to the following two. In the first one the ith element a_i of the sequence a is the output of a DFAO when taking as input the k-ary notation of i. The second one is similar, but then the reverse of the k-ary notation of i is taken as input. It is natural to consider the minimal size of a corresponding DFAO as the complexity measure of the automatic sequence, for both variants, and we denote them by $\|a\|_k$ and $\|a\|_k^R$. These complexity measures are the main topic of this paper. We show how they relate to other characterizations; in particular, $\|a\|_k^R$ is closely related to the size of the *kernel* of a, and $\|a\|_k$ is closely related to the size of the smallest alphabet needed to describe a as a *morphic* sequence with respect to a k-uniform morphism. In doing so, we follow constructions as presented in [1] for which we investigate the precise effect on the measures $\|a\|_k$ and $\|a\|_k^R$.

© Springer Nature Switzerland AG 2020
A. Leporati et al. (Eds.): LATA 2020, LNCS 12038, pp. 260–271, 2020.
https://doi.org/10.1007/978-3-030-40608-0_18

A first result states that there is an exponential gap between both measures: there exist sequences of automatic sequences a, b for which $\|a\|_k^R$ is exponential in $\|a\|_k$, and $\|b\|_k$ is exponential in $\|b\|_k^R$.

A next natural question is about the effect of taking basic operations on sequences. For instance, for any sequence a its tail $\mathsf{tail}(a)$ is obtained by removing its first element. We show that $\|\mathsf{tail}(a)\|_k^R \le 2\|a\|_k^R$ and $\|\mathsf{tail}(a)\|_k \le (\|a\|_k)^2$ for all k-automatic sequences, and that the last inequality is sharp. Similar results hold for adding an element in front rather than removing. Also other operations are considered, like pointwise combining two sequences and taking particular subsequences. About all of these basic operations f the main observation is that their sizes do not increase more than quadratically: $\|f(a)\|_k \le (\|a\|_k)^2$ and $\|f(a)\|_k^R \le (\|a\|_k^R)^2$ for all a.

Another interesting question is what happens for periodic sequences. In the current paper we only derive a quadratic upper bound for $\|\cdot\|_k^R$ and a linear upper bound for $\|\cdot\|_k$, so opposite to the effect of tail. Whether and when these upper bounds are reached is a much more involved question that is investigated in [2]. The research project on this topic is a joined project of Wieb Bosma and the current author; as this analysis for periodic sequences requires arguments of a completely different combinatorial flavor than the automata based arguments in this paper, we decided to present the current paper and [2] separately.

Throughout the paper we make several claims about the exact values of $\|a\|_k$ and $\|a\|_k^R$ for particular sequences a. To compute these values we wrote a program to search for a DFAO of minimal size n having the corresponding property for a_i for all $i < N$ for N being typically around 2^{10}. This was done by expressing the requirements as a satisfiability problem and then call a SAT solver. The smallest n for which the formula is satisfiable then is given. As only the requirements for $i < N$ are checked, this only yields a lower bound, but for N large enough it gives the exact value. According to [6], corollary 3.1 (page 59) two states in a DFAO of n states are equivalent are equivalent if and only if for every string of length $\le n - 1$ they produce the same output. This can be improved to $\le n - 2$. Applying this for the union of the found automaton and the real automaton with bounds derived in this paper, this shows that for $N = 2^{n-2}$ the exact value is obtained.

This paper is organized as follows. In Sect. 2 we give the basic definitions and a general lemma for proving lower bounds. In Sect. 3 we investigate the exponential gap between $\|\cdot\|_k$ and $\|\cdot\|_k^R$. In Sect. 4 we define the kernel of an automatic sequence and investigate its relationship with $\|\cdot\|_k^R$. In Sect. 5 we present how to define automatic sequences as morphic sequences with respect to uniform morphisms, and investigate the relationship with $\|\cdot\|_k$. In Sect. 6 we investigate the effect of basic operations like tail on $\|\cdot\|_k$ and $\|\cdot\|_k^R$. In Sect. 7 we give the upper bounds of $\|\cdot\|_k$ and $\|\cdot\|_k^R$ for periodic sequences. We conclude in Sect. 8.

2   Basic Definitions

Let $k \geq 2$ and $\Sigma_k = \{0, 1, \ldots, k - 1\}$.

The set of infinite sequences $a = a_0 a_1 a_2 a_3 \cdots$ over a finite alphabet Γ is denoted by $\Gamma^{\mathbb{N}}$.

A DFA M with output (DFAO) is defined to be a tuple $M = (Q, \Sigma, \delta, q_0, \Gamma, \tau)$, where

- Q is the finite set of states,
- Σ is the finite input alphabet,
- $\delta : Q \times \Sigma \to Q$ is the transition function,
- $q_0 \in Q$ is the initial state,
- Γ is the finite output alphabet,
- $\tau : Q \to \Gamma$ is the output function.

DFAOs are denoted by states and arrows just as is usual for DFAs; the extra information that $\tau(q) = x$ is denoted by writing q/x in the state q.

As in DFAs, δ extends to $\delta : Q \times \Sigma^* \to Q$ by $\delta(q, \epsilon) = q$, $\delta(q, xu) = \delta(\delta(q, x), u)$. A DFAO M defines a function $f_M : \Sigma^* \to \Gamma$ defined by $f_M(u) = \tau(\delta(q_0, u))$. A function $f : \Sigma^* \to \Gamma$ is called a *finite state function* if a DFAO M exists such that $f = f_M$. For every finite state function f there exists a unique (up to renaming of states) DFAO M with a minimal number of states such that $f = f_M$.

A DFAO of which the input alphabet Σ is equal to $\Sigma_k = \{0, 1, \ldots, k - 1\}$, is called a k-DFAO.

Every natural number n has a unique representation $(n)_k \in \Sigma_k^*$, where $(0)_k = \epsilon$ and

$$(n)_k = d_0 d_1 \cdots d_r \iff n = d_0 k^r + d_1 k^{r-1} + \cdots + d_{r-1} k + d_r \wedge d_0 > 0$$

for $n > 0$. So $(0)_2 = \epsilon$ and $(11)_2 = 1011$. Note that non-empty strings of which the leftmost symbol is 0 do not occur as $(n)_k$ for some number n.

Conversely, every $u \in \Sigma_k^*$ represents a number $[u]_k$:

$$[d_0 d_1 \cdots d_r]_k = d_0 k^r + d_1 k^{r-1} + \cdots + d_{r-1} k + d_r.$$

For any Σ and any string $u \in \Sigma^*$ the reverse u^R of u is defined by $(u_1 u_2 \cdots u_n)^R = u_n u_{n-1} \cdots u_1$.

An infinite sequence $a \in \Gamma^{\mathbb{N}}$ is called k-automatic if a k-DFAO $M = (Q, \Sigma_k, \delta, q_0, \Gamma, \tau)$ exists such that $a_{[w]_k} = \tau(\delta(q_0, w))$ for all $w \in \Sigma_k^*$. According to Theorem 5.2.1 from [1] a is k-automatic if and only if a k-DFAO $M = (Q_M, \Sigma_k, \delta_M, q_0, \Gamma, \tau_M)$ exists such that $\tau_M(\delta_M(q_0, (i)_k)) = a_i$ for all $i \in \mathbb{N}$. According to Theorem 5.2.3 from [1] a is k-automatic if and only if a k-DFAO $M = (Q_M, \Sigma_k, \delta_M, q_0, \Gamma, \tau_M)$ exists such that $\tau_M(\delta_M(q_0, (i)_k^R)) = a_i$ for all $i \in \mathbb{N}$.

Now we are ready to define the two natural measures $\|.\|_k$, $\|.\|_k^R$ for k-automatic sequences that we investigate in this paper.

Definition 1. *For any k-automatic sequence $a = a_0 a_1 a_2 a_3 \cdots$ its size $\|a\|_k$ is defined to be the size of a smallest k-DFAO $M = (Q_M, \Sigma_k, \delta_M, q_0, \Gamma, \tau_M)$ such that $\tau_M(\delta_M(q_0, (i)_k)) = a_i$ for all $i \in \mathbb{N}$.*

For any k-automatic sequence $a = a_0 a_1 a_2 a_3 \cdots$ its reversed size $\|a\|_k^R$ is defined to be the size of a smallest k-DFAO $M = (Q_M, \Sigma_k, \delta_M, q_0, \Gamma, \tau_M)$ such that $\tau_M(\delta_M(q_0, (i)_k^R)) = a_i$ for all $i \in \mathbb{N}$.

Conversely, every k-DFAO $M = (Q_M, \Sigma_k, \delta_M, q_0, \Gamma, \tau_M)$ defines two infinite sequences $\mathsf{seq}_k(M)$ and $\mathsf{seq}_k^R(M)$ over Γ:

$$\mathsf{seq}_k(M)_i = \tau_M(\delta_M(q_0, (i)_k)) \text{ and } \mathsf{seq}_k^R(M)_i = \tau_M(\delta_M(q_0, (i)_k^R))$$

for all $i \in \mathbb{N}$. From the above definition it is immediate that $\|\mathsf{seq}_k(M)\|_k \leq |Q_M|$ and $\|\mathsf{seq}_k^R(M)\|_k^R \leq |Q_M|$.

The *Thue-Morse sequence* $\mathsf{thue} = 0110100110010110\cdots$ is defined by $\mathsf{thue}_i = 0$ if the number of 1s in $(i)_2$ is even, and $\mathsf{thue}_i = 1$ if the number of 1s in $(i)_2$ is odd, see, e.g., [1] Section 1.6, or OEIS A010060. We have $\|\mathsf{thue}\|_2 = \|\mathsf{thue}\|_2^R = 2$, both justified by the DFAO on the right.

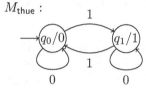

The *regular paper-folding sequence* $\mathsf{paper} = 001001100011011\cdots$ (or *dragon curve sequence* is defined by $\mathsf{paper}_i = m \bmod 2$ for every $i \geq 0$ for the unique representation $i = (2m+1)2^j - 1$, see, e.g., [1] Example 5.16., or OEIS A014577. We have $\|\mathsf{paper}\|_2 = \|\mathsf{paper}\|_2^R = 4$, respectively justified by the following two DFAOs.

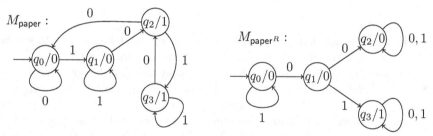

The following lemma is the basic tool for lower bounds on $\|a\|_k$ and $\|a\|_k^R$.

Lemma 1. *Let a be a k-automatic sequence, and $m_1, \ldots, m_n \in \mathbb{N}$ such that for every $i \neq j$ there exists $v \in \Sigma_k^*$ satisfying $a_{[(m_i)_k v]_k} \neq a_{[(m_j)_k v]_k}$, then $\|a\|_k \geq n$.*

Let a be a k-automatic sequence, and $m_1, \ldots, m_n \in \mathbb{N}$ such that for every $i \neq j$ there exists $v \in \Sigma_k^*$ satisfying $a_{[v(m_i)_k]_k} \neq a_{[v(m_j)_k]_k}$, then $\|a\|_k^R \geq n$.

Proof. For the first claim let $M = (Q_M, \Sigma_k, \delta_M, q_0, \Gamma, \tau_M)$ be a smallest k-DFAO such that $\tau_M(\delta_M(q_0, (i)_k)) = a_i$ for all $i \in \mathbb{N}$. For $i = 1, 2, \ldots, n$ define $q_i = \delta_M(q_0, (m_i)_k)$. For $i \neq j$ from the assumption we obtain $\tau_M(\delta_M(q_i, v)) \neq \tau_M(\delta_M(q_j, v))$, so $q_i \neq q_j$. This shows $|Q| \geq n$, so $\|a\|_k \geq n$.

The proof of the second claim is similar. □

3   The Exponential Gap

The following theorem shows that there can be an exponential gap between $\|a\|_k$ and $\|a\|_k^R$, in both directions. Its proof is inspired by the folklore result that the language $(0+1) * 1(0+1)^{n-1}$ has an NFA of size $n+1$, and its reverse has a DFA of size $n+1$, but its smallest DFA has size at least 2^n. We found it in [8], Sect. 3.2, page 67, exercise 3. Many similar results on state complexity are known, e.g., in [7], it is proved that all values until 2^n can be reached as sizes.

Theorem 1. *For every $n > 1$ there exist k-automatic sequences a, b such that $\|a\|_k \leq n+k$ and $\|a\|_k^R \geq (k-1)k^{n-1}$, and $\|b\|_k^R \leq n+k$ and $\|b\|_k \geq (k-1)k^{n-1}$.*

Proof. Define a by $a_i = 0$ for $i < k^n$, and $a_i = j$ if and only if the nth digit of $(i)_k$ is j, for $j = 0, 1, \ldots, k-1$, $i \geq k^n$. The following DFAO satisfies $\tau_M(\delta_M(q_0, (i)_k)) = a_i$ by construction:

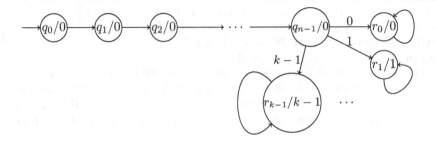

in which all unlabeled arrows are assumed to be labeled by all symbols $0, 1, \ldots, k-1$. Since this DFAO has $n+k$ states we obtain $\|a\|_k \leq n+k$.

For proving $\|a\|_k^R \geq (k-1)k^{n-1}$ we apply Lemma 1. For $i = 1, 2, \ldots, (k-1)k^{n-1}$ define $m_i = k^n + i - 1$, so the numbers m_i are exactly the numbers of k-ary length n, starting in a digit $\neq 0$. For any two distinct such numbers m_i and m_j there is a position p on which they differ, so by choosing $v = 1^{n-p}$, the strings $v(m_i)_k$ and $v(m_j)_k$ differ in their n-th position. So the condition of Lemma 1 holds and we conclude $\|a\|_k^R \geq (k-1)k^{n-1}$.

Define b by $b_i = 0$ for $i < k^n$, and $a_i = j$ if and only if the nth element of $(i)_k^R$ is j, for $j = 0, 1, \ldots, k-1$, $i \geq k^n$. A similar argument using the same automaton proves the claim for b. $\qquad\square$

4   The k-kernel

For $j \in \Sigma_k$ we define $p_j(a) = a_j a_{k+j} a_{2k+j} a_{3k+j} \cdots$ by $(p_j(a))_i = a_{ik+j}$ for all $i \in \mathbb{N}$. So for $k = 2$ we have $p_0(a) = \text{even}(a) = a_0 a_2 a_4 \cdots$ and $p_1(a) = \text{odd}(a) = a_1 a_3 a_5 \cdots$.

For an infinite sequence $a = a_0 a_1 a_2 a_3 \cdots$ over Γ we define its k-kernel $K_k(a)$ to be the smallest set $K_k(a) \subseteq \Gamma^{\mathbb{N}}$ such that

- $a \in K_k(a)$,
- for every $b \in K_k(a)$ and every $j \in \Sigma_k$ we have $p_j(b) \in K_k(a)$.

We recall from [4], Prop. V.3.3, or [1], Theorem 6.6.2, that a is k-automatic if and only if $K_k(a)$ is finite.

For a k-automatic sequence $a = a_0 a_1 a_2 a_3 \cdots$ over the alphabet Γ its k-*kernel* $K_k(a)$ has a natural DFAO structure: the DFAO $\mathcal{K}_k(a) = (K_k(a), \Sigma_k, \delta, a, \Gamma, \tau)$, where

- the input alphabet is Σ_k,
- $K_k(a)$ is the set of states,
- $\delta : K_k(a) \times \Sigma_k \to Q$ is defined by $\delta(q, j) = p_j(q)$,
- a is the initial state,
- the output alphabet is Γ,
- the output function $\tau : K_k(a) \to \Sigma_k$ is defined by $\tau(b_0 b_1 b_2 \cdots) = b_0$.

Recall that for $k = 2$ we have $p_0 = $ even and $p_1 = $ odd, so in $K_2(a)$ the 0-steps describe even and the 1-steps describe odd. For thue the 2-kernel exactly coincides with the DFAO M_{thue} given in Sect. 2, in which q_0 coincides with thue and q_1 coincides with the sequence obtained from thue by swapping symbols 0 and 1. For paper the 2-kernel exactly coincides with the given DFAO M_{paper^R}, in which q_0 coincides with paper, q_1 with $(01)^\omega = 010101 \cdots$, q_2 with $0^\omega = 000 \cdots$ and q_3 with $1^\omega = 111 \cdots$.

The following theorem is straightforwardly proved by induction on i:

Theorem 2. *For every k-automatic sequence $a = a_0 a_1 a_2 a_3 \cdots$ and every $i \in \mathbb{N}$ we have $\tau(\delta(a, (i)_k^R)) = a_i$ where τ, δ refer to $\mathcal{K}_k(a) = (K_k(a), \Sigma_k, \delta, a, \Gamma, \tau)$.*

As a consequence, by only giving the DFAO $\mathcal{K}_k(a)$ the sequence a is fully defined.

Theorem 3. *The DFAO $\mathcal{K}_k(a)$ is the unique DFAO of minimal size such that $\tau(\delta(a, (i)_k^R 0^j)) = a_i$ for every $i, j \in \mathbb{N}$.*

Proof. Let $\mathcal{K}_k(a) = (K_k(a), \Sigma_k, \delta, a, \Gamma, \tau)$. Combining Theorem 2 with the fact that $\tau(q) = \tau(\delta(q, 0))$ for all $q \in K_k(a)$ yields $\tau(\delta(a, (i)_k^R 0^j)) = a_i$ for every $i, j \in \mathbb{N}$. Assume it is not of minimal size with this property. Then there are two distinct states q, q' such that $\tau(\delta(q, u)) = \tau(\delta(q', u))$ for all $u \in \Sigma_k^*$. Since q, q' are sequences over Σ_k, applying Theorem 2 to $\mathcal{K}_k(q)$ and $\mathcal{K}_k(q')$ yield $q_i = q_i'$ for all $i \in \mathbb{N}$. But then q, q' are equal as sequences, contradicting that they are distinct. $\square$

Recall that $\|a\|_k^R$ is the minimal size $|Q|$ for which a DFAO $M = (Q, \Sigma, \delta, q_0, \Gamma, \tau)$ exists such that $\tau(\delta(q_0, (i)_k^R)) = a_i$ for every $i \in \mathbb{N}$. We observe that a DFAO with this property does not need to be unique. For instance, for $a = 01^\omega$ the DFAO $\mathcal{K}_k(a)$ is a minimal DFAO with this property, having two states a and $b = 1^\omega$, and $\delta(a, 0) = a, \delta(a, 1) = \delta(b, 0) = \delta(b, 1) = b$, $\tau(a) = 0$, $\tau(b) = 1$. But the DFAO with the same two states a, b and $\delta(b, 0) = a, \delta(a, 0) = \delta(a, 1) = \delta(b, 1) = b$, $\tau(a) = 0$, $\tau(b) = 1$ produces the same sequence $a = 01^\omega$.

Next we observe that $\|a\|_k^R$ can be strictly smaller than $|K_k(a)|$, the size of the state space of $K_k(a)$. Define $a_i = 1$ if the number of zeros in $(i)_2$ is odd, and $a_i = 0$ if this number is even. Clearly it admits the following DFAO, in which as usual $\tau(q) = x$ is denoted by q/x in the state q:

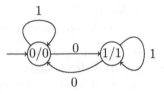

Hence $\|a\|_k^R \le 2$; we obtain $\|a\|_k^R = 2$ since the sequence contains both 0 and 1. However, $|K_k(a)| = 4$, since $K_k(a)$ is the following DFAO:

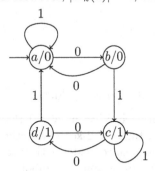

The sequences a, b, c, d are as follows:

$$a = 001001101 \cdots, \quad b = 010110010 \cdots,$$

$$c = 110110010 \cdots, \quad d = 101001101 \cdots.$$

Observe that a and d differ only at the first position, and similarly for b and c. The next lemma states that this always occurs if $|K_k(a)|$ is greater then $\|a\|_k^R$.

Lemma 2. *Let a be an infinite sequence over Γ with kernel $K_k(a) = (K_k(a), \Sigma_k, \delta, a, \Gamma, \tau)$. Let $(Q_M, \Sigma_k, \delta_M, q_0, \Gamma, \tau_M)$ such that $\tau_M(\delta_M(q_0, (i)_k^R)) = a_i$ for all $i \in \mathbb{N}$. Assume that $\delta_M(q_0, u) = \delta_M(q_0, v)$ for $u, v \in \Sigma_k^*$. Then*

$$\delta(a, u)_i = \delta(a, v)_i \text{ for all } i > 0.$$

Proof. Let $i > 0$. For any $w \in \Sigma_k^*$ define the numbers m_w by $(m_w)_k = (i)_k w^R$; this is possible since $(i)_k w^R$ does not start in 0 since $i > 0$. For any $b \in K_k(a)$ we obtain $b_i = \tau(\delta(b, (i)_k^R))$ by considering $K_k(b)$. Hence

$$\delta(a, w)_i = \tau(\delta(\delta(a, w), (i)_k^R)) = \tau(\delta(a, w(i)_k^R)) = \tau(\delta(a, (m_w)_k^R)) = a_{m_w}.$$

We obtain: $\quad \delta(a, u)_i = a_{m_u} = \tau_M(\delta_M(q_0, (m_u)_k^R))$
$$= \tau_M(\delta_M(q_0, u(i)_k^R))$$
$$= \tau_M(\delta_M(\delta_M(q_0, u), (i)_k^R))$$
$$= \tau_M(\delta_M(\delta_M(q_0, v), (i)_k^R))$$
$$= \tau_M(\delta_M(q_0, (m_v)_k^R)) = a_{m_v} = \delta(a, v)_i.$$

$\square$

Theorem 4. *Let a be a k-automatic sequence over an alphabet Γ. Then*

$$\|a\|_k^R \le |K_k(a)| \le |\Gamma| * \|a\|_k^R.$$

Moreover, if a is periodic then $\|a\|_k^R = |K_k(a)|$.

Proof. The inequality $\|a\|_k^R \le |K_k(a)|$ holds since the automaton $K_k(a)$ satisfies $\tau(\delta(a, (i)_k^R)) = a_i$ for every $i \in \mathbb{N}$. For the other inequality let $M = (Q, \Sigma, \delta, q_0, \Gamma, \tau)$ be a DFAO of minimal size $\|a\|_k^R$ such that $\tau(\delta(q_0, (i)_k^R)) = a_i$

for every $i \in \mathbb{N}$. For every $b \in K_k(a)$ choose $u_b \in \Sigma_K^*$ such that $b = \delta(a, u_b)$. Define $\sim$ on $K_k(a)$ by $b \sim c \iff \delta_M(q_0, u_b) = \delta_M(q_0, u_c)$.

According to Lemma 2 $b \sim c$ implies that $b_i = c_i$ for all $i > 0$, so the difference between b and c may only be caused by $b_0 \neq c_0$. Hence every equivalence class of $\sim$ has at most $|\Gamma|$ elements, while the number of equivalence classes is $|Q| = \|a\|_k^R$. This proves $|K_k(a)| \leq |\Gamma| * \|a\|_k^R$.

In case a is periodic then all elements of $K_k(a)$ are periodic too, and $b_i = c_i$ for all $i > 0$ implies $b = c$. Hence in that case all equivalence classes consist of a single element, proving $\|a\|_k^R = |K_k(a)|$. □

5 Morphic Sequences

Recall that $\|a\|_k = |Q_M|$ for the smallest Q_M being the set of states of a DFAO $M = (Q_M, \Sigma_k, \delta_M, q_0, \Gamma, \tau_M)$ for which $\tau_M(\delta_M(q_0, (i)_k)) = a_i$ for every $i \in \mathbb{N}$. Again this DFAO of minimal size is not unique: for $a = 01^\omega$ the DFAO $\mathcal{K}_k(a)$ as given above also satisfies $\tau_M(\delta_M(q_0, (i)_k)) = a_i$ for all $i \in \mathbb{N}$, but after changing $\delta(a, 0) = a$ to $\delta(a, 0) = b$ this property still holds, since $(i)_k$ never starts by 0.

Just like $\|a\|_k^R$ is strongly related to the kernel of a as described in Theorem 4, $\|a\|_k$ is strongly related to the number of symbols needed to describe a as a morphic sequence with respect to a k-uniform morphism. A sequence a over an alphabet Γ is called *morphic* with respect to a morphism $h : \Delta \to \Delta^*$ and a coding $\tau : \Delta \to \Gamma$ if $a = \tau(h^\omega(x))$ for some $x \in \Delta$ satisfying $h(x) = xu$, by which $h^\omega(x) = xuh(u)h^2(u)h^3(u)\cdots$ is a fixed point of h. The morphism $h : \Delta \to \Delta^*$ is called k-uniform if the string $h(y) \in \Delta^*$ has length k for every $y \in \Delta$. It is well-known (Cobham [3], see also [1] Theorem 6.3.2) that a is k-automatic if and only if it is morphic with respect to a k-uniform morphism. For instance, thue $= h^\omega(0)$ for $h(0) = 01, h(1) = 10$, and paper $= \tau(g^\omega(0))$ for $g(0) = 02, g(1) = 31, g(2) = 32, g(3) = 01, \tau(0) = \tau(2) = 0, \tau(1) = \tau(3) = 1$.

Theorem 5. *Let a be a k-automatic sequence. Let $d(a)$ be the minimal size of the alphabet Δ such that $a = \tau(h^\omega(x))$ for a k-uniform morphism $h : \Delta \to \Delta^*$ and a coding $\tau : \Delta \to \Gamma$. Then $\|a\|_k \leq d(a) \leq \|a\|_k + 1$.*

Proof. The k-DFAO $M = (\Delta, \Sigma_k, \delta, q_0, \Gamma, \tau)$ with $q_0 = x$ and $\delta(q, y) = h(q)_y$, where we write $h(q) = h(q)_0 \cdots h(q)_{k-1}$, satisfies $\tau(\delta(q_0, (i)_k)) = a_i$ for all $i \geq 0$ as is showed in the proof of Theorem 6.3.2 of [1]. As $\|a\|_k$ is the smallest size of a k-DFAO with this property we obtain $\|a\|_k \leq d(a)$.

Conversely, if $M = (Q_M, \Sigma_k, \delta_M, q_0, \Gamma, \tau_M)$ is a k-DFAO of size $\|a\|_k$ with $\tau_M(\delta_M(q_0, (i)_k)) = a_i$ for all $i \geq 0$, then by choosing a fresh state q_0' and defining $Q = Q_M \cup \{q_0'\}$, $\delta(q, y) = \delta_M(q, y)$ for $q \in Q_M$, $\delta(q_0', 0) = q_0'$, $\delta(q_0', y) = \delta_M(q_0, y)$ for $y \neq 0$, $\tau(q_0') = \tau_M(q_0)$, $\tau(q) = \tau_M(q)$ for $q \in Q_M$, we obtain the k-DFAO $(Q, \Sigma_k, \delta, q_0', \Gamma, \tau)$ of size $\|a\|_k + 1$ with $\tau(\delta(q_0', (i)_k)) = a_i$ for all $i \geq 0$. Using the fact that $\delta(q_0', 0) = q_0'$ we obtain $a = \tau(h^\omega(q_0'))$ for h defined by $h(q) = \delta(q, 0)\delta(q, 1)\cdots\delta(q, k-1)$ as is shown in the proof of Theorem 6.3.2 of [1]. Hence $d(a) \leq \|a\|_k + 1$. □

6   The Effect of Basic Operations

For any sequence $a = a_0a_1a_2a_3\cdots$ we define its tail $\mathrm{tail}(a) = a_1a_2a_3a_4\cdots$ by $(\mathrm{tail}(a))_i = a_{i+1}$ for all $i \in \mathbb{N}$.

Theorem 6. *For any k-automatic sequence a we have* $\|\mathrm{tail}(a)\|_k^R \leq 2\|a\|_k^R$ *and* $\|\mathrm{tail}(a)\|_k \leq (\|a\|_k)^2$. *For every $n > 1$ there exists a k-automatic sequence a such that* $\|a\|_k = n$ *and* $\|\mathrm{tail}(a)\|_k = n^2$.

Proof. For the first claim take a DFAO $M = (Q, \Sigma_k, \delta, q_0, \Gamma, \tau)$ of size $\|a\|_k^R$ with $\tau(\delta(q_0, (i)_k^R)) = a_i$ for all $i \geq 0$. Let $m \leq \|a\|_k^R$ be the smallest number $m > 0$ such that $j < m$ exists with $\delta(q_0, 0^m) = \delta(q_0, 0^j)$. Introduce fresh states $r_0, \ldots, r_{m-1}$ and define the DFAO $M' = (Q \cup \{r_0, \ldots, r_{m-1}\}, \Sigma_k, \delta', r_0, \Gamma, \tau')$ by

$$\delta'(q, x) = \delta(q, x) \text{ for } q \in Q, x \in \Sigma_k,$$

$$\delta'(r_i, k - 1) = r_{i+1} \text{ for } i = 1, \ldots, m - 2,$$

$$\delta'(r_{m-1}, k - 1) = r_j \text{ for } j < m \text{ with } \delta(q_0, 0^m) = \delta(q_0, 0^j),$$

$$\delta'(r_i, x) = \delta(q_0, 0^i(x + 1)) \text{ for } i = 0, \ldots, m - 1, x < k - 1.$$

By construction we have $\delta'(r_0, (k-1)^i x) = \delta(q_0, 0^i(x+1))$ for all $i \in \mathbb{N}$, $x < k-1$. So by defining $\tau'(q) = \tau(q)$ for $q \in Q$ and $\tau'(r_i) = \tau(\delta(q_0, 0^i))$ for $i = 0, \ldots, m-1$ we obtain

$$\tau'(\delta'(r_0, (vx(k-1)^i)^R)) = \tau(\delta(q_0, (v(x+1)0^i)^R))$$

and

$$\tau'(\delta'(r_0, (k-1)^i)) = \tau(\delta(q_0, (10^i)^R))$$

for all $i \in \mathbb{N}$, $v \in \Sigma_k^*$. Since $[vx(k-1)^i]_k + 1 = [v(x+1)0^i]_k$, and $[(k-1)^i]_k + 1 = [10^i]_k$, and every number in $\mathbb{N}$ is either of the shape $[vx(k-1)^i]_k$ or $[(k-1)^i]_k$, this proves that M' is a DFAO for $\mathrm{tail}(a)$. Since $|Q \cup \{r_0, \ldots, r_{m-1}\}| \leq 2|Q|$ this yields $\|\mathrm{tail}(a)\|_k^R \leq 2\|a\|_k^R$.

For the second claim take a DFAO $M = (Q, \Sigma_k, \delta, q_0, \Gamma, \tau)$ of size $\|a\|_k$ with $\tau(\delta(q_0, (i)_k)) = a_i$ for all $i \geq 0$. Define the DFAO $\overline{M} = (Q \times Q, \Sigma_k, \overline{\delta}, \overline{q_0}, \Gamma, \overline{\tau})$ of size $(\|a\|_k)^2$ by

$$\overline{q_0} = (q_0, \delta(q_0, 1)), \quad \overline{\tau}(q, q') = \tau(q'),$$

$$\overline{\delta}((q, q'), k - 1) = (\delta(q, k - 1), \delta(q', 0)),$$

$$\overline{\delta}((q, q'), x) = (\delta(q, x), \delta(q', x + 1)),$$

for all $q, q' \in Q$, $x < k - 1$. For every $i \in \mathbb{N}$ we have either $(i)_k = (k - 1)^m$ or $(i)_k = vx(k - 1)^m$, for some $m \geq 0$, $v \in \Sigma_k^*$, $x < k - 1$. In the first case we have $(i + 1)_k = 10^m$, in the second case $(i + 1)_k = v(x + 1)0^m$. The DFAO $\overline{M}$ has been constructed in such a way that $\overline{\tau}(\overline{\delta}(\overline{q_0}, (k - 1)^m) = \tau(\delta(q_0, 10^m)$ and $\overline{\tau}(\overline{\delta}(\overline{q_0}, vx(k - 1)^m) = \tau(\delta(q_0, v(x + 1)0^m)$. Hence for all $i \in \mathbb{N}$ we have $\overline{\tau}(\overline{\delta}(\overline{q_0}, (i)_k) = \tau(\delta(q_0, (i + 1)_k)) = a_{i+1} = \mathrm{tail}(a)_i$, proving the second claim.

As $\|\mathrm{tail}(a)\|_k \leq n^2$, for the last claim it suffices to prove $\|\mathrm{tail}(a)\|_k \geq n^2$. We define a by $a_i = 1$ if the number of zeros in $(i)_k$ is divisible by n, and

$a_i = 0$ otherwise. A DFAO consisting of a single n-cycle easily produces a, so $\|a\|_k \leq n$, and since a smaller one is not possible we obtain $\|a\|_k = n$. Let $b = \text{tail}(a)$, so $b_i = a_{i+1}$ for all $i \in \mathbb{N}$. We prove $\|\text{tail}(a)\|_k \geq n^2$ by Lemma 1. Choose $m_1, m_2, \ldots, m_{n^2}$ to be the numbers $[10^p(k-1)^q]_k$ for $p, q = 1, \ldots, n$. Let $m_i = [10^p(k-1)^q]_k$ and $m_j = [10^{p'}(k-1)^{q'}]_k$ for $i \neq j$, then $(p, q) \neq (p', q')$.

First we consider the case where $p + q$ and $p' + q'$ are distinct modulo n, choose r such that $p + q + r - 1$ is divisible by n and $p' + q' + r - 1$ is not. Choose $v = (k-1)^r$. Then $b_{[(m_i)_k v]_k} = a_{[(m_i)_k v]_k + 1} = a_{[10^{p-1}10^{q+r}]_k} = 1 \neq 0 = a_{[10^{p'-1}10^{q'+r}]_k} = b_{[(m_j)_k v]_k}$.

In the remaining case $p + q$ and $p' + q'$ are equal modulo n, and since $(p, q) \neq (p', q')$ we obtain that p and p' are distinct modulo n. Choose r such that $p + r$ is divisible by n and $p' + r$ is not. Choose $v = 0^{r+1}$, then $b_{[(m_i)_k v]_k} = a_{[(m_i)_k v]_k + 1} = a_{[10^p(k-1)^q 0^r 1]_k} = 1 \neq 0 = a_{[10^{p'}(k-1)^{q'} 0^r 1]_k} = b_{[(m_j)_k v]_k}$.

So the conditions of Lemma 1 hold, and $\|\text{tail}(a)\|_k \geq n^2$. □

For our examples thue and paper we have $\|\text{tail}(\text{thue})\|_2 = 4$, $\|\text{tail}(\text{thue})\|_2^R = 3$, $\|\text{tail}(\text{paper})\|_2 = 8$ and $\|\text{tail}(\text{paper})\|_2^R = 6$.

For any sequence $a = a_0 a_1 a_2 a_3 \cdots$ over Γ, and $x \in \Gamma$ the sequence $x \cdot a = x a_0 a_1 a_2 a_3 \cdots$ is defined by $(x \cdot a)_0 = x$ and $(x \cdot a)_i = a_{i-1}$ for all $i > 0$. The next theorem states that the effect of $x \cdot$ is similar to tail.

Theorem 7. *For any k-automatic sequence a over Γ, and $x \in \Gamma$ we have $\|x \cdot a\|_k^R \leq 2\|a\|_k^R$ and $\|x \cdot a\|_k \leq (\|a\|_k)^2$. For every $n > 1$ there exists a k-automatic sequence a such that $\|a\|_k = n$ and $\|x \cdot a\|_k \geq n^2$.*

Proof. Similar to the proof of Theorem 6, with the roles of the symbols 0 and $k - 1$ swapped, exploiting the property $[vx0^i]_k - 1 = [v(x-1)(k-1)^i]_k$ for any string v and any $x > 0$. □

For our examples thue and paper we have $\|0 \cdot \text{thue}\|_2 = 4$, $\|0 \cdot \text{thue}\|_2^R = 4$, $\|0 \cdot \text{paper}\|_2 = 4$ and $\|0 \cdot \text{paper}\|_2^R = 4$.

Recall that for $j \in \Sigma_k$ the operator p_j on sequences a is defined by $(p_j(a))_i = a_{ik+j}$ for all $i \in \mathbb{N}$.

Theorem 8. *For any k-automatic sequence a and $j \in \Sigma_k$ we have $\|p_j(a)\|_k \leq \|a\|_k$ and $\|p_j(a)\|_k^R \leq \|a\|_k^R$.*

Proof. Let $M = (Q, \Sigma_k, \delta, q_0, \Gamma, \tau)$ be a DFAO of size $\|a\|_k$ with $\tau(\delta(q_0, (i)_k)) = a_i$ for all $i \geq 0$. Define $M' = (Q, \Sigma_k, \delta, q_0, \Gamma, \tau')$ by $\tau'(q) = \tau(\delta(q, j))$ for all $q \in Q$. Then

$$(p_j(a))_i = a_{ki+j} = \tau(\delta(q_0, (i)_k j)) = \tau(\delta(\delta(q_0, (i)_k), j)) = \tau'(\delta(q_0, (i)_k))$$

for all $i \in \mathbb{N}$, so M' is a DFAO of size $\|a\|_k$ producing $p_j(a)$, so $\|p_j(a)\|_k \leq \|a\|_k$.

For the other claim let $M = (Q, \Sigma_k, \delta, q_0, \Gamma, \tau)$ be a DFAO of size $\|a\|_k^R$ with $\tau(\delta(q_0, (i)_k^R)) = a_i$ for all $i \geq 0$. Define $M' = (Q, \Sigma_k, \delta, \delta(q_0, j), \Gamma, \tau)$. Then

$$(p_j(a))_i = a_{ki+j} = \tau(\delta(q_0, j(i)_k^R)) = \tau(\delta(\delta(q_0, j), (i)_k^R))$$

for all $i \in \mathbb{N}$, so M' is a DFAO of size $\|a\|_k^R$ producing $p_j(a)$, so $\|p_j(a)\|_k \leq \|a\|_k$. □

For our examples thue and paper we have $\|\mathsf{even(thue)}\|_2 = 2$, $\|\mathsf{odd(thue)}\|_2^R = 2$, $\|\mathsf{even(paper)}\|_2 = 2$ and $\|\mathsf{odd(paper)}\|_2^R = 4$.

When applying an operator $f : \Gamma_1 \times \Gamma_2 \to \Gamma_3$ on two sequences $a \in \Gamma_1^{\mathbb{N}}$, $b \in \Gamma_2^{\mathbb{N}}$, by $f(a,b) \in \Gamma_3^{\mathbb{N}}$ we mean the sequence defined by $f(a,b)_i = f(a_i, b_i)$ for all $i \in \mathbb{N}$. For instance, $\wedge$ applied on boolean sequences denotes the elementwise conjunction of the two boolean sequences.

Theorem 9. *For any two k-automatic sequences $a \in \Gamma_1^{\mathbb{N}}$, $b \in \Gamma_2^{\mathbb{N}}$ and every function $f : \Gamma_1 \times \Gamma_2 \to \Gamma_3$ we have $\|f(a,b)\|_k \le \|a\|_k \|b\|_k$ and $\|f(a,b)\|_k^R \le \|a\|_k^R \|b\|_k^R$.*

Proof. Let $(Q_1, \Sigma_k, \delta_1, q_{10}, \Gamma_1, \tau_1)$ be a DFAO of size $\|a\|_k$ with $\tau_1(\delta(q_{10}, (i)_k)) = a_i$ for all $i \ge 0$. Let $(Q_2, \Sigma_k, \delta_2, q_{20}, \Gamma_2, \tau_2)$ be a DFAO of size $\|b\|_k$ with $\tau_2(\delta(q_{20}, (i)_k)) = b_i$ for all $i \ge 0$. Then $(Q_1 \times Q_2, \Sigma_k, \delta, (q_{10}, q_{20}), \Gamma_3, \tau)$ for δ, τ defined by $\delta((q_1, q_2), x) = (\delta_1(q_1, x), \delta_2(q_2, x))$ and $\tau(q_1, q_2) = f(\tau_1(q_1), \tau_2(q_2))$ for all $q_1 \in Q_1, q_2 \in Q_2, x \in \Sigma_k$, is a DFAO of size $\|a\|_k \|b\|_k$ for $f(a,b)$. The proof for the reversed version is similar. $\square$

Combining our examples thue and paper we have $\|\mathsf{thue} \wedge \mathsf{paper}\|_2 = 8$ and $\|\mathsf{thue} \wedge \mathsf{paper}\|_2^R = 7$.

7   Periodic Sequences

Theorem 10. *Let $a = v^{\omega}$ be a periodic sequence with $|v| = n$. Then $\|a\|_k \le n$ and $\|a\|_k^R \le n(n-1)$.*

Proof. Writing $v = v_0 v_1 \cdots v_{n-1}$ we obtain $a_i = v_{i \bmod n}$ for all $i \in \mathbb{N}$. Define $(Q, \Sigma_k, \delta, q_0, \Gamma, \tau)$ by $Q = \{0, 1, \ldots, n-1\}$, $q_0 = 0$, $\delta(q, x) = (kq + x) \bmod n$, $\tau(q) = v_q$, for all $q \in Q, x \in \Sigma_k$. Then by induction on the length of $(i)_k$ one proves that $\delta(q_0, (i)_k) = (i \bmod n)$ for every $i \in \mathbb{N}$. Hence $\tau(\delta(q_0, (i)_k)) = \tau(i \bmod n) = v_{i \bmod n} = a_i$ for all $i \in \mathbb{N}$, proving that $\|a\|_k \le n$.

For the other claim we prove that $|K_k(a)| \le n(n-1)$, then the result follows from Theorem 4. The states of $K_k(a)$ are sequences b for which there are numbers q, j such that $b_i = a_{ik^q + j} = v_{(ik^q + j) \bmod n}$ for all $i \in \mathbb{N}$. We have to show that there are at most $n(n-1)$ such sequences b. This follows from the fact that this only i depends on the n values for $(j \bmod n)$ and the at most $n - 1$ values for $(k^q \bmod n)$. The latter follows since if k, n are relatively prime, then the values of $(k^q \bmod n)$ are among the $n - 1$ values $1, \ldots, n-1$, and otherwise there is some $p > 1$ dividing both n and k, and the values are among the n/p multiples of p modulo n. $\square$

A natural question is for which cases the bounds of Theorem 10 can be reached, in particular the quadratic bound for $\|a\|_k^R$. This question is beyond the scope of this paper, but has been addressed in [2]. A main result of [2] is that if $n > 5$ is prime and 2 is a primitive root modulo n (on which Artin's conjecture states that this holds for infinitely many primes), then $\|v^{\omega}\|_k^R = n(n-1)$ for $v = 10110^{n-4}$.

8   Conclusions

We investigated two natural complexity measures for a k-automatic sequence a: $\|a\|_k$ closely related to the alphabet size required to present a as a morphic sequence with respect to a k-uniform morphism, and $\|a\|_k^R$ closely related to the size of the kernel of a. We saw how there can be an exponential gap between $\|a\|_k$ and $\|a\|_k^R$, but basic operations like tail, adding an element in front, or applying a binary operator elementwise, never increases $\|\cdot\|_k$ or $\|\cdot\|_k^R$ by more than a quadratic factor. Many other operations, like changing the tenth element of a sequence, can be obtained by combining such basic operations, and hence yield a polynomial upper bound too. Probably these polynomial bounds can be improved strongly. Other open questions include a further investigation of when these upper bounds can be reached. Conversely, our SAT based tool provides values that are likely to be exact, but formally are only lower bounds. It would make sense to further investigate how to be sure to have the exact value, either depending on particular ways to define automatic sequences, or by giving general criteria for exactness depending on known upper bounds.

On periodic sequences this paper only contains some very basic observations; more involved observations are given in [2].

We want to thank Wieb Bosma for fruitful collaboration on this topic and careful proof reading. We want to thank Jeffrey Shallit for giving pointers to state complexity.

References

1. Allouche, J.P., Shallit, J.: Automatic Sequences: Theory, Applications, Generalizations. Cambridge University Press, Cambridge (2003)
2. Bosma, W.: Complexity of periodic sequences (2019). https://www.math.ru.nl/~bosma/pubs/periodic.pdf
3. Cobham, A.: Uniform tag sequences. Math. Systems Theory **6**, 164–192 (1972)
4. Eilenberg, S.: Automata, Languages and Machines, vol. A. Academic Press, New York (1974)
5. Endrullis, J., Grabmayer, C., Hendriks, D.: Mix-automatic sequences. In: Dediu, A.-H., Martín-Vide, C., Truthe, B. (eds.) LATA 2013. LNCS, vol. 7810, pp. 262–274. Springer, Heidelberg (2013). https://doi.org/10.1007/978-3-642-37064-9_24
6. Gill, A.: Introduction to the Theory of Finite-State Machines. McGraw-Hill, New York (1962)
7. Jiraskova, G.: The ranges of state complexities for complement, star and reversal of regular languages. Int. J. Found. Comput. Sci. **25**(1), 101–124 (2014)
8. Lawson, M.V.: Finite Automata. Chapman and Hall/CRC, Boca Raton (2004)
9. Shallit, J.: Decidability and enumeration for automatic sequences: a survey. In: Bulatov, A.A., Shur, A.M. (eds.) CSR 2013. LNCS, vol. 7913, pp. 49–63. Springer, Heidelberg (2013). https://doi.org/10.1007/978-3-642-38536-0_5

Grammars

Context-Sensitive Fusion Grammars Are Universal

Aaron Lye[✉]

Department of Mathematics, University of Bremen,
P.O.Box 33 04 40, 28334 Bremen, Germany
lye@math.uni-bremen.de

Abstract. Context-sensitive fusion grammars are a special case of context-dependent fusion grammars where a rule has only a single positive context condition instead of finite sets of positive and negative context conditions. They generate hypergraph languages from start hypergraphs via successive applications of context-sensitive fusion rules and multiplications of connected components, as well as a filtering mechanism to extract terminal hypergraphs from derived hypergraphs in a certain way. The application of a context-sensitive fusion rule consumes two complementarily labeled hyperedges and identifies corresponding attachment vertices provided that the context condition holds. In this paper, we show that the Post correspondence problem can be formulated very intuitively by such a grammar. Furthermore, we prove that these grammars can generate all recursively enumerable string languages (up to representation of strings as graphs) and are universal in this respect.

Keywords: Graph transformation · Context-sensitive fusion grammars · Recursively enumerable languages · Chomsky grammar · Post correspondence problem

1 Introduction

In 2017 we introduced fusion grammars as generative devices on hypergraphs (cf. [2]). They are motivated by the observation, that one encounters various fusion processes in various scientific fields like DNA computing, chemistry, tiling, fractal geometry, visual modeling and others. The common principle is that a few small entities may be copied and fused to produce more complicated entities. Besides hypergraph language generation they can be used to model and solve interesting decision problems, e.g., in [3] it is shown that the Hamiltonian path problem can be solved efficiently by a respective fusion grammar due to the massive parallelism in a way that mimics Adleman's famous experiment in DNA computing (cf. [1]). In this paper, we show that the Post correspondence problem (PCP, cf. [6]), which is well-known to be undecidable, can be expressed very intuitively by means of fusion and its solvability by using context-sensitive fusion rules. Hence, undeciability results carry over to context-sensitive fusion grammars. Recently, we showed that context-dependent fusion grammars (introduced in [4]) are powerful enough to simulate Turing machines (cf. [5]). In this

© Springer Nature Switzerland AG 2020
A. Leporati et al. (Eds.): LATA 2020, LNCS 12038, pp. 275–286, 2020.
https://doi.org/10.1007/978-3-030-40608-0_19

paper, we show that one can do much better. We show that rules with a single positive context condition are sufficient. To prove this, a known result of formal language theory is used, which is, that each recursively enumerable string language is a (left) quotient of two linear languages. In our construction we employ the same recognition mechanism as the one for PCP. Throughout in the proofs we are actually operating on graphs. As graphs are a subclass of hypergraphs the results hold for the general case.

The paper is organized as follows. In Sect. 2, basic notions and notations of hypergraphs are recalled. Section 3 introduces the notions of context-sensitive fusion grammars. In Sect. 4 we present a reduction of the Post correspondence problem to the membership and emptiness problem for context-sensitive fusion grammars. Afterwards, we prove that context-sensitive fusion grammars can generate all recursively enumerable string languages (up to representation) in Sect. 5. Section 6 concludes the paper pointing out some open problems.

2   Preliminaries

A *hypergraph* over a given label alphabet Σ is a system $H = (V, E, s, t, lab)$ where V is a finite set of *vertices*, E is a finite set of *hyperedges*, $s, t: E \to V^*$ are two functions assigning to each hyperedge a sequence of *sources* and *targets*, respectively, and $lab: E \to \Sigma$ is a function, called *labeling*. The components of $H = (V, E, s, t, lab)$ may also be denoted by V_H, E_H, s_H, t_H, and lab_H respectively. The class of all hypergraphs over Σ is denoted by $\mathcal{H}_\Sigma$.

Let $H \in \mathcal{H}_\Sigma$, and let $\equiv$ be an equivalence relation on V_H. Then the *fusion of the vertices in H with respect to* $\equiv$ yields the (quotient) hypergraph $H/\equiv = (V_H/\equiv, E_H, s_{H/\equiv}, t_{H/\equiv}, lab_H)$ with the set of equivalence classes $V_H/\equiv = \{[v] \mid v \in V_H\}$ and $s_{H/\equiv}(e) = [v_1] \cdots [v_{k_1}]$, $t_{H/\equiv}(e) = [w_1] \cdots [w_{k_2}]$ for each $e \in E_H$ with $s_H(e) = v_1 \cdots v_{k_1}$, $t_H(e) = w_1 \cdots w_{k_2}$.

Given $H, H' \in \mathcal{H}_\Sigma$, a *hypergraph morphism* $g: H \to H'$ consists of two mappings $g_V: V_H \to V_{H'}$ and $g_E: E_H \to E_{H'}$ such that $s_{H'}(g_E(e)) = g_V^*(s_H(e))$, $t_{H'}(g_E(e)) = g_V^*(t_H(e))$ and $lab_{H'}(g_E(e)) = lab_H(e)$ for all $e \in E_H$, where $g_V^*: V_H^* \to V_{H'}^*$ is the canonical extension of g_V, given by $g_V^*(v_1 \cdots v_n) = g_V(v_1) \cdots g_V(v_n)$ for all $v_1 \cdots v_n \in V_H^*$.

Given $H, H' \in \mathcal{H}_\Sigma$, H is a *subhypergraph* of H', denoted by $H \subseteq H'$, if $V_H \subseteq V_{H'}$, $E_H \subseteq E_{H'}$, $s_H(e) = s_{H'}(e)$, $t_H(e) = t_{H'}(e)$, and $lab_H(e) = lab_{H'}(e)$ for all $e \in E_H$.

Let $H' \in \mathcal{H}_\Sigma$ as well as $V \subseteq V_{H'}$ and $E \subseteq E_{H'}$. Then the *removal* of (V, E) from H' given by $H = H' - (V, E) = (V_{H'} - V, E_{H'} - E, s_H, t_H, lab_H)$ with $s_H(e) = s_{H'}(e)$, $t_H(e) = t_{H'}(e)$ and $lab_H(e) = lab_{H'}(e)$ for all $e \in E_{H'} - E$ defines a subgraph $H \subseteq H'$ if $s_{H'}(e), t_{H'}(e) \in (V_{H'} - V)^*$ for all $e \in E_{H'} - E$. We will use removals of the form $(\emptyset, E)$ below.

Let $H \in \mathcal{H}_\Sigma$ and let $att(e)$ be the set of source and target vertices for $e \in E_H$. H is *connected* if for each $v, v' \in V_H$, there exists a sequence of triples $(v_1, e_1, w_1) \ldots (v_n, e_n, w_n) \in (V_H \times E_H \times V_H)^*$ such that $v = v_1, v' = w_n$ and $v_i, w_i \in att(e_i)$ for $i = 1, \ldots, n$ and $w_i = v_{i+1}$ for $i = 1, \ldots, n-1$. A subgraph

C of H is a *connected component* of H if it is connected and there is no larger connected subgraph, i.e., $C \subseteq C' \subseteq H$ and C' connected implies $C = C'$. The set of connected components of H is denoted by $\mathcal{C}(H)$.

Given $H, H' \in \mathcal{H}_\Sigma$, the *disjoint union* of H and H' is denoted by $H + H'$. It is defined by the disjoint union of the underlying sets (also denoted by $+$). The disjoint union of H with itself k times is denoted by $k \cdot H$. We use the *multiplication* of H defined by means of $\mathcal{C}(H)$ as follows. Let $m \colon \mathcal{C}(H) \to \mathbb{N}$ be a mapping, called *multiplicity*, then $m \cdot H = \sum\limits_{C \in \mathcal{C}(H)} m(C) \cdot C$.

A string is represented by a simple path where the sequence of labels along the path equals the given string. Let Σ be a label alphabet. Let $w = x_1 \ldots x_n \in \Sigma^*$ for $n \geq 1$ and $x_i \in \Sigma$ for $i = 1, \ldots, n$. Then the *string graph* of w is defined by $sg(w) = (\{0\} \cup [n], [n], s_w, t_w, lab_w)$ with $s_w(i) = i - 1, t_w(i) = i$ and $lab(i) = x_i$ for $i = 1, \ldots, n$. The string graph of the empty string λ, denoted by $sg(\lambda)$, is the discrete graph with a single node 0. Obviously, there is a one-to-one correspondence between Σ^* and $sg(\Sigma^*) = \{sg(w) \mid w \in \Sigma^*\}$. For technical reasons, we need the extension of a string graph $sg(w)$ for some $w \in \Sigma^*$ by a s-labeled edge bending from the begin node 0 to the end node n, where n is the length of w. The resulting graph is denoted by $sg(w)_s$.

3   Context-Sensitive Fusion Grammars

In this section, we introduce context-sensitive fusion grammars. These grammars generate hypergraph languages from start hypergraphs via successive applications of context-sensitive fusion rules, multiplications of connected components, and a filtering mechanism. Such a rule is applicable if the positive context-condition holds. Its application consumes the two hyperedges and fuses the sources of the one hyperedge with the sources of the other as well as the targets of the one with the targets of the other.

Definition 1. $F \subseteq \Sigma$ *is a fusion alphabet if it is accompanied by a complementary fusion alphabet* $\overline{F} = \{\overline{A} \mid A \in F\} \subseteq \Sigma$, *where* $F \cap \overline{F} = \emptyset$ *and* $\overline{A} \neq \overline{B}$ *for* $A, B \in F$ *with* $A \neq B$ *and a type function* $type \colon F \cup \overline{F} \to (\mathbb{N} \times \mathbb{N})$ *with* $type(A) = type(\overline{A})$ *for each* $A \in F$.

For each $A \in F$, *the fusion rule* $fr(A)$ *is the hypergraph with* $V_{fr(A)} = \{v_i, v'_i \mid i = 1, \ldots, k_1\} \cup \{w_j, w'_j \mid j = 1, \ldots, k_2\}$, $E_{fr(A)} = \{e, \overline{e}\}$, $s_{fr(A)}(e) = v_1 \cdots v_{k_1}$, $s_{fr(A)}(\overline{e}) = v'_1 \cdots v'_{k_1}$, $t_{fr(A)}(e) = w_1 \cdots w_{k_2}$, $t_{fr(A)}(\overline{e}) = w'_1 \cdots w'_{k_2}$, *and* $lab_{fr(A)}(e) = A$ *and* $lab_{fr(A)}(\overline{e}) = \overline{A}$.

The application of $fr(A)$ *to a hypergraph* $H \in \mathcal{H}_\Sigma$ *proceeds according to the following steps: (1) Choose a* matching *hypergraph morphism* $g \colon fr(A) \to H$. *(2) Remove the images of the two hyperedges of* $fr(A)$ *yielding* $X = H - (\emptyset, \{g(e), g(\overline{e})\})$. *(3) Fuse the corresponding source and target vertices of the removed hyperedges yielding the hypergraph* $H' = X/\equiv$ *where* $\equiv$ *is generated by the relation* $\{(g(v_i), g(v'_i)) \mid i = 1, \ldots, k_1\} \cup \{(g(w_j), g(w'_j)) \mid j = 1, \ldots, k_2\}$. *The application of* $fr(A)$ *to* H *is denoted by* $H \underset{fr(A)}{\Longrightarrow} H'$ *and called a* direct derivation.

A context-sensitive fusion rule *is a tuple csfr* $= (fr(A), c\colon fr(A) \to C)$ *for some* $A \in F$ *where* c *is a hypergraph morphism with domain* $fr(A)$ *mapping into a finite context* C.

The rule *csfr* *is applicable to some hypergraph* H *via a matching morphism* $g\colon fr(A) \to H$ *if there exists a hypergraph morphism* $h\colon C \to H$ *such that* h *is injective on the set of hyperedges and* $h \circ c = g$.

If *csfr* *is applicable to* H *via* g, *then the direct derivation* $H \underset{csfr}{\Longrightarrow} H'$ *is the*

direct derivation $H \underset{fr(A)}{\Longrightarrow} H'$.

Remark 1. 1. In this paper, we only make use of the case where every hyperedge has one source and one target vertex. Hence, fusion rules are of the form $\bullet\!\to\!\boxed{A}\!\to\!\bullet$ $\bullet\!\to\!\boxed{\overline{A}}\!\to\!\bullet$. The *type* is therefore omitted throughout the paper.
2. The applications of $fr(A)$ and $(fr(A), id)$ are equivalent. We use the first as an abbreviation for the latter. We call these rules *context-free fusion rules*.

Example 1. Let $F = \{a_1, a_2, a_3\}$. Define $reduce(x) = (fr(x), fr(x) \to \begin{smallmatrix} c_1 \to \boxed{x}\to \bullet c_2 \\ \boxed{x}\to \bullet c_3 \end{smallmatrix})$ for each $x \in F$ where the morphism is uniquely defined by the labels and maps the vertices as follows: $v_1 \mapsto c_1, v_2 \mapsto c_1, w'_1 \mapsto c_2, w_1 \mapsto c_3$. Consider the

graph $G = \begin{smallmatrix} g_1 \nearrow \boxed{\overline{a_1}}\xrightarrow{g_2}\bullet\boxed{\overline{a_2}}\xrightarrow{g_4}\bullet\boxed{\overline{a_3}}\xrightarrow{g_6}\bullet \\ \searrow \boxed{a_1}\xrightarrow{g_3}\bullet\boxed{a_3}\xrightarrow{g_5}\bullet\boxed{a_2}\xrightarrow{g_7}\bullet \end{smallmatrix}$. Only $reduce(a_1)$ is applicable because the other complementarily labeled edges do not share a common source vertex. The matching morphism g maps the edges labeled $a_1, \overline{a}_1$, resp. in $fr(a_1)$ to the a_1-labeled (resp. $\overline{a}_1$-labeled) edges in G; vertices are mapped respectively: $v_1 \mapsto g_1, v_2 \mapsto g_1, w'_1 \mapsto g_2, w_1 \mapsto g_3$. The morphism $h\colon C \to G$ exists (inclusion

morphism). Then $G \underset{reduce(a_1)}{\Longrightarrow} \begin{smallmatrix} [g_1]\bullet [g_2]\nearrow \boxed{\overline{a_2}}\xrightarrow{[q_4]}\bullet\boxed{\overline{a_3}}\xrightarrow{[q_6]}\bullet \\ \searrow \boxed{a_3}\xrightarrow{[g_5]}\bullet\boxed{a_2}\xrightarrow{[g_7]}\bullet \end{smallmatrix}$ where $g_2 \equiv g_3$. Afterwards, no further context-sensitive fusion rule is applicable.

Given a finite hypergraph, the set of all possible successive fusions is finite as fusion rules never create anything. To overcome this limitation, arbitrary multiplications of disjoint components within derivations are allowed. The generated language consists of the terminal part of all resulting connected components that contain no fusion symbols and at least one marker symbol, where marker symbols are removed in the end. These marker symbols allow us to distinguish between wanted and unwanted terminal components.

Definition 2. *A* context-sensitive fusion grammar *is a system* $CSFG = (Z, F, M, T, P)$ *where* $Z \in \mathcal{H}_{F \cup \overline{F} \cup T \cup M}$ *is a start hypergraph consisting of a finite number of connected components,* F *is a finite fusion alphabet,* M *with* $M \cap (F \cup \overline{F}) = \emptyset$ *is a finite set of* markers, T *with* $T \cap (F \cup \overline{F}) = \emptyset = T \cap M$ *is a finite set of* terminal labels, *and* P *is a finite set of context-sensitive fusion rules.*

A direct derivation $H \Longrightarrow H'$ *is either a context-sensitive fusion rule appli-* *cation* $H \underset{csfr}{\Longrightarrow} H'$ *for some csfr* $\in P$ *or a multiplication* $H \underset{m}{\Longrightarrow} m \cdot H$ *for some* *multiplicity* $m \colon \mathcal{C}(H) \to \mathbb{N}$. *A derivation* $H \overset{n}{\Longrightarrow} H'$ *of length* $n \geq 0$ *is a sequence* *of direct derivations* $H_0 \Longrightarrow H_1 \Longrightarrow \ldots \Longrightarrow H_n$ *with* $H = H_0$ *and* $H' = H_n$. *If* *the length does not matter, we may write* $H \overset{*}{\Longrightarrow} H'$.

$L(CSFG) = \{rem_M(Y) \mid Z \overset{*}{\Longrightarrow} H, Y \in \mathcal{C}(H) \cap (\mathcal{H}_{T \cup M} \setminus \mathcal{H}_T)\}$ *is the gener-* ated language *where* $rem_M(Y)$ *is the terminal hypergraph obtained by removing* *all hyperedges with labels in* M *from* Y.

Remark 2. Let $CSFG = (Z, F, M, T, P)$ *be a context-sensitive fusion grammar.* *If for every* $A \in F$ *a rule in* P *exists and every rule is context-free, then all rules* *are specified* F *and* $CSFG$ *is a fusion grammar as defined in* [2]. P *is obsolete.*

4   A Context-Sensitive Fusion Grammar for the Post Correspondence Problem

In this section, we model Post correspondence problems (PCPs) by means of context-sensitive fusion grammars in such a way that a PCP is solvable if the generated language of the corresponding grammar consists of a single vertex and that a PCP is not solvable if the language is empty. Therefore, it turns out that the emptiness problem and the membership problem for context-sensitive fusion grammars are undecidable.

The Post correspondence problem is defined as follow. Given a finite set of pairs $\{(u_1, v_1), (u_2, v_2), \ldots, (u_k, v_k)\}$ with $u_i, v_i \in \Sigma^*$ for some finite alphabet Σ. Does there exist a sequence of indices $i_1 \cdots i_n$ with $n > 0$ such that $u_{i_1} \cdots u_{i_n} = v_{i_1} \cdots v_{i_n}$? In terms of fusion, the pairs may be copied and fused in order to concatenate the strings. However, one needs a recognition mechanism to decide whether $u_{i_1} \cdots u_{i_n} = v_{i_1} \cdots v_{i_n}$ or not. This recognition procedure is expressible by means of context-sensitive fusion.

Construction 1. *Let* $S = \{(u_1, v_1), (u_2, v_2), \ldots, (u_k, v_k)\}$ *with* $k \in \mathbb{N}$, $u_i, v_i \in$ Σ^* *be an instance of PCP. Let* $F = \Sigma + \{A\}$ *be a fusion alphabet with* $\overline{A} \notin \Sigma$. *Let* $P = \{fr(A)\} \cup \{reduce(x) \mid x \in \Sigma\}$ *where* $reduce(x)$ *be as in Example 1. For* *each* $(a, b) \in \Sigma^* \times \Sigma^*$ *where* $a = a_1 \cdots a_n$ *and* $b = b_1 \cdots b_m$ *define* $init(a, b) =$

and $cont(a, b) =$

. *Let*

$A_\mu =$ *and* $Z_S = \sum_{(a,b) \in S} init(a, b) + cont(a, b) + A_\mu$. *Then* $CSFG(S) =$

$(Z_S, F, \{\mu\}, \emptyset, P)$ *is the to* S *corresponding context-sensitive fusion grammar.*

Theorem 1. *1.* $\bullet \in L(CSFG(S))$ *if and only if there exists a solution to* S. *2.* $L(CSFG(S))$ *is either* $\{\bullet\}$ *or* $\emptyset$.

Corollary 1. *The membership and the emptiness problem for context-sensitive* *fusion grammars are undecidable.*

The proof of the theorem is based on the following lemmata.

Lemma 1. *Let $G = dsg(u_1 \cdots u_n, \overline{u}_1 \cdots \overline{u}_n)$ be the hypergraph consisting of two string graphs $sg(u_1 \cdots u_n)$ and $sg(\overline{u}_1 \cdots \overline{u}_n)$ with $u_1, \ldots, u_n \in \Sigma$ where the first vertex of both string graphs is the same. i.e.,*

$$\begin{array}{c} \boxed{\overline{u}_1}\!\!\rightarrow\!\bullet\!\rightarrow \cdots \rightarrow\!\bullet\!\rightarrow\boxed{\overline{u}_n}\!\!\rightarrow\!\bullet \\ \blacktriangleleft \\ \boxed{u_1}\!\!\rightarrow\!\bullet\!\rightarrow \cdots \rightarrow\!\bullet\!\rightarrow\boxed{u_n}\!\!\rightarrow\!\bullet \end{array}. \text{ Then}$$

$G \overset{n}{\Longrightarrow} [n+1]$ by applying $reduce(u_1), \ldots, reduce(u_n)$, where $[n+1]$ denotes the discrete graph with $n+1$ vertices and no edges.

Proof. Induction base: $n = 0$. $dsg(\lambda, \lambda) = [1]$ because by definition $sg(\lambda)$ is the discrete graph $[1]$ by construction of dsg these two vertices are identified yielding the discrete graph $[1]$. Hence, $dsg(\lambda, \lambda) \overset{0}{\Longrightarrow} [1]$.

Induction step: Given $G = dsg(u_1 \cdots u_{n+1}, \overline{u}_1 \cdots \overline{u}_{n+1})$. Then $reduce(u_1)$ can be applied because by construction of $dsg(u_1 \cdots u_{n+1}, \overline{u}_1 \cdots \overline{u}_{n+1})$ the two complementary u_1- and $\overline{u}_1$-labeled hyperedges share a common source vertex yielding

$$G' = \bullet \blacktriangleleft \begin{array}{c} \boxed{\overline{u}_2}\!\!\rightarrow\!\bullet\!\rightarrow \cdots \rightarrow\!\bullet\!\rightarrow\boxed{\overline{u}_{n+1}}\!\!\rightarrow\!\bullet \\ \boxed{u_2}\!\!\rightarrow\!\bullet\!\rightarrow \cdots \rightarrow\!\bullet\!\rightarrow\boxed{u_{n+1}}\!\!\rightarrow\!\bullet \end{array} = [1] + dsg(u_2 \cdots u_{n+1}, \overline{u}_2 \cdots \overline{u}_{n+1})$$

. Then by induction hypothesis $G' \overset{n}{\Longrightarrow} [1] + [n+1] = [n+2]$. $\square$

Lemma 2. *Let $X_1 \underset{reduce(x)}{\Longrightarrow} X_2 \underset{fr(A)}{\Longrightarrow} X_3$ be a derivation in $CSFG(S)$. Then the two direct derivations can be interchanged yielding $X_1 \underset{fr(A)}{\Longrightarrow} X_2' \underset{reduce(x)}{\Longrightarrow} X_3$ for some X_2'.*

Proof. The statement follows directly from the fact that the two rules do not share fusion symbols such that they matches are hyperedge disjoint and that the context conditions of $reduce(x)$ only requires a commonly shared source for the two hyperedges. $\square$

Proof (of Theorem 1). Let $S = \{(u_1, v_1), (u_2, v_2), \ldots, (u_k, v_k)\}$. Let $i_1 \cdots i_n$ be a solution to S, i.e., $u_{i_1} \cdots u_{i_n} = v_{i_1} \cdots v_{i_n}$. Let $m_1, \ldots, m_k$ be the number of occurrences of (u_j, v_j) in the sequence except the first. Then there exists a derivation

$$Z_S \underset{m}{\Longrightarrow} init(u_{i_1}, v_{i_1}) + cont(u_{i_2}, v_{i_2}) + \ldots + cont(u_{i_n}, v_{i_n}) + A_\mu$$

$$\underset{fr(A)}{\overset{n-1}{\Longrightarrow}} init(u_{i_1} u_{i_2} \cdots u_{i_n}, v_{i_1} v_{i_2} \cdots v_{i_n}) + A_\mu \underset{fr(A)}{\Longrightarrow} \blacktriangleleft \begin{array}{c} \boxed{\overline{x}_1}\!\!\rightarrow\!\bullet\!\rightarrow \cdots \rightarrow\!\bullet\!\rightarrow\boxed{\overline{x}_w}\!\!\rightarrow\!\bullet\!\rightharpoondown \mu \\ \boxed{x_1}\!\!\rightarrow\!\bullet\!\rightarrow \cdots \rightarrow\!\bullet\!\rightarrow\boxed{x_w}\!\!\rightarrow\!\bullet \end{array}$$

$$\underset{reduce(x_1)}{\Longrightarrow} \cdots \underset{reduce(x_w)}{\Longrightarrow} [w] + \mu \circlearrowleft\bullet$$

where (1) $m(c) = 1$ for $c \in \{init(u_{i_1}, v_{i_1}), A_\mu\}, m(cont(u_j, v_j)) = m_j$ for $1 \leq j \leq k$ and $m(c) = 0$ otherwise; (2) the order in which the connected components are fused by applications of $fr(A)$ does not matter; (3) $x_1 \cdots x_w = u_{i_1} \cdots u_{i_n} = v_{i_1} \cdots v_{i_n}$ with $x_j \in \Sigma$ because $i_1 \ldots i_n$ is a solution to S; and (4) the two connected complementary strings graphs can be erased by successive applications of $reduce(x)$ for suitable x due to Lemma 1. Hence, $\bullet \in L(CSFG(S))$.

Now let $\bullet \in L(CSFG(S))$. Then there exists a derivation $Z_S \stackrel{*}{\Longrightarrow} X + \mu\,\text{⚬}\!\!\!\bullet$ for some hypergraph X. A_μ is the only connected component with marker in the start hypergraph, therefore, $\mu\,\text{⚬}\!\!\!\bullet$ must stem from A_μ. The only possibility to get rid of the A-hyperedge without attaching a new one is the application of $fr(A)$ to A_μ and some $init(x_1 x_2 \cdots x_{w_1}, y_1 y_2 \cdots y_{w_2})$ with $x_j, y_j \in \Sigma$ where the latter connected component is obtained from respective multiplications and the successive fusion wrt $fr(A)$ to some $init(u_{i_1}, v_{i_1}) + cont(u_{i_2}, v_{i_2}) + \ldots + cont(u_{i_n}, v_{i_n})$ for some n and possibly applications of $reduce(x)$ for suitable x. Due to Lemma 2 all the applications of $reduce(x)$ can be shifted behind the applications of $fr(A)$ and due to [2, Corollary 1] all the multiplications can be done as initial derivation step. To obtain $\mu\,\text{⚬}\!\!\!\bullet$ the two connected complementary strings graphs must be erased by successive applications of $reduce(x_1), \ldots, reduce(x_{w_1})$. If $x_1 \cdots x_{w_1}$ is a proper prefix of $y_1 \cdots y_{w_2}$, i.e., $y_1 \cdots y_{w_2} = x_1 \cdots x_{w_1} y_{w_1+1} \cdots y_{w_2}$, then one gets $\mu\,\text{⚬}\!\!\!\bullet\!\!\rightarrow\!\boxed{y_{w_1+1}}\!\rightarrow\!\bullet\!\rightarrow \cdots \rightarrow\!\bullet\!\rightarrow\!\boxed{y_{w_2}}\!\rightarrow\!\bullet$, and analogously if $y_1 \cdots y_{w_2}$ is a proper prefix of $x_1 \cdots x_{w_1}$, then one gets $\bullet\!\rightarrow\!\boxed{\overline{x}_{w_2+1}}\!\rightarrow\!\bullet\!\rightarrow \cdots \rightarrow\!\bullet\!\rightarrow\!\boxed{\overline{x}_{w_1}}\!\rightarrow\!\bullet\,\text{⚬}\,\mu$. This implies $w_1 = w_2$ and $y_i = x_i$ for $1 \leq i \leq w_1$ must hold. Because $x_1 \cdots x_{w_1} = u_{i_1} \cdots u_{i_n} = v_{i_1} \cdots v_{i_n}$ and $n > 0$, $i_1 \cdots i_n$ is a solution to S.

The second statement is a direct consequence of the first. Other connected components do not contribute to the language due to the lack of μ-hyperedges. $\square$

5   Transformation of Chomsky Grammars into Context-Sensitive Fusion Grammars

In this section, we prove that context-sensitive fusion grammars can generate all recursively enumerable string languages. For every Chomsky grammar one can construct a corresponding context-sensitive fusion grammar such that the generated languages of the corresponding grammars coincide up to representation.

Construction 2. *Let $G = (N, T, P, S)$ be a Chomsky grammar. Let $T' = \{t' \mid t \in T\}$. Then $CSFG(G) = (Z, \{Y_0, Y_1, X_0, X_1, X_2, X_3, c\} + N + T', \{\mu\}, T, R)$ is the corresponding context-sensitive fusion grammar where*

$$Z = dsg(X_0, Y_0)_\mu + Z_= + Z_P,\ dsg(X_0, Y_0)_\mu = \bullet\!\leftarrow\!\boxed{Y_0}\!\leftarrow\!\bullet\!\rightarrow\!\boxed{X_0}\!\rightarrow\!\bullet\,\text{⚬}\,\mu,$$

$$Z_= = sg(Y_1 \overline{ccc})_{\overline{Y_0}} + sg(\overline{c}S\overline{cc})_{\overline{Y_1}} + \sum_{x \in N \cup T \cup \{c\}} sg(\overline{x}Y_1\overline{x})_{\overline{Y_1}},$$

$$Z_P = \sum_{i=0}^{1} \sum_{x \in T} sg(x'X_i x)_{\overline{X_i}} + \sum_{\substack{u ::= v \in P, v \in T^* \\ u = u_1 \cdots u_n \\ v = v_1 \cdots v_m}} sg(u_1 \cdots u_n X_1 v_m \cdots v_1)_{\overline{X_0}}$$

$$+\ sg(cX_2ccc)_{\overline{X_1}} + \sum_{i=2}^{3} \sum_{x \in N \cup T} sg(xX_i x)_{\overline{X_i}} + \sum_{\substack{u ::= v \in P \\ u = u_1 \cdots u_n \\ v = v_1 \cdots v_m}} sg(u_1 \cdots u_n X_3 v_m \cdots v_1)_{\overline{X_2}}$$

$$+\ sg(cX_3c)_{\overline{X_2}} + sg(cc)_{\overline{X_3}}\quad and$$
$$R = \{fr(A) \mid A \in \{Y_0, Y_1, X_0, X_1, X_2, X_3\}\} \cup \{reduce(x) \mid x \in N \cup T' \cup \{c\}\}.$$

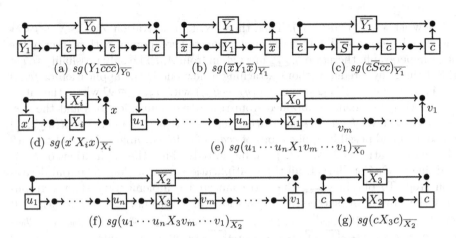

Fig. 1. Schematic drawings of some connected components of the start hypergraph of CSFG(G)

Schematic drawings of some connected components of the start hypergraph are depicted in Fig. 1.

Theorem 2. $L(CSFG(G)) = \{sg(w) \mid w \in L(G)\}$.

The proof is based on the following fact. We recall some details of the proof because we will refer to them in the proof of Theorem 2.

Fact 1. *Any recursively enumerable string language L_0 is left quotient of two linear languages $L_P, L_=$, i.e., $L_0 = L_P \backslash L_= = \{x \mid y \in L_P \wedge yx \in L_=\}$ (cf. [7, Theorem 3.13.]).*

Remark 3. $L_0 = rev(rev(L_0)) = rev(L(G)) = L_= \backslash L_P$, where $rev(L_0) = \{r(w) \mid w \in L_0\}$ where $r(w) = x_n \cdots x_1$ for $w = x_1 \cdots x_n$ and $G = (N, T, P, S)$ is a Chomsky grammar with $L(G) = rev(L_0)$.

$$L_= = \{z_m c \ldots c z_1 c S c c r(z_1) c \ldots c r(z_m) c c c \mid m \geq 1, z_i \in (N \cup T)^*, i = 1, \ldots, m\}$$
$$L_P = \{x_n u_n y_n c \ \ldots \ c x_1 u_1 y_1 c c r(y_1) r(v_1) r(x_1) c \ \ldots$$
$$\ldots \ c r(y_{n-1}) r(v_{n-1}) r(x_{n-1}) c c c r(y_n) r(v_n) r(x_n) \mid$$
$$n \geq 2, x_i, y_i \in (N \cup T)^*, u_i :: = v_i \in P, i = 1, \ldots, n-1, x_n v_n y_n \in T^*\}$$

where $c \notin N \cup T$. The basic idea is that for each $w \in L(G)$ exists a derivation $S = w_1 \rightarrow w_2 \rightarrow \cdots \rightarrow w_{n-1} \rightarrow w_n \rightarrow w_{n+1} = w$ with $w_i = x_i u_i y_i$ and

$w_{i+1} = x_i v_i y_i$ where $u_i:: = v_i \in P$ for $i = 1, \ldots, n$, i.e., $S = x_1 u_1 y_1 \to x_1 v_1 y_1 = x_2 u_2 y_2 \to \cdots \to x_{n-1} v_{n-1} y_{n-1} = x_n u_n y_n \to x_n v_n y_n = w$. $L_=$ captures the relation $x_i v_i y_i = x_{i+1} u_{i+1} y_{i+1}$ and L_P captures the relation $x_i u_i y_i \to x_i v_i y_i$.[1]

$L_=$ and L_P are linear. The following grammars generate them.

$$G_= = (\{Y_0, Y_1\}, N \cup T \cup \{c\}, P_=, Y_0) \text{ with}$$
$$P_= = \{Y_0:: = Y_1 ccc, Y_1:: = cScc\} \cup \{Y_1:: = xY_1 x \mid x \in N \cup T \cup \{c\}\}$$
$$G_P = (\{X_0, X_1.X_2, X_3\}, N \cup T \cup \{c\}, P_P, X_0) \text{ with}$$
$$P_P = \{X_0:: = xX_0 x \mid x \in T\} \cup \{X_0:: = uX_1 r(v) \mid u:: = v \in P, v \in T^*\}$$
$$\cup \{X_1:: = xX_1 x \mid x \in T\} \cup \{X_1:: = cX_2 ccc\}$$
$$\cup \{X_2:: = xX_2 x \mid x \in N \cup T\} \cup \{X_2:: = uX_3 r(v) \mid u:: = v \in P\}$$
$$\cup \{X_3:: = xX_3 x \mid x \in N \cup T\} \cup \{X_3:: = cX_2 c, X_3:: = cc\}.$$

Example 2. Let $G = (\{A\}, \{a.b\}, \{(A:: = aAb), (A:: = ab)\}, A)$. Then

$$G_= = (\{Y_0, Y_1\}, \{A, a, b, c\}, P_=, Y_0)$$
$$P_= = \{Y_0:: = Y_1 ccc, Y_1:: = cAcc \mid aY_1 a \mid bY_1 b \mid AY_1 A \mid cY_1 c\}$$
$$G_P = (\{X_0, X_1.X_2, X_3\}, \{A, a, b, c\}, P_P, X_0)$$
$$P_P = \{X_0:: = aX_0 a \mid bX_0 b \mid AX_1 ba\}$$
$$\cup \{X_1:: = aX_1 a \mid bX_0 b \mid cX_2 ccc\}$$
$$\cup \{X_2:: = aX_2 a \mid bX_2 b \mid AX_2 A \mid AX_3 bAa \mid AX_3 ba\}$$
$$\cup \{X_3:: = aX_3 a \mid bX_3 b \mid AX_3 A \mid cX_2 c \mid cc\}$$

Two derivations may be $X_0 \Longrightarrow aX_0 a \Longrightarrow aAX_1 baa \Longrightarrow aAbX_1 bbaa \Longrightarrow aAbcX_2 cccbbaa \Longrightarrow aAbcAX_3 bAacccbbaa \Longrightarrow aAbcAccbAacccbbaa = d$ and $Y_0 \Longrightarrow Y_1 ccc \Longrightarrow aY_1 accc \Longrightarrow aAY_1 Aaccc \Longrightarrow aAbY_1 bAaccc \Longrightarrow aAbcAccbAaccc = z$. Removing the prefix z from d yields $bbaa$.

Every context-free string grammars can be transformed into fusion grammars generating the same language up to representation of strings as graphs as the following construction shows.

Construction 3. *Let* $G = (N, T, P, S)$ *be a context-free string grammar. Then* $FG(G) = (sg_\mu(S) + \sum_{r \in P} hgr(r), N, \{\mu\}, T)$ *with* $sg_\mu(S) = \mu \circlearrowright \bullet \to \boxed{S} \to \bullet$, $hgr(r) = sg(u)_{\overline{A}}$ *for* $r = (A:: = u) \in P$ *and* $\mu \notin N \cup T$ *is the corresponding fusion grammar.*

---

[1] 1. W.l.o.g. assume $(S:: = S) \in P$ such that each derivation is of length ≥ 2.

2. For technical reasons each word contains the derivation twice, the middle is separated by cc, w_{n+1} is separated by ccc, the first is in reverse order and the second is reversed. This yields $w_n cw_{n-1} c \ldots cw_2 cw_1 ccr(w_2) cr(w_3) c \ldots cr(w_n) cccr(w_{n+1})$. String in L_P are of the form $d = (w_n cw_{n-1} c \ldots cw_2 cw_1 ccr(w_2) c \ldots cr(w_n) cccr(w_{n+1}))$, where $n \geq 2$, $w_i \to w_{i+1}$ in G and $w_{n+1} \in T^*$; and strings in $L_=$ are of the form $z = (z_m c \ldots cz_2 cScr(z_2) c \ldots cr(z_m) ccc)$, where $z_i \in (N \cup T)^*$. Therefore, $d = zz'$ for some z' if and only if $n = m + 1$, $S = w_1$, $z_i = w_i$ for $i = 1, \ldots, m$ and $z' = r(w_{n+1})$. Consequently, $r(w) = r(w_{n+1}) = r(y_n) r(v_n) r(x_n) \in L_= \backslash L_P$.

Example 3. Let $G = (\{A\}, \{a.b\}, \{r_1, r_2\}, A)$ with $r_1 = (A:: = aAb)$ and $r_2 = (A:: = ab)$. Then the rules are represented by $hgr(r_1) = sg(aAb)_{\overline{A}}$ and $(Z, \{A\}, \{\mu\}, \{a, b\})$ with $Z = sg_\mu(A) + sg(aAb)_{\overline{A}} + sg(ab)_{\overline{A}}$ is the corresponding fusion grammar.

Lemma 3. *1.* $L(FG(G)) = L(G)$.

2. A derivation $w_1 \to \cdots \to w_n$ *in* G *exists if and only if a derivation* $Z \underset{m}{\Longrightarrow} m \cdot$
     $\underset{r_1}{} \quad \underset{r_{n-1}}{}$
$Z = sg_\mu(w_1) + hgr(r_1) + \ldots + hgr(r_{n-1}) \Longrightarrow sg_\mu(w_2) + hgr(r_2) + \ldots + hgr(r_{n-1}) \Longrightarrow \ldots \Longrightarrow sg_\mu(w_n)$ *in* $FG(G)$ *exists.*

Proof. 1. Each context-free string grammar G can be transformed into a hyper-edge replacement grammar with connected right hand sides. Hence, the transformation of hyperedge replacement grammars into fusion grammars (cf. [2]) can be applied yielding $FG(G)$.

2. Proof by induction on the length of the derivation.   □

Remark 4. The connected components in the start hypergraphs of the context-sensitive fusion grammar in Construction 2 are hypergraph representation of the rules of the two linear string grammars (cf. Construction 3) slightly modified. The connected components in $Z_=$ are constructed for the linear rules in $G_=$ such that each symbol in $N \cup T \cup \{c\}$ is complemented and for each T-symbol the primed copy is used instead. The connected components for the linear rules in G_P containing X_0 and X_1 are constructed such that they contain fusion symbols left and terminal symbols right of the X_i-labeled hyperedge. Again for each terminal symbol the primed copy is used instead. The other connected components use the standard construction and are therefore only fusion symbol labeled (replacing also terminal symbols by their primed copy).

Proof (of Theorem 2). Let $w \in L(G)$. Then $w \in L_=\backslash L_P$ by Fact 1 and there are derivations in $G_=$ and G_P with $Y_0 \overset{*}{\to} u$ and $X_0 \overset{*}{\to} uw$ with $u = u_1 \cdots u_n$ and $w = w_1 \cdots w_m$. For each of these derivations exists by Lemma 3 a derivation in the corresponding fusion grammar $(FG(G_=), FG(G_P)$, resp. where $G_=$ and G_P are defined in Remark 3). Because the nonterminal alphabets of $G_=$ and G_P are disjoint and the connected component $dsg(X_0, Y_0)_\mu$ contains two hyperedges one labeled with each start symbol of the two linear string grammars there is a derivation

$$Z \overset{*}{\Longrightarrow} \boxed{\overline{u_1}} \to \bullet \leftrightarrow \cdots \to \bullet \leftrightarrow \boxed{\overline{u_n}} \to \bullet \atop \boxed{X_0} \to \bullet \multimap \mu \quad + Z_P \overset{*}{\Longrightarrow} \boxed{\overline{u_1}} \to \bullet \leftrightarrow \cdots \to \bullet \leftrightarrow \boxed{\overline{u_n}} \to \bullet \atop \boxed{u_1} \to \bullet \leftrightarrow \cdots \to \bullet \leftrightarrow \boxed{u_n} \to \bullet \leftrightarrow \cdots \underset{w_1 \qquad w_m}{\to \bullet \multimap \mu} = H$$

applying context-free fusion rules[2]. Then the two complementary strings graphs can be erased by successive applications of $reduce(x)$ for suitable x due to Lemma 1,

i.e., $\quad H \underset{reduce(u_1)}{\Longrightarrow} \cdots \underset{reduce(u_n)}{\Longrightarrow} \underset{w_1 \qquad w_m}{\bullet \to \cdots \to \bullet \multimap} \mu + [n]$. Consequently, $sg(w_1 \cdots w_m) \in L(CSFG(G))$.

---

[2] Applying first $fr(A)$ with $A \in \{Y_0, Y_1\}$ and then $A \in \{X_0, X_1, X_2, X_3\}$ is arbitrary. The rules may be applied in any order.

Now, let $X \in L(CSFG(G))$. Then there is a derivation $Z \overset{*}{\Longrightarrow} H$ with $X = rem_M(Y), Y \in \mathcal{C}(H) \cap (\mathcal{H}_{T \cup M} \setminus \mathcal{H}_T)\}$. Because only $dsg(X_0, Y_0)_\mu$ contains a μ-hyperedge this connected component is substantial for some derived connected component contributing to the generated language. W.l.o.g. one can assume that $dsg(X_0, Y_0)_\mu$ is never multiplied due to the following reasoning. Let C be a connected component derivable from Z. Let $\#_\mu \colon \mathcal{H}_\Sigma \to \mathbb{N}$ be a mapping of hypergraphs over Σ to the number of μ-labeled hyperedges in the respective hypergraph. Then $\#_\mu(C) \leq 1$, i.e., no two or more copies of $dsg(X_0, Y_0)_\mu$ contribute to C as the following reasoning indicates. For each $C \in \mathcal{C}(Z)$ $\#_\mu(C) \leq 1$ by construction. For each $C \notin \mathcal{C}(Z)$ assume $Z \overset{*}{\Longrightarrow} C_1 + C_2 + [k] \underset{r}{\Longrightarrow} C + [l]$ for some $k, l \in \mathbb{N}$ where C_1 and C_2 are two connected components and $\#_\mu(C_i) \geq 1$ for $i = 1, 2$. $\#_\mu(C_i) \geq 1$ implies $C_i \neq [1]$. Hence, $Z \overset{*}{\Longrightarrow} C_i, i = 1, 2$. Further, r must be a context-free fusion rule because the positive context conditions of $reduce(x)$ restrict that both hyperedges must be attached to a common source vertex which is not possible if C_1 and C_2 are two connected components. Let $fr(A)$ be the applied context-free fusion rule, $A \in \{Y_0, Y_1, X_1, X_2, X_3, X_4\}$. W.l.o.g. let A be the label of the hyperedge in C_1 and let $\overline{A}$ be the label of the hyperedge in C_2. Furthermore, it is sufficient to analyze the case $\#_\mu(C_i) = 1$ for $i = 1, 2$. However, $\#_\mu(C_i) = 1$ implies that $dsg(X_0, Y_0)_\mu$ contributes to C_i but because the linear structure of the rules in $P_=$ and P_P carries over to the connected components C_2 cannot contain both a μ- and a $\overline{A}$-labeled hyperedge. Hence, the assumption must be false.

The fusion rules wrt $Y_0, Y_1, X_0, X_1, X_2, X_3$ are context free and thus one connected component or two connected components with two complementarily labeled hyperedges from this subset can be fused arbitrarily. This may produce connected components without markers where all the hyperedges labeled with $Y_0, \overline{Y_0}, Y_1, \ldots, X_3, \overline{X_3}$ are fused. E.g. $sg(\overline{x}Y_1\overline{x})_{\overline{Y_1}}$ may be multiplied several times and all the complementary Y_1- and $\overline{Y_1}$-hyperedges can be fused yielding two circles. However this connected component is not fusible to some other connected component because now it is only labeled with fusion symbols $\{N \cup T \cup \{c\}\}$ but for these symbols the fusion is restricted to take only place if the two complementary hyperedges are attached to the same vertex. A similar argument can be applied to other cases wrt connected components with X_i-hyperedges.

The direct derivations steps can be interchanged[3] in such a way that one gets a derivation of the following form:

$$Z \underset{m}{\Longrightarrow} dsg(X_0, Y_0)_\mu + m' \cdot Z_= + m'' \cdot Z_P \qquad \text{for some multiplicities } m', m''$$

$$\underset{fr(A)}{\overset{*}{\Longrightarrow}} \quad \text{with } A \in \{Y_0, Y_1, X_0, X_1, X_2, X_3\}$$

$$\underset{reduce(u_1)}{\Longrightarrow} \cdots \underset{reduce(u_n)}{\Longrightarrow} \quad \mu + [n] = H.$$

---

[3] For the case of two context-free fusion rules see [2]; for the case involving $reduce$ see Lemma 2. All multiplications can be done initially (using the same argument as in [2]).

Hence, $Y = sg(w_1 \cdots w_m)_\mu$. The linear structure of the connected components gives us $w_1 \cdots w_m \in L(G)$. □

6 Conclusion

In this paper, we have continued the research on context-dependent fusion grammars. We have introduced context-sensitive fusion grammars and have showed that the Post correspondence problem can be formulated very intuitively by such a grammar. Afterwards, we have showed that every Chomsky grammar can be simulated by a corresponding context-sensitive fusion grammar. Hence, they can generate all recursively enumerable string languages (up to representation of strings as graphs). This improves the previous result presented in [5] showing that context-dependent fusion grammars (with positive and negative context-conditions) are another universal computing model. However, further research is needed including the following open question. Is it true, that fusion grammars without context-conditions are not universal? Are also only negative context conditions powerful enough to simulate Chomsky grammars? If so is also a single negative context-condition sufficient? One may also investigate fusion grammar with other regulations like priorities or regular expressions.

Acknowledgment. We are grateful to Hans-Jörg Kreowski and Sabine Kuske for valuable discussions. We also thank the reviewers for their valuable comments.

References

1. Adleman, L.M.: Molecular computation of solutions to combinatorial problems. Science **266**, 1021–1024 (1994)
2. Kreowski, H.-J., Kuske, S., Lye, A.: Fusion grammars: a novel approach to the generation of graph languages. In: de Lara, J., Plump, D. (eds.) ICGT 2017. LNCS, vol. 10373, pp. 90–105. Springer, Cham (2017). https://doi.org/10.1007/978-3-319-61470-0_6
3. Kreowski, H.-J., Kuske, S., Lye, A.: Relating DNA computing and splitting/fusion grammars. In: Guerra, E., Orejas, F. (eds.) ICGT 2019. LNCS, vol. 11629, pp. 159–174. Springer, Cham (2019). https://doi.org/10.1007/978-3-030-23611-3_10
4. Kreowski, H.-J., Kuske, S., Lye, A.: Transformation of petri nets into context-dependent fusion grammars. In: Martín-Vide, C., Okhotin, A., Shapira, D. (eds.) LATA 2019. LNCS, vol. 11417, pp. 246–258. Springer, Cham (2019). https://doi.org/10.1007/978-3-030-13435-8_18
5. Lye, A.: Transformation of turing machines into context-dependent fusion grammars. In: Post-Proceedings of 10th International Workshop on Graph Computation Models, (GCM 2019). Electronic Proceedings in Theoretical Computer Science (EPTCS) (2019). https://doi.org/10.4204/EPTCS
6. Post, E.L.: A variant of a recursively unsolvable problem. Bull. Am. Math. Soc. **52**, 264–269 (1946). https://doi.org/10.1090/s0002-9904-1946-08555-9
7. Păun, G., Rozenberg, G., Salomaa, A.: DNA Computing – New Computing Paradigms. Springer, Heidelberg (1998). https://doi.org/10.1007/978-3-662-03563-4

Cyclic Shift on Multi-component Grammars

Alexander Okhotin[1]([✉])[ID] and Alexey Sorokin[2,3][ID]

[1] St. Petersburg State University, Saint Petersburg, Russia
alexander.okhotin@spbu.ru
[2] Moscow State University, Moscow, Russia
alexey.sorokin@list.ru
[3] Moscow Institute of Physics and Technology, Dolgoprudny, Russia

Abstract. Multi-component grammars, known in the literature as "multiple context-free grammars" and "linear context-free rewriting systems", describe the structure of a string by defining the properties of k-tuples of its substrings, in the same way as ordinary formal grammars (Chomsky's "context-free") define properties of substrings. It is shown that, for every fixed k, the family of languages described by k-component grammars is closed under the cyclic shift operation. On the other hand, the subfamily defined by well-nested k-component grammars is not closed under the cyclic shift, yet their cyclic shifts are always defined by well-nested $(k + 1)$-component grammars.

1 Introduction

The cyclic shift operation on formal languages, defined as $\text{SHIFT}(L) = \{vu \mid uv \in L\}$ for a language L, is notable for several interesting properties. The closure of the class of regular languages under this operation is likely folklore, and proving it is a standard exercise in automata theory [2, Exercise 3.4(c)]. An interesting detail is that the cyclic shift incurs a huge blow-up in the number of states in a DFA, which is of the order $2^{n^2+n\log n - O(n)}$. [3,9] An analogous (quite an unobvious one) result for context-free grammars was first discovered by Maslov [10] and by Oshiba [12], and a direct construction of a grammar was later presented in the textbook by Hopcroft and Ullman [2, Exercise 6.4(c)]. In their proof, a grammar describing a language L is transformed to a grammar for the cyclic shift of L, and the transformation *turns the grammar inside out*, so that each parse tree in the new grammar simulates a parse tree in the original grammar, while reversing the order of nodes on one of its paths.

In contrast to this remarkable closure result, all noteworthy subfamilies of the ordinary grammars—that is, unambiguous, LR, LL, linear, input-driven, etc.—are not closed under the cyclic shift. A non-closure result for the linear conjunctive languages [11] was established by Terrier [17]. For conjunctive grammars [11], whether they are closed under the cyclic shift, remains an open

Research supported by Russian Science Foundation, project 18-11-00100.

A. Leporati et al. (Eds.): LATA 2020, LNCS 12038, pp. 287–299, 2020.
https://doi.org/10.1007/978-3-030-40608-0_20

problem. A summary of these results can be found in a fairly recent survey [11, Sect. 8.2].

This paper investigates the cyclic shift operation on one of the most well-known families of formal grammars, the *multi-component grammars*. These grammars describe the syntax of a string by defining the properties of k-tuples of its substrings, in the same way as ordinary formal grammars and their basic variants, such as conjunctive grammars, define properties of individual substrings. In their modern form, multi-component grammars were independently introduced by Seki, Matsumura, Fujii and Kasami [14] (as "multiple context-free grammars", MCFG), and by Vijay-Shankar, Weir and Joshi [18] (as "linear context-free rewriting systems", LCFRS). These grammars are subject to much ongoing research [1,7,8,19]. Also much attention is given to their special case: the *well-nested multi-component grammars*, in which all components of any intermediate k-tuple are listed in the order, in which they occur in the final string, and the grammar rules combine these k-tuples. This family is believed to correspond to the natural language syntax better than other grammar formalisms.

The first result of this paper is the closure of the language family defined by k-component grammars under the cyclic shift operation. The proof, presented in Sect. 3, proceeds by transforming an arbitrary k-component grammar to another k-component grammar describing the cyclic shift of the original language.

However, this construction does not preserve well-nestedness. A new construction adapted for well-nested grammars is presented in Sect. 4, and it incurs the increase of the number of components by one. In the final Sect. 5, it is shown that, whereas the language $\{a_1^m b_1^n c_1^n d_1^m \ldots a_k^m b_k^n c_k^n d_k^m \mid m, n \geqslant 0\}$ is defined by a well-nested k-component grammar, its cyclic shift is defined by no grammar from this class, and accordingly requires $k + 1$ components. This points out a peculiar difference between the general and the well-nested cases of multi-component grammars.

2   Multi-component Grammars

Definition 1. (Vijay-Shankar et al. [18]; Seki et al. [14]). *A multi-component grammar is a quintuple* $G = (\Sigma, N, \dim, R, S)$, *where*

- Σ *is the alphabet of the language being described;*
- N *is the set of syntactic categories defined in the grammar, usually called "nonterminal symbols";*
- $\dim \colon N \to \mathbb{N}$ *is a function that defines the number of components in each nonterminal symbol, so that if* $\dim A = k$, *then* A *describes* k-*tuples of substrings;*
- R *is a set of grammar rules, each of the form*

$$A(\alpha_1, \ldots, \alpha_{\dim A}) \leftarrow B_1(x_{1,1}, \ldots, x_{1,\dim B_1}), \ldots, B_\ell(x_{\ell,1}, \ldots, x_{\ell,\dim B_\ell}), \quad (*)$$

where $\ell \geqslant 0$, *the variables* $x_{i,j}$ *are pairwise distinct,* $\alpha_1, \ldots, \alpha_{\dim A}$ *are strings over symbols from* Σ *and variables* $x_{i,j}$, *and each variable* $x_{i,j}$ *occurs in* $\alpha_1 \ldots \alpha_{\dim A}$ *exactly once;*

- a nonterminal symbol $S \in N$ of dimension 1 is the "initial symbol", that is, the category of all well-formed sentences defined by the grammar.

A grammar is a logical system for proving elementary propositions of the form $A(w_1, \ldots, w_k)$, with $k = \dim A$ and $w_1, \ldots, w_k \in \Sigma^*$, meaning that the given k-tuple of strings has the property A. A proof proceeds using the rules in R, with each rule (*) treated as a schema for derivation rules, for any strings substituted for all variables $x_{i,j}$.

$$B_1(x_{1,1}, \ldots, x_{1,\dim B_1}), \ldots, B_\ell(x_{\ell,1}, \ldots, x_{\ell,\dim B_\ell}) \vdash A(\alpha_1, \ldots, \alpha_{\dim A})$$

The language generated by the grammar, denoted by $L(G)$, is the set of all such strings w that the proposition $S(w)$ can be derived in one or more such steps.

Whenever a string w is generated by G, the derivation of a proposition $S(w)$ forms a *parse tree*. Each node in the tree is labelled with a proposition $A(w_1, \ldots, w_k)$, where $k = \dim A$ and $w_1, \ldots, w_k$ are substrings of w. Every node has a corresponding rule (*), by which the proposition is derived, and the direct successors of this node are labelled with $B_1(x_{1,1}, \ldots, x_{1,\dim B_1})$, $\ldots$, $B_\ell(x_{\ell,1}, \ldots, x_{\ell,\dim B_\ell})$, as in the definition of a derivation step.

The dimension of a grammar, $\dim G$, is the largest dimension of a nonterminal symbol. A multi-component grammar of dimension k shall be called a k-component grammar.

A special case of these grammars are *well-nested multi-component grammars*, in which, whenever multiple constituents are joined in a single rule, their components cannot be intertwined, unless one's components are completely embedded within another's components. Thus, patterns such as $A(x_1 y_1, x_2 y_2) \leftarrow B(x_1, x_2)C(y_1, y_2)$ are prohibited.

Definition 2. A *multi-component grammar* is called *well-nested*, if every rule (*), satisfies the following conditions.

1. (non-permuting condition) For every i, the variables $x_{i,1}, \ldots, x_{i,\dim B_i}$ occur inside $\alpha_1 \ldots \alpha_{\dim A}$ in this particular order.
2. For all i, i' the concatenation $\alpha_1 \ldots \alpha_{\dim A}$ satisfies one of the following patterns:
   - $\ldots x_{i,d_i} \ldots x_{i',1} \ldots$
   - $\ldots x_{i',d_{i'}} \ldots x_{i,1} \ldots$
   - $\ldots x_{i,r} \ldots x_{i',1} \ldots x_{i',d_{i'}} \ldots x_{i,r+1} \ldots$

Example 1. A language $L = \{a^m b^n c^m d^n \mid m, n \in \mathbb{N}\}$ is defined by a 2-component grammar with the rules

$$S(x_1 y_1 x_2 y_2) \leftarrow A(x_1, x_2), B(y_1, y_2),$$
$$A(a x_1, c x_2) \leftarrow A(x_1, x_2),$$
$$B(b y_1, d y_2) \leftarrow B(y_1, y_2).$$

A well-nested 2-component grammar for the same language is

$$S(x_1x_2) \leftarrow A(x_1, x_2),$$
$$A(x_1, bx_2d) \leftarrow A(x_1, x_2),$$
$$A(x_1, x_2) \leftarrow B(x_1, x_2),$$
$$B(ax_1, cx_2) \leftarrow B(x_1, x_2).$$

A well-nested multi-component grammar can be transformed to the following form resembling the Chomsky normal form.

Proposition 1. ([15], Thm. 1). *Each well-nested k-component grammar is equivalent to a well-nested k-component grammar, in which all rules are of the following form.*

$$A(x_1, \ldots, x_{m-1}, x_m y_1, y_2, \ldots, y_n) \leftarrow B(x_1, \ldots, x_m), C(y_1, \ldots, y_n)$$
$$A(x_1, \ldots, x_i, x_i y_1, y_2, \ldots y_n x_{i+1}, x_{i+2}, \ldots, x_m) \leftarrow B(x_1, \ldots, x_m), C(y_1, \ldots, y_n)$$
$$A(a) \leftarrow$$
$$S(\varepsilon) \leftarrow$$

Rules of the first kind generalize the concatenation. The operation implemented in the rules of the second kind, defined for $i \in \{1, \ldots, m-1\}$, is known as **displacement** *or* **discontinuous product**.

A multi-component grammar of dimension 1 is an *ordinary grammar*, or "context-free" in Chomsky's terminology. A well-nested multi-component grammar of dimension 2 is known in the literature as a "head grammar" [13]; these grammars are equivalent in power to tree-adjoining grammars [4].

3   Cyclic Shift on k-component Grammars

Let G be a non-permuting k-component grammar, the goal is to construct a new k-component grammar G' that describes the language $\text{SHIFT}(L(G))$.

Whenever G generates a string w, G' should generate vu for every partition $w = uv$. Consider a parse tree of uv according to G, that is, a proof tree of the proposition $S(uv)$. Each node in the tree is labelled with a proposition $A(w_1, \ldots, w_k)$, where $k = \dim A$ and $w_1, \ldots, w_k$ are substrings of w. We call a node *split*, if one of its components w_s spans over the boundary between u and v, that is, contains both the last symbol of u and the first symbol of v.

In the proposed construction of a grammar for the cyclic shift, each split node $A(w_1, \ldots, w_k)$ is represented by another node of dimension k, which, however, specifies an entirely different k-tuple of strings. Consider that, whenever the original split node $A(w_1, \ldots, w_k)$ is used in a parse tree of a string uv, this string contains $w_1, \ldots, w_k$ as substrings, in any order. The corresponding node in the parse tree of vu according to the grammar for the cyclic shift shall contain all symbols of uv *except* the symbols in $w_1, \ldots, w_k$. For the moment, assume that $w_1, \ldots, w_k$ occur in uv in the order listed, and that some w_s spans over the boundary between u and v. Then, $uv = y_0 w_1 y_1 w_2 y_2 \ldots y_{k-1} w_k y_k$, and the symbols not in $w_1, \ldots, w_k$ are arranged into $k+1$ substrings $y_0, \ldots, y_k$. However, note that in the string vu generated by the new grammar, y_k and y_0 come concatenated as a single substring $y_k y_0$, and there is no need to represent them as separate components. Therefore, the new grammar can represent this split node $A(w_1, \ldots, w_k)$ by another node $\widetilde{A}(y_k y_0, y_1, \ldots, y_{k-1})$ of the same dimension k, where $\widetilde{A}$ is a new nonterminal symbol representing *the whole string with a gap for a k-tuple generated by A.*

To see how this transformation can be done, the structure of split nodes in the original parse tree ought to be examined, As long as $u \neq \varepsilon$ and $v \neq \varepsilon$, the root $S(uv)$ is split. Each split node has at most one split node among its immediate successors, because the last symbol of u and the first symbol of v cannot be in two successors at once. If a node is not split, then none of its successors are split. Thus, split nodes form a path in a parse tree, beginning in the root and ending somewhere inside the tree. This path shall be called the *main path*, and the new grammar G' retraces this path using the nonterminal symbols of the form $\widetilde{A}$.

In the original grammar, whenever a rule $A(\ldots) \leftarrow B(\ldots), C(\ldots)$ is used in one of the nodes on the main path, where B is the next node along the path, shorter substrings described by B are concatenated to something taken from C to form longer substrings described by A. In the new grammar, a nonterminal symbol $\widetilde{A}$ generates all symbols of the string *except* those generated by A, whereas $\widetilde{B}$ generates all symbols except the symbols generated by B. Therefore, $\widetilde{B}$ can be defined by a rule that partially fills the gap for A in $\widetilde{A}$, replacing it with a smaller gap for B in $\widetilde{B}$. This is achieved by a rule $\widetilde{B}(\ldots) \leftarrow \widetilde{A}(\ldots), C(\ldots)$. The node $\widetilde{B}$ is accordingly higher up than $\widetilde{A}$ in the parse tree of vu, and the main path of the original parse tree is retraced in the reverse direction. Each rule along the path is inverted, and the parse tree is effectively *turned inside out*.

Theorem 1. *For every k-component grammar G with n nonterminal symbols, there exists another k-component grammar with at most $(k! + 1)n$ nonterminal symbols that describes the language* SHIFT$(L(G))$.

Proof. Let $G = (\Sigma, N, \dim, R, S)$, The new grammar is defined as $G' = (\Sigma, N \cup \widetilde{N} \cup \{S'\}, \dim, R \cup R', S')$, where every new nonterminal symbol in $\widetilde{N}$ is of the form $\widetilde{A}_{p_1, \ldots, p_k}$, where $A \in N$ is a symbol of dimension k, and $(p_1, \ldots, p_k)$ is a permutation of $(1, \ldots, k)$; the dimension of this new symbol is also k.

Each symbol from N is defined in G' by the same rules as in G, and hence $L_{G'}(A) = L_G(A)$ for all $A \in N$. For each new symbol $\widetilde{A}_{p_1, \ldots, p_k}$ in $\widetilde{N}$, with $k = \dim A$, the intention is that it generates all such k-tuples $(w_0, \ldots, w_{k-1})$ that, for some partition $w_0 = v_0 u_0$, a proposition $S(u_0 x_{p_1} w_1 x_{p_2} w_2 \ldots w_{k-1} x_{p_k} v_0)$ can be derived using an assumption $A(x_1, \ldots, x_k)$. In other words, a k-tuple generated by $\widetilde{A}_{p_1, \ldots, p_k}$ is a string from $L(G)$ with k gaps, which should be filled by a k-tuple generated by A, Note that the components of $\widetilde{A}_{p_1, \ldots, p_k}(w_0, w_1, \ldots, w_{k-1})$ occur in the final string generated by the grammar G exactly in the given order, though w_0 is split into a suffix and a prefix. On the other hand, the components of $A(x_1,\ldots,x_k)$ may occur in the final string in $L(G)$ in any order, and this order is specified in the permutation $p_1,\ldots,p_k$.

The grammar G' has three kinds of rules for the new symbols. The **first** rule creates an empty string with one gap for a string generated by S.

$$\widetilde{S}_1(\varepsilon) \leftarrow \tag{1}$$

Indeed, using an assumption $S(x)$, one can derive $S(x)$ in zero steps.

For the **second** type of rules in G', consider any rule in G, which defines a symbol A of dimension k, and fix any nonterminal symbol B on its right-hand side. Let $y_1,\ldots,y_\ell$ be the variables of B. Denote the remaining nonterminal symbols referenced in this rule by $C_1,\ldots,C_q$.

$$A(\alpha_1,\ldots,\alpha_k) \leftarrow B(y_1,\ldots,y_\ell), C_1(\ldots),\ldots,C_q(\ldots)$$

For every i-th argument of A, consider all occurrences of variables $y_1,\ldots,y_\ell$ in α_i, and accordingly let $\alpha_i = \beta_{i,0} y_{r_{i,1}} \beta_{i,1} \ldots \beta_{i,m_i-1} y_{r_{i,m_i}} \beta_{i,m_i}$, where $m_i \geqslant 0$ is the number of these occurrences, $\beta_{i,j}$ are strings over the alphabet Σ and over the variables of $C_1,\ldots,C_q$, and $r_{i,j} \in \{1,\ldots,\ell\}$, for each i. Since each variable is referenced exactly once, $m_1+\ldots+m_k = \ell$ and $(r_{1,1},\ldots,r_{1,m_1},\ldots,r_{1,j},\ldots,r_{k,m_k})$ is a permutation of $(1,\ldots,\ell)$.

To see how to transform this rule, consider any proposition $\widetilde{A}_{p_1,\ldots,p_k}(w_0,w_1,\ldots,w_{w-1})$, where $(p_1,\ldots,p_k)$ is a permutation of $(1,\ldots,k)$. This symbol represents a full string generated by G, with a gap for A. If A is derived from B and $C_1,\ldots C_q$ using the above rule for A, then the substrings obtained from $C_1,\ldots,C_q$ partially fill the gaps for A, leaving smaller gaps for B. The resulting symbol $\widetilde{B}_{p'_1,\ldots,p'_\ell}$ has ℓ gaps for B, and the permutation $(p'_1,\ldots,p'_\ell)$ of $(1,\ldots,\ell)$ is defined by listing the numbers of the variables of B in the order they occur as gaps: the sequence $y_{r_{p_1,1}},\ldots,y_{r_{p_1,m_{p_1}}},\ldots,y_{r_{p_k,1}},\ldots,y_{r_{p_k,m_{p_k}}}$ is the same as $p'_1,\ldots,p'_\ell$.

The corresponding transformed rule in the new grammar has to fill the gaps in the right order. Let $z_0,z_1,\ldots,z_{w-1}$ be the variables of $\widetilde{A}_{p_1,\ldots,p_k}$. Then the circular sequence $z_0\alpha_{p_1}z_1\ldots z_{k-1}\alpha_{p_k}$ containing variables of $\widetilde{A}_{p_1,\ldots,p_k}$, B and $C_1,\ldots,C_j$ represents the entire string, and every occurrence of a variable of B becomes a gap in the new rule. Accordingly, the sequence between any two subsequent variables of B forms an argument of $\widetilde{B}_{p'_1,\ldots,p'_\ell}$. The first argument is the one containing z_0. The variables of B become gaps between the variables of $\widetilde{B}_{p'_1,\ldots,p'_\ell}$, and the resulting rule is defined as follows.

$$\widetilde{B}_{p'_1,\ldots,p'_\ell}(\beta_{p_k,m_{p_k}} z_0 \beta_{p_1,0},\ \beta_{p_1,1},\ \ldots,\ \beta_{p_1,m_{p_1}-1},\ \beta_{p_1,m_{p_1}} z_1 \beta_{p_2,0},\ \beta_{p_2,1},\ \ldots,$$
$$\beta_{p_{k-1},m_{p_{k-1}}-1},\ \beta_{p_{k-1},m_{p_{k-1}}} z_{k-1} \beta_{p_k,0},\ \beta_{p_k,1},\ \ldots,\beta_{p_k,m_{p_k}-1}) \leftarrow$$
$$\leftarrow \widetilde{A}_{p_1,\ldots,p_k}(z_0,\ldots,z_{k-1}), C_1(\ldots),\ldots,C_q(\ldots) \tag{2}$$

Rules of the **third** and the last type are defined for the initial symbol of the new grammar. They correspond to the bottom split node on the main path of the parse tree in G, where the last symbol of u and the first symbol of v

are finally assigned to different substrings. Denote the bottom split node by $A(x_1, \ldots, x_k)$, and let $u_0 x_{p_1} w_1 x_{p_2} w_2 \ldots w_{k-1} x_{p_k} v_0$ be the entire string generated by the original grammar. In the new grammar, the node $A(x_1, \ldots, x_k)$ is represented by a proposition $\tilde{A}_{p_1, \ldots, p_k}(v_0 u_0, w_1, \ldots, w_{k-1})$. Let x_{p_s}, with $s \in \{1, \ldots, k\}$, be the split component of $A(x_1, \ldots, x_k)$. The plan is to fill the gaps in $\tilde{A}_{p_1, \ldots, p_k}(v_0 u_0, w_1, \ldots, w_{k-1})$ with the symbols in the subtree of $A(x_1, \ldots, x_k)$. However, it is not possible to do this directly in a rule of the form $S'(\ldots) \leftarrow \tilde{A}_{p_1, \ldots, p_k}(\ldots), A(x_1, \ldots, x_k)$, because the component x_{p_s} is split.

Consider the rule used to derive $A(x_1, \ldots, x_k)$ in the new grammar, and let $C_1, \ldots, C_\ell$ be all nonterminal symbols on its right-hand side.

$$A(\alpha_1, \ldots, \alpha_k) \leftarrow C_1(\ldots), \ldots, C_q(\ldots)$$

The split component α_{p_s} generates a substring $x_{p_s} = \hat{x}_1 \hat{x}_2$, where the first part $\hat{x}_1$ is a suffix of u and the second part $\hat{x}_2$ is a prefix of v. Let $\alpha_{p_s} = \eta \theta$ be a partition of α_{p_s} into the symbols generating $\hat{x}_1$ and the symbols generating $\hat{x}_2$. Then the new grammar has the following rule, where the components of A are inserted into the gaps in $\tilde{A}_{p_1, \ldots, p_k}$, and the resulting string is cyclically shifted to begin in the middle of the component α_{p_s}.

$$S'(\theta z_s \alpha_{p_{s+1}} z_{s+1} \ldots z_{k-1} \alpha_{p_k} z_0 \alpha_{p_1} z_1 \ldots z_{s-2} \alpha_{p_{s-1}} z_{s-1} \eta) \leftarrow$$
$$\leftarrow \tilde{A}_{p_1, \ldots, p_k}(z_0, \ldots, z_{k-1}), C_1(\ldots), \ldots, C_q(\ldots) \qquad (3)$$

Overall, for every two strings u and v, the string uv is in $L(G)$ if and only if vu belongs to $L(G')$.

It can be easily observed that our construction does not preserve well-nestedness. Consider the well-nested rule $A(x_1, a x_2 b) \leftarrow A(x_1, x_2)$, by our construction it produces the rule $S'(a x_2 b y_2 x_1 y_1) \leftarrow A(x_1, x_2), \tilde{A}_{(12)}(y_1, y_2)$, which is not well-nested.

4 Cyclic Shift on Well-Nested k-component Grammars

The construction for the cyclic shift in the case of well-nested grammars is generally easier, since it does not involve turning parse trees inside out. All paths in the transformed trees continue in the same direction, at the expense of using one extra component. On the other hand, special care has to be taken to preserve the order of components and their well-nestedness.

Theorem 2. *If a language is defined by a well-nested k-component grammar, then its cyclic shift can be defined by a well-nested $(k+1)$-component grammar.*

Proof. Assume that all rules in the original grammar G are as in Proposition 1. If G defines a string $w = uv$, the new grammar G' should generate vu. In the parse tree of uv according to G, a node $A(w_1, \ldots, w_k)$ is *split*, if one of its components w_s spans over the boundary between u and v. Let $w_s = w_s' w_s''$, where u ends with

w'_s, and v begins with w''_s. Then, the new grammar shall have a new nonterminal symbol $\widehat{A}_s$, which defines a $(k+1)$-tuple $\widehat{A}_s(w''_s, w_{s+1}, \ldots, w_k, w_1, \ldots, w_{s-1}, w'_s)$.

For a non-split node, let $w_1, \ldots, w_s$ be in u and let $w_{s+1}, \ldots w_k$ be in v. Then the new grammar has a new nonterminal symbol A_s with defines a shifted k-tuple $A_s(w_{s+1}, \ldots, w_k, w_1, \ldots, w_s)$. In particular, the nonterminal $\widehat{S}_1$, where S is the initial symbol of G, generates the language $L_{G'}(\widehat{S}_1) = \{(v, u) \mid uv \in L, u, v \neq \varepsilon\}$. Adding a new initial nonterminal S' and the rules $S'(xy) \leftarrow \widehat{S}_1(x, y)$ and $S'(w) \leftarrow S_1(w)$ then yields the grammar for the language $\textsc{shift}(L(G))$. What remains is to equip the newly introduced nonterminals with the rules that match their definitions.

For each concatenation rule $A(x_1, \ldots, x_{m-1}, x_m y_1, y_2, \ldots, y_n) \leftarrow B(x_1, \ldots, x_m), C(y_1, \ldots, y_n)$ in the original grammar, first, there are $m + n - 1$ non-split shifts, which simply rotate the order of the components. They are using the rules below corresponding to different shifts; note that in each case one of B, C remains unshifted, and the other is shifted and wrapped around it.

$$A_i(x_{i+1}, \ldots, x_{m-1}, x_m y_1, y_2, \ldots, y_n, x_1, \ldots, x_i) \leftarrow$$
$$B_i(x_{i+1}, \ldots, x_m, x_1, \ldots, x_i), C(y_1, \ldots, y_n) \qquad (i < m)$$
$$A_{m+i}(y_{i+1}, \ldots, y_n, x_1, \ldots, x_{m-1}, x_m y_1, y_2, \ldots, y_i) \leftarrow$$
$$B(x_1, \ldots, x_m), C_i(y_{i+1}, \ldots, y_n, y_1, \ldots, y_i) \qquad (i \geqslant 1)$$

Secondly, the cyclic shift may split one of the components of this $(m + n - 1)$-tuple. This is implemented in $\widehat{A}_i$: then, one of B, C is unshifted, and the other is split. There are the following cases.

$$\widehat{A}_i(x''_i, x_{i+1}, \ldots, x_{m-1}, x_m y_1, y_2, \ldots, y_n, x_1, \ldots, x_{i-1}, x'_i) \leftarrow$$
$$\widehat{B}_i(x''_i, x_{i+1}, \ldots, x_m, x_1, \ldots, x_{i-1}, x'_i), C(y_1, \ldots, y_n) \qquad (i < m)$$
$$\widehat{A}_{m+i}(y''_i, y_{i+1}, \ldots, y_n, x_1, \ldots, x_{m-1}, x_m y_1, y_2, \ldots, y_{i-1}, y'_i) \leftarrow$$
$$B(x_1, \ldots, x_m), \widehat{C}_i(y''_i, y_{i+1}, \ldots, y_n, y_1, \ldots, y_{i-1}, y'_i) \qquad (1 \leqslant i \leqslant n)$$

Consider a displacement rule $A(x_1, \ldots, x_{j-1}, x_j y_1, \ldots y_n x_{j+1}, \ldots, x_m) \leftarrow B(x_1, \ldots, x_m), C(y_1, \ldots, y_n)$ in G, with $j \in \{1, \ldots, m - 1\}$. Again, there are non-split and split shifts. Non-split shifts fall into the following three cases.

$$A_i(x_{i+1}, \ldots, x_{j-1}, x_j y_1, y_2, \ldots y_n x_{j+1}, x_{j+2}, \ldots, x_m, x_1, \ldots, x_i) \leftarrow$$
$$B_i(x_{i+1}, \ldots, x_m, x_1, \ldots, x_i), C(y_1, \ldots, y_n) \qquad (i < j)$$
$$A_{j+i}(y_{i+1}, \ldots, y_n, x_{j+1}, \ldots, x_m, x_1, \ldots, x_i, y_1, y_2, \ldots, y_i) \leftarrow$$
$$B(x_1, \ldots, x_m), C_i(y_{i+1}, \ldots, y_n, y_1, \ldots, y_i) \qquad (1 \leqslant i \leqslant n)$$
$$A_{m-1+i}(x_{i+1}, \ldots, x_m, x_1, \ldots, x_j y_1, y_2, \ldots y_n x_{j+1}, \ldots, x_{i-1}) \leftarrow$$
$$B_i(x_{i+1}, \ldots, x_m, x_1, \ldots, x_i), C(y_1, \ldots, y_n) \qquad (i > j)$$

If one of the components is split, the corresponding rule for $\widehat{A}_i$ is one of the following.

$$\widehat{A}_i(x_i'', x_{i+1}, \ldots, x_j y_1, y_2, \ldots y_n x_{j+1}, \ldots, x_m, x_1, \ldots, x_{i-1}, x_i') \leftarrow$$
$$\widehat{B}_i(x_i'', x_{i+1}, \ldots, x_m, x_1, \ldots, x_{i-1}, x_i'), C(y_1, \ldots, y_n) \qquad (i < j)$$

$$\widehat{A}_{m+i}(y_i'', y_{i+1}, \ldots, y_n x_{j+1}, \ldots, x_m, x_1, \ldots, x_j y_1, \ldots, y_{n-1}, y_i') \leftarrow$$
$$B(x_1, \ldots, x_m), \widehat{C}_i(y_i'', y_{i+1}, \ldots, y_n, y_1, \ldots, y_{i-1}, y_i') \quad (1 \leqslant i \leqslant n)$$

$$\widehat{A}_i(x_i'', x_{i+1}, \ldots, x_m, x_1, \ldots, x_j y_1, y_2, \ldots y_n x_{j+1}, \ldots, x_{i-1}, x_i') \leftarrow$$
$$\widehat{B}_i(x_i'', x_{i+1}, \ldots, x_m, x_1, \ldots, x_{i-1}, x_i'), C(y_1, \ldots, y_n) \qquad (i > j)$$

A correctness proof for the construction proceeds by induction on the size of derivations in the respective grammars, formalizing the above explanations. $\square$

5   Number of Components in Well-Nested Grammars[1]

Theorem 2 shows how to represent the cyclic shift of a well-nested k-component grammar by a well-nested $(k+1)$-component grammar. On the other hand, without the well-nestedness restriction, a k-component grammar can be constructed by Theorem 1. The growth in the number of components is caused by keeping a split substring as two components. The question is, whether this weakness is an artefact of the construction, or is determined by the fundamental properties of well-nested grammars. In this section we prove, that for any $k \geqslant 2$, there exists a well-nested k-component grammar, whose cyclic shift lies outside this class; thus the result of the previous section cannot be strengthened.

As such a counterexample, we take a very simple language EmbBal$(2, k)$, containing all the strings of the form $a_1^m b_1^n c_1^n d_1^m \ldots a_k^m b_k^n c_k^n d_k^m$, with $m, n \geqslant 0$, which is defined by a well-nested k-component grammar (see Example 2). It is claimed that the cyclic shift of this language cannot be represented by a well-nested k-component grammar. Since this language family is closed under rational transductions, it suffices to demonstrate that the language NonEmbBal$(2, k) = \{a_1^m b_1^n c_1^n d_1^n \ldots a_k^m b_k^m c_k^n d_k^n \mid m, n > 0\}$ cannot be generated by a well-nested k-component grammar, because this language is obtained from CyclicShift(EmbBal$(2, k)$) by intersection with a regular language $b_1^+ \Sigma^* a_1^+$, and with a circular letter renaming $b_i \to a_i, c_i \to b_i, d_i \to c_i, a_i \to d_{i-1}, a_1 \to d_k$.

Example 2. The language EmbBal$(2, k)$, containing all the strings of the form $a_1^m b_1^n c_1^n d_1^m \ldots a_k^m b_k^n c_k^n d_k^m$, with $m, n \geqslant 0$, is defined by the following well-nested k-component grammar.

$$S(x_1 \ldots x_k) \leftarrow A(x_1, \ldots, x_k)$$
$$A(a_1 x_1 d_1, \ldots, a_k x_k d_k) \leftarrow A(x_1, \ldots, x_k)$$
$$A(x_1, \ldots, x_k) \leftarrow B(x_1, \ldots, x_k)$$
$$B(b_1 x_1 c_1, \ldots, b_k x_k c_k) \leftarrow B(x_1, \ldots, x_k)$$
$$B(\varepsilon, \ldots, \varepsilon) \leftarrow$$

---

[1] Most of the proofs are omitted due to space restrictions.

The definitions below are taken from Kanazawa [5].

Definition 3. *An* r*-pump* D *is a nonempty derivation of the form* $D\colon A(x_1,\ldots,x_r) \vdash A(y_1,\ldots,y_r)$.

Note that in case of a well-nested grammar in Chomsky normal form, $x_1\ldots x_r$ is a proper subsequence of $y_1\ldots y_r$. For each pump D, we define the sequence of its pumping strings: $\text{strings}(D) = \bigcup_{i=1}^{r}[w_{i,j}|y_i = w_{i,0}x_s w_{i,1}\ldots x_{s+t}w_{i,t}]$. For example, the derivation $A(x_1,x_2,x_3) \vdash A(ax_1bcx_2,a,bx_2)$ produces the pumping sequence $[a, bc, \varepsilon, a, b, \varepsilon]$. Informally, the pumping strings are maximal contiguous strings that the pump subtree injects into the derived string. It is easy to prove that the pumping sequence of an r-pump consists of exactly $2r$ strings.

Definition 4. *An even* r*-pump is a nonempty derivation of the form* $D\colon A(x_1,\ldots,x_r) \vdash A(u_1x_1v_1,\ldots,u_rx_rv_r)$.

Obviously, for an even pump D the pumping strings are $\text{strings}(D) = [u_1, v_1, \ldots, u_n, v_n]$.

We use the term "pump" not only for derivations, but also for derivation trees. Given a derivation tree, we call a letter occurrence *covered* if it occurs in the yield of some pump, and *evenly covered* if this pump is even.

In what follows we consider only grammars in the Chomsky normal form, as in Proposition 1. The following lemma is a mathematical folklore for context-free grammars, the proof for well-nested multicomponent grammars is the same.

Lemma 1. *For every language* L *defined by a well-nested grammar, there exists a number* p, *such that for every* $w \in L$ *at most* $p-1$ *letters are not covered.*

In the case of ordinary grammars (well-nested 1-component grammars), this lemma implies a weak version of the Ogden property [6,16] However, as shown by Kanazawa and Salvati [8], that is not the case for well-nested grammars of higher dimensions. Namely, the existence of an uneven pump does not imply the k-pumping lemma. However, in our case we may get rid of uneven pumps.

Definition 5. *A language is called bounded if it is a subset of the language* $a_1^+\ldots a_m^+$, *for some symbols* $a_1,\ldots,a_m \in \Sigma$. *A language is strictly bounded if all the symbols* $a_1,\ldots,a_m$ *are distinct.*

For a bounded language $L \subseteq a_1^+\ldots a_m^+$, its *decoration* is the language $\text{Dec}(L) = \{a_1^{r_1}\$_1 a_2^{r_2}\$_2 \ldots a_m^{r_m}|a_1^{r_1}a_2^{r_2}\ldots a_m^{r_m} \in L\}$. We call decorations of bounded languages *decorated bounded* and decorations of strictly bounded languages *decorated strictly bounded*. Obviously, $\text{Dec}(L)$ is rationally equivalent to L. Therefore, in what follows we consider the decorated strictly bounded language $\text{NonEmbBal}_D(2,k) = \text{Dec}(\text{NonEmbBal}(2,k))$.

Lemma 2. *Let* G *be a grammar in Chomsky normal form without useless nonterminals for a decorated strictly bounded language. Let* $\tau_L(w) = i$ *if* $w[0] \in \{a_i,\$_i\}$, *and* $\tau_R(w) = i$ *if* $w[-1] \in \{a_i,\$_{i-1}\}$ *(both functions are undefined for the empty string). Let* $A \vdash_G (u_1,\ldots,u_r)$ *and* $A \vdash_G (v_1,\ldots,v_r)$. *Then, for every* j, *it holds that*

1. *if $v_j \neq \varepsilon$ and $u_j \neq \varepsilon$, then $\tau_L(u_j) = \tau_L(v_j)$ and $\tau_R(u_j) = \tau_R(v_j)$;*
2. *if $u_j = \varepsilon$, then $v_j = a_i^k$ for some i and k.*

Lemma 3. *If there exists a well-nested k-component grammar for $\mathrm{NonEmbBal}_D(2, k)$ in Chomsky normal form without useless nonterminals, then its derivations contain only even pumps.*

The next result follows from the definition of well-nestedness by simple geometrical considerations.

Lemma 4. *Let $\vdash_G A(u_1, \ldots, u_r) \vdash_G S(w_0 u_0 w_1 \ldots u_r w_r)$ and $\vdash_G B(u'_1, \ldots, u'_s) \vdash_G S(w'_0 u'_0 w'_1 \ldots u'_s w'_s)$ be two derivations corresponding to the same derivation tree of the string $w = w_0 u_0 w_1 \ldots u_r w_r = w'_0 u'_0 w'_1 \ldots u'_s w'_s$. Then one of the following is the case:*

1. *$u_0 w_1 \ldots w_{r-1} u_r$ is a substring of $u'_0 w'_1 \ldots w'_{s-1} u'_s$.*
2. *$u'_0 w'_1 \ldots w'_{s-1} u'_s$ is a substring of $u_0 w_1 \ldots w_{r-1} u_r$.*
3. *$u_0 w_1 \ldots w_{r-1} u_r$ and $u'_0 w'_1 \ldots w'_{s-1} u'_s$ are two disjunct substrings of w.*

Informally speaking, the "continuous spans" of two constituents either are embedded or do not intersect. Now we are ready to prove our main theorem.

Theorem 3. *The language $L = \mathrm{NonEmbBal}_D(2, k)$ is not defined by any well-nested k-component grammar.*

Proof. Assuming the contrary, let such a grammar exist. Then, by Lemma 1, there exists a number p such that at most $p - 1$ letters in every string $w \in L$ are uncovered. For the string $w = a_1^p b_1^p c_1^p d_1^p \ldots a_1^p b_1^p c_1^p d_1^p \in L$, at least one c_1 in this string is covered by some pump D_1. By Lemma 3, this pump must be of the form

$$A(c_1^{m_1} d_1^{n_1}, \ldots, c_k^{m_k} d_k^{n_k}) \vdash A(c_1^{m_1+r} d_1^{n_1+r}, \ldots, c_k^{m_k+r} d_k^{n_k+r}) \vdash S(w)$$

for some nonterminal A, and natural numbers $m_j, n_j \geqslant 0$ and $r > 0$. By analogous arguments applied to the occurrences of a_1, we obtain another derivation

$$A(a_1^{m'_1} b_1^{n'_1}, \ldots, a_k^{m'_k} b_k^{n'_k}) \vdash A(a_1^{m'_1+r} b_1^{n'_1+r}, \ldots, a_k^{m'_k+r} b_k^{n'_k+r}) \vdash S(w).$$

However, the continuous spans of these two derivations contradict Lemma 4.

Theorem 4. *The family defined by well-nested k-component grammars is not closed under the cyclic shift.*

6   Conclusion

This paper has settled the closure under the cyclic shift for both general and well-nested multi-component grammars, as well as pointed out an interesting difference between these two grammar families. This contributes to the general knowledge on multi-component grammars.

This result has an interesting consequence: since the identity language of any group is closed under cyclic shift, and rational transformations preserve this closure property, no group identity language can be a rational generator of well-nested k-component grammars, for any $k \geqslant 2$. This is not the case for $k = 1$, where the Chomsky-Schützenberger theorem states that any such language can be obtained from the language D_2, that includes the words equal to 1 in a free group with two generators, by a composition of intersection with regular language and a homomorphism.

References

1. Clark, A., Yoshinaka, R.: An algebraic approach to multiple context-free grammars. In: Asher, N., Soloviev, S. (eds.) LACL 2014. LNCS, vol. 8535, pp. 57–69. Springer, Heidelberg (2014). https://doi.org/10.1007/978-3-662-43742-1_5
2. Hopcroft, J.E., Ullman, J.D.: Introduction to Automata Theory, Languages and Computation. Adison-Wesley, Reading (1979)
3. Jirásková, G., Okhotin, A.: State complexity of cyclic shift. RAIRO-Theoret. Inform. Appl. **42**(2), 335–360 (2008)
4. Joshi, A.K., Levy, L.S., Takahashi, M.: Tree adjunct grammars. J. Comput. Syst. Sci. **10**(1), 136–163 (1975)
5. Kanazawa, M.: The pumping lemma for well-nested multiple context-free languages. In: Diekert, V., Nowotka, D. (eds.) DLT 2009. LNCS, vol. 5583, pp. 312–325. Springer, Heidelberg (2009). https://doi.org/10.1007/978-3-642-02737-6_25
6. Kanazawa, M.: Ogden's lemma, multiple context-free grammars, and the control language hierarchy. Inf. Comput. (2019)
7. Kanazawa, M., Kobele, G.M., Michaelis, J., Salvati, S., Yoshinaka, R.: The failure of the strong pumping lemma for multiple context-free languages. Theory Comput. Syst. **55**(1), 250–278 (2014)
8. Kanazawa, M., Salvati, S.: Mix is not a tree-adjoining language. In: Proceedings of the 50th Annual Meeting of the Association for Computational Linguistics (Volume 1: Long Papers), pp. 666–674 (2012)
9. Maslov, A.N.: Estimates of the number of states of finite automata. Dokl. Akad. Nauk **194**(6), 1266–1268 (1970)
10. Maslov, A.N.: Cyclic shift operation for languages. Problemy Peredachi Informatsii **9**(4), 81–87 (1973)
11. Okhotin, A.: Conjunctive and Boolean grammars: the true general case of the context-free grammars. Comput. Sci. Rev. **9**, 27–59 (2013)
12. Oshiba, T.: Closure property of family of context-free languages under cyclic shift operation. Electron. Commun. Jpn **55**(4), 119–122 (1972)
13. Pollard, C.J.: Generalized phrase structure grammars, head grammars, and natural language. Ph.D. dissertation, Stanford University (1984)
14. Seki, H., Matsumura, T., Fujii, M., Kasami, T.: On multiple context-free grammars. Theoret. Comput. Sci. **88**(2), 191–229 (1991)
15. Sorokin, A.: Normal forms for multiple context-free languages and displacement Lambek grammars. In: Artemov, S., Nerode, A. (eds.) LFCS 2013. LNCS, vol. 7734, pp. 319–334. Springer, Heidelberg (2013). https://doi.org/10.1007/978-3-642-35722-0_23

16. Sorokin, A.: Ogden property for linear displacement context-free grammars. In: Artemov, S., Nerode, A. (eds.) LFCS 2016. LNCS, vol. 9537, pp. 376–391. Springer, Cham (2016). https://doi.org/10.1007/978-3-319-27683-0_26

17. Terrier, V.: Closure properties of cellular automata. Theoret. Comput. Sci. **352**(1–3), 97–107 (2006)

18. Vijay-Shanker, K., Weir, D.J., Joshi, A.K.: Characterizing structural descriptions produced by various grammatical formalisms. In: Proceedings of the 25th Annual Meeting on Association for Computational Linguistics, pp. 104–111. Association for Computational Linguistics (1987)

19. Yoshinaka, R., Kaji, Y., Seki, H.: Chomsky-Schützenberger-type characterization of multiple context-free languages. In: Dediu, A.-H., Fernau, H., Martín-Vide, C. (eds.) LATA 2010. LNCS, vol. 6031, pp. 596–607. Springer, Heidelberg (2010). https://doi.org/10.1007/978-3-642-13089-2_50

Languages

The Automatic Baire Property and an Effective Property of ω-Rational Functions

Olivier Finkel$^{(\boxtimes)}$ (iD)

Institut de Mathématiques de Jussieu - Paris Rive Gauche,
CNRS et Université Paris 7, Paris, France
Olivier.Finkel@math.univ-paris-diderot.fr

Abstract. We prove that ω-regular languages accepted by Büchi or Muller automata satisfy an effective automata-theoretic version of the Baire property. Then we use this result to obtain a new effective property of rational functions over infinite words which are realized by finite state Büchi transducers: for each such function $F : \Sigma^\omega \to \Gamma^\omega$, one can construct a deterministic Büchi automaton $\mathcal{A}$ accepting a dense $\mathbf{\Pi}_2^0$-subset of Σ^ω such that the restriction of F to $L(\mathcal{A})$ is continuous.

Keywords: Decision problems · Regular languages of infinite words · Infinitary rational relations · ω-rational functions · Topology · Automatic Baire property · Points of continuity

1 Introduction

Infinitary rational relations were first studied by Gire and Nivat [8, 10]. The ω-rational functions over infinite words, whose graphs are (functional) infinitary rational relations accepted by 2-tape Büchi automata, have been studied by several authors [1, 4, 16, 18].

In this paper we are mainly interested in the question of the continuity of such ω-rational functions. Recall that Prieur proved that one can decide whether a given ω-rational function is continuous [16, 17]. On the other hand, Carton, Finkel and Simonnet proved that one cannot decide whether a given ω-rational function f has at least one point of continuity [3]. Notice that this decision problem is actually Σ_1^1-complete, hence highly undecidable [6]. It was also proved in [3] that one cannot decide whether the continuity set of a given ω-rational function f (its set of continuity points) is a regular (respectively, context-free) ω-language. Notice that the situation was shown to be quite different in the case of *synchronous* functions. It was proved in [3] that if $f : A^\omega \to B^\omega$ is an ω-rational synchronous function, then the continuity set $C(f)$ of f is ω-rational. Moreover, if X is an ω-rational $\mathbf{\Pi}_2^0$ subset of A^ω, then X is the continuity set $C(f)$ of some rational synchronous function f of domain A^ω. Notice that these previous works on the continuity of ω-rational functions had shown that decision

© Springer Nature Switzerland AG 2020
A. Leporati et al. (Eds.): LATA 2020, LNCS 12038, pp. 303–314, 2020.
https://doi.org/10.1007/978-3-030-40608-0_21

problems in this area may be decidable or not, while it is well known that most problems about regular languages accepted by finite automata are decidable.

We establish in this paper a new effective property of rational functions over infinite words. We first prove that ω-regular languages accepted by Büchi or Muller automata satisfy an effective automata-theoretic version of the Baire property. Then we use this result to obtain a new effective property of rational functions over infinite words which are realized by finite state Büchi transducers: for each such function $F : \Sigma^\omega \to \Gamma^\omega$, one can construct a deterministic Büchi automaton $\mathcal{A}$ accepting a dense $\mathbf{\Pi}_2^0$-subset of Σ^ω such that the restriction of F to this dense set $L(\mathcal{A})$ is continuous.

The paper is organized as follows. We recall basic notions on automata and on the Borel hierarchy in Sect. 2. The automatic Baire property for regular ω-languages is proved in Sect. 3. We prove our main new result on ω-rational functions in Sect. 4. Some concluding remarks are given in Sect. 5.

2   Recall of Basic Notions

We assume the reader to be familiar with the theory of formal (ω)-languages [18,20]. We recall some usual notations of formal language theory.

When Σ is a finite alphabet, a *non-empty finite word* over Σ is any sequence $x = a_1 \ldots a_k$, where $a_i \in \Sigma$ for $i = 1, \ldots, k$, and k is an integer ≥ 1. The length of x is $|x| = k$. The *set of finite words* (including the empty word ε whose length is zero) over Σ is denoted $\Sigma^\star$.

The *first infinite ordinal* is ω. An *ω-word* over Σ is an ω-sequence $a_1 \ldots a_n \ldots$, where for all integers $i \geq 1$, $a_i \in \Sigma$. When σ is an ω-word over Σ, we write $\sigma = \sigma(1)\sigma(2)\ldots\sigma(n)\ldots$, where for all i, $\sigma(i) \in \Sigma$, and $\sigma[n] = \sigma(1)\sigma(2)\ldots\sigma(n)$.

The usual concatenation product of two finite words u and v is denoted $u \cdot v$ and sometimes just uv. This product is extended to the product of a finite word u and an ω-word v. The infinite word $u \cdot v$ is then the ω-word such that: $(u \cdot v)(k) = u(k)$ if $k \leq |u|$, and $(u \cdot v)(k) = v(k - |u|)$ if $k > |u|$. The concatenation product can be extended in an obvious way to the concatenation of an infinite sequence of finite words. The concatenation of a set U of finite words with a set V of infinite words is the set of infinite words $U \cdot V = \{u.v \mid u \in U \text{ and } v \in V\}$. If u is a finite word and V is a set of infinite words then $u \cdot V = \{u \cdot v \mid v \in V\}$.

The *set of ω-words* over the alphabet Σ is denoted by Σ^ω. An *ω-language* over an alphabet Σ is a subset of Σ^ω.

Definition 1. *A finite state machine (FSM) is a quadruple* $\mathcal{M} = (K, \Sigma, \delta, q_0)$, *where K is a finite set of states, Σ is a finite input alphabet, $q_0 \in K$ is the initial state and δ is a mapping from $K \times \Sigma$ into 2^K. A FSM is called deterministic iff: $\delta : K \times \Sigma \to \{\{q\} \mid q \in K\}$. (As usual, by a clear identification, we might consider in that case that $\delta : K \times \Sigma \to K$).*

A Büchi automaton (BA) is a 5-tuple $\mathcal{A} = (K, \Sigma, \delta, q_0, F)$ *where* $\mathcal{M} = (K, \Sigma, \delta, q_0)$ *is a finite state machine and $F \subseteq K$ is the set of final states.*

A Muller automaton (MA) is a 5-tuple $\mathcal{A} = (K, \Sigma, \delta, q_0, \mathcal{F})$ *where* $\mathcal{M} = (K, \Sigma, \delta, q_0)$ *is a FSM and $\mathcal{F} \subseteq 2^K$ is the collection of designated state sets.*

A *Büchi or Muller automaton is said to be deterministic if the associated FSM is deterministic.*

Let $\sigma = a_1 a_2 \ldots a_n \ldots$ be an ω-word over Σ.

A sequence of states $r = q_1 q_2 \ldots q_n \ldots$ is called an (infinite) run of $\mathcal{M} = (K, \Sigma, \delta, q_0)$ on σ, starting in state p, iff: 1) $q_1 = p$ and 2) for each $i \geq 1$, $q_{i+1} \in \delta(q_i, a_i)$.

In case a run r of $\mathcal{M}$ on σ starts in state q_0, we call it simply "a run of $\mathcal{M}$ on σ". For every (infinite) run $r = q_1 q_2 \ldots q_n \ldots$ of $\mathcal{M}$, In(r) is the set of states in K entered by $\mathcal{M}$ infinitely many times during run r: $\text{In(r)} = \{q \in K \mid \exists^\infty i \geq 1 \ q_i = q\}$.

For $\mathcal{A} = (K, \Sigma, \delta, q_0, F)$ a BA, the ω-language accepted by $\mathcal{A}$ is:
$L(\mathcal{A}) = \{\sigma \in \Sigma^\omega \mid \text{ there exists a run } r \text{ of } \mathcal{A} \text{ on } \sigma \text{ such that } \text{In(r)} \cap F \neq \emptyset\}$.
For $\mathcal{A} = (K, \Sigma, \delta, q_0, \mathcal{F})$ a MA, the ω-language accepted by $\mathcal{A}$ is:
$L(\mathcal{A}) = \{\sigma \in \Sigma^\omega \mid \text{ there exists a run } r \text{ of } \mathcal{A} \text{ on } \sigma \text{ such that } \text{In(r)} \in \mathcal{F}\}$.

By R. Mc Naughton's Theorem, see [15], the expressive power of deterministic MA (DMA) is equal to the expressive power of non deterministic MA which is also equal to the expressive power of non deterministic BA.

Theorem 2. *For any ω-language $L \subseteq \Sigma^\omega$, the following conditions are equivalent:*

1. *There exists a DMA that accepts L.*
2. *There exists a MA that accepts L.*
3. *There exists a BA that accepts L.*

An ω-language L satisfying one of these conditions is called a regular ω-language.

Recall that, from a Büchi (respectively, Muller) automaton $\mathcal{A}$, one can effectively construct a deterministic Muller (respectively, non-deterministic Büchi) automaton $\mathcal{B}$ such that $L(\mathcal{A}) = L(\mathcal{B})$.

A way to study the complexity of ω-languages accepted by various automata is to study their topological complexity.

We assume the reader to be familiar with basic notions of topology which may be found in [11,15,18]. If X is a finite alphabet containing at least two letters, then the set X^ω of infinite words over X may be equipped with the product topology of the discrete topology on X. This topology is induced by a natural metric which is called the *prefix metric* and is defined as follows. For $u, v \in X^\omega$ and $u \neq v$ let $\delta(u, v) = 2^{-l_{\text{pref}(u,v)}}$ where $l_{\text{pref}(u,v)}$ is the first integer n such that $u(n+1)$ is different from $v(n+1)$. The topological space X^ω is a Cantor space. The open sets of X^ω are the sets of the form $W \cdot X^\omega$, where $W \subseteq X^\star$. A set $L \subseteq X^\omega$ is a closed set iff its complement $X^\omega - L$ is an open set. Closed sets are characterized by the following:

Proposition 3. *A set $L \subseteq X^\omega$ is a closed set of X^ω iff for every $\sigma \in X^\omega$, $[\forall n \geq 1, \exists u \in X^\omega$ such that $\sigma[n] \cdot u \in L]$ implies that $\sigma \in L$.*

Define now the next classes of the Borel hierarchy:

Definition 4. *The classes* Σ_n^0 *and* Π_n^0 *of the Borel Hierarchy on the topological space* X^ω *are defined as follows:* Σ_1^0 *is the class of open sets of* X^ω, Π_1^0 *is the class of closed sets of* X^ω. *And for any integer* $n \geq 1$: Σ_{n+1}^0 *is the class of countable unions of* Π_n^0-*subsets of* X^ω, *and* Π_{n+1}^0 *is the class of countable intersections of* Σ_n^0-*subsets of* X^ω.

Remark 5. *The hierarchy defined above is the hierarchy of Borel sets of finite rank. The Borel Hierarchy is also defined for transfinite levels (see [11]) but we shall not need this in the sequel. Recall that the class of Borel subsets of a Cantor space is the closure of the class of open sets under countable unions and countable intersections.*

It turns out that there is a characterization of Π_2^0-subsets of X^ω, involving the notion of W^δ which we now recall, see [15,18].

Definition 6. *For* $W \subseteq X^\star$, *we set:* $W^\delta = \{\sigma \in X^\omega \mid \exists^\infty i \text{ such that } \sigma[i] \in W\}$. *($\sigma \in W^\delta$ iff σ has infinitely many prefixes in W.)*

Then we can state the following proposition.

Proposition 7. *A subset* L *of* X^ω *is a* Π_2^0-*subset of* X^ω *iff there exists a set* $W \subseteq X^\star$ *such that* $L = W^\delta$.

It is easy to see, using the above characterization of Π_2^0-sets, that every ω-language accepted by a deterministic Büchi automaton is a Π_2^0-set. Thus every regular ω-language is a finite Boolean combination of Π_2^0-sets, because it is accepted by a deterministic Muller automaton and this implies that it is a finite boolean combination of ω-languages accepted by deterministic Büchi automata.

Landweber studied the topological properties of regular ω-languages in [13]. He characterized the regular ω-languages in each of the Borel classes Σ_1^0, Π_1^0, Σ_2^0, Π_2^0, and showed that one can decide, for an effectively given regular ω-language L, whether L is in $\Sigma_1^0, \Pi_1^0, \Sigma_2^0$, or Π_2^0. In particular, it turned out that a regular ω-language is in the class Π_2^0 iff it is accepted by a deterministic Büchi automaton.

Recall that, from a Büchi or Muller automaton $\mathcal{A}$, one can construct some Büchi or Muller automata $\mathcal{B}$ and $\mathcal{C}$, such that $L(\mathcal{B})$ is equal to the topological closure of $L(\mathcal{A})$, and $L(\mathcal{C})$ is equal to the topological interior of $L(\mathcal{A})$, see [15,18].

3   The Automatic Baire Property

In this section we are going to prove an automatic version of the result stating that every Borel (and even every analytic) set has the Baire property.

We firstly recall some basic definitions about meager sets, see [11]. In a topological space $\mathcal{X}$, a set $A \subseteq \mathcal{X}$ is said to be *nowhere dense* if its closure $\bar{A}$ has empty interior, i.e. $\text{Int}(\bar{A}) = \emptyset$. A set $A \subseteq \mathcal{X}$ is said to be *meager* if it is the union of countably many nowhere dense sets, or equivalently if it is included in a countable union of closed sets with empty interiors. This means that A is meager if there exist countably many closed sets A_n, $n \geq 1$, such that $A \subseteq \bigcup_{n \geq 1} A_n$ where for every integer $n \geq 1$, $\mathrm{Int}(A_n) = \emptyset$. A set is *comeager* if its complement is meager, i.e. if it contains the intersection of countably many dense open sets. Notice that the notion of a *meager* set is a notion of a *small* set, while the notion of a *comeager* set is a notion of a *big* set.

Recall that a Baire space is a topological space $\mathcal{X}$ in which every intersection of countably many dense open sets is dense, or equivalently in which every countable union of closed sets with empty interiors has also an empty interior. It is well known that every Cantor space Σ^ω is a Baire space. In the sequel we will consider only Cantor spaces.

We now recall the notion of Baire property. For any sets $A, B \subseteq \Sigma^\omega$, we denote by $A \Delta B$ the symmetric difference of A and B, and we write $A =^\star B$ if and only if $A \Delta B$ is meager.

Definition 8. *A set $A \subseteq \Sigma^\omega$ has the Baire property (BP) if there exists an open set $U \subseteq \Sigma^\omega$ such that $A =^\star U$.*

An important result of descriptive set theory is the following result, see [11, page 47].

Theorem 9. *Every Borel set of a Cantor space has the Baire property.*

We are going to prove an automatic version of the above theorem. We first give the following definition.

Definition 10. *Let $L = L(\mathcal{A}) \subseteq \Sigma^\omega$ be a regular ω-language accepted by a Büchi or Muller automaton $\mathcal{A}$. The ω-language L is said to have the automatic Baire property if one can construct from $\mathcal{A}$ some Büchi automata $\mathcal{B}$ and $\mathcal{C}$ such that $L(\mathcal{B}) \subseteq \Sigma^\omega$ is open, $L(\mathcal{C}) \subseteq \Sigma^\omega$ is a countable union of closed sets with empty interior, i.e. a meager Σ_2^0-set, and $L(\mathcal{A}) \Delta L(\mathcal{B}) \subseteq L(\mathcal{C})$.*

We already know that the regular ω-languages have the Baire property since they are Borel. We now state the following theorem which gives an automatic version of this result.

Theorem 11. *Let $L = L(\mathcal{A}) \subseteq \Sigma^\omega$ be a regular ω-language accepted by a Büchi or Muller automaton $\mathcal{A}$. Then one can construct Büchi automata $\mathcal{B}$ and $\mathcal{C}$ such that $L(\mathcal{B}) \subseteq \Sigma^\omega$ is open, $L(\mathcal{C}) \subseteq \Sigma^\omega$ is a meager Σ_2^0-set, and $L(\mathcal{A}) \Delta L(\mathcal{B}) \subseteq L(\mathcal{C})$, i.e. the ω-language $L(\mathcal{A})$ has the automatic Baire property.*

In order to prove this result, we first prove the following lemmas.

Lemma 12. *Every regular ω-language which is open or closed has the automatic Baire property.*

Proof. Let $L = L(\mathcal{A}) \subseteq \Sigma^\omega$ be a regular ω-language accepted by a Büchi or Muller automaton $\mathcal{A}$.

If $L = L(\mathcal{A})$ is an open set then we immediately see that we get the result with $\mathcal{B} = \mathcal{A}$ and $\mathcal{C}$ is any Büchi automaton accepting the empty set.

If $L = L(\mathcal{A})$ is a closed set then $L \setminus \text{Int}(L)$ is a closed set with empty interior. Moreover it is known that one can construct from the Büchi automaton $\mathcal{A}$ another Büchi automaton $\mathcal{B}$ accepting $\text{Int}(L)$, and then also a Büchi automaton $\mathcal{C}$ accepting $L \setminus \text{Int}(L)$. Then we have $L(\mathcal{A})\Delta L(\mathcal{B}) = L \setminus \text{Int}(L) = L(\mathcal{C})$, with $L(\mathcal{B})$ open and $L(\mathcal{C})$ is a closed set with empty interior. $\qquad\square$

Lemma 13. *Every regular ω-language which is a Σ_2^0-set has the automatic Baire property.*

Lemma 14. *Let $L \subseteq \Sigma^\omega$ be a regular ω-language which has the automatic Baire property. Then its complement $\Sigma^\omega \setminus L$ has also the automatic Baire property.*

Lemma 15. *The class of regular ω-languages having the automatic Baire property is closed under finite union and under finite intersection.*

End of Proof of Theorem 11. We now return to the general case of a regular ω-language $L \subseteq \Sigma^\omega$, accepted by a Büchi or Muller automaton. We know that we can construct a deterministic Muller automaton $\mathcal{A} = (K, \Sigma, \delta, q_0, \mathcal{F})$ accepting L. Recall that $\mathcal{F} \subseteq 2^K$ is here the collection of designated state sets. For each state $q \in K$, we now denote by $\mathcal{A}^{(q)}$ the automaton $\mathcal{A}$ but viewed as a (deterministic) Büchi automaton with the single accepting state q, i.e. $\mathcal{A}^{(q)} = (K, \Sigma, \delta, q_0, \{q\})$. We know that the languages $L(\mathcal{A}^{(q)})$ are Borel Π_2^0-sets and thus satisfy the automatic Baire property by Lemmas 13 and 14. Moreover we have the following equality:

$$L(\mathcal{A}) = \bigcup_{F \in \mathcal{F}} [\bigcap_{q \in F} L(\mathcal{A}^{(q)}) \setminus \bigcup_{q \notin F} L(\mathcal{A}^{(q)})]$$

This implies, from the previous lemmas about the preservation of the automatic Baire property by Boolean operations, that we can construct Büchi automata $\mathcal{B}$ and $\mathcal{C}$, such that $L(\mathcal{B})$ is open and $L(\mathcal{C})$ is a meager Σ_2^0-set, which satisfy $L(\mathcal{A})\Delta L(\mathcal{B}) \subseteq L(\mathcal{C})$. Thus the ω-language L has the automatic Baire property. $\qquad\square$

Corollary 16. *On can decide, for a given Büchi or Muller automaton $\mathcal{A}$, whether $L(\mathcal{A})$ is meager.*

Proof. Let $\mathcal{A}$ be a Büchi or Muller automaton. The ω-language $L(\mathcal{A})$ has the automatic Baire property and we can construct Büchi automata $\mathcal{B}$ and $\mathcal{C}$, such that $L(\mathcal{B})$ is open and $L(\mathcal{C})$ is a countable union of closed sets with empty interiors, which satisfy $L(\mathcal{A})\Delta L(\mathcal{B}) \subseteq L(\mathcal{C})$. It is easy to see that $L(\mathcal{A})$ is meager if and only if $L(\mathcal{B})$ is empty, since any non-empty open set is non-meager, and it can be decided from the automaton $\mathcal{B}$ whether $L(\mathcal{B})$ is empty. $\qquad\square$

Remark 17. *The above Corollary followed already from Staiger's paper [19], see also [14]. So we get here another proof of this result, based on the automatic Baire property.*

4   An Application to ω-Rational Functions

4.1   Infinitary Rational Relations

We now recall the definition of infinitary rational relations, via definition by
Büchi transducers:

Definition 18. *A 2-tape Büchi automaton is a 6-tuple* $\mathcal{T} = (K, \Sigma, \Gamma, \Delta, q_0, F)$,
*where K is a finite set of states, Σ and Γ are finite sets called the input and the
output alphabets, Δ is a finite subset of $K \times (\Sigma \cup \varepsilon) \times (\Gamma \cup \varepsilon) \times K$ called the set
of transitions, q_0 is the initial state, and $F \subseteq K$ is the set of accepting states.
A computation $\mathcal{C}$ of the automaton $\mathcal{T}$ is an infinite sequence of consecutive transitions*

$$(q_0, u_1, v_1, q_1), (q_1, u_2, v_2, q_2), \ldots (q_{i-1}, u_i, v_i, q_i), (q_i, u_{i+1}, v_{i+1}, q_{i+1}), \ldots$$

*The computation is said to be successful iff there exists a final state $q_f \in F$
and infinitely many integers $i \geq 0$ such that $q_i = q_f$. The input word and output
word of the computation are respectively $u = u_1.u_2.u_3 \ldots$ and $v = v_1.v_2.v_3 \ldots$
The input and the output words may be finite or infinite. The infinitary rational
relation $R(\mathcal{T}) \subseteq \Sigma^\omega \times \Gamma^\omega$ accepted by the 2-tape Büchi automaton $\mathcal{T}$ is the set
of pairs $(u, v) \in \Sigma^\omega \times \Gamma^\omega$ such that u and v are the input and the output words
of some successful computation $\mathcal{C}$ of $\mathcal{T}$.*

*The 2-tape Büchi automaton $\mathcal{T} = (K, \Sigma, \Gamma, \Delta, q_0, F)$ is said to be synchronous
if the set of transitions Δ is a finite subset of $K \times \Sigma \times \Gamma \times K$, i.e. if each transition
is labelled with a pair $(a, b) \in \Sigma \times \Gamma$. An infinitary rational relation recognized by
a synchronous 2-tape Büchi automaton is in fact, via the natural identification
of $\Sigma^\omega \times \Gamma^\omega$ with $(\Sigma \times \Gamma)^\omega$, an ω-language over the product alphabet $\Sigma \times \Gamma$ which
is accepted by a Büchi automaton. It is called a synchronous infinitary rational
relation. An infinitary rational relation is said to be asynchronous if it can not
be recognized by any synchronous 2-tape Büchi automaton.*

Remark 19. *In the above definition, we could have defined the set of transitions
Δ as a subset of $K \times \Sigma^\star \times \Gamma^\star \times K$. We have chosen to define Δ as a finite subset
of $K \times (\Sigma \cup \varepsilon) \times (\Gamma \cup \varepsilon) \times K$ to simplify the proofs. However this is done without
loss of generality because it is easy to see that this convention does not change
the class of infinitary rational relations.*

If $R(\mathcal{T}) \subseteq \Sigma^\omega \times \Gamma^\omega$ is an infinitary rational relation recognized by the 2-tape
Büchi automaton $\mathcal{T}$ then we denote

$$Dom(R(\mathcal{T})) = \{u \in \Sigma^\omega \mid \exists v \in \Gamma^\omega \ (u, v) \in R(\mathcal{T})\}$$

and

$$Im(R(\mathcal{T})) = \{v \in \Gamma^\omega \mid \exists u \in \Sigma^\omega (u, v) \in R(\mathcal{T})\}.$$

It is well known that, for each infinitary rational relation $R(\mathcal{T}) \subseteq \Sigma^\omega \times \Gamma^\omega$, the
sets $Dom(R(\mathcal{T}))$ and $Im(R(\mathcal{T}))$ are regular ω-languages and that one can construct, from the Büchi transducer $\mathcal{T}$, some (non-deterministic) Büchi automata
$\mathcal{A}$ and $\mathcal{B}$ accepting the ω-languages $Dom(R(\mathcal{T}))$ and $Im(R(\mathcal{T}))$.

Recall now the following undecidability result of Frougny and Sakarovitch.

Theorem 20 ([7]). *One cannot decide whether a given infinitary rational relation is synchronous.*

We proved in [5] that many decision problems about infinitary rational relations are highly undecidable. In fact many of them, like the universality problem, the equivalence problem, the inclusion problem, the cofiniteness problem, the unambiguity problem, are Π_2^1-complete, hence located at the second level of the analytical hierarchy.

4.2   Continuity of ω-Rational Functions

Recall that an infinitary rational relation $R(\mathcal{T}) \subseteq \Sigma^\omega \times \Gamma^\omega$ is said to be functional iff it is the graph of a function, i.e. iff

$$[\forall x \in Dom(R(\mathcal{T}))\ \exists! y \in Im(R(\mathcal{T}))\ (x, y) \in R(\mathcal{T})].$$

Then the functional relation $R(\mathcal{T})$ defines an ω-rational (partial) function $F_\mathcal{T} : Dom(R(\mathcal{T})) \to \Gamma^\omega$ by: for each $u \in Dom(R(\mathcal{T}))$, $F_\mathcal{T}(u)$ is the unique $v \in \Gamma^\omega$ such that $(u, v) \in R(\mathcal{T})$.

An ω-rational (partial) function $f : \Sigma^\omega \to \Gamma^\omega$ is said to be synchronous if there is a synchronous 2-tape Büchi automaton $\mathcal{T}$ such that $f = F_\mathcal{T}$.

An ω-rational (partial) function $f : \Sigma^\omega \to \Gamma^\omega$ is said to be asynchronous if there is no synchronous 2-tape Büchi automaton $\mathcal{T}$ such that $f = F_\mathcal{T}$.

Recall the following previous decidability result.

Theorem 21 (Gire [9]). *One can decide whether an infinitary rational relation recognized by a given 2-tape Büchi automaton $\mathcal{T}$ is a functional infinitary rational relation.*

It is very natural to consider the notion of continuity for ω-rational functions defined by 2-tape Büchi automata.

We recall that a function $f : Dom(f) \subseteq \Sigma^\omega \to \Gamma^\omega$, whose domain is $Dom(f)$, is said to be continuous at point $x \in Dom(f)$ if :

$$\forall n \geq 1\ \ \exists k \geq 1\ \ \forall y \in Dom(f)\ \ [\ \delta(x, y) < 2^{-k} \Rightarrow \delta(f(x), f(y)) < 2^{-n}\ ]$$

The continuity set $C(f)$ of the function f is the set of points of continuity of f. Notice that the continuity set $C(f)$ of a function $f : \Sigma^\omega \to \Gamma^\omega$ is always a Borel Π_2^0-subset of Σ^ω, see [3].

The function f is said to be continuous if it is continuous at every point $x \in Dom(f)$, i. e. if $C(f) = Dom(f)$.

Prieur proved the following decidability result.

Theorem 22 (Prieur [16,17]). *One can decide whether a given ω-rational function is continuous.*

On the other hand the following undecidability result was proved in [3].

Theorem 23 (see [3]). *One cannot decide whether a given ω-rational function f has at least one point of continuity.*

The exact complexity of this undecidable problem was given in [6]. It is Σ_1^1-complete to determine whether a given ω-rational function f has at least one point of continuity.

We now consider the continuity set of an ω-rational function and its possible complexity. The following undecidability result was proved in [3].

Theorem 24 (see [3]). *One cannot decide whether the continuity set of a given ω-rational function f is a regular (respectively, context-free) ω-language.*

The situation is quite different in the case of *synchronous* functions. The following results were proved in [3].

Theorem 25 ([3]). *Let $f : A^\omega \to B^\omega$ be a rational synchronous function. The continuity set $C(f)$ of f is rational.*

Theorem 26 ([3]). *Let X be a rational $\mathbf{\Pi}_2^0$ subset of A^ω. Then X is the continuity set $C(f)$ of some rational synchronous function f of domain A^ω.*

We are now going to prove another effective result about ω-rational functions.

We first recall the following result of descriptive set theory, in the particular case of Cantor spaces Σ^ω and Γ^ω. A Borel function $f : \Sigma^\omega \to \Gamma^\omega$ is a function for which the inverse image of any Borel subset of Γ^ω, or equivalently of any open set of Γ^ω, is a Borel subset of Σ^ω.

Theorem 27 (see Theorem 8.38 of [11]). *Let Σ and Γ be two finite alphabets and $f : \Sigma^\omega \to \Gamma^\omega$ be a Borel function. Then there is a dense $\mathbf{\Pi}_2^0$-subset G of Σ^ω such that the restriction of f to G is continuous.*

We now state an automatic version of this theorem.

Theorem 28. *Let Σ and Γ be two finite alphabets and $f : \Sigma^\omega \to \Gamma^\omega$ be an ω-rational function. Then one can construct, from a 2-tape Büchi automaton accepting the graph of the function f, a deterministic Büchi automaton accepting a dense $\mathbf{\Pi}_2^0$-subset G of Σ^ω such that the restriction of f to G is continuous.*

Proof. Let Σ and Γ be two finite alphabets and $f : \Sigma^\omega \to \Gamma^\omega$ be an ω-rational function whose graph is accepted by a 2-tape Büchi automaton $\mathcal{A} = (K, \Sigma, \Gamma, \Delta, q_0, F)$.

Notice that one can also consider the 2-tape automaton $\mathcal{A}$ reading pairs of finite words $(v, u) \in \Sigma^\star \times \Gamma^\star$. A partial computation of the 2-tape automaton $\mathcal{A}$ reading such a pair (v, u) is simply a finite sequence of consecutive transitions

$$(q_0, a_1, b_1, q_1), (q_1, a_2, b_2, q_2), \ldots (q_{i-1}, a_i, b_i, q_i), (q_i, a_{i+1}, b_{i+1}, q_{i+1})$$

such that $v = a_1 a_2 \ldots a_{i+1}$ and $u = b_1 b_2 \ldots b_{i+1}$. This computation ends in state q_{i+1}.

We assume that we have an effective enumeration of the finite words over the alphabet Γ given by $(u_n)_{n \geq 1}$, $u_n \in \Gamma^*$. For $q \in K$ we also denote $\mathcal{A}_q$ the automaton $\mathcal{A}$ in which we have changed the initial state so that the initial state of $\mathcal{A}_q$ is q instead of q_0.

Let us now consider the basic open set of the space Γ^ω given by $U_n = u_n \cdot \Gamma^\omega$. We first describe $f^{-1}(U_n)$. An ω-word $x \in \Sigma^\omega$ belongs to the set $f^{-1}(U_n)$ iff x can be written in the form $x = v \cdot y$ for some words $v \in \Sigma^*$ and $y \in \Sigma^\omega$, and there is a partial computation of the automaton $\mathcal{A}$ reading (v, u_n) for which $\mathcal{A}$ is in state q after having read the initial pair $(v, u_n) \in \Sigma^* \times \Gamma^*$ (where the finite words v and u_n might have different lengths if the automaton $\mathcal{A}$ is not synchronous), and $y \in Dom(R(\mathcal{A}_q))$. Recall that $R(\mathcal{A}_q) \subseteq (\Sigma \times \Gamma)^\omega$ is an infinitary rational relation and that $Dom(R(\mathcal{A}_q))$ is then a regular ω-language and that one can construct from $\mathcal{A}$ a deterministic Muller automaton accepting this ω-language $Dom(R(\mathcal{A}_q))$ which will be denoted L_q. We also denote $T(u_n, q)$ the set of finite words v over Σ such that the automaton $\mathcal{A}$ may be in state q after having read the initial pair $(v, u_n) \in \Sigma^* \times \Gamma^*$. Then the following equality holds:

$$f^{-1}(U_n) = \bigcup_{q \in K} T(u_n, q) \cdot L_q$$

We can now apply the automatic Baire property stated in the above Theorem 11. Then for each regular ω-language L_q, one can construct a deterministic Muller automaton accepting an open set O_q and a deterministic Muller automaton accepting a countable union W_q of closed sets with empty interiors, such that for each $q \in K$,

$$L_q \Delta O_q \subseteq W_q$$

Now we set

$$V_n = \bigcup_{q \in K} T(u_n, q) \cdot O_q \quad \text{and} \quad F_n = \bigcup_{q \in K} T(u_n, q) \cdot W_q$$

Notice that each set $T(u_n, q)$ is countable and that for each finite word $u \in T(u_n, q)$ it is easy to see that the set $u \cdot O_q$ is open and that the set $u \cdot W_q$ is a countable union of closed sets with empty interiors. Thus it is easy to see that V_n is open, and that F_n is a countable union of closed sets with empty interiors. Moreover it is easy to see that V_n and F_n are regular ω-languages since each set $T(u_n, q)$ is a regular language of finite words over the alphabet Σ. Moreover it holds that:

$$f^{-1}(U_n) \Delta V_n \subseteq F_n$$

We now prove that $F = \bigcup_{n \geq 1} F_n$ is itself a regular ω-language. It holds that

$$F = \bigcup_{n \geq 1} F_n = \bigcup_{n \geq 1} \bigcup_{q \in K} T(u_n, q) \cdot W_q = \bigcup_{q \in K} \bigcup_{n \geq 1} T(u_n, q) \cdot W_q$$

Consider now the 2-tape automaton $\mathcal{B}_q$ which is like the 2-tape automaton $\mathcal{A}$ but reads only pairs of finite words in $\Sigma^* \times \Gamma^*$ and has the state q as unique accepting state. Let then $\mathcal{C}_q$ be a finite automaton which reads only finite words over the alphabet Σ and such that $L(\mathcal{C}_q) = \text{Proj}_{\Sigma^\star}(L(\mathcal{B}_q))$ is the projection of the language $L(\mathcal{B}_q)$ on $\Sigma^\star$. We can construct, from the automaton $\mathcal{A}$, the automata $\mathcal{B}_q$ and $\mathcal{C}_q$ for each $q \in K$. Now it holds that:

$$F = \bigcup_{n \geq 1} F_n = \bigcup_{q \in K} \bigcup_{n \geq 1} T(u_n, q) \cdot W_q = \bigcup_{q \in K} L(\mathcal{C}_q) \cdot W_q$$

On the other hand, for each finite word $u \in \Sigma^\star$, the set $u \cdot W_q$ is a meager Σ_2^0-set, since W_q is a meager Σ_2^0-set. Thus the set

$$F = \bigcup_{q \in K} L(\mathcal{C}_q) \cdot W_q$$

is also a countable union of closed sets with empty interiors, since K is finite and each language $L(\mathcal{C}_q)$ is countable. Moreover the ω-language F is regular and we can construct, from the automata $\mathcal{C}_q$ and from the deterministic Muller automata accepting the ω-languages W_q, a deterministic Muller automaton accepting F.

We can now set $G_n = \Sigma^\omega \setminus F_n$ and $G = \bigcap_{n \geq 1} G_n = \Sigma^\omega \setminus \bigcup_{n \geq 1} F_n = \Sigma^\omega \setminus F$. Then G is a countable intersection of dense open subsets of Σ^ω, hence also a dense $\mathbf{\Pi}_2^0$-subset G of Σ^ω. Moreover we can construct a deterministic Muller automaton and even a deterministic Büchi automaton (since G is a $\mathbf{\Pi}_2^0$-set, see [15, page 41]) accepting G. We can now see that the restriction f_G of the function f to G is continuous. This follows from the fact that the inverse image of every basic open set of Γ^ω by the function f_G is an open subset of G because for each integer $n \geq 1$, it holds that $f_G^{-1}(U_n) = f^{-1}(U_n) \cap G = V_n \cap G$. $\square$

Remark 29. *The above dense $\mathbf{\Pi}_2^0$-subset G of Σ^ω is comeager and thus Theorem 28 shows that one can construct a deterministic Büchi automaton accepting a "big" ω-rational subset of Σ^ω on which the function f is continuous.*

5   Concluding Remarks

We have proved a new effective property of ω-rational functions. We hope this property will be useful for further studies involving ω-rational functions. For instance an ω-automatic structure is defined via synchronous infinitary rational relations, see [2,12]. On the other hand, any (synchronous) infinitary rational relation is uniformizable by a (synchronous) ω-rational function, see [4]. Thus we can expect that our result will be useful in particular in the study of ω-automatic structures.

We also hope that the automatic Baire property will be useful in other studies involving regular ω-languages like the study of infinite games specified by automata.

References

1. Béal, M.P., Carton, O., Prieur, C., Sakarovitch, J.: Squaring transducers: an efficient procedure for deciding functionality and sequentiality. Theor. Comput. Sci. **292**(1), 45–63 (2003)
2. Blumensath, A., Grädel, E.: Finite presentations of infinite structures: automata and interpretations. Theory Comput. Syst. **37**(6), 641–674 (2004)
3. Carton, O., Finkel, O., Simonnet, P.: On the continuity set of an omega rational function. Theor. Inform. Appl. **42**(1), 183–196 (2008)
4. Choffrut, C., Grigorieff, S.: Uniformization of rational relations. In: Karhumäki, J., Maurer, H.A., Paun, G., Rozenberg, G. (eds.) Jewels are Forever, Contributions on Theoretical Computer Science in Honor of Arto Salomaa, pp. 59–71. Springer, Heidelberg (1999). https://doi.org/10.1007/978-3-642-60207-8_6
5. Finkel, O.: Highly undecidable problems for infinite computations. RAIRO-Theor. Inform. Appl. **43**(2), 339–364 (2009)
6. Finkel, O.: Three applications to rational relations of the high undecidability of the infinite Post correspondence problem in a regular ω-language. Int. J. Found. Comput. Sci. **23**(7), 1481–1498 (2012)
7. Frougny, C., Sakarovitch, J.: Synchronized rational relations of finite and infinite words. Theor. Comput. Sci. **108**(1), 45–82 (1993)
8. Gire, F.: Relations rationnelles infinitaires. Ph.D. thesis, Université Paris VII (1981)
9. Gire, F.: Two decidability problems for infinite words. Inf. Process. Lett. **22**(3), 135–140 (1986)
10. Gire, F., Nivat, M.: Relations rationnelles infinitaires. Calcolo **XXI**, 91–125 (1984)
11. Kechris, A.S.: Classical Descriptive Set Theory. Springer, New York (1995). https://doi.org/10.1007/978-1-4612-4190-4
12. Kuske, D., Lohrey, M.: First-order and counting theories of omega-automatic structures. J. Symb. Logic **73**(1), 129–150 (2008)
13. Landweber, L.: Decision problems for ω-automata. Math. Syst. Theory **3**(4), 376–384 (1969)
14. Michalewski, H., Mio, M., Skrzypczak, M.: Monadic second order logic with measure and category quantifiers. Logical Methods Comput. Sci. **14**(2) (2018)
15. Perrin, D., Pin, J.E.: Infinite Words, Automata, Semigroups, Logic and Games, Pure and Applied Mathematics, vol. 141. Elsevier, Amsterdam (2004)
16. Prieur, C.: How to decide continuity of rational functions on infinite words. Theor. Comput. Sci. **250**(1–2), 71–82 (2001)
17. Prieur, C.: How to decide continuity of rational functions on infinite words. Theor. Comput. Sci. **276**(1–2), 445–447 (2002)
18. Staiger, L.: ω-languages. In: Rozenberg, G., Salomaa, A. (eds.) Handbook of Formal Languages, vol. 3, pp. 339–387. Springer, Heidelberg (1997). https://doi.org/10.1007/978-3-642-59126-6_6
19. Staiger, L.: Rich ω-words and monadic second-order arithmetic. In: Nielsen, M., Thomas, W. (eds.) CSL 1997. LNCS, vol. 1414, pp. 478–490. Springer, Heidelberg (1998). https://doi.org/10.1007/BFb0028032
20. Thomas, W.: Automata on infinite objects. In: van Leeuwen, J. (ed.) Handbook of Theoretical Computer Science. Formal Models and Semantics, vol. B, pp. 135–191. Elsevier, Amsterdam (1990)

The Power of Programs over Monoids in J

Nathan Grosshans[1,2]([✉])

[1] DI ENS, ENS, CNRS, PSL University, Paris, France
nathan.grosshans@polytechnique.edu
[2] Inria, Paris, France
https://www.di.ens.fr/~ngrosshans/

Abstract. The model of programs over (finite) monoids, introduced by Barrington and Thérien, gives an interesting way to characterise the circuit complexity class NC^1 and its subclasses and showcases deep connections with algebraic automata theory. In this article, we investigate the computational power of programs over monoids in $\mathbf{J}$, a small variety of finite aperiodic monoids. First, we give a fine hierarchy within the class of languages recognised by programs over monoids from $\mathbf{J}$, based on the length of programs but also some parametrisation of $\mathbf{J}$. Second, and most importantly, we make progress in understanding what regular languages can be recognised by programs over monoids in $\mathbf{J}$. We show that those programs actually can recognise all languages from a class of restricted dot-depth one languages, using a non-trivial trick, and conjecture that this class suffices to characterise the regular languages recognised by programs over monoids in $\mathbf{J}$.

1 Introduction

In computational complexity theory, many hard still open questions concern relationships between complexity classes that are expected to be quite small in comparison to the mainstream complexity class P of tractable languages. One of the smallest such classes is NC^1, the class of languages decided by Boolean circuits of polynomial length, logarithmic depth and bounded fan-in, a relevant and meaningful class, that has many characterisations but whose internal structure still mostly is a mystery. Indeed, among its most important subclasses, we count AC^0, CC^0 and ACC^0: all of them are conjectured to be different from each other and strictly within NC^1, but despite many efforts for several decades, this could only be proved for the first of those classes.

In the late eighties, Barrington and Thérien [3], building on Barrington's celebrated theorem [2], gave an interesting viewpoint on those conjectures, relying on algebraic automata theory. They defined the notion of a program over a monoid M: a sequence of instructions (i, f), associating through function f some element of M to the letter at position i in the input of fixed length. In that way, the program outputs an element of M for every input word, by multiplying out the elements given by the instructions for that word; acceptance or rejection then depends on that outputted element. A language of words of arbitrary length

© Springer Nature Switzerland AG 2020
A. Leporati et al. (Eds.): LATA 2020, LNCS 12038, pp. 315–327, 2020.
https://doi.org/10.1007/978-3-030-40608-0_22

is consequently recognised in a non-uniform fashion, by a sequence of programs over some fixed monoid, one for each possible input length; when that sequence is of polynomial length, it is said that the monoid p-recognises that language. Barrington and Thérien's discovery is that NC^1 and almost all of its significant subclasses can each be exactly characterised by p-recognition over monoids taken from some suitably chosen variety of finite monoids (a class of finite monoids closed under basic operations on monoids). For instance, NC^1, AC^0, CC^0 and ACC^0 correspond exactly to p-recognition by, respectively, finite monoids, finite aperiodic monoids, finite solvable groups and finite solvable monoids. Understanding the internal structure of NC^1 thus becomes a matter of understanding what finite monoids from some particular variety are able to p-recognise.

It soon became clear that regular languages play a central role in understanding p-recognition: McKenzie, Péladeau and Thérien indeed observed [12] that finite monoids from a variety $\mathbf{V}$ and a variety $\mathbf{W}$ p-recognise the same languages if and only if they p-recognise the same regular languages. Otherwise stated, most conjectures about the internal structure of NC^1 can be reformulated as a statement about where one or several regular languages lie within that structure. This is why a line of previous works got interested into various notions of tameness, capturing the fact that for a given variety of finite monoids, p-recognition does not offer much more power than classical morphism-recognition when it comes to regular languages (see [8,10,11,13,14,20–22]).

This paper is a contribution to an ongoing study of what regular languages can be p-recognised by monoids taken from "small" varieties, started with the author's Ph.D. thesis [7]. In a previous paper by the author with McKenzie and Segoufin [8], a novel notion of tameness was introduced and shown for the "small" variety of finite aperiodic monoids $\mathbf{DA}$. This allowed them to characterise the class of regular languages p-recognised by monoids from $\mathbf{DA}$ as those recognised by so called quasi-$\mathbf{DA}$ morphisms and represented a first small step towards a new proof that the variety $\mathbf{A}$ of finite aperiodic monoids is tame. This is a statement equivalent to Furst's, Saxe's, Sipser's [6] and Ajtai's [1] well-known lower bound result about AC^0. In [8], the authors also observed that, while $\mathbf{DA}$ "behaves well" with respect to p-recognition of regular languages, the variety $\mathbf{J}$, a subclass of $\mathbf{DA}$, does, in contrast, "behave badly" in the sense that monoids from $\mathbf{J}$ do p-recognise regular languages that are not recognised by quasi-$\mathbf{J}$ morphisms.

Now, $\mathbf{J}$ is a well-studied and fundamental variety in algebraic automata theory (see, e.g., [15,16]), corresponding through classical morphism-recognition to the class of regular languages in which membership depends on the presence or absence of a finite set of words as subwords. This paper is a contribution to the understanding of the power of programs over monoids in $\mathbf{J}$, a knowledge that certainly does not bring us closer to a new proof of the tameness of $\mathbf{A}$ (as we are dealing with a strict subvariety of $\mathbf{DA}$), but that is motivated by the importance of $\mathbf{J}$ in algebraic automata theory and the unexpected power of programs over monoids in $\mathbf{J}$. The results we present in this article are twofold: first, we exhibit a fine hierarchy within the class of languages p-recognised by monoids from $\mathbf{J}$, depending on the length of those programs and on a parametrisation of $\mathbf{J}$;

second, we show that a whole class of regular languages, that form a subclass of dot-depth one languages [15], are p-recognised by monoids from **J** while, in general, they are not recognised by any quasi-**J** morphism. This class roughly corresponds to dot-depth one languages where detection of a given factor does work only when it does not appear too often as a subword. We actually even conjecture that this class of languages with additional positional modular counting (that is, letters can be differentiated according to their position modulo some fixed number) corresponds exactly to all those p-recognised by monoids in **J**, a statement that is interesting in itself for algebraic automata theory.

Organisation of the Paper. Following the present introduction, Sect. 2 is dedicated to the necessary preliminaries. In Sect. 3, we present the results about the fine hierarchy and in Sect. 4 we expose the results concerning the regular languages p-recognised by monoids from **J**. Section 5 gives a short conclusion.

Note. This article is based on unpublished parts of the author's Ph.D. thesis [7].

2 Preliminaries

2.1 Various Mathematical Materials

We assume the reader is familiar with the basics of formal language theory, semigroup theory and recognition by morphisms, that we might designate by classical recognition; for those, we only specify some things and refer the reader to the two classical references of the domain by Eilenberg [4,5] and Pin [16].

General Notations and Conventions. Let $i, j \in \mathbb{N}$. We shall denote by $[\![i, j]\!]$ the set of all $n \in \mathbb{N}$ verifying $i \leq n \leq j$. We shall also denote by $[i]$ the set $[\![1, i]\!]$. Given some set E, we shall denote by $\mathfrak{P}(E)$ the powerset of E. All our alphabets and words will always be finite; the empty word will be denoted by ε.

Varieties and Languages. A *variety of monoids* is a class of finite monoids closed under submonoids, Cartesian product and morphic images. A *variety of semigroups* is defined similarly. When dealing with varieties, we consider only finite monoids and semigroups, each having an *idempotent power*, a smallest $\omega \in \mathbb{N}_{>0}$ such that $x^{\omega} = x^{2\omega}$ for any element x. To give an example, the variety of finite aperiodic monoids, denoted by **A**, contains all finite monoids M such that, given ω its idempotent power, $x^{\omega} = x^{\omega+1}$ for all $x \in M$.

To each variety **V** of monoids or semigroups we associate the class $\mathcal{L}(\mathbf{V})$ of languages such that, respectively, their syntactic monoid or semigroup belongs to **V**. For instance, $\mathcal{L}(\mathbf{A})$ is well-known to be the class of star-free languages.

*Quasi **V** Languages.* If S is a semigroup we denote by S^1 the monoid S if S is already a monoid and $S \cup \{1\}$ otherwise.

The following definitions are taken from [17]. Let φ be a surjective morphism from Σ^* to a finite monoid M. For all k consider the subset $\varphi(\Sigma^k)$ of M (where

Σ^k is the set of words over Σ of length k). As M is finite there is a k such that $\varphi(\Sigma^{2k}) = \varphi(\Sigma^k)$. This implies that $\varphi(\Sigma^k)$ is a semigroup. The semigroup given by the smallest such k is called the *stable semigroup of* φ. If S is the stable semigroup of φ, S^1 is called *the stable monoid of* φ. If $\mathbf{V}$ is a variety of monoids or semigroups, then we shall denote by $\mathbf{QV}$ the class of such surjective morphisms whose stable monoid or semigroup, respectively, is in $\mathbf{V}$ and by $\mathcal{L}(\mathbf{QV})$ the class of languages whose syntactic morphism is in $\mathbf{QV}$.

Programs over Monoids. Programs over monoids form a non-uniform model of computation, first defined by Barrington and Thérien [3], extending Barrington's permutation branching program model [2]. Let M be a finite monoid and Σ an alphabet. A *program P over M on Σ^n* is a finite sequence of instructions of the form (i, f) where $i \in [n]$ and $f \in M^\Sigma$; said otherwise, it is a word over $([n] \times M^\Sigma)$. The *length* of P, denoted by $|P|$, is the number of its instructions. The program P defines a function from Σ^n to M as follows. On input $w \in \Sigma^n$, each instruction (i, f) outputs the monoid element $f(w_i)$. A sequence of instructions then yields a sequence of elements of M and their product is the output $P(w)$ of the program. A language $L \subseteq \Sigma^n$ is consequently recognised by P whenever there exists $F \subseteq M$ such that $L = P^{-1}(F)$.

A language L over Σ is *recognised* by a sequence of programs $(P_n)_{n \in \mathbb{N}}$ over some finite monoid M if for each n, the program P_n is on Σ^n and recognises $L^{=n} = L \cap \Sigma^n$. We say $(P_n)_{n \in \mathbb{N}}$ is of length $s(n)$ for $s \colon \mathbb{N} \to \mathbb{N}$ whenever $|P_n| = s(n)$ for all $n \in \mathbb{N}$ and that it is of length at most $s(n)$ whenever there exists $\alpha \in \mathbb{R}_{>0}$ verifying $|P_n| \leq \alpha \cdot s(n)$ for all $n \in \mathbb{N}$.

For $s \colon \mathbb{N} \to \mathbb{N}$ and $\mathbf{V}$ a variety of monoids, we denote by $\mathcal{P}(\mathbf{V}, s(n))$ the class of languages recognised by sequences of programs over monoids in $\mathbf{V}$ of length at most $s(n)$. The class $\mathcal{P}(\mathbf{V}) = \bigcup_{k \in \mathbb{N}} \mathcal{P}(\mathbf{V}, n^k)$ is then the class of languages p-recognised by a monoid in $\mathbf{V}$, i.e. recognised by sequences of programs over monoids in $\mathbf{V}$ of polynomial length.

The following is an important property of $\mathcal{P}(\mathbf{V})$.

Proposition 1 ([12, **Corollary 3.5**]). *Let $\mathbf{V}$ be a variety of monoids, then $\mathcal{P}(\mathbf{V})$ is closed under Boolean operations.*

Given two alphabets Σ and Γ, a Γ-program on Σ^n for $n \in \mathbb{N}$ is defined just like a program over some finite monoid M on Σ^n, except that instructions output letters from Γ and thus that the program outputs words over Γ. Let now $L \subseteq \Sigma^*$ and $K \subseteq \Gamma^*$. We say that L *program-reduces to* K if and only if there exists a sequence $(\Psi_n)_{n \in \mathbb{N}}$ of Γ-programs (the program-reduction) such that Ψ_n is on Σ^n and $L^{=n} = \Psi_n^{-1}(K^{=|\Psi_n|})$ for each $n \in \mathbb{N}$. The following proposition shows closure of $\mathcal{P}(\mathbf{V})$ also under program-reductions.

Proposition 2 ([7, **Proposition 3.3.12 and Corollary 3.4.3**]). *Let Σ and Γ be two alphabets. Let $\mathbf{V}$ be a variety of monoids. Given $K \subseteq \Gamma^*$ in $\mathcal{P}(\mathbf{V}, s(n))$ for $s \colon \mathbb{N} \to \mathbb{N}$ and $L \subseteq \Sigma^*$ from which there exists a program-reduction to K of length $t(n)$, for $t \colon \mathbb{N} \to \mathbb{N}$, we have that $L \in \mathcal{P}(\mathbf{V}, s(t(n)))$. In particular, when K is recognised (classically) by a monoid in $\mathbf{V}$, we have that $L \in \mathcal{P}(\mathbf{V}, t(n))$.*

2.2   Tameness and the Variety J

We won't introduce any of the proposed notions of tameness but will only state that the main consequence for a variety of monoids **V** to be tame in the sense of [8] is that $\mathcal{P}(\mathbf{V}) \cap \mathcal{R}eg \subseteq \mathcal{L}(\mathbf{QV})$. This consequence has far-reaching implications from a computational-complexity-theoretic standpoint when $\mathcal{P}(\mathbf{V})$ happens to be equal to a circuit complexity class. For instance, tameness for **A** implies that $\mathcal{P}(\mathbf{A}) \cap \mathcal{R}eg \subseteq \mathcal{L}(\mathbf{QA})$, which is equivalent to the fact that AC^0 does not contain the language MOD_m of words over $\{0,1\}$ containing a number of 1s not divisible by m for any $m \in \mathbb{N}, m \geq 2$ (a central result in complexity theory [1,6]).

Let us now define the variety of monoids **J**. A finite monoid M of idempotent power ω belongs to **J** if and only if $(xy)^{\omega} = (xy)^{\omega}x = y(xy)^{\omega}$ for all $x, y \in M$. It is a strict subvariety of the variety **DA**, containing all finite monoids M of idempotent power ω such that $(xy)^{\omega} = (xy)^{\omega}x(xy)^{\omega}$ for all $x, y \in M$, itself a strict subvariety of **A**. The variety **J** is a "small" one, well within **A**.

We now give some specific definitions and results about **J** that we will use, based essentially on [9], but also on [16, Chapter 4, Section 1].

For some alphabet Σ and each $k \in \mathbb{N}$, let us define the equivalence relation $\sim_k$ on Σ^* by $u \sim_k v$ if and only if u and v have the same set of k-subwords (subwords of length at most k), for all $u, v \in \Sigma^*$. The relation $\sim_k$ is a congruence of finite index on Σ^*. For an alphabet Σ and a word $u \in \Sigma^*$, we shall write $u \sqcup\!\sqcup \Sigma^*$ for the language of all words over Σ having u as a subword. In the following, we consider that $\sqcup\!\sqcup$ has precedence over $\cup$ and $\cap$ (but of course not over concatenation).

We define the *class of piecewise testable languages* $\mathcal{PT}$ as the class of regular languages such that for every alphabet Σ, we associate to Σ^* the set $\mathcal{PT}(\Sigma^*)$ of all languages over Σ that are Boolean combinations of languages of the form $u \sqcup\!\sqcup \Sigma^*$ where $u \in \Sigma^*$. In fact, $\mathcal{PT}(\Sigma^*)$ is the set of languages over Σ equal to a union of $\sim_k$-classes for some $k \in \mathbb{N}$ (see [18]). Simon showed [18] that a language is piecewise testable if and only if its syntactic monoid is in **J**, i.e. $\mathcal{PT} = \mathcal{L}(\mathbf{J})$.

We can define a hierarchy of piecewise testable languages in a natural way. For $k \in \mathbb{N}$, let the *class of k-piecewise testable languages* $\mathcal{PT}_k$ be the class of regular languages such that for every alphabet Σ, we associate to Σ^* the set $\mathcal{PT}_k(\Sigma^*)$ of all languages over Σ that are Boolean combinations of languages of the form $u \sqcup\!\sqcup \Sigma^*$ where $u \in \Sigma^*$ with $|u| \leq k$. We then have that $\mathcal{PT}_k(\Sigma^*)$ is the set of languages over Σ equal to a union of $\sim_k$-classes. Let us define $\mathbf{J_k}$ the inclusion-wise smallest variety of monoids containing the quotients of Σ^* by $\sim_k$ for any alphabet Σ: we have that a language is k-piecewise testable if and only if its syntactic monoid belongs to $\mathbf{J_k}$, i.e. $\mathcal{PT}_k = \mathcal{L}(\mathbf{J_k})$. (See [9, Section 3].)

3   Fine Hierarchy

The first part of our investigation of the computational power of programs over monoids in **J** concerns the influence of the length of programs on their computational capabilities.

We say two programs over a same monoid on the same set of input words are *equivalent* if and only if they recognise the same languages. Tesson and Thérien proved in [23] that for any monoid M in $\mathbf{DA}$, there exists some $k \in \mathbb{N}$ such that for any alphabet Σ there is a constant $c \in \mathbb{N}_{>0}$ verifying that any program over M on Σ^n for $n \in \mathbb{N}$ is equivalent to a program over M on Σ^n of length at most $c \cdot n^k$. Since $\mathbf{J} \subset \mathbf{DA}$, any monoid in $\mathbf{J}$ does also have this property. However, this does not imply that there exists some $k \in \mathbb{N}$ working for all monoids in $\mathbf{J}$, i.e. that $\mathcal{P}(\mathbf{J})$ collapses to $\mathcal{P}(\mathbf{J}, n^k)$.

In this section, we show on the one hand that, as for $\mathbf{DA}$, while $\mathcal{P}(\mathbf{J}, s(n))$ collapses to $\mathcal{P}(\mathbf{J})$ for any super-polynomial function $s \colon \mathbb{N} \to \mathbb{N}$, there does not exist any $k \in \mathbb{N}$ such that $\mathcal{P}(\mathbf{J})$ collapses to $\mathcal{P}(\mathbf{J}, n^k)$; and on the other hand that $\mathcal{P}(\mathbf{J_k})$ does optimally collapse to $\mathcal{P}(\mathbf{J_k}, n^{\lceil k/2 \rceil})$ for each $k \in \mathbb{N}$.

3.1   Strict Hierarchy

Given $k, n \in \mathbb{N}$, we say that σ is a k-*selector over* n if σ is a function of $\mathfrak{P}([n])^{[n]^k}$ that associates a subset of $[n]$ to each vector in $[n]^k$. For any sequence $\Delta = (\sigma_n)_{n \in \mathbb{N}}$ such that σ_n is a k-selector over n for each $n \in \mathbb{N}$—a sequence we will call a *sequence of k-selectors*—, we set $L_\Delta = \bigcup_{n \in \mathbb{N}} K_{n,\sigma_n}$, where for each $n \in \mathbb{N}$, the language K_{n,σ_n} is the set of words over $\{0,1\}$ of length $(k+1) \cdot n$ that can be decomposed into $k+1$ consecutive blocks $u^{(1)}, u^{(2)}, \ldots, u^{(k)}, v$ of n letters where the first k blocks each contain 1 exactly once and uniquely define a vector ρ in $[n]^k$, where for all $i \in [k]$, ρ_i is given by the position of the only 1 in $u^{(i)}$ (i.e. $u_{\rho_i}^{(i)} = 1$) and v is such that there exists $j \in \sigma_n(\rho)$ verifying that v_j is 1. Observe that for any k-selector σ_0 over 0, we have $K_{0,\sigma_0} = \emptyset$.

We now proceed similarly to what has been done in Subsection 5.1 in [8] to show, on one hand, that for all $k \in \mathbb{N}$, there is a monoid M_k in $\mathbf{J_{2k+1}}$ such that for any sequence of k-selectors Δ, the language L_Δ is recognised by a sequence of programs over M_k of length at most n^{k+1}; and, on the other hand, that for all $k \in \mathbb{N}$ there is a sequence of k-selectors Δ such that for any finite monoid M and any sequence of programs $(P_n)_{n \in \mathbb{N}}$ over M of length at most n^k, the language L_Δ is not recognised by $(P_n)_{n \in \mathbb{N}}$.

We obtain the following proposition.

Proposition 3. *For all $k \in \mathbb{N}$, we have $\mathcal{P}(\mathbf{J}, n^k) \subset \mathcal{P}(\mathbf{J}, n^{k+1})$. More precisely, for all $k \in \mathbb{N}$ and $d \in \mathbb{N}, d \le \lceil \frac{k}{2} \rceil - 1$, we have $\mathcal{P}(\mathbf{J_k}, n^d) \subset \mathcal{P}(\mathbf{J_k}, n^{d+1})$.*

3.2   Collapse

Looking at Proposition 3, it looks at first glance rather strange that, for each $k \in \mathbb{N}$, we can only prove strictness of the hierarchy inside $\mathcal{P}(\mathbf{J_k})$ up to exponent $\lceil \frac{k}{2} \rceil$. We now show, in a way similar to Subsection 5.2 in [8], that in fact $\mathcal{P}(\mathbf{J_k})$ does collapse to $\mathcal{P}(\mathbf{J_k}, n^{\lceil k/2 \rceil})$ for all $k \in \mathbb{N}$, showing Proposition 3 to be optimal in some sense.

Proposition 4. *Let $k \in \mathbb{N}$. Let $M \in \mathbf{J_k}$ and Σ be an alphabet. Then there exists a constant $c \in \mathbb{N}_{>0}$ such that any program over M on Σ^n for $n \in \mathbb{N}$ is equivalent to a program over M on Σ^n of length at most $c \cdot n^{\lceil k/2 \rceil}$.*

In particular, $\mathcal{P}(\mathbf{J_k}) = \mathcal{P}(\mathbf{J_k}, n^{\lceil k/2 \rceil})$ for all $k \in \mathbb{N}$.

4   Regular Languages in $\mathcal{P}(\mathbf{J})$

The second part of our investigation of the computational power of programs over monoids in **J** is dedicated to understanding exactly what regular languages can be p-recognised by monoids in **J**.

4.1   Non-tameness of J

It is shown in [8] that $\mathcal{P}(\mathbf{J}) \cap \mathcal{R}eg \not\subseteq \mathcal{L}(\mathbf{QJ})$, thus giving an example of a well-known subvariety of **A** for which p-recognition allows to do unexpected things when recognising a regular language. How far does this unexpected power go?

The first thing to notice is that, though none of them is in $\mathcal{L}(\mathbf{QJ})$, all languages of the form $\Sigma^* u$ and $u \Sigma^*$ for Σ an alphabet and $u \in \Sigma^+$ are in $\mathcal{P}(\mathbf{J})$. Indeed, each of them can be recognised by a sequence of constant-length programs over the syntactic monoid of $u \sqcup \Sigma^*$: for every input length, just output the image, through the syntactic morphism of $u \sqcup \Sigma^*$, of the word made of the $|u|$ first or last letters. So, informally stated, programs over monoids in **J** can check for some constant-length beginning or ending of their input words.

But they can do much more. Indeed, the language $(a+b)^* ac^+$ does not belong to $\mathcal{L}(\mathbf{QJ})$ (compute the stable monoid), yet it is in $\mathcal{P}(\mathbf{J})$. The crucial insight is that it can be program-reduced in linear length to the piecewise testable language of all words over $\{a, b, c\}$ having ca as a subword but not the subwords cca, caa and cb by using the following trick (that we shall call "feedback-sweeping") for input length $n \in \mathbb{N}$: read the input letters in the order $2, 1, 3, 2, 4, 3, 5, 4, \ldots, n, n-1$, output the letters read. This has already been observed in [8, Proposition 5].

Lemma 1. $(a + b)^* ac^+ \in \mathcal{P}(\mathbf{J}, n)$.

Using variants of the "feedback-sweeping" reading technique, we can prove that the phenomenon just described is not an isolated case.

Lemma 2. *The languages* $(a + b)^* ac^+$, $(a + b)^* ac^+ a(a + b)^*$, $c^+ a(a + b)^* ac^+$, $(a + b)^* bac^+$ *and* $(a + b)^* ac^+ (a + b)^* ac^+$ *do all belong to* $\mathcal{P}(\mathbf{J}) \setminus \mathcal{L}(\mathbf{QJ})$.

Hence, we are tempted to say that there are "much more" regular languages in $\mathcal{P}(\mathbf{J})$ than just those in $\mathcal{L}(\mathbf{QJ})$, even though it is not clear to us whether $\mathcal{L}(\mathbf{QJ}) \subseteq \mathcal{P}(\mathbf{J})$ or not. But can we show any upper bound on $\mathcal{P}(\mathbf{J}) \cap \mathcal{R}eg$? It turns out that we can, relying on two known results.

First, since $\mathbf{J} \subseteq \mathbf{DA}$, we have $\mathcal{P}(\mathbf{J}) \subseteq \mathcal{P}(\mathbf{DA})$, so Theorem 6 in [8], that states $\mathcal{P}(\mathbf{DA}) \cap \mathcal{R}eg = \mathcal{L}(\mathbf{QDA})$, implies that $\mathcal{P}(\mathbf{J}) \cap \mathcal{R}eg \subseteq \mathcal{L}(\mathbf{QDA})$.

Second, let us define an important superclass of the class of piecewise testable languages. Let Σ be an alphabet and $u_1, \ldots, u_k \in \Sigma^+$ ($k \in \mathbb{N}_{>0}$); we define $[u_1, \ldots, u_k] = \Sigma^* u_1 \Sigma^* \cdots \Sigma^* u_k \Sigma^*$. The *class of dot-depth one languages* is the class of Boolean combinations of languages of the form $\Sigma^* u$, $u \Sigma^*$ and $[u_1, \ldots, u_k]$ for Σ an alphabet, $k \in \mathbb{N}_{>0}$ and $u, u_1, \ldots, u_k \in \Sigma^+$. The inclusion-wise smallest variety of semigroups containing all syntactic semigroups of dot-depth one languages is denoted by $\mathbf{J} * \mathbf{D}$ and verifies that $\mathcal{L}(\mathbf{J} * \mathbf{D})$ is exactly the class of dot-depth one languages. (See [11,15,19].) It has been shown in [11, Corollary 8] that $\mathcal{P}(\mathbf{J} * \mathbf{D}) \cap \mathcal{R}eg = \mathcal{L}(\mathbf{Q}(\mathbf{J} * \mathbf{D}))$ (if we extend the program-over-monoid formalism in the obvious way to finite semigroups). Now, we have $\mathbf{J} \subseteq \mathbf{J} * \mathbf{D}$, so that $\mathcal{P}(\mathbf{J}) \subseteq \mathcal{P}(\mathbf{J} * \mathbf{D})$ and hence $\mathcal{P}(\mathbf{J}) \cap \mathcal{R}eg \subseteq \mathcal{L}(\mathbf{Q}(\mathbf{J} * \mathbf{D}))$.

To summarise, we have the following.

Proposition 5. $\mathcal{P}(\mathbf{J}) \cap \mathcal{R}eg \subseteq \mathcal{L}(\mathbf{QDA}) \cap \mathcal{L}(\mathbf{Q}(\mathbf{J} * \mathbf{D}))$.

In fact, we conjecture that the inverse inclusion does also hold.

Conjecture 1. $\mathcal{P}(\mathbf{J}) \cap \mathcal{R}eg = \mathcal{L}(\mathbf{QDA}) \cap \mathcal{L}(\mathbf{Q}(\mathbf{J} * \mathbf{D}))$.

Why do we think this should be true? Though, for a given alphabet Σ, we cannot decide whether some word $u \in \Sigma^+$ of length at least 2 appears as a factor of any given word w in Σ^* with programs over monoids in $\mathbf{J}$ (because $\Sigma^* u \Sigma^* \notin \mathcal{L}(\mathbf{QDA})$), Lemma 2 and the possibilities offered by the "feedback-sweeping" technique give the impression that we can do it when we are guaranteed that u appears at most a fixed number of times in w, which seems somehow to be what dot-depth one languages become when restricted to belong to $\mathcal{L}(\mathbf{QDA})$. This intuition motivates the definition of *threshold dot-depth one languages*.

4.2   Threshold Dot-Depth One Languages

The idea behind the definition of threshold dot-depth one languages is that we take the basic building blocks of dot-depth one languages, of the form $[u_1, \ldots, u_k]$ for an alphabet Σ, for $k \in \mathbb{N}_{>0}$ and $u_1, \ldots, u_k \in \Sigma^+$, and restrict them so that, given $l \in \mathbb{N}_{>0}$, membership of a word does really depend on the presence of a given word u_i as a factor if and only if it appears less than l times as a subword.

Definition 1. *Let Σ be an alphabet. For all $u \in \Sigma^+$ and $l \in \mathbb{N}_{>0}$, we define $[u]_l$ to be the language of words over Σ containing u^l as a subword or u as a factor, i.e. $[u]_l = \Sigma^* u \Sigma^* \cup u^l \sqcup \Sigma^*$. Then, for all $u_1, \ldots, u_k \in \Sigma^+$ ($k \in \mathbb{N}, k \geq 2$) and $l \in \mathbb{N}_{>0}$, we define $[u_1, \ldots, u_k]_l = [u_1]_l \cdots [u_k]_l$.*

Obviously, for each Σ an alphabet, $k \in \mathbb{N}_{>0}$ and $u_1, \ldots, u_k \in \Sigma^+$, the language $[u_1, \ldots, u_k]_1$ equals $u_1 \cdots u_k \sqcup \Sigma^*$. Over $\{a, b, c\}$, the language $[ab, c]_3$ contains all words containing a letter c verifying that in the prefix up to that letter, $ababab$ appears as a subword or ab appears as a factor. Finally, the language $(a + b)^* a c^+$ over $\{a, b, c\}$ of Lemma 1 is equal to $[c, a]_2^\complement \cap [c, b]_2^\complement \cap [ac]_2$.

We then define a *threshold dot-depth one language* as any Boolean combination of languages of the form $\Sigma^* u$, $u \Sigma^*$ and $[u_1, \ldots, u_k]_l$ for Σ an alphabet, for $k, l \in \mathbb{N}_{>0}$ and $u, u_1, \ldots, u_k \in \Sigma^+$.

Confirming the intuition briefly given above, the technique of "feedback-sweeping" can indeed be pushed further to prove that the whole class of threshold dot-depth one languages is contained in $\mathcal{P}(\mathbf{J})$, and we dedicate the remainder of this section to prove it. Concerning Conjecture 1, our intuition leads us to believe that, in fact, the class of threshold dot-depth one languages with additional positional modular counting is exactly $\mathcal{L}(\mathbf{QDA}) \cap \mathcal{L}(\mathbf{Q}(\mathbf{J} * \mathbf{D}))$. We simply refer the interested reader to Section 5.4 of the author's Ph.D. thesis [7], that contains a partial result supporting this belief, too technical and long to be presented here.

Let us now move on to the proof of the following theorem.

Theorem 1. *Every threshold dot-depth one language belongs to* $\mathcal{P}(\mathbf{J})$.

As $\mathcal{P}(\mathbf{J})$ is closed under Boolean operations (Proposition 1), our goal is to prove, given an alphabet Σ, given $l \in \mathbb{N}_{>0}$ and $u_1, \ldots, u_k \in \Sigma^+$ ($k \in \mathbb{N}_{>0}$), that $[u_1, \ldots, u_k]_l$ is in $\mathcal{P}(\mathbf{J})$; the case of $\Sigma^* u$ and $u\Sigma^*$ for $u \in \Sigma^+$ is easily handled (see the discussion at the beginning of Subsect. 4.1). To do this, we need to put $[u_1, \ldots, u_k]_l$ in some normal form. It is readily seen that $[u_1, \ldots, u_k]_l = \bigcup_{q_1, \ldots, q_k \in \{1, l\}} L^{(l)}_{(u_1, q_1)} \cdots L^{(l)}_{(u_k, q_k)}$ where the $L^{(l)}_{(u_i, q_i)}$'s are defined thereafter.

Definition 2. *Let Σ be an alphabet.*

For all $u \in \Sigma^+$, $l \in \mathbb{N}_{>0}$ and $\alpha \in [l]$, set $L^{(l)}_{(u, \alpha)} = \begin{cases} \Sigma^* u \Sigma^* & \text{if } \alpha < l \\ u^l \sqcup\!\sqcup \Sigma^* & \text{otherwise} \end{cases}$.

Building directly a sequence of programs over a monoid in **J** that decides $L^{(l)}_{(u_1, q_1)} \cdots L^{(l)}_{(u_k, q_k)}$ for some alphabet Σ and $q_1, \ldots, q_k \in \{1, l\}$ seems however tricky. We need to split things further by controlling precisely how many times each u_i for $i \in [k]$ appears in the right place when it does less than l times. To do this, we consider, for each $\alpha \in [l]^k$, the language $R^\alpha_l(u_1, \ldots, u_k)$ defined below.

Definition 3. *Let Σ be an alphabet.*

For all $u_1, \ldots, u_k \in \Sigma^+$ ($k \in \mathbb{N}_{>0}$), $l \in \mathbb{N}_{>0}$, $\alpha \in [l]^k$, we set

$$R^\alpha_l(u_1, \ldots, u_k) = (u_1{}^{\alpha_1} \cdots u_k{}^{\alpha_k}) \sqcup\!\sqcup \Sigma^* \cap \bigcap_{i \in [k], \alpha_i < l} \left(((u_1{}^{\alpha_1} \cdots u_i{}^{\alpha_i+1} \cdots u_k{}^{\alpha_k}) \sqcup\!\sqcup \Sigma^*) \right)^{\mathsf{C}}.$$

Now, for a given $\alpha \in [l]^k$, we are interested in the words of $R^\alpha_l(u_1, \ldots, u_k)$ such that for each $i \in [k]$ verifying $\alpha_i < l$, the word u_i indeed appears as a factor in the right place. We thus introduce a last language $S^\alpha_l(u_1, \ldots, u_k)$ defined as follows.

Definition 4. *Let Σ be an alphabet.*

For all $u_1, \ldots, u_k \in \Sigma^+$ ($k \in \mathbb{N}_{>0}$), $l \in \mathbb{N}_{>0}$, $\alpha \in [l]^k$, we set

$$S^\alpha_l(u_1, \ldots, u_k) = \bigcap_{i \in [k], \alpha_i < l} ((u_1{}^{\alpha_1} \cdots u_{i-1}{}^{\alpha_{i-1}}) \sqcup\!\sqcup \Sigma^*) u_i ((u_{i+1}{}^{\alpha_{i+1}} \cdots u_k{}^{\alpha_k}) \sqcup\!\sqcup \Sigma^*).$$

We now have the normal form we were looking for to prove Theorem 1: $[u_1, \ldots, u_k]_l$ is equal to the union, over all $\alpha \in [l]^k$, of the intersection of $R^\alpha_l(u_1, \ldots, u_k)$ and $S^\alpha_l(u_1, \ldots, u_k)$. Though rather intuitive, the correctness of this decomposition is not so straightforward to prove and, actually, we can only prove it when for each $i \in [k]$, the letters in u_i are all distinct.

Lemma 3. *Let Σ be an alphabet, $l \in \mathbb{N}_{>0}$ and $u_1, \ldots, u_k \in \Sigma^+$ ($k \in \mathbb{N}_{>0}$) such that for each $i \in [k]$, the letters in u_i are all distinct. Then,*

$$\bigcup_{q_1,\ldots,q_k \in \{1,l\}} L^{(l)}_{(u_1,q_1)} \cdots L^{(l)}_{(u_k,q_k)} = \bigcup_{\alpha \in [l]^k} \left(R^\alpha_l(u_1,\ldots,u_k) \cap S^\alpha_l(u_1,\ldots,u_k) \right).$$

Our goal now is to prove, given an alphabet Σ, given $l \in \mathbb{N}_{>0}$ and $u_1, \ldots, u_k \in \Sigma^+$ ($k \in \mathbb{N}_{>0}$) such that for each $i \in [k]$, the letters in u_i are all distinct, that for any $\alpha \in [l]^k$, the language $R^\alpha_l(u_1, \ldots, u_k) \cap S^\alpha_l(u_1, \ldots, u_k)$ is in $\mathcal{P}(\mathbf{J})$; closure of $\mathcal{P}(\mathbf{J})$ under union (Proposition 1) consequently entails that $[u_1, \ldots, u_k]_l \in \mathcal{P}(\mathbf{J})$. The way $R^\alpha_l(u_1, \ldots, u_k)$ and $S^\alpha_l(u_1, \ldots, u_k)$ are defined allows us to reason as follows. For each $i \in [k]$ verifying $\alpha_i < l$, let L_i be the language of words w over Σ containing $x_{i,1} u_i{}^{\alpha_i} x_{i,2}$ as a subword but not $x_{i,1} u_i{}^{\alpha_i+1} x_{i,2}$ and such that $w = y_1 u_i y_2$ with $y_1 \in x_{i,1} \amalg \Sigma^*$ and $y_2 \in x_{i,2} \amalg \Sigma^*$, where $x_{i,1} = u_1{}^{\alpha_1} \cdots u_{i-1}{}^{\alpha_{i-1}}$ and $x_{i,2} = u_{i+1}{}^{\alpha_{i+1}} \cdots u_k{}^{\alpha_k}$. If we manage to prove that for each $i \in [k]$ verifying $\alpha_i < l$ we have $L_i \in \mathcal{P}(\mathbf{J})$, we can conclude that $R^\alpha_l(u_1, \ldots, u_k) \cap S^\alpha_l(u_1, \ldots, u_k) = (u_1{}^{\alpha_1} \cdots u_k{}^{\alpha_k}) \amalg \Sigma^* \cap \bigcap_{i \in [k], \alpha_i < l} L_i$ does belong to $\mathcal{P}(\mathbf{J})$ by closure of $\mathcal{P}(\mathbf{J})$ under intersection, Proposition 1. The lemma that follows, the main lemma in the proof of Theorem 1, exactly shows this. The proof crucially uses the "feedback sweeping" technique, but note that we actually don't know how to prove it when we do not enforce that for each $i \in [k]$, the letters in u_i are all distinct.

Lemma 4. *Let Σ be an alphabet and $u \in \Sigma^+$ such that its letters are all distinct. For all $\alpha \in \mathbb{N}_{>0}$ and $x_1, x_2 \in \Sigma^*$, we have*

$$(x_1 u^\alpha x_2) \amalg \Sigma^* \cap \left((x_1 u^{\alpha+1} x_2) \amalg \Sigma^* \right)^{\complement} \cap (x_1 \amalg \Sigma^*) u (x_2 \amalg \Sigma^*) \in \mathcal{P}(\mathbf{J}) .$$

Proof (Sketch). Let Σ be an alphabet and $u \in \Sigma^+$ such that its letters are all distinct. Let $\alpha \in \mathbb{N}_{>0}$ and $x_1, x_2 \in \Sigma^*$. We let

$$L = (x_1 u^\alpha x_2) \amalg \Sigma^* \cap \left((x_1 u^{\alpha+1} x_2) \amalg \Sigma^* \right)^{\complement} \cap (x_1 \amalg \Sigma^*) u (x_2 \amalg \Sigma^*) .$$

If $|u| = 1$, the lemma follows trivially because L is piecewise testable and hence belongs to $\mathcal{L}(\mathbf{J})$, so we assume $|u| > 1$.

For each letter $a \in \Sigma$, we shall use $2|u| - 1$ distinct decorated letters of the form $a^{(i)}$ for some $i \in [\![0, 2|u| - 2]\!]$, using the convention that $a^{(0)} = a$; of course, for two distinct letters $a, b \in \Sigma$, we have that $a^{(i)}$ and $b^{(j)}$ are distinct for all $i, j \in [\![0, 2|u| - 2]\!]$. We denote by A the alphabet of these decorated letters. The main idea of the proof is, for a given input length $n \in \mathbb{N}$, to build an A-program Ψ_n over Σ^n such that, given an input word $w \in \Sigma^n$, it first ouputs the $|u| - 1$ first letters of w and then, for each i going from $|u|$ to n, outputs w_i, followed by $w_{i-1}^{(1)} \cdots w_{i-|u|+1}^{(|u|-1)}$ (a "sweep" of $|u| - 1$ letters backwards down to position $i - |u| + 1$, decorating the letters incrementally) and finally by $w_{i-|u|+2}^{(|u|)} \cdots w_i^{(2|u|-2)}$ (a "sweep" forwards up to position i, continuing the incremental decoration of the letters). The idea behind this way of rearranging and decorating letters is that, given an input word $w \in \Sigma^n$, as long as we make sure that w and thus

$\Psi_n(w)$ do contain $x_1 u^{\alpha} x_2$ as a subword but not $x_1 u^{\alpha+1} x_2$, then $\Psi_n(w)$ can be decomposed as $\Psi_n(w) = y_1 z y_2$ where $y_1 \in x_1 \sqcup \Sigma^*$, $y_2 \in x_2 \sqcup \Sigma^*$, and $|y_1|, |y_2|$ are minimal, with z containing $u^{\beta} u_{|u|-1}^{(1)} \cdots u_1^{(|u|-1)} u_2^{(|u|)} \cdots u_{|u|}^{(2|u|-2)} u^{\alpha-\beta}$ as a subword for some $\beta \in [\alpha]$ if and only if $w \in (x_1 \sqcup \Sigma^*) u (x_2 \sqcup \Sigma^*)$. This means we can check whether $w \in L$ by testing whether w belongs to some fixed piecewise testable language over A.

As explained before stating the previous lemma, we can now use it to prove the result we were aiming for.

Proposition 6. *Let Σ be an alphabet, $l \in \mathbb{N}_{>0}$ and $u_1, \ldots, u_k \in \Sigma^+$ ($k \in \mathbb{N}_{>0}$) such that for each $i \in [k]$, the letters in u_i are all distinct. For all $\alpha \in [l]^k$, we have $R_l^{\alpha}(u_1, \ldots, u_k) \cap S_l^{\alpha}(u_1, \ldots, u_k) \in \mathcal{P}(\mathbf{J})$.*

We thus derive the awaited corollary.

Corollary 1. *Let Σ be an alphabet, $l \in \mathbb{N}_{>0}$ and $u_1, \ldots, u_k \in \Sigma^+$ ($k \in \mathbb{N}_{>0}$) such that for each $i \in [k]$, the letters in u_i are all distinct. Then, $[u_1, \ldots, u_k]_l \in \mathcal{P}(\mathbf{J})$.*

However, what we really want to obtain is that $[u_1, \ldots, u_k]_l \in \mathcal{P}(\mathbf{J})$ without putting any restriction on the u_i's. But, in fact, to remove the constraint that the letters must be all distinct in each of the u_i's, we simply have to decorate each of the input letters with its position minus 1 modulo a big enough $d \in \mathbb{N}_{>0}$. This finally leads to the following proposition.

Proposition 7. *Let Σ be an alphabet, $l \in \mathbb{N}_{>0}$ and $u_1, \ldots, u_k \in \Sigma^+$ ($k \in \mathbb{N}_{>0}$). Then $[u_1, \ldots, u_k]_l \in \mathcal{P}(\mathbf{J})$.*

This finishes to prove Theorem 1 by closure of $\mathcal{P}(\mathbf{J})$ under Boolean combinations (Proposition 1) and by the discussion at the beginning of Subsect. 4.1.

5 Conclusion

Although $\mathcal{P}(\mathbf{J})$ is very small compared to AC^0, we have shown that programs over monoids in **J** are an interesting subject of study in that they allow to do quite unexpected things. The "feedback-sweeping" technique allows one to detect presence of a factor thanks to such programs as long as this factor does not appear too often as a subword: this is the basic principle behind threshold dot-depth one languages, that our article shows to belong wholly to $\mathcal{P}(\mathbf{J})$.

Whether threshold dot-depth one languages with additional positional modular counting do correspond exactly to the languages in $\mathcal{L}(\mathbf{QDA}) \cap \mathcal{L}(\mathbf{Q}(\mathbf{J} * \mathbf{D}))$ seems to be a challenging question, that we leave open. In his Ph.D. thesis [7], the author proved that all strongly unambiguous monomials (the basic building blocks in $\mathcal{L}(\mathbf{DA})$) that are imposed to belong to $\mathcal{L}(\mathbf{J} * \mathbf{D})$ at the same time are in fact threshold dot-depth one languages. However, the proof looks much too complex and technical to be extended to, say, all languages in $\mathcal{L}(\mathbf{DA}) \cap \mathcal{L}(\mathbf{J} * \mathbf{D})$. New techniques are probably needed, and we might conclude by saying that proving (or disproving) this conjecture could be a nice research goal in algebraic automata theory.

Acknowledgements. The author thanks the anonymous referees for their helpful comments and suggestions.

References

1. Ajtai, M.: Σ_1^1-formulae on finite structures. Ann. Pure Appl. Logic **24**(1), 1–48 (1983)
2. Barrington, D.A.M.: Bounded-width polynomial-size branching programs recognize exactly those languages in NC^1. J. Comput. Syst. Sci. **38**(1), 150–164 (1989)
3. Barrington, D.A.M., Thérien, D.: Finite monoids and the fine structure of NC^1. J. ACM **35**(4), 941–952 (1988)
4. Eilenberg, S.: Automata, Languages, and Machines, vol. A. Academic Press, New York (1974)
5. Eilenberg, S.: Automata, Languages, and Machines, vol. B. Academic Press, New York (1976)
6. Furst, M.L., Saxe, J.B., Sipser, M.: Parity, circuits, and the polynomial-time hierarchy. Math. Syst. Theory **17**(1), 13–27 (1984)
7. Grosshans, N.: The limits of Nečiporuk's method and the power of programs over monoids taken from small varieties of finite monoids. Ph.D. thesis, University of Paris-Saclay, France (2018)
8. Grosshans, N., McKenzie, P., Segoufin, L.: The power of programs over monoids in DA. In: MFCS 2017, Aalborg, Denmark, 21–25 August 2017, pp. 2:1–2:20 (2017)
9. Klíma, O., Polák, L.: Hierarchies of piecewise testable languages. Int. J. Found. Comput. Sci. **21**(4), 517–533 (2010)
10. Lautemann, C., Tesson, P., Thérien, D.: An algebraic point of view on the Crane Beach property. In: Ésik, Z. (ed.) CSL 2006. LNCS, vol. 4207, pp. 426–440. Springer, Heidelberg (2006). https://doi.org/10.1007/11874683_28
11. Maciel, A., Péladeau, P., Thérien, D.: Programs over semigroups of dot-depth one. Theor. Comput. Sci. **245**(1), 135–148 (2000)
12. McKenzie, P., Péladeau, P., Thérien, D.: NC^1: the automata-theoretic viewpoint. Comput. Complex. **1**, 330–359 (1991)
13. Péladeau, P.: Classes de circuits booléens et variétés de monoïdes. Ph.D. thesis, Université Pierre-et-Marie-Curie (Paris-VI), Paris, France (1990)
14. Péladeau, P., Straubing, H., Thérien, D.: Finite semigroup varieties defined by programs. Theor. Comput. Sci. **180**(1–2), 325–339 (1997)
15. Pin, J.: The dot-depth hierarchy, 45 years later. In: The Role of Theory in Computer Science - Essays Dedicated to Janusz Brzozowski, pp. 177–202 (2017)
16. Pin, J.: Varieties of Formal Languages. Plenum Publishing Co., New York (1986)
17. Pin, J., Straubing, H.: Some results on $\mathcal{C}$-varieties. ITA **39**(1), 239–262 (2005)
18. Simon, I.: Piecewise testable events. In: Brakhage, H. (ed.) GI-Fachtagung 1975. LNCS, vol. 33, pp. 214–222. Springer, Heidelberg (1975). https://doi.org/10.1007/3-540-07407-4_23
19. Straubing, H.: Finite semigroup varieties of the form $V * D$. J. Pure Appl. Algebra **36**, 53–94 (1985)
20. Straubing, H.: When can one finite monoid simulate another? In: Birget, J.C., Margolis, S., Meakin, J., Sapir, M. (eds.) Algorithmic Problems in Groups and Semigroups, pp. 267–288. Springer, Boston (2000). https://doi.org/10.1007/978-1-4612-1388-8_15
21. Straubing, H.: Languages defined with modular counting quantifiers. Inf. Comput. **166**(2), 112–132 (2001)

22. Tesson, P.: Computational complexity questions related to finite monoids and semigroups. Ph.D. thesis, McGill University, Montreal (2003)
23. Tesson, P., Thérien, D.: The computing power of programs over finite monoids. J. Autom. Lang. Comb. **7**(2), 247–258 (2001)

Geometrically Closed Positive Varieties of Star-Free Languages

Ondřej Klíma[1] and Peter Kostolányi[2(⊠)] (iD)

[1] Department of Mathematics and Statistics, Masaryk University,
Kotlářská 2, 611 37 Brno, Czech Republic
klima@math.muni.cz

[2] Department of Computer Science, Comenius University in Bratislava,
Mlynská dolina, 842 48 Bratislava, Slovakia
kostolanyi@fmph.uniba.sk

Abstract. A recently introduced operation of geometrical closure on formal languages is investigated. It is proved that the geometrical closure of a language from the positive variety $\mathcal{V}_{3/2}$, the level $3/2$ of the Straubing-Thérien hierarchy of star-free languages, always falls into the variety $\mathcal{R}_{LT}$, which is a new variety consisting of specific R-trivial languages. As a consequence, each class of regular languages lying between $\mathcal{R}_{LT}$ and $\mathcal{V}_{3/2}$ is geometrically closed.

Keywords: Language varieties · Geometrical closure ·
Straubing-Thérien hierarchy · R-trivial monoid

1 Introduction

A *geometrical closure* is an operation on formal languages introduced recently by Dubernard, Guaiana, and Mignot [8]. It is defined as follows: Take any language L over some k-letter alphabet and consider the set called the *figure* of L in [8], which consists of all elements of $\mathbb{N}^k$ corresponding to Parikh vectors of prefixes of words from L. The *geometrical closure* of L is the language $\gamma(L)$ of all words w such that the Parikh vectors of all the prefixes of w lie in the figure of L. This closure operator was inspired by the previous works of Blanpain, Champarnaud, and Dubernard [4] and Béal et al. [3], in which *geometrical languages* are studied – using the terminology from later paper [8], these can be described as languages whose prefix closure is equal to their geometrical closure. Note that this terminology was motivated by the fact that a geometrical language is completely determined by its (geometrical) figure. In the particular case of binary alphabets, these (geometrical) figures were illustrated by plane diagrams in [8].

The class of all regular languages can be easily observed not to be geometrically closed – that is, one can find a regular language such that its geometrical

The first author was supported by Grant 19-12790S of the Grant Agency of the Czech Republic. The second author was supported by the grant VEGA 2/0165/16.

A. Leporati et al. (Eds.): LATA 2020, LNCS 12038, pp. 328–340, 2020.
https://doi.org/10.1007/978-3-030-40608-0_23

closure is not regular [8] (see also the end of Sect. 2). One possible research aim could be to characterise regular languages L for which $\gamma(L)$ is regular, or to describe some robust classes of languages with this property. Another problem posed in [8] is to find some subclasses of regular languages that are geometrically closed. As we explain in Sect. 3, non-empty group languages have their geometrical closure equal to the universal language Σ^*. For this reason, it makes sense to look for more interesting geometrically closed subclasses among *star-free* languages, which are known to be "group-free". More precisely, a language L is *star-free* if and only if the syntactic monoid M_L of L is *aperiodic*, that is, if M_L does not contain non-trivial groups as subsemigroups.

It is well known that the star-free languages are classified into the *Straubing-Thérien hierarchy* based on polynomial and Boolean operations. In particular, the variety $\mathcal{V}_1$ (*i.e.*, the variety of languages of level 1) is formed by piecewise testable languages and the positive variety $\mathcal{V}_{3/2}$ is formed by polynomials built from languages of level 1. We refer to the survey paper by Pin [12] for an introduction to the Straubing-Thérien hierarchy of star-free languages and the algebraic theory of regular languages in general. This theory is based on Eilenberg correspondence between varieties of regular languages and pseudovarieties of finite monoids. Note that one well-known instance of Eilenberg correspondence, which plays an essential role in our contribution, is given by the pseudovariety of finite R-trivial monoids, for which the corresponding variety of languages is denoted by $\mathcal{R}$. Nevertheless, we emphasise that our contribution is rather elementary, and it does not use sophisticated tools developed in the algebraic theory of regular languages.

It was proved by Dubernard, Guaiana, and Mignot [8] that the class of all binary languages from the positive variety $\mathcal{V}_{3/2}$ is geometrically closed. They have obtained this result by decomposing the plane diagram of the figure of a given language into specific types of basic subdiagrams, and using this decomposition to construct a regular expression for the language $\gamma(L)$.

We prove a generalisation of the above mentioned result in this contribution. Our approach is to concentrate on the form of languages that may arise as $\gamma(L)$ for L taken from $\mathcal{V}_{3/2}(\Sigma)$. In other words, we do not construct a concrete regular expression for $\gamma(L)$, but we determine what kind of expression exists for such a language. In particular, we introduce a new variety of languages $\mathcal{R}_{LT}$, which is a subvariety of the variety $\mathcal{R}$. Note that there is a transparent description of languages from $\mathcal{R}$ and also an effective characterisation via the so-called acyclic automata (both are recalled in Sect. 4). The variety of languages $\mathcal{R}_{LT}$ is then characterised in the same manner: a precise description by specific regular expressions and also an automata-based characterisation are given. The letters LT in the notation $\mathcal{R}_{LT}$ refer to a characteristic property of acyclic automata in which "loops are transferred" along paths.

We show that the geometrical closure of a language from the positive variety $\mathcal{V}_{3/2}$ always falls into the variety $\mathcal{R}_{LT}$. As a consequence, each class of regular languages lying between $\mathcal{R}_{LT}$ and $\mathcal{V}_{3/2}$ is geometrically closed. In particular, the positive variety $\mathcal{V}_{3/2}$ is geometrically closed regardless of the alphabet, as well as is the variety $\mathcal{R}$.

2 Preliminaries

All automata considered in this paper are understood to be deterministic and finite. An *automaton* is thus a five-tuple $\mathcal{A} = (Q, \Sigma, \cdot, \iota, F)$, where Q is a finite set of states, Σ is a non-empty finite alphabet, $\cdot : Q \times \Sigma \rightarrow Q$ is a complete transition function, $\iota \in Q$ is the unique initial state, and $F \subseteq Q$ is the set of final states. The minimal automaton of a given language L is denoted by $\mathcal{D}_L$.

By a (positive) variety of languages, we always understand what is called a (positive) $*$-variety in [12]. We recall this notion for a reader's convenience briefly. A *class of languages* $\mathcal{C}$ is an operator, which determines, for each finite non-empty alphabet Σ, a set $\mathcal{C}(\Sigma^*)$ of languages over Σ. A *positive variety* is a class of regular languages $\mathcal{V}$ such that $\mathcal{V}(\Sigma^*)$ is closed under quotients, finite unions and intersections, and the whole class is closed under preimages in homomorphisms. A positive variety $\mathcal{V}$ is a *variety* if each $\mathcal{V}(\Sigma^*)$ is closed under complementation. Note that an alphabet could be fixed in our contribution, so homomorphisms among different alphabets play no role, and we could consider lattices of languages [9] instead of varieties of languages. However, we prefer to stay in the frame of the theory of (positive) varieties of languages as a primary aim of this paper is to describe robust classes closed under geometrical closure.

Given words u, v over an alphabet Σ, we write $u \leq v$ if u is a prefix of v. We also write, for each $L \subseteq \Sigma^*$,

$$\mathrm{pref}^{\uparrow}(L) := \{u \in \Sigma^* \mid \exists w \in L : u \leq w\} = L \cdot (\Sigma^*)^{-1},$$

$$\mathrm{pref}^{\downarrow}(L) := \{w \in \Sigma^* \mid \forall u \in \Sigma^* : u \leq w \implies u \in L\}.$$

We call these languages the *prefix closure* and the *prefix reduction* of L, respectively. Both are prefix-closed, while $\mathrm{pref}^{\uparrow}(L) \supseteq L$ and $\mathrm{pref}^{\downarrow}(L) \subseteq L$.

Proposition 1. *Each positive variety $\mathcal{V}$ is closed under the operator $\mathrm{pref}^{\uparrow}$.*

Proof. It is well known that each regular language has finitely many right quotients by words. Thus, for each alphabet Σ and each $L \in \mathcal{V}(\Sigma^*)$, the language

$$\mathrm{pref}^{\uparrow}(L) = L \cdot (\Sigma^*)^{-1} = \bigcup_{w \in \Sigma^*} Lw^{-1}$$

is a finite union of right quotients of L, and its membership to $\mathcal{V}(\Sigma^*)$ follows. $\square$

Let $\Sigma = \{a_1, \ldots, a_k\}$ be a linearly ordered alphabet. The *Parikh vector* of a word w in Σ^* is then given by $\Psi(w) = (|w|_{a_1}, \ldots, |w|_{a_k})$, where $|w|_a$ denotes the number of occurrences of the letter a in w. This notation extends naturally to languages: we write $\Psi(L) = \{\Psi(w) \mid w \in L\}$ for $L \subseteq \Sigma^*$. We denote by $[w]$ the equivalence class of the kernel relation of Ψ, *i.e.* $[w] = \{u \in \Sigma^* \mid \Psi(u) = \Psi(w)\}$. Then we also write, for each language $L \subseteq \Sigma^*$,

$$[L] = \bigcup_{w \in L} [w] = \{u \in \Sigma^* \mid \Psi(u) \in \Psi(L)\}$$

and we call $[L]$ the *commutative closure* of L. A language L such that $L = [L]$ is called *commutative*. A class of languages $\mathcal{C}$ is said to be *closed under commutation* if for each alphabet Σ, the language $[L]$ belongs to $\mathcal{C}(\Sigma^*)$ whenever $L \in \mathcal{C}(\Sigma^*)$.

In the previous paragraph we consider the mapping $\Psi \colon \Sigma^* \to \mathbb{N}^k$, where $\mathbb{N}$ is the set of all non-negative integers. Following the ideas of [8], we introduce some technical notations concerning $\mathbb{N}^k$, whose elements are called vectors. We denote by $\mathbf{0}$ the null vector of $\mathbb{N}^k$. Let $\mathbf{x} = (x_1, \dots, x_k)$ and $\mathbf{y} = (y_1, \dots, y_k)$ be vectors and $s \in \{1, \dots, k\}$ be an index. We write $\mathbf{x} \to_s \mathbf{y}$ if $y_s - x_s = 1$ and, at the same time, $y_i = x_i$ for all $i \neq s$. Moreover, $\mathbf{x} \to \mathbf{y}$ means that $\mathbf{x} \to_s \mathbf{y}$ for some index s. A *path* in $\mathbb{N}^k$ is a finite sequence $\pi = [\mathbf{x}_0, \dots, \mathbf{x}_n]$ of vectors from $\mathbb{N}^k$ such that $\mathbf{x}_0 = \mathbf{0}$ and $\mathbf{x}_{i-1} \to \mathbf{x}_i$ for $i = 1, \dots, n$; more specifically, we say that π is a *path leading to* $\mathbf{x}_n$. This means that a path always begins in $\mathbf{0}$ and each other vector of the path is obtained from the previous one by incrementing exactly one of its coordinates by one. If in addition $\mathbf{x}_0, \dots, \mathbf{x}_n$ all belong to a set $F \subseteq \mathbb{N}^k$, we say that π is a *path in* F and write $\pi \subseteq F$.

Given a word $w = a_{i_1} \dots a_{i_n}$ in Σ^*, we write $\pi(w)$ for the unique path $[\mathbf{x}_0, \dots, \mathbf{x}_n]$ in $\mathbb{N}^k$ such that $\mathbf{0} = \mathbf{x}_0 \to_{i_1} \mathbf{x}_1 \to_{i_2} \dots \to_{i_n} \mathbf{x}_n$. Conversely, for each path $\pi = [\mathbf{x}_0, \dots, \mathbf{x}_n]$ in $\mathbb{N}^k$, there is a unique word w such that $\pi(w) = \pi$. We denote this unique word w by $\|\pi\|$. For each $F \subseteq \mathbb{N}^k$, we denote $\|F\|$ the set $\{\|\pi\| \mid \pi \subseteq F\}$. Note that the language $\|F\|$ is prefix-closed.

Moreover, we put $\mathrm{fig}(L) = \Psi(\mathrm{pref}^\uparrow(L))$ for each $L \subseteq \Sigma^*$. The set $\mathrm{fig}(L) \subseteq \mathbb{N}^k$ is a *connex figure* in the sense of [8], *i.e.*, for each $\mathbf{x} \in \mathrm{fig}(L)$, there is a path π leading to $\mathbf{x}$ such that $\pi \subseteq \mathrm{fig}(L)$.

Finally, the *geometrical closure* of L is a language $\gamma(L) = \|\mathrm{fig}(L)\|$. A class of languages $\mathcal{C}$ is said to be *geometrically closed* if the language $\gamma(L)$ belongs to $\mathcal{C}(\Sigma^*)$ whenever L does, for each alphabet Σ.

Note that the class of all regular languages is *not* geometrically closed, as observed in [8]. For instance, the language $L = a^*(ab)^*$ is regular, while its geometrical closure $\gamma(L) = \{w \in \{a, b\}^* \mid \forall u \leq w : |u|_a \geq |u|_b\}$ is the prefix closure of the Dyck language.

3   A Characterisation of the Geometrical Closure

We now characterise the operation of geometrical closure via three simpler operations: the prefix closure, the commutative closure, and the prefix reduction. This characterisation is a key to our later considerations.

Proposition 2. *If L is a language over Σ, then $\gamma(L) = \mathrm{pref}^\downarrow \left(\left[\mathrm{pref}^\uparrow(L) \right] \right)$.*

Proof. By definition,

$$\gamma(L) = \|\mathrm{fig}(L)\| = \left\| \Psi(\mathrm{pref}^\uparrow(L)) \right\|.$$

If $w \in \gamma(L)$, then there is a path $\pi = [\mathbf{x}_0, \ldots, \mathbf{x}_n] \subseteq \Psi(\text{pref}^\uparrow(L))$ such that $w = \|\pi\|$. For an arbitrary prefix u of w, we have $\pi(u) = [\mathbf{x}_0, \ldots, \mathbf{x}_m]$ for some $m \leq n$. It follows that $\Psi(u) = \mathbf{x}_m$ belongs to $\Psi(\text{pref}^\uparrow(L))$. Hence $u \in [\text{pref}^\uparrow(L)]$ and w belongs to $\text{pref}^\downarrow([\text{pref}^\uparrow(L)])$.

On the other hand, if w belongs to $\text{pref}^\downarrow([\text{pref}^\uparrow(L)])$, then all prefixes u of w belong to $[\text{pref}^\uparrow(L)]$. Thus $\Psi(u)$ is in $\Psi(\text{pref}^\uparrow(L))$ for each $u \leq w$, and $\pi(w)$ is a path in $\Psi(\text{pref}^\uparrow(L))$, implying that w is in $\|\Psi(\text{pref}^\uparrow(L))\| = \gamma(L)$.   □

As a direct consequence of Propositions 1 and 2, we obtain the following sufficient condition, under which a positive variety of languages is geometrically closed.

Corollary 3. *Each positive variety of regular languages closed under prefix reduction and commutation is geometrically closed.*

Some positive varieties of languages $\mathcal{V}$ are geometrically closed for trivial reasons – for instance all $\mathcal{V}$ such that $\gamma(L) = \Sigma^*$ for all non-empty $L \in \mathcal{V}(\Sigma^*)$. Let us observe that this is the case for L whenever $\text{pref}^\uparrow(L) = \Sigma^*$. The proof of the following lemma is easy to see. We just note that by an *absorbing state* we mean a state p satisfying $p \cdot a = p$ for every $a \in \Sigma$.

Lemma 4. *Let L be a regular language over an alphabet Σ and $\mathcal{D}_L$ be the minimal automaton of L. Then the following conditions are equivalent:*

(i) $\text{pref}^\uparrow(L) = \Sigma^*$;
(ii) for each state p in $\mathcal{D}_L$, there exists a final state reachable from p;
(iii) every absorbing state p in $\mathcal{D}_L$ is final.

The conditions of Lemma 4 are satisfied in particular for all non-empty group languages. The variety $\mathcal{G}$, consisting of all languages L such that the syntactic monoid M_L is a group, is geometrically closed as a consequence. This result can be extended to languages of the form $L = L_0 a_1 L_1 \ldots a_\ell L_\ell$, where each a_i is a letter, and each L_i is a non-empty group language. Indeed, for every $u \in \Sigma^*$, there is some $w \in L_0$ such that $u \leq w$, and one can find at least one $w_i \in L_i$ for every $i = 1, \ldots, \ell$. Then u is a prefix of the word $wa_1 w_1 \ldots a_\ell w_\ell \in L$. This implies that $\text{pref}^\uparrow(L) = \Sigma^*$. We may thus conclude that the variety $\mathcal{G}_{1/2}$, consisting of languages of level $1/2$ in the group hierarchy, is geometrically closed. (The reader not familiar with the group hierarchy is referred to [12]).

In the rest of the paper, we move our attention to star-free languages.

4   Languages Recognised by LT-acyclic Automata

We now introduce the class of languages $\mathcal{R}_{LT}$, which plays a central role in our main result. For every alphabet Σ, the set $\mathcal{R}_{LT}(\Sigma^*)$ consists of languages which are finite unions of languages of the form

$$L = \Sigma_0^* a_1 \Sigma_1^* a_2 \ldots a_n \Sigma_n^*, \tag{1}$$

where $\Sigma_0 \subseteq \Sigma_1 \subseteq \ldots \subseteq \Sigma_n \subseteq \Sigma$ and $a_i \in \Sigma \setminus \Sigma_{i-1}$ for $i = 1, \ldots, n$.

The previous definition is similar to definitions of other classes of languages that have already been studied in literature. First of all, if we omit the condition $\Sigma_0 \subseteq \Sigma_1 \subseteq \ldots \subseteq \Sigma_n$, we get a definition of languages from the variety $\mathcal{R}$ corresponding to R-trivial monoids, which we recall in more detail later. Let us conclude here just that $\mathcal{R}_{LT} \subseteq \mathcal{R}$. Secondly, if we also require $a_i \in \Sigma_{i+1}$ in (1) for $i = 1, \ldots, n-1$, then we obtain a variety of languages considered by Pin, Straubing, and Thérien [13] and corresponding to a pseudovariety of finite monoids denoted $\mathbf{R_1}$. Finally, if we drop in (1) the condition $a_i \notin \Sigma_{i-1}$ and then we generate a variety, then we obtain the variety of languages corresponding to the pseudovariety $\mathbf{JMK}$ considered by Almeida [1, p. 236].

Since we want to characterise languages from $\mathcal{R}_{LT}$ in terms of automata, we recall the characterisation of languages from $\mathcal{R}$ first. An automaton $\mathcal{A} = (Q, \Sigma, \cdot, \iota, F)$ is *acyclic* if every cycle in $\mathcal{A}$ is a loop. This means that if $p \cdot w = p$ for some $p \in Q$ and $w \in \Sigma^*$, then also $p \cdot a = p$ for every letter a occurring in w. The defining condition means that one can number the states in Q as $1, \ldots, |Q|$ in such a way that the state $p \cdot a$, with $p \in Q$ and $a \in \Sigma$, is always greater than or equal to p. For this reason, these automata are called *extensive* in [11, p. 93]. It is known that they recognise precisely R-trivial languages [6].

We say that an acyclic automaton $\mathcal{A} = (Q, \Sigma, \cdot, \iota, F)$ has a *loop transfer* property, if $p \cdot a = p$ implies $(p \cdot b) \cdot a = p \cdot b$ for every $p \in Q$ and $a, b \in \Sigma$. We then call $\mathcal{A}$ an *LT-acyclic automaton* for short. This means that if there is an a-labelled loop in a state p in an LT-acyclic automaton, then there is also an a-labelled loop in each state reachable from p. We may thus equivalently take $b \in \Sigma^*$ in the previous definition. The first aim of this section is to show that languages recognised by LT-acyclic automata are precisely those from $\mathcal{R}_{LT}$. We do so via a series of elementary lemmas.

Lemma 5. *For a language L of the form (1), the automaton $\mathcal{D}_L$ is LT-acyclic.*

Proof. Let L be a language $L = \Sigma_0^* a_1 \Sigma_1^* a_2 \ldots a_n \Sigma_n^*$ of the form (1). For every $i = 1, \ldots, n$, we denote $\Gamma_{i-1} = \Sigma \setminus (\Sigma_{i-1} \cup \{a_i\})$ and we also put $\Gamma_n = \Sigma \setminus \Sigma_n$. Then it is an easy exercise to show that the automaton in Fig. 1 is the minimal automaton of L and that it is an LT-acyclic automaton. □

Lemma 6. *Let L, K be languages over an alphabet Σ recognised by LT-acyclic automata. Then $L \cup K$ is also recognised by an LT-acyclic automaton.*

Proof. The language $L \cup K$ can be recognised by the direct product of a pair of automata that recognise the languages L and K. It is a routine to check that a finite direct product of LT-acyclic automata is an LT-acyclic automaton. □

The previous two lemmas show that every language from $\mathcal{R}_{LT}$ is recognised by an LT-acyclic automaton. The following lemma strengthens this observation by implying that the *minimal* automaton of a language from $\mathcal{R}_{LT}$ is LT-acyclic.

Lemma 7. *Let L be a language recognised by an LT-acyclic automaton. Then the minimal automaton of L is also LT-acyclic.*

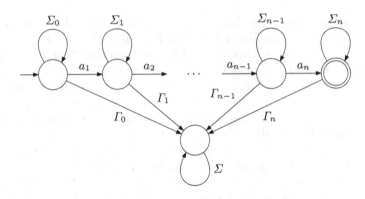

Fig. 1. An LT-acyclic automaton for the language of the form (1).

Proof. Let $\mathcal{A} = (Q, \Sigma, \cdot, \iota, F)$ be an LT-acyclic automaton such that $\|\mathcal{A}\| = L$. The minimal automaton $\mathcal{D}_L$ is a homomorphic image of some subautomaton of $\mathcal{A}$ [14]. It is clear that a subautomaton of an LT-acyclic automaton is LT-acyclic. Thus we may assume that $\mathcal{A}$ has all states reachable from the initial state ι.

Let $\varphi \colon Q \to P$ be a surjective mapping, which is a homomorphism from the automaton $\mathcal{A}$ onto an automaton $\mathcal{B} = (P, \Sigma, \bullet, \varphi(\iota), \varphi(F))$. We claim that $\mathcal{B}$ is acyclic. To prove this claim, let $p \in P$ and $w \in \Sigma^*$ be such that $p \bullet w = p$. Then we choose some state q' from $\varphi^{-1}(p)$. For that q', we have $q' \cdot w^m \in \varphi^{-1}(p)$ for every natural number m. Since the sequence $q', q' \cdot w, q' \cdot w^2, \dots$ contains only finitely many states, there are natural numbers n and m such that $q' \cdot w^{n+m} = q' \cdot w^n = q$. Since $\mathcal{A}$ is acyclic, we have $q \cdot a = q$ for every letter a occurring in w. Consequently, $p \bullet a = \varphi(q) \bullet a = \varphi(q \cdot a) = \varphi(q) = p$. We showed that $\mathcal{B}$ is acyclic.

Now let $p \in P$ and $a \in \Sigma$ be such that $p \bullet a = p$. It follows from the previous paragraph that there is $q \in \varphi^{-1}(p)$ such that $q \cdot a = q$. Since $\mathcal{A}$ is LT-acyclic, we see that $(q \cdot b) \cdot a = q \cdot b$ for every $b \in \Sigma$. Thus $p \bullet ba = \varphi(q \cdot ba) = \varphi(q \cdot b) = p \bullet b$. We showed that $\mathcal{B}$ is an LT-acyclic automaton. In particular, it is true for $\mathcal{D}_L$. $\square$

Let us also prove a converse to the statements established above.

Lemma 8. *Let $\mathcal{A}$ be an LT-acyclic automaton over an alphabet Σ. Then $\|\mathcal{A}\|$ belongs to $\mathcal{R}_{LT}(\Sigma^*)$.*

Proof. Let $\mathcal{A} = (Q, \Sigma, \cdot, \iota, F)$ and let R be the set of all valid runs in the automaton $\mathcal{A}$, which do not use loops:

$$R = \{(q_0, a_1, q_1, a_2, \dots, a_n, q_n) \mid n \in \mathbb{N}; \; q_0, \dots, q_n \in Q; \; a_1, \dots, a_n \in \Sigma;$$
$$q_0 = \iota; \; q_n \in F; \forall j \in \{1, \dots, n\} \colon q_{j-1} \neq q_j \land q_{j-1} \cdot a_j = q_j\}.$$

We see that the set R is finite. Moreover, for each q in Q, let Σ_q denote the alphabet $\Sigma_q = \{c \in \Sigma \mid q \cdot c = q\}$. Then

$$L_w := \Sigma_{q_0}^* a_1 \Sigma_{q_1}^* a_2 \ldots a_n \Sigma_{q_n}^* \subseteq \|\mathcal{A}\|$$

is a language of the form (1) for each $w = (q_0, a_1, q_1, a_2, \ldots, a_n, q_n)$ in R and

$$\|\mathcal{A}\| = \bigcup_{w \in R} L_w.$$

Hence the language $\|\mathcal{A}\|$ belongs to $\mathcal{R}_{LT}(\Sigma^*)$. □

The following theorem provides a summary of the previous lemmas.

Theorem 9. *For a language $L \subseteq \Sigma^*$, the following statements are equivalent:*

(i) L belongs to $\mathcal{R}_{LT}(\Sigma^*)$.
(ii) L is recognised by an LT-acyclic automaton.
(iii) The minimal automaton of L is LT-acyclic.

Proof. The statement (i) implies (ii) by Lemmas 5 and 6. The statement (ii) implies (iii) by Lemma 7. Finally, (iii) implies (i) by Lemma 8. □

One may prove that $\mathcal{R}_{LT}$ is a variety of languages in several different ways. It is possible to prove directly that the class $\mathcal{R}_{LT}$ is closed under basic language operations. It is also possible to prove that the class of LT-acyclic automata forms a variety of actions in the sense of [7]. Here we complete the previous characterisation by showing the algebraic counterpart of the class $\mathcal{R}_{LT}$; namely, we characterise the corresponding pseudovariety of finite monoids by pseudoidentities. We do not want to recall the notion of pseudoidentities in general. Let us only recall the implicit operation x^ω here. If we substitute for x some element s in a finite monoid M, then the image of x^ω is s^ω, which is a unique idempotent in the subsemigroup of M generated by s. It could be useful to know that, for a fixed finite monoid M, there is a natural number m such that $s^\omega = s^m$ for each $s \in M$.

Theorem 10. *Let Σ be an alphabet, $L \subseteq \Sigma^*$, and M_L the syntactic monoid of L. The following statements are equivalent:*

(i) L belongs to $\mathcal{R}_{LT}(\Sigma^*)$.
(ii) M_L satisfies the pseudoidentities $(xy)^\omega x = (xy)^\omega$ and $x^\omega yx = x^\omega y$.
(iii) M_L satisfies the pseudoidentity $(xy)^\omega zx = (xy)^\omega z$.

Proof. Let $\mathcal{D}_L = (Q, \Sigma, \cdot, \iota, F)$ be the minimal automaton of the language L. Then M_L can be viewed as the transition monoid of $\mathcal{D}_L$ (see [12, p. 692]). Elements of M_L are thus transitions of $\mathcal{D}_L$ determined by words from Σ^*. More formally, for $u \in \Sigma^*$, we denote by f_u the transition given by the rule $p \mapsto p \cdot u$ for each $p \in Q$. Let m be a natural number such that $s^\omega = s^m$ for each s in M_L.

Let us prove that (i) implies (ii). Suppose that L belongs to $\mathcal{R}_{LT}(\Sigma^*)$. Then $\mathcal{D}_L$ is an LT-acyclic automaton by Theorem 9. In particular, the language L is R-trivial as we already mentioned. Hence, the monoid M_L is R-trivial, *i.e.*, M_L satisfies the pseudoidentity $(xy)^\omega x = (xy)^\omega$. Next, let x, y be mapped to elements in M_L which are given by words $v, w \in \Sigma^*$. We now need to check that $f_{v^m} f_w f_v = f_{v^m} f_w$. Since $\mathcal{D}_L$ is acyclic, we have $(p \cdot v^m) \cdot a = p \cdot v^m$ for every $p \in Q$ and $a \in \Sigma$ occurring in v. Since $\mathcal{D}_L$ is an LT-acyclic automaton, the loop labelled by a in state $p \cdot v^m$ is transferred to every state reachable from $p \cdot v^m$. In particular, for every letter a occurring in v, there is a loop labelled by a in the state $(p \cdot v^m) \cdot w$. The equality $f_{v^m} f_w f_v = f_{v^m} f_w$ follows.

Next, let us show that the pseudoidentity $(xy)^\omega zx = (xy)^\omega z$ is a consequence of pseudoidentities from item (ii). We may interpret x, y, z as arbitrary elements of any finite monoid M satisfying these pseudoidentities. Let m be such that $s^\omega = s^m$ for each $s \in M$. Then we use the second pseudoidentity from (ii) repetitively, and we get

$$(xy)^\omega z = (xy)^\omega zxy = (xy)^\omega z(xy)^2 = \ldots = (xy)^\omega z(xy)^m = (xy)^\omega z(xy)^\omega. \quad (2)$$

By the first pseudoidentity from (ii), we get $(xy)^\omega z(xy)^\omega = (xy)^\omega z(xy)^\omega x$. Then we obtain $(xy)^\omega z(xy)^\omega x = (xy)^\omega zx$ using the equality (2). Thus we get $(xy)^\omega z = (xy)^\omega z(xy)^\omega = (xy)^\omega z(xy)^\omega x = (xy)^\omega zx$.

Finally, in order to prove that (iii) implies (i), suppose that M_L satisfies the pseudoidentity $(xy)^\omega zx = (xy)^\omega z$. Taking $z = 1$, it follows that M_L satisfies the pseudoidentity $(xy)^\omega x = (xy)^\omega$. Hence, L is R-trivial and $\mathcal{D}_L$ is acyclic. Moreover, let $p \in Q$ and $a \in \Sigma$ be such that $p \cdot a = p$, and take arbitrary $b \in \Sigma$. Then $f_{a^\omega} f_b$ in M_L maps p to $p \cdot b$. Similarly, $f_{a^\omega} f_b f_a$ in M_L maps p to $p \cdot ba$. However, taking $x \mapsto a$, $y \mapsto 1$, and $z \mapsto b$ in $(xy)^\omega zx = (xy)^\omega z$ gives us $f_{a^\omega} f_b f_a = f_{a^\omega} f_b$. Therefore, $p \cdot ba = p \cdot b$. So, we see that there is a loop labelled by a in the state $p \cdot b$. We proved that $\mathcal{D}_L$ is an LT-acyclic automaton and L belongs to $\mathcal{R}_{LT}(\Sigma^*)$ by Theorem 9. □

Corollary 11. *The class* $\mathcal{R}_{LT}$ *is a variety of languages corresponding to the pseudovariety of finite monoids* $\mathbf{R}_{LT}$ *given by*

$$\mathbf{R}_{LT} = [\![(xy)^\omega zx = (xy)^\omega z]\!] = [\![(xy)^\omega x = (xy)^\omega, x^\omega yx = x^\omega y]\!].$$

Let us also note that $[\![x^\omega yx = x^\omega y]\!]$ is known to describe the pseudovariety of finite monoids $\mathbf{MK}$; cf. Almeida [1, p. 212], who attributes this result to Pin. Therefore, $\mathbf{R}_{LT} = \mathbf{R} \cap \mathbf{MK}$.

5   The Main Result

Let us now return to the geometrical closure and prove the main result of this paper: *each class of languages lying between the variety of languages* $\mathcal{R}_{LT}$ *and the positive variety* $\mathcal{V}_{3/2}$ *is geometrically closed.* This strengthens the result from [8] mentioned in the Introduction.

The route that we take to this result (Theorem 16) consists of three steps:

1. We recall that the class $\mathcal{V}_{3/2}$ is closed under commutation [5,10]. Although it is not necessary to obtain our main result, we refine this observation by proving that a commutative closure of a $\mathcal{V}_{3/2}$-language is piecewise testable.
2. We prove that each commutative $\mathcal{V}_{3/2}$-language belongs to $\mathcal{R}_{LT}$.
3. We observe that the variety $\mathcal{R}_{LT}$ is closed under prefix reduction.

These three observations imply that the geometrical closure of a $\mathcal{V}_{3/2}$-language belongs to $\mathcal{R}_{LT}$, from which our main result follows easily.

Recall the result of Arfi [2], according to which a language belongs to $\mathcal{V}_{3/2}$ if and only if it is given by a finite union of languages $\Sigma_0^* a_1 \Sigma_1^* a_2 \ldots a_n \Sigma_n^*$, where $a_1, \ldots, a_n$ are letters from Σ and $\Sigma_0, \ldots, \Sigma_n$ are subalphabets of Σ. It follows by a more general result of Guaiana, Restivo, and Salemi [10], or of Bouajjani, Muscholl, and Touili [5] that $\mathcal{V}_{3/2}$ is closed under commutation, and this observation is a first step to Theorem 16.

Let us show that a commutative closure of a $\mathcal{V}_{3/2}$-language is in fact piecewise testable.

Lemma 12. *A commutative closure of a $\mathcal{V}_{3/2}$-language is piecewise testable.*

Proof. Let an alphabet Σ be fixed. It is clear that if $L_1, \ldots, L_m \subseteq \Sigma^*$ are languages, then

$$\left[\bigcup_{i=1}^m L_i \right] = \bigcup_{i=1}^m [L_i].$$

As a result, it is enough to prove piecewise testability of $[L]$ for all languages $L = \Sigma_0^* a_1 \Sigma_1^* a_2 \ldots a_n \Sigma_n^*$, with $a_1, \ldots, a_n \in \Sigma$ and $\Sigma_0, \ldots, \Sigma_n \subseteq \Sigma$.

Let L be of this form. Denote $\Sigma' = \Sigma_0 \cup \ldots \cup \Sigma_n$, and $x = a_1 \ldots a_n$. We claim that

$$[L] = \{ w \in \Sigma^* \mid \forall a \in \Sigma' : |w|_a \geq |x|_a; \ \forall b \in \Sigma \setminus \Sigma' : |w|_b = |x|_b \}. \quad (3)$$

Indeed, if w is in $[L]$, then $\Psi(w) = \Psi(u)$ for some $u \in L$, while clearly $|u|_a \geq |x|_a$ for each a in Σ', and $|u|_b = |x|_b$ for each b in $\Sigma \setminus \Sigma'$. Conversely, let w in Σ^* be such that $|w|_a \geq |x|_a$ for each a in Σ', and $|u|_b = |x|_b$ for each b in $\Sigma \setminus \Sigma'$. Then $\Psi(w) = \Psi(v)$ for v in Σ^* given by $v = v_0 a_1 v_1 a_2 \ldots a_n v_n$, where v_i $(i = 0, \ldots, n)$ is given as follows: if $\Sigma_i \setminus (\Sigma_0 \cup \ldots \cup \Sigma_{i-1}) = \{b_1, \ldots, b_j\}$, then

$$v_i = b_1^{|w|_{b_1} - |x|_{b_1}} \ldots b_j^{|w|_{b_j} - |x|_{b_j}}.$$

The word v is in L by construction, hence w belongs to $[L]$.

It remains to observe that the language $[L]$ given by (3) is piecewise testable. However, this language is equal to

$$[L] = \bigcap_{a \in \Sigma'} (\Sigma^* a)^{|x|_a} \Sigma^* \cap \bigcap_{b \in \Sigma \setminus \Sigma'} \left((\Sigma^* b)^{|x|_b} \Sigma^* \cap \left((\Sigma^* b)^{|x|_b + 1} \Sigma^* \right)^C \right). \quad (4)$$

The language on the right-hand side of (4) is piecewise testable. $\square$

We now proceed to prove that the geometrical closure of each language from $V_{3/2}$ belongs to $\mathcal{R}_{LT}$.

Lemma 13. *Every commutative language L from $V_{3/2}$ belongs to $\mathcal{R}_{LT}$.*

Proof. If we take into account the proof of Lemma 12 and the fact that $\mathcal{R}_{LT}$ is closed under finite unions, it is enough to prove that every language of the form (3) belongs to $\mathcal{R}_{LT}$. We may also use the expression (4) for that language. For each letter $a \in \Sigma$ and a natural number m, we may write $(\Sigma^* a)^m \Sigma^* = ((\Sigma \setminus \{a\})^* a)^m \Sigma^*$. This shows that the language $(\Sigma^* a)^m \Sigma^*$ belongs to $\mathcal{R}_{LT}$. Since $\mathcal{R}_{LT}$ is a variety, we see that also the language $((\Sigma^* a)^m \Sigma^*)^C$ belongs to $\mathcal{R}_{LT}$. Altogether, the language (4) belongs to the variety $\mathcal{R}_{LT}$. $\square$

Finally, let us observe that the variety $\mathcal{R}_{LT}$ is closed under prefix reduction.

Lemma 14. *Let L be a language from $\mathcal{R}_{LT}(\Sigma^*)$ for some alphabet Σ. Then $\mathrm{pref}^{\downarrow}(L)$ belongs to $\mathcal{R}_{LT}(\Sigma^*)$ as well.*

Proof. Let L be recognised by some LT-acyclic automaton $\mathcal{A} = (Q, \Sigma, \cdot, \iota, F)$. If $\iota \notin F$, then L does not contain the empty word, and consequently $\mathrm{pref}^{\downarrow}(L) = \emptyset$, which belongs to $\mathcal{R}_{LT}(\Sigma^*)$. So we may assume that $\iota \in F$.

Now, simply saying, we claim that the language $\mathrm{pref}^{\downarrow}(L)$ is recognised by the automaton $\mathcal{A}'$ constructed from $\mathcal{A}$ by replacing all non-final states with a single absorbing non-final state τ. More precisely, we construct an automaton $\mathcal{A}' = (F \cup \{\tau\}, \Sigma, \bullet, \iota, F)$, where τ is a new state, for which we define $\tau \bullet a = \tau$ for each $a \in \Sigma$. Furthermore, for each $p \in F$ and $a \in \Sigma$, we put $p \bullet a = p \cdot a$ if $p \cdot a \in F$, and $p \bullet a = \tau$ otherwise. As $\mathcal{A}$ contains no cycle other than a loop, the constructed automaton $\mathcal{A}'$ has the same property. Moreover, any state of $\mathcal{A}'$ reachable in $\mathcal{A}'$ from some p in $F \cup \{\tau\}$ is either reachable from p in $\mathcal{A}$, or equal to τ. As $\tau \bullet c = \tau$ for each c in Σ, this implies that $\mathcal{A}'$ is an LT-acyclic automaton and $\mathrm{pref}^{\downarrow}(L)$ belongs to $\mathcal{R}_{LT}(\Sigma^*)$ by Theorem 9. $\square$

Theorem 15. *Let Σ be an alphabet and $L \in V_{3/2}(\Sigma^*)$. Then $\gamma(L) \in \mathcal{R}_{LT}(\Sigma^*)$.*

Proof. We have $\gamma(L) = \mathrm{pref}^{\downarrow}([\mathrm{pref}^{\uparrow}(L)])$ by Proposition 2. As $V_{3/2}$ is a positive variety of languages, $\mathrm{pref}^{\uparrow}(L)$ belongs to $V_{3/2}(\Sigma^*)$ whenever L belongs to this set by Proposition 1. The language $[\mathrm{pref}^{\uparrow}(L)]$ is thus a commutative $V_{3/2}$-language by [5,10]. (Note that the language $[\mathrm{pref}^{\uparrow}(L)]$ is actually commutative piecewise testable, by Lemma 12.) It follows by Lemma 13 that $[\mathrm{pref}^{\uparrow}(L)]$ belongs to $\mathcal{R}_{LT}(\Sigma^*)$, and by Lemma 14 that the language $\gamma(L) = \mathrm{pref}^{\downarrow}([\mathrm{pref}^{\uparrow}(L)])$ belongs to $\mathcal{R}_{LT}(\Sigma^*)$ as well. $\square$

We are now prepared to state the main result of this article merely as an alternative formulation of the theorem above.

Theorem 16. *Let C be a class of languages containing $\mathcal{R}_{LT}$, which is contained in $\mathcal{V}_{3/2}$. Then C is geometrically closed.*

There are many important (positive) varieties studied in the literature for which the main result can be applied.

Corollary 17. *The following classes are geometrically closed: the positive variety $\mathcal{V}_{3/2}$, the variety $\mathcal{R}$, the variety $\mathcal{R}_{LT}$, the variety of all **JMK**-recognisable languages, the variety of all **DA**-recognisable languages.*

The variety of all **DA**-recognisable languages coincides with the intersection of $\mathcal{V}_{3/2}$ and its dual. This class has a natural interpretation in terms of logical descriptions of levels in Straubing-Thérien hierarchy (see Section 5 in [15]).

6 Conclusions

We have introduced a new variety of languages $\mathcal{R}_{LT}$ and we have proved that geometrical closures of languages from $\mathcal{V}_{3/2}$ fall into $\mathcal{R}_{LT}$. As a consequence, we have seen that many natural classes of star-free languages are geometrically closed, namely those between the variety $\mathcal{R}_{LT}$ and the positive variety $\mathcal{V}_{3/2}$. On the contrary, the variety of all piecewise testable languages $\mathcal{V}_1$ is not geometrically closed. The example is not included in the paper due to space limitations.

There are some interesting questions in connection to the paper. First of all, one may ask how to effectively construct a regular expression for the geometrical closure $\gamma(L)$ for a given language L from $\mathcal{V}_{3/2}$. Note that it is effectively testable, for a given deterministic finite automaton $\mathcal{A}$, whether the language $\|\mathcal{A}\|$ belongs to $\mathcal{V}_{3/2}$ (see [12, p. 725]). It is not clear to us whether a regular expression for $\|\mathcal{A}\|$ can be effectively computed from $\mathcal{A}$.

Nevertheless, the main open question related to the topic is to clarify the behaviour of the geometrical closure outside the class $\mathcal{V}_{3/2}$.

References

1. Almeida, J.: Finite Semigroups and Universal Algebra. World Scientific, Singapore (1994)
2. Arfi, M.: Opérations polynomiales et hiérarchies de concaténation. Theor. Comput. Sci. **91**(1), 71–84 (1991)
3. Béal, M.-P., Champarnaud, J.-M., Dubernard, J.-P., Jeanne, H., Lombardy, S.: Decidability of geometricity of regular languages. In: Yen, H.-C., Ibarra, O.H. (eds.) DLT 2012. LNCS, vol. 7410, pp. 62–72. Springer, Heidelberg (2012). https://doi.org/10.1007/978-3-642-31653-1_7
4. Blanpain, B., Champarnaud, J.M., Dubernard, J.P.: Geometrical languages. In: LATA 2007, pp. 127–138 (2007)
5. Bouajjani, A., Muscholl, A., Touili, T.: Permutation rewriting and algorithmic verification. Inf. Comput. **205**(2), 199–224 (2007)
6. Brzozowski, J.A., Fich, F.E.: Languages of $\mathscr{R}$-trivial monoids. J. Comput. Syst. Sci. **20**(1), 32–49 (1980)

7. Chaubard, L., Pin, J.É., Straubing, H.: Actions, wreath products of C-varieties and concatenation product. Theor. Comput. Sci. **356**(1–2), 73–89 (2006)
8. Dubernard, J.-P., Guaiana, G., Mignot, L.: Geometrical closure of binary $V_{3/2}$ languages. In: Martín-Vide, C., Okhotin, A., Shapira, D. (eds.) LATA 2019. LNCS, vol. 11417, pp. 302–314. Springer, Cham (2019). https://doi.org/10.1007/978-3-030-13435-8_22
9. Gehrke, M., Grigorieff, S., Pin, J.É.: Duality and equational theory of regular languages. In: Aceto, L., Damgård, I., Goldberg, L.A., Halldórsson, M.M., Ingólfsdóttir, A., Walukiewicz, I. (eds.) ICALP 2008, (Track B). LNCS, vol. 5126, pp. 246–257. Springer, Heidelberg (2008). https://doi.org/10.1007/978-3-540-70583-3_21
10. Guaiana, G., Restivo, A., Salemi, S.: On the trace product and some families of languages closed under partial commutations. J. Autom. Lang. Comb. **9**(1), 61–79 (2004)
11. Pin, J.É.: Varieties of Formal Languages. North Oxford Academic Publishers, London (1986)
12. Pin, J.-E.: Syntactic semigroups. In: Rozenberg, G., Salomaa, A. (eds.) Handbook of Formal Languages, pp. 679–746. Springer, Heidelberg (1997). https://doi.org/10.1007/978-3-642-59136-5_10
13. Pin, J.É., Straubing, H., Thérien, D.: Small varieties of finite semigroups and extensions. J. Aust. Math. Soc. **37**(2), 269–281 (1984)
14. Sakarovitch, J.: Elements of Automata Theory. Cambridge University Press, Cambridge (2009)
15. Tesson, P., Thérien, D.: Diamonds are forever: the variety DA. In: Semigroups, Algorithms, Automata and Languages, pp. 475–499. World Scientific (2002)

Intersection and Union Hierarchies of Deterministic Context-Free Languages and Pumping Lemmas

Tomoyuki Yamakami$^{(\boxtimes)}$

Faculty of Engineering, University of Fukui, 3-9-1 Bunkyo, Fukui 910-8507, Japan
TomoyukiYamakami@gmail.com

Abstract. We study the computational complexity of finite intersections and unions of deterministic context-free languages. Earlier, Wotschke (1978) demonstrated that intersections of $(d+1)$ deterministic context-free languages are in general more powerful than intersections of d deterministic context-free languages for any positive integer d based on the hierarchy separation of Liu and Weiner (1973). The argument of Liu and Weiner, however, works only on bounded languages of particular forms, and therefore Wotschke's result cannot be extended to disprove any other language to be written in the form of an intersection of d deterministic context-free languages. To deal with the non-membership of a wide range of languages, we circumvent their proof argument and instead devise a new, practical technical tool: a pumping lemma for finite unions of deterministic context-free languages. Since the family of deterministic context-free languages is closed under complementation, this pumping lemma enables us to show a non-membership relation of languages made up with finite intersections of even non-bounded languages as well. We also refer to a relationship to Hibbard's limited automata.

Keywords: Deterministic pushdown automata · Intersection and union hierarchies · Pumping lemma · Limited automata

1 A Historical Account and an Overview of Contributions

1.1 Intersection and Union Hierarchies and Historical Background

In formal language theory, context-free languages constitute a fundamental family CFL, which is situated in between the family REG of regular languages and that of context-sensitive languages. It has been well known that this family CFL is closed under an operation of union but not closed under intersection. As a quick example, the language $L_{abc} = \{a^n b^n c^n \mid n \geq 0\}$ is not context-free but it can be expressed as an intersection of two context-free languages. This non-closure property can be further generalized to any intersection of d (≥ 1) context-free languages. For later notational convenience, we here write $\mathrm{CFL}(d)$ for the family of such languages, namely, the d intersection closure of CFL (see,

© Springer Nature Switzerland AG 2020
A. Leporati et al. (Eds.): LATA 2020, LNCS 12038, pp. 341–353, 2020.
https://doi.org/10.1007/978-3-030-40608-0_24

e.g., [13]). With this notation, the above language L_{abc} belongs to $\mathrm{CFL}(2) - \mathrm{CFL}$. Similarly, the language $L_d = \{a_1^{n_1} a_2^{n_2} \cdots a_d^{n_d} b_1^{n_1} b_2^{n_2} \cdots b_d^{n_d} \mid n_1, n_2, \ldots, n_d \geq 0\}$ over an alphabet $\{a_1, a_2, \ldots, a_d, b_1, b_2, \ldots, b_d\}$ falls into $\mathrm{CFL}(d)$ because L_d can be expressed as an intersection of d context-free languages of the form $\{a_1^{n_1} a_2^{n_2} \cdots a_d^{n_d} b_1^{m_1} b_2^{m_2} \cdots b_d^{m_d} \mid n_1, n_2, \ldots, n_d, m_1, m_2, \ldots, m_d \geq 0, n_k = m_k\}$ $(1 \leq k \leq d)$. In 1973, Liu and Weiner [8] gave a contrived proof to their key statement that (*) L_d *is outside of* $\mathrm{CFL}(d-1)$ *for any index* $d \geq 2$. Therefore, the collection $\{\mathrm{CFL}(d) \mid d \geq 1\}$ truly forms an infinite hierarchy.

Deterministic context-free (dcf) languages have been a focal point in CFL since a systematic study of Ginsburg and Greibach [1]. The importance of such languages can be exemplified by the facts that dcf languages are easy to parse and that every context-free language is simply the homomorphic image of a dcf language. Unlike CFL, the family DCFL of dcf languages is closed under neither union nor intersection. We use the terms of *d-intersection deterministic context-free (dcf) languages* and *d-union deterministic context-free (dcf) languages* to express intersections of d dcf languages and unions of d dcf languages, respectively. For brevity, we write $\mathrm{DCFL}(d)$ and $\mathrm{DCFL}[d]$ respectively for the family of all d-intersection dcf languages and that of all d-union dcf languages, while Wotschke [11,12] earlier referred $\mathrm{DCFL}(d)$ to the d-intersection closure of DCFL. In particular, we obtain $\mathrm{DCFL}(1) = \mathrm{DCFL}[1] = \mathrm{DCFL}$. Since DCFL is closed under complementation, it follows that the complement of $\mathrm{DCFL}(d)$ coincides with $\mathrm{DCFL}[d]$. For our convenience, we call two hierarchies $\{\mathrm{DCFL}(d) \mid d \geq 1\}$ and $\{\mathrm{DCFL}[d] \mid d \geq 1\}$ the *intersection and union hierarchies of dcf languages*, respectively. Concerning these hierarchies, we set $\mathrm{DCFL}(\omega)$ to be the intersection closure of DCFL, which is $\bigcup_{d \geq 1} \mathrm{DCFL}(d)$. In a similar way, we write $\mathrm{DCFL}[\omega]$ for the union closure of DCFL, that is, $\bigcup_{d \geq 1} \mathrm{DCFL}[d]$.

Wotschke [11,12] noted that the aforementioned result (*) of Liu and Weiner leads to the conclusion that $\{\mathrm{DCFL}[d] \mid d \geq 1\}$ truly forms an infinite hierarchy. To be more precise, since the language L_d belongs to $\mathrm{DCFL}(d)$, the statement (*) implies $\mathrm{DCFL}(d) \not\subseteq \mathrm{CFL}(d-1)$, which instantly yields $\mathrm{DCFL}(d-1) \neq \mathrm{DCFL}(d)$. Wotschke's argument, nonetheless, heavily relies on the separation result of Liu and Weiner, who employed a notion of *stratified semi-linear set* to prove the statement (*). Notice that the proof technique of Liu and Weiner was developed only for a particular form of *bounded languages*[1] and it is therefore applicable to specific languages, such as L_d. In fact, the key idea of the proof of Liu and Weiner for L_d is to focus on the number of the occurrences of each base symbol in $\{a_1, \ldots, a_d, b_1, \ldots, b_d\}$ appearing in each given string w and to translate L_d into a set $\Psi(L_d)$ of *Parikh images* $(\#_{a_1}(w), \#_{a_2}(w), \ldots, \#_{a_d}(w), \#_{b_1}, \ldots, \#_{b_d}(w))$ in order to exploit the semi-linearity of $\Psi(L_d)$, where $\#_\sigma(w)$ expresses the total number of symbols σ in a string w.

Because of the aforementioned limitation of Liu and Weiner's proof technique, the scope of their proof cannot be extended to other forms of languages. Simple examples of such languages include $L_d^{(\leq)} = \{a_1^{n_1} \cdots a_d^{n_d} b_1^{m_1} \cdots b_d^{m_d} \mid \forall i \in [d](n_i \leq m_i)\}$, where $[d]$ denotes the set $\{1, 2, \ldots, d\}$. This is a bounded

---

[1] A bounded language satisfies $L \subseteq w_1^* w_2^* \cdots w_k^*$ for fixed strings $w_1, w_2, \ldots, w_k$.

language expanding L_d but its Parikh images do not have semi-linearity. As another example, let us take a look at a "non-palindrome" language $NPal_d^{\#} = \{w_1\#w_2\#\cdots\#w_d\#v_1\#v_2\#\cdots\#v_d \mid \forall i \in [d](w_i, v_i \in \{0,1\}^* \wedge v_i \neq w_i^R)\}$, where w_i^R expresses the *reversal* of w_i. This $NPal_d^{\#}$ is not even a bounded language. Therefore, Liu and Weiner's argument is not directly applicable to verify that neither $L_d^{(\leq)}$ nor $NPal_d^{\#}$ belongs to CFL($d-1$) unless we dextrously pick up its core strings that form a certain bounded language. With no such contrived argument, how can we prove $L_d^{(\leq)}$ and $NPal_d^{\#}$ to be outside of DCFL(d)? Moreover, given a language, how can we verify that it is not in DCFL(ω)? We can ask similar questions for d-union dcf languages and the union hierarchy of dcf languages. Ginsburg and Greibach [1] remarked *with no proof* that the context-free language $Pal = \{ww^R \mid w \in \Sigma^*\}$ for any non-unary alphabet Σ is not in DCFL[ω]. It is natural to call for a formal proof of the remark of Ginsburg and Greibach. Using a quite different language $L_{wot} = \{wcx \mid w, x \in \{a,b\}^*, w \neq x\}$, however, Wotschke [11,12] actually proved that L_{wot} does not belong to DCFL(ω) (more strongly, the Boolean closure of DCFL) by employing the closure property of DCFL(d) under inverse gsm mappings as well as complementation and intersection with regular languages. Wotschke's proof relies on the following two facts. (i) The language L_{d+1} can be expressed as the inverse gsm map of the language $Dup_c = \{wcw \mid w \in \{a,b\}^*\}$, restricted to $a_1^+ a_2^+ \cdots a_{d+1}^+ a_1^+ a_2^+ \cdots a_{d+1}^+$. (ii) Dup_c is expressed as the complement of L_{wot}, restricted to a certain regular language. Together with these facts, the final conclusion comes from the aforementioned result (*) of Liu and Weiner because $Dup_c \in$ DCFL(d) implies $L_{d+1} \in$ DCFL(d) by (i) and (ii). To our surprise, the fundamental results on DCFL(d) that we have discussed so far are merely "corollaries" of the main result (*) of Liu and Weiner!

For further study on DCFL(d) and answering more general non-membership questions to DCFL(d), we need to divert from Liu and Weiner's contrived argument targeting the statement (*) and to develop a completely different, new, more practical technical tool. The sole purpose of this exposition is, therefore, set to (i) develop a new proof technique, which can be applicable to many other languages, (ii) present an alternative proof for the fact that the intersection and union hierarchies of DCFL are infinite hierarchies, and (iii) present other languages in CFL that do not belong to DCFL(ω) (in part, verifying Ginsburg and Greibach's remark for the first time).

In relevance to the union hierarchy of dcf languages, there is another known extension of DCFL using a different machine model called *limited automata*,[2] which are originally invented by Hibbard [3] and later discussed extensively in, e.g., [9,14]. Of all such machines, a *d-limited deterministic automaton* (or a *d-lda*, for short) is a deterministic Turing machine that can rewrite each tape cell in between two endmarkers only during the first d visits (except that making a

---

[2] Hibbard [3] actually defined a rewriting system, called "scan-limited automata." Later, Pighizzini and Pisoni [9] re-formulated Hibbard's system as restricted linear automata.

turn of a tape head counts as double visits). We can raise a question of whether there is any relationship between the union hierarchy and d-lda's.

1.2 Overview of Main Contributions

In Sect. 1.1, we have noted that fundamental properties associated with DCFL(d) heavily rely on the single separation result (*) of Liu and Weiner. However, Liu and Weiner's technical tool that leads to their main result does not seem to withstand a wide variety of direct applications. It is thus desirable to develop a new, simple, and practical technical tool that can find numerous applications for a future study on DCFL(d) and DCFL[d]. Thus, our main contribution of this exposition is to present a simple but powerful, practical technical tool, called the *pumping lemma* of languages in DCFL[d] with $d \geq 1$, which also enriches our understanding of DCFL[d] as well as DCFL(d). Notice that there have been numerous forms of so-called pumping lemmas (or iteration theorems) for variants of context-free languages in the past literature, e.g., [2,4–7,10,15]. Our pumping lemma is a crucial addition to the list of such lemmas.

For a string x of length n and any number $i \in [n]$, $x[i]$ stands for the ith symbol of x and x^i for the i repetitions of x.

Lemma 1 (Pumping Lemma for DCFL[d]). *Let d be any positive integer and let L be any d-union dcf language over an alphabet Σ. There exist a constant $c > 0$ such that, for any $d + 1$ strings $w_1, w_2, \ldots, w_{d+1} \in L$, if w_i has the form $xy^{(i)}$ for strings $x, y^{(i)} \in \Sigma^*$ with $|x| > c$ and $y^{(i)}[1] = y^{(j)}[1]$ for any pair $i, j \in [d + 1]$, then there exists two distinct indices $j_1, j_2 \in [d + 1]$ for which the following conditions (1)–(2) hold. Let $k \in [d + 1]$.*

1. *If $k \notin \{j_1, j_2\}$, then either (a) or (b) holds.*
   (a) *There is a factorization $x = u_1u_2u_3u_4u_5$ with $|u_2u_4| \geq 1$ and $|u_2u_3u_4| \leq c$ such that $u_1u_2^iu_3u_4^iu_5y^{(k)}$ is in L for any number $i \geq 0$.*
   (b) *There are two factorizations $x = u_1u_2u_3$ and $y^{(k)} = y_1y_2y_3$ with $|u_2| \geq 1$ and $|u_2u_3| \leq c$ such that $u_1u_2^iu_3y_1y_2^iy_3$ is in L for any number $i \geq 0$.*
2. *In the case of $k \in \{j_1, j_2\}$, either (a) or (b) holds.*
   (a) *There is a factorization $x = u_1u_2u_3u_4u_5$ with $|u_2u_4| \geq 1$ and $|u_2u_3u_4| \leq c$ such that, for each $z \in \{y^{(j_1)}, y^{(j_2)}\}$, $u_1u_2^iu_3u_4^iu_5z$ is in L for any $i \geq 0$.*
   (b) *Let $x'y = xy^{(j_1)}$ and $x'\hat{y} = xy^{(j_2)}$. There are three factorizations $x' = u_1u_2u_3$, $y = y_1y_2y_3$, and $\hat{y} = z_1z_2z_3$ with $|u_2| \geq 1$ and $|u_2u_3| \leq c$ such that $u_1u_2^iu_3y_1y_2^iy_3$ and $u_1u_2^iu_3z_1z_2^iz_3$ are in L for any number $i \geq 0$.*

As a special case of $d = 1$, we obtain Yu's pumping lemma [15, Lemma 1] from Lemma 1. Since there have been few machine-based analyses to prove various pumping lemmas in the past literature, one of the important aspects of this exposition is a clear demonstration of the *first alternative proof* to Yu's pumping lemma, which is solely founded on an analysis of behaviors of 1dpda's instead of derivation trees of LR(k) grammars as in [15]. The proof of Lemma 1, in fact, exploits early results of [14] on an *ideal shape* form (Sect. 2.3) together with a new approach of ε-*enhanced machines* by analyzing transitions of *crossing state-stack pairs* (Sect. 2.4). These notions will be explained in Sect. 2 and their basic properties will be explored therein.

Using our pumping lemma (Lemma 1), we can expand the scope of the statement (*) of Liu and Weiner [8] targeting specific bounded languages to other types of languages, including $L_d^{(\le)}$ and $NPal_d^{\#}$ for each index $d \ge 2$.

Theorem 1. *Let $d \ge 2$ be any index.*

1. *The language $L_d^{(\le)}$ is not in* DCFL($d-1$).
2. *The language $NPal_d^{\#}$ is not in* DCFL($d-1$).

Since Lemma 1 concerns with DCFL[d], in our proof of Theorem 1, we first take the complements of the above languages, restricted to suitable regular languages, and we then apply Lemma 1 appropriately to them. The proof sketch of this theorem will be given in Sect. 3. From Theorem 1, we instantly obtain the following consequences of Wotschke [11,12].

Corollary 1. [11,12] *The intersection hierarchy of dcf languages and the union hierarchy of dcf languages are both infinite hierarchies.*

Concerning the limitation of DCFL(ω) and DCFL[ω] in recognition power, since all *unary* context-free languages are also regular languages and the family REG of regular languages is closed under intersection, all unary languages in DCFL(ω) are regular as well. It is thus easy to find languages that are not in DCFL(ω). Such languages, nevertheless, cannot serve themselves to separate CFL from DCFL(ω) $\cup$ DCFL[ω]. As noted in Sect. 1.1, Ginsburg and Greibach [1] remarked *with no proof* that the context-free language $Pal = \{ww^R \mid w \in \{0,1\}^*\}$ does not belong to DCFL(ω) (as well as DCFL[ω]). As another direct application of our pumping lemma, we give a formal written proof of their remark.

Theorem 2. *The context-free language Pal is not in* DCFL(ω) $\cup$ DCFL[ω].

As an immediate consequence of the above theorem, we obtain Wotschke's separation of DCFL(ω) from CFL. Here, we stress that, unlike the work of Wotschke [11,12], our proof does not depend on the main result (*) of Liu and Weiner.

Corollary 2. [11,12] CFL $\nsubseteq$ DCFL(ω) *and* DCFL[ω] $\subsetneq$ CFL.

We turn our interest to limited automata. Let us write d-LDA for the family of all languages recognized by d-limited deterministic automata, in which their tape heads are allowed to rewrite tape symbols only during the first d accesses (except that, in the case of tape heads making a turn, we treat each turn as double visits). Hibbard [3] demonstrated that d-LDA $\ne$ ($d-1$)-LDA for any $d \ge 3$. A slightly modified language of his, which separates d-LDA from ($d-1$)-LDA, also belongs to the 2^{d-2}-th level of the union hierarchy of dcf languages but not in the ($2^{d-2}-1$)-th level. We thus obtain the following separation.

Proposition 1. *For any $d \geq 3$, d-LDA $\cap$ DCFL$[2^{d-2}] \not\subseteq (d-1)$-LDA $\cup$ DCFL$[2^{d-2} - 1]$.*

The proofs of all the above assertions will be given after introducing necessary notions and notation in the subsequent section.

2   Preparations: Notions and Notation

2.1   Fundamental Notions and Notation

The set of all *natural numbers* (including 0) is denoted by $\mathbb{N}$. An *integer interval* $[m, n]_{\mathbb{Z}}$ for two integers m, n with $m \leq n$ is the set $\{m, m+1, m+2, \ldots, n\}$. In particular, for any integer $n \geq 1$, $[1, n]_{\mathbb{Z}}$ is abbreviated as $[n]$. For any string x, $|x|$ indicates the total number of symbols in x. The special symbol ε is used to denote the *empty string* of length 0. For a language L over alphabet Σ, $\overline{L}$ denotes $\Sigma^* - L$, the *complement* of L. Given a family $\mathcal{F}$ of languages, co-$\mathcal{F}$ expresses the *complement family*, which consists of languages $\overline{L}$ for any $L \in \mathcal{F}$.

2.2   Deterministic Pushdown Automata

A *one-way deterministic pushdown automaton* (or a 1dpda, for short) M is a tuple $(Q, \Sigma, \{\mathcal{c}, \$\}, \Gamma, \delta, q_0, Z_0, Q_{acc}, Q_{rej})$, where Q is a finite set of inner states, Σ is an input alphabet with $\check{\Sigma} = \Sigma \cup \{\varepsilon, \mathcal{c}, \$\}$, Γ is a stack alphabet, δ is a deterministic transition function from $Q \times \check{\Sigma} \times \Gamma$ to $Q \times \Gamma^*$, q_0 is the initial state in Q, Z_0 is the bottom marker in Γ, and Q_{acc} and Q_{rej} are subsets of Q. The symbols $\mathcal{c}$ and $\$$ respectively express the left-endmarker and the right-endmarker. Let $\Gamma^{(-)} = \Gamma - \{Z_0\}$. We assume that, if $\delta(p, \varepsilon, a)$ is defined, then $\delta(p, \sigma, a)$ is undefined for all symbols $\sigma \in \check{\Sigma} - \{\varepsilon\}$. Moreover, we require $\delta(q, \sigma, Z_0) \neq (p, \varepsilon)$ for any $p, q \in Q$ and $\sigma \in \check{\Sigma}$. Each content of a stack is expressed as $a_1 a_2 \cdots a_k$ in which a_1 is the topmost stack symbol, a_k is the bottom marker Z_0, and all others are placed in order from the top to the bottom of the stack.

Given $d \in \mathbb{N}^+$, a *d-intersection deterministic context-free (dcf) language* is an intersection of d deterministic context-free (dcf) languages. Let DCFL(d) denote the family of all d-intersection dcf languages. Similarly, we define *d-union dcf languages* and DCFL$[d]$ by substituting "union" for "intersection" in the above definitions. Note that DCFL$[d] =$ co-(DCFL(d)) because DCFL $=$ co-DCFL.

For two language families $\mathcal{F}_1$ and $\mathcal{F}_2$, the notation $\mathcal{F}_1 \wedge \mathcal{F}_2$ (resp., $\mathcal{F}_1 \vee \mathcal{F}_2$) denotes the family of all languages L for which there are two languages $L_1 \in \mathcal{F}_1$ and $L_2 \in \mathcal{F}_2$ over the same alphabet satisfying $L = L_1 \cap L_2$ (resp., $L = L_1 \cup L_2$).

Lemma 2. [11,12] *DCFL(d) is closed under union, intersection with* REG. *In other words,* DCFL$(d) \wedge$ REG $\subseteq$ DCFL(d) *and* DCFL$(d) \vee$ REG $\subseteq$ DCFL(d). *A similar statement holds for* DCFL$[d]$.

Lemma 3. *Let $d \geq 1$ be any natural number.*

1. *DCFL$(d) =$ DCFL$(d+1)$ iff DCFL$[d] =$ DCFL$[d+1]$.*
2. *If $L \in$ DCFL(d), then it follows that $A \cap \overline{L} \in$ DCFL$[d]$ for any $A \in$ REG.*

From Lemma 3(1) follows Corollary 1, provided that Theorem 1 is true. The-orem 1 itself will be proven in Sect. 3.

2.3 Ideal Shape

Let us recall from [14] a special "pop-controlled form" (called an *ideal shape*), in which the pop operations always take place by first reading an input symbol and then making a series (one or more) of the pop operations without reading any further input symbol. This notion was originally introduced for *one-way probabilistic pushdown automata* (or 1ppda's); however, in this exposition, we apply this notion only to 1dpda's. To be more formal, a 1dpda *in an ideal shape* is a 1dpda restricted to take only the following transitions. (1) Scanning $\sigma \in \Sigma$, preserve the topmost stack symbol (called a *stationary operation*). (2) Scanning $\sigma \in \Sigma$, push a new symbol u ($\in \Gamma^{(-)}$) without changing any other symbol in the stack. (3) Scanning $\sigma \in \Sigma$, pop the topmost stack symbol. (4) Without scanning an input symbol (i.e., ε-*move*), pop the topmost stack symbol. (5) The stack operations (4) comes only after either (3) or (4).

It was shown in [14] that any 1ppda can be converted into its "error-equivalent" 1ppda in an ideal shape. In Lemma 4, we restate this result for 1dpda's. We say that two 1dpda's are *(computationally) equivalent* if, for any input x, their acceptance/rejection coincide. The *push size* of a 1ppda is the maximum length of any string pushed into a stack by any single move.

Lemma 4 (Ideal Shape Lemma for 1dpda's). (cf. [14]) *Let $n \in \mathbb{N}^+$. Any n-state 1dpda M with stack alphabet size m and push size e can be converted into another (computationally) equivalent 1dpda N in an ideal shape with $O(en^2m^2(2m)^{2enm})$ states and stack alphabet size $O(enm(2m)^{2enm})$.*

2.4 Boundaries and Crossing State-Stack Pairs

We want to define two basic notions of boundaries and crossing state-stacks. For this purpose, we visualize a *single move* of a 1dpda M as three consecutive actions: (i) firstly replacing the topmost stack symbol, (ii) updating an inner state, and (iii) thirdly either moving a tape head or staying still.

A *boundary* is a borderline between two consecutive tape cells. We index all such boundaries from 0 to $|\text{¢}x\$|$ as follows. The boundary 0 is located at the left of cell 0 and boundary $i+1$ is in between cell i and $i+1$ for every index $i \geq 0$. When a string xy is written in $|xy|$ consecutive cells, the (x, y)-*boundary* indicates the boundary $|x| + 1$, which separates between x and y. A *boundary block* between boundaries t_1 and t_2 with $t_1 \leq t_2$ is a consecutive series of boundaries between t_1 and t_2 (including t_1 and t_2). These t_1 and t_2 are called *ends* of this boundary block. For brevity, we write $[t_1, t_2]$ to denote a boundary block between t_1 and t_2. For two boundaries t_1, t_2 with $t_1 < t_2$, the (t_1, t_2)-*region* refers to the consecutive cells located in the boundary block $[t_1, t_2]$. When an input string x is written in the (t_1, t_2)-region, we conveniently call this region the x-*region* unless the region is unclear from the context.

The *stack height* of M at boundary t is the length of the stack content while passing the boundary t. E.g., a stack content $a_1 a_2 \cdots a_k$ has stack height k.

A boundary block $[t_1, t_2]$ is called *convex* if there is a boundary s between t_1 and t_2 (namely, $s \in [t_1, t_2]$) such that there is no pop operation in the (t_1, s)-region and there is no push operation in the (s, t_2)-region. A boundary block $[t_1, t_2]$ is *flat* if the stack height does not change in the (t_1, t_2)-region. A boundary block $[t_1, t_2]$ with $t_1 < t_2$ is *pseudo-convex* if the stack height at every boundary $s \in [t_1, t_2]$ does not go below $h_2 - \frac{h_1 - h_2}{t_2 - t_1}(s - t_1)$, where h_i is the stack height at boundary t_i for any $i \in \{1, 2\}$. By their definitions, either convex or flat boundary blocks are also pseudo-convex.

A *peak* is a boundary t such that the stack heights at the boundaries $t-1$ and $t+1$ are smaller than the stack height at the boundary t. A *plateau* is a boundary block $[t, t']$ such that any stack height at a boundary $i \in [t, t']$ is the same. A *hill* is a boundary block $[t, t']$ such that (i) the stack height at the boundary t and the stack height at the boundary t' coincide, (ii) there is at least one peak at a certain boundary $i \in [t, t']$, and (iii) both $[t, i]$ and $[i, t']$ are convex. The *height* of a hill is the difference between the topmost stack height and the lowest stack height.

Given strings over alphabet Σ, *ε-enhanced strings* are strings over the extended alphabet $\Sigma_\varepsilon = \Sigma \cup \{\varepsilon\}$, where ε is treated as a special input symbol expressing the absence of symbols in Σ. An *ε-enhanced 1dpda* (or an *ε-1dpa*, for short) is a 1dpda that takes ε-enhanced strings and works as a standard 1dpda except that a tape head always moves to the right without stopping. This tape head movement is sometimes called "real time".

Lemma 5. *For any 1dpda M, there exists an ε-1dpda N such that, for any input string x, there is an appropriate ε-enhanced string $\hat{x}$ for which M accepts (resp., rejects) x iff N accepts (resp., rejects) $\hat{x}$. Moreover, $\hat{x}$ is identical to x except for the ε symbol and is uniquely determined from x and M.*

Let M be either a 1dpda or an ε-1dpda, and assume that M is in an ideal shape. A *crossing state-stack pair* at boundary i is a pair (q, γ) of inner state q and stack content γ. In a computation of M on input x, a crossing state-stack pair (q, γ) at boundary i refers to the machine's current status where (1) M is reading an input symbol, say, σ at cell $i - 1$ in a certain state, say, p with the stack content $a\gamma'$ and then M changes its inner state to q, changing a by either pushing another symbol b satisfying $\gamma = ba\gamma'$ or popping a with $\gamma = \gamma'$. Any computation of M on x can be expressed as a series of crossing state-stack pairs at every boundary in the $\text{¢}x\$$-region.

Two boundaries t_1 and t_2 with $t_1 < t_2$ are *mutually correlated* if there are two crossing state-stack pairs (q, γ) and (p, γ) at the boundaries t_1 and t_2, respectively, for which the boundary block $[t_1, t_2]$ is pseudo-convex. Moreover, assume that $t_1 < t_2 < t_3 < t_4$. Two boundary blocks $[t_1, t_2]$ and $[t_3, t_4]$ are *mutually correlated* if (i) $[t_1, t_2]$, $[t_2, t_3]$, and $[t_3, t_4]$ are all pseudo-convex, (ii) (q, γ) and $(p, \alpha\gamma)$ are crossing state-stack pairs at the boundaries t_1 and t_2, respectively, and (iii) $(s, \alpha\gamma)$ and (r, γ) are also crossing state-stack pairs at the boundaries t_3 and t_4, respectively, for certain $p, q, r, s \in Q$, $\gamma \in (\Gamma^{(-)})^* Z_0$, and $\alpha \in (\Gamma^{(-)})^*$.

If an ε-1dpda is in an ideal shape, then it pops exactly one stack symbol whenever it reads a single symbol of a given ε-enhanced input string.

Lemma 6. *Let w be any string.*

1. *Let $t_1, t_2 \in \mathbb{N}$ with $1 \le t_1 < t_2 \le |w| + 1$. Let $w = x_1 x_2 x_3$ be a factorization such that t_1 is the (x_1, x_2)-boundary and t_2 is the (x_2, x_3)-boundary. If the boundaries t_1 and t_2 are mutually correlated and inner states at the boundaries t_1 and t_2 coincide, then it follows that $w \in L$ iff $x_1 x_2^i x_3 \in L$ for any $i \in \mathbb{N}$.*
2. *Let $t_1, t_2, t_3, t_4 \in \mathbb{N}$ with $1 \le t_1 < t_2 < t_3 < t_4 \le |w| + 1$. Let $w = x_1 x_2 x_3 x_4 x_5$ such that each t_i is (x_i, x_{i+1})-boundary for each $i \in [4]$. If two boundary blocks $[t_1, t_2]$ and $[t_3, t_4]$ are mutually correlated, inner states at the boundaries t_1 and t_2 coincide, and inner states at the boundaries t_3 and t_4 coincide, then it follows that $w \in L$ iff $x_1 x_2^i x_3 x_4^i x_5 \in L$ for any number $i \in \mathbb{N}$.*

3   Proof Sketches of Three Separation Claims

We intend to present the proof sketches of three separation claims (Theorems 1 and 2 and Proposition 1) before verifying the pumping lemma. To understand our proofs better, we demonstrate a simple and easy example of how to apply Lemma 1 to obtain a separation between DCFL[d] and DCFL[$d - 1$].

Proposition 2. *Let $d \ge 2$ and let $L_{(d)} = \{a^n b^{kn} \mid k \in [d], n \ge 0\}$. It then follows that $L_{(d)} \in \mathrm{DCFL}[d] - \mathrm{DCFL}[d - 1]$.*

Proof. Let $d \ge 2$. Clearly, $L_{(d)}$ belongs to DCFL[d]. Assuming $L_{(d)} \in \mathrm{DCFL}[d - 1]$, we apply the pumping lemma (Lemma 1) to $L_{(d)}$. There is a constant $c > 0$ that satisfies the lemma. Let $n = c + 1$ and consider $w_i = a^n b^{in}$ for each index $i \in [d]$. Since each w_i belongs to $L_{(d)}$, we can take an index pair $j, k \in [d]$ with $j < k$ such that w_j and w_k satisfy the conditions of the lemma.

Since Condition (1) of the lemma is immediate, we hereafter consider Condition (2). Let $x' = a^n b^{jn-1}$, $y = b$, and $\hat{y} = b^{(k-j)n+1}$. Firstly, we consider Case (a) with a factorization $x' = x_1 x_2 x_3 x_4 x_5$ with $|x_2 x_4| \ge 1$ and $|x_2 x_3 x_4| \le c$. Since $x_1 x_2^i x_3 x_4^i x_5 y \in L_{(d)}$ for any number $i \in \mathbb{N}$, we conclude that $x_2 \in \{a\}^*$ and $x_4 \in \{b\}^*$. Let $x_2 = a^m$ and $x_4 = b^r$ for certain numbers $m, r \in [c]$. Note that $x_1 x_2^i x_3 x_4^i x_5 y$ equals $a^{n+(i-1)m} b^{jn+(i-1)r}$. Hence, $n + (i - 1)m = g(jn + (i - 1)r)$ for a certain $g \in [d]$. This implies that $(jg - 1)n = (m - gr)(i - 1)$. We then obtain $jg - 1 = m - gr = 0$, which further implies that $j = g = 1$ and $m = r$. Similarly, from $x_1 x_2^i x_3 x_4^i x_5 \hat{y} \in L_{(d)}$, it follows that $n + (i - 1)m = g'(kn + (i - 1)r)$. Thus, $(kg' - 1)n = (m - g'r)(i - 1)$. This implies $k = g' = 1$ and $m = r$. Since $j \ne k$, we obtain a contradiction.

Next, we consider Case (b) with appropriate factorizations $x' = x_1 x_2 x_3$, $y = y_1 y_2 y_3$, and $\hat{y} = z_1 z_2 z_3$ with $|x_2| \ge 1$ and $|x_2 x_3| \le c$ such that $x_1 x_2^i x_3 y_1 y_2^i y_3 \in L_{(d)}$ and $x_1 x_2^i x_3 z_1 z_2^i z_3 \in L_{(d)}$ for any number $i \in \mathbb{N}$. Since $|x_2 x_3| \le c$, we obtain $x_2 \in \{b\}^*$. Assume that $x_2 = b^m$ for a certain number $m \in [c]$. This is impossible because $x_1 x_2^i x_3 y_1 y_2^i y_3$ has the form $a^n b^{jn+(i-1)m}$ and the exponent of b is not of the form rn for any number $r \in [d]$.

Proof Sketch of Theorem 1(1). Let $d \geq 2$ be any integer and consider $L_d^{(\leq)}$ over $\Sigma_d = \{a_1, a_2, \ldots, a_{d,1}, b_2, \ldots, b_d\}$. It is not difficult to check that $L_d^{(\leq)} \in$ DCFL(d). Our goal is, therefore, to show that $L_d^{(\leq)}$ is not in DCFL($d-1$). To lead to a contradiction, we assume that $L_d^{(\leq)} \in$ DCFL($d-1$).

Take $A = a_1^* a_2^* \cdots a_d^* b_1^* b_2^* \cdots b_d^*$ in REG and consider $L' = A \cap (\Sigma_d^* - L_d^{(\leq)})$, that is, $L' = \{a_1^{n_1} \cdots a_d^{n_d} b_1^{m_1} \cdots b_d^{m_d} \mid \exists i \in [d](n_i > m_i)\}$. Note by Lemma 3(2) that, since $L_d^{(\leq)} \in$ DCFL($d-1$), we obtain $L' \in$ DCFL[$d-1$]. Take a pumping-lemma constant $c > 0$ that satisfies Lemma 1. We set $n = c+1$ and consider the set $\{xy^{(k)} \mid k \in [d]\}$, where $x = a_1^n a_2^{2n} \cdots a_d^{dn}$ and $y^{(k)} = b_1^n b_2^{2n} \cdots b_{k-1}^{(k-1)n} b_k^{kn-1} b_{k+1}^{(k+1)n} \cdots b_d^{dn}$ for each index $k \in [d]$. Lemma 1 guarantees the existence of a specific distinct pair $\{j_1, j_2\}$ with $1 \leq j_1 < j_2 \leq d$.

By Lemma 1, since $|x'| > c$, there are two conditions to consider separately. Condition (1) is not difficult. Next, we consider Condition (2). Let $x' = a_1^n \cdots a_d^{dn} b_1^n \cdots b_{j_1-1}^{(j_1-1)n} b_{j_1}^{j_1n-1}$, $y = b_{j_1} b_{j_1+1}^{(j_1+1)n} \cdots b_d^{dn}$, and $\hat{y} = b_{j_1+1}^{(j_1+1)n} \cdots b_{j_2-1}^{(j_2-1)n} b_{j_2}^{j_2n-1} b_{j_2+1}^{(j_2+1)n} \cdots b_d^{dn}$. Note that $x'y = xy^{(j_1)}$ and $x'\hat{y} = xy^{(j_2)}$. There are three factorizations $x' = u_1 u_2 u_3$ with $|u_2| \geq 1$ and $|u_2 u_3| \leq c$, $y = y_1 y_2 y_3$, and $\hat{y} = z_1 z_2 z_3$ satisfying both $u_1 u_2^i u_3 y_1 y_2^i y_3 \in L'$ and $u_1 u_2^i u_3 z_1 z_2^i z_3 \in L'$ for any number $i \in \mathbb{N}$. From $|u_2 u_3| \leq c$ follows $u_2 \in \{b_{j_1}\}^+$. Let $u_2 = b_{j_1}^e$ for a certain $e \geq 1$. In particular, take $i = 2$. Note that $u_1 u_2^2 u_3 y_1 y_2^2 y_3$ has factors $a_{j_1}^{j_1 n}$ and $b_{j_1}^{j_1 n-1+2e}$. Thus, we obtain $j_1 n = j_1 n + 2e - 1$, a clear contradiction. $\square$

We omit from this exposition the proofs of Theorems 1(2), 2, and Proposition 1. These proofs will be included in its complete version.

4   Proof Sketch of the Pumping Lemma for DCFL[d]

We are now ready to provide the proof of the pumping lemma for DCFL[d] (Lemma 1). Our proof has two different parts depending on the value of d. The first part of the proof targets the basis case of $d = 1$. This special case directly corresponds to Yu's pumping lemma [15, Lemma 1]. To prove his lemma, Yu utilized a so-called *left-part theorem* of his for LR(k) grammars. We intend to re-prove Yu's lemma using only 1dpda's with no reference to LR(k) grammars. Our proof argument is easily extendable to *one-way nondeterministic pushdown automata* (or 1npda's) and thus to the pumping lemma for CFL. The second part of the proof deals with the general case of $d \geq 2$. Hereafter, we give the sketches of these two parts.

Basis Case of $d = 1$: Let Σ be any alphabet and take any infinite dcf language L over Σ. Let us consider an appropriate ε-1dpda $M = (Q, \Sigma, \{\mathcal{c}, \$\}, \Gamma, \delta, q_0, Z_0, Q_{acc}, Q_{rej})$ in an ideal shape that recognizes L by Lemmas 4–5. For the desired constant c, we set $c = 2^{|Q|}$. Firstly, we take two arbitrary strings xy and $x\hat{y}$ over Σ with $y[1] = \hat{y}[1] = a$ and $|x| > c$.

Our goal is to show that Condition (2) in the basis case of $d = 1$ holds. There are four distinct cases to deal with. Hereafter, we intend to discuss them separately. Note that, since M is one-way, every crossing state-stack pair at any boundary in the x-region does not depend on the choice of y and $\hat{y}$.

Case 1: Consider the case where there are two boundaries t_1, t_2 with $1 \leq t_1 < t_2 \leq |xa|$ and $|t_2 - t_1| \leq c$ such that (i) the boundaries t_1 and t_2 are mutually correlated and (ii) inner states at the boundaries t_1 and t_2 coincide. In this case, we factorize x into $x_1 x_2 x_3$ so that $t_1 = |x_1|$ and $t_2 = |x_1 x_2|$. By Lemma 6(1), it then follows that, for any number $i \in \mathbb{N}$, $x_1 x_2^i x_3 y \in L$ and $x_1 x_2^i x_3 \hat{y} \in L$.

Case 2: Consider the case where there are four boundaries t_1, t_2, t_3, t_4 with $1 \leq t_1 < t_2 < t_3 < t_4 \leq |xa|$ and $|t_4 - t_1| \leq c$ and there are $p, q \in Q$, $\gamma \in (\Gamma^{(-)})^* Z_0$, and $\alpha \in (\Gamma^{(-)})^*$ for which (i) (q, γ) and $(q, \alpha\gamma)$ are the crossing state-stack pairs respectively at the boundaries t_1 and t_2, (ii) $(p, \alpha\gamma)$ and (p, γ) are the crossing state-stack pairs respectively at the boundaries t_3 and t_4, and (iii) the boundary block $[t_i, t_{i+1}]$ for each index $i \in [3]$ is pseudo-convex. We then take a factorization $x = x_1 x_2 x_3 x_4 x_5$ such that $t_i = |x_1 x_2 \cdots x_i|$ for each $i \in [4]$. Note that $|x_2 x_4| \geq 2$ because of $t_1 < t_2$ and $t_3 < t_4$. By an application of Lemma 6(2), we conclude that, for any $z \in \{y, \hat{y}\}$, $x_1 x_2^i x_3 x_4^i x_5 z \in L$ for all $i \in \mathbb{N}$.

Case 3: Assume that Cases 1–2 fail. For brevity, we set $R = (|xa| - c, |xa|)$. Consider the case where there is no pop operation in the R-region. Since R-region contains more than $|Q|^3$ boundaries, the R-region includes a certain series of boundaries $s_1, s_2, \ldots, s_m$ such that, for certain $q \in Q$, $\gamma \in (\Gamma^{(-)})^* Z_0$, and $\alpha_1', \ldots, \alpha_{m-1}' \in (\Gamma^{(-)})^*$, there are crossing state-stack pairs of the form $(q, \gamma), (q, \alpha_1' \gamma), \ldots, (q, \alpha_{m-1}' \cdots \alpha_1 \gamma)$ at the boundaries $s_1, s_2 \ldots, s_m$, respectively. Note that the boundary blocks $[s_1, s_2], [s_2, s_3], \ldots, [s_{m-1}, s_m]$ are all convex. Clearly, $m > |Q|^2$. We choose $\{t_i\}_{i \in [m]}$ and $\{r_i\}_{i \in [m]}$ so that (i) for each index $i \in [m]$, t_i and r_i are boundaries in the y-region and in the $\hat{y}$-region, respectively, satisfying that $t_1 < t_2 < \cdots < t_m$ and $r_1 < r_2 < \cdots < r_m$, and (ii) for each index $i \in [m-1]$, $[s_i, s_{i+1}]$ is mutually correlated to $[t_i, t_{i+1}]$ in the y-region and also to $[r_i, r_{i+1}]$ in the $\hat{y}$-region. Note that the boundary blocks $[t_1, t_2], \ldots, [t_{m-1}, t_m]$, $[r_1, r_2], \ldots, [r_{m-1}, r_m]$ are all pseudo-convex. Since $m > |Q|^2$, it follows that there is a pair $j_1, j_2 \in [m]$ with $j_1 < j_2$ such that inner states at the boundaries r_{j_1} and r_{j_2} coincide. Using Lemma 6(2), we can obtain the desired conclusion.

Case 4: Assume that Cases 1–3 fail. In this case, we define a notion of "true gain" in the R-region and estimate its value. Choose s_1 and s_2 so that $|xa| - c \leq s_1$, $s_2 \leq |xa|$, and the boundary block $[s_1, s_2]$ is pseudo-convex. Let $G(s_1, s_2)$ denote the set of boundary blocks $[t_1, t_1'], [t_2, t_2'], \ldots, [t_m, t_m']$ with $s_1 \leq t_1, t_m' \leq s_2$, $t_i < t_i'$ for every $i \in [m]$, and $t_j' < t_{j+1}$ for every $j \in [m-1]$ such that (i) $[t_i, t_i']$ is pseudo-convex but cannot be flat, (ii) $[t_j', t_{j+1}]$ is pseudo-convex (and could be flat), (iii) there are crossing state-stack pairs $(q_i, \gamma), (q_i', \gamma)$ at the boundaries t_i, t_i' for every $i \in [m]$, (iv) the stack height at the boundary t_i' is higher than the stack height at the boundary t_i, (v) the boundary t_i is a pit (i.e., the lowest point within its small vicinity). Define the *true gain* $tg(s_1, s_2)$ to be $\sum_{i=1}^{m} |t_i' - t_i|$. It is possible to prove that $tg(s_1, s_2) > |Q|^3$. Using this inequality, we can employ an argument similar to Case 3 to obtain the lemma.

General Case of $d \geq 2$: We begin with proving this case by considering d 1dpda's $M_1, M_2, \ldots, M_d$. The language recognized by each machine M_i is denoted by $L(M_i)$. Let us assume that $L = \bigcup_{i=1}^{d} L(M_i)$. Take $d+1$ strings $w_1, w_2, \ldots, w_{d+1}$ in L and assume that each w_k has the form $xy^{(k)}$ with $|x| > c$. Since all w_k's are in L, define a function f as follows. Let $f(k)$ denote the minimal index i_k satisfying that $w_k \in L(M_{i_k})$ but $w_k \notin L(M_j)$ for all $j \neq i_k$. Since there are at most d different languages, there are two distinct indices $j_1, j_2 \in [d+1]$ such that $f(j_1) = f(j_2)$. In what follows, we fix such a pair (j_1, j_2).

Consider the case of $w = xy^{(j_1)}$ and $w' = xy^{(j_2)}$. Take arbitrary factorizations $w = x'y$ and $w' = x'\hat{y}$. We apply the basis case of $d = 1$ again and obtain one of the following (a)–(b). (a) There is a factorization $x = x_1 x_2 x_3 x_4 x_5$ with $|x_2 x_4| \geq 1$ and $|x_2 x_3 x_4| \leq c$ such that $x_1 x_2^i x_3 x_4^i x_5 y \in L$ and $x_1 x_2^i x_3 x_4^i x_5 y \in L$ for any number $i \in \mathbb{N}$. (b) There are factorizations $x' = x_1 x_2 x_3$, $y = y_1 y_2 y_3$, and $\hat{y} = z_1 z_2 z_3$ such that $|x_2| \geq 1$, $|x_2 x_3| \leq c$, $x_1 x_2^i x_3 y_1 y_2^i y_3 \in L$, and $x_1 x_2^i x_3 z_1 z_2^i z_3 \in L$ for any number $i \in \mathbb{N}$.

References

1. Ginsburg, S., Greibach, S.: Deterministic context free languages. Inf. Control **9**, 620–648 (1966)
2. Harrison, M.A.: Iteration theorems for deterministic families of languages. Fundamenta Informaticae **9**, 481–508 (1986)
3. Hibbard, T.N.: A generalization of context-free determinism. Inf. Control **11**, 196–238 (1967)
4. Igarashi, Y.: A pumping lemma for real-time deterministic context-free languages. Theor. Comput. Sci. **36**, 89–97 (1985)
5. King, K.N.: Iteration theorems for families of strict deterministic languages. Theor. Comput. Sci. **10**, 317–333 (1980)
6. Kutrib, M., Malcher, A., Wotschke, D.: The Boolean closure of linear context-free languages. Acta Inform. **45**, 177–191 (2008)
7. Li, M., Vitányi, P.: An Introduction to Kolmogorov Complexity and Its Applications. Springer, New York (1994)
8. Liu, L.Y., Weiner, P.: An infinite hierarchy of intersections of context-free languages. Math. Syst. Theory **7**, 185–192 (1973)
9. Pighizzini, G., Pisoni, A.: Limited automata and regular languages. Int. J. Found. Comput. Sci. **25**, 897–916 (2014)
10. Wise, D.S.: A strong pumping lemma for context-free languages. Theor. Comput. Sci. **3**, 359–369 (1976)
11. Wotschke, D.: The Boolean closures of the deterministic and nondeterministic context-free languages. In: Brauer, W. (ed.) GI Gesellschaft für Informatik e. V. LNCS, pp. 113–121. Springer, Heidelberg (1973). https://doi.org/10.1007/978-3-662-41148-3_11
12. Wotschke, D.: Nondeterminism and Boolean operations in pda's. J. Comput. Syst. Sci. **16**, 456–461 (1978)
13. Yamakami, T.: Oracle pushdown automata, nondeterministic reducibilities, and the hierarchy over the family of context-free languages. In: Geffert, V., Preneel, B., Rovan, B., Štuller, J., Tjoa, A.M. (eds.) SOFSEM 2014. LNCS, vol. 8327, pp. 514–525. Springer, Cham (2014). https://doi.org/10.1007/978-3-319-04298-5_45. A complete version is found at arXiv:1303.1717 under a slightly different title

14. Yamakami, T.: Behavioral Strengths and weaknesses of various models of limited automata. In: Catania, B., Královič, R., Nawrocki, J., Pighizzini, G. (eds.) SOF-SEM 2019. LNCS, vol. 11376, pp. 519–530. Springer, Cham (2019). https://doi.org/10.1007/978-3-030-10801-4_40
15. Yu, S.: A pumping lemma for deterministic context-free languages. Inf. Process. Lett. **31**, 47–51 (1989)

Trees and Graphs

On the Weisfeiler-Leman Dimension
of Fractional Packing

Vikraman Arvind[1], Frank Fuhlbrück[2(✉)], Johannes Köbler[2],
and Oleg Verbitsky[2]

[1] The Institute of Mathematical Sciences (HBNI), Chennai, India
arvind@imsc.res.in
[2] Humboldt-Universität zu Berlin, Unter den Linden 6, 10099 Berlin, Germany
{fuhlbfra,koebler,verbitsky}@informatik.hu-berlin.de

Abstract. The k-dimensional Weisfeiler-Leman procedure (k-WL) has proven to be immensely fruitful in the algorithmic study of Graph Isomorphism. More generally, it is of fundamental importance in understanding and exploiting symmetries in graphs in various settings. Two graphs are k-WL-equivalent if dimention k does not suffice to distinguish them. 1-WL-equivalence is known as fractional isomorphism of graphs, and the k-WL-equivalence relation becomes finer as k increases.

We investigate to what extent standard graph parameters are preserved by k-WL-equivalence, focusing on fractional graph packing numbers. The integral packing numbers are typically NP-hard to compute, and we discuss applicability of k-WL-invariance for estimating the integrality gap of the LP relaxation provided by their fractional counterparts.

Keywords: Computational complexity · The Weisfeiler-Leman algorithm · Fractional packing

1 Introduction

The 1-dimensional version of the Weisfeiler-Leman procedure is the classical *color refinement* applied to an input graph G. Each vertex of G is initially colored by its degree. The procedure refines the color of each vertex $v \in V(G)$ in rounds, using the multiset of colors of vertices u in the neighborhood $N(v)$ of the vertex v. In the 2-dimensional version [25], all vertex pairs $xy \in V(G) \times V(G)$ are classified by a similar procedure of coloring them in rounds. The extension of this procedure to a classification of all k-tuples of G is due to Babai (see historical overview in [4,5]) and is known as the *k-dimensional Weisfeiler-Leman procedure*, abbreviated as k-WL. Graphs G and H are said to be k-WL *-equivalent* (denoted $G \equiv_{k\text{-WL}} H$) if they are indistinguishable by k-WL.

The WL Invariance of Graph Parameters. Let π be a *graph parameter*. By definition, $\pi(G) = \pi(H)$ whenever G and H are isomorphic (denoted $G \cong H$).

O. Verbitsky was supported by DFG grant KO 1053/8–1. He is on leave from the IAPMM, Lviv, Ukraine.

A. Leporati et al. (Eds.): LATA 2020, LNCS 12038, pp. 357–368, 2020.
https://doi.org/10.1007/978-3-030-40608-0_25

We say that π is a k-WL *-invariant* graph parameter if the equality $\pi(G) = \pi(H)$ is implied even by the weaker condition $G \equiv_{k\text{-WL}} H$. The smallest such k will be called the *Weisfeiler-Leman (WL) dimension* of π.

If no such k exists, we say that the WL dimension of π is *unbounded*. Knowing that a parameter π has unbounded WL dimension is important because this implies that π cannot be computed by any algorithm expressible in fixed-point logic with counting (FPC), a robust framework for study of *encoding-invariant* (or *"choiceless"*) *computations*; see the survey [7].

The focus of our paper is on graph parameters with *bounded* WL dimension. If π is the indicator function of a graph property $\mathcal{P}$, then k-WL-invariance of π precisely means that $\mathcal{P}$ is definable in the infinitary $(k + 1)$-variable counting logic $C^{k+1}_{\infty\omega}$. While minimizing the number of variables is a recurring theme in descriptive complexity, our interest in the study of k-WL-invariance has an additional motivation: If we know that a graph parameter π is k-WL-invariant, this gives us information not only about π but also *about k-WL*. For example, the largest eigenvalue of the adjacency matrix has WL dimension 1 (see [24]), and the whole spectrum of a graph has WL dimension 2 (see [8,13]), which implies that 2-WL subsumes distinguishing non-isomorphic graphs by spectral methods.

Fractional Graph Parameters. In this paper, we mainly consider *fractional* graph parameters. Algorithmically, a well-known approach to tackling intractable optimization problems is to consider an appropriate linear programming (LP) relaxation. Many standard integer-valued graph parameters have fractional real-valued analogues, obtained by LP-relaxation of the corresponding 0–1 linear program; see, e.g., the monograph [24]. The fractional counterpart of a graph parameter π is denoted by π_f. While π is often hard to compute, π_f provides, sometimes quite satisfactory, a polynomial-time computable approximation of π.

The WL dimension of a natural fractional parameter π_f is a priori bounded, where *natural* means that π_f is determined by an LP which is logically interpretable in terms of an input graph G. A striking result of Anderson, Dawar, Holm [1] says that the optimum value of an interpretable LP is expressible in FPC. It follows from the known immersion of FPC into the finite-variable infinitary counting logic $C^\omega_{\infty\omega} = \bigcup_{k=2}^\infty C^k_{\infty\omega}$ (see [21]), that each such π_f is k-WL-invariant for some k. While this general theorem is applicable to many graph parameters of interest, it is not easy to extract an explicit value of k from this argument, and in any case such value would hardly be optimal.

We are interested in *explicit* and, possibly, *exact* bounds for the WL dimension. A first question here would be to pinpoint which fractional parameters π_f are 1-WL-invariant. This natural question, using the concept of fractional isomorphism [24], can be recast as follows: Which *fractional* graph parameters are invariant under *fractional* isomorphism? It appears that this question has not received adequate attention in the literature. The only earlier result we could find is the 1-WL-invariance of the fractional domination number γ_f shown in the Ph.D. thesis of Rubalcaba [23].

We show that the fractional matching number ν_f is also a fractional parameter preserved by fractional isomorphism. Indeed, the matching number is an instance of the F-*packing number* π^F of a graph, corresponding to $F = K_2$. Here and throughout, we use the standard notation K_n for the complete graphs, P_n for the path graphs, and C_n for the cycle graph on n vertices. In general, $\pi^F(G)$ is the maximum number of vertex-disjoint subgraphs F' of G that are isomorphic to the fixed pattern graph F. While the matching number is computable in polynomial time, computing π^F is NP-hard whenever F has a connected component with at least 3 vertices [19], in particular, for $F \in \{P_3, K_3\}$. Note that K_3-packing is the optimization version of the archetypal NP-complete problem Partition Into Triangles [14, GT11]. We show that the fractional P_3-packing number $\nu_f^{P_3}$, like $\nu_f = \pi_f^{K_2}$, is 1-WL-invariant, whereas the WL dimension of the fractional triangle packing is 2.

In fact, we present a general treatment of fractional F-packing numbers π_f^F. We begin in Sect. 2 with introducing a concept of equivalence between two linear programs L_1 and L_2 ensuring that equivalent L_1 and L_2 have equal optimum values. Next, in Sect. 3, we consider the standard optimization versions of Set Packing and Hitting Set [14, SP4 and SP8], two of Karp's 21 NP-complete problems. These two generic problems generalize F-Packing and Dominating Set respectively. Their fractional versions have thoroughly been studied in hypergraph theory [12,20]. We observe that the LP relaxations of Set Packing (or Hitting Set) are equivalent whenever the incidence graphs of the input set systems are 1-WL-equivalent. This general fact readily implies Rubalcaba's result [23] on the 1-WL-invariance of the fractional domination number and also shows that, if the pattern graph F has ℓ vertices, then the fractional F-packing number π_f^F is k-WL-invariant for some $k < 2\ell$. This bound for k comes from a logical definition of the instance of Set Packing corresponding to F-Packing in terms of an input graph G (see Corollary 6). Though the bound is quite decent, it does not need to be optimal. We elaborate on a more precise bound, where we need to use additional combinatorial arguments even in the case of the fractional matching. We present a detailed treatment of the fractional matching in this exposition (Theorem 4), while the proof of our general result on the fractional F-packing numbers (Theorem 5), which includes the aforementioned cases of $F = K_3, P_3$, is postponed to the full version of the paper [2].

The *edge-disjoint* version of F-Packing is another problem that has intensively been studied in combinatorics and optimization. Since it is known to be NP-hard for any pattern F containing a connected component with at least 3 edges [10], fractional relaxations have received much attention in the literature [17,26]. We show that our techniques work well also in this case. In particular, the WL dimension of the fractional edge-disjoint triangle packing number $\rho_f^{K_3}$ is 2 (Theorem 7).

Integrality Gap via Invariance Ratio. Furthermore, we discuss the *approximate* invariance of *integral* graph parameters expressible by integer linear programs. For a first example, recall Lovász's inequality [12, Theorem 5.21] $\nu_f(G) \leq \frac{3}{2}\nu(G)$. As ν_f is 1-WL-invariant, it follows that $\nu(G)/\nu(H) \leq 3/2$

for any pair of nonempty 1-WL-equivalent graphs G and H. This bound is tight, as seen for the 1-WL-equivalent graphs $G = C_{6s}$ and $H = 2s\,C_3$. Consequently, the above relation between $\nu(G)$ and $\nu_f(G)$ is also tight. This simple example demonstrates that knowing, first, the exact value k of the WL dimension of a fractional parameter π_f and, second, the discrepancy of the integral parameter π over k-WL-invariant graphs implies a lower bound for the precision of approximating π by π_f.

Specifically, recall that the maximum $\max_G \frac{\pi_f(G)}{\pi(G)}$, (respectively $\max_G \frac{\pi(G)}{\pi_f(G)}$ for minimization problems) is known as the *integrality gap* of π_f. The integrality gap is important for a computationally hard graph parameter π, as it bounds how well the polynomial-time computable parameter π_f approximates π.

On the other hand, we define the k-WL-*invariance ratio* for the parameter π as $\max_{G,H} \frac{\pi(G)}{\pi(H)}$, where the quotient is maximized over all k-WL-equivalent graph pairs (G, H). If π is k-WL-invariant, then the k-WL-invariance ratio bounds the integrality gap from below. The following question suggests itself: How tight is this lower bound? In this context, we now consider the fractional domination number γ_f.

A general bound by Lovász [20] on the integrality gap of the fractional covering number for hypergraphs implies that the integrality gap for the domination number is at most logarithmic, specifically, $\frac{\gamma(G)}{\gamma_f(G)} \leq 1 + \ln n$ for a non-empty graph G with n vertices. This results in an LP-based algorithm for approximation of $\gamma(G)$ within a logarithmic factor, which is essentially optimal as $\gamma(G)$ is hard to approximate within a sublogarithmic factor assuming NP $\neq$ P [22]. As shown by Rubalcaba [23], γ_f is 1-WL-invariant. Along with the Lovász bound, this implies that the 1-WL-invariance ratio of γ is at most logarithmic. On the other hand, Chappell et al. [6] have shown that the logarithmic upper bound for the integrality gap of γ_f is tight up to a constant factor. In Sect. 6 we prove an $\Omega(\log n)$ lower bound even for the 1-WL-invariance ratio of γ over n-vertex graphs. This implies the integrality gap lower bound [6], reproving it from a different perspective. In Sect. 6 we also discuss the *additive* integrality gap of the fractional edge-disjoint triangle packing.

Related Work. Atserias and Dawar [3] have shown that the 1-WL-invariance ratio for the vertex cover number τ is at most 2. Alternatively, this bound also follows from the 1-WL-invariance of ν_f (which implies the 1-WL-invariance of τ_f as $\tau_f = \nu_f$ by LP duality) combined with a standard rounding argument. The approach of [3] uses a different argument, which alone does not yield 1-WL-invariance of the fractional vertex cover τ_f.

The bound of 2 for the 1-WL-invariance ratio of τ is optimal. Atserias and Dawar [3] also show that the k-WL-invariance ratio for τ is at least 7/6 for each k. This implies an unconditional inapproximability result for Vertex Cover in the model of encoding-invariant computations expressible in FPC.

Notation and Formal Definitions. For $\bar{x} = (x_1, \ldots, x_k)$ in $V(G)^k$, let $\mathrm{WL}_k^0(G, \bar{x})$ be the $k \times k$ matrix $(m_{i,j})$ with $m_{i,j} = 1$ if $x_i x_j \in E(G)$, $m_{i,j} = 2$ if $x_i = x_j$ and $m_{i,j} = 0$ otherwise. We also augment $\mathrm{WL}_k^0(G, \bar{x})$

by the vector of the colors of $x_1, \ldots, x_k$ if the graph G is vertex-colored. $\mathrm{WL}_k^0(G, \bar{x})$ encodes the ordered isomorphism type of $\bar{x}$ in G and serves as an initial coloring of $V(G)^k$ for k-WL. In each refinement round, 1-WL computes $\mathrm{WL}_1^{r+1}(G, x) = (\mathrm{WL}_1^r(G, x), \{\!\{\mathrm{WL}_1^r(G, y) : y \in N(x)\}\!\})$, where $N(x)$ is the neighborhood of x and $\{\!\{\ \}\!\}$ denotes a multiset. If $k \geq 2$, k-WL refines the coloring by $\mathrm{WL}_k^{r+1}(G, x) = (\mathrm{WL}_k^r(G, \bar{x}), \{\!\{(\mathrm{WL}_k^r(G, \bar{x}_1^u), \ldots, \mathrm{WL}_k^r(G, \bar{x}_k^u) : u \in V(G)\}\!\})$, where $\bar{x}_i^u$ is the tuple $(x_1, \ldots, x_{i-1}, u, x_{i+1}, \ldots, x_k)$. If G has n vertices, the color partition stabilizes in at most n^k rounds. We define $\mathrm{WL}_k(G, \bar{x}) = \mathrm{WL}_k^{n^k}(G, \bar{x})$ and $\mathrm{WL}_k(G) = \{\!\{\mathrm{WL}_k(G, \bar{x}) : \bar{x} \in V(G)^k\}\!\}$. Now, $G \equiv_{k\text{-WL}} H$ if $\mathrm{WL}_k(G) = \mathrm{WL}_k(H)$.

The color partition of $V(G)$ according to $\mathrm{WL}_1(G, x)$ is *equitable*: for any color classes C and C', each vertex in C has the same number of neighbors in C'. Moreover, if G is vertex-colored, then the original colors of all vertices in each C are the same. If $V(G) = V(H)$, then $G \equiv_{k\text{-WL}} 1H$ exactly when G and H have a common equitable partition [24, Theorem 6.5.1].

Let G and H be graphs with vertex set $\{1, \ldots, n\}$, and let A and B be the adjacency matrices of G and H, respectively. Then G and H are isomorphic if and only if $AX = XB$ for some $n \times n$ permutation matrix X. The linear programming relaxation allows X to be a doubly stochastic matrix. If such an X exists, G and H are said to be *fractionally isomorphic*. If G and H are colored graphs with the same partition of the vertex set into color classes, then it is additionally required that $X_{u,v} = 0$ whenever u and v are of different colors. It turns out that two graphs are indistinguishable by color refinement if and only if they are fractionally isomorphic [24, Theorem 6.5.1].

2   Reductions Between Linear Programs

A *linear program (LP)* is an optimization problem of the form "maximize (or minimize) $a^t x$ subject to $Mx \leq b$", where $a \in \mathbb{R}^n$, $b \in \mathbb{R}^m$, M is an $m \times n$ matrix $M \in \mathbb{R}^{m \times n}$, and x varies over all vectors in $\mathbb{R}^n$ with nonnegative entries (which we denote by $x \geq 0$). Any vector x satisfying the constraints $Mx \leq b$, $x \geq 0$ is called a *feasible solution* and the function $x \mapsto a^t x$ is called the *objective function*. We denote an LP with parameters a, M, b by $LP(a, M, b, opt)$, where $opt = \min$, if the goal is to minimize the value of the objective function, and $opt = \max$, if this value has to be maximized. The optimum of the objective function over all feasible solutions is called the *value* of the program $L = LP(a, M, b, opt)$ and denoted by $val(L)$. Our goal now is to introduce an equivalence relation between LPs ensuring equality of their values.

Equivalence of LPs. Let $L_1 = LP(a, M, b, opt)$ and $L_2 = LP(c, N, d, opt)$ be linear programs (in general form), where $a, c \in \mathbb{R}^n$, $b, d \in \mathbb{R}^m$, $M, N \in \mathbb{R}^{m \times n}$ and $opt \in \{\min, \max\}$. We say that L_1 *reduces to* L_2 ($L_1 \leq L_2$ for short), if there are matrices $Y \in \mathbb{R}^{m \times m}$ and $Z \in \mathbb{R}^{n \times n}$ such that

- $Y, Z \geq 0$
- $a^t Z \diamond c^t$, where $\diamond = \begin{cases} \leq, & opt = \min \\ \geq, & opt = \max \end{cases}$

– $MZ \leq YN$
– $Yd \leq b$

L_1 and L_2 are said to be *equivalent* ($L_1 \equiv L_2$ for short) if $L_1 \leq L_2$ and $L_2 \leq L_1$.

Theorem 1. *If* $L_1 \equiv L_2$, *then* $val(L_1) = val(L_2)$.

Proof. Let $L_1 = LP(a, M, b, opt)$ and $L_2 = LP(c, N, d, opt)$ and assume $L_1 \leq L_2$ via (Y, Z). We show that for any feasible solution x of L_2 we get a feasible solution $x' = Zx$ of L_1 with $a^t x' \Diamond c^t x$, where $\Diamond$ is as in the definition:

$$Mx' = \underbrace{MZ}_{\leq YN} x \leq Y \underbrace{Nx}_{\leq d} \leq Yd \leq b \text{ and } a^t x' = \underbrace{a^t Z}_{\Diamond c^t} x \Diamond c^t x.$$

Thus, $L_1 \leq L_2$ implies $val(L_1) \Diamond val(L_2)$ and the theorem follows.   □

LPs with Fractionally Isomorphic Matrices. Recall that a square matrix $X \geq 0$ is *doubly stochastic* if its entries in each row and column sum up to 1. We call two $m \times n$ matrices M and N *fractionally isomorphic* if there are doubly stochastic matrices $Y \in \mathbb{R}^{m \times m}$ and $Z \in \mathbb{R}^{n \times n}$ such that

$$MZ = YN \text{ and } NZ^t = Y^t M. \tag{1}$$

Grohe et al. [16, Eqs. (5.1)–(5.2) in arXiv version] discuss similar definitions. They use fractional isomorphism fractional isomorphism to reduce the dimension of linear equations and LPs. The meaning of (1) will be clear from the proof of Theorem 3 below.

Lemma 2. *If* M *and* N *are fractionally isomorphic* $m \times n$ *matrices, then*

$$LP(\mathbb{1}_n, M, \mathbb{1}_m, opt) \equiv LP(\mathbb{1}_n, N, \mathbb{1}_m, opt),$$

where $\mathbb{1}_n$ *denotes the* n-*dimensional all-ones vector.*

Proof. Since the matrices Y and Z in (1) are doubly stochastic, $Y\mathbb{1}_m = \mathbb{1}_m$ and $\mathbb{1}_n^t Z = \mathbb{1}_n^t$. Along with the first equality in (1), these equalities imply that $L_1 \leq L_2$. The reduction $L_2 \leq L_1$ follows similarly from the second equality in (1) as Y^t and Z^t are doubly stochastic.   □

3   Fractional Set Packing

The *Set Packing* problem is, given a family of sets $\mathcal{S} = \{S_1, \ldots, S_n\}$, where $S_j \subset \{1, \ldots, m\}$, to maximize the number of pairwise disjoint sets in this family. The maximum is called in combinatorics the *matching number of hypergraph* $\mathcal{S}$ and denoted by $\nu(\mathcal{S})$. The fractional version is given by $LP(\mathcal{S}) = LP(\mathbb{1}_n, M, \mathbb{1}_m, \max)$ where M is the $m \times n$ incidence matrix of $\mathcal{S}$, namely

$$\max \sum_{i=1}^{n} x_i \quad \text{under}$$

$$x_i \geq 0 \text{ for every } i \leq n,$$

$$\sum_{i : S_i \ni j} x_i \leq 1 \text{ for every } j \leq m.$$

The optimum value $\nu_f(\mathcal{S}) = val(LP(\mathcal{S}))$ is called the *fractional matching number* of $\mathcal{S}$.

Let $I(\mathcal{S})$ denote the incidence graph of $\mathcal{S}$. Specifically, this is the vertex-colored bipartite graph with biadjacency matrix M on two classes of vertices; m vertices are colored red, n vertices are colored blue, and a red vertex j is adjacent to a blue vertex i if $j \in S_i$.

Theorem 3. *Let $\mathcal{S}_1$ and $\mathcal{S}_2$ be two families each consisting of n subsets of the set $\{1, \ldots, m\}$. If $I(\mathcal{S}_1) \equiv_{1\text{-WL}} I(\mathcal{S}_2)$, then $\nu_f(\mathcal{S}_1) = \nu_f(\mathcal{S}_2)$.*

Proof. Denote the incidence matrices of $\mathcal{S}_1$ and $\mathcal{S}_2$ by M and N respectively. Let

$$A_1 = \begin{pmatrix} 0 & M \\ M^t & 0 \end{pmatrix} \text{ and } A_1 = \begin{pmatrix} 0 & N \\ N^t & 0 \end{pmatrix}$$

be the adjacency matrices of $I(\mathcal{S}_1)$ and $I(\mathcal{S}_2)$ respectively. Since $I(\mathcal{S}_1)$ and $I(\mathcal{S}_2)$ are indistinguishable by color refinement, by [24, Theorem 6.5.1] we conclude that these graphs are fractionally isomorphic, that is, there is a doubly stochastic matrix X such that

$$A_1 X = X A_2 \tag{2}$$

and $X_{uv} = 0$ whenever u and v are from different vertex color classes. The latter condition means that X is the direct sum of an $n \times n$ doubly stochastic matrix Y and an $n \times n$ doubly stochastic matrix Z, that is, Equality (2) reads

$$\begin{pmatrix} 0 & M \\ M^t & 0 \end{pmatrix} \begin{pmatrix} Y & 0 \\ 0 & Z \end{pmatrix} = \begin{pmatrix} Y & 0 \\ 0 & Z \end{pmatrix} \begin{pmatrix} 0 & N \\ N^t & 0 \end{pmatrix},$$

yielding $MZ = YN$ and $M^t Y = ZN^t$. Thus, M and N are fractionally isomorphic. Lemma 2 implies that $LP(\mathcal{S}_1) \equiv LP(\mathcal{S}_2)$. Therefore, these LPs have equal values by Theorem 1. □

4   1-WL-invariance of the Fractional Matching Number

Recall that a set of edges $M \subseteq E(G)$ is a *matching* in a graph G if every vertex of G is incident to at most one edge from M. The *matching number* $\nu(G)$ is the maximum size of a matching in G. Note that this terminology and notation agrees with Sect. 3 when graphs are considered hypergraphs with hyperedges of size 2. Fractional Matching is defined by the LP

$$\max \sum_{uv \in E(G)} x_{uv} \quad \text{under}$$

$$x_{uv} \geq 0 \text{ for every } uv \in E(G),$$

$$\sum_{v \in N(u)} x_{uv} \leq 1 \text{ for every } u \in V(G),$$

whose value is the *fractional matching number* $\nu_f(G)$. The above LP is exactly the linear program $LP(\mathcal{S}_G)$ for the instance $\mathcal{S}_G = E(G)$ of Fractional Set Packing formed by the edges of G as 2-element subsets of $V(G)$, that is, $\nu_f(G) = \nu_f(\mathcal{S}_G)$.

Theorem 4. *The fractional matching number is 1-WL-invariant.*

Proof. Given $G \equiv_{1\text{-WL}} H$, we have to prove that $\nu_f(G) = \nu_f(H)$ or, equivalently, $\nu_f(\mathcal{S}_G) = \nu_f(\mathcal{S}_H)$ where $\mathcal{S}_G$ is as defined above. By Theorem 3, it suffices to show that $I(\mathcal{S}_G) \equiv_{1\text{-WL}} I(\mathcal{S}_H)$. To this end, we construct a common equitable partition of $I(\mathcal{S}_G)$ and $I(\mathcal{S}_H)$, appropriately identifying their vertex sets. Recall that $V(I(\mathcal{S}_G)) = V(G) \cup E(G)$ and a red vertex $x \in V(G)$ is adjacent to a blue vertex $e \in E(G)$ if $x \in e$.

For $x \in V(G)$, let $c_G(x) = \mathrm{WL}_1(G, x)$ and define c_H on $V(H)$ similarly. First, we identify $V(G)$ and $V(H)$ (i.e., the red parts of the two incidence graphs) so that $c_G(x) = c_H(x)$ for every x in $V(G) = V(H)$, which is possible because 1-WL-equivalent graphs have the same color palette after color refinement. The color classes of c_G now form a common equitable partition of G and H.

Next, extend the coloring c_G to $E(G)$ (the blue part of $I(\mathcal{S}_G)$) by $c_G(\{x, y\}) = \{c_G(x), c_G(y)\}$, and similarly extend c_H to $E(H)$. Denote the color class of c_G containing $\{x, y\}$ by $C_G(\{x, y\})$, the color class containing x by $C_G(x)$ etc. Note that $|C_G(\{x, y\})|$ is equal to the number of edges in G between $C_G(x)$ and $C_G(y)$ (or the number of edges within $C_G(x)$ if $c_G(x) = c_G(y)$). Since $\{C_G(x)\}_{x \in V(G)}$ is a common equitable partition of G and H, we have $|C_G(\{x, y\})| = |C_H(\{x', y'\})|$ whenever $c_G(\{x, y\}) = c_H(\{x', y'\})$ (note that $\{x, y\}$ does not need to be an edge in H, nor $\{x', y'\}$ needs to be an edge in G). This allows us to identify $E(G)$ and $E(H)$ so that $c_G(e) = c_H(e)$ for every e in $E(G) = E(H)$.

Now, consider the partition of $V(G) \cup E(G)$ into the color classes of c_G (or the same in terms of H) and verify that this is an equitable partition for both $I(\mathcal{S}_G)$ and $I(\mathcal{S}_H)$. Indeed, let $C \subseteq V(G)$ and $D \subseteq E(G)$ be color classes of c_G such that there are $x \in C$ and $e \in D$ adjacent in $I(\mathcal{S}_G)$, that is, $e = \{x, y\}$ for some vertex y of G. Note that, if considered on $V(H) \cup E(H)$, the classes C and D also must contain $x' \in C$ and $e' = \{x', y'\} \in D$ adjacent in $I(\mathcal{S}_H)$ (take $x' = x$ and any y' adjacent to x in H such that $c_H(y') = c_G(y)$). Denote $C' = C_G(y)$ (it is not excluded that $C' = C$). The vertex x has exactly as many D-neighbors in $I(\mathcal{S}_G)$ as it has C'-neighbors in G. This number depends only on C and C' or, equivalently, only on C and D. The same number is obtained also while counting the D-neighbors of x' in $I(\mathcal{S}_H)$.

On the other hand, e has exactly one neighbor x in C if $C' \neq C$ and exactly two C-neighbors x and y if $C' = C$. What is the case depends only on D and C, and is the same in $I(\mathcal{S}_G)$ and $I(\mathcal{S}_H)$. Thus, we do have a common equitable partition of $I(\mathcal{S}_G)$ and $I(\mathcal{S}_H)$. □

As was discussed in Sect. 1, we are able to generalize Theorem 4 to any fractional F-packing number π_f^F. For a graph G, let $\mathcal{S}_{F,G}$ be the family of subsets of $V(G)$ consisting of the vertex sets $V(F')$ of all subgraphs F' of G isomorphic to the pattern graph F. Now, $\pi_f^F(G) = \nu_f(\mathcal{S}_{F,G})$. Dell et al. [9] establish a close connection between homomorphism counts and k-WL equivalence, which motivates the following definition. The *homomorphism-hereditary treewidth* of a graph F, denoted by $htw(F)$, is the maximum treewidth $tw(F')$ over all homomorphic images F' of F. The proof of the following result can be found in the full version of the paper [2].

Theorem 5. *If $htw(F) \leq k$, then π_f^F is k-WL-invariant.*

First-Order Interpretability. Our approach to proving Theorem 4 was, given an instance graph G of Fractional Matching Problem, to define an instance $\mathcal{S}_G$ of Fractional Set Packing Problem having the same LP value. The following definition concerns many similar situations. Given a correspondence $G \mapsto \mathcal{S}_G$, we say that an istance $\mathcal{S}_G$ of Fractional Set Packing is definable over a graph G with *excess* e if $G \equiv_{(1+e)\text{-WL}} H$ implies $I(\mathcal{S}_G) \equiv_{1\text{-WL}} I(\mathcal{S}_H)$.

This definition includes a particular situation when $I(\mathcal{S}_G)$ is first-order *interpretable* in G in the sense of [11, Chapter 12.3], which means that for the color predicates (to be red or blue respectively) as well as for the adjacency relation of $I(\mathcal{S}_G)$ we have first order formulas defining them on $V(G)^k$ for some k in terms of the adjacency relation of G. The number k is called *width* of the interpretation. In this case, if there is a first-order sentence over s variables that is true on $I(\mathcal{S}_G)$ but false on $I(\mathcal{S}_H)$, then there is a first-order sentence over sk variables that is true on G but false on H. Cai, Fürer, and Immerman [5] showed that two structures are $\equiv_{k\text{-WL}}$-equivalent iff they are equivalent in the $(k+1)$-variable counting logic C^{k+1}. Therefore, Theorem 3 has the following consequence.

Corollary 6. *Let π_f be a fractional graph parameter such that $\pi_f(G) = \nu_f(\mathcal{S}_G)$, where $\mathcal{S}_G$ admits a first-order interpretation of width k in G (even possibly with counting quantifiers). Under these conditions, $\mathcal{S}_G$ is definable over G with excess $2(k-1)$ and, hence, π_f is $(2k-1)$-WL-invariant.*

To obtain 1-WL-invariance via Corollary 6, we would need an interpretation of width 1. This is hardly possible in the case of the fractional matching number, and an interpretation of width 2 could only give us 3-WL-invariance of ν_f. Thus, our purely combinatorial argument for Theorem 4 is preferable here.

5 Fractional Edge-Disjoint Triangle Packing

We now show that the approach we used in the proof of Theorem 4 works as well for edge-disjoint packing. Given a graph G, let $T(G)$ denote the family of all sets $\{e_1, e_2, e_3\}$ consisting of the edges of a triangle subgraph in G. We regard $T(G)$ as a family $\mathcal{S}_G$ of subsets of the edge set $E(G)$. The optimum value of Set Packing Problem on $\mathcal{S}_G$, which we denote by $\rho^{K_3}(G)$, is equal to the maximum number of edge-disjoint triangles in G. Let $\rho_f^{K_3}(G) = \nu_f(\mathcal{S}_G)$ be the corresponding fractional parameter.

Theorem 7. *The fractional packing number $\rho_f^{K_3}$ is 2-WL-invariant.*

Proof. Given a graph G, we consider the coloring c_G of $E(G) \cup T(G)$ defined by $c_G(\{x, y\}) = \{WL_2(G, x, y), WL_2(G, y, x)\}$ on $E(G)$ and $c_G(\{e_1, e_2, e_3\}) = \{c_G(e_1), c_G(e_2), c_G(e_3)\}$ on $T(G)$. Like in the proof of Theorem 4, the upper case notation $C_G(w)$ will be used to denote the color class of $w \in E(G) \cup T(G)$.

Suppose that $G \equiv_{2\text{-WL}} H$. This condition means that we can identify the sets $E(G)$ and $E(H)$ so that $c_G(e) = c_H(e)$ for every e in $E(G) = E(H)$.

Moreover, the 2-WL-equivalence of G and H implies that $|C_G(t)| = |C_H(t')|$ for any $t \in T(G)$ and $t' \in T(H)$ with $c_G(t) = c_H(t')$. This allows us to identify $T(G)$ and $T(H)$ so that $c_G(t) = c_H(t)$ for every t in $T(G) = T(H)$. As in the proof of Theorem 4, it suffices to argue that $\{C_G(w)\}_{w \in E(G) \cup T(G)}$ is a common equitable partition of the incidence graphs $I(\mathcal{S}_G)$ and $I(\mathcal{S}_H)$. The equality $\rho_f^{K_3}(G) = \rho_f^{K_3}(H)$ will then follow by Theorem 3.

Let $C \subseteq E(G)$ and $D \subseteq T(G)$ be color classes of c_G such that there is an edge between them in $I(\mathcal{S}_G)$, that is, there are $e \in C$ and $t \in D$ such that $t = \{e, e_2, e_3\}$. If considered on $E(H) \cup T(H)$, the classes C and D also must contain $e' \in C$ and $t' = \{e', e_2', e_3'\} \in D$ adjacent in $I(\mathcal{S}_H)$ (take, for example, the edge $e' = e$ of H and extend it to a triangle with other two edges e_2' and e_3' such that $c_H(e_2') = c_G(e_2)$ and $c_H(e_3') = c_G(e_3)$, which must exist in H because H and G are 2-WL-equivalent). Denote $C' = C_G(e_2)$ and $C'' = C_G(e_3)$ (it is not excluded that some of the classes C, C', and C'' coincide).

Let x, y, and z be the vertices of the triangle t in G, and suppose that $e = \{x, y\}$. The number of D-neighbors that e has in $I(\mathcal{S}_G)$ is equal to the number of vertices z' such that $(\mathrm{WL}_2(G, x, z'), \mathrm{WL}_2(G, z', y))$ is one of the 8 pairs in $(c_G(\{x, z\}) \times c_G(\{y, z\})) \cup (c_G(\{y, z\}) \times c_G(\{x, z\}))$, like $(\mathrm{WL}_2(G, z, y), \mathrm{WL}_2(G, x, z))$ (some of these pairs can coincide). Since the partition of $V(G)^2$ by the coloring $\mathrm{WL}_2(G, \cdot, \cdot)$ is not further refined by 2-WL, this number depends only on C and D. We obtain the same number also while counting the D-neighbors of e' in $I(\mathcal{S}_H)$.

On the other hand, t has exactly one neighbor e in C if C differs from both C' and C'', exactly two C-neighbors if C coincides with exactly one of C' and C'', and exactly three C-neighbors e, e_2, and e_3 if $C = C' = C''$. Which of the three possibilities occurs depends only on D and C, and is the same in $I(\mathcal{S}_G)$ and $I(\mathcal{S}_H)$. This completes our verification that we really have a common equitable partition. $\qquad\square$

6 Invariance Ratio and Integrality Gap

Recall the discussion in the introduction about the domination number $\gamma(G)$.

Theorem 8. *For infinitely many n, there are n-vertex 1-WL-equivalent graphs G and H such that $\gamma(G)/\gamma(H) > \frac{1}{20} \ln n - 1$.*

Proof. It suffices to show that the variation of the domination number among n-vertex d-regular graphs is logarithmic for an appropriate choice of the degree function $d = d(n)$.

Assuming that dn is even, let $\mathbb{R}(n, d)$ denote a random d-regular graph on n vertices. Given $p \in (0, 1)$, let $\mathbb{G}(n, p)$ denote the Erdős–Rényi random graph with edge probability p. Kim and Vu [18] proved for certain degree functions $d = d(n)$ that the distribution $\mathbb{R}(n, d)$ can be approximated from below and above, with respect to the subgraph relation, by distributions $\mathbb{G}(n, p_1)$ and $\mathbb{G}(n, p_2)$ with $p_1 = (1 - o(1))\frac{d}{n}$ and $p_2 = (1 + o(1))\frac{d}{n}$. We need the part of this sandwiching result about the approximation from above.

For our purposes, we consider pairs n, d such that $n = (2d)^4$ and, thus, $d = n^{1/4}/2$. Applied to this case, the Kim-Vu theorem says that there is a joint distribution of $\mathbb{R}(n, d)$ and $\mathbb{G}(n, p)$ with $p = (1 + o(1))\frac{d}{n} = (\frac{1}{2} + o(1))n^{-3/4}$ such that $\Delta(\mathbb{R}(n, d) \setminus \mathbb{G}(n, p)) \leq 4$ with probability $1 - o(1)$ as n increases. It follows that

$$\gamma(\mathbb{G}(n, p)) \leq 5\gamma(\mathbb{R}(n, d))$$

with probability $1 - o(1)$. Glebov et al. [15] proved that $\gamma(\mathbb{G}(n, p)) = \frac{\ln(np)}{p}(1 + o(1))$ with probability $1 - o(1)$ whenever $p \to 0$ and $pn \to \infty$. Hence $\gamma(\mathbb{R}(n, d)) \geq \frac{1}{5}\frac{n}{d}\ln d$ with probability $1 - o(1)$. As a consequence, there is an n-vertex d-regular graph G with $\gamma(G) \geq \frac{1}{5}\frac{n}{d}\ln d$.

On the other hand, consider $H = \frac{n}{2d}K_{d,d}$, where $K_{s,t}$ stands for the complete bipartite graph with vertex classes of size s and t, and note that $\gamma(H) = \frac{n}{d}$. Therefore, $\gamma(G)/\gamma(H) \geq \frac{1}{5}\ln d$, which readily gives us the desired bound. $\square$

We conclude with a discussion of Edge-Disjoint Triangle Packing. Haxell and Rödl [17] proved that ρ^{K_3} is well approximated by $\rho_f^{K_3}$ on dense graphs as $\rho_f^{K_3}(G) - \rho^{K_3}(G) = o(n^2)$ for n-vertex G. On the other hand, Yuster [26] showed that $\rho_f^{K_3}(G) - \rho^{K_3}(G) = \Omega(n^{1.5})$ for infinitely many G, and it is open whether this lower bound is tight. Define the *invariance discrepancy* of ρ^{K_3} as the function $D_{K_3}(n) = \max|\rho^{K_3}(G) - \rho^{K_3}(H)|$ where the maximum is taken over 2-WL-equivalent n-vertex graphs G and H. As follows from Theorem 7, this function provides a lower bound for the maximum integrality gap $\rho_f^{K_3}(G) - \rho^{K_3}(G)$ over n-vertex graphs. In this respect, it is reasonable to ask what the asymptotics of $D_{K_3}(n)$ is. The following fact is a step towards this goal.

Proposition 9. $D_{K_3}(n) = \Omega(n)$.

Proof. Consider $G = tS$ and $H = tR$, where S and R are the Shrikhande and 4×4 rook's graphs respectively. Both have vertex set $\mathbb{Z}_4 \times \mathbb{Z}_4$, and (i, j) and (i', j') are adjacent in S if ($i = i'$ and $j' = j + 1$) or ($j = j'$ and $i' = i + 1$) or ($i' = i+1$ and $j' = j+1$), where equality is in $\mathbb{Z}_4$, while they are adjacent in R if $i = i'$ (row 4-clique) or $j = j'$ (column 4-clique). S is completely decomposable into edge-triangles $\{(i, j), (i + 1, j), (i + 1, j + 1)\}$ and, hence, $\rho^{K_3}(S) = 16$. On the other hand, in R the edges of each K_3 all belong to the same row or column 4-clique. Since a packing can take at most one K_3 from each row/column K_4, we have $\rho^{K_3}(R) = 8$. This yields $\rho^{K_3}(G) - \rho^{K_3}(H) = 8t$ as desired. $\square$

References

1. Anderson, M., Dawar, A., Holm, B.: Solving linear programs without breaking abstractions. J. ACM **62**(6), 48:1–48:26 (2015)
2. Arvind, V., Fuhlbrück, F., Köbler, J., Verbitsky, O.: On the Weisfeiler-Leman dimension of Fractional Packing. Technical report, arxiv.org/abs/1910.11325 (2019)
3. Atserias, A., Dawar, A.: Definable inapproximability: new challenges for duplicator. In: Proceedings of CSL 2018. LIPIcs, vol. 119, pp. 7:1–7:21 (2018)

4. Babai, L.: Graph isomorphism in quasipolynomial time. In: Proceedings of STOC 2016, pp. 684–697 (2016)
5. Cai, J., Fürer, M., Immerman, N.: An optimal lower bound on the number of variables for graph identifications. Combinatorica **12**(4), 389–410 (1992)
6. Chappell, G., Gimbel, J., Hartman, C.: Approximations of the domination number of a graph. J. Combin. Math. Combin. Comput. **104**, 287–297 (2018)
7. Dawar, A.: The nature and power of fixed-point logic with counting. SIGLOG News **2**(1), 8–21 (2015)
8. Dawar, A., Severini, S., Zapata, O.: Pebble games and cospectral graphs. Electron. Notes Discrete Math. **61**, 323–329 (2017)
9. Dell, H., Grohe, M., Rattan, G.: Lovász meets Weisfeiler and Leman. In: Proceedings of ICALP 2018. LIPIcs, vol. 107, pp. 40:1–40:14 (2018)
10. Dor, D., Tarsi, M.: Graph decomposition is NP-complete: a complete proof of Holyer's conjecture. SIAM J. Comput. **26**(4), 1166–1187 (1997)
11. Ebbinghaus, H.D., Flum, J.: Finite Model Theory. Springer Monographs in Mathematics. Springer, Berlin (2006)
12. Füredi, Z.: Matchings and covers in hypergraphs. Graphs Comb. **4**(1), 115–206 (1988)
13. Fürer, M.: On the power of combinatorial and spectral invariants. Linear Algebra Appl. **432**(9), 2373–2380 (2010)
14. Garey, M.R., Johnson, D.S.: Computers and Intractability: A Guide to the Theory of NP-Completeness. W. H. Freeman, San Francisco (1979)
15. Glebov, R., Liebenau, A., Szabó, T.: On the concentration of the domination number of the random graph. SIAM J. Discrete Math. **29**(3), 1186–1206 (2015)
16. Grohe, M., Kersting, K., Mladenov, M., Selman, E.: Dimension reduction via colour refinement. In: Schulz, A.S., Wagner, D. (eds.) ESA 2014. LNCS, vol. 8737, pp. 505–516. Springer, Heidelberg (2014). https://doi.org/10.1007/978-3-662-44777-2_42. arXiv version: arxiv.org/abs/1307.5697
17. Haxell, P.E., Rödl, V.: Integer and fractional packings in dense graphs. Combinatorica **21**(1), 13–38 (2001)
18. Kim, J., Vu, V.: Sandwiching random graphs: universality between random graph models. Adv. Math. **188**(2), 444–469 (2004)
19. Kirkpatrick, D.G., Hell, P.: On the complexity of general graph factor problems. SIAM J. Comput. **12**(3), 601–609 (1983)
20. Lovász, L.: On the ratio of optimal integral and fractional covers. Discrete Math. **13**(4), 383–390 (1975)
21. Otto, M.: Bounded Variable Logics and Counting: A Study in Finite Models. Lecture Notes in Logic, vol. 9. Cambridge University Press, Cambridge (2017)
22. Raz, R., Safra, S.: A sub-constant error-probability low-degree test, and a sub-constant error-probability PCP characterization of NP. In: Proceedings of STOC 1997, pp. 475–484. ACM (1997)
23. Rubalcaba, R.R.: Fractional domination, fractional packings, and fractional isomorphisms of graphs. Ph.D. thesis, Auburn University (2005)
24. Scheinerman, E.R., Ullman, D.H.: Fractional Graph Theory. A Rational Approach to the Theory of Graphs. Wiley, Hoboken (1997)
25. Weisfeiler, B., Leman, A.: The reduction of a graph to canonical form and the algebra which appears therein. NTI Ser. 2 **9**, 12–16 (1968). English translation is available at https://www.iti.zcu.cz/wl2018/pdf/wl_paper_translation.pdf
26. Yuster, R.: Integer and fractional packing of families of graphs. Random Struct. Algorithms **26**(1–2), 110–118 (2005)

Input Strictly Local Tree Transducers

Jing Ji[(✉)] and Jeffrey Heinz

The Department of Linguistics and The Institute of Advanced
Computational Science, Stony Brook University, Stony Brook, USA
{jing.ji,jeffrey.heinz}@stonybrook.edu

Abstract. We generalize the class of input strictly local string functions
(Chandlee et al. 2014) to tree functions. We show they are characterized
by a subclass of frontier-to-root, deterministic, linear tree transducers.
We motivate this class from the study of natural language as it provides
a way to distinguish local syntactic processes from non-local ones. We
give examples illustrating this kind of analysis.

Keywords: Strictly local · Computational syntax · Tree transducers

1 Introduction

Locally Testable sets of strings in the strict sense (Strictly Local, SL) are a
subclass of the regular languages with interesting properties [16,20]. Rogers [18]
presents a generalization of SL to sets of trees and shows they characterize the
derivations of context-free languages. Chandlee et al. [2,3] generalize SL formal
languages in another direction. They present classes of strictly local string-to-
string functions. In this paper, we generalize the SL class to a class of functions
over trees. In particular, we present a characterization in terms of frontier-to-
root, deterministic, linear tree transducers [5,7].

One motivation comes from computational and theoretical linguistics, where
the goal of one program is to identify and understand the minimally powerful
classes of formal grammars which can describe aspects of natural language [4].
To this end, subregular sets and functions over strings have been used to distinguish and characterize phonological generalizations [11]. More recent research
has begun studying natural language syntax from the perspective of subregular
sets and functions over trees, as opposed to strings [9,10].

One rationale for studying subclasses of regular string/tree sets and relations
is that it is known that finite-state methods are sufficient to describe aspects
of natural language. For phonology and morphology, finite-state methods over
strings appear sufficient [1,17]. For syntax, finite-state methods over trees similarly appear sufficient. Rogers [19] showed that a syntactic theory of English
can be understood in terms of Monadic Second Order (MSO) definable constraints over trees. Languages with more complex constructions can be understood in terms of regular tree languages undergoing regular tree transductions

© Springer Nature Switzerland AG 2020
A. Leporati et al. (Eds.): LATA 2020, LNCS 12038, pp. 369–381, 2020.
https://doi.org/10.1007/978-3-030-40608-0_26

[8,14]. Tree transducers also have found broad application in machine translation [13,15]. It remains an open question, however, whether the full power of regular computations are necessary [11].

Another rationale for identifying subregular classes of languages is that learning problems may be easier to solve in the sense of requiring less and time and resources than otherwise [12].

By defining and characterizing the Input Strictly Local class of tree transducers, we hope to take a first step in developing a more fine-grained perspective on the syntactic transformations present in natural languages. The structure of the paper is as follows.

Section 2 defines trees and associated properties and functions based on their recursive structure. In this way we follow the tree transducer literature [5,7]. However, we note that we do *not* adopt the convention of ranked alphabets. Instead we obtain their effects by bounding the largest number of children a tree in some tree set can have and by requiring that the pre-image of the transition function of the tree automata is finite. While this is unconventional, we believe it simplifies our presentation and proofs. Section 2 also reviews strictly local treesets and reviews the proof of the abstract characterization of them [18].

Section 3 presents the main theoretical results. Deterministic, frontier-to-root, finite-state, linear tree transducers (abbreviated DFT) are defined, Input Strictly Local (ISL) tree functions are defined abstractly and then characterized in terms DFTs. Section 4 concludes.

2   Preliminaries

Assume a finite alphabet Σ and let Σ^* denote the set of all strings of finite length that can be obtained via concatenation of the elements of Σ. We denote the empty string with λ.

Consider an alphabet Σ and symbols $[\,]$ which do not belong to it. A tree is defined inductively as follows:

- **Base Case:** For each $a \in \Sigma$, $a[\,]$ is a tree. The tree $a[\,]$ is also called a *leaf*. We also write $a[\lambda]$ for $a[\,]$.
- **Inductive Case:** If $a \in \Sigma$ and $t_1 t_2 \ldots t_n$ is a string of trees of length n (n $\geq$ 1), then $a[t_1 t_2 \ldots t_n]$ is a tree.

For a trees $t = a[t_1 t_2 \ldots t_n]$, the trees $t_1, t_2, \ldots t_n$ are the *children* of t and t_i denotes the ith child. Σ^T denotes the set of all trees of finite size from Σ.

The depth, size, yield, root, branch, and the set of subtrees of a tree t, written $\mathtt{dp}(t)$, $|t|$, $\mathtt{yld}(t)$, $\mathtt{root}(t)$, $\mathtt{branch}(t)$ and $\mathtt{sub}(t)$, respectively, are defined as follows. For all $a \in \Sigma$:

- If $t = a[\,]$, then $\mathtt{dp}(t) = 1$, $|t| = 1$, $\mathtt{yld}(t) = a$, $\mathtt{root}(t) = a$, $\mathtt{branch}(t) = 0$, and $\mathtt{sub}(t) = \{t\}$.
- If $t = a[t_1 t_2 \ldots t_n]$ then $\mathtt{dp}(t) = \max\{\mathtt{dp}(t_i)|1 \leq i \leq n\} + 1$, and $|t| = 1 + \sum_{i=1}^{n}|t_i|$, and $\mathtt{yld}(t) = \mathtt{yld}(t_1)\mathtt{yld}(t_2)\ldots\mathtt{yld}(t_n)$, and $\mathtt{root}(t) = a$, and $\mathtt{branch}(t) = n$, and $\mathtt{sub}(t) = \bigcup\{\mathtt{sub}(t_i)|1 \leq i \leq n\} \cup \{t\}$.

The roots of the subtrees of a tree t are called *nodes*. The root of a tree is also called its *root node*. Leaves are also called *frontier nodes*.

The branching degree of a tree t is $\mathtt{branch\_degree}(t) = \max\{\mathtt{branch}(u) \mid u \in \mathtt{sub}(t)\}$. Let Σ_n^T denotes the set of trees $\{t \in \Sigma^T \mid \mathtt{branch\_degree}(t) \leq n\}$.

Example 1. Suppose $\Sigma = \{S, a, b\}$. $S[a\, S[a\, b]\, b]$ denotes a tree rooted in S with $\mathtt{branch\_degree}$ of 3.

Let N^* be the set of all sequences of finite length of positive natural numbers. For $\vec{n} = \langle n_1, n_2, \ldots, n_m \rangle \in N^*$ ($m \geq 1$), the subtree of t at $\vec{n}$ is written $t.\vec{n}$, and it is defined inductively:

- **Base Case:** $t.\vec{n} = t$ iff $\vec{n} = \lambda$.
- **Inductive Case:** Suppose $t = a[t_1 t_2 \ldots t_n]$ and $\vec{n} \neq \lambda$. Then $t.\vec{n} = t.\langle n_1, n_2 \ldots n_m \rangle = t_{n_1}.\langle n_2, n_3 \ldots n_m \rangle$.
- **Note:** $t.\vec{n}$ is undefined otherwise.

These sequences are the Gorn addresses of the subtrees of t. For example, The first child of t is given by $t.\langle 1 \rangle$ (if it exists); the second child by $t.\langle 2 \rangle$ (if it exists); the second child of the first child by $t.\langle 1, 2 \rangle$ (if it exists); and of course $t.\langle\ \rangle = t$.

The Gorn addresses provide a natural ordering of the subtrees of t in terms of the length-lexicographic ordering. For distinct $\vec{n} = \langle n_1, n_2, \ldots, n_k \rangle$, $\vec{m} = \langle m_1, m_2, \ldots, m_\ell \rangle$, $\vec{n}$ precedes $\vec{m}$ iff either $k < \ell$, or $k = \ell$ and $n_1 < m_1$, or $k = \ell$ and $n_1 = m_1$ and $\langle n_2, \ldots, n_k \rangle < \langle m_2, \ldots, m_\ell \rangle$. This essentially orders subtrees of t such that the ones closer to the root of t are ordered earlier, and those 'on the same level' in t are ordered 'left to right.' We make use of this ordering in our proof of Theorem 1.

The largest common subtrees of a set of trees T, denoted $\mathtt{lcs}(T)$, is $\{d \in \bigcap_{t \in T} \mathtt{sub}(t) \mid \forall d' \in \bigcap_{t \in T} \mathtt{sub}(t), |d'| \leq |d|\}$.

The k-stem ($k \geq 1$) of a tree t, written $\mathtt{stem}_k(t)$, is defined as follows.

- **Base Case:** For all $a \in \Sigma$, if $t = a[\,]$, then $\mathtt{stem}_k(t) = a[\,]$.
- **Inductive Case:** For all $a \in \Sigma$, if $t = a[t_1 t_2 \ldots t_n]$, then
  - $\mathtt{stem}_1(t) = \mathtt{root}(t)[\,]$, and
  - $\mathtt{stem}_k(t) = a[\mathtt{stem}_{k-1}(t_1)\mathtt{stem}_{k-1}(t_2) \ldots \mathtt{stem}_{k-1}(t_n)]$.

The stems of a tree t, denoted $\mathtt{stem}(t)$ is the set $\{\mathtt{stem}_k(t) \mid k \geq 1\}$.

Example 2. The 2-stems of the tree in Example 1 is $\{S[a\, S\, b], S[a\, b], a[\,], b[\,]\}$.

It is useful to incorporate boundary markers into the roots and leaves of trees. Informally, given a Σ-tree t, boundary markers are added above the root and below the leaves. Formally, we employ symbols $\rtimes, \ltimes \notin \Sigma$ for this purpose. We let $\hat{\Sigma} = \Sigma \cup \{\rtimes, \ltimes\}$.

Thus for all $a \in \Sigma$, $t \in \Sigma^T$, let $\mathtt{add}\_\rtimes(t) = \rtimes[t]$, and $\mathtt{add}\_\ltimes(a[\,]) = a[\ltimes[\,]]$, and $\mathtt{add}\_\ltimes(a[t_1 \ldots t_n]) = a[\ltimes(t_1) \cdots \ltimes(t_n)]$. Then for any Σ-tree t, its augmented counterpart $\hat{t} = \mathtt{add}\_\rtimes(\mathtt{add}\_\ltimes(t))$.

The k-factors of a tree t are defined as the set of k-depth stems of subtrees of $\hat{t}$. For all $t \in \Sigma^T$, let $F_k(t) = \bigcup\{\mathtt{stem}_k(u) \mid u \in \mathtt{sub}(\hat{t})\}$.

We lift the definition of k-factors to treesets in the natural way. For all $T \subseteq \Sigma^T$, $F_k(T) = \bigcup_{t \in T} F_k(t)$.

Example 3. The 2-factors of the tree in Example 1 is the set $\{\ltimes[S[\,]],$ $S[a[\,]S[\,]b[\,]], S[a[\,]b[\,]], a[\ltimes[\,]], b[\ltimes[\,]], \ltimes[\,]\}$.

A strictly k-local grammar $G = (\Sigma, S)$ where S is a finite subset of $F_k(\Sigma^T)$ and the tree language of G is defined as: $\mathbb{L}((\Sigma, S)) = \{t \mid F_k(t) \subseteq S\}$.

Note that since S is finite, there exists a smallest number n such that $S \subseteq \hat{\Sigma}_n^T$. It follows that $\mathbb{L}((\Sigma, S))$ is of branching degree n. A treeset $T \subseteq \Sigma^T$ is strictly k-local if there exists a k and a strictly k-local grammar G such that $\mathbb{L}(G) = T$. Such treesets form exactly strictly k-local treesets (SL_k). Strictly local stringsets are a special case of strictly local treesets where all the branching degree is 1; so every node (except leaves) are unary branching.

Strictly 2-local treesets have been called local treesets in previous literature [18]. Every Strictly 2-local tree language can be generated by a context free grammar [7,18].

Comparable to the characterization of strictly local string sets, which is Suffix Substitution Closure [20], each strictly 2-local tree language satisfies Subtree Substitution Closure[18]. To explain this characterization, we first introduce the notion of subtree-substitution.

For $t, s \in \Sigma^T$ and $\vec{n} = \langle n_1, n_2, \ldots, n_m \rangle \in N^*$ (m $\geq$ 1), the operation of substituting the subtree of t at $\vec{n}$ by s, written as $t.\vec{n} \leftarrow s$, is defined as follows.

- **Base Case:** $t.\vec{n} \leftarrow s = s$ iff $\vec{n} = \lambda$.
- **Inductive Case:** If t $= a[t_1 t_2 \ldots t_n]$ then $t.\vec{n} \leftarrow s = a[t_1 t_2 \ldots (t_{n_1}.$ $\langle n_2, n_3 \ldots n_m \rangle \leftarrow s) \ldots t_n]$.

We also define substitution of all the subtrees of t rooted at x ($x \in \Sigma$) by s, which we write as $t \overset{x}{\leftarrow} s$.

- **Base Case:** If root(t) $=$ x, $t \overset{x}{\leftarrow} s = $ s.
- **Base Case:** If root(t) $\neq$ x and t $= a[\,]$ (a $\in \Sigma$), $t \overset{x}{\leftarrow} s = $ t.
- **Inductive Case:** If root(t) $\neq$ x and t $= a[t_1 t_2 \ldots t_n]$ (a $\in \Sigma$), $t \overset{x}{\leftarrow} s = $ $a[s_1 s_2 \ldots s_n]$ where $s_i = t_i \overset{x}{\leftarrow} s$ ($1 \leq i \leq n$).

Rogers [18] proves the following result and we repeat the proof to set the stage for the sequel.

Theorem 1 (Subtree Substitution Closure). *A treeset $T \subseteq \Sigma^T$ is strictly 2-local iff there is n such that T is of branching degree n and for all $A, B \in T$, whenever there exist two vectors $\vec{n_1}, \vec{n_2} \in \vec{N}$, such that $\text{root}(A.\vec{n_1}) = \text{root}(B.\vec{n_2})$ then $A.\vec{n_1} \leftarrow B.\vec{n_2} \in T$.*

Proof. If T is strictly 2-local, then there exists a corresponding strictly 2-local grammar G that satisfies $\mathbb{L}(G) = T$. Thus there exists a finite set $S \subset F_k(\Sigma^T)$ such that $\mathbb{L}((\Sigma, S)) = T$.

Consider any $A, B \in T$ and $\vec{n_1}, \vec{n_2} \in \vec{N}$ such that $\text{root}(A.\vec{n_1}) = \text{root}(B.\vec{n_2})$. Let $t = A.\vec{n_1} \leftarrow B.\vec{n_2}$. We show $t \in T$. First notice that $F_2(A) \subseteq S$ and $F_2(B) \subseteq S$ because $A, B \in T$ and $T = \mathbb{L}((\Sigma, S))$. Next consider any element $u \in F_2(t)$. By definition of t and 2-factor, u must be a 2-stem of a subtree of

$A.\vec{n_1} \leftarrow B.\vec{n_2}$. If u is the 2-stem of a subtree of $B.\vec{n_2}$ then $u \in F_2(B) \subset S$. If not, then u is a 2-stem of a subtree of A and so $u \in F_2(A) \subset S$. Either way, $u \in S$ and so $F_2(t) \subseteq S$. It follows that $t \in T$.

Conversely, consider a treeset T such that whenever there exist two vectors $\vec{n_1}, \vec{n_2} \in \vec{N}$, such that $\text{root}(A.\vec{n_1}) = \text{root}(B.\vec{n_2})$ then $A.\vec{n_1} \leftarrow B.\vec{n_2} \in T$. We refer to this property as the SSC. To show T is Strictly 2-Local, we present a finite set $S \subset F_k(\Sigma^T)$ such that $\mathbb{L}((\Sigma, S)) = T$. Let $S = F_2(T)$. Since T is of branching degree n, S is finite. In order to prove $\mathbb{L}((\Sigma, S)) = T$, we need to show both $\mathbb{L}((\Sigma, S)) \subseteq T$ and $T \subseteq \mathbb{L}((\Sigma, S))$. It is obvious that $T \subseteq \mathbb{L}((\Sigma, S))$ because for any $t \in T$, $F_2(t) \subseteq S = F_2(T)$.

The following proves that $\mathbb{L}((\Sigma, S)) \subseteq T$ by recursive application of SSC. Consider any $t \in \mathbb{L}((\Sigma, S))$. Let $t_1 = t.\vec{n_1}, t_2 = t.\vec{n_2}, \ldots t_m = t.\vec{n_m}$ be an enumeration of the m subtrees of t by their Gorn addresses in length-lexicographic order. (Note that $t_1 = t$).

The base step of the induction is to choose a tree $s_0 \in T$ that has the same root as t. Such a $s_0 \in T$ exists because $\rtimes[\text{root}(t)[\,]] \in S$.

Next we assume by the induction hypothesis that $s_{i-1} \in T$ and we will construct s_i which is also in T. For each $1 \leq i \leq m$, if t_i is a leaf then let $u = t_i[\rtimes[\,]]$, otherwise let $u = \text{stem}_2(t_i)$. Choose a tree $x \in T$ such that $u \in F_2(x)$. Such a tree $x \in T$ exists because $u \in S = F_2(T)$. It follows there is $\vec{m}$ such that $\text{stem}_2(x.\vec{m}) = u$. Let $s_i = s_{i-1}.\vec{n_i} \leftarrow x.\vec{m}$. Since $\text{root}(s_{i-1}.\vec{n_i}) = \text{root}(x.\vec{m})$ and $s_{i-1}, x \in T$, it follows that $s_i \in T$ by SSC. Informally, this construction ensures the nodes and children of s_i are identical to those of t from the root of t to the root of the subtree t_i.

Since each s_i is built according to s_{i-1} and $s_0 \in T$ we conclude that $s_m \in T$. Furthermore, since the subtrees are ordered length-lexicographically and we substitute a 2-stem of a subtree of t to build s_i, it follows that $s_m = t$. As t was arbitrary in $\mathbb{L}((\Sigma, S))$, we obtain $\mathbb{L}((\Sigma, S)) \subseteq T$. □

The catenation operation of two trees $u \cdot t$ is defined by substitution in the leaves. Let \$ be a new symbol, i.e., \$ $\notin \Sigma$. Let $\Sigma_{\$}^T$ denote the set of all trees over $\Sigma \cup$ \$ which contain exactly one occurrence of label \$ in the leaves. The operation of catenation is defined inductively:

- **Base Case:** For $t \in \Sigma^T$, \$$[\,] \cdot t = t$.
- **Base Case:** For all $a \in \Sigma$, if $u = a[\,]$, $u \cdot t = a[\,]$.
- **Inductive Case:** For all $a \in \Sigma$, if $u = a[t_1 t_2 \ldots t_n]$, $u \cdot t = a[(t_1 \cdot t)(t_2 \cdot t) \ldots (t_n \cdot t)]$.

Example 4. Suppose $\Sigma = \{\text{S, a, b}\}$. Let $u = \text{S}[\text{a}[\,]\$[\,]\text{b}[\,]]$ and $t = \text{S}[\text{a}[\,]\text{b}[\,]]$. $u \cdot t = \text{S}[(\text{a}[\,]\cdot t)(\$[\,]\cdot t)(\text{b}[\,]\cdot t)] = \text{S}[\text{a}[\,]\text{S}[\text{a}[\,]\text{b}[\,]]\text{b}[\,]]$.

Notice that the classical catenation of strings can be viewed as a special case of catenation of trees with unary branching. This operation can also be used to represent subtrees. For $t \in \Sigma^T \cup \Sigma_{\$}^T$, if $t = u \cdot s$, then s is a subtree of t.

If $U \subseteq \Sigma_{\$}^T$ and $T \subseteq \Sigma^T \cup \Sigma_{\$}^T$, then $U \cdot T = \{u \cdot t \mid u \in U, t \in T\}$. Furthermore, for any $t \in T$ and any tree language $T \subseteq \Sigma^T$, the quotient of t w.r.t. T is defined

374 J. Ji and J. Heinz

as $\mathsf{qt}_T(t) = \{u \in \Sigma_\$^T \mid u \cdot t \in T\}$. Canonical finite-state tree recognizers can be defined in terms of these quotients.

3 Input Strictly Local Tree Transducers

In this section we define functions that map trees to trees. After reviewing some basic terminology, we introduce deterministic, frontier-to-root, linear, finite-state Tree Transducers (DFT). We then define Input Strictly Local Tree Transducers (ISLTT) in a grammar-independent way, and then prove they correspond exactly to a type of DFTs. Examples are provided along the way.

A function f with domain X and co-domain Y can be written $f : X \to Y$. The image of f is the set $\{f(x) \in Y \mid x \in X, f(x) \text{ is defined}\}$ and the pre-image of f is the set $\{x \in X \mid f(x) \text{ is defined}\}$. Tree transducers compute functions that map trees to trees $f : \Sigma_n^T \to \Gamma^T$.

DFTs are defined as a tuple $(Q, \Sigma, \Gamma, F, \delta)$, where Q is a finite set of states, $F \subseteq Q$ is a set of final states, and δ is a transition function that maps a sequence of states paired with an element of Σ to a state and a *variably-leafed tree*. A variably-leafed tree is a tree which may include variables in the leaves of the tree. Let $X = \{x_1, x_2, \ldots\}$ be a countable set of variables. If Σ is a finite alphabet then $\Sigma^T[X]$ denotes the set of trees t formed with the alphabet $\Sigma \cup X$ such that if the root of a subtree s of t is a variable then s is a leaf (so variables are only allowed in leaves). Thus formally the transition function is $\delta : Q^* \times \Sigma \to \Gamma^T[X] \times Q$. Importantly, the pre-image of the transition function must be finite. We sometimes write $(q_1 q_2 \ldots q_m, a, t, q) \in \delta$ to mean $\delta(q_1 q_2 \ldots q_m, a) = (t, q)$.

In the course of computing a tree transduction, the variables in variably-leafed trees are substituted with trees. Assume $t_1, t_2, \ldots t_m \in \Gamma^T$ and $s \in \Gamma^T[X]$, which is a variable leafed tree with any subset of the variables $\{x_1, x_2, \ldots, x_m\}$. We define a substitution function ϕ such that $\phi(t_1 t_2 \ldots t_m, s) = s \overset{x_i}{\leftarrow} t_i$ for $1 \le i \le m$.

We define the process of transducing a tree recursively using a function π, which maps Σ_n^T to $Q \times \Gamma^T$, which itself is defined inductively with δ.

- **Base Case:** $\pi(a[\,]) = (q, v)$ iff $\delta(\lambda, a) = (v, q)$
- **Inductive Case:** $\pi(a[t_1 t_2 \ldots t_m]) = (q, \phi(v_1 v_2 \ldots v_m, s))$ iff $\delta(q_1 q_2 \ldots q_m, a) = (s, q)$ and $\pi(t_i) = (q_i, v_i)$ for each $1 \le i \le m$.

The tree-to-tree function the transducer M recognizes is the set of pairs $\mathbb{L}(M) = \{(t, s) \mid t \in \Sigma_n^T, s \in \Gamma^T, \pi(t) = (q, s), q \in F\}$. We also write $M(t) = s$ whenever $(t, s) \in \mathbb{L}(M)$.

A DFT is *linear* provided whenever $\delta(q_1 q_2 \ldots q_m, a) = (s, q)$, no variable occurs more than once in s.

Example 5. Wh-movement refers to a syntactic analysis of question words such as English *what* and *who*. It is common to analyze this as a relation between tree structures [21]. The input structure describes the relation of the wh-word to its verb (cf. "John thinks Mary believes Bill buys what?") and the yield of the output structure reflects the pronunciation (cf. "What does John think Mary believe Bill buys").

We use a simplified transformation to make the point. In the alphabet, S represents the root node of a input tree, W stands for a wh-word and P for everything else (P is for phrase). A transducer of wh-movement can be constructed as a tuple $M_{wh} = (Q, \Sigma, F, \delta)$ where $Q = \{q_w, q_p, q_s\}$, $F = \{q_s\}$, $\Sigma = \{S, P, W\}$, and $\delta = \{(\lambda, P, P[\,], q_p), (\lambda, W, W[\,], q_w), (q_p q_p, P, P[x_1 x_2], q_p), (q_w q_p, P, P[x_1 x_2], q_w),$ $(q_p q_w, P, P[x_1 x_2], q_w), (q_p q_w, S, S[W[\,]S[x_1 x_2]], q_s), (q_w q_p, S, S[W[\,]S[x_1 x_2]], q_s),$ $(q_p q_p, S, S[x_1 x_2], q_s)\}$.

Figure 1 illustrates some of the transformations computed by the finite-state machine M_{wh}. The tree with a wh-word in Fig. (1a) is transformed into the tree in Fig. (1b). (M_{wh} keeps the original wh-word in-situ but it could easily be removed or replaced with a trace). The trees in Fig. (1c) and (d) are the same because there is no wh-word in the input tree and so M_{wh} leaves it unchanged.

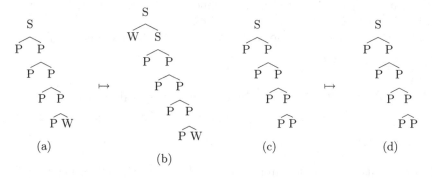

Fig. 1. M_{wh} maps the tree in (a) to the tree in (b) and likewise maps the tree in (c) to itself in (d).

Next we describe the canonical form of deterministic tree transducers. The *quotient* of a tree $t \in \Sigma^T$ with respect to a tree-to-tree function $f : \Sigma^T \to \Gamma^T$ is a key idea. It will be useful to develop some notation for the *largest common subtree of the image under f of the set of trees which includes t as a subtree.* Let $\mathrm{lcsi}_f(t) = \mathrm{lcs}\left(f(\Sigma_\$^T \cdot \{t\})\right)$. When f is understood from context, we just write $\mathrm{lcsi}(t)$. Then the quotient is defined as follows:

$$\mathrm{qt}_f(t) = \left\{(u, v) \mid f(u \cdot t) = v \cdot s, s = \mathrm{lcsi}_f(t)\right\}. \tag{1}$$

When f is clear from context, we write $\mathrm{qt}(t)$ instead of $\mathrm{qt}_f(t)$.

It is worth noting that for a tree $t \in \Sigma_n^T$, the largest common subtree of the image of a linear transducer with the input of $\Sigma_\$^T \cdot \{t\}$ is unique if it exists because if there is more than one tree that belongs to $\mathrm{lcs}(f(\Sigma_\$^T \cdot \{t\}))$, they must be produced by copying, which is not allowed by linear DFT. If trees $t_1, t_2 \in \Sigma^T$

have the same quotient with respect to a function f, they are quotient-equivalent with respect to f and we write $t_1 \sim_f t_2$. Clearly, $\sim_f$ is an equivalence relation which partitions Σ^T.

As in the string case, to each regular tree language T, there is a canonical DFT accepting T. The characterization given by the Myhill-Nerode theorem can be transferred to the tree case [6]. For any treeset T, the quotients of trees w.r.t. T can be used to partition Σ^T into a finite set of equivalence classes.

Analogous to the smallest subsequential finite state transducer for a subsequential function, we can construct the smallest linear DFT for a deterministic tree-to-tree function f and refer to this transducer as the canonical transducer for f, Ψ_f^c. For $t_1, t_2, \ldots, t_m \in \Sigma_n^T$ ($m \leq n$) and $a \in \Sigma$, let the contribution of a w.r.t. $t_1 t_2 \ldots t_m$ be $\mathrm{cont}_f(a, t_1 t_2 \ldots t_m) = v \in \Gamma^T[X]$, which satisfies

$$\phi\Big(\mathrm{lcsi}(t_1)\mathrm{lcsi}(t_2)\ldots\mathrm{lcsi}(t_m), v\Big) = \mathrm{lcsi}\Big(a[t_1 t_2 \ldots t_m]\Big). \tag{2}$$

The term $\mathrm{cont}_f(a, t_1 t_2 \ldots t_m)$ is well-defined since each $\mathrm{lcsi}(t_1), \mathrm{lcsi}(t_2), \ldots$ $\mathrm{lcsi}(t_m)$, and $\mathrm{lcsi}(a[t_1 t_2 \ldots t_m])$ are unique.

Then the canonical DFT for a deterministic tree-to-tree function f is:

- $Q = \{\mathrm{qt}_f(t) \mid \in \Sigma_n^T\}$,
- $F \subseteq Q$,
- For $a \in \Sigma$, there exists $v \in \Gamma^T$ that satisfies $(\lambda, a, v, \mathrm{qt}_f(a[\,])) \in \delta$,
- For $t_1, t_2, \ldots, t_m \in \Sigma_n^T (m \leq n)$ and $a \in \Sigma$, $\Big(\mathrm{qt}_f(t_1)\,\mathrm{qt}_f(t_2)\ldots\mathrm{qt}_f(t_m),$
  $a, \mathrm{cont}_f(a, t_1 t_2 \ldots t_m), \mathrm{qt}_f(a[t_1 t_2 \ldots t_m])\Big) \in \delta$.

The presentation here differs from Friese et al. [6], but the only thing we require in the proof of Theorem 2 below is the existence of the canonical DFT whenever $\sim_f$ is of finite index.

We define ISLTT as a subclass of linear DFTs.

Definition 1 (Input Strictly Local Tree-to-tree Function). *A function f is Input Strictly Local (ISL) if there is a k and n such that for all $t_1, t_2 \in \Sigma_n^T$, if $\mathrm{stem}_{k-1}(t_1) = \mathrm{stem}_{k-1}(t_2)$ then $\mathrm{quotient}_f(t_1) = \mathrm{quotient}_f(t_2)$.*

In the same way ISL string functions can be used to probe the locality properties of phonological processes, ISL tree functions can used to probe the locality properties of syntactic transformations.

To show that a syntactic transformation is *not* ISL one need only construct a counterexample to Definition 1.

Example 6. We can show the function computed by $M_w h$ from Example 5 is not ISL for any k because there is no bound on the distance the wh-word can 'travel.' Suppose there is a k and n such that for all $t_1, t_2 \in \Sigma_n^T$, if $\mathrm{stem}_{k-1}(t_1) = \mathrm{stem}_{k-1}(t_2)$ then $\mathrm{qt}_f(t_1) = \mathrm{qt}_f(t_2)$. Let $u_1 = u_2 \ldots = u_{k-1} = P[P\$]$. Also let $u_k = \mathrm{P}\ [\mathrm{P}\ \mathrm{P}]$, $s = S[P\$]$ and $w = P[PW]$. We construct two sentence structures: $s \cdot t_1$ and $s \cdot t_2$, where $t_1 = u_1 \cdot u_2 \ldots u_{k-1} \cdot w$ and $t_2 = u_1 \cdot u_2 \ldots u_{k-1} \cdot u_k$.

It is obvious that $\mathtt{stem}_{k-1}(t_1) = \mathtt{stem}_{k-1}(t_2)$. However, $\mathtt{qt}_f(t_1) \neq \mathtt{qt}_f(t_2)$ since $(s, s) \in \mathtt{qt}_f(t_2)$ but $(s, s) \notin \mathtt{qt}_f(t_1)$. As we can always find such a pair of trees t_1 and t_2 for any k, it is thus proved that wh-movement is not ISL for any k.

Our main result, Theorem 2 below, establishes an automata-theoretic characterization of ISL tree-to-tree functions. As we illustrate after the proof, one can show that a tree transformation is ISL using this theorem.

Theorem 2 (ISL Tree Transducers). *A function f is ISL iff there is some k and n such that f can be described with a DFT for which*

1. $Q = \{\mathtt{stem}_{k-1}(t) \mid t \in \Sigma_n^T)\}$ and $F \subseteq Q$,
2. $\forall q_1 q_2 \ldots q_m \in Q^* (1 \leq m \leq n)$, $a \in \Sigma$, $u \in \Gamma^T[X]$, *it is the case that* $(q_1 q_2 \ldots q_m, a, u, q') \in \delta \Rightarrow q' = \mathtt{stem}_{k-1}(a[q_1 q_2 \ldots q_m])$.

The transducer is finite since Σ is finite and n bounds the branching degree of the pre-image of f which ensures the finiteness of both Q and δ.

Before our proof of the Theorem, we prove a lemma based on these remarks.

Remark 1. For all k,m $\in \mathbb{N}$ with k $\leq$ m, and for all $t \in \Sigma_n^T$, $\mathtt{stem}_k(\mathtt{stem}_m(t)) = \mathtt{stem}_k(t)$ since both t and $\mathtt{stem}_m(t)$ share the same k-stem from the root.

Remark 2. For all $k \in \mathbb{N}$, and for all $a \in \Sigma$ and $t_1, t_2, \ldots t_m \in \Sigma_n^T (m \leq n)$, $\mathtt{stem}_{k-1}(a[t_1 t_2 \ldots t_m]) = \mathtt{stem}_{k-1}(a[\mathtt{stem}_{k-1}(t_1)\,\mathtt{stem}_{k-1}(t_2) \ldots \mathtt{stem}_{k-1}(t_m)])$. This is a direct consequence of Remark 1.

Lemma 1. *Let Ψ be a ISLTT with the properties defined in Theorem 2. If $t \in \Sigma_n^T$ and $u \in \Gamma^T$, $\pi(t) = (q, u)$, then $q = \mathtt{stem}_{k-1}(t)$.*

Proof. The proof is by induction on the depth of the trees to which π is applying. The base case follows from the facts that for $(\lambda, a, v, q) \in \delta$ iff $\pi(a[\,]) = (q, v)$ and $q = \mathtt{stem}_{k-1}(a[\,])$.

Next assume for all $t_1, t_2, \ldots, t_m \in \Sigma_n^T$ ($m \leq n$) and $v_1, v_2 \ldots, v_m \in \Gamma^T$ such that $\pi(t_1) = (q_1, v_1)$ implies $q_1 = \mathtt{stem}_{k-1}(t_1)$, $\pi(t_2) = (q_2, v_2)$ implies $q_2 = \mathtt{stem}_{k-1}(t_2), \ldots, \pi(t_m) = (q_m, v_m)$ implies $q_m = \mathtt{stem}_{k-1}(t_m)$. We show that $\forall a \in \Sigma$ that there is a $v \in \Gamma^T[X]$ such that $\pi(a[t_1 t_2 \ldots t_m]) = (q, \phi(v_1 v_2 \ldots v_m, v))$ and $q = \mathtt{stem}_{k-1}(a[t_1 t_2 \ldots t_m])$. Based on the assumption, we know that $\pi(t_1) = (\mathtt{stem}_{k-1}(t_1), v_1)$, $\pi(t_2) = (\mathtt{stem}_{k-1}(t_2), v_2)$, $\ldots$, $\pi(t_m) = (\mathtt{stem}_{k-1}(t_m), v_m)$, so there exists $v \in \Gamma^T[X]$ such that $(\mathtt{stem}_{k-1}(t_1)\mathtt{stem}_{k-1}(t_2)\mathtt{stem}_{k-1}(t_m), a, v, q) \in \delta$. By the construction, q is defined to be equal to $\mathtt{stem}_{k-1}(a[\mathtt{stem}_{k-1}(t_1)\mathtt{stem}_{k-1}(t_2)\mathtt{stem}_{k-1}(t_m)])$, which by Remark 2, equals $\mathtt{stem}_{k-1}(a[t_1 t_2 \ldots t_m])$.

Now we can prove the theorem.

Proof (Theorem 2). ($\Leftarrow$) Assume $k \in \mathbb{N}$ and let f be a function described by $\Psi = \{Q, \Sigma, \Gamma, F, \delta\}$ constructed as in Theorem. Let $t_1, t_2 \in \Sigma_n^T$ such that $\mathtt{stem}_{k-1}(t_1) = \mathtt{stem}_{k-1}(t_2)$. By Lemma 1, both t_1 and t_2 lead to the same state, so $\mathtt{qt}_f(t_1) = \mathtt{qt}_f(t_2)$. Therefore, f is k-ISL.

($\Rightarrow$) Consider any ISL tree-to-tree function f. Then there is some k and n such that $\forall t_1, t_2 \in \Sigma_n^T$, we have $\mathtt{stem}_{k-1}(t_1) = \mathtt{stem}_{k-1}(t_2) \Rightarrow \mathtt{qt}_f(t_1) = \mathtt{qt}_f(t_2)$. We show that the corresponding ISL tree transducer Ψ_f^{ISL} exists. Since $\mathtt{stem}_{k-1}(\Sigma_n^T)$ is a finite set, the equivalence relation $\sim_f$ partitions Σ^T into at most $\mathtt{stem}_{k-1}(\Sigma_n^T)$ blocks. Thus there exists a canonical linear DFT $\Psi_f^c = \{Q_c, F_c, \Sigma, \Gamma, \delta_c\}$. π_c is the process function derived from δ_c that maps Σ_n^T to $Q_c \times \Gamma^T$.

Construct $\Psi = \{Q, F, \Sigma, \Gamma, \delta\}$ as follows:

- $Q = \mathtt{stem}_{k-1}(\Sigma_n^T)$
- $\forall q \in Q, q \in F$ iff $\mathtt{qt}(q) \in F_c$.
- For $a \in \Sigma$ and $v \in \Gamma^T[X]$, $(\lambda, a, v, q) \in \delta$ iff $(\lambda, a, v, \mathtt{qt}(q)) \in \delta_c$.
- $\forall q_1 q_2 \ldots q_m \in Q^* (1 \leq m \leq n), a \in \Sigma, u \in \Gamma^T[X]$, we have $(q_1 q_2 \ldots q_m, a, v, \mathtt{stem}_{k-1}(a[q_1 q_2 \ldots q_m])) \in \delta$ if and only if $(\mathtt{qt}(q_1)\mathtt{qt}(q_2) \ldots \mathtt{qt}(q_m), a, v, \mathtt{qt}(a[q_1 q_2 \ldots q_m])) \in \delta_c$.

Ψ is ISL by construction, as the states and transitions of Ψ meet requirements (1) and (2) of Theorem 2.

The following proof show that Ψ computes the same function as Ψ_f^c by showing that Ψ and Ψ_f^c generate the same function. In other words we show $\forall t \in \Sigma_n^T$, $u \in \Gamma^T$, $\pi(t) = (\mathtt{stem}_{k-1}(t), u)$ iff $\pi_c(t) = (\mathtt{qt}(t), u)$ and $\mathtt{stem}_{k-1}(t) \in F$ iff $\mathtt{qt}(t) \in F_c$.

First, we show that $\pi(t) = (\mathtt{stem}_{k-1}(t), u)$ iff $\pi_c(t) = (\mathtt{qt}(t), u)$. Clearly, the base case is satisfied. For all $a \in \Sigma$ and $v \in \Gamma^T[X]$, $(\lambda, a, v, q) \in \delta$ iff $(\lambda, a, v, \mathtt{qt}(q)) \in \delta_c$. Thus $\pi_c(a[\,]) = (\mathtt{qt}(a[\,]), v)$ and $\pi(a[\,]) = (\mathtt{stem}_{k-1}(a[\,]), v)$.

Next assume that there exist $t_1, t_2, \ldots, t_m \in \Sigma_n^T$ and $u_1, u_2, \ldots, u_m \in \Gamma^T$ such that $\pi(t_i) = (\mathtt{stem}_{k-1}(t_i), u_i)$ iff $\pi_c(t_i) = (\mathtt{qt}(t_1), u_i)$ for each $1 \leq i \leq m$. We show $\forall a \in \Sigma$ and $\forall v \in \Sigma^T[X]$ such that $\pi(a[t_1 t_2 \ldots t_m]) = (\mathtt{stem}_{k-1}(a[t_1 t_2 \ldots t_m]))$, we have $(\phi(u_1 u_2 \ldots u_m], v))$ iff $\pi_c(a[t_1 t_2 \ldots t_m]) = (\mathtt{qt}(a[t_1 t_2 \ldots t_m]), \phi(u_1 u_2 \ldots u_m], v))$.

Suppose $\pi_c(a[t_1 t_2 \ldots t_m]) = (\mathtt{qt}(a[t_1 t_2 \ldots t_m]), (\phi(u_1 u_2 \ldots u_m, v)))$. By assumption, $\pi_c(t_i) = (\mathtt{qt}(t_1), u_i)$ for each $1 \leq i \leq m$. Hence, $(\mathtt{qt}(t_1) \ldots \mathtt{qt}(t_m), a, v, \mathtt{qt}(a[t_1 t_2 \ldots t_m])) \in \delta_c$.

Let $q_i = \mathtt{stem}_{k-1}(t_i)$ for each $1 \leq i \leq m$. Observe that each $\mathtt{stem}_{k-1}(t_i) = \mathtt{stem}_{k-1}(q_i)$ by Remark 1. Consequently, since f is k-ISL, $\mathtt{qt}(t_i) = \mathtt{qt}(q_i)$. Similarly, $\mathtt{stem}_{k-1}(a[t_1 t_2 \ldots t_m]) = \mathtt{stem}_{k-1}(a[q_1 q_2 \ldots q_m])$ and so $\mathtt{qt}(a[t_1 t_2 \ldots t_m]) = \mathtt{qt}(a[q_1 q_2 \ldots q_m])$. By substitution then, we have $\pi_c(t_i) = (\mathtt{qt}(q_i), u_i)$ for each $1 \leq i \leq m$ and $(\mathtt{qt}(q_1)\mathtt{qt}(q_2) \ldots \mathtt{qt}(q_m), a, v, \mathtt{qt}(a[q_1 q_2 \ldots q_m])) \in \delta_c$.

By construction of Ψ, $(q_1 q_2 \ldots q_m, a, x, \mathtt{stem}_{k-1}(a[q_1 q_2 \ldots q_m])) \in \delta$. Since $\pi(t_i) = (\mathtt{stem}_{k-1}(t_i), u_i)$ for each $1 \leq i \leq m$, it follows that $\pi(a[t_1 t_2 \ldots t_m]) = (\mathtt{stem}_{k-1}(a[q_1 q_2 \ldots q_m]), (\phi(u_1 u_2 \ldots u_m, v)))$ which equals $(\mathtt{stem}_{k-1}(a[t_1 t_2 \ldots t_m]), (\phi(u_1 u_2 \ldots u_m, v)))$.

Conversely, consider any $a \in \Sigma$ and $v \in \Sigma^T[X]$ and suppose $\pi(a[t_1 t_2 \ldots t_m]) = (\mathtt{stem}_{k-1}(a[t_1 t_2 \ldots t_m]), (\phi(u_1 u_2 \ldots u_m], v)))$. By assumption, $\pi(t_i)$ equals $(\mathtt{stem}_{k-1}(t_i), u_i)$ for each $1 \leq i \leq m$. Thus $(\mathtt{stem}_{k-1}(t_1)\mathtt{stem}_{k-1}(t_2) \ldots$

$\mathtt{stem}_{k-1}(t_m), a, v, \mathtt{stem}_{k-1}(a[t_1 t_2 \ldots t_m])) \in \delta$. Let $q_i = \mathtt{stem}_{k-1}(t_i)$ for each $1 \leq i \leq m$ as before. It follows that $\mathtt{stem}_{k-1}(t_i) = \mathtt{stem}_{k-1}(q_i)$, so $\mathtt{qt}(t_i) = \mathtt{qt}(q_i)$. Likewise, $\mathtt{stem}_{k-1}(a[t_1 t_2 \ldots t_m]) = \mathtt{stem}_{k-1}(a[q_1 q_2 \ldots q_m])$, so $\mathtt{qt}(a[t_1 t_2 \ldots t_m]) = \mathtt{qt}(a[q_1 q_2 \ldots q_m])$. Therefore, $(\mathtt{stem}_{k-1}(q_1)\mathtt{stem}_{k-1}(q_2) \ldots \mathtt{stem}_{k-1}(q_m), a, v, \mathtt{stem}_{k-1}(a[q_1 q_2 \ldots q_m])) \in \delta$.

By construction of Ψ, this means $(\mathtt{qt}(q_1)\mathtt{qt}(q_2) \ldots \mathtt{qt}(q_m), a, v,$ $\mathtt{qt}(a[q_1 q_2 \ldots q_n])) \in \delta_c$. Since $\pi_c(t_i) = (\mathtt{qt}(t_i), u_i)$ for each i by assumption, it follows that $\pi_c(a[t_1 t_2 \ldots t_m]) = (\mathtt{qt}(a[q_1 q_2 \ldots q_n]), (\phi(u_1 u_2 \ldots u_n, v))$.

We need to further show that $\mathtt{stem}_{k-1}(t) \in F$ iff $\mathtt{qt}(t) \in F_c$. By construction, we know that $q \in F$ iff $\mathtt{qt}(q)$ belongs to F_c. Thus $\mathtt{stem}_{k-1}(t) \in F$ iff $\mathtt{qt}(\mathtt{stem}_{k-1}(t)) \in F_c$. By Remark 1, $\mathtt{qt}(t) = \mathtt{stem}_{k-1}(\mathtt{stem}_{k-1}(t))$. Hence $\mathtt{qt}(t) = \mathtt{qt}(\mathtt{stem}_{k-1}(t))$. Therefore, $\mathtt{stem}_{k-1}(t) \in F$ iff $\mathtt{qt}(t) \in F_c$.

This concludes the proof that Ψ and Ψ_f^c generate the same function. □

As mentioned earlier, the value of Theorem 2 is that it can be used to establish that certain tree transformations are ISL by presenting a transducer for the transformation which satisfies the properties specified by the theorem.

Example 7. This example shows that reversing the branch order of a regular tree set $T \subseteq \Sigma_n^T$ is ISL. We illustrate with the classic tree language whose yield is the string language $a^n b^n$. In other words we wish to show that the transformation that maps $t_1 = S[a[\,]b[\,]]$ to $t_1' = S[b[\,]a[\,]]$ and $S[a[\,]t_1 b[\,]]$ to $S[b[\,]t_1' a[\,]]$ and so on is ISL.

The DFT can be represented as a tuple (Q, Σ, F, δ) where the states are expressed by the 1-stems of the subtrees of the pre-image: $Q = \{a[\,], b[\,], S[\,]\}$, and $F = \{S[\,]\}$, and $\Sigma = \{a, b, S\}$, and $\delta = \{(\lambda, a, a[\,], a[\,]), (\lambda, b, b[\,], b[\,]), (a[\,]b[\,], S, S[x_2, x_1], S[\,]), (a[\,]S[\,]b[\,], S, S[x_3 x_2 x_1], S[\,])\}$.

The reader can verify that this transducer correctly reverses the branch order of the trees in its pre-image. Further, this construction shows the function is ISL since it satisfies the requirements in Theorem 2.

4   Conclusion

This paper took a first step in characterizing local syntactic transformations by generalizing Input Strictly Local string functions to trees. Future work includes defining Output SL tree functions (cf. [3]) and studying whether these classes of tree functions can be learned more quickly and with fewer resources, and characterizing subclasses of tree transducers which characterize the types of non-local processes found in syntax and machine translation.

References

1. Beesley, K., Kartunnen, L.: Finite State Morphology. CSLI Publications, Stanford (2003)

2. Chandlee, J., Eyraud, R., Heinz, J.: Learning strictly local subsequential functions. Trans. Assoc. Comput. Linguist. **2**, 491–503 (2014)

3. Chandlee, J., Eyraud, R., Heinz, J.: Output strictly local functions. In: Kuhlmann, M., Kanazawa, M., Kobele, G.M. (eds.) Proceedings of the 14th Meeting on the Mathematics of Language (MoL 2015), Chicago, USA, pp. 112–125, July 2015

4. Chomsky, N.: The Minimalist Program. The MIT Press, Cambridge (1995)

5. Comon, H., et al.: Tree automata techniques and applications (2007). http://tata.gforge.inria.fr/. Release 12 Oct 2007

6. Friese, S., Seidl, H., Maneth, S.: Minimization of deterministic bottom-up tree transducers. In: Gao, Y., Lu, H., Seki, S., Yu, S. (eds.) DLT 2010. LNCS, vol. 6224, pp. 185–196. Springer, Heidelberg (2010). https://doi.org/10.1007/978-3-642-14455-4_18

7. Gécseg, F., Steinby, M.: Tree Automata. Akadémiai Kiadó, Budapest (2015). http://arxiv.org/abs/1509.06233. Originally published in 1984

8. Graf, T.: Closure properties of minimalist derivation tree languages. In: Pogodalla, S., Prost, J.-P. (eds.) LACL 2011. LNCS (LNAI), vol. 6736, pp. 96–111. Springer, Heidelberg (2011). https://doi.org/10.1007/978-3-642-22221-4_7

9. Graf, T.: Curbing feature coding: strictly local feature assignment. In: Proceedings of the Society for Computation in Linguistics (SCiL) 2020 (2020, to appear)

10. Graf, T., Shafiei, N.: C-command dependencies as TSL string constraints. In: Jarosz, G., Nelson, M., O'Connor, B., Pater, J. (eds.) Proceedings of SCiL 2019, pp. 205–215 (2019)

11. Heinz, J.: The computational nature of phonological generalizations. In: Hyman, L., Plank, F. (eds.) Phonological Typology, Chap. 5, pp. 126–195. Phonetics and Phonology, De Gruyter Mouton (2018)

12. Heinz, J., de la Higuera, C., van Zaanen, M.: Grammatical Inference for Computational Linguistics. Synthesis Lectures on Human Language Technologies, Morgan and Claypool (2015)

13. Knight, K., May, J.: Applications of weighted automata in natural language processing. In: Droste, M., Kuich, W., Vogler, H. (eds.) Handbook of Weighted Automata, Chap. 14. EATCS, pp. 571–596. Springer, Heidelberg (2009). https://doi.org/10.1007/978-3-642-01492-5_14

14. Kobele, G.M.: Minimalist tree languages are closed under intersection with recognizable tree languages. In: Pogodalla, S., Prost, J.-P. (eds.) LACL 2011. LNCS (LNAI), vol. 6736, pp. 129–144. Springer, Heidelberg (2011). https://doi.org/10.1007/978-3-642-22221-4_9

15. Maletti, A.: Survey: tree transducers in machine translation. In: Bordihn, H., Freund, R., Hinze, T., Holzer, M., Kutrib, M., Otto, F. (eds.) Proceedings of the 2nd International Workshop on Non-Classical Models of Automata and Applications. books@ocg.at, vol. 263, pp. 11–32. Österreichische Computer Gesellschaft (2010)

16. McNaughton, R., Papert, S.: Counter-Free Automata. MIT Press, Cambridge (1971)

17. Roark, B., Sproat, R.: Computational Approaches to Morphology and Syntax. Oxford University Press, Oxford (2007)

18. Rogers, J.: Strict LT$_2$: regular :: local : recognizable. In: Retoré, C. (ed.) LACL 1996. LNCS, vol. 1328, pp. 366–385. Springer, Heidelberg (1997). https://doi.org/10.1007/BFb0052167

19. Rogers, J.: A Descriptive Approach to Language-Theoretic Complexity. CSLI Publications, Stanford (1998)

20. Rogers, J., Pullum, G.: Aural pattern recognition experiments and the subregular hierarchy. J. Log. Lang. Inf. **20**, 329–342 (2011)
21. Sportiche, D., Koopman, H., Stabler, E.: An Introduction to Syntactic Analysis and Theory. Wiley, Hoboken (2013)

Words and Codes

Lyndon Words versus Inverse Lyndon Words: Queries on Suffixes and Bordered Words

Paola Bonizzoni[1] , Clelia De Felice[2] , Rocco Zaccagnino[2],
and Rosalba Zizza[2(✉)]

[1] Dipartimento di Informatica, Sistemistica e Comunicazione,
Università degli Studi di Milano - Bicocca, Viale Sarca 336, Milano, Italy
bonizzoni@disco.unimib.it
[2] Dipartimento di Informatica, Università degli Studi di Salerno,
Via Giovanni Paolo II 132, Fisciano (Salerno), Italy
{cdefelice,rzaccagnino,rzizza}@unisa.it

Abstract. The Lyndon factorization of a word has been extensively studied in different contexts and several variants of it have been proposed. In particular, the canonical inverse Lyndon factorization ICFL, introduced in [5], maintains the main properties of the Lyndon factorization since it can be computed in linear time and it is uniquely determined. In this paper we investigate new properties of this factorization with the purpose of exploring its use in string queries.

As a main result, we prove an upper bound on the length of the longest common extension (or longest common prefix) for two factors of a word w. This bound is at most the maximum length of two consecutive factors of ICFL(w). A tool used in the proof is a property that we state for factors with nonempty borders in ICFL(w): a nonempty border of a factor m_i cannot be a prefix of the next factor m_{i+1}. Another interesting result relates sorting of global suffixes, i.e., suffixes of a word w, and sorting of local suffixes, i.e., suffixes of the factors in ICFL(w).

Finally, given a word w and a factor x of w, we prove that their Lyndon factorizations share factors, except for the first and last term of the Lyndon factorization of x. This property suggests that, given two words sharing a common overlap, their Lyndon factorizations could be used to capture the common overlap of these two words.

Keywords: Lyndon words · Lyndon factorization · Combinatorial algorithms on words

1 Introduction

The Lyndon factorization CFL(w) of a word w is the unique factorization of w into a sequence of Lyndon words in nonincreasing lexicographic ordering. This factorization is one of the most well-known and extensively studied in different

© Springer Nature Switzerland AG 2020
A. Leporati et al. (Eds.): LATA 2020, LNCS 12038, pp. 385–396, 2020.
https://doi.org/10.1007/978-3-030-40608-0_27

contexts, from formal languages to algorithmic stringology and string compression. In particular the notion of a Lyndon word has been shown to be useful in theoretical applications, such as the well known proof of the *Runs Theorem* [2] as well as in string compression analysis. A connection between the Lyndon factorization and the Lempel-Ziv (LZ) factorization has been given in [18], where it is shown that in general the size of the LZ factorization is larger than the size of the Lyndon factorization, and in any case the size of the Lyndon factorization cannot be larger than a factor of 2 with respect to the size of LZ. This result has been further extended in [28] to overlapping LZ factorizations. The Lyndon factorization has recently revealed to be a useful tool also in investigating queries related to suffixes of a word and sorting such suffixes [25] with strong potentialities [26] for string comparison that have not been completely explored and understood. Relations between Lyndon words and the Burrows-Wheeler Transform (BWT) have been discovered first in [11, 23] and, more recently, in [19]. The main interest in such a factorization is also due to the fact that it can be efficiently computed. Linear-time algorithms for computing this factorization can be found in [15, 16] whereas an $\mathcal{O}(\lg n)$-time parallel algorithm has been proposed in [1, 13].

Most recently, variants of the Lyndon factorization have been introduced and investigated with different motivations. In [5], the notion of an inverse Lyndon word (a word which is strictly greater than each of its proper suffixes) has been introduced to define new factorizations, called *inverse Lyndon factorizations*. An inverse Lyndon factorization has the property that a word is factorized in a sequence of inverse Lyndon words, in an increasing and *prefix-order-free* lexicographic ordering, where prefix-order-free means that a factor cannot be a prefix of the next one. A word w which is not an inverse Lyndon word may have several inverse Lyndon factorizations but it admits a *canonical inverse Lyndon factorization*. This special inverse Lyndon factorization has been introduced in [5] and denoted ICFL(w) because it is the counterpart of the Lyndon factorization CFL(w) of w, when we use (I)inverse words as factors. Indeed, in [5] it has been proved that ICFL(w) can be computed in linear time and it is uniquely determined for a word w.

In this paper we further investigate ICFL(w). The main results stated here are the following: (1) we find un upper bound on the length of the longest common prefix of two distinct factors in ICFL(w), namely the maximal length of two consecutive factors in ICFL(w) (Proposition 6), (2) we are able to relate sorting of global suffixes, i.e., suffixes of the word w, and local suffixes, i.e., suffixes of the factors in ICFL(w) (Lemma 3).

Differently from Lyndon words, inverse Lyndon words may be bordered. As an intermediate result, we show that if a factor m_i in ICFL(w) has a nonempty border, then such a border cannot be inherited by the next factor, since it cannot be the prefix of the next factor m_{i+1} (Proposition 5). This result is proved by a further investigation on the connection between the Lyndon factorization and the canonical inverse Lyndon factorization of a word, given in [5] through the *grouping* property. Indeed, given a word w which is not an inverse Lyndon word, the factors in ICFL(w) are obtained by grouping together consecutive factors of the anti-Lyndon factorization of w that form a chain for the prefix order (Proposition 7.7 in [5]).

Another natural question is the following.

Given two words having a common overlap, can we use their Lyndon factorizations to capture the similarity of these words?

A partial positive answer to this question is provided here: given a word w and a factor x of w, we prove that their Lyndon factorizations share factors, except for the first and last term of the Lyndon factorization of x.

For the detailed proofs of the results in this paper we refer the reader to [6].

2   Words, Lyndon Words and the Lyndon Factorization

Throughout this paper we follow [4,10,20,22,27] for the notations. We fix the finite non-empty (totally ordered) alphabet Σ. We denote by Σ^* the *free monoid* generated by Σ and we set $\Sigma^+ = \Sigma^* \setminus 1$, where 1 is the empty word. For a word $w \in \Sigma^*$, we denote by $|w|$ its *length*. A word $x \in \Sigma^*$ is a *factor* of $w \in \Sigma^*$ if there are $u_1, u_2 \in \Sigma^*$ such that $w = u_1 x u_2$. If $u_1 = 1$ (resp. $u_2 = 1$), then x is a *prefix* (resp. *suffix*) of w. A factor (resp. prefix, suffix) x of w is *proper* if $x \neq w$. Given a language $L \subseteq A^*$, we denote by $\mathrm{Pref}(L)$ the set of all prefixes of its elements. Two words x, y are *incomparable* for the prefix order if neither x is a prefix of y nor y is a prefix of x. Otherwise, x, y are *comparable* for the prefix order. We write $x \leq_p y$ if x is a prefix of y and $x \geq_p y$ if y is a prefix of x. We recall that, given a nonempty word w, a *border* of w is a word which is both a proper prefix and a suffix of w [12]. The longest proper prefix of w which is a suffix of w is also called *the border* of w [12,22]. A word $w \in \Sigma^+$ is *bordered* if it has a nonempty border. Otherwise, w is *unbordered*. A nonempty word w is *primitive* if $w = x^k$ implies $k = 1$. An unbordered word is primitive. A *sesquipower* of a word x is a word $w = x^n p$ where p is a proper prefix of x and $n \geq 1$.

The *lexicographic* (or *alphabetic order*) $\prec$ on $(\Sigma^*, <)$ is defined by setting $x \prec y$ if x is a proper prefix of y, or $x = ras$, $y = rbt$, $a < b$, for $a, b \in \Sigma$ and $r, s, t \in \Sigma^*$. For two nonempty words x, y, we write $x \ll y$ if $x \prec y$ and x is not a proper prefix of y [3]. We also write $y \succ x$ if $x \prec y$. Two words x, y are called *conjugate* if there exist words u, v such that $x = uv, y = vu$. The conjugacy relation is an equivalence relation. A conjugacy class is a class of this equivalence relation. A Lyndon word $w \in \Sigma^+$ is a word which is primitive and the smallest one in its conjugacy class for the lexicographic order. A class of conjugacy is also called a *necklace* and often identified with the minimal word for the lexicographic order in it. Thus, a nonempty word is a necklace if and only if it is a power of a Lyndon word. A *prenecklace* is a prefix of a necklace, hence any nonempty prenecklace w has the form $w = (uv)^k u$, where uv is a Lyndon word, $u \in \Sigma^*$, $v \in \Sigma^+$, $k \geq 1$, that is, w is a sesquipower of a Lyndon word uv. A characterization of the structure of the prefixes of the Lyndon words is given in [15]. It states that a word is a nonempty prefix of a Lyndon word if and only if it is a sesquipower of a Lyndon word distinct of the maximal letter.

It is known that each Lyndon word w is unbordered. Moreover, a word $w \in \Sigma^+$ is a Lyndon word if and only if $w \prec s$, for each nonempty proper suffix s of w. Different characterizations and variations of Lyndon words are given [3,14,21]. In the following $L = L_{(\Sigma^*,<)}$ will be the set of Lyndon words, totally ordered by the relation $\prec$ on $(\Sigma^*, <)$. We know that any word $w \in \Sigma^+$ can be written in a unique way as a nonincreasing product $w = \ell_1 \ell_2 \cdots \ell_h$ of Lyndon words, i.e., in the form $w = \ell_1 \ell_2 \cdots \ell_h$, with $\ell_j \in L$ and $\ell_1 \succeq \ell_2 \succeq \ldots \succeq \ell_h$ [9]. The sequence $\mathrm{CFL}(w) = (\ell_1, \ldots, \ell_h)$ is called the *Lyndon decomposition* (or *Lyndon factorization*) of w. Uniqueness of the above factorization is proved in [15] and allows us to state a recursive definition of $\mathrm{CFL}(w)$, for a nonempty word w. Precisely, if w is not a Lyndon word, then $\mathrm{CFL}(w) = (\ell_1, \ell_1', \ldots, \ell_h')$, where $(\ell_1', \ldots, \ell_h') = \mathrm{CFL}(w')$, $w = \ell_1 w'$ and ℓ_1 is the longest prefix of w which is a Lyndon word. Sometimes we need to emphasize consecutive equal factors in CFL. We write $\mathrm{CFL}(w) = (\ell_1^{n_1}, \ldots, \ell_r^{n_r})$ to denote a tuple of $n_1 + \ldots + n_r$ Lyndon words, where $r > 0$, $n_1, \ldots, n_r \geq 1$. Precisely $\ell_1 \succ \ldots \succ \ell_r$ are Lyndon words, also named *Lyndon factors* of w. There is a linear time algorithm to compute the pair (ℓ_1, n_1) and thus, by iteration, the Lyndon factorization of w [16,22]. Linear time algorithms may also be found in [15] and in the more recent paper [17].

3   Anti-Lyndon Words, Inverse Lyndon Words and Anti-prenecklaces

The *inverse lexicographic* or *inverse alphabetic order* on $(\Sigma^*, <)$, denoted $\prec_{in}$, is the lexicographic order on $(\Sigma^*, <_{in})$. Here $<_{in}$ means that the order of the alphabet is reversed, that is $b <_{in} a \Leftrightarrow a < b$, for all $a, b \in \Sigma$. We denote by $L_{in} = L_{(\Sigma^*,<_{in})}$ the set of the Lyndon words on Σ^* with respect to the inverse lexicographic order. A word $w \in L_{in}$ will be named an *anti-Lyndon word*. Correspondingly, an *anti-prenecklace* will be a prefix of an *anti-necklace*, which in turn will be a necklace with respect to the inverse lexicographic order. We have that a word $w \in \Sigma^+$ is in L_{in} if and only if w is primitive and $w \succ vu$, for each $u, v \in \Sigma^+$ such that $w = uv$. Alternatively, a word $w \in \Sigma^+$ is in L_{in} if and only if w is unbordered and $w \succ v$, for each proper nonempty suffix v. We denote by $\mathrm{CFL}_{in}(w)$ the Lyndon factorization of w with respect to the inverse order $<_{in}$. The following definition plays a fundamental role in our results.

Definition 1. *A word $w \in \Sigma^+$ is an inverse Lyndon word if $s \prec w$, for each nonempty proper suffix s of w.*

It is easy to see that a, b, $aaaaa$, $bbba$, $baaab$, $bbaba$ and $bbababbaa$ are inverse Lyndon words on $\{a, b\}$, with $a < b$. On the contrary, $aaba$ is not an inverse Lyndon word since $aaba \prec ba$. Moreover, $baaab$ is not an anti-Lyndon word since it is bordered. In [5] it has been proved that a nonempty word is an anti-Lyndon word if and only if it is an unbordered inverse Lyndon word. Finally, the set of the inverse Lyndon words coincides with the set of the anti-prenecklaces, hence any nonempty prefix of an inverse Lyndon word is still an inverse Lyndon word [5].

4   A Canonical Inverse Lyndon Factorization: ICFL(w)

For the material in this section see [5]. An inverse Lyndon factorization of a word $w \in \Sigma^+$ is a sequence $(m_1, \ldots, m_k)$ of inverse Lyndon words such that $m_1 \cdots m_k = w$ and $m_i \ll m_{i+1}$, $1 \le i \le k - 1$. A word may have different inverse Lyndon factorizations (see Example 2) but it has a unique canonical inverse Lyndon factorization, denoted ICFL(w). If w is an inverse Lyndon word, then ICFL(w) = w. Otherwise, ICFL(w) is recursively defined. The first factor of ICFL(w) is obtained by a special factorization of the shortest nonempty prefix z of w such that z is not an inverse Lyndon word.

Definition 2 [5]. *Let $w \in \Sigma^+$, let p be an inverse Lyndon word which is a nonempty proper prefix of $w = pv$. The bounded right extension $\overline{p}$ of p (relatively to w), if it exists, is a nonempty prefix of v such that:*

(1) $\overline{p}$ is an inverse Lyndon word,
(2) pz' is an inverse Lyndon word, for each proper nonempty prefix z' of $\overline{p}$,
(3) $p\overline{p}$ is not an inverse Lyndon word,
(4) $p \ll \overline{p}$.

Moreover, we set $\mathrm{Pref}_{bre}(w) = \{(p, \overline{p}) \mid p$ *is an inverse Lyndon word which is a nonempty proper prefix of w.*

It has been proved that $\mathrm{Pref}_{bre}(w)$ is empty if and only if w is an inverse Lyndon word (Proposition 4.2 in [5]). If w is not an inverse Lyndon word, then $\mathrm{Pref}_{bre}(w)$ contains only one pair and the description of this pair is given below (Propositions 4.1 and 4.3 in [5]).

Proposition 1. *Let $w \in \Sigma^+$ be a word which is not an inverse Lyndon word. Let z be the shortest nonempty prefix of w which is not an inverse Lyndon word. Then,*

(1) $z = p\overline{p}$, with $(p, \overline{p}) \in \mathrm{Pref}_{bre}(w)$.
(2) $p = ras$ and $\overline{p} = rb$, where $r, s \in \Sigma^*$, $a, b \in \Sigma$ and r is the shortest prefix of $p\overline{p}$ such that $p\overline{p} = rasrb$, with $a < b$.

Example 1. Let $\Sigma = \{a, b\}$ with $a < b$. Let us consider $w = babaaabb$ and the prefixes $p_1 = bab$ and $p_2 = babaaa$ of w. First, w is not an inverse Lyndon word. Thus, $\mathrm{Pref}_{bre}(w)$ contains only one pair. Moreover each proper nonempty prefix of w is an inverse Lyndon word. By item (1) in Proposition 1, we have $w = p\overline{p}$. By item (2) in Proposition 1, the bounded right extension of $p_1 = bab$ does not exist (we should have $\overline{p_1} = aaabb$ in contradiction with $p_1 \ll \overline{p_1}$). Since w starts with b, the shortest common prefix r of p and $\overline{p}$ has a positive length. Indeed, $p = p_2 = babaaa$ and $\overline{p} = \overline{p_2} = bb$.

The canonical inverse Lyndon factorization has been also recursively defined.

Definition 3. *Let $w \in \Sigma^+$.*
(Basis Step) *If w is an inverse Lyndon word, then* ICFL$(w) = (w)$.
(Recursive Step) *If w is not an inverse Lyndon word, let $(p, \bar{p}) \in \text{Pref}_{bre}(w)$ and let $v \in \Sigma^*$ such that $w = pv$. Let* ICFL$(v) = (m'_1, \ldots, m'_k)$ *and let $r, s \in \Sigma^*$, $a, b \in \Sigma$ such that $p = ras$, $\bar{p} = rb$ with $a < b$.*

$$\text{ICFL}(w) = \begin{cases} (p, \text{ICFL}(v)) & \text{if } \bar{p} = rb \leq_p m'_1 \\ (pm'_1, m'_2, \ldots, m'_k) & \text{if } m'_1 \leq_p r \end{cases}$$

Example 2 [5]. *Let $\Sigma = \{a, b, c, d\}$ with $a < b < c < d$, $w = dabadabdabdadac$. We have* CFL$_{in}(w) = (daba, dab, dab, dadac)$, ICFL$(w) = (daba, dabdab, dadac)$. Another inverse Lyndon factorizations of w is $(dabadab, dabda, dac)$. Consider $z = dabdadacddbdc$. It is easy to see that $(dab, dadacd, db, dc)$, $(dabda, dac, ddbdc)$, $(dab, dadac, ddbdc)$ are all inverse Lyndon factorizations of z. The first factorization has four factors whereas the others have three factors. Moreover ICFL$(z) = $ CFL$_{in}(z) = (dab, dadac, ddbdc)$.

5   Groupings and Borders

Let $w \in \Sigma^+$ be a word which is not an inverse Lyndon word, let ICFL$(w) = (m_1, \ldots, m_k)$. The aim of this section is to state that any nonempty border of m_i is not a prefix of m_{i+1}, $1 \leq i \leq k-1$ (Proposition 5). The proof of this result is strongly based on a property of ICFL(w), proved in [5] and defined through the notion of *groupings* of CFL$_{in}(w)$.

Let CFL$_{in}(w) = (\ell_1, \ldots, \ell_h)$, where $\ell_1 \succeq_{in} \ell_2 \succeq_{in} \cdots \succeq_{in} \ell_h$. Consider the partial order $\geq_p$, where $x \geq_p y$ if y is a prefix of x. Recall that a *chain* is a set of a pairwise comparable elements. We say that a chain is maximal if it is not strictly contained in any other chain. A non-increasing *(maximal) chain* in CFL$_{in}(w)$ is the sequence corresponding to a (maximal) chain in the multiset $\{\ell_1, \ldots, \ell_h\}$ with respect to $\geq_p$. We denote by $\mathcal{PMC}$ a non-increasing maximal chain in CFL$_{in}(w)$. Looking at the definition of the (inverse) lexicographic order, it is easy to see that a $\mathcal{PMC}$ is a sequence of consecutive factors in CFL$_{in}(w)$. Moreover CFL$_{in}(w)$ is the concatenation of its $\mathcal{PMC}$. Formally, if $\mathcal{C}$ is a $\mathcal{PMC}$ in CFL$_{in}(w)$, then there are indexes r, s with $1 \leq r < s \leq h$ such that $\mathcal{C} = (\ell_r, \ldots, \ell_s)$, with $\ell_r \geq_p \ell_{r+1} \geq_p \cdots \geq_p \ell_s$, and $\ell_{r-1} \not\geq_p \ell_r$ if $r > 1$, $\ell_s \not\geq_p \ell_{s+1}$ if $s < h$.

Example 3 [5]. *Let $\Sigma = \{a, b, c, d\}$ with $a < b < c < d$, $w = dabadabdabdadac$. In Example 2, we observed that* CFL$_{in}(w) = (daba, dab, dab, dadac)$. This sequence has two $\mathcal{PMC}$, namely $(daba, dab, dab)$, $(dadac)$. Let $z = dabdadacddbdc$. Then CFL$_{in}(z) = (dab, dadac, ddbdc)$ has three $\mathcal{PMC}$: (dab), $(dadac)$, $(ddbdc)$.

A *grouping* of CFL$_{in}(w)$ is an inverse Lyndon factorization $(m_1, \ldots, m_k)$ of w such that any factor is a product of consecutive factors in a $\mathcal{PMC}$ of CFL$_{in}(w)$. ICFL(w) is always a grouping of CFL$_{in}(w)$ but, as showed below, it is not always its unique grouping.

Example 4 [5]. Let $\Sigma = \{a, b, c, d\}$, $a < b < c < d$, and $w = dabadabdabdadac$. We have $\mathrm{CFL}_{in}(w) = (daba, dab, dab, dadac)$, $\mathrm{ICFL}(w) = (daba, dabdab, dadac)$ (see Example 2). $\mathrm{ICFL}(w)$ is a grouping of $\mathrm{CFL}_{in}(w)$ but $(dabadab, dabda, dac)$ is not a grouping. Next, let $y = dabadabdabdabdadac$. We have $\mathrm{CFL}_{in}(y) = (daba, dab, dab, dab, dadac)$ and $\mathrm{ICFL}(w) = (daba, (dab)^3, dadac)$. The inverse Lyndon factorization $(dabadab, (dab)^2, dadac)$ is another grouping of $\mathrm{CFL}_{in}(y)$.

The proof of Proposition 5 is organized as follows. We firstly state that any nonempty border x of a non-increasing chain in $\mathrm{CFL}_{in}(w)$ cannot cut any ℓ_i and admits a shortest border.

Proposition 2. *Let $w \in \Sigma^+$, let $\mathrm{CFL}_{in}(w) = (\ell_1, \ldots, \ell_h)$ and let $(\ell_r, \ldots, \ell_s)$, $1 \le r < s \le h$, be a non-increasing chain in $\mathrm{CFL}_{in}(w)$. For any nonempty border x of $y = \ell_r \cdots \ell_s$ there is t, $r \le t < s$, such that $x = \ell_{t+1} \cdots \ell_s$. Consequently, ℓ_s is a nonempty border of any other nonempty border of $\ell_r \cdots \ell_s$.*

The next step is to prove that p in the pair $(p, \bar{p}) \in \mathrm{Pref}_{bre}(w)$ has a grouping-like property. Indeed we show that p is always a product of consecutive factors in a $\mathcal{PMC}$ of $\mathrm{CFL}_{in}(w)$. Thus, thanks to Proposition 2, p has a shortest border. This shortest border determines the relation $p \ll \bar{p}$.

Proposition 3. *Let $w \in \Sigma^+$ be a word which is not an inverse Lyndon word, let $(p, \bar{p}) \in \mathrm{Pref}_{bre}(w)$ and let $\mathrm{ICFL}(w) = (m_1, \ldots, m_k)$. Let $\mathrm{CFL}_{in}(w) = (\ell_1^{n_1}, \ldots, \ell_h^{n_h})$, with $h > 0$, $n_1, \ldots, n_h \ge 1$ and let $(\ell_1^{n_1}, \ldots, \ell_q^{n_q})$ be a $\mathcal{PMC}$ in $\mathrm{CFL}_{in}(w)$, $1 \le q \le h$. Then the following properties hold.*

(1) $p = \ell_1^{n_1} \cdots \ell_g^{n_g}$, for some g, $1 \le g \le q$.
(2) $\ell_g = u_g v_g = u_g a_g v_g'$, $\bar{p} = u_g b$, $a_g < b$.

Now, we can state that, for each nonempty border z of $p = ras$, we have that z and $\bar{p} = rb$ are incomparable for the prefix order. We use the same notations as in Propositions 2, 3. The word $\bar{p}$ cannot be a prefix of z because $\bar{p}$ is not a prefix of p. Thus z should be a prefix of $\bar{p}$. By Proposition 2, the shortest border $\ell_g = u_g a_g v_g'$ of p should be a prefix of z, thus of $\bar{p} = u_g b$, $a_g < b$, a contradiction.

Proposition 4. *Let $w \in \Sigma^+$ be a word which is not an inverse Lyndon word and let $(p, \bar{p}) \in \mathrm{Pref}_{bre}(w)$. For each nonempty border z of p, one has that z and $\bar{p}$ are incomparable for the prefix order.*

Finally, we can explicitly prove, by induction on $|w|$, that if z is a nonempty border of m_1, then z is not a prefix of m_2. We use the recursive definition of $\mathrm{ICFL}(w)$, with the same notations as in Definition 3, and a proof by induction. We distinguish the two cases $m_1 = p$ and $m_1 = pm_1'$. In the first case, $\bar{p}$ is a prefix of $m_1' = m_2$. Thus, if z were a prefix of m_2, we would be in contradiction with Proposition 4. In the second case, we have $m_2 = m_2'$ and again two cases: $|z| \ge |m_1'|$ or $|z| < |m_1'|$. If z were a prefix of m_2 with $|z| \ge |m_1'|$, m_1' would be a prefix of m_2' in contradiction with $m_1' \ll m_2'$. If z were a prefix of m_2 with $|z| < |m_1'|$, z would be a border of m_1', in contradiction with the induction hypothesis. Then, again by induction on $|w|$, we extend this argument to prove the general result stated below.

Proposition 5. *Let $w \in \Sigma^+$ be a word which is not an inverse Lyndon word and let* $\mathrm{ICFL}(w) = (m_1, \ldots, m_k)$. *If z is a nonempty border of m_i, then z is not a prefix of m_{i+1}, $1 \leq i \leq k - 1$.*

6   A Bound on the Length of the Longest Common Prefix

Given a word w and two factors x, y of w, we denote by $\mathrm{lcp}(x, y)$ the *longest common prefix* of x, y and we set $\mathrm{LCP}(x, y) = |\mathrm{lcp}(x, y)|$. Proposition 5 in the previous section is extremely useful to obtain a bound on the length of the longest common prefix of two factors of a word w, when w is not an inverse Lyndon word (Proposition 6). Precisely, we state that $\mathrm{LCP}(x, y)$ is at most the maximum length of two consecutive factors in $\mathrm{ICFL}(w)$. As a direct corollary, we obtain the same bound for $\mathrm{LCP}(x, y)$, when x, y are suffixes of w [6].

We also follow the notations used in [5,24,25]. Let $w, x, u, v \in \Sigma^*$, and let x be a nonempty factor of $w = uxv$. Let $first(x)$ and $last(x)$ denote the position of the first and the last symbol of x in w, respectively. If $w = a_1 \cdots a_n$, $a_i \in \Sigma$, $1 \leq i \leq j \leq n$, then we also set $w[i, j] = a_i \cdots a_j$. A *local suffix* of w is a suffix of a factor of w, specifically $suf_x(i) = w[i, last(x)]$ denotes the *local suffix* of w at the position i with respect to x, $i \geq first(x)$. The corresponding *global suffix* $suf_x(i)v$ of w at the position i is denoted by $suf_w(i) = w[i, last(w)]$ (or simply $suf(i)$ when it is understood). We say that $suf_x(i)v$ is *associated* with $suf_x(i)$.

When we consider $\mathrm{ICFL}(w) = (m_1, \ldots, m_k)$, given a factor m_j of $\mathrm{ICFL}(w)$ we have that a local suffix x of m_j is a suffix of m_j and the associated global suffix x_w of w is $x \cdot m_{j+1} \ldots m_k$. The following lemmas are crucial for proving our upper bound. Lemma 1 shows that, given two local suffixes x and y of the same factor m_{i-1}, then the longest common prefix of the associated global suffixes is the longest common prefix between xr and yr. Here r is the longest common prefix between m_{i-1} and m_i. Lemma 2 handles the case of local suffixes x and y of different factors. In this case the result leads to a bound on $\mathrm{LCP}(x_w, y_w)$.

Lemma 1. *Let $w \in \Sigma^+$ be a word which is not an inverse Lyndon word. Let* $\mathrm{ICFL}(w) = (m_1, \ldots, m_k)$. *Let $r, s, t \in \Sigma^*$, $a, b \in \Sigma$ be such that $m_{i-1} = ras$, $m_i = rbt$, $a < b$, $1 < i \leq k$. If x, y are nonempty suffixes of m_{i-1}, then* $\mathrm{lcp}(x_w, y_w) = \mathrm{lcp}(xr, yr)$.

Lemma 2. *Let $w \in \Sigma^+$ be a word which is not an inverse Lyndon word and let* $\mathrm{ICFL}(w) = (m_1, \ldots, m_k)$. *Let i, j be integers such that $1 < i < j \leq k$. If x is a nonempty suffix of m_{i-1} and y is a nonempty suffix of m_{j-1}, then $\mathrm{lcp}(x_w, y_w)$ is a prefix of ym_j.*

Let $w \in \Sigma^+$ be a word which is not an inverse Lyndon word and let $\mathrm{ICFL}(w) = (m_1, \ldots, m_k)$. We set $\mathcal{M} = \max\{|m_i m_{i+1}| \mid 1 \leq i < k\}$. As a main consequence of the previous lemmas, we state that $\mathcal{M}$ is an upper bound on $\mathrm{LCP}(u, v)$, where u, v are factors of w.

Proposition 6. *Let $w \in \Sigma^+$ be a word which is not an inverse Lyndon word and let $\mathrm{ICFL}(w) = (m_1, \ldots, m_k)$. For each nonempty proper factors u, v of w, we have $\mathrm{LCP}(u, v) = |\mathrm{lcp}(u, v)| \leq \mathcal{M}$.*

Observe that Lemmas 1 and 2 could lead to a more specialized version of the compatibility property, proved in [5,24,25], which relates sorting local suffixes of a concatenation of factors to sorting the corresponding global suffixes (see Theorem 1). Indeed the above mentioned lemmas could be applied to sort suffixes of a word by sorting factors of w of bounded size.

We recall that the sorting of the nonempty local suffixes of w with respect to a nonempty factor x is *compatible* with the sorting of the corresponding nonempty global suffixes of w if for all i, j with $first(x) \leq i < j \leq last(x)$, $suf_x(i) \prec suf_x(j) \iff suf(i) \prec suf(j)$.

Theorem 1 [24,25]. *Let $w \in \Sigma^+$ and let $\mathrm{CFL}(w) = (\ell_1, \ldots, \ell_h)$ be its Lyndon factorization. Then, for any r, s, $1 \leq r \leq s \leq h$, the sorting of the nonempty local suffixes of w with respect to $x = \ell_r \cdots \ell_s$ is compatible with the sorting of the corresponding nonempty global suffixes of w.*

Lemma 3 states a property similar to the compatibility property when we deal with $\mathrm{ICFL}(w)$. Shortly speaking, consider $\mathrm{ICFL}(w) = (m_1, m_2, \ldots, m_k)$ and take two indexes j_1, j_2 both contained in $x = m_r m_{r+1} \cdots m_s$, $1 \leq r < s \leq k$. Consider the local suffixes starting from j_1, j_2 and let us compare them with respect to $\prec$. If $suf_x(j_1) \prec suf_x(j_2)$, then two cases are possible: $suf_x(j_1) \ll suf_x(j_2)$ or $suf_x(j_1) \in \mathrm{Pref}(suf_x(j_2))$. In the first case obviously $suf(j_1) \ll suf(j_2)$. Lemma below covers both the cases.

Lemma 3. *Let $w \in \Sigma^+$ be a word which is not an inverse Lyndon word and let $\mathrm{ICFL}(w) = (m_1, \ldots, m_k)$. Let $x = m_i m_{i+1} \cdots m_h$ with $1 \leq i < h \leq k$. Assume that $suf_x(j_1) \prec suf_x(j_2)$, where $first(x) \leq j_1 \leq last(x)$, $first(x) \leq j_2 \leq last(x)$, $j_1 \neq j_2$. If $suf_x(j_1)$ is a proper prefix of $suf_x(j_2)$ and $h < k$ then $suf(j_2) \prec suf(j_1)$, otherwise $suf(j_1) \prec suf(j_2)$.*

Example 5. Let $w = a^{12}bbab \in \{a, b\}^+$ with $a < b$. We have $\mathrm{ICFL}(w) = (m_1, m_2) = (a^{12}, bbab)$. Let $x = m_1 = a^{12}$. Consider $suf_x(4) = a^9$ and $suf_x(12) = a$. We have $suf_x(12) = a \prec a^9 = suf_x(4)$. We are in the first case of Lemma 3 and then $suf(4) = a^9bbab \prec abbab = suf(12)$.

Example 6. Let $w = dabadabdabdadac \in \{a, b, c, d\}^+$ with $a < b < c < d$. We have $\mathrm{ICFL}(w) = (m_1, m_2, m_3) = (daba, dabdab, dadac)$. Let $x = m_2$. Consider $suf_{m_2}(8) = dab$ and $suf_{m_2}(5) = dabdab$. We have $suf_{m_2}(8) = dab \prec suf_{m_2}(5) = dabdab = (dab)^2$. We are in the first case of Lemma 3 and then $suf(5) = dabdabdadac \prec suf(8) = dabdadc$. Consider now $suf_{m_2}(9) = ab \prec suf_{m_2}(8) = dab$. Since $suf_{m_2}(9)$ is not a proper prefix of $suf_{m_2}(8)$), we are in the second case of Lemma 3 and we have $suf(9) = abdadac \prec suf(8) = dabdadac$.

7   Lyndon Factorizations of Factors of a Word and Overlapping Factors

Let $w \in \Sigma^+$ be a word and let $\mathrm{CFL}(w) = (\ell_1, \ldots, \ell_k)$ be its Lyndon factorization, $k \geq 1$. Let x be a proper factor (resp. prefix, suffix) of w. We say that x is a *simple* factor of w if, for each occurrence of x as a factor of w, there is j, with $1 \leq j \leq k$, such that x is a factor of ℓ_j. Informally speaking, every occurrence of x needs to be within some ℓ_j. We say that x is a *simple* prefix (resp. suffix) of w if x is a proper prefix (resp. suffix) of ℓ_1 (resp ℓ_k). In this section we compare the Lyndon factorization of w and that of its non-simple factors. Lemma 4 handles a trivial case: if $x = \ell_i \ell_{i+1} \cdots \ell_j$ is a concatenation of consecutive factors of CFL(w), then CFL(x) is the sequence $(\ell_i, \ell_{i+1}, \ldots, \ell_j)$.

Lemma 4. *Let $w \in \Sigma^+$ be a word and let CFL(w) $= (\ell_1, \ldots, \ell_k)$ be its Lyndon factorization. For any i, j, with $1 \leq i \leq j \leq k$, one has CFL($\ell_i \ell_{i+1} \cdots \ell_j$) $= (\ell_i, \ell_{i+1}, \ldots, \ell_j)$.*

If x is a non-simple factor of w and x does not satisfy the hypotheses of Lemma 4, then there are i, j with $1 \leq i < j \leq k$, a suffix ℓ_i'' of ℓ_i and a prefix ℓ_j' of ℓ_j, with $\ell_i'' \ell_j' \neq 1$, such that $x = \ell_i'' \ell_{i+1} \cdots \ell_{j-1} \ell_j'$, where it is understood that if $j = i + 1$, then $\ell_{i+1}, \cdots, \ell_{j-1} = 1$ and $\ell_i'' \neq 1$, $\ell_j' \neq 1$, $\ell_i'' \ell_j' \neq \ell_i \ell_j$. We say that the sequence $\ell_i'', \ell_{i+1}, \ldots, \ell_{j-1}, \ell_j'$ is *associated* with x. The following result gives relations between CFL(x) and CFL(w).

Lemma 5. *Let $w \in \Sigma^+$ be a word and let CFL(w) $= (\ell_1, \ldots, \ell_k)$ be its Lyndon factorization. Let x be a non-simple factor of w such that x does not satisfy the hypotheses of Lemma 4 and let $\ell_i'', \ell_{i+1}, \ldots, \ell_{j-1}, \ell_j'$ be the sequence associated with x. Let CFL(ℓ_i'') $= (g_1, \ldots, g_{k''})$ and CFL(ℓ_j') $= (g_1', \ldots, g_{k'}')$ We have*

$$\text{CFL}(x) = (g_1, \ldots, g_{k''}, \ell_{i+1}, \ldots, \ell_{j-1}, g_1', \ldots, g_{k'}')$$

where it is understood that if $\ell_i'' = 1$ (resp. $\ell_j' = 1$), then the first k'' terms (resp. last k' terms) in CFL(x) vanish.

Let $x, y, z, w, w' \in \Sigma^+$. Lemma 5 gives relations between the Lyndon factorizations of two overlapping words w, w', i.e., such that $w = xy$, $w' = yz$, and the Lyndon factorization of the overlap y, when y is non-simple (as a suffix of w and as a prefix of w'). Indeed observe that both w and w' are substrings of the same word xyz. As a consequence of Lemma 5, the words w, w' may share common Lyndon factors between them and with xyz. Moreover, some of these factors may be in y. More precisely, let CFL(w) $= (\ell_1, \ldots, \ell_k)$ and CFL(w') $= (f_1, f_2, \ldots, f_h)$. If y is a non-simple suffix of w and a non-simple prefix of w', then there are indexes i, j, with $1 \leq i < k$, $1 < j \leq h$, such that $y = \ell_i'' \ell_{i+1} \cdots \ell_k = f_1 \cdots f_{j-1} f_j'$, where ℓ_i'' is a suffix of ℓ_i and f_j' is a prefix of f_j. Let CFL(ℓ_i'') $= (g_1, \ldots, g_{k''})$ and CFL(f_j') $= (g_1', \ldots, g_{k'}')$. By Lemma 5 we have CFL(y) $= (g_1, \ldots, g_{k''}, \ell_{i+1}, \ldots, \ell_k) = (f_1, \ldots, f_{j-1}, g_1', \ldots, g_{k'}')$. Since the Lyndon factorization can be computed in linear time, the above result could lead to efficient measures of similarities between words. These measures could be used to capture words that may be overlapping.

8   Conclusions and Open Problems

In this paper we investigate new properties of the Lyndon factorization and of the canonical inverse Lyndon factorization, aimed to answer to string queries by using these factorizations. Our main result, Proposition 6, gives an upper bound on the length of the longest common prefix of two factors of a word and this upper bound has relationships with the factors in ICFL. This result could also be applied to investigate parallel approaches to sorting suffixes of a word w with a nontrivial inverse Lyndon factorization. Indeed, the above mentioned bound could relate sorting suffixes of w to sorting factors of w of bounded length. In addition, we state a property showing that substrings of the same word could share common factors of the Lyndon factorization (Lemma 5). This property could be extended to two words that share a common overlap to capture the suffix-prefix relationship between them. It is an open problem if Lemma 5 extends to ICFL(w). This extension, if it exists, may be of interest in the well known problem of efficient computation of the suffix-prefix relationship. This is an interesting problem in the analysis of sequencing data [7,8] and in the construction of overlap graphs for a collection of strings. We believe that the above results could shed new light in further applications of the Lyndon and the inverse Lyndon factorization and this is the goal of our future research work.

Acknowledgments. The authors thank the anonymous referees for their helpful suggestions.

References

1. Apostolico, A., Crochemore, M.: Fast parallel Lyndon factorization with applications. Math. Syst. Theory **28**(2), 89–108 (1995)
2. Bannai, H., Tomohiro, I., Inenaga, S., Nakashima, Y., Takeda, M., Tsuruta, K.: The "Runs" theorem. SIAM J. Comput. **46**(5), 1501–1514 (2017)
3. Bannai, H., Tomohiro, I., Inenaga, S., Nakashima, Y., Takeda, M., Tsuruta, K.: A new characterization of maximal repetitions by Lyndon trees. In: Proceedings of the Twenty-Sixth Annual ACM-SIAM Symposium on Discrete Algorithms, SODA 2015, San Diego, CA, USA, 4–6 January 2015, pp. 562–571 (2015)
4. Berstel, J., Perrin, D., Reutenauer, C.: Codes and Automata. Encyclopedia of Mathematics and its Applications, vol. 129. Cambridge University Press, Cambridge (2009)
5. Bonizzoni, P., De Felice, C., Zaccagnino, R., Zizza, R.: Inverse Lyndon words and inverse Lyndon factorizations of words. Adv. Appl. Math. **101**, 281–319 (2018)
6. Bonizzoni, P., De Felice, C., Zaccagnino, R., Zizza, R.: Lyndon words versus inverse Lyndon words: queries on suffixes and bordered words. CoRR abs/1911.01851 (2019). http://arxiv.org/abs/1911.01851
7. Bonizzoni, P., Della Vedova, G., Pirola, Y., Previtali, M., Rizzi, R.: An external-memory algorithm for string graph construction. Algorithmica **78**(2), 394–424 (2017)
8. Bonizzoni, P., Della Vedova, G., Pirola, Y., Previtali, M., Rizzi, R.: FSG: fast string graph construction for de novo assembly. J. Comput. Biol. **24**(10), 953–968 (2017)
9. Chen, K.T., Fox, R.H., Lyndon, R.C.: Free differential calculus, IV. The quotient groups of the lower central series. Ann. Math. **68**, 81–95 (1958)
10. Choffrut, C., Karhumäki, J.: Combinatorics of words. In: Rozenberg, G., Salomaa, A. (eds.) Handbook of Formal Languages, pp. 329–438. Springer, Heidelberg (1997). https://doi.org/10.1007/978-3-642-59136-5_6

11. Crochemore, M., Désarménien, J., Perrin, D.: A note on the Burrows-Wheeler transformation. Theoret. Comput. Sci. **332**(1), 567–572 (2005)
12. Crochemore, M., Hancart, C., Lecroq, T.: Algorithms on Strings. Cambridge University Press, Cambridge (2007)
13. Daykin, J.W., Iliopoulos, C.S., Smyth, W.F.: Parallel RAM algorithms for factorizing words. Theor. Comput. Sci. **127**(1), 53–67 (1994)
14. Dolce, F., Restivo, A., Reutenauer, C.: On generalized Lyndon words. Theor. Comput. Sci. **777**, 232–242 (2019)
15. Duval, J.: Factorizing words over an ordered alphabet. J. Algorithms **4**(4), 363–381 (1983)
16. Fredricksen, H., Maiorana, J.: Necklaces of beads in k colors and k-ary de Brujin sequences. Discrete Math. **23**(3), 207–210 (1978)
17. Ghuman, S.S., Giaquinta, E., Tarhio, J.: Alternative algorithms for Lyndon factorization. In: Proceedings of the Prague Stringology Conference 2014, Prague, Czech Republic, 1–3 September 2014, pp. 169–178 (2014)
18. Kärkkäinen, J., Kempa, D., Nakashima, Y., Puglisi, S.J., Shur, A.M.: On the size of Lempel-Ziv and Lyndon factorizations. In: 34th Symposium on Theoretical Aspects of Computer Science, STACS 2017, Hannover, Germany, 8–11 March 2017, pp. 45:1–45:13 (2017)
19. Kufleitner, M.: On bijective variants of the Burrows-Wheeler transform. In: Proceedings of the Prague Stringology Conference 2009, Prague, Czech Republic, 31 August–2 September 2009, pp. 65–79 (2009)
20. Lothaire, M.: Algebraic Combinatorics on Words. Encyclopedia of Mathematics and its Applications, vol. 90. Cambridge University Press, Cambridge (1997)
21. Lothaire, M.: Combinatorics on Words. Cambridge University Press, Cambridge (1997)
22. Lothaire, M.: Applied Combinatorics on Words. Cambridge University Press, Cambridge (2005)
23. Mantaci, S., Restivo, A., Rosone, G., Sciortino, M.: An extension of the Burrows-Wheeler transform. Theor. Comput. Sci. **387**(3), 298–312 (2007)
24. Mantaci, S., Restivo, A., Rosone, G., Sciortino, M.: Sorting suffixes of a text via its Lyndon factorization. In: Proceedings of the Prague Stringology Conference 2013, Prague, Czech Republic, 2–4 September 2013, pp. 119–127 (2013)
25. Mantaci, S., Restivo, A., Rosone, G., Sciortino, M.: Suffix array and Lyndon factorization of a text. J. Discrete Algorithms **28**, 2–8 (2014)
26. Mucha, M.: Lyndon words and short superstrings. In: Proceedings of the Twenty-Fourth Annual ACM-SIAM Symposium on Discrete Algorithms, SODA 2013, New Orleans, Louisiana, USA, 6–8 January 2013, pp. 958–972 (2013)
27. Reutenauer, C.: Free lie algebras. Oxford University Press (1993)
28. Urabe, Y., Kempa, D., Nakashima, Y., Inenaga, S., Bannai, H., Takeda, M.: On the size of overlapping Lempel-Ziv and Lyndon factorizations. In: 30th Annual Symposium on Combinatorial Pattern Matching, CPM 2019, 18–20 June 2019, Pisa, Italy. LIPIcs, vol. 128, pp. 29:1–29:11. Schloss Dagstuhl - Leibniz-Zentrum fuer Informatik (2019)

Reducing the Ambiguity
of Parikh Matrices

Jeffery Dick, Laura K. Hutchinson$^{(\boxtimes)}$, Robert Mercaş, and Daniel Reidenbach

Department of Computer Science, Loughborough University, Loughborough, UK
{J.Dick,L.Hutchinson,R.G.Mercas,D.Reidenbach}@lboro.ac.uk

Abstract. The Parikh matrix mapping allows us to describe words using matrices. Although compact, this description comes with a level of ambiguity since a single matrix may describe multiple words. This work looks at how considering the Parikh matrices of various transformations of a given word can decrease that ambiguity. More specifically, for any word, we study the Parikh matrix of its Lyndon conjugate as well as that of its projection to a smaller alphabet. Our results demonstrate that ambiguity can often be reduced using these concepts, and we give conditions on when they succeed.

Keywords: Combinatorics · Parikh matrix · Ambiguity · Lyndon conjugate

1 Introduction

An approach for a more compact representation of data can be provided by histograms, which are also a well established statistical tool used in a wide range of applications. The concept of a Parikh vector [15] represents a type of such histograms that is specific to the analysis of sequences of symbols (or: words), considering the number of occurrences of each letter that exists in a word.

Parikh vectors can be easily computed and are guaranteed to be logarithmic in the size of the word they represent, but they are ambiguous; that is, multiple words typically share the same Parikh vector. Following this, in [14] the authors look at a refinement of the vector notion which is meant to reduce this ambiguity, and introduce an extension for it in the form of a Parikh matrix. A Parikh matrix not only contains the Parikh vector of the word, but also information regarding some of the word's (scattered) subwords. Such a matrix has the same asymptotic compactness as a Parikh vector and is associated to a significantly smaller number of words. However, it does not normally remove ambiguity entirely.

The bulk of the work done on the Parikh matrix mapping concerns the ambiguity that Parikh matrices exhibit. A lot of effort is spent on identifying an alternative to the Parikh matrix concept that would make a mapping from a word injective, or less ambiguous in general [1,2,8–11,18]. These include even more refined versions of the matrices by inclusion of polynomials, various extensions on the mappings, or both. For Parikh matrices explicitly, due to the difficulty

A. Leporati et al. (Eds.): LATA 2020, LNCS 12038, pp. 397–411, 2020.
https://doi.org/10.1007/978-3-030-40608-0_28

arising from this ambiguity, the primary focus was on investigating this property on binary [4–7,17] and ternary [3,13,16,19] alphabets, leaving alphabets of size greater than three relatively unexplored.

In terms of reducing the ambiguity of a *word*, the investigation was based on either gathering more information about the specific word by altering the order of the alphabet, known as the dual order [6,14], or by considering the reverse image of the word [6]. Hence an under-studied aspect that may reduce the ambiguity of a matrix concerns the information acquired by altering the word itself, or considering other alterations of the alphabet. In this work we present and investigate two different methods that reduce the ambiguity of the original Parikh matrices in the form of $\mathbb{P}$-Parikh matrices and $\mathbb{L}$-Parikh matrices.

The first of the two transformations, the $\mathbb{P}$-Parikh matrix mapping, considers the Parikh matrices associated to a projection morphism of the initial word, where the considered alphabet is reduced to the subset of the alphabet used within the defined transformation. These represent a particular case of the extended mapping presented in [18], where we only consider a subset of the original alphabet. For example, consider the words *abcaabaac* and *abacabcaa*. It is easy to see that both share the same number of letters, and subwords *ab*, *bc* and *abc*, respectively, making their Parikh matrices equal and therefore ambiguous. The $\mathbb{P}$-Parikh matrices associated to them with respect to $\{a, c\}$ consider the number of subwords *ac*, which is 6 in the former, but only 5 in the latter of the words. Hence, there exist $\mathbb{P}$-Parikh matrices not shared by the words.

We show that, using $\mathbb{P}$-Parikh matrices, we can reduce the ambiguity of the vast majority of words. We also explore when $\mathbb{P}$-Parikh matrices do not reduce ambiguity, as well as provide some insight into the types of words that cannot be uniquely described by a $\mathbb{P}$-Parikh matrix.

However, since $\mathbb{P}$-Parikh matrices are defined for a subset of the initial alphabet, they prove useless when dealing with binary sequences. We therefore consider an alternative transformation of words: the Lyndon conjugate, first introduced in [20], which is defined as the lexicographically smallest circular rotation of a word. Lyndon conjugates were used previously as a tool for ambiguity reduction. In [17], the authors define the Lyndon image of a Parikh matrix as the lexicographically smallest word describing such a matrix. Hence every Parikh matrix has exactly one distinct Lyndon image, which therefore allows each Parikh matrix to be described uniquely. In the context of this paper, we use the Lyndon conjugate differently, i.e., we consider the Parikh matrix of the Lyndon conjugate of a word, and we call the resulting matrix the $\mathbb{L}$-Parikh matrix of the original word.

Consider the Parikh matrix of the Lyndon conjugates of the two previously given words. Observe that *aabaacabc* has 7 occurrences of *ab*, whereas *aaabacabc* has 8, making their Parikh matrices different. Hence, the ambiguity of their Parikh matrix can be reduced using $\mathbb{L}$-Parikh matrices.

While $\mathbb{L}$-Parikh matrices are a useful concept for any alphabet size, we focus on the cases where they reduce ambiguity in the binary alphabet and show that this happens in most cases. We give specific conditions of when $\mathbb{L}$-Parikh matrices do not help reduce the ambiguity of the given word, and investigate the words for which these criteria apply. This leads us to our main result of the paper, a characterisation of words whose ambiguity can be reduced using $\mathbb{L}$-Parikh matrices.

We end this section with a brief breakdown of our paper. In Sect. 2 we present some basic definitions and notions. Section 3 examines the first of the two notions we introduce, the $\mathbb{P}$-Parikh matrix, establishing conditions for when they can or cannot achieve ambiguity reduction. In Sect. 4, we study equivalent questions for $\mathbb{L}$-Parikh matrices, largely focusing on binary alphabets in some cases. We end our paper with conclusions as well as directions for future work.

2   Preliminaries

It is assumed the reader is familiar with the basics of combinatorics on words. If needed, [12] can be consulted. Throughout this paper, $\mathbb{N}$ refers to the set of natural numbers starting with 1.

We refer to a string of arbitrary letters as a *word* which is formed by concatenation of letters. The set of all letters used to create our words is called an *alphabet*. We represent an *ordered alphabet* as $\Sigma_k = \{a_1 < \cdots < a_k\}$, where $k \in \mathbb{N}$ is the *size* of the alphabet, and by convention a_i is the ith letter in the Latin alphabet. Whenever the alphabet size is irrelevant or understood, we omit this from notation using only Σ. All alphabets referred to in this paper have an order imposed on them.

We define the concatenation of two words u and v as uv. The *length* of a word is the total number of not necessarily distinct letters it contains and the *empty word* of length zero is denoted ε. The *Kleene star*, denoted $*$, is the operation that, once applied to a given alphabet, generates the set of all finite words that result from concatenating any words in that alphabet. Further, we denote the ith letter in a word w as $w[i]$.

The *reversal* of a word, denoted rev, is defined as $rev(w) = w[m]w[m-1]\cdots w[1]$, where $w = w[1]w[2]\cdots w[m]$ is a word with $w[i] \in \Sigma$. We say that a *factor* v is in w if and only if w can be written as $w = w_1 v w_2$, where $w_1, w_2 \in \Sigma^*$. We say that $u = u[1]u[2]\cdots u[m]$ is a *subword* of v if we have a factorisation $v = v_0 u[1] v_1 u[2] \cdots v_{m-1} u[m] v_m$ where $v_0, \ldots, v_m \in \Sigma^*, u[1], \ldots, u[m] \in \Sigma$. We use $|v|_u$ to denote the number of distinct occurrences of u as a subword in v.

The *Parikh vector* [15] ϕ associated with a word w is obtained through a mapping $\phi : \Sigma^* \to \mathbb{N}^k$, defined as $\phi(w) = [|w|_{a_1}, |w|_{a_2}, \ldots, |w|_{a_k}]$. For a matrix M of size $k \times k$, the *j-diagonal* is defined as all elements of M that are in the position $M_{i,i+j}$ for $i = 1, \ldots, k - j$. A word is *associated* with a matrix, called its Parikh matrix, if the matrix is obtained from that word following the process detailed in the following explanatory definition. For a technical version of the definition we refer to [14].

Definition 1 (Explanatory). *Let $w \in \Sigma_k^*$. The Parikh matrix, denoted $\Psi(w)$, that w is associated with has size $(k+1) \times (k+1)$. The diagonal of the matrix is* *populated with* 1*'s and all elements below it are* 0. *The count of all subwords that consist of consecutive letters in* Σ_k *and are of length* n *in the word are found on the* n-*diagonal, for* $1 \leq n \leq k$.

One notion we introduce in this paper relies on a change in alphabet size. As such, to emphasise the size n of the alphabet used for a Parikh matrix, we write $\Psi_n(w)$. We say that a Parikh matrix *describes* a word if the word is associated to the matrix. Notice that due to the associativity of matrix multiplication, the Parikh matrix of a word can be constructed from the Parikh matrices of its factors. For a word $w = u_1 u_2$, we have $\Psi_n(w) = \Psi_n(u_1)\Psi_n(u_2)$.

Example 1. Consider the word $w = abca$ defined over the alphabet $\Sigma_3 = \{a < b < c\}$. Then by definition our Parikh matrix is of size 4×4 and we have

$$\Psi(abca) = \begin{pmatrix} 1&1&0&0 \\ 0&1&0&0 \\ 0&0&1&0 \\ 0&0&0&1 \end{pmatrix} \cdot \begin{pmatrix} 1&0&0&0 \\ 0&1&1&0 \\ 0&0&1&0 \\ 0&0&0&1 \end{pmatrix} \cdot \begin{pmatrix} 1&0&0&0 \\ 0&1&0&0 \\ 0&0&1&1 \\ 0&0&0&1 \end{pmatrix} \cdot \begin{pmatrix} 1&1&0&0 \\ 0&1&0&0 \\ 0&0&1&0 \\ 0&0&0&1 \end{pmatrix} = \begin{pmatrix} 1&2&1&1 \\ 0&1&1&1 \\ 0&0&1&1 \\ 0&0&0&1 \end{pmatrix}.$$

For the rest of this work we refine our notation for a Parikh matrix where we remove the elements not depending on the associated word. By definition a Parikh matrix is an upper triangular matrix with 1's on the diagonal regardless of the word described. For aesthetics, removing the redundant part leaves us with a triangular structure that holds the same information as the original matrix,

$$\Psi(abca) = \left\langle \begin{smallmatrix} 2&1&1 \\ &1&1 \\ &&1 \end{smallmatrix} \right\rangle.$$ ◁

Two words w and w' are *conjugates* if we can write $w = uv$ and $w' = vu$. For a word w, we say that the *conjugacy class of* w, denoted $C(w)$ is the class of all of its possible conjugates. A *conjugacy class is associated to a Parikh matrix* if at least one word belonging to that class is associated to the matrix.

Example 2. The matrix $\left\langle \begin{smallmatrix} 4&4 \\ &2 \end{smallmatrix} \right\rangle$ has only the words $aabbaa, abaaba, baaaab$ associated to it. The words $aabbaa$ and $baaaab$ are members of the same conjugacy class, while $abaaba$ belongs to a different conjugacy class. Hence this matrix has two conjugacy classes associated to it.   ◁

A Parikh matrix can be associated to multiple words, as seen above, although cases exist where a matrix describes a single word, e.g., $aabb$ is the unique word associated to $\left\langle \begin{smallmatrix} 2&4 \\ &2 \end{smallmatrix} \right\rangle$. We say that two words are *amiable* if they are associated to the same Parikh matrix. If two or more words are associated to a single Parikh matrix, we say that the matrix is *ambiguous*. Later in this paper, we reduce the ambiguity of a word using both its Parikh matrix and the Parikh matrix of an altered form of that word to describe it. As such, we introduce a formal definition of the *ambiguity* that multiple functions may have based on the set of all words that satisfy all functions. We are then able to use this when considering the ambiguity of the notions we introduce later.

Definition 2. *For a word* w *and functions* $f_1, \ldots, f_n$ *we define* $\mathcal{A}(w, f_1, \ldots, f_n) = \{v \mid f_i(v) = f_i(w)$ *for* $1 \leq i \leq n\}$. *If* $|\mathcal{A}(w, f_1, \ldots, f_n)| = 1$, *then we* *call w unambiguous on $f_1, \ldots, f_n$, and say that $f_1(w), \ldots, f_n(w)$ uniquely define w. However, if $|\mathcal{A}(w, f_1, \ldots, f_n)| > |\mathcal{A}(w, f_1, \ldots, f_m)|$ for $m > n$ and functions $f_{n+1}, \ldots, f_m$, then we say that $f_{n+1}, \ldots, f_m$ reduce the ambiguity of w on $f_1, \ldots, f_n$.*

Observe that we always have $|\mathcal{A}(w, f_1, \ldots, f_n)| \geq |\mathcal{A}(w, f_1, \ldots, f_m)|$. Furthermore, if $|\mathcal{A}(w, f_1, \ldots, f_n)| = |\mathcal{A}(w, f_1, \ldots, f_m)| = 1$, then $\mathcal{A}(w, f_1, \ldots, f_n)$ is unambiguous and it is not possible to further reduce ambiguity.

First we introduce the $\mathbb{P}$-Parikh matrix. This matrix is in essence the Parikh matrix of a projection of a word, and represents a particular case of the extension of the Parikh matrix mapping presented in [19]. For $n \in \mathbb{N}$, $w \in \Sigma_n^*$ and $S \subset \Sigma_n$, the $\mathbb{P}$-Parikh matrix of w with respect to S is defined as follows.

Definition 3. *For $m, n \in \mathbb{N}$ with $1 \leq m \leq n$, let $S \subset \Sigma_n$ such that $S = \{a_{k_1}, a_{k_2}, \ldots a_{k_m}\}$, where $0 < k_1 < \cdots < k_m \leq n$. We define the $\mathbb{P}$-Parikh matrix of the word w with respect to S as $\Psi_n^S(w) := \Psi_{|S|}(\pi_S(w))$, where the morphism $\pi : \Sigma_n^* \to \Sigma_m^*$ is defined as*

$$\pi_S(a_j) := \begin{cases} a_i & : a_j = a_{k_i} \\ \varepsilon & : a_j \notin S \end{cases}.$$

To gain some intuition about the above definition, consider an example.

Example 3. Let $\Sigma_5 = \{a, b, c, d, e\}$, $S = \{a, d, e\}$, and $w = bacbebda$. For the index sequence of S, since a is the lexicographically smallest letter in S, we obtain $k_1 = 1$, $k_2 = 4$ and $k_3 = 5$. Hence $\pi_S(a) = a$, $\pi_S(d) = b$ and $\pi_S(e) = c$.

With the transformation defined we apply this to the word, and calculate the corresponding $\mathbb{P}$-Parikh matrix as the Parikh matrix of the transformed word,

$$\pi_S(w) = \pi_S(b)\pi_S(a)\pi_S(c)\pi_S(b)\pi_S(e)\pi_S(b)\pi_S(d)\pi_S(a) = \varepsilon a\varepsilon\varepsilon c\varepsilon ba = acba$$

$$\Psi_5^{\{a,d,e\}}(bacbebda) = \Psi_3(\pi_{\{a,d,e\}}(bacbebda)) = \Psi_3(acba) = \left\langle \begin{smallmatrix} 2 & 1 & 0 \\ & 1 & 0 \\ & & 1 \end{smallmatrix} \right\rangle. \triangleleft$$

The *Lyndon conjugate* of a word is the conjugate that is lexicographically smallest based on the order on the alphabet. The Lyndon conjugate of a word w is denoted $L(w)$. In an attempt to reduce the ambiguity of Parikh matrices, we modify the original Parikh matrix mapping to gain more information about a given word. Next, we introduce the $\mathbb{L}$-Parikh matrix associated to a word.

Definition 4. *Given a word w, we define its $\mathbb{L}$-Parikh matrix, Ψ_L, as the Parikh matrix associated with its Lyndon conjugate, $L(w)$.*

It was shown in [4] that there exist transformations that, when applied to a word, create a new word that is amiable with the original. For non-binary alphabets, a Type 1 transformation is given.

Lemma 1 ([4]). *Let $w, w' \in \Sigma_n^*$ with $n \geq 3$. Then w transforms into w' using a Type 1 transformation if $w = u_1 a_i a_j u_2$ and $w' = u_1 a_j a_i u_2$, where $u_1, u_2 \in \Sigma_n^*$, $a_i, a_j \in \Sigma_n$, and $|i - j| \geq 2$.*

For binary alphabets, a second type of transformation is described, referred to as a Type 2, that allows us to check if certain words are amiable without constructing their matrices.

Lemma 2 ([4]). *Let $w, w' \in \Sigma_2^*$. Then w transforms into w' through a Type 2 transformation if $w = xa_1a_2ya_2a_1z$ and $w' = xa_2a_1ya_1a_2z$, or vice-versa, where $x, y, z \in \Sigma_2^*$ and $a_1, a_2 \in \Sigma_2$.*

3   P-Parikh Matrices

In this section, we examine when and how much P-Parikh matrices reduce the ambiguity of a given word. When we refer to a reduction in ambiguity using P-Parikh matrices, we mean that the number of words described by the original Parikh matrix and their respective P-Parikh matrices is strictly less than the total number of words described by the original Parikh matrix alone, i.e., $|\mathcal{A}\{w, \Psi_n, \Psi_n^S\}| < |\mathcal{A}\{w, \Psi_n\}|$, for some $S \subset \Sigma_n$. First we present an example of P-Parikh matrices removing the ambiguity of a Parikh matrix entirely.

Example 4. Consider the word $w = abca$ from Example 1, which is amiable with the word $w' = abac$ and no others. Then we choose our set $S = \{a, c\}$, and get that: $\Psi_3^{\{a,c\}}(w) = \Psi_2(aba) = \langle\,^2\,_1^1\,\rangle$ and $\Psi_3^{\{a,c\}}(w') = \Psi_2(aab) = \langle\,^2\,_1^2\,\rangle$. Thus w and w' have different P-Parikh matrices and we can uniquely describe them.   ◁

We first introduce some terms that are useful when describing how effective a given P-Parikh matrix is at reducing ambiguity.

Definition 5. *Given a word $w \in \Sigma_n^*$, we call $\Psi(w)$ P-distinguishable if either $|\mathcal{A}(w, \Psi)| = 1$ or there exists a word $u \in \Sigma_n^*$ and a set $S \subset \Sigma_n$ such that $\Psi(w) = \Psi(u)$ and $\Psi_n^S(w) \neq \Psi_n^S(u)$. In the latter case we say that w and u are P-distinct. Furthermore, we call w P-unique if there exist sets $S_1, S_2, \ldots, S_m \subset \Sigma_n$ such that $|\mathcal{A}(w, \Psi, \Psi_n^{S_1}, \Psi_n^{S_2}, \ldots, \Psi_n^{S_m})| = 1$.*

Now we use these terms to examine words whose ambiguity can be reduced using P-Parikh matrices, namely those that contain any length two factor where those two letters are not equal or consecutive in the alphabet.

Proposition 1. *For any word $w \in \Sigma_n^*$ with a factor a_ia_j where $|i - j| > 1$, we have that $\Psi(w)$ is P-distinguishable.*

Proof. Since $|i - j| > 1$, if $w = u_1a_ia_ju_2$ where $u_1, u_2 \in \Sigma_n^*$, then $w' = u_1a_ja_iu_2$ is also associated to w, following Lemma 1. Without loss of generality, take $S = \{a_i < a_j\}$. Then $\Psi_n^S(w) \neq \Psi_n^S(w')$, since $|w|_{a_ia_j}$ and $|w'|_{a_ia_j}$ are elements in $\Psi_n^S(w)$ and $\Psi_n^S(w')$, respectively, and $|w|_{a_ia_j} \neq |w'|_{a_ia_j}$.   □

It is simple to identify words that have such factors by comparing adjacent positions in the word. We can use this to find a lower bound for the proportion of words that are uniquely identified for a given alphabet and word length.

Proposition 2. *The number of words of length m in Σ_n that are reduced in ambiguity by $\mathbb{P}$-Parikh matrices is bounded below by $(n^m) - (n \times 3^{m-1})$.*

Notice especially that as n and m get larger, the proportion of words which are reduced in ambiguity by $\mathbb{P}$-Parikh matrices also gets larger. We therefore conclude that the use of $\mathbb{P}$-Parikh matrices reduces ambiguity for a larger ratio of words for bigger alphabets rather than smaller.

There also exist words for which $\mathbb{P}$-Parikh matrices do not reduce ambiguity. Our following result says that if our choice of a subset consists of only consecutive letters of the initial alphabet, the $\mathbb{P}$-Parikh matrices are not $\mathbb{P}$-distinguishable.

Remark 6. *If all elements of the set $S \subset \Sigma_n$ are consecutive in the alphabet Σ_n, then $|\mathcal{A}(w, \Psi_n)| = |\mathcal{A}(w, \Psi_n, \Psi_n^S)|$.*

The result of Remark 6 strengthens the one of Proposition 1 by telling us that the ambiguity of words defined over binary alphabets is not reducible by $\mathbb{P}$-Parikh matrices.

Corollary 1. *There does not exist a Parikh matrix that describes binary words whose ambiguity can be reduced by $\mathbb{P}$-Parikh matrices.*

Furthermore, there exist non-binary words for which $\mathbb{P}$-Parikh matrices do not remove ambiguity, namely those that are not $\mathbb{P}$-unique. Finally, we end this section by giving two classes of words which are not uniquely described by $\mathbb{P}$-Parikh matrices, no matter how we choose the set S.

Proposition 3. *Take two words $w, w' \in \Sigma_n^*$ with the form $w = u_1 a_i a_j v a_j a_i u_2$ and $w' = u_1 a_j a_i v a_i a_j u_2$, where $a_i \leq a_j \in \Sigma_n$ and $u_1, u_2 \in \Sigma_n^*$. If $v \in \{a_k \in \Sigma_n | a_i \leq a_k \leq a_j\}^*$, then for all $S \subseteq \Sigma_n$, we have $\Psi_n^S(w) = \Psi_n^S(w')$.*

Proof. Firstly, if $a_i = a_k = a_j$, equivalence follows, as $w = w'$. Now, let $a_i < a_j$.

In the case where S contains either a_i or a_j, then $\pi_S(w) = \pi_S(w')$ since a_i and a_j are the only letters that swap places in w' compared to w. Since $\pi_S(w) = \pi_S(w')$, clearly $\Psi_n^S(w) = \Psi_n^S(w')$ follows.

If $S = \{a_i, a_j\}$, then $\pi_S(w)$ is a binary word and can be transformed via a Type 2 transformation, from Lemma 2, into $\pi_S(w')$, so $\Psi_n^S(w) = \Psi_n^S(w')$.

Next consider that $\{a_i, a_j\} \subset S$, $|S| > 2$, and S has no elements between a_i and a_j. Then $\pi_S(w) = \pi_S(u_1) a_i a_j a_j a_i \pi_S(u_2)$ and $\pi_S(w') = \pi_S(u_1) a_j a_i a_i a_j \pi_S(u_2)$. Using an extension from [3] of the Type 2 transformations we can transform $\pi_S(w)$ into $\pi_S(w')$, and get that $\Psi_n^S(w) = \Psi_n^S(w')$.

Finally, consider the case where S contains a_i, a_j, and at least one letter that comes lexicographically between a_i and a_j. Then, $\pi_S(w)$ can be transformed into $\pi_S(w')$ via two Type 1 transformations on a_i and a_j, since a_i and a_j are not lexicographically adjacent in S (see Lemma 1). $\qquad\square$

The ideas from Proposition 3 give rise to another class of words that are not $\mathbb{P}$-unique, by loosening the condition on v and extending the length of the word.

Proposition 4. *Take two words of the form* $w = u_1 a_i a_j v_1 a_j a_i a_j a_i v_2 a_i a_j u_2$, *and* $w' = u_1 a_j a_i v_1 a_i a_j a_i a_j v_2 a_j a_i u_2$, *where* $a_i < a_j \in \Sigma_n$ *and* $u_1, u_2, v_1, v_2 \in \Sigma_n^*$. *Let* $v_1 = v_1[1]v_1[2] \cdots v_1[x]$ *and* $v_2 = v_2[1]v_2[2] \cdots v_2[y]$. *Then,* w *and* w' *are not* $\mathbb{P}$-*distinct if and only if* $|v_1|_{a_\ell} = |v_2|_{a_\ell}$ *for all* $a_\ell \notin \{a_k | a_i \leq a_k \leq a_j\}$, *and at least one of the following conditions is true:*

1. $v_1, v_2 \in \{a_k | a_k \leq a_j\}^*$, *and for* $\ell < p$, *if* $v_2[p], v_2[\ell] \in \{a_k | a_k < a_i\}$, *then* $v_2[p] \leq v_2[\ell]$, *and if* $v_1[p], v_1[\ell] \in \{a_k | a_k < a_i\}$, *then* $v_1[p] \geq v_1[\ell]$;
2. $v_1, v_2 \in \{a_k | a_k \geq a_i\}^*$, *and for* $\ell < p$, *if* $v_2[p], v_2[\ell] \in \{a_k | a_k > a_j\}$, *then* $v_2[p] \geq v_2[\ell]$, *and if* $v_1[p], v_1[\ell] \in \{a_k | a_k > a_j\}$, *then* $v_1[p] \leq v_1[\ell]$.

In other words, the above statement says that two words are not $\mathbb{P}$-distinct if both v_1 and v_2 are defined on the subset of the alphabet which is either lexicographically bigger than a_i or smaller than a_j, and they share the same Parikh vector for the subset of letters which are not in between a_i and a_j. Furthermore, if $v_1 \in \{a_{i+1}, \ldots, a_n\}^*$, then all the letters which are lexicographically greater than a_j must occur in v_1 in decreasing lexicographical order and in v_2 in increasing order. On the other hand, if $v_1 \in \{a_1, \ldots, a_{j-1}\}^*$, then all the letters which are lexicographically smaller than a_i must occur in v_1 in increasing lexicographical order and in v_2 in decreasing lexicographical order.

4   L-Parikh Matrices

Proposition 2 shows that in many cases, the set of words that share both a Parikh matrix and a $\mathbb{P}$-Parikh matrix is smaller than the set of those that share only a Parikh matrix. However, following Corollary 1 we also know that this never happens for binary alphabets. Hence we now study L-Parikh matrices as an alternative method of ambiguity reduction. While they can be effective for any non-unary alphabet, we focus on binary alphabets specifically. We begin this section by explaining the motivation for choosing the Lyndon conjugate of a word and then build to our main result where we characterise words whose ambiguity is reduced by the use of L-Parikh matrices.

As indicated by Definition 4, the concept of L-Parikh matrices is based on a modification to a word that results in a change in the order of letters. The following theorem implies that the strategy of altering a word is not always a successful method of ambiguity reduction. Note that Ψ_{rev} refers to the Parikh matrix of the reversal of a word.

Theorem 1 ([4]). *For a word* w, *we have that* $\mathcal{A}(w, \Psi) = \mathcal{A}(w, \Psi, \Psi_{\text{rev}})$.

Unlike Theorem 1, L-Parikh matrices use the conjugate of a word. The next proposition implies that such conjugates need to be chosen wisely.

Proposition 5. *Given words* $v, w \in \Sigma^*$ *with* $\Psi(v) = \Psi(w)$, *for any factorisations* $v = v_1 v_2$ *and* $w = w_1 w_2$ *such that* $|v_2| = |w_2|$, *we have that* $\Psi(v_2 v_1) = \Psi(w_2 w_1)$ *implies* $\phi(v_2) = \phi(w_2)$. *For* Σ_2, *the reverse direction also stands, namely* $\phi(v_2) = \phi(w_2)$ *implies* $\Psi(v_2 v_1) = \Psi(w_2 w_1)$.

Proof Outline. We can prove the statement that holds for every size alphabet by contradiction, by assuming that $\Psi(v) = \Psi(w), \Psi(v_2 v_1) = \Psi(w_2 w_1)$ and $\phi(v_2) \neq \phi(w_2)$. We examine the total number of ab subwords in v, w, $v_2 v_1$ and $w_2 w_1$ to obtain a set of equations. We then consider the total number of b's in v_2 and w_2 to find a contradiction within these equations.

For the statement that holds just for the binary alphabet we examine the total number of ab subwords in $v_2 v_1$, $w_2 w_1$, v_1, v_2, w_1 and w_2 and get a contradiction in the equations we obtain by initially assuming that $\phi(v_2) = \phi(w_2)$, $\Psi(v) = \Psi(w)$ and $\Psi(v_2 v_1) \neq \Psi(w_2 w_1)$. $\qquad\square$

Below example shows that $|v_2| = |w_2|$ is necessary for Proposition 5.

Example 5. Consider the words $v = aabaabbb$ with $v_2 = aabbb$ and $w = aaabbabb$ with $w_2 = abb$. One can easily find that $\Psi(v_2 v_1) = \Psi(w_2 w_1) = \left(\begin{smallmatrix} 4 & 10 \\ & 4 \end{smallmatrix}\right)$. Furthermore, we have that $\Psi(v) = \Psi(w)$, $\Psi(v_2 v_1) = \Psi(w_2 w_1)$ and $|v_2| \neq |w_2|$. However $\phi(v_2) \neq \phi(w_2)$, since $\phi(v_2) = [2, 3]$ and $\phi(w_2) = [1, 2]$, and therefore $|v_2| = |w_2|$ is a necessary condition in the context of Proposition 5. $\qquad\triangleleft$

An example for the ternary alphabet where $\Psi(v_2 v_1) \neq \Psi(w_2 w_1)$ even though we have that $\Psi(v) = \Psi(w)$ and $\phi(v_2) = \phi(w_2)$ is given below. Note that if $\phi(v_2) = \phi(w_2)$, then we must also have $|w_2| = |v_2|$. Since any alphabet of size greater than 3 would rely on the result of the ternary alphabet always being true, we can deduce that the backwards direction from Proposition 5 only holds for the binary alphabet.

Example 6. Let $v = cbbaaabb$ and $w = cabbbaab$. We have that $\Psi(v) = \Psi(w)$. Now let $v_2 = aabb$ and $w_2 = baab$. Then we have that $|w_2| = |v_2|$ and $\phi(v_2) = \phi(w_2)$. Note that $\Psi(v_2) \neq \Psi(w_2)$, since $|v_2|_{ab} = 4$ and $|w_2|_{ab} = 2$. But this gives us $\Psi(v_2 v_1) = \Psi(aabbcbba) \neq \Psi(baabcabb) = \Psi(w_2 w_1)$. $\qquad\triangleleft$

Proposition 5 shows that when looking for a modification that we can apply to a word to find a new and different Parikh matrix, we need to consider conjugates of amiable words where it is less likely that the Parikh vectors of their right factors are the same, i.e., conjugates obtained by shifting the original words a different number of times, respectively.

Let us now consider how using L-Parikh matrices reduces ambiguity. The rest of this section ignores any word w where $|\mathcal{A}(w, \Psi)| = 1$, since there is no ambiguity to be reduced here. For a word w, we calculate $\Psi(w)$ and $\Psi_L(w)$ and use both of these matrices to describe the original word. The ambiguity of a word w, with respect to its Parikh and L-Parikh matrices, according to Definition 2, is the total number of words that share a Parikh matrix and an L-Parikh matrix with w, namely $|\mathcal{A}(w, \Psi, \Psi_L)|$. We use the next definitions and propositions to build to our main result where we characterise binary words whose ambiguity is reduced using L-Parikh matrices. In line with Definition 5 we introduce the following definitions.

Definition 7. *Given a word $w \in \Sigma^*$, we call $\Psi(w)$ L-distinguishable if either $|\mathcal{A}(w, \Psi)| = 1$ or there exists a word $u \in \Sigma^*$ with $\Psi(w) = \Psi(u)$, such that*

$\Psi_L(w) \neq \Psi_L(u)$. In the latter case we say that w and u are $\mathbb{L}$-distinct. A word w is $\mathbb{L}$-unique if $|\mathcal{A}(w, \Psi, \Psi_L)| = 1$.

Note that if w and v are $\mathbb{L}$-distinct, then $\mathcal{A}(w, \Psi) = \mathcal{A}(v, \Psi)$ and $\mathcal{A}(w, \Psi, \Psi_L) \neq \mathcal{A}(v, \Psi, \Psi_L)$. The example below demonstrates the effectiveness of $\mathbb{L}$-Parikh matrices for ambiguity reduction.

Example 7. Consider the words $w = babbbaa$, $u = bbababa$ and $v = bbbaaab$ with $\Psi(w) = \Psi(u) = \Psi(v)$. However, for the conjugates $L(w) = aababbb$, $L(u) = abababb$ and $L(v) = aaabbbb$ we have that $\Psi_L(w) = \langle {}^3 \, {}^{11}_4 \rangle$, $\Psi_L(u) = \langle {}^3 \, {}^9_4 \rangle$, and $\Psi_L(v) = \langle {}^3 \, {}^{12}_4 \rangle$. Thus their $\mathbb{L}$-Parikh matrices are all different and we can uniquely describe each of the words by using $\mathbb{L}$-Parikh matrices.   ◁

$\mathbb{L}$-distinguishability is necessary for ambiguity reduction in this case.

Corollary 2. *For $w \in \Sigma^*$, $|\mathcal{A}(w, \Psi)| > |\mathcal{A}(w, \Psi, \Psi_L)|$ if and only if $\Psi(w)$ is $\mathbb{L}$-distinguishable.*

The above characterisation of ambiguity reduction leads us to investigate sufficient conditions for a matrix to be ambiguous, and therefore for any pair of words it describes not to be $\mathbb{L}$-distinct. Our next results consider the situations when the Parikh matrix of a word is not $\mathbb{L}$-distinguishable. We show that words that meet the criteria outlined in each proposition within the binary alphabet are rare either later in the paper or directly following the next proposition.

Proposition 6. *For a word $w \in \Sigma^*$, if all words in $\mathcal{A}(w, \Psi)$ belong to the same conjugacy class, then $\Psi(w)$ is not $\mathbb{L}$-distinguishable.*

Example 8. Let $w = aababa$ and $w' = abaaab$. These two words are amiable with each other and nothing else. Furthermore, $L(w) = aaabab = L(w')$, and since both words share a Lyndon conjugate, both words also share an $\mathbb{L}$-Parikh matrix. Therefore $\Psi(w)$ is not $\mathbb{L}$-distinguishable.   ◁

Now we move on to explore, for binary alphabets, the case where all words in $\mathcal{A}(w, \Psi)$ belong to the same conjugacy class in more detail. Recall that $C(w)$ refers to the conjugacy class of w.

Proposition 7. *Let $w \in \Sigma_2^*$. Then $L(u) = L(w)$, for all $u \in \mathcal{A}(w, \Psi)$, if and only if $L(w) \in \{aabb, ababbb, aababb, aabbab, aaabab\}$.*

Proof Outline. The forwards direction is proven by examining every element of the conjugacy class of w. We can first prove that if $L(u) = L(w)$, for all $u \in \mathcal{A}(w, \Psi)$, then words in the conjugacy class of w are only amiable with other conjugates of w. We then show that this is only true when $L(w)$ is in the set $\{aabb, ababbb, aababb, aabbab, aaabab\}$. For this we define a *block of a letter* to be a unary factor of a word which is not extendable to the right or left and argue that applying a Type 2 transformation to any Lyndon conjugate that is not in the above set either alters the size of the block of a's at the start of the word, or changes the total number of blocks of a's in the word altogether. This therefore gives us a word that is amiable to, but not a conjugate of, the original.

The backwards direction is proven by finding the Parikh matrices of all conjugates of words in the set $\{aabb, ababbb, aababb, aabbab, aaabab\}$. We then find that the only words described by these matrices are these conjugates. □

We now look at the case where all words associated to a Parikh matrix are the Lyndon representatives of their respective conjugacy classes, which again makes this matrix not $\mathbb{L}$-distinguishable.

Proposition 8. *For a word $w \in \Sigma^*$, if $|\mathcal{A}(w, \Psi)| \geq 2$ and $\mathcal{A}(w, \Psi) = \mathcal{A}(w, \Psi_L)$, then $\Psi(w)$ is not $\mathbb{L}$-distinguishable.*

Example 9. The words $w = aaaabaabbb$ and $w' = aaaaabbabb$ are only amiable with each other, $\Psi(w) = \Psi(w')$, and both are the Lyndon representatives of their respective conjugacy classes. Therefore, $\Psi(w) = \Psi(w') = \Psi_L(w) = \Psi_L(w')$ and $\Psi(w)$ is not $\mathbb{L}$-distinguishable. ◁

For binary alphabets, we examine in greater detail when all words in $\mathcal{A}(w, \Psi)$ are the Lyndon representatives of their conjugacy classes. The next result provides a necessary and sufficient condition, and therefore the complete characterisation, for this case to occur for the binary alphabet.

Proposition 9. *Let $w \in \Sigma_2^*$. Then the following statements are equivalent.*

- *For all $u \in \mathcal{A}(w, \Psi)$, we have that $u = L(u)$.*
- *$w = a^* v b^*$ and for $n = |v|_{ba}$ we have that $|v|_a = 2n$ and $|v|_b = n + 1$.*

Proof Outline. To show that these two statements are equivalent, we begin by showing that the second statement implies the former. We do this by first showing that if a word is of the form $w = a^* v b^*$ and, for $n = |v|_{ba}$, we have that $|v|_a = 2n$ and $|v|_b = n + 1$, then $w = L(w)$, and next move on to prove that only words of this form are described by $\Psi(w)$. We prove that $w = L(w)$ by observing that $v = L(v)$. Adding more a's to the start of v and more b's to the end means that the Lyndon conjugate is still the word itself, and hence obtain $w = L(w)$. We prove that words of the form described in the second point are only amiable with each other by calculating the total number of ab subwords in v and extrapolating this to w.

To prove that the first statement implies the second, we use the fact that our words share a Parikh matrix and that they must begin with the largest number of consecutive a's in the word and end with at least one b. We also rewrite $w = a^+ w_i' b^+$ where w_i' begins with the first occurrence of a b and ends with the last occurrence of an a in w, and examine the form that this must take given the fixed number of ab subwords we must have in w. This gives us the total number of a's and b's in a word relative to the total number of ba subwords. □

The next example shows how the above result can be used to identify the form of the words that always share a Parikh matrix with other Lyndon conjugates.

Example 10. Following Proposition 9, Lyndon representatives of different conjugacy classes share a Parikh matrix only if they are of the form a^*vb^*, where for $n = |v|_{ba}$ we have that $|v|_a = 2n$ and $|v|_b = n + 1$. Let us find all words of this form where $n = 3$. We begin by finding all binary words that contain 3 subwords ba. These are $baaa, baba$ and $bbba$. Next add a's to the front and b's to the end of each word, respectively, so that we have a total of 6 a's and 4 b's per word: $aaabaaabbb, aaaababab, aaaaabbbab$. Finally, any number of a's and b's can be added to the front and end of each word, respectively: $a^*aaabaaabbbb^*, a^*aaaababababb^*, a^*aaaaabbbabb^*$. Hence we know that any word of this form is the Lyndon representative of its conjugacy class and shares a Parikh matrix with the two other words stated above. For example, $\Psi(a^2aaabaaabbb^3) = \Psi(a^2aaaababababb^3) = \Psi(a^2aaaaabbbabb^3) = \langle\, 8\ {}^{53}_{\ 7}\,\rangle$.   ◁

Thus far, we presented sufficient conditions for two amiable words not to be $\mathbb{L}$-distinct. Our main result shows that these conditions are in fact also the necessary ones. The following lemmas are used in the proof of the final result, but are also included here as they are also interesting results on their own. The first lemma tells us that if the Parikh vectors of the proper right factors of two amiable words are different, then the size of these factors must also be unequal.

Lemma 3. *Consider the words $w = w_1w_2 = xabybaz$ and $v = v_1v_2 = xbayabz$ with $w, v \in \Sigma_2$, such that $w_1, w_2, v_1, v_2 \neq \varepsilon$ and $w_2w_1 = L(w) \neq L(v) = v_2v_1$. If $\phi(w_2) \neq \phi(v_2)$, then $|w_2| \neq |v_2|$.*

Furthermore, if two amiable binary words are not the Lyndon representatives of their conjugacy classes, then to either of them we can apply a Type 2 transformation to obtain an amiable word whose Lyndon conjugate begins in a different position from the original one.

Lemma 4. *Let $w = w_1w_2 \in \Sigma_2^*$ with $L(w) = w_2w_1 \neq w$. If $|\mathcal{A}(w, \Psi)| \geq 2$, then there exists $u = u_1u_2 \in \mathcal{A}(w, \Psi)$, where $L(u) = u_2u_1$, such that $|u_2| \neq |w_2|$.*

Proof Outline. The statement can be proven by contradiction, by first assuming that the Lyndon conjugate of every word associated to $\Psi(w)$ begins in the same position within those words. We then show that for the Lyndon conjugate to begin at any position within a given binary word, it is possible to apply a Type 2 transformation to obtain a new word whose Lyndon conjugate begins in a different position.   □

Next we show that all words that are conjugates of any word w such that $\mathcal{A}(w, \Psi) = \mathcal{A}(w, \Psi_L)$ are also amiable with a word that is not a conjugate of any of the words in $\mathcal{A}(w, \Psi)$.

Lemma 5. *Let $w, u, v \in \Sigma_2^*$, where $\mathcal{A}(w, \Psi) = \mathcal{A}(w, \Psi_L)$. For any $u \in C(w)$ there exists $v \in \mathcal{A}(u, \Psi)$ such that $\mathcal{A}(w, \Psi_L) \cap C(v) = \emptyset$.*

Proof Outline. This statement can be proven by considering every form that a word w can take, such that $\mathcal{A}(w, \Psi) = \mathcal{A}(w, \Psi_L)$, from Proposition 9 and then examining all conjugates of these words. We show that a Type 2 transformation can be applied to every conjugate to obtain a word that is not a conjugate of any word in our original set $\mathcal{A}(w, \Psi)$. □

We end this section by giving our main result that characterises all binary words whose Parikh matrix is not $\mathbb{L}$-distinguishable.

Theorem 2. *For Σ_2, a Parikh matrix is not $\mathbb{L}$-distinguishable if and only if any of the words it describes meet at least one of the following criteria:*

- *$w \in \{aabb, ababbb, aababb, aabbab, aaabab, bbabbaaa, bbbaabaa\}$*
- *$w = a^* v b^*$ and for $n = |v|_{ba}$ we have that $|v|_a = 2n$ and $|v|_b = n + 1$*

Proof Outline. For the set of words $B = \{bbabbaaa, bbbaabaa\}$, the forward direction is easily proven by finding these words' Parikh and $\mathbb{L}$-Parikh matrices, respectively. The backward direction is proved using the fact that for words $w, w' \in \Sigma_2^*$ such that w is the reverse of w' and $\mathcal{A}(w', \Psi) = \mathcal{A}(w', \Psi_L)$, then $w \in B$ if and only if $\mathcal{A}(w, \Psi) = \mathcal{A}(w, \Psi, \Psi_L)$.

For the rest of the words, the 'if' direction was mostly proven earlier when Propositions 6, 7, 8 and 9, describing these situations, were introduced.

The 'only if' direction is proven by first examining the consequences of Proposition 5, which tells us that two words are $\mathbb{L}$-distinct if their Lyndon conjugates begin in different positions, respectively. We use Lemmas 3 and 4 to conclude that no set of amiable binary words exists where the Lyndon conjugates of all words in the set begin in the same position of each word, respectively. Hence all Parikh matrices would be $\mathbb{L}$-distinguishable if it were not for some cases that arise as a result of us using the Lyndon conjugate. These cases are namely the ones where the set of amiable words are all Lyndon conjugates, are all members of the same conjugacy class, or are all conjugates of words whose Lyndon conjugates share a Parikh matrix. We showed in Propositions 7 and 9 that the first two cases are characterised by words of the form $w = a^* v b^*$ where for $n = |v|_{ba}$ we have that $|v|_a = 2n$ and $|v|_b = n + 1$, and by words where their Lyndon conjugate is in the set $\{aabb, ababbb, aababb, aabbab, aaabab\}$, respectively. We use Lemma 5 to conclude that no words exist such that the third case is true. □

5   Conclusion and Future Work

In this paper, we have shown that using $\mathbb{P}$-Parikh matrices and $\mathbb{L}$-Parikh matrices reduces the ambiguity of a word in most cases. From Corollary 1, we learn that $\mathbb{P}$-Parikh matrices cannot reduce the ambiguity of a Parikh matrix that describes words in a binary alphabet, but are very powerful when it comes to reducing the ambiguity of words in larger alphabets (Proposition 2). On the other hand, we find that $\mathbb{L}$-Parikh matrices reduce the ambiguity of most binary words, with the few exceptions from Theorem 2, which have all been shown to be rare occurrences within the binary alphabet. Thus, using both tools together leads to a reduction in ambiguity in most cases.

Going forward, we wish to characterise words that are described uniquely by both types of matrices, respectively, as well as quantifying the ambiguity reduction permitted by both notions. Theorem 2 tells us that there are very few binary words whose Parikh matrix ambiguity cannot be reduced by $\mathbb{L}$-Parikh matrices. Future research on $\mathbb{L}$-Parikh matrices could also include an analysis similar to the one done in Proposition 2.

Finally we present a conjecture on the types of words that might be described by a Parikh matrix that is $\mathbb{P}$-distinguishable. We know that the presence of a certain type of factor, described in Proposition 1, in a word means that its Parikh matrix is $\mathbb{P}$-distinguishable. This conjecture implies that the presence of this factor is the *only* way that the ambiguity of a word could be reduced by $\mathbb{P}$-Parikh matrices.

Conjecture 8. *For any word $w \in \Sigma_n^*$, if $\Psi(w)$ is $\mathbb{P}$-distinguishable, then there exists a word amiable with w which contains a factor $a_i a_j$, where $|i - j| > 1$.*

References

1. Alazemi, H.M.K., Černý, A.: Counting subwords using a trie automaton. Int. J. Found. Comput. Sci. **22**(6), 1457–1469 (2011)
2. Alazemi, H.M.K., Černý, A.: Several extensions of the Parikh matrix L-morphism. J. Comput. Syst. Sci. **79**(5), 658–668 (2013)
3. Atanasiu, A.: Parikh matrix mapping and amiability over a ternary alphabet. In: Discrete Mathematics and Computer Science, pp. 1–12 (2014)
4. Atanasiu, A., Atanasiu, R., Petre, I.: Parikh matrices and amiable words. Theoret. Comput. Sci. **390**(1), 102–109 (2008)
5. Atanasiu, A., Martín-Vide, C., Mateescu, A.: Codifiable languages and the Parikh matrix mapping. J. UCS **7**, 783–793 (2001)
6. Atanasiu, A., Martín-Vide, C., Mateescu, A.: On the injectivity of the Parikh matrix mapping. Fund. Inform. **49**(4), 289–299 (2002)
7. Atanasiu, A., Teh, W.C.: A new operator over Parikh languages. Int. J. Found. Comput. Sci. **27**(06), 757–769 (2016)
8. Bera, S., Mahalingam, K.: Some algebraic aspects of Parikh q-matrices. Int. J. Found. Comput. Sci. **27**(4), 479–500 (2016)
9. Egecioglu, Ö.: A q-matrix encoding extending the Parikh matrix mapping. Technical report 14, Department of Computer Science at UC Santa Barbara (2004)
10. Egecioglu, O., Ibarra, O.H.: A matrix q-analogue of the Parikh map. In: Levy, J.-J., Mayr, E.W., Mitchell, J.C. (eds.) TCS 2004. IIFIP, vol. 155, pp. 125–138. Springer, Boston (2004). https://doi.org/10.1007/1-4020-8141-3_12
11. Egecioglu, Ö., Ibarra, O.H.: A q-analogue of the Parikh matrix mapping. In: Formal Models, Languages and Applications [this volume commemorates the 75th birthday of Prof. Rani Siromoney]. In: Series in Machine Perception and Artificial Intelligence, vol. 66, pp. 97–111 (2007)
12. Lothaire, M.: Combinatorics on Words. Cambridge University Press, Cambridge (1997)
13. Mahalingam, K., Subramanian, K.G.: Product of Parikh matrices and commutativity. Int. J. Found. Comput. Sci. **23**(01), 207–223 (2012)

14. Mateescu, A., Salomaa, A., Salomaa, K., Yu, S.: On an extension of the Parikh mapping. Turku Centre for Computer Science (2000)
15. Parikh, R.J.: On context-free languages. J. ACM **13**(4), 570–581 (1966)
16. Poovanandran, G., Teh, W.C.: Strong (2·t) and strong (3·t) transformations for strong M-equivalence. Int. J. Found. Comput. Sci. **30**(05), 719–733 (2019)
17. Salomaa, A., Yu, S.: Subword occurrences, Parikh matrices and Lyndon images. Int. J. Found. Comput. Sci. **21**, 91–111 (2010)
18. Şerbănuţă, T.F.: Extending Parikh matrices. Theor. Comput. Sci. **310**(1–3), 233–246 (2004)
19. Şerbănuţă, V.N.: On Parikh matrices, ambiguity, and prints. Int. J. Found. Comput. Sci. **20**(01), 151–165 (2009)
20. Širšov, A.I.: Subalgebras of free Lie algebras. Mat. Sbornik N.S. **33**(75), 441–452 (1953)

On Collapsing Prefix Normal Words

Pamela Fleischmann[1](✉), Mitja Kulczynski[1], Dirk Nowotka[1],
and Danny Bøgsted Poulsen[2]

[1] Department of Computer Science, Kiel University, Kiel, Germany
{fpa,mku,dn}@informatik.uni-kiel.de
[2] Department of Computer Science, Aalborg University, Aalborg, Denmark
dannybpoulsen@cs.aau.dk

Abstract. Prefix normal words are binary words in which each prefix has at least the same number of 1s as any factor of the same length. Firstly introduced in 2011, the problem of determining the index (amount of equivalence classes for a given word length) of the prefix normal equivalence relation is still open. In this paper, we investigate two aspects of the problem, namely prefix normal palindromes and so-called collapsing words (extending the notion of critical words). We prove characterizations for both the palindromes and the collapsing words and show their connection. Based on this, we show that still open problems regarding prefix normal words can be split into certain subproblems.

1 Introduction

Two words are called abelian equivalent if the amount of each letter is identical in both words, e.g. *rotor* and *torro* are abelian equivalent albeit *banana* and *ananas* are not. Abelian equivalence has been studied with various generalisations and specifications such as abelian-complexity, k-abelian equivalence, avoidability of (k-)abelian powers and much more (cf. e.g., [6,10,11,13,17,22–24]). The number of occurrences of each letter is captured in the Parikh vector (also known as Parikh image or Parikh mapping) [21]: given a lexicographical order on the alphabet, the ith component of this vector is the amount of the ith letter of the alphabet in a given word. Parikh vectors have been studied in [12,16,19] and are generalised to Parikh matrices for saving more information about the word than just the amount of letters (cf. eg., [20,25]).

A recent generalisation of abelian equivalence, for words over the binary alphabet $\{0, 1\}$, is prefix normal equivalence (pn-equivalence) [14]. Two binary words are pn-equivalent if their maximal numbers of 1s in any factor of length n are equal for all $n \in \mathbb{N}$. Burcsi et al. [5] showed that this relation is indeed an equivalence relation and moreover that each class contains exactly one uniquely determined representative - called a *prefix normal word*. A word w is said to be prefix normal if the prefix of w of any length has at least the number of 1s as any of w's factors of the same length. For instance, the word 110101 is prefix normal but 101101 is not, witnessed by the fact that 11 is a factor but not a prefix. Both words are pn-equivalent. In addition to being representatives of the

© Springer Nature Switzerland AG 2020
A. Leporati et al. (Eds.): LATA 2020, LNCS 12038, pp. 412–424, 2020.
https://doi.org/10.1007/978-3-030-40608-0_29

pne-classes, prefix normal words are also of interest since they are connected to Lyndon words, in the sense that every prefix normal word is a pre-necklace [14]. Furthermore, as shown in [14], the indexed jumbled pattern matching problem (see e.g. [2,4,18]) is connected to prefix normal forms: if the prefix normal forms are given, the indexed jumbled pattern matching problem can be solved in linear time $\mathcal{O}(n)$ of the word length n. The best known algorithm for this problem has a run-time of $\mathcal{O}(n^{1.864})$ (see [7]). Consequently there is also an interest in prefix normal forms from an algorithmic point of view. An algorithm for the computation of all prefix normal words of length n in run-time $\mathcal{O}(n)$ per word is given in [8]. Balister and Gerke [1] showed that the number of prefix normal words of length n is $2^{n-\Theta(\log^2(n))}$ and the class of a given prefix normal word contains at most $2^{n-O(\sqrt{n\log(n)})}$ elements. A closed formula for the number of prefix normal words is still unknown. In "OEIS" [15] the number of prefix normal words of length n (A194850), a list of binary prefix normal words (A238109), and the maximum size of a class of binary words of length n having the same prefix normal form (A238110), can be found. An extension to infinite words is presented in [9].

Our Contribution. In this work we investigate two conspicuities mentioned in [3,14]: palindromes and extension-critical words. Generalising the result of [3] we prove that prefix normal palindromes (pnPal) play a special role since they are not pn-equivalent to any other word. Since not all palindromes are prefix normal, as witnessed by 101101, determining the number of pnPals is an (unsolved) sub-problem. We show that solving this sub-problem brings us closer to determining the index, i.e. number of equivalence classes w.r.t. a given word length, of the pn-equivalence relation. Moreover we give a characterisation based on the maximum-ones function for pnPals. The notion of extension-critical words is based on an iterative approach: compute the prefix normal words of length $n + 1$ based on the prefix normal words of length n. A prefix normal word w is called extension-critical if $w1$ is not prefix normal. For instance, the word 101 is prefix normal but 1011 is not and thus 101 is called extension-critical. This means that all non-extension-critical words contribute to the class of prefix normal words of the next word-length. We investigate the set of extension-critical words by introducing an equivalence relation *collapse*, grouping all extensional-critical words that are pn-equivalent w.r.t. length $n + 1$. Finally we prove that (prefix normal) palindromes and the collapsing relation (extensional-critical words) are related. In contrast to [14] we work with suffix-normal words (least representatives) instead of prefix-normal words. It follows from Lemma 1 that both notions lead to the same results.

Structure of the Paper. In Sect. 2, the basic definitions and notions are presented. In Sect. 3, we present the results on pnPals. Finally, in Sect. 4, the iterative approach based on collapsing words is shown. This includes a lower bound and an upper bound for the number of prefix normal words, based on pnPals and the collapsing relation. Due to space restrictions all proofs are in the appendix.

2   Preliminaries

Let $\mathbb{N}$ denote the set of natural numbers starting with 1, and let $\mathbb{N}_0 = \mathbb{N} \cup \{0\}$. Define $[n] = \{1, \ldots, n\}$, for $n \in \mathbb{N}$, and set $[n]_0 = [n] \cup \{0\}$.

An alphabet is a finite set Σ, the set of all finite words over Σ is denoted by Σ^*, and the empty word by ε. Let $\Sigma^+ = \Sigma^* \backslash \{\varepsilon\}$ be the free semigroup for the free monoid Σ^*. Let $w[i]$ denote the ith letter of $w \in \Sigma^*$ that is $w = \varepsilon$ or $w = w[1] \ldots w[n]$. The *length* of a word $w = w[1] \ldots w[n]$ is denoted by $|w|$ and let $|\varepsilon| = 0$. Set $w[i..j] = w[i] \ldots w[j]$ for $1 \leq i \leq j \leq |w|$. Set $\Sigma^n = \{w \in \Sigma^* \mid |w| = n\}$ for all $n \in \mathbb{N}_0$. The number of occurrences of a letter $\mathsf{x} \in \Sigma$ in $w \in \Sigma^*$ is denoted by $|w|_\mathsf{x}$. For a given word $w \in \Sigma^n$ the *reversal* of w is defined by $w^R = w[n] \ldots w[1]$. A word $u \in \Sigma^*$ is a factor of $w \in \Sigma^*$ if $w = xuy$ holds for some words $x, y \in \Sigma^*$. If $x = \varepsilon$ then u is called a *prefix* of w and a *suffix* if $y = \varepsilon$. Let $\mathrm{Fact}(w), \mathrm{Pref}(w), \mathrm{Suff}(w)$ denote the sets of all factors, prefixes, and suffixes respectively. Define $\mathrm{Fact}_k(w) = \mathrm{Fact}(w) \cap \Sigma^k$ and $\mathrm{Pref}_k(w), \mathrm{Suff}_k(w)$ are defined accordingly. Notice that $|\mathrm{Pref}_k(w)| = |\mathrm{Suff}_k(w)| = 1$ for all $k \leq |w|$. The powers of $w \in \Sigma^*$ are recursively defined by $w^0 = \varepsilon$, $w^n = ww^{n-1}$ for $n \in \mathbb{N}$.

Following [14], we only consider binary alphabets, namely $\Sigma = \{0, 1\}$ with the fixed lexicographic order induced by $0 < 1$ on Σ. In analogy to binary numbers we call a word $w \in \Sigma^n$ *odd* if $w[n] = 1$ and *even* otherwise.

For a function $f : [n] \to \Delta$ for $n \in \mathbb{N}_0$ and an arbitrary alphabet Δ the concatenation of the images defines a finite word $\mathsf{serialise}(f) = f(1)f(2) \ldots f(n) \in \Delta^*$. Since serialise is bijective, we will identify $\mathsf{serialise}(f)$ with f and use in both cases f (as long as it is clear from the context). This definition allows us to access f's *reversed function* $g : [n] \to \Delta; k \mapsto f(n - k + 1)$ easily by f^R.

Definition 1. *The* maximum-ones functions *is defined for a word* $w \in \Sigma^*$ *by* $f_w : [|w|]_0 \to [|w|]_0; k \mapsto \max\{|v|_1 \mid v \in \mathrm{Fact}_k(w)\}$, *giving for each* $k \in [|w|]_0$ *the maximal number of* 1s *occuring in a factor of length* k. *Likewise the* prefix-ones *and* suffix-ones *functions are defined by* $p_w : [|w|]_0 \to [|w|]_0; k \mapsto |\mathrm{Pref}_k(w)|_1$ *and* $s_w : [|w|]_0 \to [|w|]_0; k \mapsto |\mathrm{Suff}_k(w)|_1$.

Definition 2. *Two words* $u, v \in \Sigma^n$ *are called* prefix-normal equivalent *(pn-equivalent,* $u \equiv_n v$*) if* $f_u = f_v$ *holds and* v*'s equivalence class is denoted by* $[v]_\equiv = \{u \in \Sigma^n \mid u \equiv_n v\}$. *A word* $w \in \Sigma^*$ *is called* prefix (suffix) normal *iff* $f_w = p_w$ *(*$f_w = s_w$ *resp.) holds. Let* $\sigma(w) = \sum_{i \in [n]} f_w(i)$ *denote the maximal-one sum of a* $w \in \Sigma^n$.

Remark 1. Notice that $s_w = p_{w^R}, f_w = f_{w^R}, p_w(i), s_w(i) \leq f_w(i)$ for all $i \in \mathbb{N}_0$. By $p_{w^R} = s_w$ and $f_w = f_{w^R}$ follows immediately that a word $w \in \Sigma^*$ is prefix normal iff its reversal is suffix normal.

Fici and Lipták [14] showed that for each word $w \in \Sigma^*$ there exists exactly one $w' \in [w]_\equiv$ that is prefix normal - the prefix normal form of w. We introduce the concept of *least representative*, which is the lexicographically smallest element of a class and thus also unique. As mentioned in [5] palindromes play a special role. Immediately by $w = w^R$ for $w \in \Sigma^*$, we have $p_w = s_w$, i.e. palindromes are the

Table 1. Prefix normal palindromes (pnPals).

Word length	Prefix normal palindromes	# prefix normal words
1	$0, 1$	2
2	$0^2, 1^2$	3
3	$0^3, 101, 1^3$	5
4	$0^4, 1001, 1^4$	8
5	$0^5, 10001, 10101, 11011, 1^5$	14
6	$0^6, 100001, 110011, 1^6$	23
7	$0^7, 10^2 10^2 1, 10^5 1, 1010101, 1^2 0101^2, 1^2 0^3 1^2, 1^3 01^3, 1^7$	41
8	$0^8, 10^6 1, 1010^2 101, 1^2 0^4 1^2, 1^2 01^2 01^2, 1^3 0^2 1^3, 1^8$	70

only words that can be prefix and suffix normal. Recall that not all palindromes are prefix normal witnessed by 101101.

Definition 3. *A palindrome is called* prefix normal palindrome *(pnPal) if it is prefix normal. Let* $\mathrm{NPal}(n)$ *denote the set of all prefix normal palindromes of length* $n \in \mathbb{N}$ *and set* $\mathrm{npal}(n) = |\mathrm{NPal}(n)|$. *Let* $\mathrm{Pal}(n)$ *be the set of all palindromes of length* $n \in \mathbb{N}$.

3   Properties of the Least-Representatives

Before we present specific properties of the least representatives (LR) for a given word length, we mention some useful properties of the maximum-ones, prefix-ones, and suffix-ones functions (for the basic properties we refer to [5,14] and the references therein). Since we are investigating only words of a specific length, we fix $n \in \mathbb{N}_0$. Beyond the relation $p_w = s_{w^R}$ the mappings p_w and s_w are determinable from each other. Counting the 1s in a suffix of length i and adding the 1s in the corresponding prefix of length $(n - i)$ of a word w, gives the overall amount of 1s of w, namely

$$p_w(n) = p_w(n - i) + s_w(i) \quad \text{and} \quad s_w(n) = p_w(i) + s_w(n - i).$$

For suffix (resp. prefix) normal words this leads to $p_w(i) = f_w(n) - f_w(n - i)$ resp. $s_w(i) = f_w(n) - f_w(n - i)$ witnessing the fact $p_w = s_w$ for palindromes (since both equation hold). Before we show that indeed pnPals form a singleton class w.r.t. $\equiv_n$, we need the relation between the lexicographical order and prefix and suffix normality.

Lemma 1. *The prefix normal form of a class is the lexicographically largest element in the class and the suffix-normal of a class is a LR.*

Lemma 1 implies that a word being prefix and suffix normal forms a singleton class w.r.t. $\equiv_n$. As mentioned $p_w = s_w$ only holds for palindromes.

Proposition 1. *For a word $w \in \Sigma^n$ it holds that $\|[w]\|_{\equiv} = 1$ iff $w \in \mathrm{NPal}(n)$.*

The general part of this section is concluded by a somewhat artificial equation which is nevertheless useful for pnPals : by $s_w(i) = p_w^R(i) - p_w^R(i+1) + s_w(i-1)$ with $p_w^R(n+1) = 0$ for $i \in [n]$ and $s_w = p_{w^R}$ we get

$$p_{w^R}(i) = p_w^R(i) - p_w^R(i+1) - p_{w^R}(i-1).$$

The rest of the section will cover properties of the LRs of a class.

Remark 2. For completeness, we mention that 0^n is the only even LR w.r.t. $\equiv_n$ and the only pnPal starting with 0. Moreover, 1^n is the largest LR. As we show later in the paper 0^n and 1^n are of minor interest in the recursive process due to their speciality.

The following lemma is an extension of [5, Lemma 1] for the suffix-one function by relating the prefix and the suffix of the word s_w for a least representative. Intuitively the suffix normality implies that the 1s are more at the end of the word w rather than at the beginning: consider for instance $s_w = 1123345$ for $w \in \Sigma^7$. The associated word w cannot be suffix normal since the suffix of length two has only one 1 ($s_w(2) = 1$) but by $s_w(5) = 3, s_w(6) = 4$, and $s_w(7) = 5$ we get that within two letters two 1s are present and consequently $f_w(2) \geq 2$. Thus, a word w is only least representative if the amount of 1s at the end of s_w does not exceed the amount of 1s at the beginning of s_w.

Lemma 2. *Let $w \in \Sigma^n$ be a LR. Then we have*

$$s_w(i) \geq \begin{cases} s_w(n) - s_w(n-i+1) & \text{if } s_w(n-i+1) = s_w(n-i), \\ s_w(n) - s_w(n-i+1) + 1 & \text{otherwise.} \end{cases}$$

The remaining part of this section presents results for prefix normal palindromes. Notice that for $w \in \mathrm{NPal}(n)$ with $w = \mathsf{x}v\mathsf{x}$ with $\mathsf{x} \in \Sigma, v$ is not necessarily a pnPal; consider for instance $w = 10101$ with $010 \in \mathrm{Pal}(3) \setminus \mathrm{NPal}(3)$. The following lemma shows a result for prefix normal palindromes which is folklore for palindromes substituting f_w by p_w or s_w.

Lemma 3. *For $w \in \mathrm{NPal}(n) \setminus \{0^n\}, v \in \mathrm{Pal}(n)$ with $w = 1v1$ we have*

$$f_w(k) = \begin{cases} 1 & \text{if } k = 1, \\ f_v(k-1) + 1 & \text{if } 1 < k \leq |w| - 1, \\ f_w(|v|+1) + 1 & \text{if } k = |w|. \end{cases}$$

In the following we give a characterisation of when a palindrome w is prefix normal depending on its maximum-ones function f_w and a derived function $\overline{f_w}$. In particular we observe that $f_w = \overline{f_w}^R$ if and only if w is a prefix normal palindrome. Intuitively $\overline{f_w}$ captures the progress of f_w in reverse order. This is an intriguing result because it shows that properties regarding prefix and suffix normality can be observed when f_w, s_w, p_w are considered in their serialised representation.

Table 2. Number of pnPals. [15] (A308465)

i	1	2	3	4	5	6	7	8	9	10	11	12	13	14	15
#	2	2	3	3	5	4	8	7	12	11	21	18	36	31	57

i	16	17	18	19	20	21	22	23	24	25	26	27	28	29	30
#	55	104	91	182	166	308	292	562	512	1009	928	1755	1697	3247	2972

Definition 4. *For $w \in \Sigma^n$ define $\overline{f}_w : [n] \to [n]$ by $\overline{f}_w(k) = \overline{f}_w(k-1) - (f_w(k-1) - f_w(k-2))$ with the extension $f_w(-1) = f_w(0) = 0$ of f and $\overline{f}_w(0) = f_w(n)$. Define $\overline{p}_w$ and $\overline{s}_w$ analogously.*

Example 1. Consider the pnPal $w = 11011$ with $f_w = 12234$. Then $\overline{f}_w$ is 43221 and we have $f_w = \overline{f}_w^R$. On the other hand for $v = 101101 \in \mathrm{Pal}(6) \backslash \mathrm{NPal}(6)$ we have $p_v = 112334$ and $f_v = 122334$ and $\overline{f}_v = 432211$ and thus $\overline{f}_v^R \neq f_v$.

The following lemma shows a connection between the reversed prefix-ones function and the suffix-ones function that holds for all palindromes.

Lemma 4. *For $w \in \mathrm{Pal}(n)$ we have $s_w \equiv \overline{p}_w^R$.*

By Lemma 4 we get $p_w \equiv \overline{p}_w^R$ since $p_w \equiv s_w$ for a palindrome w. As advocated earlier, our main theorem of this part (Theorem 1) gives a characterisation of pnPals. The theorem allows us to decide if a word is a pnPal by only looking at the maximum-ones-function, thus a comparison of all factors is not required.

Theorem 1. *Let $w \in \Sigma^n \setminus \{\, 0^n \,\}$. Then w is a pnPal if and only if $f_w = \overline{f}_w^R$.*

Table 2 presents the amount of pnPals up to length 30 These results support the conjecture in [5] that there is a different behaviour for even and odd length of the word.

4   Recursive Construction of Prefix Normal Classes

In this section we investigate how to generate LRs of length $n + 1$ using the LRs of length n. This is similar to the work of Fici and Lipták [14] except they investigated appending a letter to prefix normal words while we explore the behaviour on prepending letters to LRs. Consider the words $v = 1001$ and $w = 0011$, both being (different) LRs of length 4. Prepending a 1 to them leads to 11001 and 10011 which are pn-equivalent. We say that v and w *collapse* and denote it by $v \leftrightarrow w$. Hence for determining the index of $\equiv_n$ based on the least representatives of length $n-1$, only the least representative of one class matters.

Definition 5. *Two words $w, v \in \Sigma^n$ collapse if $1w \equiv_{n+1} 1v$ holds. This is denoted by $w \leftrightarrow v$.*

Prepending a 1 to a non LR will never lead to a LR. Therefore It is sufficient to only look at LRs. Since collapsing is an equivalence relation, denote the equivalence class w.r.t. $\leftrightarrow$ of a word $w \in \Sigma^*$ by $[w]_\leftrightarrow$. Next, we present some general results regarding the connections between the LRs of lengths n and $n+1$. As mentioned in Remark 2, 0^n and 1^n are for all $n \in \mathbb{N}$ LRs. This implies that they do not have to be considered in the recursive process.

Remark 3. By [14] a word $w0 \in \Sigma^{n+1}$ is prefix-normal if w is prefix-normal. Consequently we know that if a word $w \in \Sigma^n$ is suffix normal, $0w$ is suffix normal as well. This leads in accordance to the naïve upper bound of $2^n + 1$ to a naïve lower bound of $|\Sigma^n/\equiv_n|$ for $|\Sigma^{n+1}/\equiv_{n+1}|$.

Remark 4. The maximum-ones functions for $w \in \Sigma^*$ and $0w$ are equal on all $i \in [|w|]$ and $f_{0w}(|w|+1) = f_w(|w|)$ since the factor determining the maximal number of 1's is independent of the leading 0. Prepending 1 to a word w may result in a difference between f_w and f_{1w}, but notice that since only one 1 is prepended, we always have $f_{1w}(i) \in \{f_w(i), f_w(i)+1\}$ for all $i \in [n]$. In both cases we have $s_w(i) = s_{xw}(i)$ for $x \in \{0,1\}$ and $i \in [|w|]$ and $s_{0w}(n+1) = s_w(n)$ as well as $s_{1w}(n+1) = s_w(n) + 1$.

Firstly we improve the naïve upper bound to $2|\Sigma^n/\equiv_n|$ by proving that only LRs in Σ^n can become LRs in Σ^{n+1} by prepending 1 or 0.

Proposition 2. *Let $w \in \Sigma^n$ not be LR. Neither $0w$ nor $1w$ are LRs in Σ^{n+1}.*

By Proposition 1 prefix (and thus suffix) normal palindromes form a singleton class. This implies immediately that a word $w \in \Sigma^n$ such that $1w$ is a prefix normal palindrome, does not collapse with any other $v \in \Sigma^n\setminus\{w\}$. The next lemma shows that even prepending once a 1 and once a 0 to different words leads only to equivalent words in one case.

Lemma 5. *Let $w, v \in \Sigma^n$ be different LRs. Then $0w \equiv_n 1v$ if and only if $v = 0^n$ and $w = 0^{n-1}1$.*

By Lemma 5 and Remark 3 it suffices to investigate the collapsing relation on prepanding 1s. The following proposition characterises the LR $1w$ among the elements $1v \in [1w]_\equiv$ for all LRs $v \in \Sigma^n$ with $w \leftrightarrow v$ for $w \in \Sigma^n$.

Proposition 3. *Let $w \in \Sigma^n$ be a LR. Then $1w \in \Sigma^{n+1}$ is a LR if and only if $f_{1w}(i) = f_w(i)$ holds for $i \in [n]$ and $f_{1w}(n+1) = f_w(n) + 1$.*

Corollary 1. *Let $w \in \mathrm{NPal}(n)$. Then $f_{w1}(i) = f_w(i)$ for $i \in [n]$ and $f_{w1}(n+1) = f_w(n) + 1$. Moreover $s_{w1}(i) = s_w(i)$ for $i \in [n]$ and $s_{w1}(n+1) = s_w(n) + 1$.*

This characterization is unfortunately not convenient for determining either the number of LRs of length $n+1$ from the ones from length n or the collapsing LRs of length n. For a given word w, the maximum-ones function f_w has to be determined, f_w to be extended by $f_w(n) + 1$, and finally the associated word - under the assumption $f_{1w} \equiv s_{1w}$ has to be checked for being suffix normal.

For instance, given $w = 100101$ leads to $f_w = 11223$, and is extended to $f_{1w} = 112234$. This would correspond to 110101 which is not suffix normal and thus w is not extendable to a new LR. The following two lemmata reduce the amount of LRs that needs to be checked for extensibility.

Lemma 6. *Let $w \in \Sigma^n$ be a LR such that $1w$ is a LR as well. Then for all LRs $v \in \Sigma^n \backslash \{w\}$ collapsing with w, $f_v(i) \leq f_w(i)$ holds for all $i \in [n]$, i.e. all other LRs have a smaller maximal-one sum.*

Corollary 2. *If $w, v \in \Sigma^n$ and $1w \in \Sigma^{n+1}$ are LRs with $w \leftrightarrow v$ and $v \neq w$ then $w \leq v$.*

Remark 5. By Corollary 2 the lexicographically smallest LR w among the collapsing leads to the LR of $[1w]$. Thus if w is a LR not collapsing with any lexicographically smaller word then $1w$ is LR.

Before we present the theorem characterizing exactly the collapsing words for a given word w, we show a symmetry-property of the LRs which are not extendable to LRs, i.e. a property of words which collapse.

Lemma 7. *Let $w \in \Sigma^n$ be a LR. Then $f_{1w}(i) \neq f_w(i)$ for some $i \in [n]$ iff $f_{1w}(n - i + 1) \neq f_w(n - i + 1)$.*

By [5, Lemma 10] a word $w1$ is prefix normal if and only if $|\operatorname{Suff}_k(w)|_1 < |\operatorname{Pref}_{k+1}(w)|_1$ for all $k \in \mathbb{N}$. The following theorem extends this result for determining the collapsing words w' for a given word w.

Theorem 2. *Let $w \in \Sigma^n$ be a LR and $w' \in \Sigma^n \backslash \{w\}$ with $|w|_1 = |w'|_1 = s \in \mathbb{N}$. Let moreover $v \nleftrightarrow w$ for all $v \in \Sigma^*$ with $v \leq w$. Then $w \leftrightarrow w'$ iff*

1. $f_{w'}(i) \in \{f_w(i), f_w(i) - 1\}$ *for all $i \in [n]$,*
2. $f_{w'}(i) = f_w(i)$ *implies $f_{1w'}(i) = f_w(i)$,*
3. $f_{w'}(i) \geq \begin{cases} f_{w'}(n) - f_{w'}(n - i + 1) & \text{if } f_{w'}(n - i + 1) = f_{w'}(n - i), \\ f_{w'}(n) - f_{w'}(n - i + 1) + 1 & \text{otherwise.} \end{cases}$

Theorem 2 allows us to construct the equivalence classes w.r.t. the least representatives of the previous length but more tests than necessary have to be performed: Consider, for instance $w = 11101100111011111$ which is a smallest LR of length 17 not collapsing with any lexicographically smaller LR. For w we have $f_w = 1 \cdot 2 \cdot 3 \cdot 4 \cdot 5 \cdot 5 \cdot 6 \cdot 7 \cdot 8 \cdot 8 \cdot 8 \cdot 9 \cdot 10 \cdot 10 \cdot 11 \cdot 12 \cdot 13$ where the dots just act as separators between letters. Thus we know for any w' collapsing with w, that $f_{w'}(1) = 1$ and $f_{w'}(17) = 13$. The constraints $f_{w'}(2) \in \{f_w(2), f_w(2) + 1\}$ and $f_{w'}(2) \leq f_w(2)$ implies $f_{w'}(2) \in \{1, 2\}$. First the check that $f_{w'}(10) = 4$ is impossible excludes $f_{w'}(2) = 1$. Since no collapsing word can have a factor of length 2 with only one 1, a band in which the possible values range can be defined by the unique greatest collapsing word w'. It is not surprising that this word is connected with the prefix normal form. The following two lemmata define the band in which the possible collapsing words f_w are.

Lemma 8. *Let $w \in \Sigma^n \setminus \{0^n\}$ be a LR with $v \not\leftrightarrow w$ for all $v \in \Sigma^n$ with $v \leq w$. Set $u := (1w[1..n-1])^R$. Then $w \leftrightarrow u$ and for all LRs $v \in \Sigma^n \setminus \{u\}$ with $v \leftrightarrow w$ and all $i \in [n]$ $f_v(i) \geq f_u(i)$, thus $\sigma(u) = \sum_{i \in [n]} f_u(i) \leq \sum_{i \in [n]} f_v(i) = \sigma(v)$.*

Notice that $w' = (1w[1..n-1])^R$ is not necessarily a LR in $\Sigma^n / \equiv_n$ witnessed by the word of the last example. For w we get $u = 1110111001101111$ with $f_u(8) = f_w(8)$ and $f_u(10) = 7 \neq 8 = f_w(10)$ violating the symmetry property given in Lemma 7. The following lemma alters w' into a LR which represents still the lower limit of the band.

Lemma 9. *Let $w \in \Sigma^n$ be a LR such that $1w$ is also a LR. Let $w' \in \Sigma^n$ with $w \leftrightarrow w'$, and I the set of all $i \in [\lfloor \frac{n}{2} \rfloor]$ with*

$$(f_{w'}(i) = f_w(i) \wedge f_{w'}(n-i+1) \neq f_w(n-i+1)) \text{ or}$$
$$(f_{w'}(i) \neq f_w(i) \wedge f_{w'}(n-i+1) = f_w(n-i+1))$$

and $f_w(j) = f_{w'}(j)$ for all $j \in [n] \setminus I$. Then $\hat{w}$ defined such that $f_{\hat{w}}(j) = f_{w'}(j)$ for all $j \in [n] \setminus I$ and $f_{\hat{w}}(n-i+1) = f_{w'}(n-i+1)+1$ ($f_{\hat{w}}(i) = f_{\hat{w}}(i)+1$ resp.) for all $i \in I$ holds, collapses with w.

Remark 6. Lemma 9 applied to $(1w[1..n-1])^R$ gives the lower limit of the band. Let $\hat{w}$ denote the output of this application for a given $w \in \Sigma^n$ according to Lemma 9.

Continuing with the example, we firstly determine $\hat{w}$ for $w = 1111011\,1001101111$. We get with $u = w[n-1..1]1$ Since for all collapsing $w' \in \Sigma^n$ we have $f_{\hat{w}}(i) \leq f_{w'}(i) \leq f_w(i)$, w' is determined for $i \in [17] \setminus \{5, 9, 13\}$. Since the value for 5 determines the one for 13 there are only two possibilities, namely $f_{w'}(5) = 5$ and $f_{w'}(9) = 7$ and $f_{w'}(5) = 4$ and $f_{w'}(9) = 8$. Notice that the words w' corresponding to the generated words $f_{w'}$ are not necessarily LRs of the shorter length as witnessed by the one with $f_{w'}(5) = 5$ and $f_{w'}(9) = 7$. In this example this leads to at most three words being not only in the class but also in the list of former representatives. Thus we are able to produce an upper bound for the cardinality of the class. Notice that in any case we only have to test the first half of w''s positions by Lemma 7. This leads to the following definition.

Table 3. f for $w = 11110111001101111$.

i	1	2	3	4	5	6	7	8	9	10	11	12	13	14	15	16	17
f_w	1	2	3	4	5	5	6	7	8	8	8	9	10	10	11	12	13
f_u	1	2	3	4	4	5	6	7	7	7	8	9	9	10	11	12	13
$f_{\hat{w}}$	1	2	3	4	4	5	6	7	7	8	8	9	9	10	11	12	13

Definition 6. *Let* $h_d : \Sigma^* \times \Sigma^* \to \mathbb{N}_0$ *be the Hamming-distance. The* palindromic distance $p_d : \Sigma^* \to \mathbb{N}_0$ *is defined by* $p_d(w) = h_d(w[1..\lfloor \frac{n}{2} \rfloor], (w[\lceil \frac{n}{2} \rceil + 1..|w|])^R)$. *Define the* palindromic prefix length $p_\ell : \Sigma^* \to \mathbb{N}_0$ *by* $p_\ell(w) = \max\{ k \in [|w|] \mid \exists u \in \mathrm{Pref}_k(w) : p_d(u) = 0 \}$.

The palindromic distance gives the minimal number of positions in which a bit has to be flipped for obtaining a palindrome. Thus, $p_d(w) = 0$ for all palindromes w, and, for instance, $p_d(110011001) = 2$ since the first half of w and the reverse of the second half mismatch in two positions. The palindromic prefix length determines the length of w's longest prefix being a palindrome. For instance $p_\ell(1101) = 2$ and $p_\ell(01101) = 4$. Since a LR w determines the upper limit of the band and $w[n-1..1]1$ the lower limit, the palindromic distance of $ww[n-1..1]1$ is in relation to the positions of f_w in which collapsing words may differ from w.

Theorem 3. *If* $w \in \Sigma^n$ *and* $1w$ *are both LRs then* $|[w]_{\leftrightarrow}| \leq 2^{\lceil \frac{p_d(ww[n-1..1]1)}{2} \rceil}$.

For an algorithmic approach to determine the LRs of length n, we want to point out that the search for collapsing words can also be reduced using the palindromic prefix length. Let $w_1, \ldots, w_m$ be the LRs of length $n-1$. For each w we keep track of $|w| - p_\ell(w)$. For each w_i we check firstly if $|w_i| - p_\ell(w_i) = 1$ since in this case the prepended 1 leads to a palindrome. Only if this is not the case, $[w_i]_{\leftrightarrow}$ needs to be determined. All collapsing words computed within the band of w_i and $\hat{w}_i$ are deleted in $\{w_{i+1}, \ldots, w_m\}$.

In the remaining part of the section we investigate the set $\mathrm{NPal}(n)$ w.r.t. $\mathrm{NPal}(\ell)$ for $\ell < n$. This leads to a second calculation for an upper bound and a refinement for determining the LRs of $\Sigma^n/\equiv_n$ faster.

Lemma 10. *If* $w \in \mathrm{NPal}(n)\backslash\{1^n\}$ *then* $1w$ *is not a LR but* $w1$ *is a LR.*

Remark 7. By Lemma 10 follows that all words $w \in \mathrm{NPal}(n)$ collapse with a smaller LR. Thus, for all $n \in \mathbb{N}$, an upper bound for $|\Sigma^{n+1}/\equiv_{n+1}|$ is given by $2|\Sigma^n/\equiv_n| - \mathrm{npal}(n)$.

For a closed recursive calculation of the upper bound in Remark 7, the exact number $\mathrm{npal}(n)$ is needed. Unfortunately we are not able to determine $\mathrm{npal}(n)$ for arbitrary $n \in \mathbb{N}$. The following results show relations between prefix normal palindromes of different lengths. For instance, if $w \in \mathrm{NPal}(n)$ then $1w1$ is a prefix normal palindrome as well. The importance of the pnPals is witnessed by the following estimation.

Theorem 4. *For all* $n \in \mathbb{N}_{\geq 2}$ *and* $\ell = |\Sigma^n/\equiv_n|$ *we have*

$$\ell + \mathrm{npal}(n-1) \leq |\Sigma^{n+1}/\equiv_{n+1}| \leq \ell + \mathrm{npal}(n+1) + \frac{\ell - \mathrm{npal}(n+1)}{2}.$$

The following results only consider pnPals that are different from 0^n and 1^n. Notice for these special palindromes that $0^n0^n, 1^n1^n, 1^n11^n, 0^n00^n, 11^n1^n1, 10^n0^n1 \in \mathrm{NPal}(k)$ for an appropriate $k \in \mathbb{N}$ but $0^n10^n \notin \mathrm{NPal}(2n+1)$.

Lemma 11. *If $w \in \mathrm{NPal}(n) \backslash \{1^n, 0^n\}$ then neither ww nor $w1w$ are prefix normal palindromes.*

Lemma 12. *Let $w \in \mathrm{NPal}(n) \backslash \{0^n\}$ with $n \in \mathbb{N}_{\geq 3}$. If $w0w$ is also a prefix normal palindrome then $w = 1^k$ or $w = 1^k01u101^k$ for some $u \in \Sigma^*$ and $k \in \mathbb{N}$.*

A characterisation for $w1w$ being a pnPal is more complicated. By $w \in \mathrm{NPal}(n)$ follows that a block of 1s contains at most the number of 1s of the previous block. But if such a block contains strictly less 1s the number of 0s in between can increase by the same amount the number of 1s decreased.

Lemma 13. *Let $w \in \mathrm{NPal}(n) \backslash \{1^n, 0^n\}$. If $1ww1$ is also a prefix normal palindrome then $10 \in \mathrm{Pref}(w)$.*

Lemmas 11, 12, and 13 indicate that a characterization of prefix normal palindromes based on smaller ones is hard to determine.

5   Conclusion

Based on the work in [14], we investigated prefix normal palindromes in Sect. 3 and gave a characterisation based on the maximum-ones function. At the end of Sect. 4 results for a recursive approach to determine prefix normal palindromes are given. These results show that easy connections between prefix normal palindromes of different lengths cannot be expected. By introducing the collapsing relation we were able to partition the set of extension-critical words introduced in [14]. This leads to a characterization of collapsing words which can be extended to an algorithm determining the corresponding equivalence classes. Moreover we have shown that palindromes and the collapsing classes are related.

The concrete values for prefix normal palindromes and the index of the collapsing relation remain an open problem as well as the cardinality of the equivalence classes w.r.t. the collapsing relation. Further investigations of the prefix normal palindromes and the collapsing classes lead directly to the index of the prefix equivalence.

Acknowledgments. We would like to thank Florin Manea for helpful discussions and advice.

References

1. Balister, P., Gerke, S.: The asymptotic number of prefix normal words. J. Comb. Theory **784**, 75–80 (2019)
2. Burcsi, P., Cicalese, F., Fici, G., Lipták, Z.: Algorithms for jumbled pattern matching in strings. Int. J. Found. CS **23**(2), 357–374 (2012)
3. Burcsi, P., Fici, G., Lipták, Z., Ruskey, F., Sawada, J.: On combinatorial generation of prefix normal words. In: Kulikov, A.S., Kuznetsov, S.O., Pevzner, P. (eds.) CPM 2014. LNCS, vol. 8486, pp. 60–69. Springer, Cham (2014). https://doi.org/10.1007/978-3-319-07566-2_7

4. Burcsi, P., Fici, G., Lipták, Z., Ruskey, F., Sawada, J.: Normal, abby normal, prefix normal. In: Ferro, A., Luccio, F., Widmayer, P. (eds.) FUN 2014. LNCS, vol. 8496, pp. 74–88. Springer, Cham (2014). https://doi.org/10.1007/978-3-319-07890-8_7
5. Burcsi, P., Fici, G., Lipták, Z., Ruskey, F., Sawada, J.: On prefix normal words and prefix normal forms. TCS **659**, 1–13 (2017)
6. Cassaigne, J., Richomme, G., Saari, K., Zamboni, L.Q.: Avoiding Abelian powers in binary words with bounded Abelian complexity. Int. J. Found. CS **22**(04), 905–920 (2011)
7. Chan, T.M., Lewenstein, M.: Clustered integer 3SUM via additive combinatorics. In: 47th ACM Symposium on TOC, pp. 31–40. ACM (2015)
8. Cicalese, F., Lipták, Z., Rossi, M.: Bubble-flip—a new generation algorithm for prefix normal words. In: Klein, S.T., Martín-Vide, C., Shapira, D. (eds.) LATA 2018. LNCS, vol. 10792, pp. 207–219. Springer, Cham (2018). https://doi.org/10.1007/978-3-319-77313-1_16
9. Cicalese, F., Lipták, Z., Rossi, M.: On infinite prefix normal words. In: Proceedings of the SOFSEM, pp. 122–135 (2019)
10. Coven, E.M., Hedlund, G.A.: Sequences with minimal block growth. TCS **7**(2), 138–153 (1973)
11. Currie, J., Rampersad, N.: Recurrent words with constant Abelian complexity. Adv. Appl. Math. **47**(1), 116–124 (2011)
12. Dassow, J.: Parikh mapping and iteration. In: Calude, C.S., PĂun, G., Rozenberg, G., Salomaa, A. (eds.) WMC 2000. LNCS, vol. 2235, pp. 85–101. Springer, Heidelberg (2001). https://doi.org/10.1007/3-540-45523-X_5
13. Ehlers, T., Manea, F., Mercas, R., Nowotka, D.: k-Abelian pattern matching. J. Discrete Algorithms **34**, 37–48 (2015)
14. Fici, G., Lipták, Z.: On prefix normal words. In: Mauri, G., Leporati, A. (eds.) DLT 2011. LNCS, vol. 6795, pp. 228–238. Springer, Heidelberg (2011). https://doi.org/10.1007/978-3-642-22321-1_20
15. OEIS Foundation Inc.: The on-line encyclopedia of integer sequencess (2019). http://oeis.org/
16. Karhumäki, J.: Generalized Parikh mappings and homomorphisms. Inf. Control **47**(3), 155–165 (1980)
17. Keränen, V.: Abelian squares are avoidable on 4 letters. In: Kuich, W. (ed.) ICALP 1992. LNCS, vol. 623, pp. 41–52. Springer, Heidelberg (1992). https://doi.org/10.1007/3-540-55719-9_62
18. Lee, L.-K., Lewenstein, M., Zhang, Q.: Parikh matching in the streaming model. In: Calderón-Benavides, L., González-Caro, C., Chávez, E., Ziviani, N. (eds.) SPIRE 2012. LNCS, vol. 7608, pp. 336–341. Springer, Heidelberg (2012). https://doi.org/10.1007/978-3-642-34109-0_35
19. Mateescu, A., Salomaa, A., Salomaa, K., Yu, S.: On an extension of the Parikh mapping, 06 September 2000. http://citeseer.ist.psu.edu/440186.html
20. Mateescu, A., Salomaa, A., Yu, S.: Subword histories and Parikh matrices. J. Comput. Syst. Sci. **68**(1), 1–21 (2004)
21. Parikh, R.J.: On context-free languages. J. ACM **13**, 570–581 (1966)
22. Puzynina, S., Zamboni, L.Q.: Abelian returns in Sturmian words. J. Comb. Theory **120**(2), 390–408 (2013)

23. Richomme, G., Saari, K., Zamboni, L.Q.: Abelian complexity of minimal subshifts. J. Lond. Math. Soc. **83**(1), 79–95 (2010)
24. Richomme, G., Saari, K., Zamboni, L.Q.: Balance and Abelian complexity of the Tribonacci word. Adv. Appl. Math. **45**(2), 212–231 (2010)
25. Salomaa, A.: Connections between subwords and certain matrix mappings. TCS **340**(2), 188–203 (2005)

Simplified Parsing Expression Derivatives

Aaron Moss[✉][iD]

University of Portland, Portland, USA
mossa@up.edu

Abstract. This paper presents a new derivative parsing algorithm for parsing expression grammars; this new algorithm is both simpler and faster than the existing parsing expression derivative algorithm presented by Moss [12]. This new algorithm improves on the worst-case space and runtime bounds of the previous algorithm by a linear factor, as well as decreasing runtime by about half in practice.

Keywords: Parsing · Parsing expression grammar · Derivative parsing

1 Introduction

A derivative parsing algorithm for parsing expression grammars (PEGs) was first published by Moss [12]; this paper presents a simplified and improved algorithm, as well as a practical comparison of the two algorithms both to each other and to other PEG parsing methods. This new algorithm preserves or improves the performance bounds of the earlier algorithm, trimming a linear factor off the worst-case time and space bounds, while preserving the linear time and constant space bounds for the class of "well-behaved" inputs defined in [12].

2 Parsing Expression Grammars

Parsing expression grammars are a language formalism similar in power to the more familiar context-free grammars (CFGs). PEGs are a formalization of recursive-descent parsing with limited backtracking and infinite lookahead; Fig. 1 provides definitions of the fundamental parsing expressions. a is a *character literal*, matching and consuming a single character of input; ε is the *empty expression* which always matches without consuming any input, while $\varnothing$ is the *failure expression*, which never matches. A is a *nonterminal*, which is replaced by its corresponding parsing expression $\mathcal{R}(A)$ to provide recursive structure in the formalism. The *negative lookahead expression* $!\alpha$ provides much of the unique power of PEGs, matching only if its subexpression α does not match, but consuming no input[1]. The *sequence expression* $\alpha\beta$ matches α followed by β, while the *alternation expression* α/β matches either α or β. Unlike the unordered choice in CFGs, if its first alternative α matches, an alternation expression never backtracks to attempt its second alternative β; this *ordered choice* is responsible for the unambiguous nature of PEG parsing.

---

[1] The *positive lookahead expression* $\&\alpha$ can be expressed as $!!\alpha$.

© Springer Nature Switzerland AG 2020
A. Leporati et al. (Eds.): LATA 2020, LNCS 12038, pp. 425–436, 2020.
https://doi.org/10.1007/978-3-030-40608-0_30

$$a(\mathbf{s}) = \begin{cases} \mathbf{s}' & \mathbf{s} = \mathbf{a}\,\mathbf{s}' \\ \mathsf{fail} & \mathsf{otherwise} \end{cases} \qquad A(\mathbf{s}) = (\mathcal{R}(A))(\mathbf{s})$$

$$\varepsilon(\mathbf{s}) = \mathbf{s} \qquad\qquad\qquad \alpha\beta(\mathbf{s}) = \begin{cases} \beta(\alpha(\mathbf{s})) & \alpha(\mathbf{s}) \neq \mathsf{fail} \\ \mathsf{fail} & \mathsf{otherwise} \end{cases}$$

$$\varnothing(\mathbf{s}) = \mathsf{fail}$$

$$!\alpha(\mathbf{s}) = \begin{cases} \mathbf{s} & \alpha(\mathbf{s}) = \mathsf{fail} \\ \mathsf{fail} & \mathsf{otherwise} \end{cases} \qquad \alpha/\beta(\mathbf{s}) = \begin{cases} \alpha(\mathbf{s}) & \alpha(\mathbf{s}) \neq \mathsf{fail} \\ \beta(\mathbf{s}) & \mathsf{otherwise} \end{cases}$$

Fig. 1. Formal definitions of parsing expressions; $\mathcal{R}(A)$ is the expansion of A

Parsing expressions are functions that recognize prefixes of strings, producing either the un-consumed suffix of a match, or fail on failure. The *language* $\mathcal{L}(\varphi)$ of a parsing expression φ over strings from an alphabet Σ is the set of strings *matched* by φ; precisely, $\mathcal{L}(\varphi) = \{\mathbf{s} \in \Sigma^* : \exists \mathbf{s}' \in \Sigma^*, \varphi(\mathbf{s}) = \mathbf{s}'\}$. This paper uses the notation ϵ for the empty string (distinct from the empty expression ε) and $\mathbf{s}[i]$ for the suffix $\mathbf{s}_i \mathbf{s}_{i+1} \cdots \mathbf{s}_{n-1}$ of some string $\mathbf{s} = \mathbf{s}_0 \mathbf{s}_1 \cdots \mathbf{s}_{n-1}$.

2.1   Related Work

A number of recognition algorithms for parsing expression grammars have been presented in the literature, though none have combined efficient runtime performance with good worst-case bounds. Ford [4] introduced both the PEG formalism and two recognition algorithms: *recursive descent* (a direct translation of the functions in Fig. 1) and *packrat* (memoized recursive descent). The recursive descent algorithm has exponential worst-case runtime, though it behaves well in practice (as shown in Sect. 6); packrat improves the runtime bound to linear, but at the cost of best-case linear space usage. Ford [5] also showed that there exist PEGs to recognize non-context-free languages (*e.g.* $a^n b^n c^n$), and conjectured that some context-free languages exist for which there is no PEG. Mizushima *et al.* [11] have demonstrated the use of manually-inserted "cut operators" to trim memory usage of packrat parsing to a constant, while maintaining the asymptotic worst-case bounds; Kuramitsu [8] and Redziejowski [14] have built modified packrat parsers that use heuristic table-trimming mechanisms to achieve similar real-world performance without manual grammar modifications, but which sacrifice the polynomial worst-case runtime. Medeiros and Ierusalimschy [9] have developed a parsing machine for PEGs, similar in concept to a recursive descent parser, but somewhat faster in practice. Henglein and Rasmussen [7] have proved linear worst-case time and space bounds for their progressive tabular parsing algorithm, with some evidence of constant space usage in practice for a simple JSON grammar, but their work lacks empirical comparisons to other algorithms.

Moss [12] and Garnock-Jones *et al.* [6] have developed derivative parsing algorithms for PEGs. This paper extends the work of Moss, improving the theoretical quartic time and cubic space bounds by a linear factor each, and halving runtime in practice. Garnock-Jones *et al.* do not include empirical performance results for their work, but their approach elegantly avoids defining new parsing expressions through use of a *nullability combinator* to represent lookahead followers as later alternatives of an alternation expression.

3   Derivative Parsing

Though the backtracking capabilities of PEGs are responsible for much of their expressive power and ease-of-use, backtracking is also responsible for the worst-case resource bounds of existing algorithms. Recursive-descent parsing uses exponential time in the worst case to perform backtracking search, while packrat parsing trades this worst-case time for high best-case space usage. Derivative parsing presents a different trade-off, with low common-case memory usage paired with a polynomial time bound. A derivative parsing approach pursues all backtracking options concurrently, eliminating the repeated backtracking over the same input characteristic of worst-case recursive-descent, but also discarding bookkeeping information for infeasible options, saving space relative to packrat.

The essential idea of derivative parsing, first introduced by Brzozowski [3], is to iteratively transform an expression into an expression for the "rest" of the input. For example, given $\gamma = foo/bar/baz$, $d_b(\gamma) = ar/az$, the suffixes that can follow b in $\mathcal{L}(\gamma)$. After one derivative, the first character of the input has been consumed, and the grammar mutated to account for this missing character. Once repeated derivatives have been taken for every character in the input string, the resulting expression can be checked to determine whether or not it represents a match, *e.g.* $d_z \circ d_a \circ d_b(\gamma) = \varepsilon$, a matching result. Existing work shows how to compute the derivatives of regular expressions [3], context-free grammars [10], and parsing expression grammars [6,12]. This paper presents a simplified algorithm for parsing expression derivatives, as well as a formal proof of the correctness of this algorithm, an aspect lacking from the earlier presentations.

The difficulty in designing a derivative parsing algorithm for PEGs is simulating backtracking when the input must be consumed at each step, with no ability to re-process earlier input characters. Consider !$(ab)a$; ab and a must be parsed concurrently, and an initial match of a must be reversed if ab later matches. Alternations introduce further complications; consider $(!(ab)/a!c)a$: the final a must be parsed concurrently with !(ab), but also "held back" until after the a in $a!c$ has been matched. To track the connections among such backtracking choices, Moss [12] used a system of "backtracking generations" to label possible backtracking options for each expression, as well as a complex mapping algorithm to translate the backtracking generations of parsing expressions to the corresponding generations of their parent expressions. The key observation of the simplified algorithm presented here is that an index into the input string is sufficient to label backtracking choices consistently across all parsing expressions.

Typically [3,10,12], the derivative $d_c(\varphi)$ is a function from an expression φ and a character $c \in \Sigma$ to a derivative expression. Formally, $\mathcal{L}(d_c(\varphi)) = \{s \in \Sigma^* : cs \in \mathcal{L}(\varphi)\}$. This paper defines a derivative $d_{c,i}(\varphi)$, adding an index i for the current location in the input. This added index is used as a label to connect backtracking decisions across derivative subexpressions by annotation of certain parsing expressions. A sequence expression $\alpha\beta$ must track possible indices where α may have stopped consuming characters and β began to be parsed; to this end, $\alpha\beta$ is annotated with a list of *lookahead followers* $[\beta_{i_1} \cdots \beta_{i_k}]$, where β_{i_j} is the repeated derivative of β starting at each index i_j where α may have stopped consuming characters. To introduce this backtracking, ε and $!\alpha$, neither of which consume any characters, become ε_j, a match at index j, and $!_j\alpha$, a lookahead expression at index j. These annotated expressions are formally defined in Fig. 2; note that they produce either a string or fail under the same conditions as their equivalents in Fig. 1. Considered in isolation these extensions appear to introduce a dependency on the string $\mathbf{s}$ into the expression definition (given that $\mathbf{s}[k]$ is a suffix of $\mathbf{s}[j]$), but within the context of the derivative parsing algorithm any ε_j or $!_j$ must be in the α subexpression of a sequence expression $\alpha\beta[\beta_{i_1} \cdots \beta_{i_k}]$ and paired with a corresponding β_j lookahead follower such that $\beta(\mathbf{s}[j]) = \beta_j(\mathbf{s}[k])$, eliminating the dependency. Figure 3 defines a *normalization function* $\langle \bullet \rangle_i$ to annotate parsing expressions with their indices; derivative parsing of φ starts by taking $\langle \varphi \rangle_0$.

$$\varepsilon_j(\mathbf{s}[k]) = \mathbf{s}[j]$$

$$!_j\alpha(\mathbf{s}[k]) = \begin{cases} \mathbf{s}[j] & \alpha(\mathbf{s}[k]) = \text{fail} \\ \text{fail} & \text{otherwise} \end{cases}$$

$$\alpha\beta[\beta_{i_1} \cdots \beta_{i_k}](\mathbf{s}[k]) = \alpha\beta(\mathbf{s}[k])$$

Fig. 2. Formal definitions of added parsing expressions

$$\langle a \rangle_i = a \qquad\qquad \langle A \rangle_i = \langle \mathcal{R}(A) \rangle_i$$

$$\langle \varepsilon \rangle_i = \varepsilon_i$$
$$\langle \varnothing \rangle_i = \varnothing \qquad \langle \alpha\beta \rangle_i = \begin{cases} \langle \alpha \rangle_i \beta[\beta_i = \langle \beta \rangle_i] & \epsilon \in \mathcal{L}(\alpha) \\ \langle \alpha \rangle_i \beta[] & \text{otherwise} \end{cases}$$

$$\langle !\alpha \rangle_i = !_i \langle \alpha \rangle_i \qquad \langle \alpha/\beta \rangle_i = \langle \alpha \rangle_i / \langle \beta \rangle_i$$

Fig. 3. Definition of normalization function

Expressions that are known to always match their input provide opportunities for short-circuiting a derivative computation. For instance, if ν is an expression that is known to match, ν/β never tries the β alternative, while $!\nu$ always fails, allowing these expressions to be replaced by the simpler ν and $\varnothing$, respectively. A similar optimization opportunity arises when expressions that have stopped consuming input are later invalidated; the augmented sequence expression $\alpha\beta[\beta_{i_1} \cdots \beta_{i_k}]$ keeps an ongoing derivative β_j of β for each start position j that may be needed, so discarding unreachable β_j is essential for performance. Might *et al.* [10] dub this optimization "compaction" and demonstrate its importance to derivative performance; this work includes compaction in the derivative step based on functions *back* and *match* defined in Fig. 4 over normalized parsing expressions. By these definitions, based on [12], $back(\varphi)$ is the set of indices where φ may have stopped consuming input, while $match(\varphi)$ is the set of indices where φ matched. Note that $|match(\varphi)| \leq 1$ and the definition of $match(\alpha/\beta)$ depends on the invariant that the β alternative is discarded if α matches.

$$back(a) = \{\} \qquad\qquad match(a) = \{\}$$
$$back(\varepsilon_i) = \{i\} \qquad\qquad match(\varepsilon_i) = \{i\}$$
$$back(\varnothing) = \{\} \qquad\qquad match(\varnothing) = \{\}$$
$$back(!_i\alpha) = \{i\} \qquad\qquad match(!_i\alpha) = \{\}$$
$$back(\alpha\beta[\beta_{i_1} \cdots \beta_{i_k}]) \qquad\qquad match(\alpha\beta[\beta_{i_1} \cdots \beta_{i_k}])$$
$$= \cup_{j \in [i_1 \cdots i_k]} back(\beta_j) \qquad\qquad = \cup_{j \in match(\alpha)} match(\beta_j)$$
$$back(\alpha/\beta) = back(\alpha) \cup back(\beta) \qquad match(\alpha/\beta) = match(\beta)$$

Fig. 4. Definitions of *back* and *match*

With these preliminaries established, the derivative is defined in Fig. 5. The derivative consumes character literals, while preserving ε_j matches and $\varnothing$ failures. To a first approximation, the derivative distributes through lookahead and alternation, though match and failure results trigger expression simplification. The bulk of the work done by the algorithm is in the sequence expression $\alpha\beta$ derivative. At a high level, the sequence derivative takes the derivative of α, then updates the appropriate derivatives of β, selecting one if α matches. Any index j in $back(d_{c,i}(\alpha))$ where α may have stopped consuming input needs to be paired with a corresponding backtrack follower β_j; introducing a new follower β_i involves a normalization operation. Testing for a match at end-of-input is traditionally [3,6,10] handled in derivative parsing with a nullability combinator δ which reduces the grammar to ε or $\varnothing$; this work uses the derivative with respect to an end-of-input character $\# \notin \Sigma$ to implement this combinator. As such, if α matches at end-of-input, $d_{n,\#}(\langle\beta\rangle_n)$ must also be evaluated. As in previous work [10,12], $\langle\bullet\rangle_i$, $d_{c,i}$, *back*, and *match* are all memoized for performance.

The derivative with respect to a character can be extended to the derivative with respect to a string $\mathbf{s} = \mathbf{s}_1\mathbf{s}_2 \cdots \mathbf{s}_n$ by repeated application: $d_{\mathbf{s},i}(\varphi) = \left(d_{\mathbf{s}_n,i+n} \circ d_{\mathbf{s}_{n-1},i+n-1} \circ \cdots \circ d_{\mathbf{s}_1,i+1}\right)(\varphi)$. After augmentation with an initial normalization step and final end-of-input derivative, the overall derivative parsing

$$d_{c,i}(a) = \begin{cases} \varepsilon_i & c = \mathbf{a} \\ \varnothing & \text{otherwise} \end{cases}$$

$$d_{c,i}(\varepsilon_j) = \varepsilon_j$$

$$d_{c,i}(\varnothing) = \varnothing$$

$$d_{c,i}(!_j\alpha) = \begin{cases} \varnothing & match(d_{c,i}(\alpha)) \neq \{\} \\ \varepsilon_j & d_{c,i}(\alpha) = \varnothing \\ !_j d_{c,i}(\alpha) & \text{otherwise} \end{cases}$$

$$d_{c,i}(\alpha\beta[\beta_{i_1}\cdots\beta_{i_k}]) = \begin{cases} \varnothing & d_{c,i}(\alpha) = \varnothing \\ \langle\beta\rangle_i & d_{c,i}(\alpha) = \varepsilon_i \wedge c \neq \# \\ d_{c,i}(\langle\beta\rangle_i) & d_{c,i}(\alpha) = \varepsilon_i \wedge c = \# \\ d_{c,i}(\beta_j) & d_{c,i}(\alpha) = \varepsilon_j \wedge j < i \\ d_{c,i}(\alpha)\,\beta[\beta_j^\dagger : j \in back(d_{c,i}(\alpha))] & \text{otherwise, where} \\ & \quad \beta_i^\dagger = \langle\beta\rangle_i, \\ & \quad \beta_j^\dagger = d_{c,i}(\beta_j), j < i \end{cases}$$

$$d_{c,i}(\alpha/\beta) = \begin{cases} d_{c,i}(\beta) & d_{c,i}(\alpha) = \varnothing \\ d_{c,i}(\alpha) & d_{c,i}(\beta) = \varnothing \vee match(d_{c,i}(\alpha)) \neq \{\} \\ d_{c,i}(\alpha)\,/\,d_{c,i}(\beta) & \text{otherwise} \end{cases}$$

Fig. 5. Definition of derivative step; $\#$ is end-of-input

algorithm is then $\varphi^{(n)} = d_{\#,n+1} \circ d_{\mathbf{s},0}(\langle\varphi\rangle_0)$. If $\varphi^{(n)} = \varepsilon_j$, then $\varphi(\mathbf{s}) = \mathbf{s}[j]$, otherwise $\varphi(\mathbf{s}) = \text{fail}$. As an example, see Fig. 6.

4   Correctness

There is insufficient space in this paper to include a formal proof of the correctness of the presented algorithm. The author has produced such a proof, however; the general approach is outlined here.

$$\gamma = (!(ab)/a!c)a$$
$$\langle\gamma\rangle_0 = (!_0(ab[])/a!c[])a[\beta_0 = a]$$
$$d_{a,1}(\langle\gamma\rangle_0) = (!_0b/!_1c)a[\beta_0 = \varepsilon_1, \beta_1 = a]$$
$$d_{c,2} \circ d_{a,1}(\langle\gamma\rangle_0) = \varepsilon_1 \quad [\text{Note: } \beta_0 \text{ from } !_0b \text{ success}]$$
$$d_{\#,3} \circ d_{c,2} \circ d_{a,1}(\langle\gamma\rangle_0) = \varepsilon_1$$

Fig. 6. Derivative execution example on string ac

The proof makes extensive use of structural induction, thus it must also show that such induction terminates when applied to recursively-expanded non-terminals. If evaluation of a parsing expression involves a left-recursive call to a nonterminal, this evaluation never terminates; as such, left-recursive grammars are generally excluded from consideration. Ford [5, § 3.6] introduced the notion that a parsing expression is *well-formed* if it does not occur anywhere in its own recursive left-expansion or have any subexpression that does; Fig. 7 formalizes the immediate left-expansion LE and the recursive left-expansion LE^+ consistently with Ford's definition. The normalization step presented in this paper expands nonterminals left-recursively, eliminating recursive structure from the parsing expressions considered by the derivative algorithm; this expansion is safe for well-formed grammars.

$$LE(a) = \{\}$$
$$LE(\varepsilon) = \{\}$$
$$LE(\varepsilon_j) = \{\}$$
$$LE(\varnothing) = \{\}$$
$$LE(A) = \{\mathcal{R}(A)\}$$

$$LE(!\alpha) = \{\alpha\}$$
$$LE(!_j\alpha) = \{\alpha\}$$
$$LE(\alpha\beta) = \begin{cases} \{\alpha, \beta\} & \epsilon \in \mathcal{L}(\alpha) \\ \{\alpha\} & \text{otherwise} \end{cases}$$
$$LE(\alpha/\beta) = \{\alpha, \beta\}$$

$$LE(\alpha\beta[\beta_{i_1} \cdots \beta_{i_k}]) = \{\alpha, \beta_{i_1}, \cdots \beta_{i_k}\}$$
$$LE^+(\varphi) = LE(\varphi) \cup_{\gamma \in LE(\varphi)} LE^+(\gamma)$$

Fig. 7. Definition of LE left-expansion function and its transitive closure LE^+; LE computed by iteration to a fixed point.

To prove the equivalence of derivative parsing with recursive descent, it must be shown that normalization does not change the semantics of a parsing expression, that the derivative step performs the expected transformation of the language of an expression, and that the end-of-input derivative correctly implements the behavior of an expression on the empty string. In each of these cases, the proof proceeds by treating the relevant parsing expressions as functions over their input and proving that they produce equivalent results.

Proof of correctness of the derivative step depends on a number of invariant properties of the normalized parsing expressions (*e.g.* there is a lookahead follower β_j in $\alpha\beta[\beta_{i_1} \cdots \beta_{i_k}]$ for every ε_j that may arise from derivatives of α); these properties must be shown to be established by the $\langle \bullet \rangle_i$ function and maintained by $d_{c,i}$. Other lemmas needed to support the proof describe the dynamic behavior of the derivative algorithm (*e.g.* $match(\varphi)$ implies that the derivative of φ eventually becomes a ε_j success result).

Without appealing to a formal proof of correctness, it should be noted that the experimental results in Sect. 6 demonstrate successful matching of a large number of strings, and thus a low (possibly zero) false-negative rate for the derivative algorithm; further automated correctness tests are available with the source distribution [13].

5 Analysis

In [12], Moss demonstrated the polynomial worst-case space and time of his algorithm with an argument based on bounds on the depth and fanout of the DAG formed by his derivative expressions. These bounds, cubic space and quartic time, were improved to constant space and linear time for a broad class of "well-behaved" inputs with constant-bounded backtracking and depth of recursive invocation. This paper includes a similar analysis of the algorithm presented here, improving the worst-case bounds of the previous algorithm by a linear factor, to quadratic space and cubic time, while maintaining the optimal constant space and linear time bounds for the same class of "well-behaved" inputs.

For an input string of length n, the algorithm runs $O(n)$ derivative steps; the cost of each derivative step $d_{c,i}(\varphi)$ is the sum of the cost of the derivative algorithm in Fig. 5 on each expression node in the recursive left-expansion LE^+ of φ. Since by convention the size of the grammar is a constant, all operations on any expression γ from the original grammar (particularly $\langle \gamma \rangle_i$) run in constant time and space. It can be observed from the derivative step and index equations in Figs. 5 and 4 that once the appropriate subexpression derivatives have been calculated, the cost of a derivative step on a single expression node δ is proportional to the size of the immediate left-expansion of δ, $LE(\delta)$. Let b be the maximum $|LE(\delta)|$ over all $\delta \in LE^+(\varphi)$; by examination of Fig. 7, $|LE(\delta)|$ is bounded by the number of backtracking followers β_{i_j} in the annotated sequence expression. Since no more than one backtracking follower may be added per derivative step, $b \in O(n)$. Assuming $\langle \bullet \rangle_i$ is memoized for each i, only a constant number of expression nodes may be added to the expression at each derivative step, therefore $|LE^+(\varphi)| \in O(n)$. By this argument, the derivative parsing algorithm presented here runs in $O(n^2)$ worst-case space and $O(n^3)$ worst-case time, improving the previous space and time bounds for derivative parsing of PEGs by a linear factor each. This linear improvement over the algorithm presented in [12] is due to the new algorithm only storing $O(b)$ backtracking information in sequence nodes, rather than $O(b^2)$ as in the previous algorithm.

In practical use, the linear time and constant space results presented in [12] for inputs with constant-bounded backtracking and grammar nesting (a class that includes most source code and structured data) also hold for this algorithm. If b is bounded by a constant rather than its linear worst-case, the bounds discussed above are reduced to linear space and quadratic time. Since b is a bound on the size of $LE(\varphi)$, it can be seen from Fig. 7 that this is really a bound on sequence expression backtracking choices, which existing work including [12] has shown is often bounded by a constant in practical use.

Given that the bound on b limits the fanout of the derivative expression DAG, a constant bound on the depth of that DAG implies that the overall size of the DAG is similarly constant-bounded. Intuitively, the bound on the depth of the DAG is a bound on recursive invocations of a nonterminal by itself, applying a sort of "tail-call optimization" for right-recursive invocations such as $R_{\alpha*} := \alpha\, R_{\alpha*} \,/\, \varepsilon$. The conjunction of both of these bounds defines the class of "well-behaved" PEG inputs introduced by Moss in [12], and by the constant bound on derivative DAG size this algorithm also runs in constant space and linear time on such inputs.

6   Experimental Results

In addition to being easier to implement than the previous derivative parsing algorithm, the new parsing expression derivative also has superior performance.

To test this performance, the simplified parsing expression derivative (SPED) algorithm was compared against the parser-combinator-based recursive descent (Rec.) and packrat (Pack.) parsers used in [12], as well as the parsing expression derivative (PED) implementation from that paper. The same set of XML, JSON, and Java inputs and grammars used in [12] are used here; the inputs originally come from [11]. Code and test data are available online [13]. All tests were compiled with g++ 6.2.0 and run on a Windows system with 8 GB of RAM, a 2.6 GHz processor, and SSD main storage.

Figure 8 shows the runtime of all four algorithms on all three data sets, plotted against the input size; Fig. 9 shows the memory usage of the same runs, also plotted against the input size, but on a log-log scale.

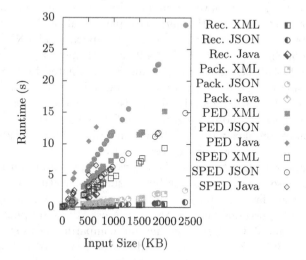

Fig. 8. Algorithm runtime with respect to input size; lower is better.

Contrary to its poor worst-case asymptotic performance, the recursive descent algorithm is actually best in practice, running most quickly on all tests,

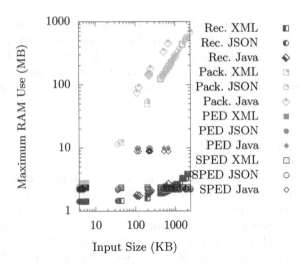

Fig. 9. Maximum algorithm memory use with respect to input size; lower is better.

and using the least memory on all but the largest inputs (where the derivative parsing algorithms' ability to not buffer input gives them an edge). Packrat parsing is consistently slower than recursive descent, while using two orders of magnitude more memory. The two derivative parsing algorithms have significantly slower runtime, but memory usage closer to recursive descent than packrat.

Though on these well-behaved inputs all four algorithms run in linear time and space (constant space for the derivative parsing algorithms), the constant factor differs by both algorithm and grammar complexity. The XML and JSON grammars are of similar complexity, with 23 and 24 nonterminals, respectively, and all uses of lookahead expressions $!\alpha$ and $\&\alpha$ eliminated by judicious use of the more specialized negative character class, end-of-input, and until expressions described in [12]. It is consequently unsurprising that the parsers have similar runtime performance on those two grammars. By contrast, the Java grammar is significantly more complex, with 178 nonterminals and 54 lookahead expressions, and correspondingly poorer runtime performance.

Both the packrat algorithm and the derivative parsing algorithm presented here trade increased space usage for better runtime. Naturally, this trade-off works more in their favour for more complex grammars, particularly those with more lookahead expressions, as suggested by Moss [12]. Grouping the broadly equivalent XML and JSON tests together and comparing mean speedup, recursive descent is 3.3x as fast as packrat and 18x as fast as SPED on XML and JSON, yet only 1.6x as fast as packrat and 3.7x as fast as SPED for Java. Packrat's runtime advantage over SPED also decreases from 5.5x to 2.3x between XML/JSON and Java.

Though the packrat algorithm is a modest constant factor faster than the derivative parsing algorithm across the test suite, it uses as much as 300x as much peak memory on the largest test cases, with the increases scaling linearly in the input size. Derivative parsing, by contrast, maintains a grammar-dependent constant memory usage across all the (well-behaved) inputs tested. This constant memory usage is within a factor of two on either side of the memory usage of the recursive descent implementation on all the XML and JSON inputs tested, and 3–5x more on the more complex Java grammar. The higher memory usage on Java is likely due to the lookahead expressions, which are handled with runtime backtracking in recursive descent, but extra concurrently-processed expressions in derivative parsing.

Derivative parsing in general is known to have poor runtime performance [1, 10], as these results also demonstrate. However, this new algorithm does provide a significant improvement on the current state of the art for parsing expression derivatives, with a 40% speedup on XML and JSON, a 50% speedup on Java, and an up to 13% decrease in memory usage. This improved performance may be beneficial for use cases that specifically require the derivative computation, such as the modular parsers of Brachthäuser *et al.* [2] or the sentence generator of Garnock-Jones *et al.* [6].

7   Conclusion and Future Work

This paper has introduced a new derivative parsing algorithm for PEGs based on the previously-published algorithm in [12]. Its key contributions are simplification of the earlier algorithm and empirical comparison of this new algorithm to previous work. The simplified algorithm also improves the worst-case space and time bounds of the previous algorithm by a linear factor. The author has produced a formal proof of correctness for this simplified algorithm, but was unable to include it in this paper due to space constraints.

While extension of this recognition algorithm to a parsing algorithm remains future work, any such extension may rely on the fact that successfully recognized parsing expressions produce a ε_e expression in this algorithm, where e is the index where the last character was consumed. As one approach, $\langle \bullet \rangle_b$ might annotate parsing expressions with b, the index where they began to consume characters. By collecting subexpression matches and combining the two indices b and e on a successful match, this algorithm should be able to return a parse tree on match, rather than simply a recognition decision. The parser derivative approach of Might *et al.* [10] may be useful here, with the added simplification that PEGs, unlike CFGs, have no more than one valid parse tree, and thus do not need to store multiple possible parses in a single node.

References

1. Adams, M.D., Hollenbeck, C., Might, M.: On the complexity and performance of parsing with derivatives. In: Proceedings of the 37th ACM SIGPLAN Conference on Programming Language Design and Implementation, PLDI 2016, pp. 224–236. ACM, New York (2016)

2. Brachthäuser, J.I., Rendel, T., Ostermann, K.: Parsing with first-class derivatives. In: Proceedings of the 2016 ACM SIGPLAN International Conference on Object-Oriented Programming, Systems, Languages, and Applications, OOPSLA 2016, pp. 588–606. ACM, New York (2016)
3. Brzozowski, J.A.: Derivatives of regular expressions. J. ACM (JACM) **11**(4), 481–494 (1964)
4. Ford, B.: Packrat parsing: a practical linear-time algorithm with backtracking. Master's thesis, Massachusetts Institute of Technology, September 2002
5. Ford, B.: Parsing expression grammars: a recognition-based syntactic foundation. In: ACM SIGPLAN Notices, vol. 39, no. 1, pp. 111–122. ACM (2004)
6. Garnock-Jones, T., Eslamimehr, M., Warth, A.: Recognising and generating terms using derivatives of parsing expression grammars. arXiv preprint arXiv:1801.10490 (2018)
7. Henglein, F., Rasmussen, U.T.: PEG parsing in less space using progressive tabling and dynamic analysis. In: Proceedings of the 2017 ACM SIGPLAN Workshop on Partial Evaluation and Program Manipulation, PEPM 2017, pp. 35–46. ACM, New York (2017)
8. Kuramitsu, K.: Packrat parsing with elastic sliding window. J. Inf. Process. **23**(4), 505–512 (2015)
9. Medeiros, S., Ierusalimschy, R.: A parsing machine for PEGs. In: Proceedings of the 2008 Symposium on Dynamic Languages, DLS 2008, pp. 2:1–2:12. ACM, New York (2008)
10. Might, M., Darais, D., Spiewak, D.: Parsing with derivatives: a functional pearl. In: ACM SIGPLAN Notices, vol. 46, no. 9, pp. 189–195. ACM (2011)
11. Mizushima, K., Maeda, A., Yamaguchi, Y.: Packrat parsers can handle practical grammars in mostly constant space. In: Proceedings of the 9th ACM SIGPLAN-SIGSOFT workshop on Program analysis for software tools and engineering. pp. 29–36. ACM (2010)
12. Moss, A.: Derivatives of parsing expression grammars. In: Proceedings of the 15th International Conference on Automata and Formal Languages, AFL 2017, Debrecen, Hungary, 4–6 September 2017, pp. 180–194 (2017). https://doi.org/10.4204/EPTCS.252.18
13. Moss, A.: Egg (2018). https://github.com/bruceiv/egg/tree/deriv
14. Redziejowski, R.R.: Parsing expression grammar as a primitive recursive-descent parser with backtracking. Fundam. Inform. **79**(3–4), 513–524 (2007)

Complete Variable-Length Codes: An Excursion into Word Edit Operations

Jean Néraud$^{(\boxtimes)}$ [iD]

Université de Rouen, Laboratoire d'Informatique, de Traitement de l'Information et
des Systèmes, Avenue de l'Université, 76800 Saint-Étienne-du-Rouvray, France
jean.neraud@univ-rouen.fr, neraud.jean@gmail.com
http://neraud.jean.free.fr

Abstract. Given an alphabet A and a binary relation $\tau \subseteq A^* \times A^*$, a
language $X \subseteq A^*$ is *τ-independent* if $\tau(X) \cap X = \emptyset$; X is *τ-closed* if
$\tau(X) \subseteq X$. The language X is *complete* if any word over A is a factor
of some concatenation of words in X. Given a family of languages $\mathcal{F}$
containing X, X is maximal in $\mathcal{F}$ if no other set of $\mathcal{F}$ can strictly contain
X. A language $X \subseteq A^*$ is a *variable-length* code if any equation among
the words of X is necessarily trivial. The study discusses the relationship
between maximality and completeness in the case of τ-independent or
τ-closed variable-length codes. We focus to the binary relations by which
the images of words are computed by deleting, inserting, or substituting
some characters.

Keywords: Closed · Code · Complete · Deletion · Detection ·
Dependent · Distribution · Edition · Embedding · Independent ·
Insertion · Levenshtein · Maximal · String · Substitution · Substring ·
Subword · Variable-length · Word

1 Introduction

In formal language theory, given a property $\mathcal{F}$, the *embedding problem* with
respect to $\mathcal{F}$ consists in examining whether a language X satisfying $\mathcal{F}$ can be
included into some language $\hat{X}$ that is *maximal* with respect to $\mathcal{F}$, in the sense
that no language satisfying $\mathcal{F}$ can strictly contain $\hat{X}$. In the literature, maximality is often connected to completeness: a language X over the alphabet A is
complete if any string in the free monoid A^* (the set of the words over A) is a
factor of some word of X^* (the submonoid of all concatenations of words in X).
Such connection takes on special importance for codes: a language X over the
alphabet A is a *variable-length code* (for short, a *code*) if every equation among
the *words* (i.e. *strings*) of X is necessarily trivial.

A famous result due to M.P. Schützenberger states that, for the family of the
so-called *thin* codes (which contains *regular* codes and therefore also finite ones),
being maximal is equivalent to being complete. In connection with these two
concepts lots of challenging theoretical questions have been stated. For instance,

© Springer Nature Switzerland AG 2020
A. Leporati et al. (Eds.): LATA 2020, LNCS 12038, pp. 437–448, 2020.
https://doi.org/10.1007/978-3-030-40608-0_31

to this day the problem of the existence of a finite maximal code containing a given finite one is not known to be decidable. From this latter point of view, in [16] the author asked the question of the existence of a regular complete code containing a given finite one: a positive answer was brought in [4], where was provided a now classical formula for embedding a given regular code into some complete regular one. Famous families of codes have also been concerned by those studies: we mention *prefix* and *bifix* codes [2, Theorem 3.3.8, Proposition 6.2.1], codes with a *finite deciphering delay* [3], *infix* [10], *solid* [11], or *circular* [13].

Actually, with each of those families, a so-called *dependence system* can be associated. Formally, such a system is a family $\mathcal{F}$ of languages constituted by those sets X that contain a non-empty finite subset in $\mathcal{F}$. Languages in $\mathcal{F}$ are $\mathcal{F}$-*dependent*, the other ones being $\mathcal{F}$-*independent*. A special case corresponds to binary words relations $\tau \subseteq A^* \times A^*$, where a dependence systems is constituted by those sets X satisfying $\tau \cap (X \times X) \neq \emptyset$: X is τ-*independent* if we have $\tau(X) \cap X = \emptyset$ (with $\tau(X) = \{y : \exists x \in X, (x,y) \in \tau\}$). *Prefix codes* certainly constitute the best known example: they constitute those codes that are independent with respect to the relation obtained by removing each pair (x,x) from the famous *prefix* order. Bifix, infix or solid codes can be similarly characterized.

As regards to dependence, some extremal condition corresponds to the so-called *closed* sets: given a word relation $\tau \subseteq A^* \times A^*$, a language X is closed under τ (τ-*closed*, for short) if we have $\tau(X) \subseteq X$. Lots of topics are concerned by the notion. We mention the framework of prefix order where a one-to-one correspondence between independent and closed sets is provided in [2, Proposition 3.1.3] (cf. also [1,18]). Congruences in the free monoid are also concerned [15], as well as their connections to DNA computing [7]. With respect to morphisms, involved topics are also provided by the famous L-systems [17] and, in the case of one-to-one (anti)-automorphisms, the so-called *invariant* sets [14].

As commented in [6], maximality and completeness concern the economy of a code. If X is a complete code then every word occurs as part of a message, hence no part of X^* is potentially useless. The present paper emphasizes the following questions: given a regular binary relation $\tau \subseteq A^* \times A^*$, in the family of regular τ-independent (-closed) codes, are maximality and completeness equivalent notions? Given a non-complete regular τ-independent (-closed) code, is it embeddable into some complete one?

Independence has some peculiar importance in the framework of coding theory. Informally, given some concatenation of words in X, each codeword $x \in X$ is transmitted via a channel into a corresponding $y \in A^*$. According to the combinatorial structure of X, and the type of channel, one has to make use of codes with prescribed error-detecting constraints: some minimum-distance restraint is generally applied. In this paper, where we consider variable length codewords, we address to the Levenshtein metric [12]: given two different words x, y, their distance is the minimal total number of elementary edit operations that can transform x into y, such operation consisting in a one character *deletion*, *insertion*, or *substitution*. Formally, it is the smallest integer p such that we have $y \in \Lambda_p(x)$, with $\Lambda_p = \bigcup_{1 \leq k \leq p}(\delta_1 \cup \iota_1 \cup \sigma_1)^k$, where δ_k, ι_k, σ_k are further defined below.

From the point of view of error detection, X being Λ_p-independent guarantees that $y \in \Lambda_p(x)$ implies $y \neq x$. In addition, a code satisfies the property of error correction if its elements are such that $\Lambda_p(x) \cap \Lambda_p(y) = \emptyset$ unless $x = y$: according to [9, chap. 6], the existence of such codes is decidable. Denote by $\mathrm{Subw}(x)$ the set of the subsequences of x:

- δ_k, the k-*character deletion*, associates with every word $x \in A^*$, all the words $y \in \mathrm{Subw}(x)$ whose length is $|x| - k$. The *at most p-character deletion* is $\Delta_p = \bigcup_{1 \leq k \leq p} \delta_k$;
- ι_k, the k-*character insertion*, is the converse relation of δ_k and we set $I_p = \bigcup_{1 \leq k \leq p} \iota_k$ (*at most p-character insertion*);
- σ_k, the k-*character substitution*, associates with every $x \in A^*$, all $y \in A^*$ with length $|x|$ such that y_i (the letter of position i in y), differs of x_i in exactly k positions $i \in [1, |x|]$; we set $\Sigma_p = \bigcup_{1 \leq k \leq p} \sigma_k$;
- We denote by $\underline{\Lambda}_p$ the antireflexive relation obtained by removing all pairs (x, x) from Λ_p (we have $\Lambda_1 = \underline{\Lambda}_1$).

For short, we will refer the preceding relations to *edit relations*. For reasons of consistency, in the whole paper we assume $|A| \geq 2$ and $k \geq 1$. In what follows, we draw the main contributions of the study:

Firstly, we prove that, given a positive integer k, the two families of languages that are independent with respect to δ_k or ι_k are identical. In addition, for $k \geq 2$, no set can be Λ_k-independent. We establish the following result:

Theorem A. *Let A be a finite alphabet, $k \geq 1$, and $\tau \in \{\delta_k, \iota_k, \sigma_k, \Delta_k, I_k, \Sigma_k, \underline{\Lambda}_k\}$. Given a regular τ-independent code $X \subseteq A^*$, X is complete if, and only if, it is maximal in the family of τ-independent codes.*

A code X is $\underline{\Lambda}_k$-independent if the Levenshtein distance between two distinct words of X is always larger than k: from this point of view, Theorem A states some noticeable characterization of maximal k-error detecting codes in the framework of the Levenshtein metric.

Secondly, we explore the domain of closed codes. A noticeable fact is that for any k, there are only finitely many δ_k-closed codes and they have finite cardinality. Furthermore, one can decide whether a given non-complete δ_k-closed code can be embedded into some complete one. We also prove that no closed code can exist with respect to the relations ι_k, Δ_k, I_k.

As regard to substitutions, beforehand, we focus to the structure of the set $\sigma_k^*(w) = \bigcup_{i \in \mathbb{N}} \sigma_k^i$. Actually, excepted for two special cases (that is, $k = 1$ [5,19], or $k = 2$ with $|A| = 2$ [8, ex. 8, p.77]), to our best knowledge, in the literature no general description is provided. In any event we provide such a description; furthermore we establish the following result:

Theorem B. *Let A be a finite alphabet and $k \geq 1$. Given a complete σ_k-closed code $X \subseteq A^*$, either every word in X has length not greater than k, or a unique integer $n \geq k + 1$ exists such that $X = A^n$. In addition for every $\Sigma_k (\Lambda_k)$-closed code X, some positive integer n exists such that $X = A^n$.*

In other words, no σ_k-closed code can simultaneously possess words in $A^{\leq k}$ and words in $A^{\geq k+1}$. As a consequence, one can decide whether a given non-complete σ_k-closed code $X \subseteq A^*$ is embeddable into some complete one.

2   Preliminaries

We adopt the notation of the free monoid theory. Given a word w, we denote by $|w|$ its length; for $a \in A$, $|w|_a$ denotes the number of occurrences of the letter a in w. The set of the words whose length is not greater (not smaller) than n is denoted by $A^{\leq n}$ ($A^{\geq n}$). Given $x \in A^*$ and $w \in A^+$, we say that x is a *factor* of w if words u, v exist such that $w = uxv$; a *subword* of w consists in any (perhaps empty) subsequence $w_{i_1} \cdots w_{i_n}$ of $w = w_1 \cdots w_{|w|}$. We denote by $\mathrm{F}(X)$ ($\mathrm{Subw}(X)$) the set of the words that are factor (subword) of some word in X (we have $X \subseteq \mathrm{F}(X) \subseteq \mathrm{Subw}(X)$). A pair of words w, w' is *overlapping-free* if no pair u, v exist such that $uw' = wv$ or $w'u = vw$, with $1 \leq |u| \leq |w| - 1$ and $1 \leq |v| \leq |w'| - 1$; if $w = w'$, we say that w itself is overlapping-free.

It is assumed that the reader has a fundamental understanding with the main concepts of the theory of variable-length codes: we suggest, if necessary, that he (she) report to [2]. A set X is a *variable-length code* (a *code* for short) if for any pair of sequences of words in X, say $(x_i)_{1 \leq i \leq n}$, $(y_j)_{1 \leq j \leq p}$, the equation $x_1 \cdots x_n = y_1 \cdots y_p$ implies $n = p$, and $x_i = y_i$ for each integer i (equivalently the submonoid X^* is *free*). The two following results are famous ones from the variable-length codes theory:

Theorem 1. Schützenberger [2, Theorem 2.5.16] *Let $X \subseteq A^*$ be a regular code. Then the following properties are equivalent:*

 (i) *X is complete;*
 (ii) *X is a maximal code;*
 (iii) *a positive Bernoulli distribution π exists such that $\pi(X) = 1$;*
 (iv) *for every positive Bernoulli distribution π we have $\pi(X) = 1$.*

Theorem 2. [4]   *Given a non-complete code X, let $y \in A^* \setminus \mathrm{F}(X^*)$ be an overlapping-free word and $U = A^* \setminus (X^* \cup A^*yA^*)$. Then $Y = X \cup y(Uy)^*$ is a complete code.*

With regard to word relations, the following statement comes from the definitions:

Lemma 3. *Let $\tau \in A^* \times A^*$ and $X \subseteq A^*$. Each of the following properties holds:*

 (i) *X is τ-independent if, and only if, it is τ^{-1}-independent (τ^{-1} denotes the converse relation of τ).*
 (ii) *X is $\delta_k(\Delta_k)$-independent if, and only if, it is $\iota_k(I_k)$-independent.*
 (iii) *X is τ-closed if, and only if, it is τ^*-closed.*

3   Complete Independent Codes

We start by providing a few examples:

Example 4. For $A = \{a, b\}$, $k = 1$, the prefix code $X = a^*b$ is not δ_k-independent (we have $a^{n-1}b \in \delta_k(a^n b)$), whereas the following codes are δ_1-independent:

- the regular code: $Y = \{a^2\}^+ \{b, aba, abb\}$. Note that since it contains $\{a^2\}^+$, $\delta_1(Y)$ is not a code.
- the non-complete finite bifix code $Z = \{ab^2, ba^2\}$: actually, $\delta_1(Z)$ is the complete uniform code A^2.
- for every pair of different integers $n, p \geq 2$, the prefix code $T = aA^n \cup bA^p$. We have $\delta_1(T) = A^n \cup A^p$, which is not a code, although it is complete.

In view of establishing the main result of Sect. 3, we will construct some peculiar word:

Lemma 5. *Let $k \geq 1$, $i \in [1, k]$, $\tau \in \{\delta_i, \iota_i, \sigma_i\}$. Given a non-complete code $X \subseteq A^*$ some overlapping-free word $y \in A^* \setminus F(X^*)$ exists such that $\tau(y)$ does not intersect X and $y \notin \tau(X)$.*

Proof. Let X be a non-complete code, and let $w \in A^* \setminus F(X^*)$. Trivially, we have $w^{k+1} \notin F(X^*)$. Moreover, in a classical way a word $u \in A^*$ exists such that $y = w^{k+1}u$ is overlapping-free (e.g. [2, Proposition 1.3.6]). Since we assume $i \in [1, k]$, each word in $\tau(y)$ is constructed by deleting (inserting, substituting) at most k letters from y, hence by construction it contains at least one occurrence of w as a factor. This implies $\tau(y) \cap F(X^*) = \emptyset$, thus $\tau(y)$ does not intersect X.

By contradiction, assume that a word $x \in X$ exists such that $y \in \tau(x)$. It follows from $\delta_k^{-1} = \iota_k$ and $\sigma_k^{-1} = \sigma_k$ that $y = w^{k+1}u$ is obtained by deleting (inserting, substituting) at most k letters from x: consequently at least one occurrence of w appears as a factor of $x \in X \subseteq F(X^*)$: this contradicts $w \notin F(X^*)$, therefore we obtain $y \notin \tau(X)$ (cf. Fig. 1).   □

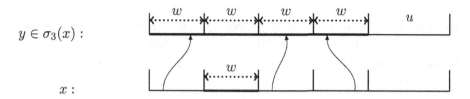

$y \in \sigma_3(x)$:

x :

Fig. 1. Proof of Lemma 5: $y \in \tau(X)$ implies $w \in F(X)$; for $i = k = 3$ and $y = w^4 u$, the action of the substitution $\tau = \sigma_3$ is represented in some extremal condition.

As a consequence, we obtain the following result:

Theorem 6. *Let $k \geq 1$ and $\tau \in \{\delta_k, \iota_k, \sigma_k\}$. Given a regular τ-independent code $X \subseteq A^*$, X is complete if, and only if, it is maximal as a τ-independent codes.*

Proof. According to Theorem 1, every complete τ-independent code is a maximal code, hence it is maximal in the family of τ-independent codes. For proving the converse, we make use of the contrapositive. Let X be a non-complete τ-independent code, and let $y \in A^* \setminus F(X^*)$ satisfying the conditions of Lemma 5. With the notation of Theorem 2, necessarily $X \cup \{y\}$, which is a subset of $Y = X \cup y(Uy)^*$, is a code. According to Lemma 5, we have $\tau(y) \cap X = \tau(X) \cap \{y\} = \emptyset$. Since X is τ-independent and τ antireflexive, this implies $\tau(X \cup \{y\}) \cap (X \cup \{y\}) = \emptyset$, thus X non-maximal as a τ-independent code. $\square$

We notice that for $k \geq 2$ no Λ_k-independent set can exist (indeed, we have $x \in \sigma_1^2(x) \subseteq \Lambda_k(x)$). However, the following result holds:

Corollary 7. *Let $\tau \in \{\Delta_k, I_k, \Sigma_k, \underline{\Lambda}_k\}$. Given a regular τ-independent code $X \subseteq A^*$, X is complete if, and only if, it is maximal as a τ-independent code.*

Proof. As indicated above, if X is complete, it is maximal as a τ-independent code. For the converse, once more we argue by contrapositive that is, with the notation of Lemma 5, we prove that $X \cup \{y\}$ remains independent. By definition, for each $\tau \in \{\Delta_k, I_k, \Sigma_k, \underline{\Lambda}_k\}$, we have $\tau \subseteq \bigcup_{1 \leq i \leq k} \tau_i$, with $\tau_i \in \{\delta_i, \iota_i, \sigma_i\}$. According to Lemma 5, since τ_i is antireflexive, for each $i \in [1, k]$ we have $\tau_i(X \cup \{y\}) \cap (X \cup \{y\}) = \emptyset$: this implies $(X \cup \{y\}) \cap \bigcup_{1 \leq i \leq k} \tau_i(X \cup \{y\}) = \emptyset$, thus $X \cup \{y\}$ is τ-independent. $\square$

With regard to the relation $\underline{\Lambda}_k$, Corollary 7 expresses some interesting property in term of error detection. Indeed, as indicated in Sect. 1, every code is $\underline{\Lambda}_k$-independent if the Levenshtein distance between its (distinct) elements is always larger than k. From this point of view, Corollary 7 states some characterization of the maximality in the family of such codes.

It should remain to develop some method in view of embedding a given non-complete $\underline{\Lambda}_k$-code into a complete one. Since the construction from the proof Theorem 2 does not preserve independence, this question remains open.

4   Complete Closed Codes with Respect to Deletion or Insertion

We start with the relation δ_k. A noticeable fact is that corresponding closed codes are necessarily finite, as attested by the following result:

Proposition 8. *Given a δ_k-closed code X, and $x \in X$, we have $|x| \in [1, k^2 - k - 1] \setminus \{k\}$.*

Proof. It follows from $\varepsilon \notin X$ and X being δ_k-closed that $|x| \neq k$. By contradiction, assume $|x| \geq (k-1)k$ and let q, r be the unique pair of integers such that $|x| = qk + r$, with $0 \leq r \leq k - 1$. Since we have $0 \leq rk \leq (k-1)k \leq |x|$, an integer $s \geq 0$ exists such that $|x| = rk + s$, thus words $x_1, \cdots, x_k, y$ exist such that $x = x_1 \cdots x_k y$, with $|x_1| = \cdots = |x_k| = r$ and $|y| = s$. By construction, every word $t \in \mathrm{Sub}(x)$ with $|t| \in \{r, s\}$ belongs to $\delta_k^*(x) \subseteq X$ (indeed, we have $r = |x| - qk$ and $s = |x| - rk$). This implies $x_1, \cdots, x_k, y \in X$, thus $x \in X^{k+1} \cap X$: a contradiction with X being a code. $\square$

Example 9. (1) According to Proposition 8, no code can be δ_1-closed. This can
be also drawn from the fact that, for every set $X \subseteq A^+$ we have $\varepsilon \in \delta_1^*(X)$.
(2) Let $A = \{a, b\}$ and $k = 3$. According to Proposition 8, every word in any
δ_k-closed code has length not greater than 5. It is straightforward to verify
that $X = \{a^2, ab, b^2, a^4b, ab^4\}$ is a δ_k-closed code. In addition, a finite number
of examinations lead to verify that X is maximal as a δ_k-closed code. Taking
for π the uniform distribution we have $\pi(X) = 3/4 + 1/16 < 1$: thus X is
non-complete.

According to Example 9(2), no result similar to Theorem 6 can be stated in the
framework of δ_k-closed codes. We also notice that, in Proposition 8 the bound
does not depend of the size of the alphabet, but only depends of k.

Corollary 10. *Given a finite alphabet A and a positive integer k, one can decide
whether a non-complete δ_k-closed code $X \subseteq A^*$ is included into some complete
one. In addition there are a finite number of such complete codes, all of them
being computable, if any.*

Proof. According to Proposition 8 only a finite number of δ_k-closed codes over
A can exist, each of them being a subset of $A^{\leq k^2 - k - 1} \setminus A^k$. □

We close the section by considering the relations Δ_k, ι_k and I_k:

Proposition 11. *No code can be ι_k-closed, Δ_k-closed, nor I_k-closed.*

Proof. By contradiction assume that some ι_k-closed code $X \subseteq A^*$ exists. Let
$x \in X$, $n = |x|$ and $u, v \in A^*$ such that $x = uv$. It follows from $|(vu)^k| = kn$,
that $u(vu)^k v \in \iota_k^*(x)$. According to Lemma 3(iii), we have $\iota_k^*(X) \subseteq X$, thus
$u(vu)^k v \in X$. Since $u(vu)^k v = (uv)^{k+1} = x^{k+1} \in X^{k+1}$, we have $X^{k+1} \cap X \neq$
$\emptyset$: a contradiction with X being a code. Consequently no I_k-closed codes can
exist. According to Example 9(1), given a code $X \subseteq A^*$, we have $\delta_1(X) \not\subseteq X$:
this implies $\Delta_k(X) \not\subseteq X$, thus X not Δ_k-closed. □

5 Complete Codes Closed Under Substitutions

Beforehand, given a word $w \in A^+$, we need a thorough description of the set
$\sigma_k^*(w)$. Actually, it is well known that, over a binary alphabet, all n-bit words can
be computed by making use of some Gray sequence [5]. With our notation, we
have $A^n = \sigma_1^*(w)$. Furthermore, for every finite alphabet A, the so-called $|A|$-
arity Gray sequences allow to generate A^n [8,19]: once more we have $\sigma_1^*(w) =$
A^n. In addition, in the special case where $k = 2$ and $|A| = 2$, it can be proved
that we have $|\sigma_2(w)| = 2^{n-1}$ [8, Exercise 8, p. 28]. However, except in these
special cases, to the best of our knowledge no general description of the structure
of $\sigma_k^*(w)$ appears in the literature. In any event, in the next paragraph we provide
an exhaustive description of $\sigma_k(w)$. Strictly speaking, the proofs, that we have
reported in Sect. 5.2, are not involved in σ_k-closed codes: we suggest the reader
that, in a first reading, after Sect. 5.1 he (she) directly jumps to Sect. 5.3.

5.1 Basic Results Concerning $\sigma_k^*(w)$

Proposition 12. *Assume $|A| \geq 3$. For each $w \in A^{\geq k}$, we have $\sigma_k^*(w) = A^{|w|}$.*

In the case where A is a binary alphabet, we set $A = \{0,1\}$: this allows a well-known algebraic interpretation of σ_k. Indeed, denote by $\oplus$ the addition in the group $\mathbb{Z}/2\mathbb{Z}$ with identity 0, and fix a positive integer n; given $w, w' \in A^n$, define $w \oplus w'$ as the unique word of A^n such that, for each $i \in [1,n]$, the letter of position i in $w \oplus w'$ is $w_i \oplus w_i'$. With this notation the sets A^n and $(\mathbb{Z}/2\mathbb{Z})^n$ are in one-to-one correspondence. Classically, we have $w' \in \sigma_1(w)$ if, and only if, some $u \in A^n$ exists such that $w' = w \oplus u$ with $|u|_1 = 1$ (thus $|u|_0 = n-1$). From the fact that $\sigma_k(w) \subseteq \sigma_1^k(w)$, the following property holds:

$$w' \in \sigma_k(w) \Longleftrightarrow \exists u \in A^n : w = w' \oplus u, \ |u|_1 = k. \tag{1}$$

In addition $w \oplus u = w'$ is equivalent to $u = w \oplus w'$. Let $d = |\{i \in [1,n] : w_i = w_i' = 1\}|$. The following property follows from $|u|_1 = (|w|_1 - d) + (|w'|_1 - d)$ and $|w|_1 + |w'|_1 = |w_1| + |w'|_1 - 2|w'|_1 \pmod 2$:

$$|w|_1 + |w'|_1 = |w_1| - |w'|_1 \pmod 2 = |u|_1 \pmod 2. \tag{2}$$

Finally, for $a \in A$ we denote by $\bar{a}$ its complementary letter that is, $\bar{a} = a \oplus 1$; for $w \in A^n$ we set $\overline{w} = \overline{w}_1 \cdots \overline{w}_n$.

Lemma 13. *Let $A = \{0,1\}$, $n \geq k+1$. Given $w, w' \in A^n$ the two following properties hold:*

(i) *If k is even and $w' \in \sigma_k^*(w)$ then $|w'|_1 - |w|_1$ is an even integer;*
(ii) *If $|w'|_1 - |w|_1$ is even then we have $w' \in \sigma_k^*(w)$, for every $k \geq 1$.*

Given a positive integer n, we denote A_0^n (A_1^n) the set of the words $w \in A^n$ such that $|w|_1$ is even (odd).

Proposition 14. *Assume $|A| = 2$. Given $w \in A^{\geq k}$ exactly one of the following conditions holds:*

(i) $|w| \geq k+1$, k *is even, and* $\sigma_k^*(w) \in \{A_0^{|w|}, A_1^{|w|}\}$;
(ii) $|w| \geq k+1$, k *is odd, and* $\sigma_k^*(w) = A^{|w|}$;
(iii) $|w| = k$ *and* $\sigma_k^*(w) = \{w, \overline{w}\}$.

5.2 Proofs of the Statements 12, 13 and 14

Actually, Proposition 12 is a consequence of the following property:

Lemma 15. *Assume $|A| \geq 3$. For every word $w \in A^{\geq k}$ we have $\sigma_1(w) \subseteq \sigma_k^2(w)$.*

Proof. Let $w' \in \sigma_1(w)$ and $n = |w| = |w'| \geq k$. We prove that $w'' \in A^*$ exists with $w'' \in \sigma_k(w)$ and $w' \in \sigma_k(w'')$. By construction, $i_0 \in [1,n]$ exists such that:

(a) $w_i' = w_i$ if, and only if, $i \neq i_0$.

It follows from $k \leq n$ that some $(k-1)$-element subset $I \subseteq [1,n] \setminus \{i_0\}$ exists. Since we have $|A| \geq 3$, some letter $c \in A \setminus \{w_{i_0}, w_{i_0}'\}$ exists. Let $w'' \in A^n$ such that:

(b) $w_{i_0}'' = c$ and, for each $i \neq i_0$: $w_i'' \neq w_i$ if, and only if, $i \in I$.

By construction we have $w'' \in \sigma_k(w)$, moreover $c \neq w_{i_0}'$ implies $w_{i_0}' \neq w_{i_0}''$. According to (a) and (b), we obtain:

(c) $w_{i_0}' \neq c = w_{i_0}''$,

(d) $w_i' = w_i \neq w_i''$ if $i \in I$, and:

(e) $w_i' = w_i = w_i''$ if $i \notin I \cup \{i_0\}$.

Since we have $|I \cup \{i_0\}| = k$, this implies $w' \in \sigma_k(w'')$.   □

Proof of Proposition 12. Let $w' \in A^n \setminus \{w\}$: we prove that $w' \in \sigma_k^*(w)$. Let $I = \{i_0, \cdots, i_p\} = \{i \in [1,n] : w_i' \neq w_i\}$ and let $(w^{(i_j)})_{0 \leq j \leq p}$ be a sequence of words such that $w = w^{(i_0)}$, $w^{(i_p)} = w'$ and, for each $j \in [0, p-1]$: $w_\ell^{(i_{j+1})} \neq w_\ell^{(i_j)}$ if, and only if, $\ell = i_{j+1}$. Since we have $w^{(i_{j+1})} \in \sigma_1(w^{(i_j)})$ $(1 \leq j < p)$, by induction over j we obtain $w' \in \sigma_1^*(w)$ thus, according to Lemma 15: $w' \in \sigma_k^*(w)$.   □

In view of proving Lemma 13 and Proposition 14, we need some new lemma:

Lemma 16. *Assume* $|A| = 2$. *For every* $w \in A^{\geq k+1}$, *we have* $\sigma_2(w) \subseteq \sigma_k^2(w)$.

Proof. Set $A = \{0,1\}$. It follows from $\sigma_2 \subseteq \sigma_1^2$ that the result holds for $k = 1$. Assume $k \geq 2$ and let $n = |w|$, $w' \in \sigma_2(w)$. By construction, there are distinct integers $i_0, j_0 \in [1,n]$ such that the following holds:

(a) $w_i' = \overline{w_i}$ if, and only if, $i \in \{i_0, j_0\}$.

Since some $(k-1)$-element set $I \subseteq [1,n] \setminus \{i_0, j_0\}$ exists, $w'', w''' \in A^n$ exist with:

(b) $w_i'' = \overline{w_i}$ if, and only if, $i \in \{i_0\} \cup I$, and:

(c) $w_i''' = \overline{w_i''}$ if, and only if, $i \in \{j_0\} \cup I$.

By construction, we have $w'' \in \sigma_k(w)$ and $w''' \in \sigma_k(w'')$, thus $w''' \in \sigma_k^2(w)$. Moreover, the fact that we have $w''' = w'$ is attested by the following equations:

(d) $w_{j_0}''' = \overline{w_{j_0}''} = \overline{w_{j_0}} = w_{j_0}'$,

(e) $w_{i_0}''' = w_{i_0}'' = \overline{w_{i_0}} = w_{i_0}'$, and:

(f) for $i \notin \{i_0, j_0\}$: $w_i''' = \overline{w_i''} = w_i = w_i'$ if, and only if, $i \in I$.   □

Proof of Lemma 13. Assume k even. According to Property (1) we have $w' = w \oplus u$ with $|u|_1 = k$. According to (2), $|w'|_1 - |w|_1$ is even: hence (i) follows. Conversely, assume $|w'|_1 - |w|_1$ even and let $u = w \oplus w'$. According to (2), $|u|_1$ is also even, moreover according to (1) we obtain $w' = \sigma_{|u|_1}(w)$: this implies $w' \in \sigma_2^*(w)$. According to Lemma 16, we have $w' \in \sigma_k^*(w)$: this establishes (ii).   □

Proof of Proposition 14. Let $w \in A^{\geq k}$ and $n = |w|$. (iii) is trivial and (i) follows from Lemma 13(i): indeed, since k is even, $\sigma_k^*(w)$ is the set of the words $w' \in A^n$

such that $|w'|_1 - |w|_1$ is even. Assume k odd, and let $w' \in A^n \setminus \{w\}$; we will prove that $w' \in \sigma_k^*(w)$. If $|w'|_1 - |w|_1$ is even, the result comes from Lemma 13(ii). Assume $|w'|_1 - |w|_1$ odd and let $t \in \sigma_1(w')$, thus $w' \in \sigma_1(t) \subseteq \sigma_k \circ \sigma_{k-1}(t)$ that is, $w' \in \sigma_k(t')$ for some $t' \in \sigma_{k-1}(t)$. It follows from $w' \in \sigma_1(t)$ that $|t|_1 - |w'|_1$ is odd, whence $|t|_1 - |w|_1 = (|t|_1 - |w'|_1) + (|w'|_1 - |w|_1)$ is even: according to Lemma 13(ii), this implies $t \in \sigma_k^*(w)$. But since $k - 1$ is even, we have $t' \in \sigma_{k-1}(t) \subseteq \sigma_2^*(t)$: according to Lemma 16, this implies $t' \in \sigma_k^*(t)$ (we have $|t| = |w'| = n$). We obtain $w' \in \sigma_k(t') \subseteq \sigma_k^*(t) \subseteq \sigma_k^*(\sigma_k^*(w)) = \sigma_k^*(w)$: this completes the proof. □

5.3   The Consequences for σ-Closed Codes

Given a σ_k-closed code $X \subseteq A^*$, we say that the tuple (k, A, X) satisfies Condition (3) if each of the three following properties holds:

$$(a)\ k\ is\ even, \quad (b)\ |A| = 2, \quad (c)\ X \nsubseteq A^{\leq k}.$$

We start by proving the following technical result:

Lemma 17. *Assume $|A| = 2$ and k even. Given a pair of words $v, w \in A^+$, if $|w| \geq \max\{|v| + 1, k + 1\}$ then the set $\sigma_k^*(w) \cup \{v\}$ cannot be a code.*

Proof. Let $v, w \in A^+$, and $n = |w| \geq \max\{|v| + 1, k + 1\}$ (hence $v \notin \sigma_k^*(w) \subseteq A^{|w|}$). By contradiction, we assume that $\sigma_k^*(w) \cup \{v\}$ is a code. We are in Condition (i) of Proposition 14 that is, we have $\sigma_k^*(w) \in \{A_0^n, A_1^n\}$. On a first hand, since A^{n-1} is a right-complete prefix code [2, Theorem 3.3.8], it follows from $|v| \leq n - 1$ that a (perhaps empty) word s exists such that $vs \in A^{n-1}$. On another hand, it follows from $A^{n-1}A = A^n = A_0^n \cup A_1^n$ that, for each $u \in A^{n-1}$, a unique pair of letters a_0, a_1, exists such that $ua_0 \in A_0^n$, $ua_1 \in A_1^n$ with $a_1 = \overline{a_0}$ that is, $a \in A$ exists with $vsa \in \sigma_k^*(w)$. According to Lemma 13(i), $|sav|_1 - |w|_1 = |vsa|_1 - |w|_1$ is even; according to Lemma 13(ii), this implies $sav \in \sigma_k^*(w)$. Since we have $(vsa)v = v(sav)$, the set $\sigma_k^*(w) \cup \{v\}$ cannot be a code. □

As a consequence of Lemma 17, we obtain the following result:

Lemma 18. *Given a σ_k-closed code $X \subseteq A^*$, if (k, A, X) satisfies Condition (3) then either we have $X \subseteq A^{\leq k}$, or we have $X \in \{A_0^n, A_1^n, A^n\}$ for some $n \geq k+1$.*

Proof. Firstly, consider two words $v, w \in X \cap A^{\geq k+1}$ and by contradiction, assume $|v| \neq |w|$ that is, without loss of generality $|v| + 1 \leq |w|$. Since X is σ_k-closed, we have $\sigma_k^*(w) \subseteq X$, whence the set $\sigma_k^*(w) \cup \{v\}$, which a subset of X is a code: this contradicts the result of Lemma 17. Consequently, we have $X \subseteq A^{\leq k} \cup A^n$, with $n = |v| = |w| \geq k+1$. Secondly, once more by contradiction assume that words $v \in X \cap A^{\leq k}$, $w \in X \cap A^{\geq k+1}$ exist. As indicated above, since X is σ_k-closed, $\sigma_k^*(w) \cup \{v\}$ is a code: since we have $|w| \geq k+1$ and $|w| \geq |v|+1$, once more this contradicts the result of Lemma 17. As a consequence, necessarily we have $X \subseteq A^n$, for some $n \geq k+1$. With such a condition, according to Proposition 14 for each pair of words $v, w \in X$, we have $\sigma_k^*(v), \sigma_k^*(w) \in \{A_0^n, A_1^n\}$: this implies $X \in \{A_0^n, A_1^n, A^n\}$. □

According to Lemma 18, with Condition (3) no σ_k-closed code can simultaneously possess words in $A^{\leq k}$ and words in $A^{\geq k+1}$.

Lemma 19. *Given a σ_k-closed code $X \subseteq A^*$, if (k, A, X) does not satisfy Condition (3) then either we have $X \subseteq A^{\leq k}$, or we have $X = A^n$, with $n \geq k + 1$.*

Proof. If Condition (3) doesn't hold then exactly one of the three following conditions holds:

(a) $X \subseteq A^{\leq k}$;
(b) $X \not\subseteq A^k$ and $|A| \geq 3$;
(c) $X \not\subseteq A^{\leq k}$ with $|A| = 2$ and k odd.

With each of the two last conditions, let $w \in X \cap A^{\geq k+1}$. Since X is σ_k-closed, according to the propositions 12 and 14(ii), we have $A^n = \sigma_k^*(w) \subseteq \sigma_k^*(X)$. Since A^n is a maximal code, it follows from Lemma 3(iii) that $X = A^n$. $\qquad\square$

As a consequence, every σ_k-closed code is finite. In addition, we state:

Theorem 20. *Given a complete σ_k (Σ_k, Λ_k)-closed code X, exactly one of the following conditions holds:*

(i) *X is a subset of $A^{\leq k}$;*
(ii) *a unique integer $n \geq k + 1$ exists such that $X = A^n$.*

In addition, every $\Sigma_k(\Lambda_k)$-closed code is equal to A^n, for some $n \geq 1$.

Proof. Let X be a complete σ_k-closed code. If Condition (3) does not hold, the result is expressed by Lemma 19. Assume that Condition (3) holds. According to Lemma 18, in any case some integer $n \geq k+1$ exists such that $X \in \{A_0^n, A_1^n, A^n\}$. Taking for π the uniform distribution, we have $\pi(A_0^n) = \pi(A_1^n) = 1/2$ and $\pi(A^n) = 1$ thus, according to Theorem 1: $X = A^n$. Recall that we have $\sigma_1^*(w) = A^{|w|}$ (e.g. [8]). Assume X Σ_k-closed, and let $w \in X$, $n = |w|$: we have $A^n = \sigma_1^*(X) \subseteq \Sigma_k^*(X) \subseteq X$ thus $X = A^n$ (indeed, A^n is a maximal code). Since $\Sigma_k \subseteq \Lambda_k$, if X is Λ_k-closed then it is Σ_k-closed, thus we have $X = A^n$. $\qquad\square$

As a corollary, in the family of $\Sigma_k(\Lambda_k)$-closed codes, maximality and completeness are equivalent notions. With regard to σ_k-closed codes, things are otherwise: indeed, as shown in [16], there are finite codes that have no finite completion. Let X be one of them, and $k = \max\{|x| : x \in X\}$. By definition X is σ_k-closed. Since every σ_k-closed code is finite, no complete σ_k-closed code can contain X.

Proposition 21. *Let X be a (finite) non-complete σ_k-closed code. Then one can decide whether some complete σ_k-closed code containing X exists. More precisely, there is only a finite number of such codes, each of them being computable, if any.*

Proof Sketch. We draw the scheme of an algorithm that allows to compute every complete σ_k-closed code $\hat{X}$ containing X. In a first step, we compute $Y = X \cap A^{\leq k}$. If $Y = X$, according to Theorem 20, we have $\hat{X} \subseteq A^{\leq k}$: $\hat{X}$, if any, can be computed in a finite number of steps. Otherwise, $\hat{X}$ exists if, and only if, for some $n \geq k + 1$ we have $X \subseteq A^n$: this can be straightforwardly checked. $\square$

Acknowledgment. We would like to thank the anonymous reviewers for their fruitful suggestions and comments.

References

1. Berstel, J., Felice, C.D., Perrin, D., Reutenauer, C., Rindonne, G.: Bifix codes and Sturmian words. J. Algebra **369**, 146–202 (2012)
2. Berstel, J., Perrin, D., Reutenauer, C.: Codes and Automata. Cambridge University Press, New York (2010)
3. Bruyère, V., Wang, L., Zhang, L.: On completion of codes with finite deciphering delay. Eur. J. Comb. **11**, 513–521 (1990)
4. Ehrenfeucht, A., Rozenberg, S.: Each regular code is included in a regular maximal one. RAIRO Theoret. Inf. Appl. **20**, 89–96 (1986)
5. Ehrlich, G.: Loopless algorithms for generating permutations, combinations, and other combinatorial configurations. J. ACM **20**, 500–513 (1973)
6. Jürgensen, H., Konstantinidis, S.: Codes[1]. In: Rozenberg, G., Salomaa, A. (eds.) Handbook of Formal Languages, pp. 511–607. Springer, Heidelberg (1997). https://doi.org/10.1007/978-3-642-59136-5_8
7. Kari, L., Păun, G., Thierrin, G., Yu, S.: At the crossroads of linguistic, DNA computing and formal languages: characterizing RE using insertion-deletion systems. In: Proceedings of Third DIMACS Workshop on DNA Based Computing, pp. 318–333 (1997)
8. Knuth, D.: The Art of Computer Programming, Volume 4, Fascicule 2 : Generating All Tuples and Permutations. Addison Wesley, Boston (2005)
9. Konstantinidis, S.: Error correction and decodability. Ph.D. thesis, The University of Western Ontario, London, Canada (1996)
10. Lam, N.: Finite maximal infix codes. Semigroup Forum **61**, 346–356 (2000)
11. Lam, N.: Finite maximal solid codes. Theoret. Comput. Sci. **262**, 333–347 (2001)
12. Levenshtein, V.: Binary codes capable of correcting deletions, insertion and reversals. Sov. Phys. Dokl. **163**, 845–848 (1965). (Engl. trans. in: Dokl. Acad. Nauk. SSSR)
13. Néraud, J.: Completing circular codes in regular submonoids. Theoret. Comp. Sci. **391**, 90–98 (2008)
14. Néraud, J., Selmi, C.: Embedding a θ-invariant code into a complete one. Theoret. Comput. Sci. **806**, 28–41 (2020). https://doi.org/10.1016/j.tcs.2018.08.022
15. Nivat, M., et al.: Congruences parfaites et semi-parfaites. Séminaire Dubreil. Algèbre et théorie des nombres **25**, 1–9 (1971)
16. Restivo, A.: On codes having no finite completion. Discrete Math. **17**, 309–316 (1977)
17. Rozenberg, G., Salomaa, A.: The Mathematical Theory of L-Systems. Academic Press, New York (1980)
18. Rudi, K., Wonham, W.M.: The infimal prefix-closed and observable superlanguage of a given language. Syst. Control Lett. **15**, 361–371 (1990)
19. Savage, C.: A survey of combinatorial gray codes. SIAM Rev. **39**(4), 605–629 (1997)

Author Index

Printed in the United States
By Bookmasters